Y0-BQP-632

A HISTORY OF
JEWISH LITERATURE

Volume I

A HISTORY OF
JEWISH LITERATURE

Volume I

From the Close of the Canon
to the End of the Twelfth Century

by

MEYER WAXMAN

THOMAS YOSELOFF

New York • London

FERNALD LIBRARY
COLBY-SAWYER COLLEGE
NEW LONDON, N. H. 03257

Copyright © 1960, by Meyer Waxman

THOMAS YOSELOFF, *Publisher*
11 East 36th Street
New York 16, N. Y.

THOMAS YOSELOFF LTD.
123 New Bond Street
London W. 1, England

PJ
5008
W 323
vol. 1

Sf0S9

Printed in the United States of America

To the Memory of My Parents

MORDECAI AND SARAH

*This Volume is Dedicated as a
Token of Reverence
and Filial Piety*

PREFACE TO FIRST EDITION

The undertaking of the writing of a history of post-Biblical Jewish literature, the development of which occupies more than half of the time of the history of civilized humanity, and the extent of its distribution in space more than half of the globe, if not done by a Steinschneider or a Zunz, may be considered by many, to say the least, presumptuous. A word of explanation as to the purpose of the work may, therefore, be necessary.

The purpose of this history is to make accessible to the large lay intelligent public the results of Jewish scholarship and research in the various branches of Jewish literature, carried on during the last century; to coördinate and correlate the scattered facts and the numerous data, so as to present a complete picture of the productivity of the Jewish genius during the ages. That such a work is necessary, and in fact comes to satisfy a crying need, is evident to anyone who is even superficially acquainted with the state of the spread of Jewish knowledge.

It is deplorable, but true nevertheless, that in spite of the fact that "Jewish science" or scholarship is more than a century old, and that the literature produced by it in various languages is both extensive and of high quality, the influence it exerted upon the intelligent reading public is not proportionate to its efforts. Knowledge of Jewish literature, of its ideals and ideas, of its views of life and human conduct is comparatively scant even in the higher intellectual circles. This is true not only of non-Jews interested in matters Jewish, but of Jews as well. Even at the present, when apparently, partly due to the nationalistic movement, there seems to be a desire in many Jewish circles to acquaint themselves with the treasures of the Jewish spirit, the efforts to obtain this coveted knowledge fall far below the extent of the desire.

To ameliorate somewhat these conditions, to supply to those who want to know the content, the ideas and ideals of the great masterpieces of Jewish literature, and learn of the uninterrupted process of the literary creation of the Jewish people, adequate information, as well as a coördinated conception of the ramifications of the intellectual and spiritual activity of Jewry during the long post-Biblical period, is the aim of this book. The work may also serve as a text or reference book for all students in Jewish theological schools, teachers' seminaries and departments of Jewish studies in universities.

The aim the author had in mind was deemed by him worthy enough to brave all the difficulties and hazards connected with such a work and make the attempt. How far he succeeded in fulfilling such aim is not for him to say, but he will patiently await the judgment of the readers.

The aim determined also the character of the work. While the facts and data were obtained, sifted and tested, in accordance with the rules of scholarly research, the presentation of the content is done in a non-technical manner. For this reason, notes were reduced to a minimum, and the discussion of moot questions omitted. Furthermore, in order to make the book accessible to those who are not conversant with Hebrew, Hebrew phrases and titles of books were transliterated.

The reader who wants to continue his research in any branch of Jewish literature will find help and guidance by consulting the selected bibliography given at the end of the book. It is limited to selected books and articles, for a complete bibliography on such an extensive subject would occupy a volume in itself.

Of the two methods available for the presentation of the content, namely the chronological one and that of treating each branch of literature separately, the author chose the latter. Literature is an organic thing, and while the various organs make up one whole, each organ or branch possesses an individuality of its own and the whole can best be conceived through a study of the parts. This method has, of course, its disadvantages, for the reader may have to consult several chapters before he gets a fair conception of the literary activity of a Saadia or a Maimonides, but its advantages far outweigh the drawbacks.

Chicago, August, 1930

MEYER WAXMAN

PREFACE TO THE SECOND EDITION

This edition is, as stated in the title page, both revised and enlarged. However, as far as the text proper is concerned, the revision is more of a formal than of fundamental nature, for it is impossible to incorporate new material in a printed book without rewriting it, a task which would involve much labor and expense. Efforts were, therefore, primarily concentrated on revision of style and expression in order to make it more lucid and concise. Changes were also made in the transliteration of the numerous Hebrew titles and words bringing it in consonance with the adopted scientific principles. The bibliography, though, was rewritten and numerous works added. Likewise, was the index recast and adjusted to the changed transliteration and all inaccuracies carefully checked and corrected.

The enlargement consists of a series of appendices or additions arranged according to chapters and given at the end of the book. These additions, which bring the content of the volume up to the present state of Jewish scholarship, deal with new theories propounded or new data brought to light within the last eight years. Some of them discuss works which were either inadvertently omitted in the first edition or recently edited and published.

The author wishes to thank Mr. Benjamin Groner, who carefully read the first edition and made a number of suggestions in its revision; to his son, Mordecai, and Mr. I. W. Jacobson, for revising the index, and finally to his wife, who was of exceptional help in the preparation of this edition.

Chicago, September, 1938

Meyer Waxman

TABLE OF CONTENTS

CHAPTER I

APOCRYPHAL AND APOCALYPTIC LITERATURE

APOCALYPTIC LITERATURE

CHAPTER II

THE DEVELOPMENT OF THE HALAKAH

CHAPTER III

ORGANIZATION OF THE HALAKAH

A. Tannaim and their Method

CHAPTER IV

OTHER FORMS OF LITERATURE—HELLENISTIC LITERATURE

CHAPTER V

THE TALMUD

CHAPTER VI

THE AGADIC COLLECTIONS (MIDRASHIM)

BOOK II

CHAPTER VII

GRAMMAR AND LEXICOGRAPHY

CHAPTER VIII

BIBLE EXEGESIS

CHAPTER IX

POETRY

CHAPTER X

RABBINIC LITERATURE—COMMENTARIES, CODES AND RESPONSA

CHAPTER XI

PHILOSOPHY AND THEOLOGY

ADDITIONS

CHAPTER I

CHAPTER II

CHAPTER IV

CHAPTER VI

CHAPTER IX

CHAPTER X

CHAPTER XIV

INTRODUCTION

The literature of a people is very often described as the mirror of its soul. In it are reflected its strivings and desires, its expressions and ideals, its failures and achievements. The relation of history to literature is like unto the relation of the external action to the inner motive. Whatever actions and deeds a people performed in the course of its history were prompted by the ideals and emotions expressed in its literature, while the mere records of these acts and deeds are known as history. History without literature is, therefore, only a dry chronicle of the past life of a people. It is the literature which supplies the glow of emotion, the warmth of passion, the intelligent meaning, the connecting link to the dry series of facts and breathes into it the very breath of life, so that the past life of the particular nation rises before us as in a vision.

And if this is to be said about the literature of any historical people, so much more should the dictum be applied to Jewish literature, the mirror of the soul of that people which had long been named the "People of the Book," a people that has left but little of other permanent monuments except books, one to whom the book was a portable fatherland for many centuries. To try to understand the history of the Jews without at least a fair acquaintance with the various phases of Jewish literature is an impossibility, as it forms the very woof of which the history of this people is woven.

However, a better understanding of Jewish history is not the only compensation awaiting the student of Jewish literature. There is a higher reward in store for the toiler in this field, and that is the saturation with the beauty and fascinating charm pervading this mass of literary productions of the Jewish genius.

Post-Biblical Jewish literature is a great, wide garden, a veritable "Garden of God." In it are found the strangest and most exotic plants, culled from all lands and all climes. There, contrary to Kipling, East meets West, Jew meets Greek and a host of his successors, Roman, Arab, and all Western nations. It is a point where the spirits of all nations, which left their mark on the history of human development, commingle, and is the scene of a great spiritual panorama which has the world for its background, where the echo of all centuries and all lands is heard. It is a literature without geographic boundaries, one which grew luxuriously on the shores of the rivers of Babylon, on the banks of the Jordan, bloomed most beautifully by the rivers Tagus and Gaudalquivir (Spain and Portugal), and flourished with equal vigor on the Rhine, the Vistula, and the Dnieper.

In Jewish literature, Judaism becomes conscious of its power, and expresses itself in many ways and forms. It is true that the great bulk of that massive and voluminous literature has a religious coloring, but it is not the spirit of dogmatic religion which is embodied in its pages, but the spirit of a religion which is bubbling with life, seething with emotion, and revealing the many-sidedness of the human soul. Law has its place in that literature, and a prominent one at that, for it formed for a long time the backbone of Judaism, the shelter which protected it from many storms, still the other aspects of religion were not neglected by it; they too find their place there. In the pages of this literature, we feel the deepest expression of the yearning for God, of the longing of the soul for the Infinite, of the hope of the individual for a future life, and of the cry of a martyred people for a Messiah, a redeemer. It is all there in the long list of books known as Apocrypha, Apocalyptic, Agada, and Midrashim. And when the experiences of the nation accumulated, and in their turn clamored for expression, we have, as a result, books on history. Again, when life in general, and Jewish life in particular, became tinged with earnestness and assumed a more speculative aspect, this phase also found its expression in philosophy and ethics.

As we speed through the centuries, we encounter new currents of literary activity. The ancient lyre of Israel is struck again, and new chords are emitted by a host of singers both religious and secular. It is the Golden Age of Spanish Jewry when Jew meets Arab and cultures mingle, wide vistas and new avenues of expression open up, and science, philosophy, grammar, and lexicography come and take their place side by side with Halakah and Agada. And simultaneously, almost stealthily and unnoticed, there rises to full bloom the exotic plant of mysticism known as Kabbala. Thus, the kaleidoscopic picture changes through the ages, and through these metamorphisms tells the wonderful story of Judaism.

MAP OF
JEWISH LITERARY CENTERS DURING THE AGES

On the following map, the reader can see at a glance the countries and cities which, at one time or another, served as centers of Jewish literature.

Palestine and Babylonia, being the principal centers of literary activity, are placed at the top, and under each of these are grouped the countries which were included in its sphere of influence.

Palestine influenced directly, in the 7th and 8th centuries Italy and it in turn influenced France and Germany. Babylonia influenced Northern Africa and Spain. Provence, in the 12th century, was influenced by Spain, Italy, France and Germany together, hence its central position.

Dates of maps:

 Palestine—about 150 c. e.

 Babylonia—500 c. e.

 Italy, Provence, France and Germany—1200 c. e.

 Spain—1037 c. e.

Only such cities are placed on the map which bear on development of literature.

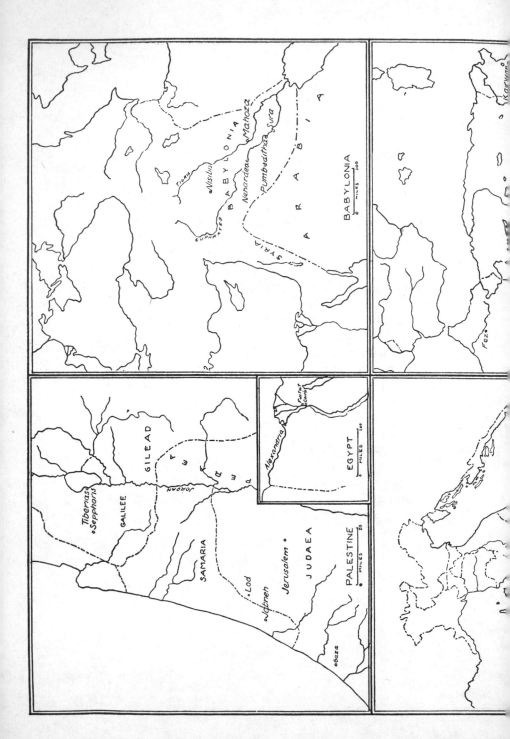

BABYLONIA

EUPHRATES
TIGRIS

Nisibis
BABYLONIA
Mahoza
Nenardea
Pumbeditha Sura
ARABIA
SYRIA

MILES
0   100

GILEAD
Tiberias
Sepphoris
GALILEE
SAMARIA
JORDAN
D
E
Lod
Jabneh
Jerusalem
JUDAEA
Gaza

PALESTINE
MILES
0   20

EGYPT
Alexandria
Fustat
Cairo

MILES
0   100

Fez

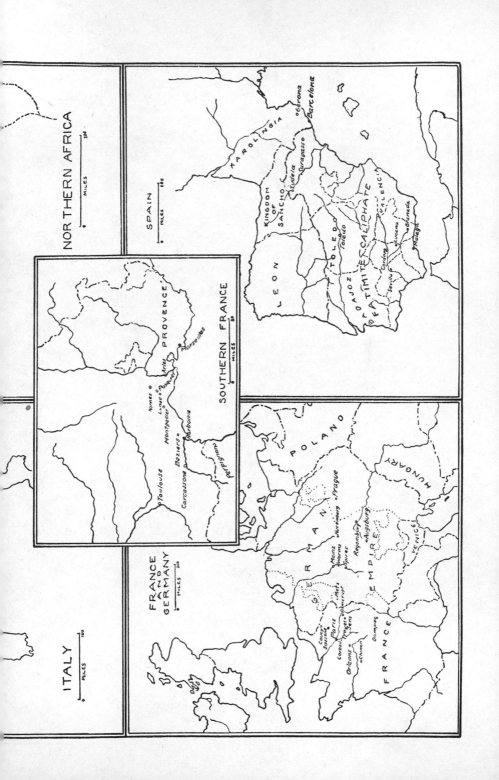

NORTHERN AFRICA

MILES

SPAIN

MILES

KAROLINGIA

Gerona
Barcelona

KINGDOM
OF
SANCHO

Tudela
Saragossa

LEON

TOLEDO

Toledo

BADAJOZ

FATIMITE CALIPHATE

VALENCIA

Murcia
Granada
Malaga

Cordova
Seville

PROVENCE

SOUTHERN FRANCE

MILES

Arles
Avignon
Marseilles

Nimes
Lunel
Montpellier
Beziers
Carcassonne
Narbonne

Toulouse

Perpignan

ITALY

MILES

FRANCE
AND
GERMANY

MILES

POLAND

HUNGARY

GERMAN

EMPIRE

Prague
Nuremberg
Regensburg
Augsburg

Mainz
Worms
Speyer

VENICE

Metz
Gorbenheim

Paris
Corbeil
Orleans
Chatres

Dijon

FRANCE

Book I

ANCIENT PERIOD
From 400 B. C. E. to 600 C. E.

ANCIENT PERIOD

CHAPTER I

APOCRYPHAL AND APOCALYPTIC LITERATURE

1. GENERAL FEATURES

The first stage of post-Biblical Jewish literature consists of the Apocryphal and Apocalyptic books. This literature fills the gap between the Bible and the Mishnah, or to be more exact, the other forms of Halakic and Agadic literature, the compilation and organization of which began somewhat earlier than the Mishnah, about the close of the first century after the destruction of the Temple which corresponds to the middle of the second century of the common era. To the Christians, it forms the link between the Old and the New Testaments. The period of this kind of literary activity extends for about three centuries, namely, from 200 B. C. E. to about 100 C. E. In view of the fact that the canon of the Old Testament was closed about 250 B. C. E., the uninterrupted activity of the genius of Israel becomes apparent.

In fact, it was really intended by the writers of this literature to be a continuation of the Bible, inasmuch as it follows along the same lines. As it is known, the Bible consists of several divisions: law, history written with a moral purpose, prophecy, religious poetry, both lyric and didactic, and reflective writings. With the exception of the element of law which is scantily represented in this kind of literature, all the other elements find there adequate representation.

The name Apocrypha given to a part of this literature is derived from the Greek word Ἀπόκρυφος which means hidden away or secret. The term, though, seems to have been applied to this group of books in three different usages. First, in the sense of having been excluded from the canon of the Old Testament, for, with the close of that canon, no more books were added to it, and all other books written either after the close or even before, but were not considered worthy of inclusion in the authorized collection, were designated as *Ḥiẓonim*—i. e. external.

I

In time, these excluded books were not as widely circulated as the
canonical and were found only in the hands of a few, hence the name
Apocrypha, hidden, on account of their rarity.[1] Second, it was used in
the sense of being hidden away from the eyes of the masses on account
of the sacred teachings and the mystic and exotic character of some of
them. Later, the name was applied to the whole group, even to the
historical books. Third, the name *hidden* was applied because some of
the books were attributed by the writers to personages of Biblical fame,
either to prophets, such as The Epistle of Jeremiah, The Book of Baruch,
or even to Solomon, such as "The Wisdom of Solomon," or as in some
of the Apocalyptic writings, which as a rule were a part of this literature,
to Abraham, Enoch, etc., and their distant origin was usually explained
by the fact that they were hidden away during the generations until
the appointed time for their revelation came.

The name Apocalypse is really another word for revelation, and
Apocalyptic means revealed. The books named Apocalyptic are akin
to the prophetic books of the Bible, especially to certain portions of some
of them, such as Daniel and Zechariah. Apocalypse and Apocalyptic
books differ from prophecy and prophetic books not only by the fact
that they are not divinely inspired but also by a number of external
characteristics which can be subsumed under the following heads: (*a*)
While the prophet dwelt on the conditions of the present, interpreting
current history with the purpose of disclosing the divine forces at work,
the Apocalypsist speaks almost entirely of the future, disparaging the
present. (*b*) In the prophetic books, symbols are only occasionally used
as a means of enforcing the message; in the Apocalyptic books, allegory
occupies the most important place and a regular symbolic machinery,
in which animal symbols predominate, is built up. (*c*) Prophecy openly
avows the name of the author; Apocalypse hides under the names of
men of antiquity—hence it is mostly pseudepigraphic—rewrites the past
in the name of some hero and makes him divine the future through
visions and oracles.

Yet, though this kind of literature is usually separated into two divisions, Apocryphal and Apocalyptic, there is really no fast line separating
them. In some collections of the Apocrypha, such as the one in the
English Bible, IV Esdras is included, while by its content and tone it

[1] In accordance with this derivative meaning, a new Hebrew term was coined for
these books—*Genuzim* instead of *Ḥizonim,* i. e. hidden or stored away, and the verb
Ganoz came to be used to denote the exclusion of books from the Canon, cf. *Babli Sabbath* 13b.

really belongs to the Apocalyptic division. On the other hand, the Book of Jubilees should be classed rather as Apocryphal than Apocalyptic.

2. TIME AND SPIRIT OF THIS LITERATURE

To understand this kind of literature, we must know the time in which it was produced and the spirit by which it was permeated. As stated above, the period of its production extends from 200 B.C.E. to 100 C.E. This period was, on the whole, one of tribulation, of suffering, strife, and subjection, with only a short span of rest and prosperity. It began with the entrance of the Jews under the dominion of the Graeco-Syrian Empire, and ended with the destruction of the Temple and the dispersion, embracing, in its midst, the years of the Hasmonean struggle as well as the eight decades of peace under the rule of the princes of that house. In general, the Second Commonwealth of the Jews presents a sorry spectacle, and in no way approaches the glories presaged by the older prophets nor even those foretold by the later, such as Haggai and Zechariah. This political background which presented a sharp incongruity between the future portrayed by the prophets and that of the present, coupled with other factors, gave rise to a number of features which together make up the peculiar spirit of this literature. These features are as follows: (*a*) Moved by deep belief that the promises of the prophets must be fulfilled, contrary state of the present notwithstanding, the heart of the faithful yearned for a better future, and the hope for it became, to all who were dissatisfied with the present, a passionate longing. No wonder then, that the old Messianic idea forms a leading note in this literature which deals primarily with the future.

(*b*) The other leading feature is the zeal for the Law of God. The people of Israel, from the time of Ezra on, was transformed from a people struggling towards religion into the religious people par excellence. The Law—Torah—became all important, the very center of life. This zeal for the Law found multifarious expression in Apocryphal and Apocalyptic literature. On the whole, though, it may be said that the zeal for the Law is expressed mainly in the Apocrypha, while the hope for the future is the primary motive in the Apocalyptic books. However, the lines are not fast drawn. Both of them were practical. The Apocrypha taught the way of life through Law, while the Apocalyptic books offered consolation to the sufferers of the present.

(*c*) Another feature which is quite prominent in this literature is the reward of the individual. In Biblical times—though it is my personal opinion that the individual did occupy a more prominent place in the religious scheme of the time than is generally assumed—the place of the individual and his hopes and strivings were very often superseded by the hope for the future destiny of the nation as a whole. At all events, the theory that the righteous are rewarded and the wicked punished was mostly expressed in terms of prosperity and suffering in this world. True, the doctrines of a future life of the individual as well as that of resurrection are referred to several times by the prophets and also in the Book of Job, but these doctrines seem to have been the share of the few and not that of the masses. For, whether it was due to the reason that the prophets addressed themselves to the masses, and therefore spoke in terms of their conception of reward and punishment which was a worldly one, or to any other cause, the fact is that these doctrines were not sufficiently emphasized by them.

As years passed by, the theory of the reward of the righteous and the punishment of the wicked in this world was put to test, and it was found wanting. Life did not bear it out, as it was full of examples to the contrary—the righteous suffered and the wicked prospered. And little by little, the cry arose, why and wherefore? Jeremiah already had asked the question, "Why is the way of the wicked successful?" (Jer. XII, 1). The problem reached its highest point in the Book of Job, where it was dealt with on a large scale, but no satisfactory solution was reached. References in the book to the hope of life after death are few and far between. As times changed and the individual came more and more into his own during the first centuries of the Second Commonwealth, and in addition, there came the persecutions of the righteous in the time of the Graeco-Syrian rule, especially under Antiochus Epiphanes, when thousands of *Hassidim,* pious men, went down to an ignominious death, the problem became exceedingly acute. Then, the old solution, which was hitherto indistinct, pressed forward, namely, that the reward of the righteous will not come in this world but in the world after death, and the punishment of the wicked was likewise postponed to that world. Thus, the old theory of the immortality of the soul of the individual and its reward and punishment in the hereafter became prevalent, and striking deep roots in the hearts of the people, found passionate expression in this literature.

(*d*) There is yet a fourth idea which affects both the individual and the nation and which was destined to become a central point in Apocalyptic literature, and that is resurrection. This idea is a kind of synthesis into which the future hope of the nation, i. e. the Messianic kingdom, and the hope of the individual coalesce. Not only will all the righteous men living at the time of the advent of the Messiah participate in its blessings, but also all the righteous of the past will be resurrected and will participate in the blessings of the great event. And thus, the righteous individual receives an additional compensation besides his reward after death, namely, the promise of a return to life at the time when his nation will be happy and blessed. In this doctrine, the good of the individual and the happiness of the nation meet.

To recapitulate, we have four great motives which underlie the spirit that prompted and animated this mass of literature which developed within three centuries, from the beginning of the second century B. C. E. to 100 C. E., the formative period of Judaism as we know it today. The first motive is to inculcate faith in the blessed future of the nation promised by the prophets of old, i. e. Messianic times, still unfulfilled, and which the conditions of the time were constantly relegating to a more distant future.

The second, a very important feature, is the zeal for the Law which became all-inclusive and all-embracing in the life of the Jew during that period. The need for inculcating that zeal received a constant impetus from the great conflict with Hellenism in which Judaism was engaged, especially with Hellenizing sects within Israel proper. All devices were used in the defense of the Law or the Torah—historical narratives, moral tales, collections of reflective proverbs, epigrams, and aphorisms, all of which proved the superiority of the Torah over other paths and philosophies of life. This part of the task was performed mostly by the Apocrypha.

The third and fourth motives are to clarify and propagate the idea of the compensation of the righteous and punishment of the wicked in the life after death, thereby consoling the individual, and to paint the glorious future when happiness will come to the nation and the righteous will arise to participate in that happiness.

The picture, however, will not be complete unless we add two other essential features which are (1) the Last Judgment, and (2) the Kingdom of God. Both of these ideas are of prophetic origin. The great judgment or, to call it by its Biblical name, the Day of God, is given a good deal of attention by Isaiah, Joel, Amos, Zephaniah, and Zechariah. Likewise is the Kingdom of God, i. e. the age when the knowledge of God will cover the earth and He will be proclaimed king everywhere, frequently spoken of by the prophets. But not only are they not clearly defined by them and are subjected to various interpretations, such as that the judgment is only partial, either of Israel (as in the case of Amos) or of the nations that oppressed Israel, but also, in prophetic utterances, these two ideas are not connected (except probably in Isaiah, Ch. II).

During the period we are dealing with, though, these two ideas became the central points and an integral part of the great hope for a better future, or the Messianic age. Besides, they were broadened and inherently connected with each other. The judgment of God became the Last Judgment of all men, Jews and Gentiles alike, and this "general assize" will be immediately followed by the introduction of the Kingdom of God. The last idea in itself became more complex, inasmuch as it included various elements. It meant, on the one hand, the inauguration of a glorious time and the establishment of Israel as a nation of supermen, and, on the other hand, it also meant the extension of the rule and knowledge of God among mankind as a whole, and the supremacy of the Saints. The last conception is more spiritual and even in its very beginning contained germs of a dangerous tendency for Judaism. On the whole, the two notions are not clearly separated from each other and are often given in the books one beside the other. But when the latter, namely, the more spiritualized conception of the Kingdom of God, began to prevail, Jewish leaders took alarm, which was probably the cause of the rejection by the Jewish authorities of the entire literature, as will be explained later (Sec. 20).

Finally, there is the aspect of the Greek influence upon this literature which requires us to take into account its relation to Greek culture and spirit. Many of the books are not only permeated with borrowed Greek ideas which were, of course, Judaized and given a different form, but were also written in Greek, and very often outside of Palestine, namely, in Egypt, where Greek was the vernacular used by the Jews. It was there, where the conflict between Judaism and Hellenism raged in its most intense form, that defense was most needed. As a result, a good number of those books assumed an apologetic and polemic character. And as in all apologetics and polemics, there is a conscious and unconscious tendency in these books to adjust the ideas of the writer to the ideas of his antagonists. In the case of apologetics especially, there is an endeavor to show that there is really no essential difference between the two sets of ideas and that the difference consists only in form. Hence, we have in this kind of literature the extensive use of symbol and allegory which intends to empty the solid content of religious ideas and fill them with a more plastic one, and hence also the prevalent use of interpretation of Biblical verses or even precepts in a different manner than the accepted one. All this makes this literature different from the great collections of authoritative books, the Bible and the Talmud, when they happen to deal with the same subject. Yet a large part of this literature, especially of the Apocrypha, was only slightly affected by Greek ideas as far as the content is concerned, so that after all, they are fine examples of pure Jewish thought and feeling and should be considered as such.

3. APOCRYPHAL BOOKS

The Apocrypha are divided according to their nature and character into four classes: (a) Historical Books, (b) Legendary and Moral Fiction, (c) Prophetic and Poetic Writings, (d) Didactic. We have then, accordingly, the following list:

(a) Historical Books

1) I or III Ezra (Esdras)
2) I Maccabees
3) II Maccabees
4) III Maccabees

(b) Legendary and Moral Fiction

5) Tobit
6) Judith
7) Bel and the Dragon (Additions to Daniel)
8) Susanna
9) Additions to Esther

(c) Prophetic and Poetic Writings

10) Prayer of Azariah and Song of the Three Children
11) Prayer of Manasses
12) Book of Baruch
13) Epistle of Jeremiah

(d) Didactic

14) Wisdom of Sirach
15) Wisdom of Solomon
16) IV Maccabees

(a) HISTORICAL

4. I EZRA (Esdras)

This book, which is designated as I Ezra by the Septuagint, i. e. the Greek translation of the Bible, and III Ezra by the Vulgate, i. e. the standard Latin translation, should, according to its content, be considered first, inasmuch as it deals with the early history of the Second Commonwealth. It practically covers the same historical events contained in the Biblical books of Ezra and Nehemiah with some additions. The additions are as follows: (*a*) It begins with the story of the Passover celebrated by King Josiah and relates the succeeding events up to the destruction of the First Temple. In this narrative, it follows closely II Chronicles, Chas. XXXV, XXXVI, 1–26. (*b*) Chas. III–V, 4 of this book contain an entirely new version of the rise of Zerubbabel as the leader of the Jews. It tells how he, when a page in the service of King Darius, competed with two others in uttering sayings of wisdom and was declared to be the wisest of the three. The contest between the pages turned on the question as to what is the strongest power in the world.

One wrote wine is the strongest; the other wrote, the king; Zerubbabel wrote, women are the strongest but "above all truth beareth away victory." His answer was declared the best. On being asked to name his reward, Zerubbabel expressed the desire to be sent to Jerusalem to help build the city and Temple. His request was granted, and he was sent to Jerusalem to head the work of restoration.

Josephus had evidently seen I Ezra for he repeats the story of the rise of Zerubbabel verbatim. This version of the coming of Zerubbabel stands in contradiction with our canonical book of Ezra according to which Zerubbabel came to Jerusalem with the first settlers in the time of Cyrus, while according to I Ezra, Zerubbabel was still in Babylon at the beginning of the reign of Darius, namely, in 522 B. C. E. and did not go to Jerusalem probably until 520. The writer was, as it seems, primarily interested in Ezra, as he does not mention Nehemiah, and the part of the story to which we find a parallel in the canonical book of Nehemiah, namely, I Ezra Ch. IX, 37–55 which otherwise agrees with Nehemiah Chas. VII, 73–VIII, 13, deals only with the reading of the law by Ezra, while the name of Nehemiah is omitted.

The date of the book is indefinite. It is not later than 100 C. E. for it was used by Josephus, but it is probably much older, as it might even have been written in the third century B. C. E. Its original language was most likely Hebrew or Aramaic. It is now found only in Greek, Latin, and Syriac versions.

5. I MACCABEES

This book covers the history of a period of forty years, from the accession of Antiochus Epiphanes (175 B. C. E.) to the death of Simon

Maccabee (135). It is the chief historical source we have of the Jewish struggle for religious and civil independence during this period. It is prefaced with a brief sketch of the story of the conquest of Alexander, the division of his empire, the rule of the Syrians, and the oppression of Antiochus Epiphanes. It also recites very briefly the events preceding the revolt, the treachery of the Hellenist party, the despoiling of the city and the Temple, and the efforts of Antiochus to destroy the religion and nationality of the Jew. After this introduction, it proceeds to tell of the uprising of Mattathias, the struggles of Judah and Jonathan, and closes with a detailed account of the reign of Simon and a brief reference to John Hyrcanus. It is quite possible that there existed short notices of the Maccabean deeds which served our author as sources.

It is impossible to assume otherwise, namely, that one who lived about two generations after Judah could remember the events so minutely, for the author lived not earlier than the reign of Hyrcanus. The book contains also a number of official documents, such as letters exchanged between Jonathan and the King of Sparta, (Ch. XII, 6–18; XII, 20–22), a copy of the Treaty of Alliance concluded in the time of Judah Maccabee between Rome and the Jews (VIII, 22–32), and others. The preservation of these documents goes to prove that records of the most important events which transpired were kept in some kind of archive, and it is these records which, as surmised, served as the sources for the writer of I Maccabees.

The standpoint of the author is that of orthodox legal Judaism. Yet it is written in a very rational way; nowhere is the victory attributed to supernatural intervention, but credit is given to the skill of the military leaders and their wisdom. It is, of course, emphasized that these princes acted with an unshaken trust in God. The author shows great historical skill in picturing the period by putting discourses into the mouths of his heroes. It is very fortunate that he used a definite era in his dating; this is the Seleucidean era beginning in the year 312 B.C.E., the date of the victory of Seleucus over Antigonus.

The time of its composition seems to have been between 137–105 B.C.E. It was written originally in Hebrew, as the grammatical peculiarities indicate, and in addition we have the testimony of Jerome and Origen for the existence of a Hebrew original. Origen even says that he saw a copy of the Hebrew text. Its original title was probably *Sefer Bet Hashmonai*. It has come down to us in the Greek and was preserved by the fact that it was incorporated in the Greek Bible. It is very strange that it does not refer to the immortality of the soul or to the resurrection of the dead in such places where reference to these matters would have been in place. It has, therefore, been concluded that the writer belonged to the Sadducean party who were deeply religious, but did not accept these doctrines. This conclusion, however, should be taken with reserve, as the failure to mention these doctrines might have been due to other causes, such as that the writer as a historian was primarily interested in merely narrating the events and not in stating doctrines.

6. II MACCABEES

The second book of Maccabees, according to the testimony of its author, is an abridgment of a longer history written by Jason of Cyrene. It is prefaced by two letters written by the Jews of Jerusalem to the Jews of Alexandria urging them to observe the Feast of Dedication, (Hanukkah) and meanwhile telling them a story about the holy fire on the Altar, how it was hidden at the time of the exile, and how it was discovered by Nehemiah.

The epitome itself relates the events of a period of fifteen years, from the attempted despoliation of the Temple by Heliodorus, the treasurer of Seleucus IV (175 B.C.E.), to the death of Nicanor (161 B.C.E.). The events related in it are similar to those told in the first book, but the narrative differs in many particulars and sometimes in the very order of events. There is a copiousness of detail, especially in the preliminary history of the Maccabean rising. It is possible that Jason derived his data from the lips of contemporaries and not from written records, for the book abounds with inaccuracies. Jason then must have written his book shortly after 160 B.C.E.

II Maccabees differs greatly from I Maccabees in the mode of narrating. It includes the supernatural element, as, for instance, the story of the intervention of angels in preventing Heliodorus from carrying out the despoliation of the Temple. It is also distinguished by several stories exalting the martyrdom of the *Hassidim,* such as that of Eliezer (Ch. VI) and that of Hannah[2] and her seven children (Ch. VII). These embellished stories are told with the express purpose of arousing the

---

[2] The name Hannah by which the mother is usually called is not given in our book, and similarly, several Talmudic and Midrashic sources simply call her the mother, or the widow. Another Mediæval source calls her Miriam, daughter of Naḥtom (Midrash to Lamentations Ch. 1, 50). But the *Yossipon,* a Mediæval historical book, calls the martyred mother Hannah and this name was adopted.

spirit of devotion to the Torah and the faith of the Fathers by inspiring emulation of the deeds of the saints and heroes. There are several references in the book to the resurrection of the dead (Ch. XII, 44, 45; XIV, 46) and the gathering of the dispersed (Kibuẓ Galuiot). It was therefore written by a Pharisee. We are, though, at a loss to understand why the narrator breaks off with the victory of Judah over Nicanor. Perhaps Jason intended to continue the story at some other time.

The date of the composition of this epitome cannot be fixed definitely but it is to be placed between the years 108 and 50 B. C. E., at any rate not later than that year. It was undoubtedly written originally in Greek by an Egyptian Jew, as its fine Greek rhetorical style indicates.

7. III MACCABEES

The third book of Maccabees, in spite of its name, has nothing to do with the Maccabean struggle and can really be considered historical only in form. In reality, it is a piece of fiction founded on an unascertainable historical fact. Its content is as follows: Ptolemy IV, after his victory over Antiochus the Great (217 B. C. E.), comes to Jerusalem and desires to enter the Temple. The Jews entreat him not to do so, but he insists, enters the Temple and is struck by the hand of God. On returning to Egypt, he wishes to wreak his vengeance upon the Jews. At first, he deprives them of their rights, and finally commands that they should be brought to Alexandria in chains. Ptolemy then orders that five hundred elephants be intoxicated and set upon the Jews. When everything is ready and the king approaches the race course with his troops, two angels appear and strike the elephants with terror, so that instead of turning upon the Jews, they turn upon the king's troops. As a result, the king changes his mind and orders the liberation of the Jews, and henceforth bestows favors upon them.

We do not know the authenticity of these facts. It is probably based on the story told by Josephus (Against Apion II, 5) about Ptolemy VII (146–117 B. C. E.) who acted towards the Jews of Alexandria, his political opponents, in a similar manner and whose attempt ended with similar results. It is possible that the story was composed at the time of the first persecution against the Jews under Caligula about 30 C. E., but this again is not certain as there are no references in the book to the character of Caligula. Its date cannot therefore be ascertained. At the earliest, it may be placed in the first century B. C. E. Its purpose was like that of all books of this kind of literature, namely, to extol the greatness of God in preserving His people from the hands of their enemies, and thus encourage them in their difficult task of battling for the existence of Judaism. A feast for the commemoration of such an event was observed in Alexandria. The original language of the book was Greek.

(b) LEGENDARY AND MORAL FICTION

8. THE BOOK OF TOBIT

The book, Tobit, is a moral story which intends to inculcate the virtues of honoring the dead and the giving of alms. It aims primarily at the individual and deals with the biography of a pious man named Tobit. The scene is laid in Nineveh, the capital of Assyria. Tobit is a captive Jew who was brought there by Shalmaneser together with all the other exiles from Israel in 722 B. C. E. He settles in Nineveh and lives there quite happily with his wife Hannah and his son Tobias. He performs good deeds, gives alms, buries the dead, and clothes the naked. Once, after performing a kind deed, he lies down to sleep in the open air and is blinded by sparrow's dung which falls into his eyes. He is sorely tried for he becomes poor and all his friends forsake him while his wife mocks at his good deeds and asks him pertinently where is his reward.

Meanwhile, Tobit reminds himself that a certain Gabael in Rages, Media, owes him money and he sends his son Tobias to collect it. In Ecbatana, there lives a Jew, Raguel, whose daughter, Sarah, had been married to seven husbands, all of whom had died on the wedding night through the agency of an evil spirit, named Asmodeus. On his way to Rages which leads through Ecbatana, Tobias is joined by a fellow traveler, who is no other than the angel Raphael, sent by God both to heal Tobit and to help Sarah in her plight. While traveling together, Tobias bathes in the Tigris and catches a fish, and at the direction of the angel, he takes out the heart, liver, and gall of the fish and preserves them. On reaching Ecbatana, Raguel recognizes him as the son of his friend Tobit, and at the advice of the disguised angel, he offers him, though reluctantly, his daughter in marriage. On entering the bridal chamber, Tobias, at the suggestion of the angel, burns the liver and heart of the fish, the smoke of which drives away the evil spirit. Contrary to the expectations of the parents of the bride, the couple are found safe and sound in the morning. Great joy reigns in the house of Raguel, and

Tobias remains at the home of his father-in-law for fourteen days, the disguised angel having meanwhile gone to collect the money from Gabael. At the termination of the fourteen days of festivity, Tobias and his wife return home, and with the gall of the fish, he cures his father's blindness. Tobit praises God for restoring his sight and lives after that one hundred years more, his life being in all one hundred and sixty-six years. He is thus rewarded for his kindness.

The plot is well laid and is skillfully interwoven. Emphasis is laid upon observance of the Law, but superstition forms an important element. It seems that the purpose of the author was to encourage the Jews of the Diaspora and to strengthen their hearts in the observance of the Law.

The date can be tolerably fixed within wide limits. It was written before the Temple of Herod was built, which was about 20 B. C. E.,[3] and we can go back about a century and a half, so that the date for the composition of the book ranges between 190 and 20 B. C. E. It has even been advanced that the book was written in Egypt at the close of the third century B. C. E. by a pious Jew. The original language must have been Aramaic. There is still an Aramaic text in existence.

9. BOOK OF JUDITH

This book belongs to the kind of literature classed as historical fiction written with a certain tendency in view. It is possible that the author of this story intended that it be regarded as founded on fact, but the object in view was not really to impart historical information but mainly to use the story as a vehicle for conveying moral and religious lessons and exhortations. From the incident narrated, which is supposed to have been taken from Jewish history, the reader is to learn that the fear of the Lord is the highest wisdom, for He delivers His children in some wonderful way, though He may bring them for a time unto trial.

Its plot is as follows: Nebuchadnezzar, king of Assyria, decides to chastise the people of Palestine because they disobeyed his commands to furnish him with troops in his war against Arphaxad, king of Media. He sends his general, Holofernes, into Judea to carry out his command.

---

[3] Ch. XIV, 5 speaks of the Temple that will be built,—which really means the one that the author knew,—will be inferior to the First Temple, i. e. that of Solomon. The Temple spoken of as inferior could only be that of Zerubbabel which was rather a small affair. The Temple of Herod, on the other hand, was a wonderful structure surpassing the Solomonic in beauty and grandeur. Hence, we must conclude that the author did not see Herod's Temple, and consequently, the book was written before 20 B. C. E.

When the Jews hear of his approach, they all rally to offer resistance and decide to meet his forces at Bethulia, a fortress near Esdraelon. Holofernes then besieges Bethulia. After a short time, the distress in the city becomes acute, and a beautiful and pious widow, Judith, undertakes to save her people by an act of daring. She gains entrance into the enemy's camp and charms the very general with her beauty. After three days, she is invited to a banquet at which Holofernes drinks to excess, and she then finds her opportunity. Seizing his own scimitar, she cuts off his head and manages to escape from camp with her ghastly trophy. In the morning, when the enemy discovers the death of the general, they flee and are destroyed by the Jews. Judith is thus hailed as the deliverer of Israel.

The tendency of the book is clear. It was written for the purpose of arousing the spirit of nationalism and patriotism in a time of national calamity. The question arises as to its historicity, as the book is full of errors. It makes Nebuchadnezzar king of Assyria at a time when Assyria was no more in existence, since it speaks of the Jews as having just returned from captivity. Nor is the name of Bethulia ever found in the list of the cities of Palestine. Some scholars attempted to identify Nebuchadnezzar with Antiochus and Assyria with Syria, and believed the story to refer to Antiochus' persecution. Others advanced the theory that the work was suggested by the campaign of Artexerxes Ochus, 350 B. C. E., against Egypt and Palestine, conducted by two generals, Holofernes and Bagoas, who, likewise, play a part in the book of Judith. Be that as it may, it is most probable that the book was written not later than the last quarter of the second century B. C. E. as all circumstances indicate that it belongs to the Greek period. The book was written either in Hebrew or Aramaic. Jerome states in his preface to the Latin version of the book that he had before him an Aramaic text of which the Greek is a translation. The standpoint of the author is thoroughly Pharasaic, as Judith is praised for the scrupulous care she took with regard to food as well as other observances.

10. BEL AND THE DRAGON (Additions to Daniel)

There are a number of stories clustering around Daniel and the events related in the book bearing his name. They were supposed to be additions to the book and are really included in the Septuagint. To these additions belong also the two stories of Bel and the Dragon. The first tells how Daniel convinced Cyrus that it was foolish to worship the god

Bel who is merely an idol and not a living God. The king argued that Bel is a mighty and powerful god, for he consumes daily a vast amount of food placed on his table. Daniel undertook to prove to the king that it is not Bel who consumes this food but somebody else. He spread ashes on the floor of the temple, and in the morning the traces of many footsteps were clearly seen in them. This was sufficient proof that the priests entered through a secret passage together with their families and consumed Bel's food. Cyrus then praised Daniel for his wisdom and rewarded him with many gifts.

The second story tells how Daniel killed the Dragon, worshipped by the Persians, by means of a device and was thrown into the den of the lions as a punishment for his act. He was, however, rescued by an angel of God. Both stories were most likely written in Hebrew.

11. SUSANNA

The story of Susanna was placed in some editions of the Septuagint at the beginning of the Book of Daniel. It tells of a certain woman Susanna (Heb. Shoshanna) who was falsely accused of unchastity by two wicked elders of the community and was brought to trial and convicted, but the clever youth, Daniel, intervened and, by skillful examination of the witnesses, proved the falsity of the accusation. The scene is laid in Babylon in the days of captivity. The first half of the story is based on a certain tradition about two wicked elders in Babylon who practiced the seduction of women. Reference to this tradition is also found in the Talmud (Bab. Tal. Sanhedrin, 93a). The second half relates to the reform in the administration of justice which was a bone of contention between the Pharisees and Sadducees. The book was probably written between the years 90–60 B.C.E. in Hebrew or Aramaic.

12. ADDITIONS TO ESTHER

The "Additions to Esther" form a group of six passages intended as embellishments on the canonical Book of Esther, so as to make this important event in Jewish history fuller and more poetic. They were incorporated at an early time in the Septuagint version of the Book of Esther, and are still found in all Greek versions of the Bible. The old Latin Bible translation followed the Greek, and had these additions inserted in the book proper. But Jerome, in the Vulgate translation of the Old Testament, relegated them to the end of the book, numbering the passages as additional chapters of Esther from ten to sixteen, and ultimately, they were placed in the Apocrypha. Thus, they are found in the English version of the Apocrypha as a separate book, though still bearing the numbers of additional chapters to Esther, i. e. from ten to sixteen.

The content of the six passages is as follows: (*a*) In the first passage, we are told how Mordecai saw in his dream two dragons fighting and making great noise and tumult. At their cry, all nations prepared to battle against the righteous people. At the same time, darkness came upon the earth, but the righteous cried unto God and a little fountain spurted forth which ultimately turned into a flood, whereupon the darkness lifted, the sun rose, and the righteous were saved. Mordecai kept this dream in mind; the following night he overheard the conspiracy of two eunuchs planning to kill the king, and he informed the king of it. (This last part is told briefly in Esther Ch. II, 21–23 with slight variation.) This addition is prefixed in the Septuagint as an introduction to the Book of Esther. In the Vulgate and the English Apocrypha, it is numbered Chas. XI, XII.

(*b*) The second section contains the text of the edict of the king ordering, at the advice of Haman, the destruction of the Jews. In the Greek version, it follows Ch. III, verse 13 of Esther; in the Latin and English Apocrypha, it is Ch. XIII, verses 1–8.

(*c*) The third contains the prayers of Mordecai and Esther, which in the Greek follow Ch. IV, verse 17 of Esther, and in the Latin and English Apocrypha it is marked Ch. XIII, verses 8–18 and Ch. XIV.

(*d*) In the fourth, the appearance of Esther before the king is described which follows in the Septuagint Ch. V, 2 of Esther and is designated Ch. XV in the Apocrypha.

(*e*) This passage gives the text of the second edict of the king canceling his former order and decreeing the protection of the Jews. It is an addition to Ch. VIII of Esther and named Ch. XVI in the Apocrypha.

(*f*) In the last section, we are given the interpretation of the dream of Mordecai mentioned above, saying that the dragons symbolized Haman and himself, and the fountain which turned into a raging flood represented Esther. In the Septuagint, the passage follows Ch. X and is so numbered in the Apocrypha. It is therefore placed before the other passages, though it is really the last.

It is possible that these additions were written by different men. They seem to bear the marks of the time of the Maccabean revolt. There is a superscription in *a,* or Ch. XI, stating that these letters were in-

terpreted by Lysimachus, son of Ptolemy of Jerusalem, and were brought
to Egypt by Dositheus, a Levite and priest, in the fourth year of Ptolemy
and Cleopatra. As there were four kings who were named Ptolemy and
whose wives were named Cleopatra, the date cannot be ascertained.
It is quite evident that these additions were written in Greek. The
purpose was to add a more religious spirit to the rather prosaic and
secular Book of Esther.[4]

(c) PROPHETIC AND POETIC WRITINGS

13. PRAYER OF AZARIAH AND THE SONG OF THE THREE CHILDREN

This excellent hymn is known by various names. Some manuscripts
call it "The Hymn of the Father" and some "The Prayer of Azariah,"
and many call it "The Song of the Three Children." It is based on the
story told in the Book of Daniel (Ch. III, 12–30) of the three friends of
Daniel, Azariah, Ḥanania, and Mishoel, who were thrown into the fiery
furnace by Nebuchadnezzar for refusing to worship idols but were
saved by the intervention of angels sent by God. It forms one of the
additions to the canonical Book of Daniel and contains the prayer of
Azariah to God in the midst of the fiery furnace, an embellishment of
the story of their rescue, and also the song of praise of the three youths.
It is quite probable that the prayer and the song were written in Hebrew
as they really fit in with the text of Ch. III of Daniel. The date of
composition cannot be definitely determined, but from all indications,
we may probably assign it to the early Maccabean period, about 165
B. C. E.

14. PRAYER OF MANASSES

To this class belongs also the short penitential prayer ascribed to
Manasses, son of Hezekiah, king of Judah. Manasses is represented in
the second book of Kings as one of the worst rulers that ever reigned
over Judah, one who committed all kinds of crimes, idolatry and bloodshed included. But in II Chronicles (Ch. XXXIII, 12), it is told that the
armies of Assyria took him captive and brought him to Babylon where
he returned to the God of his fathers, and was reinstated in his kingship.

---

[4] The prosaic character of Esther is attested by the fact that the name of God is not
mentioned.

It seems that this prayer is based on the story told in II Chronicles and purports to be the very text used by Manasses in his plea to God. It consists of three parts: (a) Verses 1–7, a characterization of the God of Abraham, Isaac, and Jacob as one who is merciful and compassionate, who appointed repentance as a means by which sinners may be saved; (b) Verses 8–10, a confession of sin; (c) Verses 11–15, a plea for forgiveness.

Both the original language and the date cannot be determined definitely. Most scholars believe it was originally written in Greek and assign it a late date, even as late as 200 c. e. There are, however, a number who claim a Hebrew or Aramaic original, and believe its date to be the Maccabean period. There is much to be said in favor of this date; inasmuch as the burden of the prayer is a call to repentance, the Maccabean period would be the most suitable for such a call. It might have been written by a Palestinian Jew as a call to the Hellenist apostates to return to the God of their fathers, and Manasses was chosen as a typical penitent.

The later Agada retained a number of stories about the penitence of Manasses which fact shows that there were numerous legends current about him in Jewish circles. It is probable that they date from early times and that the prayer formed a part of the Manasses literature.

15. BOOK OF BARUCH

The Book of Baruch belongs to the prophetic class of this literature. Baruch, the disciple of Jeremiah, who seemed to have gone into exile, is the reputed author of the book. It falls into three parts: (a) Chas. I–III, 8; (b) Ch. III, 9–Ch. IV, 4; (c) Ch. IV, 5 to the end. The first part bears a superscription stating that Baruch wrote the book after the first capture of Jerusalem by the Chaldeans when Jeconiah was exiled. It was read in the presence of Jeconiah and the nobles in exile who then sent it to Jerusalem together with offerings, accompanied by a request that their confession be read on the feast day. In the second, the cause of Israel's suffering is set forth and a short eulogy of wisdom follows; the third part is a consolation to the exiles and a promise of hope and restoration.

The language of the original is a moot point among the scholars. Some claim that the whole book was written in Greek, some admit that Hebrew was the original of part one, but assert that the other two parts were written in Greek. They thus assume a double authorship. Others, though, claim a Hebrew original for the entire book. The last opinion is the most probable. Likewise, there is a difference of opinion among scholars as to its date. Some say that it was composed early in the Maccabean period about 150 B. C. E., while others place it after the destruction of the Second Temple, arguing that the state of desolation in Jerusalem mentioned in part I symbolizes the destruction of Jerusalem by the Romans. But the arguments are not well founded and we may allow the earlier date to stand.

16. THE EPISTLE OF JEREMY

The letter which was supposed to have been written by the prophet Jeremiah to the exiles in Babylon is usually joined in the English version of the Apocrypha to the Book of Baruch as its sixth chapter, but it is really a separate composition and was always considered as such.

Its content is as follows: Jeremiah tells the exiles that they were driven out of Palestine because of their sins and that they will remain in Babylon for seven generations. He then warns them against the idolatry of their masters lest they be led to follow the ways of the pagans. With the warning as a starting point, he launches a bitter diatribe against idols and their worshippers. This satire against paganism seems to be the burden of the writer.

As for the date and original language of the work, there is a variety of opinion. One view is that it was written in Greek, in Alexandria, as an attack against heathenism and places its date about 70 B. C. E. But of late, scholars have advanced proofs for a Hebrew original and are inclined to fix its date at the end of the fourth century B. C. E. According to this point of view, the Babylon referred to is the actual Babylon, and the letter itself was addressed by a Palestinian sage to the Jews of Babylon to warn them against assimilation. Against this quite plausible theory, there militates the fact that the theme of the letter is not so much the warning to the Jews as the satire against heathenism which occupies the bulk of the Epistle (Verse 8–73 to the end). It should, therefore, be considered rather as a Jewish polemic against paganism which was more appropriate in Greek. The place of composition was probably Alexandria and the time the first half of the first century B. C. E., when the Jews began to assert themselves not only by defending Judaism but also by attacking the religion of their neighbors.

(d) DIDACTIC BOOKS

17. WISDOM OF JOSHUA, SON OF SIRACH (Ecclesiasticus)

"The Wisdom of Joshua, Son of Sirach," perhaps the most famous of the Apocrypha, belongs to that species of Jewish literature known as Wisdom writing. Three of such books, Proverbs, Job, and Ecclesiastes are included in the Old Testament canon. A few words about the Jewish conception of wisdom will, therefore, not be amiss. Wisdom, or *Hokmah,* to the Jews never meant philosophy in the Greek sense. It never dealt with pure metaphysical problems but has a wider, and in a way a double, meaning. On the one hand, it is primarily a philosophy of life, purporting to teach and guide the individual. On the other hand, it also represents or rather symbolizes the World Reason which is reflected in the creative work of God, that of life and nature. As such, it not only includes the order and harmony evidenced in life and nature, but is even more, their very source.

In this role, *Hokmah* is very often hypostatized, i.e. personified, and is given almost the guise of a personality which was present even before the creation of the world, as it says of itself, "Before the mountains were established, before the hills, was I brought forth" (Prov. VIII, 25). Of course, it is not an independent being; like all things, it is created by God, His first creation, as it continues, "Then I was by Him as one brought up with Him and I was daily His delight" (ibid. vs., 30).

But, in this form, man is unable to grasp it fully, for as it is said in Job (XXVIII, 12), "But where shall wisdom be found and where is the place of understanding?" Only God Himself knows it. What is left for man to do is to follow that kind of wisdom which is within his grasp, i.e. the fear of the Lord, "For this is wisdom, and turning away from evil is understanding" (ibid. XXVIII). Wisdom, therefore, becomes, as indicated, a philosophy of life, or still better, a means of education, not only for the child but for man and woman during their entire life. As such, the current of wisdom which flowed in Jewish literature besides the prophetic and strictly religious one, becomes an all-inclusive director of life and moral guide as well as a practical counselor in all other forms of life. Wisdom is supposed not only to show the path of good and evil, but also to lead to actual happiness. In this multifarious teaching, wisdom literature made use of the *Mashal,* the pointed pithy saying which has the simile for its basis and is easily remembered. By means of this device, it made observations on all matters of life, primarily on the life of the individual. Biblical wisdom literature is permeated by a broad humanitarian spirit, giving advice on matters pertaining to all phases of life, and is thus of an almost international character. Typical of this literature are the Proverbs of Solomon.

Similar in manner and tone to the Biblical Wisdom books are the two Apocryphal books, Ecclesiasticus and "The Wisdom of Solomon." The first one represents the more practical and moral side of wisdom, while the second, the religious—theologic and philosophic one.

In Ecclesiasticus, or "The Wisdom of Joshua, the Son of Sirach," Wisdom becomes identified with the Law, the Torah; the highest, most perfect wisdom rests in God, and man's wisdom consists in trusting and obeying Him. Yet, while this is the substratum of the book, the content is varied and broadly humanitarian. The Proverbs of Solomon are taken as the model, but in view of the fact that the age of Sirach represented a richer and fuller life, more advanced in culture, the book reflects many more phases of life, and the picture drawn in it is many-colored. We will now turn to the author and the book. The name of the author is given by all translators, Greek, Syriac, etc., as Joshua, the son of Sirach, although it is stated in many manuscripts that he was the son of Eliezer who was the son of Sirach. But he has gone down to tradition by the name of Sirach or ben Sira in Hebrew.

The age of the author and the date of the composition of the book can be determined, unlike other Apocryphal books, with definiteness. His grandson, who translated the book into Greek, states in his prologue to the translation that he completed it in the year 132 B.C.E. We can, therefore, suppose with certainty that his grandfather lived about the beginning of that century, and that the book was composed between the years 190–175 B.C.E. Joshua ben Sira was a scholar (Sofer), and as evidenced from the book, conducted a kind of college at his house of study where people came to drink of his wisdom. He was at the same time a man of the world and traveled much in his youth. In his age, the Jews came in contact with Greek culture, and many of them, saturated with that culture, became Hellenized and followed a life of pleasure with all its attendant consequences—laxity of morals, and loosening of family bonds, as well as neglect of social responsibility. Against all these evils, the book was intended. It purports to give a program in life which was intended as an antidote against Hellenism.

The outline of the book can be roughly given as follows:

Ch. I, 20, Prologue on wisdom and religion.

I, 21–IV, 11, On the conduct of the individual with relation to parents and society, and against pride.

IV, 12–VII, On steadfastness of character and praise of wisdom.

VIII–IX, On friends, family, and relation to tyrants.

X–XI, On wisdom and government.

XII–XV, On friendship false and true, and choice of action.

XVI–XVIII, On God and His providence.

XIX–XX, On carefulness in speech.

XXI–XXIII, On the evils of foolishness and anger.

XXIV, On wisdom.

XXV–XXVI, On women.

XXVII–XXIX, On greediness, right conduct in business and quarrelsomeness.

XXX–XXXI, On education, poverty, and riches.

XXXII, On feasts and song.

XXXIII, On the righteous.

XXXIV–XXXV, On duties to God.

XXXVI–XXXVII, On prayer, friends, and counselors.

XXXVIII–XLII, On life and death, and the value and uses of physicians.

XLIII–XLIX, A didactic sketch of early Jewish history.

L, A eulogy of the High Priest, Simon, the son of Onias, named The Just.

LI, the final chapter, closes the book with a beautiful prayer.

"The Wisdom of Ben Sira" was written in Hebrew, but the original was lost and the book came down to us in Greek. The Hebrew, however, was preserved for many centuries longer than the original of other books. Recently, a large portion of the Hebrew original was restored to us through the efforts of the late Dr. Solomon Schechter, who discovered these fragments in the Genizah at Cairo, Egypt, in the year 1897.

"The Wisdom of Ben Sira" forms an exception to the other Apocryphal books, inasmuch as it exerted a great influence on later Jewish literature. In spite of the fact that the later Babylonian scholar, Rab Joseph, included it among the other Apocryphal books, the reading of which was prohibited by Rabbi Akiba,[5] the book was assiduously

---

[5] *Tal B. Sanhedrin* 99b.

studied by the Talmudic scholars. The leading *Tannaim* and *Amoraim* quote his sayings. There are more than twenty proverbs of ben Sira cited in the Babylonian and Palestinian Talmuds, as well as Midrashic collections under his name, and double that number are given anonymously. Some of the quotations are even introduced by the formula usually applied to quotations from the Bible, namely, "It is written." In two places, Ben Sira is actually called *Ketubim,* the name given to the Hagiographa, the third division of the canon.

All this shows that the words of Rab Joseph were never taken seriously, and that Ecclesiasticus, both in its Hebrew and Aramaic versions, was held in great esteem by the Talmudic authorities and Agadists. In post-Talmudic literature, the sayings of Ben Sira are quoted frequently. We may add that in numerous quotations, the book is called *Mishlé Ben Sira* (The Parables or Proverbs of Ben Sira) which was undoubtedly its original Hebrew name.

18. THE WISDOM OF SOLOMON

The book called "The Wisdom of Solomon," which in common with other books of this literature, belongs to the pseudepigraphic class, namely, those that bear the name of an ancient authority as their author, resembles very closely the nature and character of its predecessor, "The Wisdom of Joshua, Son of Sirach." But, being of a later age and the product of a soil more saturated with Hellenic culture, it displays evidence of a marked influence of that culture. The fact that the author was extensively acquainted with Greek philosophy is borne out almost in every chapter. It represents the first attempt at a blending of Greek philosophy with the Jewish spirit, yet the blending is far from complete; it is still mainly a product of Jewish wisdom.

The author of "The Wisdom of Solomon," like Ben Sira, glorifies wisdom, and like him, and even in a greater degree, he considers wisdom the daughter of God, nay, even His very reflection and glory. The book, however, possesses a different tone from "The Wisdom of Ben Sira," for while the author of the former devotes himself primarily to describing the conduct of the wise men in different circumstances of life, the author of "The Wisdom of Solomon" is primarily interested in warning people against the folly of ungodliness, especially that of idolatry. The book contains also special discourses on the righteous and the wicked which are intended to inculcate the theory of reward and punishment after death, thus answering the vexing question why the wicked prosper and the righteous suffer. Yet, ungodliness seems to be its main theme. On account of his peculiar treatment of the themes in the book, the author does not adhere strictly to the prescribed form of proverb and pithy sayings, but passes often into that of connected discourse.

The book falls into three parts: The first part, Chas. I–VI, 8 deals with eschatology, namely, the doctrine of the last things, and as stated, is devoted to inculcating the belief in immortality and reward and punishment. The second part, VI, 9–X, is devoted to the glorification of wisdom. In this part, Solomon is supposed to address himself to the potentates of the world, telling them of the beauties and the glories of wisdom. Wisdom becomes here almost an independent personality by the side of God. It is, "A breath of God's power, a brightness of the everlasting light" (VII, 25, 26). It is almost intrinsically united with God, initiated into His knowledge and a chooser of His works. It is thus represented not only as the special instrument of God in ordering things in the world but also as His assistant, though originating from His very nature (Ch. VIII, 1; IX, 2). The third part, XI–XIX, is a philosophic moral Midrash, i. e. interpretation of the history of Israel with relation to the rule of wisdom, showing how wisdom and the providence of God have guided the destinies of the Jews as well as that of other nations. And from these events, the author draws conclusions as to the blessings of godliness and the curse of ungodliness. A long discourse on the folly of idolatry is inserted here (XIII–XV). This discourse possesses special interest on account of its theory on the origin of idolatry which reminds us of the Spencerian account of the origin of religion (XIV, 4–24). In this book, we find also an attempt to personify the almighty word of God, an attempt which later bore fruit in the Logos theory of Philo as well as in the Christian Apocalypse (IX, 1; XVI, 12; XVIII, 15).

The influence of Greek philosophy is evidenced not only in the application of the above epithets to wisdom, but also in the enumeration of the four cardinal virtues, temperance, prudence, justice, and fortitude, advocated by the Stoics (VIII, 7). The psychology taught by the author seems to be Platonic, inasmuch as we are told that the soul of man is preëxistent, and that if it is good, it enters an undefiled body. The body is considered by him only as a tabernacle for the soul.

The date can be fixed at some point between the years 125–100 B. C. E., and Greek was the original language, as it was undoubtedly written

by an Alexandrian Jew. Many prominent scholars claim double authorship for our book, assigning part III to a different writer. But this
question is still a moot one, and this theory cannot be said to possess
absolute certainty.

19. IV MACCABEES

To the class of philosophic and didactic Apocryphal books belongs
also the book called IV Maccabees. In its form it is really a discourse, as
the author himself states in his opening sentence that he is going to
demonstrate that pious reason is the absolute ruler over motives and
passions. He continues to tell us that by obeying reason, man cannot
only control his passions but also his emotions if they happen to be
contrary to justice. He endeavors to prove his thesis by citing facts from
Jewish history, especially the martyrdom of Eliezer and that of the
seven brethren, the very same stories related in the second book of the
Maccabees. Naturally, a large portion of the contents of the book is
devoted to the description of the martyrdom of these heroes.

It is quite evident that the author is greatly influenced by Stoicism,
as it is the Stoic morality, the rule of reason over impulse, which he
teaches. But he also deviates from Stoic teaching, inasmuch as it is not
merely reason which holds sway over passion, but pious reason, namely,
that reason which guides man to the obedience of the divine law. The
author is very close to Pharisaism, and extols the virtues of the seven
martyred brothers in their adherence to ceremonial law. He also emphasizes the theory of resurrection, but his view is somewhat different
from the current one, namely, that it amounts to eternal and blessed
life in Heaven. In this book, we likewise find the doctrine that the
martyrdom of the righteous serves as an atonement for the sins of the
generation, a view which was later adopted also in the Talmud.

IV Maccabees was most likely written in Greek at the beginning of
the first century of the common era, about the year 10 c.e.

APOCALYPTIC LITERATURE

20. GENERAL CHARACTERISTICS

We now come to the class of books which are usually called
Apocalyptic-pseudepigraphic. The first title, as stated above, explains
the chief characteristic of their form, namely, that of revelation, for,
as we already know, Apocalypse is only another term for revelation.

The author in these books is not supposed to speak his own mind, but only what is revealed to him either by direct vision, i. e. by communion with the spirit of God, or through the medium of an angel or through both. The second title is given to them on account of the fact that the revelation was not made to the real author but to a fictitious one, to one of the ancient heroes or saints of Israel. This false authorship was used for the purpose of giving to the utterings more authority, and hence the title pseudepigraphic.

Their contents deal mainly with the Eschatology—the doctrine of last things which includes the problems discussed above (Sec. 3)—the immortality of the soul of the individual after death, the Messiah, the Day of Judgment, and the new world which will come after the destruction of this world. But the dominant note in Apocalyptic literature is the problem of suffering in its double aspect, both of the individual and the nation. It can, however, be said that this literature is, or was originally at least, not as much interested in the problem of the individual Job as in that of the national Job. In other words, it deals primarily with the Job of the nations, the people of Israel. While the problem of the individual Job was more or less definitely settled by the doctrine of immortality and reward and punishment after death which was, by the second century B. C. E., almost generally accepted by the majority of the people and tacitly assumed by the Apocryphal books, the national Job problem, due to the condition of the times, assumed with every passing year a graver aspect. In time, people began to question why does this righteous nation, God's chosen one, suffer, while impious and wicked nations prosper? How long will this state continue? Of course, there was an old solution to this problem—the Messiah of the Prophets. But that Messiah has delayed his coming and something had to be done to strengthen the belief in his coming and supply it with a lasting hold upon the minds of the people. An ordinary Messiah, i. e. merely a king or a ruler, who rules his people or even a large part of the world with justice and bestows prosperity upon the nations, would not do. This Messiah ought to be a superhuman being, all powerful, whose coming should be heralded by an entirely new era. This world with its iniquity and impiety cannot be redeemed; it must be done away with altogether and a new one take its place. Thus, the whole idea was embellished and a new glamour was given to it. In addition, the craving for revenge, for retribution to the wicked and impious nations, enhanced the idea of a Day of Judgment.

But the seed imbedded in the tendency to exalt the Messiah bore exotic fruit. The investment of the Messiah with a supernatural character and the emphasizing of the new era and the Day of Judgment set in motion a mystic current, which affected both the destiny of the martyred nation and the suffering righteous. The happy days promised by the Messianic prophecies for Israel as a whole were gradually replaced by promises for the righteous only, and the righteous became the salt of the earth. This led to an identification and coalescence of the righteous man with the righteous nation. The righteous nation will consist of righteous men only, and the new world era of the righteous nation together with the resurrection will be only for the select, (Zaddikim) the righteous.

Once this current of mysticism and spiritualization set in, there was no way to stem it or control it. In time, the process of spiritualization was carried to the extreme. Material elements in the Messianic era were dropped altogether, and complete life in eternity and spiritual bliss took their place. From this conception to dropping nationality altogether and placing the righteous individual on the throne in the kingdom of God is but a succession of steps, and thus we have the curious phenomenon of a movement arising as a solution to a national problem ending by eliminating nationalism altogether.

We have outlined as briefly as possible in a general survey the contents of this literature. We will now examine its most important representative books, a list of which is hereby given.

21. THE JEWISH APOCALYPTIC BOOKS

1) Book of Enoch	6) Assumption of Moses
2) The Book of Jubilees	7) 2 or 4 Ezra (Esdras)
3) Testaments of the Twelve Patriarchs	8) Book of Adam and Eve
4) Psalms of Solomon	9) Slavonic Enoch
5) Apocalypse of Baruch	10) Sibylline Oracles

22. THE BOOK OF ENOCH

The Book of Enoch is not only the oldest of the Apocalyptic works but probably the most important one. It is not a homogeneous work but a collection of books all bearing the name Enoch as their author, though, in reality, emanating from the hands of different authors. The choice of Enoch as the supposed author of these heterogeneous writings is to be explained by the fact that the interpretation of the words in Genesis V, 24, "And Enoch walked with God, and he was not, for God took him," to mean that Enoch was translated to Heaven during his lifetime, was current among the Jews in very early times. This situation made Enoch the proper author of books where Apocalypses and prophecies regarding the last judgment, as well as an interpretation of the entire history are stated and discussed. He, who was a righteous man and who later became an angel, was the person to whom all secrets were to be entrusted. And accordingly, all these things are found in the books of Enoch.

What goes now under the name of the Book of Enoch is divided into the following sections or books: (*1*) Chas. I–XXXVI; (*2*) Chas. XXXVII–LXXI; (*3*) Chas. LXXII–LXXXII; (*4*) Chas. LXXXIII–XC; (*5*) Chas. XCI–CIV; (*6*) Chas. CV–CIX is an appendix containing extracts from an older book of Noah.

Book I opens with a description of the impending Day of Judgment, and how the earth will tremble when God will appear to judge it. It then calls upon sinners to observe the order of nature and how regularly it is carried on, and reproaches them for not having pursued the proper course of action. Doom is therefore promised to the wicked, but long life, gladness, and continuous peace to the righteous. These utterings are contained in the first seven chapters which seem to be an introduction to the whole book, for the Day of Judgment is one of the central ideas of this collection of writings. We meet with it again and again in every section of the book, no matter how different the contents may otherwise be.

In subsequent chapters, the history of sin in the world is related. It originated according to this book in the fall of the angels. The story runs that the angels under the leadership of *Semhazai,* according to one source, or *Azael* according to another, or under both, saw the daughters of men and lusted after them, and decided to descend to the earth and enjoy their company. They accordingly did so, and giant children were born unto them. These giants committed much sin, and the angels, having been disgraced by their action, stayed on earth and taught men the art of metal making and sword manufacturing, and women the art of making cosmetics and their sinful use. Thus, sin and bloodshed multiplied in the world. God then decided to bring the flood to cleanse the earth of sin and sent the angel, Raphael, to bind the leaders of the fallen *watchers* (another name for the fallen angels) and chain them to rocks to await the Day of Judgment (Chas. VII–XII). In the following chapters, Enoch comes to the fore; he is translated into Heaven and sees two visions. In the first, he tells how the *watchers* ask him to intercede on their behalf before God. He accedes to their request and presents their petition for reinstatement, but it is rejected and their doom is announced. In the second vision, Enoch is conducted through the universe; he sees everything, the pillars of the earth, the abode of the winds, visits *Sheol,* and sees spirits of men, both of the righteous who wait for reward and the wicked who wait for judgment. He even sees Paradise, as well as the accursed valley destined for the punishment of the wicked. He finally sees the abode of the stars, the portals whence they issue to run their course, as well as that of rain and dew. And thus the book ends. The story of the fall of the angels is based upon a very early interpretation of Genesis VI, 2–4, where it is briefly told how the *Benē Elohim*—literally sons of God— saw the comely daughters of men, and chose wives for themselves, of which union giants and mighty men were born—which interpretation took the words *Benē Elohim* to mean angels—[6] and hence the story of their fall.

The second section of the book (Chas. XXXVII–LXXI) is called the "Book of Parables," as it consists of three parables or visions. They deal practically with the same problem, namely, why there is so much sin in the world, and why the wicked prosper and how long that state will last. The answer runs on lines similar to that of the first book. Sin is traced again to the rebellious angels who led men astray, but were punished and are still awaiting greater punishment on the Day of Judgment. Sin continues to flourish in the world, but God or as the book calls Him, the Lord of Spirits, or the Head of Days—a name already mentioned in Daniel—will appear, and with Him the Son of Man, i. e. the Messiah, who preëxists in the world from eternity, and to him God will commit all the sinners for judgment. The *Son of Man* will judge all beings, from angels to men; he will slay the sinners with the word of his mouth, and will banish wickedness from the face of the

---

[6] The adopted Jewish tradition, however, interpreted the words *Benē Elohim* to mean simply sons of great men, or sons of the mighty. Thus, the Aramaic translation known as Onkelos, which is the standard authorized Jewish translation as it was approved of by great scholars at Jabne (90 c. e. see Ch. IV), rendered these words: The sons of the great (Benē Rabrebaia).

earth forever. The righteous and the elect of the past ages will be resurrected and together with the living righteous will enjoy both material prosperity and spiritual bliss forever.

The third section (Chas. LXXII–LXXXII) is primarily an astronomical treatise on the course of the sun, moon, and the stars. The secret of the movements of the luminaries are revealed to Enoch, who sees with his own eyes their very course, even the portals through which they enter and issue forth, in order that he may transmit this knowledge to future generations. The calendar spoken of in this book is rather a peculiar one. The author knows the difference between the lunar year of 354 days and the solar year, yet he fixes the length of the year to be 364 days instead of 365¼. As for adjusting the difference of ten days between the lunar and solar years, he seems to add to each year ten days, instead of the accepted Jewish method of adding a whole month at certain intervals.

The fourth section (Chas. LXXXIII–XC) runs along lines laid down in the first two books dealing with the problem of sin and suffering of Israel, except that it deals with them in a more concrete fashion, inasmuch as the entire history up to the time of the writer is recounted in an Apocalyptic manner. The section is divided into two visions. In the first one, Enoch recounts to his son, Methuselah, what he saw regarding the impending deluge. In the second one, the history of the world is told in a series of dramatic conflicts, but these conflicts take place among animals instead of among men. The participants are bulls, rams, and sheep as well as lions and tigers. The sheep, of course, represent Israel. The history of the sheep is told in detail, their suffering is due partly to their own sin, but primarily to the sin of seventy shepherds who were appointed to guard them. It is rather an obscure symbol, and we do not know who these seventy shepherds are, but most likely they are angels. At any rate, these shepherds proved faithless, and the flocks suffered. But the day of delivery is near; there is a family in Israel from whom a deliverer will come. The sheep turn against their assailants, and a long sword is given to them. Then the future is depicted in the usual glowing colors: God will appear, the shepherds will be judged, a new Jerusalem will be set up by God Himself, and the righteous will be raised up; the Messiah will then appear, and the age of bliss will begin.

The last section (Chas. XCI–CIV) takes no account of the origin of sin and seems to be devoted primarily to the problem of the suffering of the righteous and the prosperity of the oppressing sinners. The sinners here are represented as a party in Israel who falsify the sacred writings and deny God's providence over men. They oppress the party of the righteous, but their deeds are recorded and their punishment will come immediately after death in hell. Then follows a description of the Messianic kingdom, which differs considerably from the previous conception. The Messianic age is only preliminary to the final judgment. This age will last for a period of time, designated by the author as two world weeks, for he divides the entire time of the world into ten weeks. At the end of this time, the final judgment will take place, and then will follow the creation of a new earth and the resurrection of the righteous. The resurrected will live as spirits and angels, and not as mortals.

The dates of the various sections are approximately as follows: the first section is the oldest, and was written before the Maccabean period about 170 B.C.E.; this was succeeded by the fourth about 165–161 and followed by the third about 110. The second and the fifth sections were written most probably between the years 95–64 B.C.E. The original language of the books was Hebrew, and only a small portion was written in Aramaic. The Greek translation was lost, and it was preserved only in an Ethiopic version which is a translation of the Greek. The central ideas of the books of Enoch are the Day of Judgment, the conceptions of the Messianic age, and of the end of days. As regards the latter, there are different currents noticeable. In the first section, there is redemption but no personal Messiah. In the second and fourth sections, a Messiah appears, but in the former he is endowed with a supernatural character, while in the latter he is more human. Likewise, there are differences in the conception of the Messianic kingdom or the kingdom of God. According to the first section, it will be established on earth with Jerusalem as a center, while according to the last, the Messianic kingdom is only preliminary to the eternal spiritual kingdom which will last forever. We see here already the beginning of the conflict between these two conceptions as to the future, the one, more nationalistic, the other, a more spiritual and universal one. We will meet again and again these two conflicting views in other Apocalyptic books, and traces of this conflict are also found in the Jewish Agadic literature.

23. THE BOOK OF JUBILEES

The "Book of Jubilees," which also goes under the name of "Little Genesis" is a very interesting book. Its first name is given to it because the author uses as the chronology, for the period it covers, the system of jubilees. Each jubilee consists of forty-nine years which is again divided into seven year weeks, each year representing a day in that week. The second name is applied to it on account of the fact that it is primarily a supplement to the Biblical book of Genesis, as well as to a part of Exodus.

Its contents are supposed to have been dictated by an angel of the Presence (the highest order of angels, namely, those who are always in the presence of God) to Moses, on his ascension on Mount Sinai, and given a brief survey of the destinies of Israel in the future. The book is intended to be the secret version of the history of Israel up to the time of the giving of the Law, which supplements the revealed history related in Genesis and part of Exodus, and it was supposed to be handed down from father to son until the time of its publication.

The "Book of Jubilees" consists of two elements, the homiletic narrative and Apocalyptic, but the first element predominates. It constitutes the first attempt at systematizing the various Agadic legends and stories which began to crystallize in early times around the personages of the Patriarchs, heroes, and events related in the Bible. For this purpose, all the events from creation to the giving of the Law are told as they are found in the Bible with slight omissions, but with a lot of detail and embellishments and additional stories explaining certain apparent contradictions and inconsistencies. Thus, we are supplied with a detailed list of the other children of Adam, the names of the wives of Cain and Seth, also those of the wives of the sons of Jacob as well as other names of Biblical personages not mentioned in the Bible. We also find there detailed accounts of the building of the Tower of Babel and its destruction, of the lives of Adam, Abraham, Isaac, and Jacob, descriptions of the wars between the children of Jacob and the children of Esau, as well as between them and the kings of the Amorites. The love of the author for detail may be seen in the fact that he gives the exact date of each event, such as the day of the month on which each of the sons of Jacob was born and many other dates.

But besides these embellishments, the author has another and a higher purpose in mind, and that is the glorification of the Law. Whether he meant to fend off the attacks made by the Hellenists against the Law, or for some other reason, he teaches everlasting validity of the Law and asserts that it has been observed from eternity. The Law, according to him, was observed in its most important parts at all times in Heaven. Thus, the two highest orders of angels were created circumcised, likewise, the Sabbath was observed in Heaven by God and by the same orders of angels long before its observation was ordained to the Jews. Similarly, many other laws which were given to the Jews by Moses were observed previously by Adam, Enoch, Noah, and the Patriarchs. The law regarding purification after childbirth was instituted immediately after the creation of Adam and Eve, and the law of Jubilees was enacted by Enoch. Again, Noah was commanded to institute The Feast of Weeks (Shabuot) as well as that of the New Moon (Rosh Hodesh); Abraham observed the Feast of Tabernacles (Succot) and the giving of tithes; penalties for incestuous relations were enacted yet in the time of Jacob and Judah as well as for intermarriage with heathens. Levi was called to the priesthood by Jacob, and in this manner many more laws are traced to early times. In the description of these laws, there is observed the spirit of a rigorous Halakah, though we find there a good number of deviations from the Halakah embodied in the Mishnah.

The Apocalyptic element is quite considerable—angels and demons predominate and abound in the world. The story of the fall of the angels and their teaching of sin to the children of man is referred to. The future is pictured in a manner which we meet with quite frequently in other Apocalyptic books. The Messiah will come to Judah, but no supernatural characteristics are attributed to him. The Messianic era will be realized on earth and at that time there will be a physical and ethical transformation; pain and sin will disappear and man will live a thousand years in happiness, and after death gain immortality.

The date of the book can be almost definitely determined to be between the years 135–105 B. C. E. in the heyday of the Maccabean dynasty, namely, the reign of John Hyrcanus, as reference to the high priest being civil ruler is made, and a time of peace and prosperity is implied, and no reference to party strife between the Sadducees and Pharisees is mentioned. The original language was undoubtedly Hebrew, but that version was lost, and even the Greek translation disappeared, and like the Book of Enoch, it was preserved in the Ethiopic. The Book of Jubilees exerted great influence on later Jewish literature. Many of its stories are incorporated in later Agadic collections, and its remarks are other-

66999

FERNALD LIBRARY
COLBY-SAWYER COLLEGE
NEW LONDON, N. H. 03257

wise quoted in a number of small Midrashim. According to one source,[7] a Hebrew copy under the name of *Sefer* ha-*Yoblot* (Book of Jubilees) was still extant in the time of Saadia (tenth century).

24. THE TESTAMENTS OF THE TWELVE PATRIARCHS

The value of the book, The Testaments of the Twelve Patriarchs, or rather the collection of little books consists not so much in its Apocalyptic character as in its ethical nature, for it contains primarily exhortations and admonitions to follow in the way of righteousness and warnings to abstain from sin. These twelve Patriarchs are the twelve children of Jacob who are represented as imparting to their children before death moral testaments and ethical injunctions. In this work, there are many Christian interpolations as there are references to an incarnated Messiah, but the work is undoubtedly genuinely Jewish and was written in Hebrew. As said, it is a collection of twelve little books, one for each of the Patriarchs, yet they evidently come from one hand, as there is quite a marked uniformity in their makeup.

In each of these testaments, three different elements may be distinguished. The first one is the rehearsal by the Patriarch of the history of his own life, in which, on the one hand, he confesses his sins, and on the other hand, glorifies his virtues. These stories are very interesting in themselves, as they represent the early Agada, the folk embellishments of the lives of the Biblical heroes. We find there, therefore, a large number of details concerning the lives of the twelve children of Jacob. The second element is the moral which each Patriarch draws from his life. He exhorts his descendants to beware of that sin which was the cause of deep distress to him, and recommends them to follow and imitate his virtuous life.

The third element is the Apocalyptic. At the end of each of these Testaments, there are found certain predictions regarding the future of that particular tribe, as each Testament is addressed to one tribe by its Patriarch, e. g. Reuben or Simon, etc. In these predictions punishments for apostasies is foretold, their exile is described, and the destruction of the Temple is mentioned. They are also warned not to sever their connections with the tribes of Levi and Judah, one representing the priesthood and the other the regal power. Finally, the predictions contain numerous references to a Messiah.

[7] Commentary on Chronicles, Ch. XXIII, 3, by one of the pupils of Saadia quoted by A. Epstein in his introduction to *Midrash Tadshe,* p. 7.

These last predictions have an interesting feature. It seems that the Messiah is not to come from Judah, as all Messianic utterances have always predicted, but from Levi. However, there are also in the same book allusions to the Messiah from Judah. These contradicting statements are to be explained by the fact that the greater part of the book was written during the time of John Hyrcanus, the illustrious Maccabean prince, when he was still a Pharisee. The author looked upon him as the chosen Messiah and promised him a glorious future—hence, the Messiah from Levi, for John was a priest. But soon John broke with the Pharisees, and his descendants were far from being ideal pious Jews. The Maccabean high priests could not have become the desired Messiah, and therefore, the later additions to the Testaments reverted to the traditional Messiah from Judah. The date of the book is accordingly clearly determined. The original was written during the years 109–106 B.C.E., while the additions were written 75–50 B.C.E.

The ethical teachings of the book are of great importance. They exhibit noble sentiments on social relations, and it is quite evident that some of the plumes with which the New Testament adorns itself are borrowed from this source. Testament of Gad, Ch. VI, 3–7 reads as follows: "Love ye one another from the heart, and if a man sin against thee, cast forth the poison of hate and speak peacefully to him, and in thy soul hold not guile; and if he confess and repent, forgive him. But if he deny it, do not get into a passion with him, lest catching the poison from thee, he take to swearing and so thou sin doubly. And though he deny it, and yet have a sense of shame when reproved, give over reproving him. For he who denieth may repent, so as not again to wrong thee; yea, he may also honor and be at peace with thee. But if he be shameless and persist in his wrong doing, even so forgive him from the heart and leave to God the avenging." On comparing the passages in Matthew, Ch. VI, 12-15, or Ch. XVIII, 15-17, 35, with other passages, we can notice almost direct borrowing. Here forgiveness becomes synonymous with banishing personal resentment when wrong is done to one. The injunction, "Thou shalt love thy neighbor as thyself," which was supposed by some to be a Christian improvement upon Leviticus Ch. XIX, 18, inasmuch as it is said there, "Thy friend," is also found in the Testament Issachar Ch. V, 2 and VII, 6 in this wording. There is also no condemnation of the Gentile; their righteous will share in the glory of the Messiah. (Testament of Benjamin, Ch. V, 2-5.)

The ideas on resurrection also display some peculiarities. There is to be a gradual resurrection, first of the heroes of the Old Testament, and then of all the righteous, and finally also of the wicked. There is no new world spoken of. The earth will be the scene of the Messianic age, but the kingdom of the Messiah will last forever.

25. THE PSALMS OF SOLOMON

This collection of eighteen Psalms possesses great interest for everyone who seeks to penetrate into the soul of the pious Jew in a time of great religious fermentation, namely, the first half of the first century before the common era, and fathom its depths. Somebody has named these Psalms, the Psalms of a Pharisee. We find in them not only a soul-stirring yearning for God, but also a high moral tone, glorification of the Law, and insistence on its scrupulous observance. The Psalms denounce the last Maccabean princes, who "despise the Law" by allying themselves with the Sadducees. They tell of their punishment by God in bringing a strange man from a strange land who was not of the race of Israel, and that he struck a mighty blow at them. That this refers to Pompey, there is no doubt, for we are told that the dragon which had conquered Jerusalem was itself put to death at the seashore in Egypt (Ps. II).

It is no wonder then that there is an urgent desire for a Messiah and the belief is expressed that this Messiah will come from the House of David. There is also reference to the resurrection of the righteous, but they rise not in order to enjoy the material blessings of the Messianic kingdom but for eternal life in the spirit.

The original language was undoubtedly Hebrew, but like the others it was lost, and it is found now only in Greek. The date of its composition as indicated by references to the events of the times can be quite definitely determined. The Psalms were written between the years 63–40 B. C. E.

26. THE APOCALYPSE OF BARUCH

This Apocalypse is a beautiful and noble reflection of the feelings of the faithful Jews at the time of the destruction of the Temple and immediately after, and of what they thought of this catastrophe and how they looked towards the future. It is ascribed to Baruch, son of Nereiah, disciple of Jeremiah, and is divided into seven sections: (*1*) Chas. I–XII; (*2*) Chs. XIII–XX; (*3*) XXI–XXXIV; (*4*) XXXV–XLVI; (*5*) XLVII–LII; (*6*) LIII–LXXVI; (*7*) LXXVII–LXXXVIII.

In section I, Baruch describes the destruction of Jerusalem by the Chaldeans—it refers, of course, to the First Temple, since Baruch is the supposed writer. He tells us, however, that the Chaldeans did not really conquer the city nor burn the Temple. This work was done by four angels, who took good care to bury the most holy vessels so that they should not be profaned by the enemy. Only after the angels had deserted the city, the enemy entered and fire broke out in the Temple. The exiles are carried away and—contrary to Jeremiah XL, 2-4, according to which Jeremiah, who was among the exiles, returned to Palestine, —Jeremiah goes with them to Babylon while Baruch stays in Jerusalem to comfort the people.

In the second section, Baruch has a vision, wherein he is commanded to fast seven days, and then appear before God. After he has done so, he pours forth his complaint at the evil that has befallen his people, and asks the pertinent question: "Why do men depart while the world which was supposed to have been created for their sake stands?" He is informed of the judgment which will overtake the Gentiles too, and of the happy days the righteous will enjoy in the world to come. He is then bidden to prepare for another vision.

The third section contains the vision of Messianic times. Baruch, after being reprimanded for his doubts, is told in detail of the signs of the coming judgment and the tribulations that people will then undergo, and after that, the Messiah will appear and times of joy and glory will follow. The author is quite punctilious in telling of the incidents of that time. The magnitude of the *Behemot,* the great ox, and the Leviathan prepared for the righteous, are minutely described. Then follows an account of the remarkable productivity of the land in those times—each vine will have one thousand branches, each branch one thousand clusters, and each cluster one thousand grapes. After this, he calls the elders of the people together, tells them about the redemption, and admonishes them about the strict observance of the Law.

The fourth section relates a dream by Baruch wherein a forest of mighty trees is seen, and opposite it, a single vine. A spring issues forth from the vine, which grows into a flood, and gradually sweeps away the trees of the forest, only one cedar remaining. Finally, that cedar is burned, while the vine breaks forth into bloom. The interpretation of the dream is given, namely, the forest which is Rome will be swept away and only one part of it will remain, but even that will be destroyed by the vine which symbolizes the Messiah. Baruch then prepares for another revelation.

The fifth section is that promised revelation, but adds little to the foregoing; it only gives more details about Messianic times and resurrection.

The sixth section is complete in itself. It gives in an Apocalyptic and symbolic form the history of the world as well as a description of the future. Baruch sees a huge cloud which discharges at intervals black and clear waters, the black water predominating; then a light breaks forth which heals the earth and twelve streams arise which are controlled by the light. An interpretation is offered. The cloud is the present world, the successive black waters are the sinful generations; the clear waters are the generations of the righteous, such as that of the Patriarchs, David, and other righteous kings; the last dark water represents the time of tribulation before the Messiah appears, and the light is the Messiah, while the twelve streams are symbolic of the twelve tribes of Israel. At the close of the interpretation, Baruch is informed that his end is near.

The seventh section tells how Baruch addresses the people, and at their request, two epistles are written, one to the nine and one half tribes driven away by Shalmaneser in 722 B.C.E., and one to the exiles in Babylon. In the epistle to the nine and one half tribes, they are told of the destruction of the Temple, and also of the promised redemption, and are urged to be steadfast in the observance of the Law. The other epistle is not given.

The date is evident, as stated above, and it must have been written between the years 70–90 C.E. It was written originally in Hebrew and was later translated into Greek, but both the Hebrew and Greek versions were lost and the book was preserved only in Syriac.

The "Apocalypse of Baruch" possesses a number of interesting points besides those mentioned above. In its Messianic conception, it seems to imply a double Messianic time, a temporary restoration of Zion which will be followed by a great war, and only then the real Messiah will appear and the permanent Messianic time will be initiated. This view was later incorporated in Talmudic literature, where it is asserted that a Messiah ben Joseph is supposed to gather the Jews first into Palestine, and then Gog and Magog (Ezekiel XXXVIII–XXXIX) will come and war upon Israel, and that Messiah will be killed, and after that, the Messiah of the House of David will appear. Likewise, there are many parallels to our author's description of Messianic times in the Talmud and Midrashim.

Very important are his utterances about the Law, which means the study of the Torah. Such sayings as, "There shall not be wanting to Israel a wise man, nor a son of the Law to the race of Jacob" (XL, 4), or "Though man depart, yet the Law abideth" (LXXVII, 15), or "Zion has been taken away from us and we have nothing now save the Torah" (LXXIII, 3), are significant of the time and spirit of Rabban Johanan ben Zakkai. The last saying was parodied in a poem used in the *Neilah* liturgy of the Day of Atonement.

27. IV EZRA (Esdras)

IV Ezra, as it is found in the English Apocrypha, consists of sixteen chapters, but we have to separate the first two and the last two, namely, Chas. I, II, and XV, XVI, as these two appendices are really independent works, and are sometimes called III and V Ezra respectively. They seem to come from a much later hand, and contain clearly Christian additions as is evident from Ch. II, 34 to the end. IV Ezra proper is the portion comprising Chas. III–XIII which is divided into three parts: One, III–X inclusive, named the Apocalypse of Salthiel; two, Chas. XI, XII, Vision of the Eagle, and Ch. XIII, Vision of the Son of Man, and three, Ch. XIV, called the Ezra Piece, an extract from an older Ezra Apocalypse. These parts are again subdivided into separate visions, and the whole book is a series of them.

Our book is a pure Hebrew composition, and reflects genuine Jewish thinking. Unfortunately, the text of the English Apocrypha is very corrupt, for following the Latin version, it is full of Christian interpolations, such as in Ch. VII, 28–29 where references to Jesus which are not found in any of the versions in the other languages are inserted. IV Ezra is preserved in four versions—Latin, Syriac, Ethiopic, and Armenian. They all seem to be translations from a Greek text which is lost and which in turn was a translation of the Hebrew original.

It deals primarily with the problem of the national Job–Israel. In fact, it is a Job in miniature following along the lines of the Biblical book of Job in a number of respects. It runs, as mentioned, in a series of visions, the contents of which is as follows: Vision one, Chas. III–V, 20, relates how Ezra, being in Babylon, in the thirtieth year after the destruction of the Temple, complains to God why his chosen one, Israel, is suffering, while the pagan nations prosper. The angel, Uriel, reproves him for his complaints, and informs him that the reign of wickedness has an appointed time, and that most of the distress has already passed, and the end will be soon announced by definite signs. Ezra then fasts seven days, and prepares for a second revelation. In the second vision, Chas. V, 21–VI, 34, Ezra bewails again the bitter fate of Israel, and is rebuked and promised once more that the end of suffering is near, and the angel enumerates the signs of the approaching end more fully. The third vision, VI, 34–IX, 35, is the climax of the Salthiel Apocalypse. In it, Ezra propounds the problem in its final form. If the world was created for Israel's sake, why is Israel deprived of his inheritance? A debate between Ezra and the angel ensues, at the close of which the temporary Messianic kingdom and the end of the world are once more announced and described. The vision contains also discussions on the election of Israel, and on the saving of the righteous as well as other kindred matters. In the fourth vision, Chas. IX, 35–XI, Ezra sees a woman weeping, and on being asked for the cause of her tears, she tells him that it is because of the loss of a son. He chides her for that, and tells her to mourn for Jerusalem. The woman disappears, and in her stead there appears a city. The interpretation is then offered by the angel: the woman is Zion; the son, the Temple of Solomon; and the city, the new Jerusalem.

The fifth vision, XI–XII, relates how Ezra saw the rise of an eagle with twelve wings and three heads from the sea, and from these wings grew more wings. The eagle flew and ruled over the land. The ruling, however, was done successively by each wing and head, and as soon as the wing or head had completed its time of ruling, it disappeared and the next wing or head rose to rule. As the series of changes drew towards the end, a lion rushed forth from the woods, and roared at the eagle upon whose body only two heads remained, foretelling its doom. And as he spoke, the entire body of the eagle was consumed by fire. The interpretation of the vision is given: The eagle is the Roman Empire; the wings and heads the various kings and emperors; and the lion who foretold the doom of the eagle is the Messiah. The sixth vision, Ch. XIII, that of the Son of Man, contains a description of the coming of the Messiah. It tells how Ezra sees a man rising from the sea and at the sight of him, nations tremble and rush to attack him; he ascends a mountain, and from there he subdues them not by weapons, but by the breath of his mouth. Multitudes then surround him, rejoicing at his coming. The interpretation follows; the man is the Messiah, and the rejoicing multitudes are the returning ten tribes. The seventh vision, Ch. XIV, is the Ezra legend, where Ezra is told to write the books of wisdom for his end is near. Accordingly, then, he writes ninety-four books, twenty-four of which he is told to publish—this may refer to the twenty-four books of the Scriptures—and to hide the seventy which, of course, refer to the Apocryphal and Apocalyptic books. Ezra accomplishes, with the aid of assistants, the task assigned to him, and thus completes his mission in this world. It is quite evident that this vision is intended as an apology for the Apocryphal and Apocalyptic literature, and endeavors to prove their sacred origin.

The author of the book was a Pharisee, a careful observer of the Law and of an ascetic nature. His beliefs are that God, and God alone, is responsible for the creation of the world, and that Israel is His chosen people for whose sake the world was made.

The answers to the problem of the suffering of Israel are as follows: (1) God's ways are inscrutable; (2) human intelligence is finite and we cannot therefore comprehend them, (3) evil must run its course, but God loves Israel and the future Messianic age will solve all difficulties. In general, we are to note in our author's conception of the future age and the end of days, a blending of two currents. The one is a more material view of the glorious days of the Messiah, when prosperity for Israel will come in full measure. The other is the more spiritual one, where eternal life and bliss are promised to the elect. He accordingly divides the future age into two periods, the Messianic, which will last for four hundred years, during which time all the righteous will enjoy great prosperity, and at the end of which all, including the Messiah, will die. After an interval of seven days of silence, the second period will be ushered in by the Day of Judgment and will be followed by the resurrection and the creation of a new world (Ch. VII, 26–36). This conception of the future represents a compromise between two tendencies and an attempt to join the two current views of Yemot ha-Moshiaḥ (Days of the Messiah) and Olam ha-Ba. The duration of four hundred years for the Messianic period is unique in this literature, though it is found in Rabbinic literature.

If we add to this highly interesting content the beauty of its style, the pointed parables, and deep pathos with which it is permeated, IV Ezra becomes the most inspiring book in this particular literature.

Its date can almost be determined with precision. Its constant references to the Romans, the destruction of the Temple, and the acquaintance of the author with the succession of the Roman emperors all point to the close of the first century c. e., namely, the period between the years 81–96.

28. THE MINOR APOCALYPTIC WORKS

There are a number of other Apocalyptic books, some preserved wholly, and some partly. They are of minor importance, as they contribute but little to the trend of thought of Apocalyptic literature, and many of them were interpolated by later Christian hands, so that the Jewish element can be disentangled with difficulty. Of these, the most important are: (1) The Assumption of Moses; (2) The Book of Adam and Eve, and (3) several books of the Sibylline Oracles.

(1) "The Assumption of Moses" seems to be only a fragment of a much larger work, reference to which is found in many ancient writings. It is supposed to be the content of an address delivered by Moses to Joshua before his death. In it, the dying leader discloses to his pupil prophecies concerning the future of Israel, which he instructs him to write down and hide until the appointed time. The entire history of Israel up to the time of the author is foretold. There are evident references to the destruction of the First Temple, the persecution of Antiochus, the reign of the Hasmoneans, the division into Pharisees and Sadducees, and the reign of Herod. It ends with a promise for a happy future, when God will arise to judge the world, and inaugurate the period of happiness for Israel. There is no description, though, of the Messiah. The date of the book is evident from the content which points to the first decade after the death of Herod, namely, about 6 c. e. The original language was either Hebrew or Aramaic.

(2) "The Book of Adam and Eve" is a book of legends clustering around Adam and Eve and their descendants. It begins by telling how Adam and Eve mourn for the loss of Paradise through their fall, and how, desiring to do penance for their sins, they wade into the Jordan and stand there for days, up to their necks, in water. Satan attempts to persuade Eve to leave the water, but she refuses to listen to his advice; he then relates the story of his fall. The life of Adam and Eve is subsequently told with many embellishments. Finally, the death of Adam approaches; at first, he attempts to evade his end by sending Seth and Eve to Paradise for the healing oil, but when they are refused entrance,

he resigns himself to his fate. He assembles his family, and Eve recounts the story of their fall. Adam dies and is borne away by angels who promise his resurrection. Six days later, Eve dies and is likewise borne away by angels.

(3) The collection of oracles bearing the name of the "Sibylline Oracles" constitutes very interesting reading. The legend of the existence of a Sibyl, i. e. a woman prophetess, or rather several Sibyls, was current among many nations of antiquity, such as the Greeks, the Romans, and a number of peoples of Asia Minor. According to the story, prophecies of the Sibyl were said to have been brought to King Tarquinius Priscus (616–578 B. C. E.) in Rome and deposited in the Temple. Some Hellenized Jews of Alexandria utilized this current story for propaganda purposes, and wrote long poems in the name of the heathen Sibyl, wherein Judaism is glorified, and the fortunes and vicissitudes of the Jews foretold. In the collection of Sibylline Oracles preserved, there are twelve books, but only three, namely, the third, fourth, and fifth, emanated from Jewish writers; the rest belong to Christian writers of a later date.

In the third book, Biblical incidents, such as the building of the Tower of Babel, the establishment of the Solomonic kingdom, as well as other events of historical importance in the life of other nations are mentioned and enlarged upon, and in conclusion, a sketch of the history of the Jewish people up to the time of Cyrus is given, in which the Jews are characterized as a God-fearing nation. There follows then a series of oracles, announcing judgment against Babylon, Egypt, Gog, Magog, Troy, and Lybia for their sins and addiction to idolatry. The book contains also a number of prophecies concerning Antiochus Epiphanes, Phrygia, Cyprus, and the Hellenes, as well as other prophecies foretelling judgment upon a sinful world and terminating in the coming of the Messiah. In all these prophecies, Israel is lauded as a people which cleaves to the Law of God, and the paganism of the other nations together with their unnatural crimes are severely decried, and exhortation to the heathen for conversion to Judaism is made.

The fourth book is a bitter diatribe against heathen wickedness, and a call upon the nations of Europe and Asia to repent. It warns them that unless they do so, God will destroy the world by fire, and mete out judgment to all sinners. The siege of Jerusalem and the destruction of the Second Temple are mentioned in that book. The fifth book contains a good deal of eschatology, a fine geographical description of Judea, as well as a chronicle of events in Jewish history up to the time of Hadrian.

The dates of these books can be definitely determined from their contents. Book three is the oldest, and was written about 140 B. C. E., book four about 80 C. E., and book five about 130 C. E. These oracles were all written in Greek and constitute the boldest Jewish polemic against heathenism. They were written not only in fine Greek hexameters, but were purposely put in a heathen garb, namely, in the form of prophecies of heathen sybils, in order to give their utterances more credence.

CHAPTER II

THE DEVELOPMENT OF THE HALAKAH

29. JUDAISM IN THE 4TH AND 3RD CENTURIES B.C.E.

The shaping of the form of Judaism, as we know it today, as it was lived and practiced for the last two thousand years as a religion which embraces all phases of Jewish life—not only the life of the group but of the individual as well—begins with the return of the Jews from exile, and especially with the reformation of Ezra (period of activity 458-444 B.C.E.). It is rather a curious fact, but true nevertheless, that it was the Babylonian exile that gave the greatest impetus to the development of Judaism, to its deepening and extension. Deprived of their country, their national sanctuary, and prevented from offering sacrifices —which was until that time the strongest religious expression,—the Jews turned to religion as their only bulwark of defense which might preserve their national entity. At the same time, on account of the absence of sacrifices, which is primarily a group function, prayer became the expression of religious feeling. And as prayer is individual by nature, religion as a whole thus became more individualized and intensified—God came nearer to man. No more was His presence, even in the mind of the average Jew, associated with a definite place; He was everywhere, and the Jew could communicate with Him at any time and at any place. The deeper inner expression demanded likewise a fuller external expression of religion which ultimately resulted in a craving for more ceremonies, more detailed and strict fulfillment of religious precepts and legal enactments.

With this tendency for a more individualized and more detailed religion, the Jews returned from exile. The first century passed in struggle, both spiritual and physical, but the clouds were finally dispersed, and life in all phases, political, social, and spiritual, assumed a more settled form, thanks to the labors of Ezra and Nehemiah, the latter operating in the political and social sphere, and the former in the spiritual one.

Ezra, known as the scribe (Heb. Sofer), a name which is practically

45

synonymous with the name teacher, was the first of the great caste in Israel who follow in a long successive line through the ages under various names, but whose function was to teach and instruct in the ways of practical life. And the Jews at that time needed teachers more than preachers. With religion becoming individualized, the share of every Jew, the function of the preacher, and even the very greatest of this class, the *Nabi*—the Prophet—became inadequate, and hence prophecy was silenced. The *Nabi* left the scene and his place was taken by the scribe, the teacher.

Thus, a movement of religious, spiritual, and literary revival, the result of a happy combination of a popular demand, though it might have been inarticulate, and the existence of the proper leaders to meet that demand, had begun. The movement was not the work of one man, nor even of one generation, but continued to progress for at least two centuries. Unfortunately, the veil of secrecy is cast over this most fruitful period of spiritual activity, but when the veil is finally lifted, and the light of history shines forth upon Jewish life in the Second Commonwealth, about the close of the third century B. C. E., there is revealed to us a Judaism fully grown and firmly intrenched in the hearts of the people, one ramified in many ways, and bubbling with energy, one to which the succeeding generations have added comparatively little.

This was a peculiar period of activity, inasmuch as its traces were not left in writing but in life itself, for with the exception of a few additions to the Old Testament and the great work of organizing and closing the Canon, which most probably took place in the period under discussion, there are no literary records which tell the story of the great spiritual fermentation of the time. And well did a Jewish scholar characterize it by saying: "Religious institutions and not documents are the witnesses of development of Judaism and its activity during these two centuries; ideas and not books are the expression of the period."[1] And because of this peculiarity, the delineating of such a literature is certainly not a light task, but none the less an interesting one.

Later tradition ascribed almost the entire work of revival to Ezra, making him the central figure of this great work, and the Great Synagogue (Kenesset ha-Gedolah), the assembly of sages, merely as his assistants, thus speaking of him as the founder of many religious institutions which are at times referred to the entire assembly. In reality,

[1] G. Karpeles: *Geschichte der jüdischen Literatur*, Vol. I, p. 139.

he was merely the initiator of the movement, and many were the successors and the workers in the field of spiritual progress. Ezra's great merit is, that he inaugurated a system of popular education on a scale the like of which was never seen. The book of the Law of Moses (Torat Moshe) which in previous times was probably the share of the few became, through the activities of Ezra, the inheritance and property of every Jew. It was he who instituted public reading of the Torah on the Sabbath, festivals, and all public occasions; and it was not a mere reading, but an intelligent and interpretative one (Nehemiah, Chas. VIII, 1, 8; IX, 3; XIII, 1). These public readings and interpretations gave impetus to study which continued to call forth new activities and constant interpretations of the law which, in turn, necessitated further study. The craving for religious satisfaction brought about the establishment of synagogues in various places and these became not only centers of religious worship, but also centers of education, for the Law was read and expounded there as well as in the general public gatherings.

But the books of the Law of Moses were not the only books in the possession of the people; there were also historical works, prophecies, psalms, collections of proverbs, all of which gave inspiration and inculcated teachings and hope in the hearts of the people. These again needed interpretation and expounding, and what is more, organization and standardization into one complete body. Thus, the work of education and spiritual revival ramified and called constantly for new energy, for new zeal on the part of the men who were to direct this movement.

30. THE SOFERIM (SCRIBES) AND THE GREAT ASSEMBLY

But who were these men who guided the stream of spiritual fermentation into the proper channels and really molded Judaism into that mighty force which withstood all onslaughts through the ages? They were the men of the Great Assembly, or we should rather say, Assemblies, and what is probably more correct, a certain portion of them. It is true that we possess no written documents describing the exact nature and character of this kind of Assembly—and certainly not the transactions at their sessions, as nothing short of that would satisfy some scholars—but a persistent tradition of the existence and fruitful activity of such an Assembly is constantly reiterated in Talmudic literature and incorporated in the Mishnah (Aboth, I, 1). There is, therefore, no reason whatever to doubt the existence and extensive activity of such an Assembly, some opinions of radical scholars notwithstanding, but with one modification, namely, that it was not an occasional assembly but a permanent institution, the activity of which lasted for two centuries. In other words, it was a successive series of Assemblies.

Since we know that the Jews under Persian suzerainty possessed complete home rule which kept law and order, and that no other organ of government existed at the time, it stands to reason that this Great Assembly was that public and social organ which discharged the functions of government. But as in Judaism, civil, religious, and political laws were never separated, it follows that the same body discharged several functions at once, and acted simultaneously as a judicial, executive, and legislative body.

It originated, according to some scholars,[2] in the group of signers of the agreement drawn up by Nehemiah and Ezra in the year 444 B.C.E. wherein a popular pledge to observe the Laws of Moses was made (Nehemiah X, 1–30). The number of signers was eighty-five, and a tradition in the Palestinian Talmud actually fixes the number of the Great Assembly as eighty-five, though other traditions round the number out to one hundred and twenty. With the death of Ezra and Nehemiah, this body was constituted into a permanent assembly which through its several functions carried on the work of both leaders. But legislative work could not be carried on without study and expounding of the Law, and likewise, the supervising of the great educational movement required the proper persons for its accomplishment. Hence, the teachers and expounders formed not only an important part of the Great Assembly or Assemblies but also formed a special department within it. They then assumed the humble cognomen of their spiritual leader, Ezra, namely, *Sofer,* scribe or teacher, and were called *Soferim,* but later tradition calls them at times also the men of the Great Assembly, which, in fact, they were.

31. THE WORK OF THE SOFERIM

It was these scholars or *Soferim* who, as a step in popular education, changed the ancient Hebrew script for the Assyrian or the Syrian, the square script, which was henceforth used in transcribing the sacred Scriptures, and ultimately became the only script known to the Jews. This change was an important literary step, as the Jews after their return from exile were scarcely acquainted with the ancient script, and

---

[2] N. Krochmal, *Guide of the Perplexed in Our Time* (More Nebuké ha-Zeman), p. 42.

the adoption of the more familiar one facilitated the study of the Holy Law, and brought it within the reach of every Jew. The next great literary task of the *Soferim,* in the course of time, was the closing of the Canon of the Old Testament. We know very little of the process of this important event; all that later tradition tells us is that men of the Great Assembly had organized or edited certain collections of prophecies and other writings and finally closed the Canon. We must, however, imagine that the closing of the Canon did not take place at once but was rather a protracted process, the final step of which took place at the close of the period of the existence of the Great Assembly, namely, in the second half of the third century B. C. E., though it is not improbable that minor additions were inserted later.[3]

The *Soferim* also arranged and standardized the earliest forms of the liturgy which were rather few in number, but served as a basis for a much more extensive one in later ages. Thus, their activity extended to all phases of life. But as great as it was in all these directions, their Magnum Opus consisted not in written documents but in their role as teachers and expounders of the Law of Moses, and in a lesser degree, also the other Scriptures. This activity made Judaism what it is and laid the basis for the great literary collections known as the Mishnah and the Talmud, and the various Agadic books. Our task is, therefore, to see how it was carried on.

When the teacher began to expound the laws, there was revealed the rift between the law as stated in the Pentateuch and life as it was lived, especially in its developed form.

The Law or the Laws as embodied in the Pentateuch are, on the whole, expressed in a general way; statements are inadequate, and many phases of life are omitted. Life is always ahead of the written Law, if it be taken in its literal meaning, and Jewish law and life form no exception. Undoubtedly, there were always supplementary traditions, customs, and usages which the people employed in their everyday life. As a matter of fact, Jewish tradition asserts, and with justice, that a supplementary Law was given to Moses on Sinai which he in turn handed over to his follower, Joshua, and he again to his successors, and so on

---

[3] This is rather a conservative opinion but the one which seems to be more probable. The question of the closing of the Canon is a very complex one, and the literature on the subject is quite extensive. It would be out of place in a history of literature to analyze all the opinions and views on this matter. We will only refer the reader to the following works: Zunz, *Die Gottesdienstlichen Vorträge* p. 34; Weiss, *Dor Dor we-Dorshov* (History of Oral Law), Vol. I, p. 89, where the conservative view is ably defended.

through the generations. This body of Oral Law, besides direct Mosaic supplements, contained a number of adopted customs, old usages, and some ancient interpretations of the Written Law. But in general, the Oral Law was not spread among nor observed by the people at large during the First Commonwealth; only a small minority observed it. A large part of it might have been forgotten during the exile. It had, therefore, to be revived, and new interpretations added, new precepts grafted upon the old so as to meet the exigencies of a developed and extended life.

32. METHOD OF THE SOFERIM

The method of the *Soferim,* the scribes, in expounding the Law was a strictly analytic one. It took as its basis the view that the Torah is not to be taken as literature, where additional words or special constructions are used for rhetorical purposes, but that each word or change in construction has a special meaning. Besides, by careful analysis, they elicited interpretations from the very words themselves which gave to their contents a fuller and more detailed meaning. In addition, other devices were used, such as comparison of passages, logical analogy, and similar means of synthetic exegesis, and thus the Law was expanded, and came to embrace all phases of life.

We must not, however, assume that all this work of exegesis and interpretation really added many new laws, for as stated, the greater part of Oral Law was old, and undoubtedly was practiced in early times either as Mosaic supplements or older interpretations by the few who did observe. What the *Soferim* did was, in most cases, to show that all these forms of practice of the written laws are in reality enfolded in the Law itself. In other words, there are no new additions, but merely an unfolding of the contents of the Law. But that in their exegesis, they added new applications which widened the usage of the laws so as to embrace new conditions of life, goes without saying.

As an illustration of the insufficiency of the Written Law, if taken literally, and that if it was practiced, it must necessarily have been supplemented both by direct Mosaic instruction and by old interpretation and custom, we will cite two cases. The first is the case of the Sabbath. The Pentateuch refers several times to the prohibitions of doing any work on the Sabbath (Exodus Ch. XX, 10; XXXI, 14, 15; XXXV, 2; Lev. XXIII, 3; Deut. V, 14), and the injunction that one who desecrates the Sabbath is punished by death is likewise repeated several times, but nowhere is there a definition given as to what is meant by the term, *work*. Only three kinds of labor are specified, kindling of fire (Ex. XXXV, 3), walking beyond a certain limit (Ex. XVI, 29), and cording or hewing of wood (Num. XV, 32–36). But, it is self-evident, that there are hundreds of forms of labor which fall under the term *work*. How then could the Sabbath be observed without any supplementary instruction as to what constitutes work and what not? Undoubtedly, such instructions and supplements have existed from the very time of the giving of the Law, and they were included in the Mosaic Oral Law. The subsequent ages also added interpretations which helped to clarify the Law. As far as the Sabbath is concerned, we have direct reference to wider interpretations in ages previous to that of the *Soferim*. Nowhere in the Pentateuch is there a direct prohibition of carrying burdens on the Sabbath. Yet, we find Jeremiah reproaching the people for that very offense (Jer. XVII, 21). Again, Nehemiah enforces with a strong hand the law of cessation of business and even drove away the Gentile traders who came to Jerusalem on the Sabbath (Nehem. XXIII, 15–23), though trading on the Sabbath is nowhere prohibited in the Pentateuch.

But it was the *Soferim* who not only classified and organized all previous interpretations regarding work on the Sabbath, but actually classified and standardized the kinds of work prohibited. Moreover, by the method of exegesis, they showed that the written laws implied all these classes of work although they were not specified, and that these kinds of work were included in the general term, *Kol Melakah,* all work. Work, in general was divided into thirty-nine classes, each of which embraced a number of special labors, and they were called *Abot Melakot,* i. e. heads of classes of work. Each kind of work included in these classes may have one or more subspecies subsuming other works resembling the head species; these are denominated *Tolodot,* i. e. kindred. Thus, the number of works prohibited on the Sabbath increased considerably. Tradition asserts, though, that the thirty-nine classes of work were of Mosaic supplement. But the *Soferim* derived them from the term work, itself. They proceeded in the following manner: Starting to enlarge the term "all work" prohibited on the Sabbath, they compared it with another usage of the term in regard to the building of the Tabernacle (Ex. XXXVI, 7, 8; XXXIX, 43). There, the meaning is clear, for possessing a fair description of the building of the Tabernacle, we can safely calculate the kinds of work necessary for its construction. Upon investigation, it was found that they can be subsumed under thirty-nine classes. Consequently, by analogy, the term "all work" or "any work" employed with regard to the Sabbath also includes all these classes. And thus, the old oral supplements or instructions were brought into strict relation with the Written Law, nay, it became the very unfolding of the literal meaning of the words themselves.

Another example is the law concerning the transfer of property. The Pentateuch refers a number of times to the buying and selling of houses or estates, stating that money was paid in the transaction, and even enacts certain laws about their redemption by the seller (Lev. XXV), but nowhere are there specific statements telling of the actual way in which property was to be transferred from one person to another, or when such transfer is invalid, and when valid. We cannot imagine, however, that the Jews during the First Commonwealth continued to buy and sell property without following certain strict laws or usages in these transactions. We must, therefore, assume that supplementary Mosaic laws existed on this subject which were augmented by adopted usage. In fact, we find Jeremiah giving us a detailed description of the process of transferring property (Jer. XXXII, 9–13). But these oral laws and usages had to be solidified and systematized. This work was again done by the scribes, who, interpreting that very passage in Jeremiah, standardized these laws and usages and gave them legal solidity and they were henceforth invested with unquestionable validity.

Such examples might be multiplied considerably, for almost every precept in the Pentateuch needs supplementing and interpretation in order that it become a living practiced law. These two cases were quoted only in order to prove that the work of the scribes did not consist, as many scholars would have us believe, in building up a new system of oral laws which was grafted, by means of casuistic devices, upon a simple form of Judaism as embodied in the Pentateuch, but that a great part of what is called oral law did really exist in tradition along with the written law, even when in times of sin and waywardness, during the first period of Jewish history, it was observed only by the few. The scribes, in a time of religious revival, when the needs of the individual called for scrupulous observance of law and expansion of religion, not only standardized these ancient laws and usages, but by interpretation, both analytic and synthetic, unfolded them out of the written law. Thus, the oral laws and supplements, though still remaining oral, received the status of written laws, since the former represented the full meaning implied in the latter. Needless to say that these activities, and especially the method of interpretation, paved the way for further study which led to a deepening of the religious feeling and which in turn brought about a craving for further expansion and development of the law, thus bringing about new enactments of injunctions and regulations.

33. MIDRASH

This method of interpretation of the Bible used by the scribes, their very *modus operandi* described above, was designated by the name of *Midrash*, a word which is derived from the Hebrew root *Darosh*, i. e. to search or investigate. Its process was as follows: A verse from the Bible was quoted, and then it was commented upon, analyzed, and the new interpretation attached to it. And thus, the study of the Law was carried on for a time, namely, the practical interpretation joined together with the verse. This method of *Midrash* was applied not only to matters of law and pure religious practice, but also to ethics, theology, and belief, and thus gave rise to what is known as Agada. For this purpose, the other books of the Bible were primarily utilized, but of this later. (Secs. 50, 53.)

34. HALAKAH

But this method, useful as it may be as an instrument of interpretation and development of law, is cumbersome as a means of study, especially when study is oral and is transmitted primarily by memory. As time went on and interpretations multiplied, laws amplified, oral transmission of the whole mass of Midrashic law became unwieldy and burdened the memory of the students. In addition, there were added laws of the scribes which were of a secondary character, namely, those that were not part of the ancient Oral Law nor derived by direct interpretation, but were enacted by them either as matters of exigency in accordance with the needs of the times, or as fences around the law (Seyogim). These secondary laws added to the difficulty, and a new method was therefore adopted. The old form of motivated legal study was, to a great extent, abandoned, and the mere legal statements alone, abstracted from the interpretation and motive, began to be used. These statements were termed Halakah. The meaning of the word seems to be derived from the Hebrew root *Halok,* i. e. to go, namely, a rule of conduct which people should follow. There began to be circulated groups of statements or *Halakot,* about certain legal subjects whether religious, civil, or criminal law which stated very briefly, without reference to the Biblical verse or the enactments of the *Soferim,* what line of action was to be followed in certain matters. For purposes of making the statements easily remembered, mnemonic devices were often used, such as numbering the cases when one is allowed to do a certain thing, or on the contrary when not. The old method, however, was not entirely abandoned, and was continued through the generations, and was later even improved upon by additional rules of interpretation. But the new form began to prevail, and Halakah was transmitted from teacher to pupil. In time, the term Halakah came to denote the entire branch of practical religion. We do not exactly know the definite time when Halakah became the prevailing method of study. Some scholars would defer it to the time of Hillel, some to the end of the Maccabean period, and some to the middle of it, toward the end of the first half of the second century B. C. E.[4] But it is most probable that the first layer of the Halakah already took shape at the close of the Soferic period about the year 200.

Thus, the great period of intellectual activity of the Soferim ended, leaving a rich inheritance to the succeeding generations, which they increased and amplified but hardly changed. The saying placed at the beginning of the Mishnaic treatise *Aboth,* or "The Sayings of the Fathers," in the collective name of the Great Assembly, sums up in a measure the character and the nature of the activity of this remarkable group of men. They said: "Be deliberate in your judgment, raise many disciples, and make a fence around the Law" (Aboth, I, 1). Deliberation in judgement on all matters of law and religion is a primary necessity for any great religious activity, and certainly the *Soferim* used deliberation in their analytic method of interpretation of the Torah. The next step in their activity was to increase the number of disciples making study a popular matter and thus deepen and intensify study itself. Of equal importance was the last step, the fencing of the Law. The whole work of the men of the Great Synagogue in interpreting the Law and putting new meaning into it would have been endangered were they not to add, here and there, a fence and buttress in order to stabilize the entire structure.

35. THE ZUGOT (Pairs)

With the death of Simon the Just (d. 180 B. C. E.), the Great Assembly seemed to cease functioning, or else it assumed a different form.

[4] On this subject, see Z. Lauterbach: *Midrash and Mishnah,* Chas. I, II

The sources are scanty and we have no clear conception of the inner life of Israel during that period. The times were turbulent, party strife ran high, and Judaism was headed for a crisis. The work of the *Soferim* was about to be put to a severe test in the great struggle with Hellenism. Yet, it seems that intellectual activity on the lines laid down was carried on. In the treatise *Aboth,* there is enumerated an almost continuous chain of leading scholars, carrying on the tradition of study and religious leadership from Simon the Just to the close of the Mishnah. (210 c. e.). The leaders, from the time of Antigonus, the disciple of Simon, until after Hillel (d. 10 c. e.) are given in pairs. This period of intellectual activity is, therefore, denominated the period of the *Zugot,* i. e. pairs of leaders. We are told by later tradition that of the pairs mentioned, one was the *Nasi,* i. e. president, and the other, the *Ab Bet Din,* namely, the dean of the Sanhedrin, the highest court or religious council. Whether this Sanhedrin was modeled after the Great Assembly and embraced all functions, political and executive, as well as legislative and judicial, or it was limited to the last two functions is a matter still debated by historians. What is important for us to know is that these pairs of leading scholars carried on the literary work, and thus layer after layer of Halakah was added. There was, likewise, a constant accretion in the field of theology and ethics, and a general thickening in the crust of religious life. The work of generations of scholars was about to enter the phase of organization, but then its basic validity was challenged by powerful opponents. We do not know clearly the origin of the opposition, but it was ultimately crystallized and organized into definite opinion and a new party strife arose in Judaism.

36. PHARISEES AND SADDUCEES

When the smoke of the Maccabean wars cleared away, and the Maccabean prince, John Hyrcanus, sat securely on his throne, there came into view two parties in Jewry whose conflict of opinion left an indelible mark upon the development of Judaism; these were the Pharisees and the Sadducees.

Of the two, it is the former party that is the most important and which not only succeeded in surviving, but practically impressed entire Judaism with its stamp, and it is their literary activity which underlies the great literary structure of post-Biblical literature.

Who were the Pharisees? As a group, they were the teachers who continued to develop the views and the activity of the *Soferim.* The origin of the name (Heb., Perushim), is not quite certain. Some derive it from the root *Parosh,* meaning to interpret, which would indicate their chief attribute, namely, interpreters of the Law. Objections have been raised to this derivation. Others derive it from a similar root, *Parosh,* meaning to separate, as they kept themselves separated and distinct from the *Amé*-ha-Arazim, i. e. the lower strata of the people who were not careful in the observance of the Law. Yet, we have the testimony of Josephus,[5] that they were beloved by the people and were their leaders. The result is that while as a small group they are said to be teachers and scribes, as a party, they comprised the popular party.

The Pharisees continued to develop the Oral Law. Their fundamental point of view was like that of the *Soferim,* that all these interpretations, all these applications of the Torah to life also constituted Torah, which though not written, could still claim that title, inasmuch as a part of it was most likely given by Moses himself as an oral explanation of the written laws, while another part was implicitly embodied in the words of the Pentateuch, and by interpretation, became explicit. From this view, the interpretations themselves become Torah. To them, the Torah became the living word of God which continually gave forth new revelations, and was subject to interpretation. The supreme conception is that the Torah is more than mere law, but is the word of God, His great gift, the inexhaustible revelation of the divine truth, inasmuch as it encompasses all forms of life, individual as well as national. To the Pharisee, therefore, the performance of the precepts of the Torah was no burden but a joy. These sentiments were already beautifully expressed in Psalms XIX and CXIX, where the Torah is compared to the sun, and what the latter is in nature, the former is in the sphere of the soul of man, and the performance of the precepts is like receiving the light of the sun, pleasant.

Thus, literary activity was carried on by the leaders of the Pharisees who were invariably scholars, and slowly the Halakah grew. In a similar fashion, layers of views and opinions in the field of ethics and theology and kindred subjects were compiled, and were handed down from generation to generation. But all these teachings being oral, there arose differences of opinion, and even these differences were preserved so that the circle was widened.

In the field of speculative religion, the Pharisees taught the immortality of the soul, and thus solved the great problem of suffering, namely,

[5] *Antiquities,* Book XIII, Ch. X, 5.

that the righteous were to be rewarded in the world after death. And as we have already indicated, they also inculcated the theory of resurrection which was connected with the Messianic age.

It is very often asserted that the Pharisees disregarded politics or the welfare of the nation for the sake of religion. This assertion is not true. They were as deeply interested in the political welfare of the Jews as the other parties. No doubt, there were some extremists among them, but the fact is that the zealots, who fought so bitterly for the freedom of Palestine were all Pharisees, and so were their leaders. They were, however, not ready to make concessions to political exigencies at the expense of religion. Their emphasis was laid on the religious and moral life of the nation, as well as that of the individual.

The Sadducees belonged more to the aristocratic stratum of the people, and consisted mostly of priests, hence their name Sadducees which is probably derived from the name of the ancestor of the most important priestly family, Zadok. This supposition is not, however, certain. We also find priests who were leaders among the Pharisees, and on the contrary, the very founder of the order of the scribes, Ezra, was himself a priest. It is more preferable to accept in part the view of later tradition [6] which refers the establishment of this party to a man named Zadok, who was himself somewhat of a scholar, a disciple of Antigonus of Socho who followed in religious leadership Simon the Just, as it contains an element of truth in it. For, while the whole view stating that Sadduceism arose merely from a misinterpretation of a saying of Antigonus is untenable, the kernel of truth in it is that a man, not necessarily a priest, by the name of Zadok who was a leader among the aristocratic stratum of the population, was the founder of the party. The opposition to the teaching of the popular scholars was smoldering for a time in the hearts of certain people until Zadok gave formal expression to it. There was undoubtedly a political background to this antagonism. The leaders of the upper classes, seeing the influence the scribes, or scholars, wielded upon the populace, and desiring to wrest the power from them, planned to undermine their influence by repudiating their entire teaching. Among the aristocrats, there were, of course, quite a number of priests, but the Sadducees were not primarily a priestly party. However, the whole outlook of the Sadducees is not very clear. Their principal view seemed to have been a strict adherence to the Written Law, and a rejection of the Oral Law and its method of

[6] *Aboth di R. Nathan*, an Agadic addition to the Mishnaic treatise *Aboth*, Ch. V.

interpretation. From this point, they were really the conservative wing. But, inasmuch as they did not accept the mass of enactments and interpretations of the Oral Law, their life seemed apparently freer. They were in certain respects more ready than the Pharisces to make concessions to political exigencies, but on the whole, their view of the Torah to which they were devoted was inflexible, and as a result, with all their apparent liberality, they were unprogressive. Hence, their civil and penal law was more severe; they practiced the *lex talionis* literally. It is not to be understood, however, that the Sadducees rejected the Pharasaic tradition altogether, as the Torah without interpretation can hardly be practiced, as indicated above, but they rejected the binding force of the principles of interpretation and allowed free play of private opinion.

They also seem to have denied reward and punishment in the other world and the existence of angels and spirits. They denied the providence of God over the actions of the individual man. Yet, with all their worldliness, they did not manage to survive, and the saving of Judaism was left to the Pharisees.

This strife between the Pharisees and the Sadducees, though at times very severe, especially when the wrath of a Hasmonean prince inclined to the Sadducean view entered into it, yet, it never interrupted the Pharasaic intellectual activity. The chain of the bearers of tradition was not broken during this whole period. On the whole, there existed a more or less friendly relation between the leaders of both parties; they sat together in the Sanhedrin, and most likely there were a good number of concessions on the part of the Sadducees to the practical side of Pharasaism. We find distinct reference to such concession in the Temple worship.[7]

One of the leaders of the Pharisees and also one of the *Zugot* who is worthy of mention, as his activity extends beyond mere legal scholasticism, is Simon ben Shetaḥ. He was the brother of Queen Alexandra, and in her reign (76–69 B. C. E.) was the acclaimed leader of the people. He introduced many important institutions, but the greatest of them was the laying of the foundation of the elementary school system among the Jews. He thus supplied the very basis of the strength of Judaism.

---

[7] Tal. Bab. Yoma 18b, "Said a Sadduceean priest to his son, the high priest, 'Although we are Sadducees, we fear the Pharisees,' namely, we fear to depart from their accepted practices."

Chapter III

ORGANIZATION OF THE HALAKAH

A. Tannaim and Their Method

37. GENERAL OBSERVATIONS

Just as at the end of the period of the *Soferim* there arose, on account of the multiplicity of Midrashic interpretations of the Bible, the need to abandon to a great extent the Midrashic form of study and introduce that of Halakah, so likewise, at the end of the period of the *Zugot* (about 30 B.C.E.), there arose for similar reasons the need of putting the great mass of *Halakot*[1] which was constantly accumulating into some organized form. The need was accentuated by the fact that since the study of the law became very popular, the number of teachers as well as that of pupils greatly increased, which increase brought about differences and variations both in the method of interpretation and in the forms of transmitted *Halakot*.

As stated, the Midrashic method of study was not entirely abandoned but continued along with the study of Halakah; new interpretations were, therefore, constantly pronounced by the teachers in the schools, from which new Halakic statements were abstracted. In addition, the exigencies of life called forth new applications of older statements, which in turn became *Halakot* in themselves. All these teachings were transmitted orally by the pupils, and as all oral statements they were liable to changes and differences according to the individual transmitters. Nor were the rules of interpretation firmly established, and they were applied variously by different teachers. Besides, there were current a number of *Halakot,* the Biblical proofs for which were forgotten, but which nevertheless were accepted. This state of affairs gave rise to a twofold need, first to organize the *Halakot* proper, to give them a stabilized form, to expand them when necesssary, to harmonize con-

---

[1] The term Halakah is applied in a double sense, first as one signifying the entire legal study and discussion, second denoting a single legal statement. In the second sense it has a plural *Halakot,* i. e. legal statements.

tradictions, to choose between two different versions, and to make them at times more flexible to meet new conditions; secondly, to relate any of them back to the Bible by the old method of Midrash, which now needed a set of fast and standard rules to prevent the use of individual methods.

38. TANNAIM

As the central point of interest lay now in the organization of the Halakah which was by this time of great bulk extending to all phases of life, while interpretation or Midrash was of lesser importance, merely a means of adducing Scriptural proof for *Halakot* which did not already possess one, or even to add from time to time a new rule, the scholars from now on were, therefore, designated by the name of *Tannaim*, i. e. teachers. This name is derived from the Aramaic root *Tnē*, to tell or to teach, for the chief task of these scholars was to teach the application of the laws and rules to life, namely, what the exact form of the Halakah is and how it should be understood, and similar matters. The teachings themselves went by the name of Mishnah, which is derived from *Shano*, a Hebrew root which means to repeat, and later acquired the meaning of study. The name was used to designate the work of the scholars both as study and as an act, namely, the mere repeating of the rules, laws, and regulations as well as the introducing of proper modifications. This period lasted for about 250 years, from about 30 B. C. E. to 210 C. E., namely, from the time of Hillel to that of Judah ha-Nasi, i. e. the Prince. During this entire period, the process of organization of the great mass of Halakah went on until it culminated in the compilation of the Mishnah, the summary and sum total of the Oral Law. Many were the workers in this field, each one contributing his number of bricks to the great Edifice, but the master builders were few, and they can be limited to five, Hillel, Johanan ben Zakkai, Akiba, Rabbi Meir, and Judah the Prince. These names are the outstanding ones in the great company of *Tannaim*, and rise even from the midst of a long line of intellectual giants.

39. HILLEL

The personality of Hillel, the first of the great *Tannaim*, was a remarkable one, and, as a matter of fact, the influence of his personality equaled that of his instruction. He was a Babylonian by birth, and hailed from a very distinguished family, in fact, a descendant on his mother's side from the Davidic dynasty. The folk mind has embellished his early efforts for the study of the Law with beautiful stories, but when he is revealed to us in history, he is the full-fledged scholar. By a fortunate incident, he was elevated to the presidency of the Sanhedrin in the year 30 B. C. E. and for forty years, he guided the spiritual destinies of the Jews.

Hillel, first of all, set himself to the task of standardizing the methods of interpretation of the Law, namely, the various systems of the Midrash. After examining the rules used by previous scholars, he selected a few of these rules as logically sound, or as those that had the approval of generations, and adding some of his own he laid down a canon of seven rules of interpretation which henceforth became the adopted instruments of the Midrashic method. The introduction of this canon brought about, on the one hand, an extension of the field of study by making it possible to derive new *Halakot* from the Torah, as well as to relate new decisions to Biblical sources; on the other hand, it checked an undue growth of deriving *Halakot* from the Pentateuch, for henceforth, every new derivation was tested whether it was made according to rule. It is also possible that the rules were used retroactively, namely, that a number of *Halakot* which were current in the schools but had no sound reason for their basis were likewise tested by these rules, and if they could not be traced back to the Pentateuch were disqualified. These rules made also possible an adjustment of law to life, even when the Bible seems to be explicit on the point. The classical example of such adjustment is Hillel's institution of the *Prosboul* which enabled people to lend money to the needy without risking forfeiture of the loan at the end of the Sabbatical year (Shemitah), as such is the case according to the Biblical law of *Shemitah* (Deut. XV, 1–4). The obviation of the risk of forfeiting loans in the Sabbatical year is carried out by means of presenting to court a document signed by the lender, wherein he notifies the court that he intends to collect all the enumerated debts at any time he will see fit. This document is attested by witnesses. The name *Prosboul* is Greek, a combination of two Greek words, *Pros Bouleh,* i. e. in the presence of the council, referring to the document which is given in the presence of the court.

The legal reason for this institution is usually explained to be, that when debts are turned over to court, they are considered as collected, and hence, the law of forfeiture of debts does not apply to them, since they are already legally collected. The real reason is, however, a dexterously applied interpretation of the verses 2 and 3 in Deuteronomy Ch. XV. We thus see the role analytic interpretation played in adjustment of law to life.

The sifting and testing of older *Halaḳot* by means of the rules of interpretation, called forth, most likely, an endeavor to classify the various layers of Halakah in general, as well as to organize them according to a certain system. It is probable that Hillel began this most important work. A later Gaonic tradition [2] insists that Hillel and his colleague, Shammai, laid down the six great divisions of the Mishnah usually called Orders. But although we have no means to verify the exact nature of this tradition, nor to determine the character of that organization, there is good reason to assume that Hillel possibly with the help of Shammai, did lay the foundation of future collections.

He was also great, as stated, in his personality. He became the model of conduct and leader who personified the Jewish ideal of peace and loving-kindness. Around his name there cluster a number of stories which characterize his outstanding personality. His ethical influence was great, and he epitomized the ethics of Judaism in one famous maxim: "Do not unto others that which is hateful to thee." This saying was often misinterpreted, and even such a great and deep thinker as Immanuel Kant had taken it to be merely an injunction not to harm others. In reality, however, in spite of its negative form, the content is positive. It should be understood to mean: Do not unto others that which thou wouldst not have desired to have done unto thee if thou wert placed in the other man's position. It is thus, though taking human desires as a basis of ethics, wide and extensive including positive acts as well as negative. We will quote one instance: Suppose a man sees another in distress, it is his duty to offer him succor, for were he in the same position, he certainly would not have desired to be left without help, hence, he must not do unto the other man what he would not have desired to have done unto him, and consequently, he is to offer him help. The possible reason why Hillel put his maxim in a negative form may have been the desire to accentuate the psychological reason for doing good by offering sympathy as a motive.

Hillel's colleague, Shammai, is represented as a sterner man, and his teaching was of a more conservative nature. We do not know exactly his method of interpretation, but it seemed to have been of a

---

[2] Hai Gaon (969–1038) in a Responsum, No. 20, in the Responsa collection, *Sha'aré Teshubah*.

simpler nature, following more closely the literal meaning of the verse, hence, it was often not in agreement with a changed form of life, and consequently, his Halakah is, on the whole, though exceptions abound, a severe one. Besides, Shammai very seldom analyzed the phases of a certain prohibition or measure, but accepted it *in toto* to apply to all cases, irrespective of variation.

40. THE SCHOOLS OF HILLEL AND SHAMMAI

These two scholars founded schools which were known as Shammaites and Hillelites (Bet Shammai and Bet Hillel). The members of the schools carried the diverse teachings of the masters into practice. As the days were turbulent and the authority of the Sanhedrin declined considerably under Herod and his successor Archelaus, there was no one with sufficient authoritative power to decide between these two tendencies, and thus the divergence between the schools increased and different versions of *Halakot* multiplied. A later scholar bewails the fact that from the time of Hillel and Shammai, division arose among the scholars on account of disciples who did not study sufficiently at the feet of their masters, and thus the Torah became split into two *Torot,* i. e. two different ways of teaching.

The schools existed for about one hundred years until finally the Hillelites prevailed, as their teachings were more adaptable to life and more flexible; besides, they were also based on more logically sound methods of interpretation and analysis.

41. JOHANAN BEN ZAKKAI

A great impetus towards the strengthening of literary activity, as well as towards the organization of the Halakah, was the destruction of the Commonwealth. The political structure was shattered, the religious center was destroyed, and Israel was forced to construct another spiritual center which should radiate influence to all the scattered members of Jewry. This new center was established by R. Johanan ben Zakkai at Jamnia (Jabne) in Judea. Thither was carried all their spiritual wealth, and scholars and students sat together forging the links which were destined to bind the parts of the Jewish people into one whole. This center was not merely a university, but also the seat of the High Court—the Sanhedrin which was the central authority whence decisions went forth, affecting all forms of life. The leaders of Israel were equally as interested in civil law as in the purely religious, and they formed and molded opinions and views with the same zeal and ardor as legal interpretations. This court, which should rather be called Senate, held in its hand the threads of the spiritual life of all Jewries in exile. It fixed the calendar, it licensed the judges and teachers, and very often directed the political life, at least whatever was left of that life.

The central figure during the first decade of the existence of this center was, of course, the founder, Rabban Johanan ben Zakkai. He made a number of regulations intended to strengthen the new center, investing it with the dignity of authority formerly held by the Sanhedrin at the Temple court. But he centered his activity upon the fixation and organization of the Law. He seemed to be instrumental in making the Hillelite view prevail, being himself a disciple of Hillel.

Another step in that direction was the actual compilation of certain groups of *Halakot* which bore on Temple worship. This particular phase of law was threatened by the danger that it might be forgotten, since it was no more in use. In order to avert that danger, the older scholars, most of them priests who themselves participated in the worship, were called together and each one described from memory how certain phases of Temple worship were put into practice. Thus, we have records that the first edition of the treatise included in the Mishnah Yoma, i. e. The Day, referring to the Day of Atonement, where the details of the Temple worship on that day are given, was compiled by a scholar named Simon (Ish ha-Mizpa), who formerly acted as supervisor in the Temple court. Similarly, two other treatises, one relating to the description of the Temple itself, Midot, i. e. measurements, and the other describing the morning service and called *Tamid* after the name of the daily sacrifice, were also roughly outlined then by priests or scholars who were otherwise close to the Temple service. And so parts of the Mishnah began to be consolidated.

42. THE JABNE CENTER

The activity of Johanan ben Zakkai at Jabne was of short duration, as he was a very old man at the time of the destruction of the Temple, and it could not have lasted more than a decade. But short as it was, it was of lasting value. The impetus given by him for consolidation of the work of the Law was taken up by his disciples. There was an enormous mass of work to be accomplished before the actual structure of the Mishnah, the standard text of the Oral Law, could be constructed. First, older traditions embodied in different versions of *Halakot* had to be verified, differences between scholars straightened out, and scattered statements collected. Besides, when literary activity took a fresh start, it did not limit itself to conserve the old traditional study, but broke new paths, especially in interpretation.

A strong desire animated the Jabne scholars to find a basis for almost every Halakic statement and regulation in the Torah itself, i. e. the Pentateuch, and thus the old method of Midrash was extended. Not only were the rules of Hillel employed in their widest capacity, but new rules were added and the older ones expanded. These two tendencies, the standardization of the Halakah on the one hand, and the expansion of interpretation on the other hand, occupied the minds of the scholars at Jabne, the second generation of *Tannaim*. The leaders of that generation were: the Patriarch, Gamaliel the Second, the two disciples of Johanan, namely, Rabbi Eliezer, the son of Hyrkanus, and Rabbi Joshua, the son of Hananiah—Rabbi Eliezer represented the Shammaitic tendency, while the Patriarch and Joshua followed the Hillelites. Thus, differences were not as yet abolished. True, Rabban Gamaliel attempted to follow Johanan in making the Hillelite view prevail, but his method was somewhat harsh, and a rebellion broke out among the scholars and Gamaliel was deposed.

This rather revolutionary act was a source of blessing in disguise as it brought the work of consolidation a step nearer. A great gathering was assembled, probably about the year 90 c. e. on the occasion of the deposition of the president, Rabban Gamaliel, which met for some time, and at which the grouping and collecting of scattered statements on all parts of law and even on opinions and views was undertaken. Many doubtful cases were cleared up at this session which is usually called *Oto ha-Yom* (That Day), though as said, it met for a number of days. These doubtful cases on which decision was reached, mostly by testimony of older scholars, were compiled in one group, an enlarged edition of which was later incorporated in the Mishnah under the name of *Eduyyot,* i. e. Testimonies.

The second important work of that assembly was the revision of the various layers of the Halakah and smoothening and sifting out the outstanding differences between the two schools, the Hillelites and the Shammaites. Their opinions were tested and those which stood the test were adopted irrespective of party lines. Yet, it seems that the Hillelite view prevailed even then, though not because of any personal inclination but on account of its soundness of method. But in addition, a number of Shammaite *Halakot* were adopted when they proved to be better founded. Thus, the long party strife in the realm of the spirit came to an end. Differences, of course, still prevailed but they were more in the nature of differences between individual scholars rather than group differences.

It seems also that the second generation of *Tannaim* began to gather separate collections of Halakic statements grouped around certain subjects, so that consequently, the extensive material of the Oral Law, which was for generations in a state of flux, began to solidify in parts and form the building material for the structure which was soon to be erected. Simultaneously with the activity of standardization, the name Mishnah came more and more into vogue. It began to be used as a term for collections of ii.dividual scholars, and were usually called the Mishnah of this *Tanna,* or that *Tanna.*

B. Early Mishnaic and Other Halakic Collections

43. THE WORK OF RABBI ISHMAEL

Many and great were the scholars that made up the third generation of *Tannaim.* Each one of them contributed his share towards the organization of the Oral Law. But in the center of this generation there stand out two great personalities, and of the two, the second is the greater, these are Rabbi Ishmael and Rabbi Akiba ben Joseph. With these two, there culminated the process of interpretation which went on for generations and reached the highest point to such a degree that it practically came to an end. Both of these men also gave a strong impetus to the organization of the Halakah.

Rabbi Ishmael, in his love to relate every rule and Halakic regulation to the Bible, found it necessary, in order to meet his extended interpretation, to expand the rules of this method. He, therefore, increased the seven rules of Hillel to thirteen. He also made a collection of motivated *Halakot,* namely, where the rules are given together with their basis, the interpretation of the verse. This collection was arranged as a commentary on the Book of Exodus beginning with Chapter XII to the end of the book. This was the first collection of such motivated *Halakot* arranged in proper order, and a great part of it was incorporated in a later commentary on the same Biblical book bearing the peculiar name of *Mekilta,* i. e. measures and divisions, probably originally meaning groups, referring to the group arrangement of statements. R. Ishmael is said to be the author of the *Mekilta* which has come down to us, but as said, his collection most likely supplied only the nucleus, and the one we possess is from a much later hand. R. Ishmael's activity in compiling *Halakot* served as an example to subsequent compilers of motivated Halakah, which books are known as Tannaitic Midrashim, namely, compilation of statements derived or based on Midrash.

44. *RABBI AKIBA AND HIS DISCIPLES*

Greater than all scholars of his generation was Rabbi Akiba. He, whose life was romantic and death tragic, left his impress upon the succeeding generations, and later tradition ascribed to him unsurpassing greatness. He can be properly considered the architect of the structure of Halakah in the widest sense as embodied both in the standard collection of the unmotivated, the Mishnah, and the motivated collection of Halakah, i. e. the Midrashim. But he was more than the architect; he actually erected the frame of that building. Rabbi Akiba's activity represents first of all the zenith of extended interpretation. To him, study of the law was not only a means for practical decision, but a joy and an art. He was, therefore, carried away by his enthusiasm, and his system of interpretations was so extensive that at times it bordered on the casuistic. He is said by later generations to have interpreted every letter in the Torah, even every superfluous dot. His motive was the same as that of the other scholars, namely, to find a reason in the Bible for every legal rule and regulation, and hence it was often forced. Even his colleagues, who respected him greatly, frequently rebuked him for his strange methods of interpretation.

Yet, though Akiba with the intense ardor of his great soul was engrossed in increasing and deepening the study of the Halakah by the method of interpretation, he devoted himself, as stated, with equal zeal to the great task of its organization. It was he who, as said, erected the very frame of the Mishnah. It is told of him that he made the Oral Law like a chain of rings,[3] by which is to be understood that he introduced or more probably completed the grouping of the *Halakot* into definite divisions and subdivisions, such as books and chapters, so that it was thoroughly systematized. We are even told that he himself made an extensive Mishnaic compilation which was called the Great Mishnayot. He also stimulated the compilation of collections of motivated *Halakot,* which, like that of Rabbi Ishmael, were arranged as com-

[3] *Aboth Di Rabbi Nathan,* Ch. XVIII.

mentaries on the various books of the Bible, i. e. Halakic Midrashim. This particular work was the task of one of his disciples, as we will soon see, but he was the moving spirit in all this activity.

The spirit of Rabbi Akiba was too great to be limited to one field of endeavor, no matter how extensive it might have been. We, therefore, find that it roamed over the entire domain of the spiritual. He was as deeply interested in Agada (Sec. D) as in Halakah and his contribution to the organization and systematization of Jewish opinion and dogmatic view of Judaism was considered of such importance that it was incorporated in the Mishnah and passed as the standard opinion. And taking into consideration that in addition to this remarkable and exceptionally productive activity, Akiba possessed also a great personality, it is no wonder that the succeeding generations paid him the homage they did and spoke of him as the beacon light of the ages.

The fourth generation of *Tannaim* carried on its activity under great mental and physical stress. The times were turbulent; the disastrous war of Bar Kokhba and the subsequent Hadrianic persecutions wrought havoc in the Palestinian Jewry; for a time the schools were closed and the disciples were dispersed, and it took great effort to reopen the ancient seats of learning. At such a time, the need for completing the work of the organization of the Oral Law begun previously became a pressing one. The leaders in this work as well as in the entire intellectual activity were the disciples of Rabbi Akiba, and of them the most distinguished were R. Judah, R. Meir, R. Simon, and R. José, the son of Ḥalafta.

Rabbi Judah and Rabbi Simon were primarily interested in the work of compiling motivated Halakah, i. e. Midrashic commentaries on the books of the Pentateuch. Judah compiled such a commentary on Leviticus. He was most likely only carrying out the instructions and the rules of the great master Akiba. As in the case of the *Meḳilta* (Sec. 43), the Halakic Midrash to Leviticus which we possess, and the authorship of which is ascribed to Judah, is not really his but emanated from a later hand, and undoubtedly contains his collection as a nucleus. That collection bears the name of *Sifra*, i. e. the book, and it is possible that it is the original name of Judah's collection. Rabbi Simon collected motivated *Halaḳot* related to the Books of Numbers and Deuteronomy which likewise were incorporated in a later collection that we possess and which bears the name of *Sifrē*, i. e. the books. He also compiled a similar commentary on Exodus which seemed to have been named *Mekilta* like that of R. Ishmael.

Rabbi Meir, though resembling in mental acumen his great master Akiba, did not employ that acumen in dialectic interpretation, no matter how skilled he was in it, but devoted himself to the organization of the unmotivated Halakah, i. e. Mishnah. Working on the basis of the arrangement of Rabbi Akiba, he compiled a Mishnah of his own which seemed to have been of such nature of completeness and improvement that it is quite possible that the standard Mishnah we possess is only an improved and redacted edition of it. Rabbi Meir not only compiled Halakic statements, tested them, and sifted the material, but also attempted to decide between the different opinions, and the one which he thought best he quoted anonymously, thus indicating his approval of it. By this method, the Mishnah became a very serviceable instrument. This method was later adopted in the final Mishnah. Rabbi Meir was, like his master, a man of many parts, and possessed a great personality. He was a master of Agada and one who delved in mysteries of philosophic thought, and besides he possessed a charming style, being especially known as a fabulist. All these qualities gave him the desired influence, and his compilation became the outstanding one. The structure was almost complete, but still it lacked much, and many were the rifts and loose stones. It awaited the master builder.

C. The Mishnah

45. THE REDACTOR OF THE MISHNAH—JUDAH THE PRINCE

The one who perfected the Mishnah and perfected it in such a manner that it could weather the buffeting of the ages was Judah ha-Nasi, i. e. the Prince, whom later ages called by the title of Rabbi, master.

Judah, the son of Simon ben Gamaliel (135–219) was well fitted to undertake the task. He was the undisputed head of the Great Court, the Sanhedrin, the patriarch recognized by all Jewry and even by the Roman government as the stories, which were circulated about him of his friendly relations with the Roman Emperor, Antoninus, testify. He was rich and of extensive influence. Yet, he was modest and of pleasant character, so that his colleagues willingly submitted to his authority and cheerfully coöperated with him. In order to prepare himself for this task, he visited various academies maintained by the pupils of the great Akiba, examined their collections, and compared notes. But he spent the greater part of his time at the school of R. Meir. It was undoubtedly his collection that was taken by Judah as the basis of his Mishnah, but we would be mistaken were we to assume that all that Judah did was to edit the text of R. Meir. Judah also added a considerable amount of new material which he extracted from other collections, for, as said, he studied in various schools. Later scholars said that Judah possessed thirteen collections of *Mishnayot*. Whether the number is correct or not is immaterial, but the fact is that he practically rebuilt the Mishnah and gave it his individual impress.

There was a threefold purpose set before him. First, to bring order and unity in the activity of the development of the Oral Law so that it should not deviate into strange paths. Secondly, to give the students a text which should serve them as a guide in their studies; and thirdly, that it should become a code of laws in accordance with which the teachers shall be able to render decisions in practical cases. The Mishnah was, therefore, constructed in such a way so as to meet all these aims. It is bulky and contains all Halakic statements even on subjects which after the destruction of the Temple had no more validity, such as the laws relating to the Temple, its service and sacrifices, or laws of purity intimately connected with them. On the other hand, it is also exclusive; not all the statements were collected but only the important ones, and thousands were left out. Finally, a definite attempt was made to decide between the opinions of scholars on all matters practical, or otherwise important. This was done by quoting the accepted view anonymously (Heb. Setam). But still, we must not construe the codifying purpose strictly. It is not a mere code, for otherwise no differing opinions would be given. The Mishnah did not aim to stop study and research, and therefore contrary statements to those accepted were included, and these bear the names of their promulgators. Likewise, we very often find an opinion stated anonymously, and later a controversy about the same is given, which indicates that the former opinion must not be taken as absolutely authoritative. We meet also two contrary anonymous statements, all of which indicate that Judah left a place for liberty of research and opinion.

46. MANNER OF REDACTION

The redaction of the Mishnah was not carried out by Rabbi Judah himself, nor was it the work of a day or even a year. The process of redaction went on for some time, and it was done by a collegium among whom were the greatest scholars of the generation who worked with Judah.

47. FORM AND DIVISION OF THE MISHNAH

The entire collection is divided into six orders (Heb. Seder, pl. Sedorim); each order into tractates (Heb. Maseket, literally, a web on account of the subjects being woven together); each tractate into chapters (Heb. Perek, i. e. a joint or a link), and each chapter into sections, called Mishnah or Halakah.

The six orders are: (1). Zeraim, i. e. seeds dealing with all laws relating to agriculture and all precepts enjoining the performance of ceremonies which have any connection with the tilling of the soil or with its fruits and plants. (2). Moed, containing all laws relating to the observance of the holidays, including the Sabbath. (3). Nashim, literally women, containing all laws relating to the family, as well as laws arising from such relations. (4). Nezikin, i. e. damages, containing all civil and criminal laws including regulations concerning courts and form of court procedure. (5). Kadashim, i. e. holy things, comprising laws and regulations concerning the sacrifices, Temple service, as well as the dietary laws which were considered a form of holiness and distinction. (6). Taharot, embracing laws of purity and impurity.

The possible reason for this adopted order is as follows. The first thing in the life of man is his work, and as the chief work at the time was agriculture, it was deemed necessary to place Zeraim first. To this order is prefaced the treatise Berakot on prayer and benediction which enunciates the principle of the existence of God in a practical way by describing the form and manner of His worship. Next in order of importance in a man's life is rest, and hence Moed, containing the description and regulations of the Sabbath and holidays follows. The third step in the cycle of human life is the family life, wherefore the order of Nashim succeeds Moed. After the family, society and its relations are next in importance, and therefore Nezikin was placed after Nashim. Kadashim and Taharot, which deal with laws not practiced since the destruction of the Temple, were placed last.

48. THE CHARACTER OF THE MISHNAH

As stated, the Mishnah is both a textbook for the study of Oral Law and a code. But in its latter capacity, it was not meant to be so in the strict meaning of the term, for in giving various opinions, it left room for the later scholars to follow a different view from the one adopted by the compiler. However, as a rule, the decision of the Mishnah was usually followed. The method of decision was pointed out above, namely, quoting the adopted opinion anonymously. But the redactor or redactors used also a supplementary method and that was by stating the opinion of an individual in the name of the *wise* (Ḥakamim) which means that this opinion was considered by the redactor to be as important as if it were so pronounced by a majority. By using these devices, the editor of the Mishnah accomplished his aim to give the final form of standardization to the Halakah, without at the same time impairing its further development.

The Mishnah, however, was intended to be more than a mere combination of text and code of laws; it also aimed to standardize to a certain degree Jewish opinion, and inculcate the principles of Judaism and Jewish conduct as well as to preserve the records of ancient Jewish customs which show the sanctity of certain institutions. For this purpose, a certain number of selected Agadic *Mishnayot* were included, sixty-five in all, besides a special treatise on conduct, *Pirḳé Aboth,* i. e. The Sayings of the Fathers (on its character see below).

Of the dogmas emphasized in the Mishnah, the most important are, first of all, the unity of God—the recital of its formula (Shema) being the first subject discussed in the opening passage of the entire book. This dogma is given a good deal of prominence, and is mentioned a number of times in various ways. Along with unity, God's providence is likewise emphasized, and on several occasions it is distinctly stated that there is singleness in Providence, but that good and evil happenings both emanate from the same divine power (Berakot Ch. V, 3; IX, 5; Megillah IV, 9 and other tractates). Next in importance come reward and punishment both in this world and the hereafter, freedom of the will, the coming of the Messiah, the revealed authority of the Torah (literally Torah min ha-Shamayyim), i. e. that the Torah was given from heaven, and resurrection.

These last two dogmas were given special emphasis, and an opinion was expressed that the one who denies these two beliefs will be excluded from sharing the happiness of the last days (Olam ha-Ba, i. e. the world to come). The reason for the stringency is most likely that these beliefs were strongly impugned, at the time, by the Judæo-Christians who denied the validity of the Torah and gave a different interpretation of the resurrection and the last days. To strengthen these two cardinal beliefs, the promised penalty was included. Yet, with all attempts at standardization of opinion, no strict and close definition of some of the dogmas was fixed, and room was left for commentators and interpreters to apply a measure of latitude in their interpretation.

Of Jewish religious and social ideals, there are three outstanding ones which deserve mention. Love of God is inculcated to the extreme. Basing itself on the verse in Deut. VI, 5, "And thou shalt love thy God with all thy heart and all thy soul," it interprets the last words literally and says, "That man is to love God even when He takes away his soul, namely, no matter what great punishment is inflicted upon him, he is still to love God" (Berakot IX, 5). The second great ideal or principle inculcated is the value of the inner meaning of the performance of precepts (Kawanah). It is said, "Both the one whose offering to the Temple is much, and the one whose offering is little will be considered equally pious, provided the act of each is directed for the sake of God" (Menaḥot XIII, 2). In other words, the inner meaning of the act is the determining factor in its value. The ideal of peace is the third one emphasized. The Mishnah closes with the statement that "God has not found any other instrument of blessing for Israel except peace."

To the principles of conduct, there is devoted, as we said, a whole treatise, but there are many more statements incorporated in the Mishnah which bear on the subject. The editor had even gone so far as to include customs which illustrate the ethical character of institutions. To such a class belongs the recording of the custom of the daughters of Jerusalem who used to hold dances in the vineyards on the fifteenth of Ab and the Day of Atonement, and while dancing make pithy remarks to the young men around. The pretty ones among them eulogized beauty as the quality most desired in a woman for the purposes of marriage; the homelier who were of noble descent praised the value of family; the humble who possessed neither, sang of good character, quoting Proverbs XXXI, 30, "Favor is deceitful and vain is beauty; a God-fearing woman, she alone shall be praised." The last quality seems to be emphasized by the Mishnah, thus giving us a more or less accepted view of marriage.

49. ARRANGEMENT OF THE MISHNAH

The Mishnah, as a whole, possesses a well-defined logical arrangement of subjects. As indicated, there are six general classes of subjects,

i. e. Orders, which are divided into sixty-three subdivisions or tractates which are further divided into chapters. In each of these divisions, there is a coherence between the central theme and the subdivisions which describe a phase or a portion of the subject. Yet, in an attempt to erect a grandiose structure from a mass of single statements and decisions, it is inevitable that here and there, there should be a loose stone, a rift, and at times, even a whole section is somewhat loosely joined. Sometimes a chapter is included in a book or even a treatise in an order, merely by dint of the technical similarity of its subject rather than by strict logical classification. As for the lowest subdivision, namely, grouping the *Mishnayot* in chapters, it seems that there the technical or verbal similarity played an important part, and prominence is often given to it at the expense of unity of subject. We often find in the Mishnah groups of *Halakot,* the members of which treat of diverse subjects, their similarity consisting in a certain stereotyped phrase repeated in each of them, and hence they succeed each other irrespective of the fact that they interrupt the unity of the chapter. These groups were undoubtedly incorporated in the Mishnah from older collections where the literary formula served as a mnemonic device for the students.[4]

50. THE STYLE AND EDITIONS OF THE MISHNAH

The Mishnah represents not only a great scholarly effort, but a great literary achievement from the point of view of style, which contributed much to the development of the Hebrew language, especially Hebrew prose. Its language is comparatively pure Hebrew. It is true that we find there a considerable number of words which are not mentioned in the Scriptures, but we must not conclude that they were all borrowed or invented by the compilers. They might have been in use in the popular language, but were not quoted in the Bible on account of its limited field, for the Bible barely touches upon the everyday phases of life, while the Mishnah is all-inclusive. On the other hand, the Mishnah did borrow a number of words especially from the Aramaic and also from Greek and Latin, the other two languages current in Palestine, but in most cases, an attempt was made to Hebraize them in form. The admixture of Aramaic helped to add to the stately Hebrew a certain flexity and elasticity making it possible to express the various shades of meaning implied in the usage of legal terms.

The style of the Mishnah is not absolutely homogeneous. On the

[4] See L. Ginzberg, *"Zur Entstehungsgeschichte der Mischna,"* in Hoffman's Festschrift.

contrary, there are discerned in it the styles of the various scholars whose names are attached to the opinions quoted as well as the style of the older collections. Judah the Prince was careful to quote the opinions in their original language, but on the whole collection, there is impressed the unifying spirit of the compiler.

The style, especially in the Halakic part which constitutes the bulk of the Mishnah, is terse and concise, yet use is made of pithy sayings and legal maxims which soften the otherwise austere aspect. In the Agadic portion, the style often waxes poetic, and many an expression of the Mishnah has become a popular saying and forms a part of the vernacular of the average intelligent Jew. The Mishnah underwent two editions in the lifetime of Judah. The first was prepared by him in his younger days, and the second a revised one, in his later years. There were undoubtedly some changes introduced in the text of the Mishnah in later years, but these are comparatively slight. On the whole, it remained as it emanated from the hands of its editor. The Mishnah became the great source of the supplementary law known as Oral Law, which henceforth, was no more oral since it was written. And not in vain did many of the Christian Fathers call it the Second Scriptures, deriving the name Mishnah from the Hebrew root, i. e. *Shano,* to repeat, for it is really the second great book of the Jews after the Bible.

D. THE AGADA

51. THE GENERAL CHARACTER OF THE AGADA

We had occasion to refer several times to the Agada in the course of our narrative on the organization of the Oral Law, but as this form of Jewish literature is of such importance that without at least a general understanding of its nature and character one can hardly estimate the profoundness of the Jewish spirit, it deserves a section for itself.

Agada is the general name for the greatest diversified mass of Jewish literature which aims to complement the teachings of the Halakah, which primarily defines the practical way of living by instruction in the views, opinions, and ethical maxims touching both on the life of the individual and that of the nation in all their phases. Its character is indicated in the very name it bears literally signifying both saying and instruction, derived from the Hebrew root *Nagod,* which in its *hifhil* (causative) form *Haged* means to say or to impart instruction. The Hebrew form is *Hagada* and the Aramaic Agada.

It is encyclopaedic in character and contains a multitude of subjects including, besides matters of religion, ethics, and history, also some elements of the sciences, such as the rudiments of medicine, mathematics, and especially astronomy. Its period of development is a very long one and extends for over a thousand years; some of its early layers go back to Biblical times.

52. ELEMENTS AND CLASSES OF AGADA

In general, there are to be discerned in the Agada two elements, one contributed by the folk mind, and the other, the gift of the sage and the scholar. The first consists of stories and legends which began to cluster, in comparatively early times, about the lives of famous historical persons, or even about episodes of the past. The Bible forms, of course, the center of these embellishments. The second consists of a conscious effort on the part of the sages to make the entire Bible, not only the Pentateuch, but the historical, prophetic, and poetic parts as well, a source of inspiration for the people. This effort expressed itself in commenting upon the Bible and its interpretation.[5] The folk embellishments of history may date back to pre-exilic times, but received their developed form during the period of great activity in the Second Commonwealth when supplementary books to the Bible began to be written, i. e. those books known as Apocrypha and Apocalyptic (Ch. I). As remarked above, a great part of the older Agada is preserved there, but only a part, as the popular Agadic current was much larger. The origin of the other element may be dated back to the great religious revival under Ezra. When the Torah began to be read publicly and expounded, it was explained in two ways, from the point of view of ethical and inspirational teaching and from the point of view of law. It was thus the first expression of homiletic teaching. It was, of course, oral and employed the same method of Midrash as the Halakah. But, as the subject-matter of Agada was primarily thought and feeling, it gradually widened and swelled like a river fed by numerous springs and brooklets.

As the vicissitudes of national life multiplied during the turbulent centuries of the Second Commonwealth, as the experiences of the nation were enriched by persecution and struggle, by triumph, and hope for complete redemption, and as new ideas were increased both by

---

[5] For some elucidating remarks on the subject, see L. Ginzberg in his preface to *The Legends of the Jews*, Vol. I.

contact with other cultures and by Jewish reaction to their encroach-ment, they all found expression in the constantly growing Agada. The interpretation of the Bible in all its parts had to be strained to the ut-most to provide spiritual food for the people. It had to absorb all other elements, such as stories, proverbs, allegories, bits of metaphysics, or even science and many more forms of literature. Thus the Agada, like the Halakah, had to be divided into two parts, one which was always connected with the interpretation of the Bible, and the other which consisted of groups of stories, ethical sayings, proverbs, even general maxims on conduct bearing upon ordinary phases of life, such as preservation of health, the arts, industries, domestic economy, etc. It is possible that these groups of Agadic statements were written down in books, known as books of Agada, and were circulated among the people even before the destruction of the Second Temple. But the interpretative Agada continued to grow and increase through the activity of the preachers who delivered sermons in the synagogues on the Sabbath and festive days. The lines of division between these two kinds of Agada were often overstepped, and the two types of spiritual teaching frequently amalgamated.

With the destruction of the Temple and the intensifying of Jewish persecution, an increased demand was made upon the Agada, namely, to supply comfort to the downtrodden and inspire them with hope. This, together with other demands arising from life in exile which was constantly changing and becoming more complex, taxed the in-genuity of the preachers and the sages. And consequently, they used all methods in order to ably discharge their function as teachers and guides of the people. Using the Biblical text as a peg, they hung on it all kinds of teachings, sometimes touching on ethics, sometimes giving ex-tensively the biography of a hero, at times taking as a subject the suffer-ing of the Jews, at other times, their glorious future, and at still others, the coming doom of the oppressing nations. Thus, the web of the Agada was woven, trangressing all lines and divisions, like a parti-colored carpet where strands of many hues and shades make up an enchanting pattern.

Still the lines of division of the classes of the Agada are there, though not entirely separable. We can, therefore, divide the Agada into two main divisions, (1) general, and (2) homiletic. The general Agada can be further subdivided into (a) ethical-religious and (b) historical.

53. ETHICAL-RELIGIOUS AGADA

The ethical Agada contains a variety of subjects. It includes not only ethics proper, namely, the teaching of conduct, but also inculcates piety permeated with deep religious feeling bearing upon the relations between man and God, and embraces at times subjects of a metaphysical nature. Besides, it teaches also wisdom, both theoretical and practical, such as manners as well as observations on ordinary affairs of life culled from daily experience. As such, it appears under two aspects,[6] as a general philosophy of life, on the one hand, and as practical instruction on the other hand.

The style of this kind of Agada is at times flowery and poetic, but on the whole, it made extensive use of the half-poetic *Mashal* which includes the epigram, the maxim, and sometimes the pointed proverb, or the fable and parable. This form of expression suited its purpose best, as it made its teaching not only more intelligible by the use of the simile or antithesis, but also more easily remembered on account of its brevity and other mnemonic devices. In search for the perfection of this form, the Agadists ransacked the treasures of the Bible, popular collections of proverbs and sayings, and also drew upon the literature of other nations with whom the Jews came into contact, so that as a result, the Agada both enriched the Jewish spirit and the form of expression of the Hebrew language, as well as that of the Aramaic vernacular.

Of this ethical-religious Agada, we possess a number of collections of early times, probably the remnants of a much larger literature. To this belongs first of all the Apocryphal book "The Wisdom of Sirach," which, as we have seen (Ch. I), was written in Hebrew and translated into Aramaic. There is another collection of proverbs and maxims known as the *Aleph-Bet di Ben Sira* containing ethical sayings and maxims written in Aramaic. It has little relation with the original book of Sirach but is a much later collection. There are a few more books of a similar nature which are preserved in whole or in part. There was also, in former times, an extensive collection of ethical maxims often quoted in the Mishnah under the name of *Megillat Setorim* (Secret Scroll). But the finest example of this Agada is the treatise of *Pirké Aboth* (The Sayings of the Fathers) incorporated in the Mishnah. This treatise contains the ethical and religious teachings of the sages of Israel in chronological order (infra Sec. 56). The book has also a supplementary treatise known as *Aboth di Rabbi Nathan*, i. e. the ad-

---

[6] On this subject, see Steinschneider, *Jewish Literature* Heb. translation, p. 56 *seq.*

ditional ethical teachings of the Fathers collected by Rabbi Nathan, an older contemporary of Judah the Prince. Later, more works of this type were added, but they belong to the subsequent period. There were also collections of fables and parables. We are told that Rabbi Meir, the compiler of the earlier Mishnah, possessed a collection of three hundred fables. There are also other collections mentioned, such as "Fox Fables" and "Fables of Kubsin," which some take to be the name of a man Kubyses, a Lybian fabulist, whose fables were trans- lated.[7] These collections were lost, but their content was not lost al- together as we find hundreds of fables, parables, ethical maxims, and proverbs scattered throughout the numerous books of the great Agadic collections, as well as the Agadic part of the Talmud, and many of them are interwoven with Halakah. All these forms of teaching make up the ethical-religious Agada.

54. HISTORICAL AGADA

Historical Agada embraces embellishments both of the lives of the leading Biblical personages and of episodes of Biblical and later times, records of persecutions and miraculous redemptions, national and in- dividual, as well as genealogies of persons and families and many other subjects. Much of this Agada contains historical facts which have to be extracted from the mass of extraneous matter. This kind of Agada swelled and increased as time went on. The complex Jewish life sup- plied it with sufficient material; the persecutions, the lives of the martyrs, the activity of the great sages, all these gave the impetus for fresh Agadic productions. This class of Agada is intimately connected with the homiletic and interpretative class, as the episodes, incidents, and stories were interwoven in the sermons, and are scattered in Talmudic liter- ature and the great Agadic collections. But there seemed to have been a number of special collections frequently mentioned in the Talmud, such as *Megillat Yuḥasin* (Rolls of Genealogy) where, besides gene- alogical material proper, there were also some characterizations of the men mentioned, and undoubtedly there were more books of a dif- ferent nature. Much of this kind of Agada, especially that pertain- ing to the Biblical period, was left to us in the Apocalyptic books, as indicated before. Of special collections of this type, we possess two; the first is *Megillat Ta'anit* (The Roll of Fasts and Feasts), as early Tannaitic record of special days celebrated as minor feast days and of

[7] Joseph Jacobs, in his introduction to *Æsop's Fables*.

special fast days, commemorating certain events in later Jewish history, both joyful and sad. The second one is called the *Seder Olam* (Order of the World), the authorship of which is ascribed to José ben Ḥalafta, the disciple of Rabbi Akiba. It is a historical record of events from the creation of the world to his time (see Ch. IV for more details).

55. HOMILETIC AGADA

The homiletic interpretative Agada constitutes the bulk of Agada. Its main charactersitic is that it primarily turns around the Bible. In it, either verses or passages are actually explained or short sermons where many ideas are brought together are grouped and joined to a verse or several verses, the joining being at times logical, and at times forced. In such cases where the prime concern was the unfolding of a certain thought, or what is more probable, the forcing of the thought the preacher had in mind into the verse, the methods of interpretation were greatly diversified. Besides adapting the rules used in the Halakic Midrash, which for Agadic purposes were enlarged into thirty-two, the Agadists or preachers also employed other means, such as *Notariḳon,* namely, taking the single letters of a certain word as initials of words, thus forming a whole sentence out of one word, *Gematria,* i. e. using the letters of words as representing sums and comparing them with the sums of the letters of other words, or other devices.

Homiletic Agada reflects Jewish life closely, for it ministered to its needs. It was a part of the weekly instruction given in the synagogue, and as such, it was supposed to comment on current life, whether it was one of misery, or struggle, or peacefulness. As life became complex, so did Homiletic Agada become complex, and gradually drew in all other elements. It embellished history, it told stories about the great men of all times, it inculcated ethics and religious truths, and sometimes taught the law. In most cases, the preacher was also the great master of Halakah, and he interpreted the verse in two ways, as legal and as spiritual teaching. The sermon often began with an Halakic discussion, and then an Agadic explanation followed. Hence, we find Agada frequently interspersed with Halakic passages.

As the preaching was usually held on Sabbath afternoon, and as the afternoon service contained, besides a reading from the Pentateuch, also a portion from the Hagiographa, just as the morning service contained also a reading from the Prophets, the verses used in the sermon were drawn from all the three weekly readings. In time, these homilies

began to be collected into books arranged in the order of the books
of the Bible, but their actual compilation belong to a later period which
will be discussed in its proper place. It seems that the reducing of the
Agada to writing began much earlier than that of the Mishnah and
Talmud. Agadic books were circulated in early times, and were incorporated in the later larger collections generally known as Midrashim,
i. e. interpretative sermons (Sec. 84). About the time of the redaction
of the Mishnah or immediately after, the nucleus of the first great
Midrash on Genesis (Genesis, or Bereshit Rabba) was already in existence, though in its present form it was not completed till a few centuries
later. Likewise, there were included many Agadic passages in the
Mishnah and also in the Halakic Midrashim on the other books of the
Pentateuch (Sec. 41) the first compilation of which emanated from
the schools of Rabbis Ishmael and Akiba. Thus, the two great currents
of Jewish teaching began to be organized about the same time into
form and shape, only with this difference, that while Halakah attained
in the Mishnah the more complete definiteness of a text, Agada, on
account of its very fluidity still remained in a comparatively flowing
form until later. And even then, no one undertook to compile a text of
the Agada. There are many collections but no text, for it is essentially a
spiritual production and there are no bounds to the spirit.

56. THE SAYINGS OF THE FATHERS

As "The Sayings of the Fathers" is the most important collection of
the ethical Agada, its character deserves a few words of description.
As stated, it is a collection of proverbs bearing on the moral conduct of
the individual as well as that of society, and touches also on religious
questions, inculcating views accepted by the authorities.

It was intended to supplement the Mishnah which deals mainly with
law with a more or less coördinated view of Jewish ethics, namely,
the ethics practiced by the fathers of the Jewish tradition.

The collection retains a certain chronological order. There are,
however, some irregularities in the chronology, which are undoubtedly
due to a later arrangement. The tractate was placed in the order of
Nezikin, damages, in accordance with a very apt remark in the Talmud,
that "one who wants to be a Hassid, some say, let him study *Nezikin,*
and some say, let him study *Aboth.*" In the first instance one is advised
to study the Law and know how to avoid damaging or harming anyone. In the other, he is counseled to study *Aboth,* and know the prin-

ciples of conduct, so that he will carry out the law spontaneously.

The first four chapters contain the sayings of the leading scholars beginning with the men of the Great Synagogue and ending with Judah the Prince, his children, and their contemporaries. The fifth chapter consists mainly of anonymous statements, and the greater part of them are number maxims. The use of number in proverbs, sayings, and maxims was a well-known device with all Semites as it is very helpful to memory. It is found in the Book of Amos, the Proverbs of Solomon, and "The Wisdom of Sirach," and also in Arabic collections of proverbs. The numbers preferred in this chapter are 10, 7, 4. In general, the teachings of *Aboth* can be divided into two main divisions: (*1*) those relating to Torah and religious principles; and (*2*) those concerning the conduct of the individual and society. The second one embraces (*a*) rules of conduct for the scholar; (*b*) for the relation between pupil and teacher; (*c*) of man towards man; (*d*) of justice and its administration. The sixth chapter, added later, is entirely devoted to the Torah, its love, value, and methods of acquisition.

57. THE AGADA AND THE JEWISH PEOPLE

A word should be said finally about the place the Jewish people and its destiny occupy in the Agada. The Agada expatiates on the virtues of the Jewish people. It magnifies the idea of a chosen people, relates with many embellishments certain episodes in Jewish history, thus showing how the hand of God is manifested in it from its beginning, and inculcates innumerable times the idea that God has not forsaken Israel even in exile. The question of the suffering of the people occupies a prominent place. It is explained to be both a chastisement for sins, and a means for future reward. And above all, the Agada devotes itself to Messianic times. It pictures those times with the glowing and rich colors of Oriental phantasy. The Messiah becomes an ideal figure. His coming is described extensively and minutely. Entire collections are devoted to that end, where the sufferings that will be sustained before the redemption are described, and the glorious time painted in grotesque manner. In the description of the Messianic time, the material and the spiritual are mixed.

The Agada was the well of living waters whence the Jew in exile drank thirstily and drew inspiration and comfort in his bitter struggle. In it, he found shelter from the persecutions and insults heaped upon him by his neighbors. Borrowing a simile from Heine, we can say that it is thanks to the Agada which fortified the Jew in his miserable life and whispered to him words of comfort reminding him of his former dignity and future splendor, that the "enchanted prince" preserved inwardly his princely dignity while forced to live the life of a dog externally. In the Agada, the Jewish child found ample room for the play of his imagination, and in it he satisfied his poetic craving, so that the poetic feeling of the singer of the Psalms was kept alive in Israel, and in time bore fruit.

E. ADDITIONS TO THE MISHNAH

58. TOSEFTA

Such a grandiose work as standardizing the great mass of *Halakot* could not have been, by its very nature, complete and all-embracing. Since it was primarily a process of sifting, it was necessary that many *Halakot* should be left out. Also because it was the intention of the compiler to have the Mishnah as a textbook, brevity was desirable. On that account, not only were many *Halakot* omitted, but the shorter versions of statements were preferred to the longer ones, though the latter were more explicit. But those statements were not entirely forgotten. Even in early times, when the first compilation of the Mishnah was made by Rabbi Akiba, we find that one of his disciples, Rabbi Nehemiah, had already collected *Tosofot,* i. e. additions.

This collection most likely was more or less limited to the longer versions of the same *Halakot* incorporated in the Mishnah. In this case the earliest forms of the *Tosefta* were commentaries on the groups of *Mishnayot* collected in the standard Mishnah. But when the Mishnah was ultimately redacted by Judah the Prince, there were many of his disciples and contemporaries, such as Levi, Bar Kappara, Rabbi Ḥiyya, and Rabbi Hoshayah who busied themselves with compilations of *Halakot* which included many of the statements omitted altogether. These collections were at times known as the *Mishnayot Gedolot.* Especially active in this work were Rabbis Ḥiyya and Hoshayah, and it is probably to them and their schools that we owe the collected additions to the Mishnah known as *Tosefta.* It is arranged accordingly in the same six orders of the Mishnah, divided into tractates, chapters, and paragraphs. It consists of two elements, entirely new material which was formerly excluded altogether, and elucidation of the statements of the

Mishnah either by giving additional matter upon the subjects merely referred to there, or assigning the reasons for the pronounced opinions in the Mishnaic statements.

The *Tosefta* we have now, though, seems to have received its final form much later, probably at the close of the Talmud, as we find there many later additions. But there is no doubt that the last compiler, whoever he was, took as his basis the *Tosefta* collections of the school of Rabbis Ḥiyya and Hoshayah. The *Tosefta* contains also many Agadic statements which are either enlargements upon those quoted in the Mishnah or new ones. And just as the Mishnah contains an entire Agadic treatise, so does the *Tosefta,* and this is the *Aboth di Rabbi Nathan* which is a scholium of "The Sayings of the Fathers," where each brief saying or proverb is enlarged and commented upon.

59. BARAITOT

Even the *Tosefta* does not include the entire material. There was still a large mass of Halakic statements the collections of which were not preserved, but their material is preserved to a larger extent in the *Gemarah,* the commentary on the Mishnah. There are hundreds of such statements scattered there and are known as *Baraitot,* (sing. Baraita) namely, external, that is not of Mishnaic origin. They come, as said, from lost collections, or from groups of such statements which were committed to memory by generations of scholars.

Chapter IV

OTHER FORMS OF LITERATURE

Hellenistic Literature

60. GENERAL REMARKS

In a previous chapter, we had occasion to refer to the great Jewish literary and cultural center, Alexandria, the *nervus vivendi* of the entire Diaspora in the Hellenistic world. But while there we discussed only one phase of the literary activity emanating from that center, we wish now to complete that picture, and survey the entire spiritual heritage left to us by the savants and the literati of Egyptian Jewry who were, during three or four centuries, the spokesmen of all intelligent Jews in the Græco-Roman Diaspora.

There is a peculiar tone and character to this literature, the like of which is hardly found anywhere else. It bears the impress of two world views on its face, views opposite and harmonious at the same time. In it a wonderful amalgam between Judaism and Hellenism was effected, and as a whole, it is a testimony to the remarkable power of the Jew to penetrate into the spirit and culture of other nations, sound their depths, enrich them with his contributions, without at the same time losing his identity and spiritual aloofness. Yet, with all the inner richness it may possess as a product of two cultures, it is nevertheless stunted in its growth and limited in its extent, for it bears upon it the stamp of being the conscious expression of a minority, and a disliked minority, to say the least, at that.

Many were the Jewish communities scattered through those parts of Asia, Africa, and Europe which together constituted the Hellenistic world, and some of them even attained power, wealth, and influence. Yet, on the whole, the life of the Jews in those communities was a life of struggle, not so much a physical struggle for existence as a spiritual struggle for self-preservation. This struggle gave rise to a two-phased literary expression; on the one hand, as an attempt to defend the Judaism these dispersed Jews possessed from the constant encroachment of Greek culture and influence for the benefit of the weaklings in Jewish ranks, and on the other hand, as a means to protect it from the attacks of malice and calumny from without.

Hellenism, that powerful civilizing agent which succeeded in casting its spell in a comparatively short time upon a motley of nations differing in race, language, religion, and culture, and weld them into a uniform mass, did not leave the Jews within its sphere of influence untouched. Before long, the scattered Jewish communities in the Hellenistic Diaspora began to be Hellenized. Greek ideas, culture, and manners became part and parcel of the life of these Jews, and above all, the Greek language became their medium of speech. It was then that the inner struggle to maintain Judaism in the face of a changed environment began—a problem not unknown in our days. As all struggles of a minority, it was carried on along lines of compromise and adjustment. It was not a question of the exclusion of the ideas of the more powerful culture, but of inclusion, namely, how to include in Judaism the best that there is in that culture without at the same time injuring the tenets and principles of the former. The result was, of course, a modification of both.

Zealously and diligently went on the struggle to maintain the integrity of Judaism within the ranks, and with equal zeal and vigor was the defense of Judaism from attacks of the outside world simultaneously carried on. The latter was as necessary and as important as the first phase of the struggle, for in fact, they complemented each other. The more the honor and the dignity of Judaism was vindicated, the easier it was for the Jews to uphold and maintain it. The position of the Jews in the Diaspora was far from an enviable one. As much as the Jew adapted himself to the mode of life of his neighbors, there remained in him enough of aloofness and distinctness to make him totally different from the surrounding world. It was this aloofness which irritated the other nations, the fact that the Jews denied the right to other religions to exist, that they considered themselves a chosen people, as well as the abstractedness of their religion—all these taken together made them an object of hatred and even of contempt. They were considered a dissonance in an otherwise harmonious world, and as such, they were attacked on all sides. The educated and the literati considered it their duty to denounce the Jews and their faith; they called them either atheists, namely, disbelievers in any kind of organized religion, or barbarously superstitious. Fables were invented about the peculiar superstitions practiced by them both in the Diaspora and in the Temple at Jerusalem. Similar fables were spread about their descent and history; the nation as a whole was declared to have no culture of its own, and to have contributed little to general civilization. Such and similar slanders were circulated by the educated of all Hellenized peoples, whether Greeks, or Egyptians, or Syrians, but more than in all countries, Jew baiting was especially popular in Alexandria.

It was no wonder then, that Jews there developed a vigorous literary activity of an apologetic nature. In this literature, the Jewish writers endeavor to show the greatness of their faith, its purity and loftiness; and more, they endeavor to prove that the ideas embodied there are the very same ideas preached by Greek philosophers, that the Jewish nation is of great antiquity and that its great men, especially Moses, the Lawgiver, instructed other peoples. At times, the writers pass from defense to offense, attacking the beliefs of the pagans (Ch. I), but behind the seemingly offensive attitude, there really lurks the desire to defend and vindicate Judaism by declaring the inferiority of other cultures.

Thus, out of this double spiritual struggle, there arose an extensive literature permeated with the tendency of an attempt at adjustment on one hand, and that of apologetics on the other. And these characteristics are evident in all its expressions, stunting its free development and curtailing its extent. In general, we note in it two main currents, that of Biblical exegesis and theology and the historical-philosophical, both of which served the double purpose of the struggle, to accomplish the harmonization of Judaism with Greek culture as well as to defend it in the eyes of the world. Here and there, other forms of literature are employed, but always with the same tendency. Of course, the means used by the writers to accomplish their purpose were not always honorable; spurious names were employed, as well as other literary forgeries, but after all, these were only war measures, and in war, especially that of defense, many things are permissible.

A. Bible Translation and Exegesis

61. THE SEPTUAGINT

The beginning of this Jewish Hellenistic literature must be traced to the translation of the Bible, known as the Septuagint. It arose both as the fulfillment of a need of the Egyptian Jews for a version of the Bible in Greek, since Hebrew was no more understood by the majority of the people, and also from a desire to show the nations the beauty of the Torah. Later history, however, invested the act of translation with a halo of wonder and miracle. A subsequent Hellenist writer in a book entitled "The Letter of Aristeas" (*infra* Sec. 65) tells the story in profuse detail. According to him, King Ptolemy Philadelphus (285–247 B. C. E.) was advised by his librarian, Demetrius Phalerus, to have the laws of the Jews translated for his library. The king accordingly sent a request to the high priest, Eliezer, at Jerusalem, to procure for him suitable translators. The latter sent seventy-two elders versed both in Hebrew and Greek. When they arrived in Egypt, they were received with honors and placed in seventy-two different apartments, and each one completed a translation. When the translations were compared, they were found to be exactly alike.

This story was accepted as true for many generations, hence the name Septuagint, i. e. the translation of the seventy, as the two additional men were the leaders of the delegation, and were not included in the number. But modern scholarship has proved almost conclusively that this account is mere fiction; the only true fact which remains is the time of the translation of the Pentateuch, as the story relates only to that part of the Bible, namely, that it was translated during the reign of Ptolemy Philadelphus about the middle of the 3rd century B. C. E.

The translation, as said, was done by the Jews themselves to fill a most pressing need, and most likely, their best men participated in the work, and it probably took a number of years. After the Pentateuch was translated, a desire arose for the translation of the other books of the Bible which work was gradually carried out in a number of years by different authors. We know, though, that in the year 132 B. C. E., all the prophetic books, including the historical and many of the Hagiographa, were already translated, for the grandson of Sirach, writing in that year tells of their translation. By the beginning of the first century B. C. E., the entire Bible was translated. When the various translations were completed, they were gathered into one book, bearing one name, i. e. Septuagint, and were considered by the Jews of the Hellenic Diaspora as their text. The value of the translation for these Jews cannot be overestimated. It was their Bible; it was the translation which was most likely read in their synagogues; it was the text quoted in their books; and it was the one which they commented upon and interpreted. In short, it was the corner-stone of their thought and philosophy.

The Septuagint was a great achievement, notwithstanding many of its defects, the chief of which is its style. The Greek was Hebraized, and in many cases, the Hebrew construction was followed, and it was often difficult for a real Greek to understand its meaning. But its advantages outweigh its shortcomings. It is not a literal translation, but a commentary as well. A conscious effort is seen in it to harmonize the Torah with current ideas thus serving the purpose of reconciling Judaism with the culture of the day. Its chief characteristic, as in later translations, is the removal of anthropomorphic expressions concerning God, enhancing thereby the purity of the God conception. The translators were evidently scholars of the Law, and were conversant with the interpretation of the Bible as it was taught in Palestine, as they incorporated many Halakic and Agadic interpretations of verses. A number of other changes were obviously made to meet certain exigencies of the time. But there are many deviations in the translation from the Hebrew text which we possess and we cannot definitely know whether the translators actually had different readings in the text they possessed, or whether these deviations represent their own explanation of the words of the Bible. But be that as it may, this first translation still serves scholars as a guide for the interpretation of many a knotty passage in the Holy Scriptures.

62. AQUILA'S AND THEODOTION'S BIBLE TRANSLATIONS

Authoritative as the Septuagint was for the Jews of the Hellenic Diaspora, yet it could not be kept free from interpolations and errors of the transcribers during the ages. These began to multiply especially from the time of the advance of Christianity. The Septuagint was the only Bible the gentile Christians knew, and in the heat of polemics against Judaism, the partisan Christians did not hesitate to manipulate their Bible in such a way as to prove their doctrines. As a result, the text became corrupt. Besides, a demand arose among the more pious elements of the Diaspora for a new translation which should be more in harmony with the spirit of Judaism in the developed form it assumed in the beginning of the second century c. e. This demand was given the proper attention by the leaders of the school at Jamnia (Jabne) in Palestine, by Rabbi Eliezer, son of Hyrcanus, Joshua the son of Ḥanania, and Akiba, and soon a man was found to undertake the task.

That man was Aquila, a Jewish proselyte from Pontus. Born a Greek, he knew that language well, and having sat at the feet of the great Akiba, in Palestine, he likewise mastered Hebrew. His translation received the sanction of the Palestinian Rabbis, Eliezer and Joshua, the disciples of Johanan ben Zakkai, and it is even said to have been supervised by them. It is on the whole a very literal translation as its aim was to render every detail into Greek. He took care, of course, to incorporate the interpretations of the Rabbis, and endeavored to avoid every possibility of such dubious rendering from which a meaning not in agreement with the adopted view of Judaism could be deduced. His masters, Eliezer and Joshua, praised the translation exceedingly, and applied to Aquila the words "Thou art the fairest of men, grace is poured upon thy lips" (Ps. XLV, 3), meaning thereby that his translation possesses all possible grace. Simon, the son of Gamaliel, the Patriarch, during the subsequent generation pronounced the dictum, that after due investigation it was found that the Torah cannot be accurately translated in any other language except in Greek,[1] referring to Aquila's translation. Numerous passages of the translation are quoted in the Talmud, and from other sources we know that it was widely used by the Jews in the Diaspora for centuries. Yet, it was not preserved wholly; only fragments are preserved in the writings of the Church Fathers who used Origen's (185–254 C. E.) Hexapla, i. e. a Bible in six versions, where Aquila's version was also given.

Another translation was made half a century later, about 200 C. E., by one named Theodotion who is also said to have been a Jewish proselyte, and likewise a native of Pontus. He, however, did not make a new translation but revised the Septuagint and brought it closer to the Hebrew. His work was likewise lost; only his version of the Book of Daniel is preserved, as it was accepted by the Church and hence incorporated in the manuscripts of the Septuagint, and has supplanted the older translation of that book.

63. EXEGESIS

The attempt of the translators of the Septuagint to comment on the Pentateuch as well as to translate it, and especially their efforts to harmonize it with current ideas gave rise to a school of exegetes which carried the effort further. The more the intelligent Jew of the Diaspora became Hellenized, the stronger grew the need for a reconciliation

---

[1] Palestinian Talmud, tractate *Megillah*, Ch. I, Sec. 2.

between his Hellenic and Jewish selves. And as the Bible, chiefly the Pentateuch, was the center of his religion, for none, even the radical, dared to doubt the divine origin of the Torah, it was, of course, made the central point of the efforts at reconciliation, hence, the peculiar tendency of all exegetes and commentators. There were undoubtedly many such exegetes; unfortunately, however, their works were lost, but we possess almost the complete works of the greatest of them, and from their extent and copiousness, we cannot only learn the exact nature and character of that kind of exegesis, but also infer that his work represents the fruition of a process long used in the schools.

That great exegete is Philo Judaeus, the famous philosopher [2] (Sec. 68). The chief characteristic of that kind of exegesis is the extensive use of the allegory. Allegory and the interpretation of the hidden meaning of words were really not limited to the Jews, for as Zunz remarked long ago, "That for several centuries, we meet wherever we turn, among Jews, Syrians, Greeks, and Christians, with allegory and Midrash in interpretation of sacred writings. Everywhere there is a concerted effort to draw out from the otherwise plain words the deep and secret meaning of the text hidden therein." [3] The underlying motive of this tendency was the desire to harmonize the sacred text with current philosophical ideas. Sometimes, it was used as a means of defense against those who attacked the sacred Scriptures on account of the literal meaning of some passages. It was then endeavored to interpret the passages allegorically, to show that they contain a hidden meaning, a nobler one than the mere literal explanation of the word would convey. But primarily, it came as a philosophic need for the interpreters themselves who held the Scriptures in great respect, but were at the same time saturated with the philosophy of the time. It was thus with the Alexandrian Jews,

---

[2] Very little is left us concerning the life of this great man; only scattered remarks here and there. The year of his birth is not definitely known; it is variously placed between 30–20 B. C. E. He was a native of Alexandria and a descendant of a highly aristocratic family. His brother Alexander was the Alabarch, the head of the Jewish community of Alexandria, a high office indeed, as the number of Jews in that city reached close to a million. He was distinguished while still a youth by his zeal for study, as he says of himself, "that instead of crawling about after wealth and glory, I was carried aloft in inspiration by philosophy." It seems, though, that in spite of devotion to philosophy he took an active part in general Jewish life, for at the time of the attack on the Jews at Alexandria instigated by the Roman proconsul, Flaccus (38 C. E.), he headed a delegation of the Egyptian Jews to the mad Emperor, Cajus Caligula in 40 C. E. He was then an old man as he describes himself as such in his treatise *Legatio ad Gaium,* (The Embassy to Caius), which contains an account of his mission. He must have died a few years later.

[3] *Gottesdienstlichen Forträge,* p. 41.

and especially with Philo who was permeated with Greek culture. Such allegoristic interpretations were primarily employed when the question of the character of God was concerned, namely, when the Bible described God or His actions in a manner repulsive to the philosophic conception.

We have, for instance, Philo's interpretation of the passage in Genesis III, 8–11, where it is told that Adam and Eve hid from God, and that He asked Adam, "Where art thou?" What is really meant here is the false conception of the wicked man who hides from the voice of reason. In such interpretation, Adam, of course, becomes a symbol, not the first ancestor. What forced Philo to turn the story into allegory is the difficulty which the text involved to a philosophic mind. For how could one conceive that Adam and Eve could possibly hide from the all-seeing eye of God. Similarly, he interprets the story of the fall of man in an allegorical way. Adam and Eve represent the male and female types in the human species, and the serpent symbolizes evil desires and passions. The passage in Genesis XI, 5–9, where it is related that God descended to see the Tower of Babel which the people built and then destroyed is explained by Philo to be a warning to men that they should not pronounce judgment upon any act until they actually investigate it on the spot where it took place. It could not be taken by him literally, for God does not have to go down to investigate in order to know the truth. And thus, Philo goes on and allegorizes and interprets almost the entire Pentateuch in this wise. Even the very laws do not escape the fate of being allegorized, and are forced to yield a philosophic thought, as for instance, leaven which is forbidden on Passover (Ḥomeẓ) becomes a symbol for passion in man, and *Mazzah* stands for purity of soul.

This tendency contained an element of danger, for it led to an undervaluation of the laws. Philo was not unconscious of it, and he very often insisted that the precepts and commandments must be taken literally as well, and must be observed carefully in all detail. But that there were others who were not as scrupulous and did sublimate the Law into ethical precepts and injunctions is quite evident. Besides allegory, he used a good deal of Agada in his exegesis and especially in his treatises on the lives of great men. His Agadic interpretations resemble very much the Palestinian Agada. He also displays considerable acquaintance with Halakah, as in many interpretations of the Law he clearly reminds us of similar interpretations given in the Talmud. As it is hardly possible to assume that Philo was a pupil of the Palestinian scholars, we must, therefore, explain his extensive acquaintance with their teachings, either through the fact that these Halakic interpretations were widely current in Egypt and were the common share of intelligent Jews, or that Philo, in this case, drew from the commentaries of his predecessors. But his main object in explaining the Mosaic Law was to show its ethical and spiritual character. For this purpose, he endeavored to find an ethical meaning in every law, an intention to improve the state of human spirituality in every injunction. The apologetic tendency is evident on every step. Thus, in explaining the purpose of the dietary laws, he avers that they do not intend to foster separateness, as the vilifiers of Judaism have asserted, but on the contrary, to teach self-control. In explaining the Sabbath with its injunction to cease from all kinds of work, he launches upon a long discourse, upon the esteem in which work is held by the Jews, in order to obviate the accusation which was usually made against the Jews by pagan writers that they despise work, and emphasizes innumerable times that the Sabbath is a day devoted to study and the ennobling of the spirit. The result of such masterful apologetics was that Judaism as a whole appeared in the eyes of intelligent unprejudiced Gentiles as a highly ethical and spiritual religion. And it is possible that it is due to such exegetic works that the great proselytizing movement in the Roman Empire, during the first century c. e., took place. Thousands of Greeks in Alexandria and Romans in Rome and elsewhere became either full or semi-converts to Judaism.

Philo's exegetical works are quite extensive, even though not all of them have been preserved, and can on the whole be divided into three classes:

(1) A shorter commentary on the Pentateuch intended for popular use under the name of "Questions and Answers," as it runs in that form. It is not certain whether it really covered the entire five books or only some of them. According to the testimony of Eusebius (4th century), in his time they were only extant to Genesis and Exodus, in all, eleven books, six to the former and five to the latter. The Greek original was lost, and a large part of it, four books on Genesis and two on Exodus, was preserved only in Armenian of which a translation was made into Latin.

(2) His chief work is the large allegorical commentary on Genesis. It begins with Chapter II and runs to the end of Chapter XL. It is

voluminous and is divided into sixteen treatises which are in turn sub-divided into books. Most of the treatises bear special titles according to the subject they treat, such as *De Cherubim et flammeo gladio* (The Cherubim and the Flaming Sword), dealing with the passage in Genesis III, 24; IV, 1, or, *Quod Deus sit immutabilis* (That God is Immutable), explaining the passage Genesis VI, 4–12, where it is told that God regretted His act of creating man, a subject which required a lengthy discussion, for how could we apply regret to God since He is not susceptible to change? Other titles are: *De ebriate* (On Intoxication), referring to Noah's intoxication, Genesis IX, 21; "On Sobriety," Ibid., 24; "On The Value of Temperance;" *De migratione Abrahami* (On The Migration of Abraham), Genesis XII, 1–6, and many more subjects. These treatises are more than commentaries on the verses, but discourses on subjects where philosophy, ethics, and kindred teachings are imparted.

(3) The third class of Philo's exegetic works is what can be called an outline of the Mosaic legislation. It comprises a group of works covering the various divisions of laws arranged in systematic order. It was primarily intended for non-Jews. To this class belong the treatises: *De mundi opificio* (On The Creation of the World); "On The Life of Abraham," a philosophical treatise on the teaching of virtue, as Abraham typifies instructive virtue; "On Political Life," or "On Joseph." He, then, turns to legislation proper and begins with the treatise *De decalogo* (On The Decalogue), giving a general statement of its character and division. This is followed by the main treatise of the class *De specialibus legibus* (On The Special Laws). This is a most praiseworthy work as in it Philo tries to arrange systematically almost all Mosaic Laws under the heads of the Ten Commandments. For instance, under the first two commandments, he places all the laws connected with the worship of God, such as those concerning priests and sacrifices; under that of the Sabbath, all laws dealing with the day of rest and all festivals; under the seventh commandment (prohibition of adultery) all laws bearing on marriage and divorce; under the other three, prohibition of murder (Philo changes the order of the Commandments), stealing, coveting, and all civil and criminal laws. In addition to these, he also wrote a treatise on the three virtues: "Fortitude, Charity, and Repentance" and *De praemiis et poenis* (On Reward and Punishment). These treatises are a sort of appendices to the main work on special laws, and include also such laws which could not be grouped under the ten cate-

gories. In all these works, there is contained besides exegesis also philosophy and ethics. He wrote some other treatises, such as "On the Life of Moses," and several historical books. These as well as his philosophy will concern us in the next section.

B. HISTORY, POETRY, AND PHILOSOPHY

64. THE HISTORICAL WORKS OF DEMETRIUS EUPOLEMUS AND ARTAPANUS

The two tendencies characterizing the entire Hellenistic Jewish literature, that of harmonizing Judaism with Greek culture and the apologetic one, which were discussed above, are especially in evidence in historical-philosophical literature. One of the oft-repeated slurs against the Jews was, as we have seen, the lack of a history of their past; they were said to be a people without a culture of their own since they had no records of that culture. To refute that charge, Jewish writers began to compile histories of their people wherein the deeds of the past were greatly glorified. The first historical work of this kind, fragments of which we still possess, was one written by an historian named Demetrius, who lived in Alexandria towards the close of the third century B. C. E. The title of this work was "Concerning the Kings in Judea." It did not, however, deal with the lives of the kings but seems primarily to have been a detailed work on chronology in Jewish history. It started with reciting briefly the early history of the Patriarchs, giving special attention to dates, and continued to the time of Ptolemy IV (222–205 B. C. E.), which was most likely the time of the author. The book, as evidenced from the fragments, bristled with painstaking details about the genealogy of the leaders of Israel, and the author, in supplying all those details in both chronology and genealogy, must have drawn upon other sources besides the Bible, possibly oral Agadic elements which later found their way into the Apocryphal and Apocalyptic books.

The next historian of whose work also some fragments are preserved in the writings of Eusebius and other Church Fathers and is also mentioned by Josephus (Against Apion I, 23), is one by the name of Eupolemus. His work is mentioned under several titles but the most probable one is "The Jewish Kings," though a work on "The Prophecy of Elijah" is also ascribed to him. He really endeavored to give a narrative of Jewish history from early times, but the apologetic tendency is quite in evidence as he embellishes the lives of all the Jewish heroes with great splendor. In a preserved fragment about Moses, he makes him the inventor of alphabetical writing, transmitting it to the Jews, and they to the Phœnicians, and they in turn to the Greeks. Another lengthy fragment contains the chronology from Moses to David and tells at length of the life of the latter as well as that of Solomon. The author also gives the correspondence between Solomon and the kings, Hiram and Uaphres of Tyre and Egypt, respectively, wherein he solicits their aid in building the Temple, and likewise offers a detailed description of the Temple. The reproduction of the letters of Solomon already shows the strong tendency towards pseudepigraphy, namely, of ascribing writings to persons of antiquity in order to give them more authenticity.

The date of Eupolemus is not certain. He does mention a king, Demetrius, supposed to be Demetrius I, King of Syria, in the years 162–150 B. C. E., who most likely lived at that time. Besides, he is identified with a certain Eupolemus mentioned in I Maccabees Ch. VIII, 17, as one of the ambassadors of Judah Maccabee to Rome. If this is correct, he was a Palestinian and not an Alexandrian. This is strengthened by evidence from his writings that he used, besides the Septuagint translation, also the Hebrew Bible.

Another work of which we possess some fragments is one which bore the title "About the Jews" by an author named Artapanus. This work exhibits a propagandistic tendency, inasmuch as the writer makes Abraham, Joseph, and Moses the instructors of the Egyptians and founders of their culture. To the last-named, especially, is attributed the inventions of navigation, architecture, military science, and even the very institution of the Egyptian religion. To such degree had the apologetic tendency attained that it would even allow Moses to prescribe the rites of Apis in order to prove the indebtedness of the Egyptians to the Jews.

65. CONTEMPORARY HISTORY

We have thus far dealt with the writings of historians who aimed chiefly at glorifying the past of their people, but there were a host of others who devoted themselves to the history of their nation in their own time, writing for the purpose of showing the world the achievements of the Jews, covering either whole epochs or single episodes of special importance. To this group belongs, first of all, the work of Jason of Cyrene on the Maccabean wars in five books, of which our

II Maccabees is an abridgment. As the book is lost, we cannot judge of its character except from the abridgment which was already discussed. As for its date, it must have been written not long after the events took place which would be about 150 B. C. E., at any rate, not much later (Ch. I, Sec. 6.) Another work is one which bore the name of a famous Greek historian, Hecateus of Abdera, a contemporary of Alexander the Great and Ptolemy Lagos, but which was written by a Jew. Hecateus' work on the Jews is quoted by Josephus, and many fragments of it are still preserved. It probably dealt also with ancient Jewish history, but more with the relations of the Jews to Alexander and Ptolemy I, and described the privileges conferred by these monarchs upon them. Its whole character was of a defensive nature and the virtues of the Jews were extolled. Josephus relates in the name of Hecateus a story concerning a Jew, Messollam (Meshullam), who acted as guide to a party of Greek soldiers on a march towards the Red Sea. When the party stopped at the behest of an augur who was endeavoring to foretell the success of the march by the flight of a bird which was then circling above their heads, Mesollam inquired for the cause of the delay. On being told the reason, he silently drew his bow and hit the bird, and when chided for his sacrilegious act, he calmly remarked, "How could you expect the bird to foretell our future success when it did not even know its own fate?" (Against Apion B. II, 22.) The date of this interesting work is variously determined, some place it about 200 B. C. E. and some at the beginning of the first century B. C. E.

The famous letter of Aristeas also belongs to that class, and like the pseudo-Hecateus, it was also ascribed to a Greek writer. It deals with the episode of the translation of the Bible into Greek. Aristeas, an official at the court of Ptolemy Philadelphus (285-247 B. C. E.), writes to his brother Philocrates and tells him, in detail, of the wonderful manner in which the translation was accomplished, as related above (Sec. 59). It is evident, though, that the story of the translation was only a means for telling of the great esteem the Greek kings had for the Jewish Law and its teachings. The greater part of the book is devoted to describing the wise answers of the translators to the questions propounded by the king and his counselors. The whole story is given authenticity by making the writer, i. e. Aristeas, not only an eye-witness but the very ambassador of the king to the high priest, Eliezer, to bring the translators into Egypt. In general, the book breathes with love and admiration for Jews and Judaism and is thus one of the cleverest pieces of apologetics ever written. For centuries, the genuineness of the book was not doubted, and as stated, the very name Septuagint was given to the Greek translation of the Bible on its account. But modern research has discovered its real nature and it is a foregone conclusion that the book was written by a Jew much later than the actual translation took place. As for its date, it is usually placed between 200–96 B. C. E.

The most sober piece of contemporary Jewish history was written by Philo Judæus. It originally contained five books and described in detail the persecutions of the Jews in Alexandria under the procurators, Sejanus in the time of Tiberius, and Flaccus in the time of Caligula, and also his embassy to Caligula in the year 40 B. C. E. We, however, possess only two books, "Against Flaccus" and "The Embassy to Caius." In both works, Philo describes vividly the events of his day, and relates at length of his sad mission to Rome. It serves as a real historical source for the history of the time.

66. HISTORICAL POETRY

The desire of the Hellenistic Jewish writers to proclaim the glories and greatness of their people and to impart instruction to their own brethren was not limited to historical prose but also found expression in poetry. They used for that purpose the most common forms then in vogue in Greek literature, epic poetry and the drama. On the whole, historical poetry is the most appropriate term for this literature as it deals primarily with past deeds.

This kind of poetry must have been very extensive, but not much of it has been preserved. A number of fragments from a larger epic "On Jerusalem" by a certain poet, Philo, are quoted by Eusebius. The first one deals with Abraham, the second with Joseph, and the third where the abundance of water in the Holy City is extolled is a description of the springs and the water pipes of Jerusalem.

Another fragment of a similar epic is from one "On Sichem" (Schechem) by Theodotus. It is devoted to the geography and history of that town. Its topography is first described with enthusiasm, and then the entire history of Jacob and his settlement in that city, his alliance with Hamor, the ravaging of Dinah, and the attack of Simeon and Levi are described at length. From the fact that Sichem is made the subject of the poem and that it is called the Holy City, it can be inferred that Theodotus was a Samaritan to whom Sichem, where the Samaritan Temple stood, was the Holy City instead of Jerusalem.

The most remarkable piece of historical Jewish poetry written in Greek is a drama by the name of "Exodus" by a dramatist Ezekiel. He is called by several writers, "The Poet of Jewish Tragedies," and he must have written a number of them. In the extracts of "Exodus" preserved for us, the action begins with the flight of Moses to Midion, and opens with a monologue of Moses where he tells the story of his life up to that point. His meeting with the daughters of Jethro is then described, and is followed by the scene of the burning bush. In other scenes, an Egyptian, who escaped drowning in the Red Sea, enters and tells the sad tale, and a messenger arrives and tells Moses of the discovery of an excellent place of encampment at Elim. Thus, the entire story of Exodus is dramatized with skill and talent. The date of its composition is about 150 B. C. E.

In addition to what was mentioned, there are a number of historical works by anonymous writers as well as excerpts of Jewish Greek poetry which were interpolated by the authors into the writings of famous Greek poets, such as Æschylus, Sophocles, and many more wherein the worship of the one true God is extolled and the Jews praised. All this was the work of Jewish propagandists who used all means to glorify the Jewish name.

67. JOSEPHUS AND HIS HISTORY

The greatest Jewish historian of that period who gave us a consecutive and complete history of the Jewish people covering a period of over 2000 years was Joseph ben Matatyahu, or Matthias ha-Kohen, i. e. a priest, or as he is otherwise known, Josephus Flavius. His life was a very checkered one, and the course of his activity is full of deviations and extreme meanderings. He was born in the year 37 c. e. in Jerusalem to a father who was descended from a noble priestly family. As he tells us himself in his "Life," he was exceptionally proficient in the study of the law, and while a youth, he evinced a desire to acquaint himself with the various Jewish parties. At first, he associated himself with an Essene, Banus, and for three years, led an ascetic life, but at the age of nineteen, he returned to Jerusalem and joined the Pharisees. At twenty-six, he went to Rome on a mission to rescue some imprisoned priests, and there he made the acquaintance of the Empress Poppea, wife of Nero, who was sympathetic to Judaism. In Rome he learned both to fear and respect the Roman power and culture, and his weak nature became greatly impressed with the pomp and power of the Roman Empire.

On returning to Jerusalem in the year 66 c. e., he found Judea in a
state of seething rebellion, and he tried, together with the other peace-
loving leaders, to persuade the Jews to submit to the Roman power.
His efforts were unsuccessful, and he, either for fear lest he be considered an enemy, or for some other reason, became active in the rebellion. His activity in the war was, to say the least, of a curious character.
He himself tells, that he and two priests were sent by the Sanhedrin
to Galilee to persuade the people to lay down their arms. How came it
then, that when he arrived there, he set about to govern the province
and organize an army to fight the Romans? His unfortunate campaign
in Galilee, as well as the charge often made against him that the speedy
fall of the province was mainly due to his double dealing, are too well
known to need any comment. After his surrender in 67, he became, on
account of his prophecy that Vespasian will become emperor, the
favorite of the general. When the prophecy was fulfilled, favors were
showered upon Josephus and he was allowed to adopt the Emperor's
family name, Flavius. He accompanied Titus to Jerusalem, stayed at
the Roman camp till the fall, and afterwards settled in Rome. There he
was a court favorite through the reign of three emperors, Vespasian,
Titus, and Domitian, received a literary pension, and was granted full
Roman citizenship. At Rome, he devoted himself to literary work of
which his history is a result, and he thus partly atoned for his un-
patriotic conduct as a general in the Jewish war of liberation. The year
of his death is not known with certainty. It is generally placed at 95
c. e., though some believe that he lived until the beginning of the
second century.

His historical works consist of (1) "The Wars of the Jews," in seven
books, (2) "Jewish Antiquities," in twenty books, (3) "The Life." The
last work, though supposed to be an autobiography, dwells little on his
life proper but is devoted to a detailed survey of the war in Galilee, and
justifies his conduct in its management. His other work entitled
"Against Apion" in two books, is an apology for Jews and Judaism, and
as will be seen, constitutes his chief merit as a literary champion of
his people.

"The Wars of the Jews" were, as Josephus states in his preface, first
written in Aramaic, his native tongue, for the benefit of those whom he
calls "The Upper Barbarians," who were most likely the Jews of Babylonia, with the purpose, as it is surmised, to restrain them from instigat-
ing a revolt in the border provinces of the Roman Empire by convincing

them of the power of Rome. Later, towards the end of the reign of Vespasian about the years 75–79 c. e., he translated the work with the help of some of the Greek scholars into Greek. Yet, though it is supposed to be a translation, there can be no doubt that the first version was more favorable to the Jews, for the second version of this history bore the character of an official history of the Jewish War sanctioned by the very people who conquered the Jews, as it bore testimonies of accuracy by Vespasian, Titus, and for the sake of appearances also by the Jewish king, Agrippa II, who was more Roman than Jew.

It is true, that Josephus in his preface tells us that the main motive which actuated him to write the history of the war was the fact that the other histories did not do justice to the Jews in their struggle against the Romans, either because of flattery to the latter, or hatred towards the former. He, therefore, proposes to give a true account of this war, and though a Jew, he intends to be fair to all sides. Yet, it is doubtful whether he really carried out his promise. He was fair enough to the Romans, but hardly to the Jews. And though he apologizes to his readers for the passion he may be under in describing these affairs, and begs them to allow him "to indulge in some lamentations upon the miseries undergone by my own country," [4] he hardly displays that expected passion, and throughout the work bears the air of a scientific historian.

Of the seven books of "The Wars," the first two are devoted to a survey of the events in Jewish history from the persecution of Antiochus Epiphanes to the time of the rebellion, while the last five deal in detail with the story of the great war. At the time when Josephus wrote "The Wars," he did not plan to write a history of the Jewish people, as he says in his preface that he thinks such a task superfluous, for many Jews before him had done so, and also many Greeks had dealt with that subject. He, therefore, prefixed that survey of the period from Antiochus to the war merely as an introduction. He really covers it briefly with the exception of the reign of Herod which he narrates at length. This is to be explained by the fact that Josephus was primarily a compiler and made extensive use of previous sources, almost copying them verbatim.

The principal source for the history of the period preceding his time, which he used in "The Wars," seems to have been the writings of Nicolas of Damascus, a Greek historian who was a friend of Herod and

[4] Preface to The Wars, Sec. 4.

an official at his court. It is no wonder then that he followed his source in describing the reign of that monarch in full detail. Besides Nicolas, he must have used also other sources, such as some of the writings of the Hellenistic Jews, which dealt with the Maccabean period. Where his sources fail him as in the period between Archelaus, the son of Herod, to the War (5–66 c. e.), he is brief and disjointed.

In "The Wars of the Jews," Josephus endeavors to appear in the character of a disinterested historian who has in mind only one object, to tell the truth. He is, of course, anxious to defend himself and his patrons, Vespasian and Titus, and, except for that tendency, there is a spirit of aloofness pervading it. He gives, on the whole, a clear account of the war with a certain precision, but his history bears the character of a chronicle of events rather than a history of Jewish life. There is very little of the inner life pictured there. He gives a description of the three Jewish sects, Pharisees, Sadducees, and Essenes, which, however, is primarily limited to the last sect, inasmuch as the first two, the most important ones, are given only one or two paragraphs, a thing hardly to be expected from one who describes himself as a Pharisee and a learned priest. There is no mention of the great Jewish men of the period covered, such as Hillel and others. In addition, there are in "The Wars," especially in the first two books dealing with the period antedating the war, a number of inaccuracies which were later corrected in "The Antiquities." All this indicates that Josephus followed his non-Jewish sources too closely. Even in the description of the war itself where he is supposed to write from personal notes,[5] there are many inaccuracies in the names of places in Judea, a thing almost unpardonable for a native of that land, a priest and leader of the Jews. This again proves that Josephus followed Roman sources, such as the "Commentaries on the Jewish Wars" by Vespasian which were placed at his disposal,[6] and others. Finally, he surprises us by the total absence of feeling for the miseries of his people, in spite of his assurance that he was deeply affected by them. The description of the triumphal march of Titus in Rome, and the execution of Simon bar Giora, the Jewish general,[7] does not betray any passion on the part of Josephus, on witnessing the final humiliation of his people and the degrading death of a brave Jew who fought valiantly for the liberation of his country. This description could

---

[5] *Against Apion.* B. 1, 9.
[6] *Life,* 65.
[7] *Wars* B. VII, Ch. V.

have been given by any Roman eye-witness and need not have been written by one who professed himself a Jewish patriot. Yet, with all these defects, Josephus' history of the war is the only complete account of this period which was left to us and which managed to survive, and thus it became our only historical source.

His large historical work, "The Antiquities of the Jews," which forms a complete history of the Jews from the creation to the war, constitutes the chief glory of Josephus as an historian. It was written eighteen years after "The Wars" and published in 93 c. e. The motives for his writing the history he states to be the desire to benefit the public by informing them of matters which they did not know, and especially because of the great importance of the facts themselves.[8] He was urged to complete his task by his patron, Epaphroditus, a man of nobility and a lover of knowledge. He proposes to follow the sacred records of the Jews which, as he says, contain a history of five thousand years.[9] He speaks in the usual language of exaggeration of his time, for the matter of following records is open to doubt, as will be evident.

The character of this Magnum Opus of Josephus is of a much higher nature than that of "The Wars." The Jewish patriot in him appears quite often, and as a whole it bears an apologetic nature as he aims to show the world the glory of the Jews and the greatness of Judaism. Still, even here he pretends to keep up the appearance of a disinterested historian. For this work, he prepared himself more thoroughly than for the first. He used a great many sources, Jewish as well as non-Jewish, and he even quotes his sources by name, especially the non-Jewish. This is done, of course, to show the world how highly the Greeks thought of the Jews. Even "The Antiquities" are more in the nature of a chronicle than a real history of Jewish life, yet there is a more earnest attempt to picture the inner relations.

In relating the events of the Biblical period, he follows the Bible pretty closely, but utilizes a great deal of Agada in embellishing the events, and here and there, there is an attempt to rationalize the miraculous happenings, but on the whole, he relates them as they are stated in the Bible. In one place, he states, "I have related the things as they are contained in the Holy Writ, but my readers may accept or reject the story as they please," [10] thus showing his disinterestedness. In giving a

[8] Preface, 2.
[9] Ibid. 3.
[10] Antiquities B. II, Ch. XVI, 5.

summary of the Mosaic Code, he recounts the laws generally in accordance with Halakic interpretations, but there are quite a number of aberrations from the accepted Halakah.

With the close of the Biblical period, i. e. the return from Babylon and the resettlement in Palestine, Josephus was at a loss for sources. His account, therefore, of the two hundred and odd years between the return from Babylon to the conquest of Alexander the Great is rather meager. He utilized, however, all Jewish sources, such as the Apocryphal book of I Ezra, Additions to Esther and probably some chronicles of the High Priests, in order to add some details to the stories of Zerubbabel and Mordecai and to elucidate some events in that obscure period, such as the killing of the High Priest, John, by his brother, an event which is also mentioned in the Talmud. But there is no mention of the inner life of that period, of the activity of the *Soferim* and the Great Synagogue.

From the period of Alexander to that of the Maccabees where he had more sources, both Jewish—mostly Alexandrian—and Greek, his treatment is fuller. But from the Maccabees on where the sources grow abundant, his narrative is detailed. There he quotes in detail the Roman decrees concerning the Jews of the Diaspora and copies extensively from Greek historians, but also utilizes Jewish sources, especially the first Maccabees. Yet, though he tried to be faithful to his people, he was very often misled by his non-Jewish sources, which he followed closely from the time of the Maccabees. These sources were Strabo (30 c. e.), Nicolus of Damascus, especially the latter, and others. Thus, we see in one place when describing the Pharisees, he speaks of them, "as those who were in a capacity of greatly opposing kings," and further, "a cunning sect they were, and soon elevated to a pitch of open fighting and doing mischief." [11] Such language about the Pharisees does not tally with his other descriptions of them, and is evidently taken from the source of Nicolus of Damascus, as the passage occurs in the story of Herod whose historian he was. It proves conclusively that Josephus lacked the skill of a great historian who only utilizes his sources but does not incorporate them verbatim. The same defect noticeable in "The Wars" of omitting to mention the great Jewish sages who had little to do with politics, is evident here too. Yet, with all its defects, "The Jewish Antiquities" is a great work, especially as it is the only reliable source we possess for the long period of Jewish history until the de-

---

[11] *Antiquities*, B. XVII, Ch. II, p. 4.

struction of the Temple, and Josephus will remain the historian par excellence for that period.

His "Life" has been described as the least reliable of his historical works, having been intended primarily as an apology against his assailants, especially Justus of Tiberias who impeached his loyalty to the Romans. It thus represents a distortion of facts in his own favor, and in reality, it is an impeachment of his conduct as a Jewish patriot. Yet, it serves as a source for the details of the war in Galilee, and unfortunately the only source, for the other writings on the subject were lost. It was written towards the end of his life about 95 c. e. and served as an appendix to "The Antiquities."

Of special merit is the last writing of Josephus which goes under the title "Against Apion," in two books. The title is a misleading one, for the book does not deal with Apion only—in fact, he occupies little space there—but with all calumniators of Jews and Judaism. It is an excellent apology on behalf of his people and their faith. It can be roughly said that the first book deals with the calumniators of the Jews, and the second with those of Judaism. In a world full of hatred against the Jews, especially on the part of Greek writers who invented all kinds of calumnies against them, and who attacked the Jewish people on account of their lack of history as well as their "superstition," a book like Josephus' "Antiquities" which told in a consecutive manner and with great intelligence the long and illustrious story of the hated people, was ill received. His scholarship was doubted, his veracity impugned, and his style ridiculed. It was this clamor of the enemies which aroused Josephus to write the apology, as he himself tells us in the opening paragraphs. He might have had a personal motive, for, in defending his people, he defended himself, yet, it does not detract from the value of the work.

He opens his defense with a broadside against Greek vanity. Why, he asks, are they so proud; is it because of their antiquity? Can they prove it then? Their records go only a few hundred years back; as for older times, their own historians disagree among themselves. As for their arts, they themselves admit of learning the art of writing from the Phœnicians and other arts from other nations. He then goes on to compare the records of the Egyptians and the Chaldeans with those of the Greeks and finds the former more ancient and authentic. After this introduction, he begins his real apology and proves the antiquity of the Jews from the testimony of the Egyptians and the Phœnicians, referring here to Manetho, the Egyptian priest, whose calumnies about the Exodus he later refutes, but for the present citing him as an authority for the fact that the Jews left Egypt one thousand years before the siege of Troy. He quotes also many citations from Greek writers corroborating his statements, among whom he counts also Eupolemus (Sec. 62) whom he takes for a Greek. This is followed up by testimonies from such Greeks as Aristotle and Hecateus to the excellency of the Jewish character and purity of their religion. He then discusses in particular the falsity of the statements of the Jewish calumniators about the Exodus and Moses, the chief of whom was Manetho, the Egyptian historian. The main contention of all these falsifiers was that the Jews were driven out of Egypt on account of their affliction of leprosy, a story which has long persisted in Græco-Roman literature, and is repeated by Tacitus. Josephus, in a number of paragraphs shows the falsity of Manetho's account, its inconsistencies, and its slanderous character. With Manetho stand and fall the other writers, for they all based their stories on his records. But Josephus disposes of all of them, and thus ends the first book.

The second book begins with a refutation of the charges of Apion, the Egyptian Stoic and grammarian, who lived in the time of Philo. Apion accused the Jews of Alexandria of being strangers in Egypt and complained of their keeping aloof from their neighbors, of their being misanthropes, and many more charges. Besides, he repeated the slanders of the vilifiers of Judaism, that the Jews worship the head of an ass, and similar lies. Josephus refutes all these falsifications very skillfully one by one, and quotes Greek writers who testify to the nobility of the Jews. After this refutation, he begins his real apology of Judaism which constitutes the most exalted part of the whole work. He opens with a eulogy of Moses who is the oldest legislator. He describes the Jewish conception of God which represents Him as unbegotten and immutable through all eternity, superior to all mortal conceptions in pulchritude, and though He is known to us by His power, yet He is unknown to us through His essence.[12] This conception has indeed a fine philosophic ring. He further makes a fine point by stating that Moses did not make religion a part of virtue, but virtue a part of religion, and winds up by showing the wonderful harmony in Judaism between instruction and practice. Judaism insists on practice, while the Greeks had fine notions of virtue and even excellent laws, "but had no regard to the exercising

[12] *Against Apion* B. II, 23.

them thereto in practice," hence the Greek laxity in morals. After dwelling on the spread of education among the Jews, Josephus proceeds to a detailed exposition of the Laws. He describes the exaltedness of Jewish laws of sacrifices, purification, marriage, charity, the burial customs and duties of honor to parents. From the family law, he passes to social laws, such as those bearing on the conduct of judges, relations with strangers, care of animals, and winds up with a statement of Jewish beliefs in resurrection and reward and punishment. He ends by making an attack against paganism, showing its dark and ugly side, and thus apologizes for Jewish aloofness. It is not due to the unsociability on the part of the Jews, but to their desire to observe their own laws and guard their integrity. That this constitutes no offense, he proves by examples from Plato, who also insisted that the Commonwealth should keep itself pure from admixture as well as from numerous similar laws in other Greek states. He is not unconscious of the fact that an argument from the superiority of Jewish law will place a weapon into the hands of the enemies, and fearlessly says, "If this be the disposition we are under with regard to the excellency of our laws, let our enemies make use of this concession that our laws are more excellent." [13]

"The Apology" was the last work written by Josephus about the year 95, and in it, he gave the best that was in him to his people. In it he is once more the Jewish patriot and warm-hearted Jew that he was in his youth. His presentation of Judaism, though rather brief, is a masterly one, and because of its quality it has survived through the ages.

68. JUSTUS OF TIBERIAS

Justus of the city of Tiberias, in Palestine, was a contemporary of Josephus who also tried his hand at writing Jewish history in Greek. Unfortunately, his works were lost, though they were preserved for several centuries and are mentioned by later Christian historians. They seemed to have consisted of two separate treatises, one called "The History of the Jewish Kings from Moses to Agrippa II," and the other dealt with the Jewish war in which he also took an active part. "The History of the Kings" was, however, more in the nature of a chronicle rather than a complete history like Josephus' "Antiquities." In "The History of the War," he must have gone into detail and accused Josephus of many misdeeds, as the latter felt it necessary to enter in a long polemic with Justus in his "Life."

[13] *Ibid.* 39.

69. PHILOSOPHY

That the desire to harmonize Jewish teachings with Greek philosophy produced some kind of Jewish philosophy among the intellectuals in Hellenistic Jewry goes without saying. We know, however, only two men who attempted the creation of such a current of thought, and of one our knowledge is very scanty, as we possess merely a few fragments of his work. That one is Aristobulus who probably lived around 150 B. C. E. The work attributed to him by Eusebius and other Christian Greek writers bore the name "An Explanation of the Mosaic Laws." It was not, however, intended to be a commentary but a kind of philosophic discourse on the Law. The author had for his object to prove that the peripatetic philosophy was dependent upon the laws of Moses and other prophets. He, of course, had to employ allegories and many other devices to prove his contention and to show the similarity between the peripatetic philosophy and the teachings of the Bible. The main problem was the explaining away of the anthropomorphisms of God. Thus, in a fragment from a discourse on the creation of the world, which is still preserved, Aristobulus teaches that the words God said, "And it was," which are frequently repeated in the story of creation, mean nothing else but that things came into being by the operation of the powers or energy of God. In another fragment explaining the Sabbath, we find him extolling the power of the number seven in the Pythagorean manner.

All these statements do not prove him an original philosopher, as such notions were the stock in trade of every intelligent Hellenistic Jew, and we will see them expressed at length and with greater vigor by Philo, but to Aristobulus belongs the credit of being one of the first to attempt to formulate a philosophic conception of Judaism.

70. PHILO

The other philosopher who is really deserving of that name is Philo. We have already dealt with Philo's method of exegesis which is in itself a semi-philosophic production, and we will attempt to give a brief survey of his philosophic ideas which are scattered through his commentaries, as he never attempted to give a systematic statement of them.

We will begin with his doctrines of God and the world. Philo posits a dualism of God and the world. God is the primal ground of, or reason for everything that exists, while matter is the primal stuff. In itself, matter is without qualities and passive, and subject to the action of spirit or form. It becomes then finite and the source of imperfection. From the tenor of Philo's talk, it can be inferred that he considered matter eternal, and yet he did not commit himself explicitly. God is the absolute self-determining mind, nameless and of unknown essence, though activity seems to be an essential attribute of His. All that we can say of Him is that He *is,* but not *what* He is.

Philo, being God-intoxicated, did not adduce many proofs for the existence of God, yet here and there, some are found. He produces the argument from design, namely, that the world reflects the shadow of God by its harmony and coördination. He also appeals to man to search his own mind and observe how it rules the body, and draw the analogy that likewise is the world ruled by a universal mind. He finally appeals to mysticism. "The thirsty soul," he says, "knows God immediately by direct contact." He even claims that knowledge of God is implanted in man from his very creation, and that this is what is meant by man being endowed with "the spirit of God."

The main problem for Philo was how to explain the relation of the absolutely perfect God to an imperfect world, and this he does by bringing in intermediate causes. These are the powers of God; they are the connecting link between Him and the world. He sometimes calls them angels. These powers were created by God first before the world, though Philo is not clear as to what the creation actually means. They are, however, the manifestations of His constant active energy. The powers are many, but the principal ones are two, the regal and the creative power, or as he sometimes calls them Might and Goodness, corresponding to the Rabbinic conception of *Midat ha-Din,* i. e. justice, and *Midat ha-Raḥmim,* i. e. mercy. They may be interpreted as the fixed powers of nature, on the one hand, and that of Providence on the other. Over and above these, or rather the source of all powers, is the Logos, i. e. the word of God. The Logos which is the chief contribution of Philo is variously conceived by him. At times, he speaks of it as the sum total of all powers, as the intellect of the universe, but at times, as the bond of the universe, as the moral law. But in no wise should it be understood as a separate entity. It is only the supreme manifestation of God's activity.

It is the Logos and other powers which participated in the creation of the world and brought order into chaos. Man is created in the image of the Logos, and his soul is one of the divine powers. The body as matter is the source of evil and imperfection; it is a prison into which the spirit is banished and is set free only on death.

Yet, with all his philosophy, he clung to the sanctity of the Torah and believed in revelation at Sinai which came from God's goodness. He was the first to propound the theory that the voice of God pronouncing the Commandments was an especially created voice, a theory which was constantly repeated in Mediæval Jewish philosophy. He also believed the prophets to be the interpreters of God's spirit which degree they attained by falling into a state of ecstasy, wherein their human consciousness and sensations ceased to operate and their souls dissolved into a higher element and became one with it; hence, their power of inspiration and their source of truth.

Philo's ethics is to a great extent influenced by his view on matter and body. In man, as in the universe there is a dualism of soul and body, the soul being the source of good, the body that of evil. Yet, he does not teach, as some of his interpreters maintain, original sin. On the contrary, he claims that man is from nature neither good nor bad up to the age of seven, and the child's heart is pure and is like wax which can be molded either way.[14] He does, however, admit that man possesses an inclination towards sin, which, if not guarded against, will lead him astray. From this view of the body, it follows that the way to virtue lies through abstaining from sensual pleasures. And thus, his ethics has an ascetic ring, for he says that the fatherland of man's soul is heaven, the life of the spirit and the beautiful, and that material life is only an appearance. But here too he does not go the full length of asceticism and speaks of the body as the Temple of God. In general, his ethics on this point is contradictory, for while he speaks often in derogatory terms of life and advocates its renunciation, at times he places a high value on life. This last strain is undoubtedly due to the Jewish element in him, which kept him from following Stoicism to its extreme consequences. He does in the main advocate the cultivation of the four cardinal virtues of the Stoics, especially temperance, moderation of the passions, and proportion in action, but he adds to the four virtues two more, namely, holiness and piety which are his Jewish contribution to ethics.

The *summum bonum,* though, are not these two last virtues as in Rabbinic Judaism, but knowledge and philosophy or rather contemplation. As a matter of fact, Philo's contemplation is more a mystic union with God than logical philosophy. This is, of course, the highest virtue,

---

[14] The same idea is found in the *Midrash Tanḥuma* to Genesis, Ch. VII. It forms however an isolated view in Rabbinic literature, as the other statements all agree that the Yeẓer ha-Ra', i.e. evil desire, enters in man upon birth. May we not see in this view the influence of Philo's teaching?

the aim and goal of ethics, but in order to reach it, men must lead a virtuous life, and since will is the source of all practical virtues, hence the acquisition of a good will is the most important thing in life. Philo thus manages to agree with the ethical tenets of the Palestinian Rabbis, for though he differs from them a great deal, he seems to have succeeded in effecting a reconciliation between the Stoic conception of knowledge as leading to virtue and the Jewish idea of a good will. He differs from the Stoics in inserting the religious element. Man cannot liberate himself; he must have the help of God. The imitation of the ways of God and the striving to emulate Him became to Philo a great ethical ideal, the very ideal so frequently emphasized in Talmudic literature.

Philo also gives attention to the practical side of ethics; he places great value on duty and makes it the central point in an ethical life. Of duties, there are three classes, duties to God, to self, and to fellow-man, and the factors that bring about an ethical life are likewise three, natural inclination, education, and habit of practice. The last two are to him of the greatest importance and he emphasizes their need many times. In reality, the idea itself is Aristotelian, but Philo added the Jewish insistence on practice.

Philo, though thoroughly Jewish in spirit even if not always in ideas, did not exert great influence on Jewish thought, except probably on the mystics. The reason for that may be his theory of the Logos and inclination to asceticism, both of which ideas were fraught with danger for Judaism, as was evidenced from the fact that he became a favorite with the Christian Fathers who made much of these ideas for their own purposes. It was they who preserved his writings for posterity. Yet, he deserves an honorable place in Jewish literature, both on account of his works and his personality.

C. ARAMAIC TRANSLATIONS AND EXEGESIS

71. EARLY INTERPRETATION OF THE BIBLE IN ARAMAIC

With the return of the Jews from Babylon, there began the spread of Aramaic in Palestine as a spoken language, or as a vernacular, and thus there arose a competition between the two kindred languages, the Hebrew and the Aramaic. It seems, though, that by a kind of compromise Hebrew remained the language of literature and the more educated, and Aramaic became the language of the street and the common people. The lines were, of course, not drawn fast, and the two languages overlapped each other in their usage. Be that as it may, under the circumstances there arose a need for the use of the Aramaic in the teaching and the interpretation of the Bible to the people. Such use was introduced in very early times—probably earlier than the Maccabean period—when the scholars began to teach and expound the Bible in the synagogues. The verses of the Bible were rendered by them in an Aramaic version with explanations and commentaries, both the Halakic additions and Agadic embellishments.

These translations, however, were mostly oral, and continued so for hundreds of years. In fact, since the translations were really of an exegetic nature and contained Halakic elements, they were considered a part of Oral Law which was not supposed to be written down. Yet, since it was not strict Halakah and was mostly Agada, the prohibition was not observed and we have references to complete written translations of certain books of the Bible, especially those of the Hagiographa before the destruction of the Temple. The Septuagint translation of Job has an addition of an Agadic nature at the end of the book on the genealogy of Job taken, as it is stated, from an Aramaic translation of that book which proves that such written translations were current in early days. A story in the Talmud [15] tells us that Gamaliel the First (50 C.E.), the grandson of Hillel, saw a copy of an Aramaic version of Job which he ordered to be destroyed. Furthermore, the Talmud ascribes the Aramaic version of the prophetical books of the Bible to Jonathan, the son of Uziel, a pupil of Hillel, a statement, which even if taken in a modified form, still proves the antiquity of that translation, parts of which might have been written down in early times.

72. THE ARAMAIC TRANSLATION OF THE PENTATEUCH, PROPHETS, AND HAGIOGRAPHA

From all that has been said, it is clear that translation and exegetic activity was going on in Palestine for centuries. References to that activity abound in the Mishnah and the entire Talmudic literature. As a result, we have a number of Aramaic versions of the Pentateuch which on account of their importance received great attention at the hands of the popular interpreters.

These are: (*1*) the Aramaic version known as *Targum Onkelos*, (*2*)

[15] *Babli, Sabbath* 115a.

the *Jerusalem Targum* known as pseudo-Jonathan, (3) the fragmentary *Jerusalem Targum*.

The *Targum Onkelos*, which is the standard Aramaic version of the Pentateuch printed in almost every Hebrew Bible, is the oldest authoritative version, arranged according to the Talmud by a proselyte named Onkelos under the direction of Rabbi Eliezer and Rabbi Joshua at Jabne (about 100–130 c. e.). This Onkelos, as the Talmudic references show, was thought to have been a historic personality. But research and investigation of the sources on the part of the scholars has thrown great doubt on the existence of a man by that name, who was the author of that version. It is generally believed that this version arose from the attempt in the school at Jabne, chiefly through the influence of the great Akiba, to arrange from the various oral versions a standard one which should meet the needs of an authorized translation. The impetus for that work was, most likely, given by the Greek translation of Aquila which was sanctioned by the heads of the schools. They felt the need for a similar Aramaic version. When the task was accomplished, it was named by some the Translation of Onkelos—the Aramaic pronunciation of Aquila—namely, that it resembles the translation of Aquila in spirit and faithfulness to Jewish tradition. We are thus able to fix the time of its arrangement to be during the first half of the second century.

The Onkelos version is a Palestinian production, but as the need for an Aramaic translation was greater in Babylon, it was immediately transported there where it became the authoritative version used in all the synagogues on the Sabbaths. It became imperative upon the Jews to read the Pentateuch together with this *Targum*. The Babylonian scholars called it "Our Targum" and numerous quotations from it are found in the Talmud. In time, changes in style were introduced to suit the Eastern Aramaic dialect current in Babylon, and also some other additions. So sacred was this version considered that it was later provided with vowel points and accents like the Hebrew Pentateuch itself.

This version was executed with great skill, and besides its literary value, it possesses high exegetic value as well, for every translation is also a commentary. On the whole, it clings closely to the text and is, as the Aquilian model, literal, yet all necessary Halakic interpretations and sometimes also Agadic embellishments, are included. The main problem for the translator was to present the Pentateuch to the people at large, for whose sake the translation was made, in the most revered and dignified manner, so as to remove all gross conceptions of God and all misconceptions of other subjects, such as the character of the founders of the nation, the occurrence of certain events, etc., which a too strict literal translation may convey. He is very careful to remove all possibility of doubt concerning the unity of God, and therefore translates the two names of God, the Tetragramaton and Elohim by one name, i. e. Adonai, the usual reading of the Tetragramaton. He is especially painstaking to remove all anthromorphisms from God, and so whereever the Pentateuch speaks of God as performing human actions, he renders it in such a way as to remove even a shadow of that conception. Thus he renders instead of "And the Lord smelt a sweet savour" (Gen. VIII, 21) "And God received the sacrifice willingly;" or instead of "And God descended to see the city and the tower" (Gen. XI, 5) "And God revealed Himself to punish the builders of the city and tower;" or the expressions, "God spoke to Moses face to face" (Ex. XXXIII, II), and "My face will go with you" (Ibid. 15) by "As speaker to speaker," and "My presence will go with you." In this manner, all kinds of circumlocutions are used by the translator so as to present a pure conception of God.

As the anthropomorphic expressions are many, he uses various devices, but in general, he employs as substitutes three expressions, *Glory of God, Presence of God* (Shekinah), and *Word of God* (Memra) especially where the word God alone would imply a gross conception; for instance, instead of "And they saw the God of Israel" (Ex. XXIV, 10) he renders "And they saw the glory of the God of Israel"; instead of "And they heard the voice of God" (Gen. III, 8) "And they heard the voice of the *word* of God." The use of the word *Memra* reminds us of the Philonian Logos where *The Word* is the reflection of God (Sec. 68). He is also careful to protect the honor of the great men and women in Israel and gives dignified renderings wherever harsh expressions are used. The expressions, "And Rachel stole the *Terafim*" (Gen. XXXI, 19) "And Jacob stole the heart of Laban, the Aramean" (Ibid. 20), are rendered "And Rachel *took* the *Terafim*," and "Jacob hid his design from Laban," so as not to use unworthy expressions concerning our Patriarchs. In a similar manner, hard expressions about the people of Israel are changed. When it comes to the laws, the translator is careful to give in such places, where the literal meaning of the law may be misleading the Halakic interpretation and, at times, even an

Agadic interpretation where the verse is exceedingly difficult. We will cite one example. The verse, "Visiting the iniquity of the fathers upon the children and upon the children's children unto the third and fourth generations" (Ex. XXXIV, 7) is rendered with the addition, "When the children follow the sinful ways of their fathers," an interpretation which agrees with the explanation of the Rabbis. It intends to soften the harshness of judgment contained in the literal meaning of the verse, for why should innocent children suffer for the sins of their fathers? It, therefore, tells us that the sins of the fathers are only added when they themselves are sinful. Explanations of a similar nature are found in Onkelos in large numbers, thus making it not only a translation but a valuable commentary.

The *Jerusalem Targum,* called the pseudo-Jonathan, is a purely Palestinian version of the Pentateuch. It is not primarily a translation executed with care and exactness by one or more authors with a fixed purpose in mind, but a later compilation of free renderings of passages of the Pentateuch by the homiletists in the synagogues on the Sabbaths and holidays. As such, it has no unified character, and certain verses have several renderings. On the whole, it does not cling to the text, and contains a large element of Midrashic and Agadic embellishments. It contains also a good deal of Halakah. The date of the final compilation is late, as it mentions the city of Constantinople (founded in 330 c. e.) and the establishment of the calendar (365 c. e.) and there even the names of the wife and the daughter of Mohammed are mentioned. Its final redaction must, therefore, be placed about the end of the seventh century c. e., but not later, as we must assume that it came to fill a need in the life of the people who still spoke Aramaic. Half a century later, the Jews of Palestine and Syria already spoke Arabic, and it is hardly possible to assume that they needed an Aramaic version of the Pentateuch.

Yet, in spite of the above-named facts which point to a later date of the compilation of that version, the bulk of it hails from earlier times. There are a number of Aramaic renderings to verses of the Pentateuch mentioned in the Mishnah and the Talmud which are incorporated in this version. Moreover, some of the renderings are commented upon with disfavor by the Rabbinic authorities, and yet they found place in this version. All of which goes to prove that this *Targum* consists of various layers of renderings current in the schools and synagogues for centuries. And since it is a compilation, it is by its nature eclectic and it thus came to include renderings which were condemned by Talmudic authorities.

Its style and grammatical construction resemble greatly the language of the Palestinian Talmud, which again proves the older date of the larger part of its material which is also evidenced by the fact that the number of Greek words found in it is quite considerable, thus pointing to a time when Greek was current in Palestine. How this version was ascribed to Jonathan and was named by the first printers *Targum Jonathan* cannot be definitely explained. It is suggested, though, that since it was not widely known during the Middle Ages, the error occurred through the mistaken reading of the title by some copyists of the manuscripts. The title was undoubtedly written in abbreviated form *Taw Yod* (ת״י) meaning *Targum Yerushalmi*, i. e. *Jerusalem Targum,* and they read *Targum Jonathan,* for since the *Targum* to the prophets was ascribed to Jonathan, the transcribers thought that this version of the Pentateuch also belonged to him. The first printers, finding manuscripts distinguished by the name *Targum Jonathan,* printed the version under that title.

The fragmentary version of the Pentateuch, known in the printed Bibles as the *Targum* of Jerusalem, is only another partial recension of the main Palestinian version, for as stated, there were many renderings current and variations of many passages were frequent. It is these variations which were collected and arranged, and ultimately assumed that name.

The standard Aramaic *Targum* to the prophetical books of the Bible, i. e. from Joshua to Malachai, is ascribed by the Talmudic authorities to Jonathan, the son of Uziel, a disciple of Hillel. It would thus indicate an early date for its composition. It seems, though, that here too, as in the Onkelos version, the name does not really signify the existence of a certain person who is the author, but merely a certain tendency of standardization. This version probably followed immediately after the arrangement of the Onkelos translation of the Pentateuch, as some of the renderings of the latter are reproduced by it, and besides, it resembles in style and tendency that of *Onkelos.* On the whole, it is not as literal as Onkelos, but gives a freer rendering utilizing the current Agadas in many places. This Targum is of high exegetic value, as very often it forms a fine commentary on the text displaying deep insight into its meaning. It frequently deviates in the readings of the words from the adapted Massoretic text, and at times agrees in these readings with the Septuagint and other translations.

The Aramaic versions of the books of the Hagiographa include only Psalms, Proverbs, Job, Chronicles, and the Five Scrolls. The Books of Daniel, Ezra, and Nehemiah have no Aramaic translation as they are partly written in that language. The versions of Psalms, Job, and Chronicles follow mainly in the way of the prophetic *Targum,* namely, a more or less free translation, but on the whole, clinging to the text. They contain also a large element of Agada. They belong to an earlier period, in fact, as stated above, Aramaic versions of Job were current even in Temple times. The version of Proverbs is peculiar in its character, inasmuch as it is entirely free from Agadic embellishments and clings closely to the text. It agrees almost entirely with the Syriac translation known as the *Peshitta,* and it is most likely modeled after it. The versions of the Five Scrolls are really no translations but homiletic Midrashim. The Book of Esther has two *Targumim,* the second one being merely a collection of stories and legends, some bearing on the incidents related in the book and some having only a distant relation to the main story of Purim. The homiletic character of these translations is explained by the fact that the Scrolls were read on the holidays, and their contents were, therefore, made a subject of discussion by the preachers in the vernacular, i. e. Aramaic.

D. HISTORY

73. *MEGILLAT TA'ANIT*

The Jewish scholars of the Mishnaic age were not greatly interested in the study of history as a special subject and whatever historical knowledge we may derive from the extensive Talmudic literature has to be extracted from stray notes and isolated sayings. Whether the reason for the lack of cultivation of this branch of literature was due to the fact that these leaders were themselves engaged in creating history for their people, or to the reason given by Simon, the son of Gamaliel, namely, that were they to write down the events of their time, time would be too short to chronicle all the sufferings the nation was undergoing,[16] the fact remains that we have few historical works dating from that period. Of these, two are preserved, and several lost.

The oldest of the two is the *Megillat Ta'anit,* literally the Roll of the

---

[16] *Sabbath* 13b.

Fast Days. Curiously enough, though, the purpose of the book is opposed to what its name conveys. In reality, it gives a list of all such days, on which fasting is not permitted on account of the fact that they commemorate happy events in the history of the people. The book is arranged according to the months of the year and is thus divided into twelve chapters chronicling in each chapter the historical holidays of the month.

The Chronicle itself was written not later than the middle of the second century c. e. as it ends with the mention of the cessation of the persecution of Hadrian. It was written in very concise style and in Aramaic. Later, however, a scholium written in Hebrew, i. e. a kind of Talmudic commentary, was added to it. Both the Chronicle itself as well as the commentary contain valuable historical data for the period of the Second Commonwealth and also for the one immediately following the destruction of the Temple. Especially important are the remarks concerning the differences between the Pharisees and the Sadducees. The appendix to the book contains a list of the fast days observed by the Jewish people.

74. SEDER OLAM RABBA

The other historical book of that period is the *Seder Olam* (The Order of the World), ascribed to José, the son of Halafta, a disciple of Rabbi Akiba (130–160). It is a brief chronicle of the events in Jewish history from creation to the time of Alexander the Great, with some additional notes on later occurrences up to the destruction of the Second Temple, and is divided into thirty chapters. Its method is, on the whole, Midrashic. Opinions of various scholars are quoted and often the happenings of certain events, or their nature and characters are determined by homiletic interpretation of a verse. Yet, it has great historic value especially for the period ending with the destruction of the First Temple.

CHAPTER V

THE TALMUD

A. LITERARY ACTIVITY IN PALESTINE CULMINATING IN THE REDACTION
OF THE PALESTINIAN TALMUD

75. GENERAL CHARACTERISTICS OF THE TALMUD

Just as the Bible became the text around which there developed a
literary activity, beginning with commenting upon and interpreting
the verses and ultimately ending in an aggregate of Halakic statements,
so did the Mishnah in its turn become a text for further interpretation
and comment by the scholars of the succeeding generations. The source
of this continued scholastic activity lay in the very nature of the Mishnah, for as we have seen above, it was never intended to be a code of
laws, but a mere text for study. As all texts, its statements were not
concise, and many things were left unexplained and in doubt. Besides,
the version, though it was likely written down, was far from perfect,
and contained contradictory statements. All these reasons served as in-
centives to the scholars whose trained minds, logical acumen, and
great zeal for study craved for literary activity. And thus, the post-Mish-
naic work, which lasted for several centuries, began and ultimately
culminated in the compilation of another great book which, including
the Mishnah, is known as the Talmud of which two versions exist, one
the Babylonian, and the other the Palestinian.

The interpretations and comments upon the Mishnah are known as
Gemarah derived from a root *Gmar*, i. e. to learn, which shows the
essential nature of this activity, that it primarily came to satisfy the need
for study, not as a means but as an end in itself. It is this *Gemarah* which
constitutes the bulk of the Talmud whereas the Mishnah forms a comparatively small part. The scholars, the builders of the great edifice, the
composers of the *Gemarah*, are, in distinction to the scholars of the
preceding generations, *The Tannaim*, whose teachings are incorporated in the Mishnah, called *Amoraim*, i. e. commentators, whose chief
business was to expound the Mishnah. The name is derived from the

119

root *Amar,* which originally meant to say, but in time it acquired the meaning to explain, to comment, and to interpret.

The method followed by these interpreters, the *Amoraim,* was very similar to the one followed by the scribes, or *Soferim,* and later by the *Tannaim* in interpreting the Bible and developing the Oral Law, for it was the same subject-matter and the same purpose that animated this activity as that of the preceding generations, namely, to make the law an all-embracing way of life, and the task was not as yet completed.

These scholars, however, had a distinct advantage over the *Tannaim,* namely, they had a greater amount of material at hand, hundreds and thousands of *Halakot* which were omitted from the Mishnah, a great number of which were collected in the *Tosefta* and other compilations of individual scholars, while a large part, though not yet collected, was known to the scholars by tradition. These external Halakic statements (Baraitot) were utilized as aids in ascertaining the real meaning of the Mishnah, to correct its readings, as well as to decide between conflicting opinions or statements. These comparisons, which included also the ascertaining of the names of the *Tannaim* whose statements were embodied anonymously in the Mishnah, constitute an important part of the *Gemarah.*

Another method was the analysis of the text of the Mishnah by means of logic and application of reason. This analysis was called *Seborah* from the root *Sabar* which means to assume, to think. This was a very effective means of interpretation and was carried to the extreme. Every word of the Mishnah was scrutinized, its meaning tested in numerous ways, and as a result very often the text of the Mishnah was corrected to suit the interpretation, or the arrangement of the statements altered. As all this discussion was carried on orally, and opinions of different men were quoted and often contrasted, it assumed enormous proportions and admitted much of casuistry and extenuated analysis, hence its great bulk.

In addition, there were also added new *Halakot* by the *Amoraim* themselves, either on the basis of deduction or decisions, peculiar application of the law, changes, and variations. These new *Halakot* again required explanations, verifications, and groundings either in the words of the Mishnah or even in the Bible. Besides, these scholars were not satisfied with merely interpreting the Mishnah, but also supplied reasons for the opinions stated therein, and consequently a new Midrash developed where the old rules were used and new ones added. We must not forget either that the study carried on was not always of a practical nature, for it was not considered a means but an aim, and so hypothetical questions were often propounded, and ingenious answers sought for them. Thus, the interpretations, comments, discussions, and *Halaḳot* were ramified and constantly increased so that at the end of two centuries it reached the bulk which is contained in the Babylonian Talmud.

Both versions of the Talmud contain, besides the Halakah a great part of Agada, the Babylonian about one third, and the Palestinian about one sixth. The Agada of the Talmud is of great variance. It contains stories, proverbs, medical maxims, observations on astronomy and other sciences, and also ethics and pithy sayings on the practical ways of life. In brief, it is really a compendium of all knowledge known at the time to the scholars of the age, and not of that age alone but of the preceding ages as well.

76. THE AMORAIC SCHOOLS IN PALESTINE

Most of the scholars of the first generation of *Amoraim,* the pupils of Judah the Prince, carried on their activity at the Academy of Sepphoris in Galilee, the seat of the Patriarchate. To this generation belong Rabbi Ḥanina, son of Ḥama, who presided at the Academy; Rabbi Janai; Bar Kappara, a man of profound learning who was also endowed with a keen sense of humor and whose witticisms are preserved in the Talmud, and many others. A considerable number of scholars settled in Judea, and several schools were founded there. Of the Judean scholars, Rabbi Hoshaya, who on account of the esteem in which he was held was surnamed The Great, and Joshua, the son of Levi, were the leaders. The first generation busied themselves primarily with the explanation of the Mishnah in a plain and direct way, more in the nature of a commentary rather than the broad extensive discussion of the succeeding generations which embraced many extraneous elements. Some of the scholars occupied themselves with collecting extraneous Halakic statements and comparing them with those of the Mishnah, thus laying the basis for the extended Talmudic activity. Of the latter, Hoshaya was the most active in this kind of work and specialized in collecting groups of statements omitted, for one reason or another, from the Mishnah. Joshua, the son of Levi, also had his own collection of Halakic statements but devoted himself with greater zeal to the explanation of the Mishnah, searched to find the reasons for its opinions, and even studied assiduously its style and delved into the peculiar meaning of single expressions. He tells of himself that once when he found a difficult and foreign word in a *Baraita,* i. e. external Halakic statement, he interrogated every linguist in Palestine in order to ascertain its meaning and find the right connotation.

The condition of the Jews in Palestine in those times was not favorable to the development of learning. Persecutions, though not severe, were not infrequent. Taxes were heavy and the economic situation of the Jews became worse from year to year. Under these circumstances, the number of schools was diminished, those of Judea were closed in a short time, and the entire intellectual activity centered in one place, in the Academy at Tiberias, in Galilee, where the court of the Patriarch had its seat, moving thither from Sepphoris. The outstanding figures of the second generation of Palestinian scholars were Rabbi Johanan, son of Nafḥa, and Simon, son of Lakish. Johanan (199–279), the head of the Academy, who in his youth had studied in the school of Judah the Prince, acted as the link between the older generation of *Tannaim* and the new school. By his great store of knowledge, he contributed greatly towards the elucidation of the Mishnah, besides establishing a number of rules for its interpretation and decision between the various opinions propounded there. All these regulations contributed much towards the development of the Palestinian *Gemarah.* Rabbi Johanan was also endowed with a noble personality which distinguished him from the rest of his contemporaries. His love for the study of the Torah was unbounded, and it was he who pronounced the famous Talmudic maxim, "A scholar, though he may be illegitimately born (Mamzer) takes precedence over an ignorant high priest," thus inculcating the teaching that it is not riches nor noble descent which determine the value of a man but knowledge and scholarship.

Simon ben Lakish (200–275), the colleague and brother-in-law of Johanan, was a man of powerful character and mind. His youth is tinged with the color of legend. It is told that in his early days, being endowed with a remarkable physique, he was associated, in some capacity, with a band of lawless men, and that Johanan, making his acquaintance, persuaded Simon to give up his profession and devote himself to the study of the Torah, prophesying for him a great future in this field. The prophecy of Johanan was realized to the fullest extent. Simon ben Lakish shared with Johanan the authority at the Academy, and was known as the profoundest and most penetrating intellect of his day, so that he was given the nickname "Mountain Raiser," namely, that by his keen acumen and logical analysis he could remove all obstacles in the way of a propounded theory. His love for the Torah was no less than his mental keenness, and his assiduity in study became proverbial. His own maxim on the subject of continuous study was that the Torah says "If thou forsakest me for one day, I will forsake thee for two," namely, if a man ceases to study for one day, he forgets as much of the Law which can be acquired in two days. Ben Lakish, being a man of strong and fearless character did not hesitate to pronounce opinions of a daring nature. Thus, he ventured to say that the story of Job is only a parable intended to teach morality and not the record of an actual occurrence, and that the names of the angels are of Babylonian origin. The same daring spirit he carried into Halakic study, relying primarily upon the logical soundness of an opinion and not upon the fact that it was pronounced by many. He, therefore, gave strong impetus to the development of study in his age.

It is no wonder then that under the leadership of two such men, the Academy at Tiberias, during a large part of the third century, became a great intellectual center. Students from all parts of Palestine congregated there, and even students from Babylon flocked thither. In fact, this period of activity was the heyday of Palestinian scholarship, and a large part of Palestinian Talmud dates from this period. It is also possible that the foundation of that Talmud, its plan and organization, was laid then. Some of the older writers have even ascribed to Rabbi Johanan the redaction of the Palestinian Talmud,[1] but it cannot be taken as a fact, as we find a large part of it consisting of statements by scholars of later generations. We must, therefore, understand that statement to refer to the mapping out of its outline by the school of Rabbi Johanan.

There were three more generations of *Amoraim* in Palestine, five in all, but only the one succeeding the generation of Johanan was of importance. The luster of the predecessors had not faded as yet. The leaders of this generation were Rabbis Ami and Asi, Rabbi Eliezer, son of Pedot, the Babylonian Zeira, and a number of others. These scholars not only carried on the tradition of their predecessors, but followed more or less the Babylonian method of complicated discussion, where hypothetical questions of a casuistic nature took the place of a simple commentary. A man of outstanding ability and character of this period was Rabbi Abbahu of Cæsarea. He was the acknowledged leader of

---

[1] Maimonides in the preface to his Code.

the Jews in his day, and on account of his knowledge of Greek, their representative at the court of the proconsul, as well as an able disputant in religious controversies. Most of his disputes he carried on with the Christians whose influence in Palestine grew in strength daily. He was thus enabled by his argumentative powers and biting satire to weaken the vigorous propaganda of the early Church which carried on an extensive missionary activity in Palestine. Many of his keen remarks uttered at these disputes are preserved in both versions of the Talmud.

With the passing of this generation, Palestinian scholarship began to decline, for with Christianity becoming, from the time of Constantine, the dominant religion in the Roman Empire, the position of the Jews in Palestine changed for the worse. Persecutions became more frequent; the Church, seeing in Judaism its inveterate enemy, exerted pressure upon the Emperors to issue edict after edict against both the Jews and Judaism. Study was made difficult, the number of scholars decreased, many of them emigrated to Babylon, and the activity of the schools diminished. As conditions grew worse from day to day, the few remaining scholars decided to effect a compilation of the Talmud, to arrange in some order all the comments, additions, discussions, and remarks in both Halakah and Agada transmitted by the scholars of the preceding generations. This compilation or redaction seems to have been entrusted to one by the name of José, the son of Bun. So aggravating were the conditions of the Jews, and of such a haphazard manner was the scholastic activity at the time, that we do not even know definitely the date of the redaction of this great work, and we place it, on assumption, in the third quarter of the fourth century c. e.

B. Literary Activity in Babylon and the Babylonian Talmud

77. THE BABYLONIAN SCHOOLS

Turning to the second important center of Jews and Judaism, namely, Babylonia, we meet with a bright picture of the condition and situation of the Jews in that land. Not only did they enjoy full rights and economic prosperity, but also almost an autonomous government. The Persian rulers were liberal and respected the Jewish religion, and did not interfere with the management of the internal affairs of the Jews. These were under the charge of the Exilarch, the chief of the exile who was as a rule a descendant of the House of David. This Exilarch had broad powers and was even recognized by the king as the representative of the Jews. Such conditions were favorable towards fostering intellectual activity. But, as long as Palestine held the spiritual hegemony, the Jews of Babylonia looked towards it for guidance and knowledge, and Babylonian scholars went there to study. With the completion of the Mishnah, however, the situation changed.

Abba Areka (175–247) or, as he was later known, Rab, i. e. the master, on account of his learning and activity, himself a Babylonian, returned in the year 219 C. E. to his homeland from Palestine where he had studied under Judah the Prince. His coming marks the beginning of an epoch of intellectual activity.

Rab brought the Mishnah there, and, together with his colleague, Samuel (180–254), who conducted a school at Neardea, began to teach. Soon he founded his own school at Sura and students began to flock thither. Rab and Samuel not only expounded the Mishnah, but analyzed it, compared it with other Halakic statements, propounded questions, and gave to them various answers. Each one of them chose a special branch for specialization; Rab chose the field of religious law, and Samuel that of civil law—the statements and discussions of each preponderate in these two fields respectively. Besides, being a great Halakic scholar, Rab was also an Agadist of note, and even tried his hand at composing liturgical pieces, especially for the New Year's services which were adopted in our prayer-books. Through his personality he exerted great influence over the Jews of Babylonia, and he succeeded in raising his homeland to a seat of learning which ultimately took precedence over that of Palestine.

Samuel was distinguished by his logical mind and analytical power. He, therefore, found in the field of civil law play for his mental powers. Like his colleague, he devoted himself to the elucidation of the Mishnah, ascertaining the right reading and introducing emendations by logical research. He also deduced many new rules of interpretation and laid down a number of regulations in civil law which he propounded himself in order to facilitate the dispensing of justice. Samuel also was famed as both astronomer and physician, and applied his knowledge in these two sciences to good advantage in the study of the Torah, such as the solving of the knotty problems of calendar fixation, where astronomical knowledge is of great help, or in problems relating to *Terefah,* i. e. meat prohibited from being eaten, and kindred subjects where medical knowledge is required. These two constitute the leaders of the first generation of the Babylonian *Amoraim* who laid the foundation of the *Gemarah*.

Rab and Samuel were succeeded by Rab Huna (212–292) and Rab Judah, the son of Ezekiel (220–299), who became the leaders of the second generation of *Amoraim*. Huna presided at the Academy at Sura, and Judah founded his own Academy at Pumbedita. These were the two great Academies of Babylonia which radiated learning and culture to the Jews of the Diaspora for a period close to a thousand years. Under the successors of Rab and Samuel, studies progressed exceedingly. The number of students increased to such a degree, that the Sura school alone is said to have contained over eight hundred, beside the number attending Pumbedita and also some smaller schools presided over by other famous scholars of the period. Huna followed the methods of his master Rab, and continued to expound the Mishnah as well as to deduce new *Halaḳot*. But real keenness of mind which opened a new way of study, namely, that of dialetic and subtle reasoning, was displayed by Judah who was called "sharpminded" by his master, Samuel. This method which he introduced at the Academy at Pumbedita stimulated discussion and attracted the best minds of the day to his school. So skilled were the dialecticians of Pumbedita that they were spoken of ironically as "Pumbeditians who carry an elephant through the eye of a needle," namely, they accomplish the impossible.

Intellectual intercourse was constantly going on between Babylonia and Palestine, and scholars were going to and fro so that there was a continual interchange of opinion. The same subjects were discussed in both places, opinions of Palestinian scholars were quoted in Babylonia, and vice versa; quite frequently an answer of a Babylonian to a question of a Palestinian in a certain legal discussion was carried across by an itinerant scholar, and the latter in turn sent his refutation of the answer back to Babylonia, either by the same messenger, or by another traveling student. Thus, study increased, knowledge deepened, minds were trained and sharpened, and layers of the *Gemarah* were added. Besides Huna and Judah, there were other distinguished scholars in that generation, such as Rab Naḥman of Neardea, the disciple of Samuel, who like his master specialized in civil law, and distinguished himself by his deep analysis of law and the supplying of reasons for each decision. Another scholar was Rab Ḥisdah of Kafri, who in his old age succeeded to the presidency of the Sura Academy at the death of Huna.

The dialectic method introduced by Judah at Pumbedita, which ultimately held sway at both Academies, opened a broad way for Halakic study and research; no more was the *Gemarah* limited to a commentary or explanation of the Mishnah, but became a production in itself. Subjects upon subjects were piled up and joined together, though loosely; hypothetical cases and problems were discussed and solved, and the work grew in bulk. In this new method, the succeeding two generations of *Amoraim* led the way. The leaders of the third generation were Rabbah, the son of Naḥmani (270–332), and Joseph, the son of Ḥiyya (270–334), both presiding at the Academy at Pumbedita in succession. Rabbah was the keener mind of the two and followed in the footsteps of his teacher, Judah. His skill in dialectics attracted a crowd of students, at times said to number twelve hundred, and he was given the title of "Mountain Raiser and Grinder," i. e. a remover of all intellectual obstacles. He operated mainly with the *Seborah,* that analysis and logical interpretation of laws, opinions, and decisions, which in turn gave rise to new opinions and statements. Joseph, on the other hand, excelled in the possession of accumulated knowledge, a great stock of *Mishnayot* or *Baraitot,* and other statements transmitted by the preceding generations. He applied this knowledge to his teachings, comparing texts and contents of *Halakot,* refuting unfounded opinions propounded by overzealous dialecticians, and pronounced his own decisions always based on traditional teaching. On account of his profound learning, he was called *Sinai,* namely, one who is the treasure-house of Torah, like Mount Sinai, the place where the Torah was given.

The climax of extensive commentaries on the Mishnah, as well as on the statements of the preceding scholars and of dialectic discussion, was reached during the fourth generation of *Amoraim*. The leaders of that generation were Abaye (280–338) and Raba (299–352). The real name of Abaye was Naḥmani, being named after his grandfather, but his uncle, Rabba, called him Abaye which means my father, since he bore the same name. The name of Raba was Aba, which joined with the Rab, became Raba in the abbreviated form. Abaye succeeded Joseph as head of Pumbedita, and Raba conducted his own school at Meḥusa. These two carried the dialectic method to the extreme; their discussion touched upon every point whether it had any relation with the Mishnah or even with reality, or not. Any hypothesis in the field of Law that the human mind could grasp and discuss was a welcome subject in their schools. Sharp-mindedness and keenness of intellect was their delight. Raba used to say, "I prefer a single pungent pepper to a basketful of melons," meaning by it that a single flash of thought was preferred by him to a number of ready-made statements, though they may be correct and important. Their method of teaching received a special name, *Hawaiot de Abaye we-Raba,* i. e. the arguments of Abaye and Raba. The pair were assiduous scholars and their discussions occupy an important part of the *Gemarah.* There is hardly a page in the entire Talmud where the name of either is not mentioned.

Their successors of the fifth generation whose leaders were Papa, the son of Naḥman, Naḥman, the son of Isaac, and others, followed the way of their predecessors but lacked their ability. In general, a spirit of weakness was already noticeable in the course of study, possibly as a reaction from great mental effort. At any rate, the *Gemarah,* which contained layer upon layer of comment, interpretation, discussion, and opinion which were loosely connected with each other, and in addition, was carried around in the memories of the scholars and transmitted orally from generation to generation, was in need of arrangement and systematization, as otherwise, it was in danger of being forgotten. The burden became too heavy for any human memory. Some master mind had to come and weld its loose joints into a great production, to group the various opinions according to a system, to forge the links into one chain which should withstand the battering of time and change, so as to transmit to the future generations a complete spiritual heritage.

78. THE REDACTION OF THE TALMUD

The master mind was found; he was Ashi, the son of Shimi (352–427). He was a descendant of a noble and scholarly family, and was himself endowed with great mental ability. Besides, he was also blessed with riches and possessed great influence at the royal court. All these qualities and endowments made him the man fit to carry out the immense task. When he was elected to the presidency of the Academy at Sura at the age of twenty-three, Ashi devoted himself to his life's ambition. His fame drew to Sura a large crowd of students and this facilitated the work. Close to thirty years were spent by Ashi and his colleagues in arranging the large mass of material in the desired order, according to various tractates of the Mishnah. As there are about sixty tractates, two tractates a year were redacted, one during each study month of the academic semester. Full academic sessions were held only two months in the year, namely, *Adar* and *Elul,* which were known as *Kalah* months (probably derived from the root Klal, to crown, as these were the crowning months of the Academy). During the other months, the scholars who were business or professional men studied at home. The enormity of the task required great carefulness in revision, and Ashi determined to devote an equal number of years to revising the work, and thus the two editions consumed a period of close to sixty years.

With the death of Ashi, the Talmud was almost completed, yet there remained many things to be improved upon, gaps to be filled, weak spots to be strengthened, and other matters to be adjusted. This work of completing and perfecting the edifice was left to the successors. The work proceeded rather slowly; for sixty-eight years the scholars were engaged in the task, which consisted not only in perfecting the arrangement, but also in adding some new material occasionally. Chief among the later builders of the Talmud were Tabume, the son of Ashi, Méramor, and especially Rabina, the son of Huna, who put the final touches to the work. He died in 499, leaving the Talmud complete, and José, his successor, in the following year (500 C. E.) declared it officially closed.

As is evident from the time consumed in this arrangement and from the number of tractates edited each year, there was originally a *Gemarah* to each of the tractates of the Mishnah. But we possess *Gemarahs* only to thirty-seven tractates in the Babylonian Talmud, and to thirty-nine in the Palestinian one. What happened to the rest of the *Gemarahs* cannot be ascertained definitely. It is possible that they were lost accidentally, but more probable that the *Gemarahs* to certain tractates were purposely omitted by the *Saburaim,* the successors of the *Amoraim.* The reason for it is the fact that these tractates deal with laws and customs which are not observed since the destruction of the Temple, such as those contained in the order of *Zeraim* which, with the exception of the tractate *Berakot,* treat of the laws of tithes, Sabbatical year, and other things, or the entire order of *Taharot* dealing with laws of purification which laws ceased to be operative with the destruction of the Temple. It is also possible that the copyists were less careful in copying such tractates which did not deal with laws observed in post-exilic times. It is interesting, however, to note that the *Gemarah* to the order *Kadashim,* dealing mainly with the cult of the Temple proper, was carefully preserved in the Babylonian Talmud. It is lost, though, in the Palestinian, but earlier Jewish authorities mention its existence. The reason for the retention of these tractates may have been the hope that was alive in the heart of the Jew that at any moment the Temple may be restored and thus the discussion of its laws was of prime importance. The Palestinian Talmud has *Gemarah* to the ten tractates of the order *Zeraim* nine of which are missing in the Babylonian. There, the separating of the tithes and other practices connected with agriculture were observed even in post-exilic times.

79. THE PALESTINIAN AND THE BABYLONIAN TALMUDS

When we compare the two versions of the Talmud, the Babylonian and the Palestinian, we are astounded at the difference between them. The latter, as compared with the former, appears by its side as a man stunted in his growth beside one fully developed and grown to full size. Not only is the quantity of the Palestinian Talmud about one seventh or eighth of the Babylonian, but its quality also falls much below that of the latter. It is true that the Palestinians were more simple and direct in their interpretations, and their minds worked in a straighter line, and as a result, their remarks are very often closer to the true meaning of the Mishnah. But on the other hand, they lack the keenness of mind, the dialectic skill, the logical analysis and the wide sweep of the Babylonians. The Palestinians are too brief in their opinions and do not develop them; their remarks are stunted and cryptic. But the real difference lies in the edition. The Palestinian Talmud reflects the conditions of the times, the persecutions and sufferings that the Jews were undergoing; the work was, therefore, done with an impatient spirit, in a' haphazard way. Subjects are placed side by side without any connection; *Halakot* are brought in abruptly without introduction, or they are not even completed; quotations are not cited fully but in an abbreviated manner, so that the student remains confused and perplexed. In brief, it was edited under great stress; the persecutions pressed hard upon the scholars, and they were anxious to complete the work as speedily as possible, that the future generations should have before them a basic text to work upon and to improve. But conditions became worse, and as a result, study in the schools either ceased altogether or sank to such a low degree that no work of a creative nature could be undertaken. And thus, the Palestinian Talmud remained in its incomplete and unfinished state.

The Babylonian Talmud, on the other hand, presents an entirely different picture. It is well edited and skillfully compiled. The editors had sufficient time and leisure to do their important work. Several generations working assiduously for over a hundred years contributed to the erection of this edifice. Subjects are joined together by logical connections, though it is true that at times the connection is a bit strained and fanciful, but there is an effort to avoid abruptness, quotations are given in full, and editorial explanations or decisions abound. In general, the Babylonian method as indicated was of a more subtle, dialectic nature. It analyzed the subject under discussion to a nicety; point after point was examined and put to test, so that when the discussion was completed, there remained no dark phase on which light was not thrown. Such a method tended to make matters complex, for in elucidating a subject, comparisons were employed, analogies were used, other subjects which in turn required elucidation were included, and so the whole discussion assumed the aspect of an argumentative chain, the links of which are of different material yet present a general harmonious character.

Just as these two Talmuds differ in character so do they differ in style. The Palestinian uses a vernacular which consists of a mixture of Hebrew with the West-Aramaic dialect, while the Babylonian employed together with the Hebrew the East-Aramaic dialect which is closer to the language of the *Targum*. On the whole, there is a greater use of Hebrew in the Babylonian than in the Palestinian Talmud. The style of the Babylonian Talmud is clear and lucid, and very often tends to verbosity, and at times, it is tinged with a bit of humor which is not even wanting in discussions of a strictly legal nature. The Palestinian, on the other hand, is not only abrupt, but cryptic and generally dry, except when it comes to Agada, but even there, a sad spirit prevails. The shadow of suffering and strain rests both upon content and style.

80. THE SPIRIT OF THE TALMUD

It is almost an impossibility to convey to one who has not himself spent years in the study of this remarkably complex work—the Talmud —which took centuries for its completion, an idea of its nature and character. At the best, he can only get a glimpse of it, and the rest must be left to the imagination. The first thing which singles out the Talmud as a work *sui generis,* distinguishing it from other literary endeavors, is the completeness of its world, for it is not mere literature, where only a part of human life is reflected, but a whole world in itself, where the diverse currents of the life of a people during centuries flow side by side and, at times, mingle and cross each other. Its unity with life at the time of its making is unique; there is no rift between the two. It flowed out of life as waters gush from a bubbling well, and hence its diversity of subjects as well as its general unity. True, it deals, to a great extent, with law, but it is not the hardened law of the court and lawyer, but the law of the everyday life of the Jew, the law of social relations, the law of the family, the law of the individual in his home, in the field, in the market-place, and in the synagogue, school and assembly-place, the law describing the minutiæ of exercises and ceremonies connected with the birth of a child, its growing into manhood or womanhood, marriage and marital life, and ultimately death and burial. Perhaps, the term law is not adequate—it is in reality conduct. The Talmud deals with the complete conduct of the life of man in all its multifarious relations and phases. But complete conduct is really complete life, and life cannot be regulated. Life is ruled by spontaneous outbursts of feeling, of emotions of hope and despair, of thought and reflection. Hence, the Talmud deals not only with law but with medicine as far as it affects conduct, with astronomy and meteorology in their relations to human life and occupations, with the rules and methods of agriculture as it was practiced by the people in their daily tasks, and a host of other matters which in life are linked together directly and indirectly, with the wisdom of the everyday man culled from hard experience and expressed for brevity's sake in adages, proverbs, saws, and epigrams, and finally with the suffering of the people in the present, as well as with their hopes for a better and brighter future. This is only a partial description of the world embodied in the Talmud.

Several factors contributed to this completeness and wholeness. First, the favorable political and economic conditions of the Jews in Babylonia. True, the Jews there were in exile, but except in times of occasional persecutions, the yoke of subordination was hardly felt. They had complete autonomous government of inner affairs, their own courts, their own chiefs of the exile; whole districts were occupied by the Jews where they engaged in agriculture, trade, and commerce and Jewish life was as prevalent in the market-place as in the home and the synagogue. Nor, was there any struggle with foreign cultures. The Babylonian and Persian cultures were on a lower level than the Jewish and no foreign influence was entertained. In the districts inhabited by the Jews hardly any Persian was spoken, and Aramaic was the language of the Jews and Gentiles alike, the very same language which in the schools mixed so well with Hebrew. Under such ideal conditions, it is no wonder that Jewish life was a complete life, and that Jewish culture was whole without rifts and crevices occasioned by encroachments of foreign cultures.

The second factor was the peculiar conception of the Torah which was the very center of Jewish cultural and spiritual life. This conception, the origin of which can be traced to the prophets and which struck root in life during the Second Commonwealth when religion became the dominant factor, has many phases, but in general, they may be subsumed under two aspects: (*a*) the Torah as the sum total of all good and wisdom and (*b*) as a teaching and way of life for the group and the individual. Under the first aspect, it is almost unequaled in the history of human thought. The Torah becomes the very purpose of the existence of the world, and certainly that of man. Under the second aspect, it comprises everything which conduces to complete human conduct, law, ethics, and teachings of life. Under such conditions, the study of the Torah is not a means but an end, and there is no set limited period for its completion. All life is not sufficient for the study of the Torah. There is continual advancement, ever-growing progress.

But as great as the importance of the Torah is for the individual Jew, it is still greater for the nation as a whole. To Israel, the people of the Torah, it is the very essence of its collective life, the *raison d'être* of its existence, and the second fatherland. Has it not been expressed by the Rabbis, "God, the Torah, and Israel are one"? All this brought about a unique state of adult education which thus far has hardly been equaled anywhere else. As a result, study did not stop with the boy growing into manhood but continued to a later period. Scholarship was no profession; the Academies of Sura and Pumbedita were no universities where degrees were granted at the end of a stated period; and the students were not confined within its walls. They were men of trade and work, taking to the study of the Torah as to a labor of love, as an exercise of play and pleasure. And when the desire moved them, or at the stated months of assembly, they came to the Academy, some from the fields, some from the workshop, some from behind the counter, and even from the breweries and wine presses, to exchange opinions and decide upon intellectual and spiritual questions. Thither they brought their daily experiences of trade, agriculture, or profession, or practical medicine, or meteorological observation, and utilized this accumulated store of knowledge in various ways in the discussion, whether it be Halakah or Agada. Furthermore, these scholars, though not professionally so, were teachers of the people, and each of them preached to the congregations in the synagogues, some Halakah, and others Agada in its various phases, such as the principles of faith, ethics, rules of life, and even gave advice in matters of business and trade. These popular lectures were illustrated with stories and adages taken from everyday life. It is due to this closeness to folk life that many Agadic portions of the Talmud are steeped in the simplicity of the folk spirit, and are tinged with the exaggerated naïveté and even occasionally with the superstition of the folk mind.

The third factor was the fact that study was oral. As such, it knew no bounds, it had no limit. The discussion swelled according to the mood of the participants. It assumed the nature of mental sport and gymnastics. Whoever could display his mental keenness, his brilliancy of argumentation and sharpness of analysis was welcome to this arena of the intellect. There was only one purpose animating them all, "To increase the study of the Torah and strengthen it" (Le-Hagdil Torah we-le-Hadira). In oral discussion, all means were permissible, farfetched comparisons were brought, the bounds between Halakah and Agada were obliterated, and all faculties of the mind were brought into play. This quality of oral study might have jeopardized the logical order, the finished polish of a written work, but it added the flavor of vividness, the freshness of repartee, the scintillating wit and humor of a face-to-face discussion. In compilation, even when the Talmud was written down, no attempt was made to give it the stiff character of carefully composed treatises, but its original character was retained.

These three factors and a number of others gave to the Talmud its peculiarity and uniqueness, its encyclopaedic and all-embracing aspect. And it verily deserves the name of the *Sea* or the *Ocean* of the Talmud, for it does represent the latter with its swells and storms, its depth and expanse, its hues and colors, its exotic plants, and even its intellectual Leviathans who swam and still swim in its waters and raise the dialectic spray.

81. THE ORDER OF THE TALMUD

The *Gemarah,* as stated, is a commentary on the Mishnah and follows the order and the division of the latter. As each tractate of the Mishnah is divided into chapters, and these into sections of single *Mishnayot* dealing with a single subject at a time, so is the commentary. Each section of a chapter or a Mishnah is discussed. It is analyzed and compared, and while the discussion goes on, it broadens out when a *Baraita* is brought for comparison. The *Baraita* itself becomes a subject of interpretation and explanation and other statements are again quoted to explain the *Baraita*. These statements may in turn become a subject for discussion, and thus the argument swells, sometimes even in geometric proportion. At times, the explanatory statement of an *Amorah* is itself placed under analysis, especially if the man who pronounced it is one of the earlier scholars. Under the circumstances, the connection is a loose one and the relation strained. There was one more factor that contributed to the looseness of the connection between the parts, and that is the mnemonic devices employed by the scholars. One of these devices was the grouping together of the statements of one man. The same man might have pronounced three or four statements on different subjects, but when one was mentioned the others bearing the name of the same author were also given. It thus happens that in a heated Halakic discussion, the explanation offered by a certain *Amorah* is quoted and immediately after, the subject is interrupted, and interpretations of verses of an Agadic nature by the same author are cited. These Agadic matters require elucidation, or they may be connected with similar explanations. And thus, Agada takes the place of Halakah to the extent of a few pages or more; when the subject is exhausted, the Halakic thread is picked up again and the discussion continues. The same happens when diverse Halakic statements of one man follow in succession. The entire discourse presents the aspect of a complicated machine where wheels within wheels keep on turning all for the same purpose. When all that can be said about one Mishnah is given, the second one is taken up, and so on until the chapter is completed, and chapter follows chapter until the treatise is completed.

In completing the chapter on the Talmud, it remains for us to say a few words as to the influence of the Talmud on Jewish life. The Talmud became, next to the Bible, the Book of the Jew, and at times, its study superseded that of the Bible. It was, for generations, the only set of books in the study of which the soul of the Jew was engrossed. The Jewish youths sharpened their minds by means of its intricacies and delicate web of syllogism, and attained intellectual acumen and agility. From its mellow legends and exotic stories, the Jew drew inspiration and solace in the hard struggle of life. Its epigrams and *bon mots* became part and parcel of the daily vernacular of the Jew, and every dialect spoken by the Jews is saturated with them, and even the ignorant employ them in their speech.

CHAPTER VI

THE AGADIC COLLECTIONS

82. THE LARGE HOMILETIC MIDRASHIM

The compilation of the Talmud in its two versions which marks the end of a period of intensive literary activity gave an impetus to collectors and compilers in similar fields of literary endeavor, namely, in that of Agada. True, a large part of the Agada was also included in the Talmud, but there it lacks system and completeness, the Agadic statements are given as supplements to Halakic passages, and very often only for the reason that they happen to be stated by the same participants in the Halakic discussion. A need was, therefore, felt for the systematization and organization of the great mass of Agadic matter which had been accumulating through the generations and which was written down only to a very small extent, and mostly transmitted orally from one generation of preachers to another.

The need was especially felt in Palestine. There, where persecutions were most frequent and life for the Jew a hard and bitter struggle, the people looked for comfort and alleviation from misery. In the mild, semi-poetic, and soothing words of the Agada, they found a balsam for their bleeding hearts, and the Agadist was a very beloved person among the Jews of the Holy Land. The synagogues were thronged on Saturdays and holidays by listeners who were enchanted by the words of the preacher which carried them away into a different world far more noble and beautiful than the one in which they lived and suffered. Under these circumstances, the Agada increased and expanded. Each preacher not only repeated the words of his predecessor, but also added something of his own. However, the people were not satisfied with mere oral sermons; they wanted to have Agadic books which they should be able to read and study in their homes and schools. And thus, the compilation began.

Most important of the Agadic collections are the books known as "Large Midrashim" which are ten in number, five on the five books of the Pentateuch, and five on the Five Scrolls (Megillot), i. e. Canticles,

Ruth, Lamentations, Ecclesiastes, and Esther. They are denominated Large (Rabba) on account of their quantity, in order to distinguish them from smaller collections on these Biblical books. The time of compilation of these books lasted for several centuries, as one of these Midrashim was compiled as late as the 12th century, but as the material is ancient and only the arrangement is of later date, they all belong to the Agadic literature. Most of these Midrashim were compiled in Palestine, for it is the land of the Agada, but one or two of these books seem to have been edited in Babylonia. But it really matters little whether an Agadic book was edited in Palestine or Babylonia, as the material is of a similar nature. Agada, like Halakah, traveled from one country to the other, and the Babylonian scholars were as well versed in the Palestinian Agada as in their own, nor were the Palestinian preachers unacquainted with the Agadic statements of their Babylonian brethren. The Midrashim, therefore, contain sayings, parables, interpretations of verses, stories and proverbs of both Palestinian and Babylonian scholars alike, except that the Palestinian element predominates.

The earliest Midrash is the *Genesis Rabba;* its date of compilation can safely be placed about the beginning of the sixth century. It was composed in Palestine, and is a representative example of Palestinian Agada. *Leviticus Rabba* is likewise one of the older Midrashim, and was compiled immediately after the one on Genesis or even contemporaneously. It seems, however, that though the compiler was a Palestinian, he already made use of the Babylonian Talmud as he employed some of its technical terms.

Next in chronological sequence comes *Ekhah Rabba,* i. e. the Midrash on Lamentations, which is a purely Palestinian product, as its material is to a great extent drawn from the Palestinian Talmud and *Genesis Rabba.* It is prefaced by a long introduction (*Petiḥta*) consisting of thirty-three short homilies on the first verse of Lamentations. Of various dates but bearing the stamp and impress of Palestine are the Midrashim on the other Scrolls (Megillot) in consecutive order, Canticles, Ruth, Ecclesiastes, and Esther. The first two are of older date, not later than the end of the seventh century, while the date of the latter two cannot be determined with accuracy; they are probably earlier than the other Midrashim on the Pentateuch. Two of these Midrashim, namely, Ruth and Esther, are, like *Ekhah Rabba,* provided with an introduction which contains primarily homilies on the first verses of the respective books. The Five Scrolls were read in the synagogue on the holidays, namely, Canticles on Passover, and Ruth, Lamentations, Ecclesiastes, and Esther on the Feast of Weeks, Ninth of Ab, Tabernacles, and Purim, respectively, and as such were, of course, made the subject of interpretation and homilies; hence, the comparatively large quantity of Agadic statements and interpretations which center around these books that was ultimately collected in Midrashim.

The other Midrashim on the Pentateuch are of later date. The earliest among them is the *Exodus Rabba* which was compiled about the end of the seventh century. This is followed by *Debarim Rabba,* i. e. Midrash on Deuteronomy, which shows signs of later authorship, probably 900 c. e., and the very latest is *Bamidbar Rabba,* the one on Numbers, which most likely received its present shape not earlier than the beginning of the twelfth century, as it is not quoted by any earlier authors. The editors of these books quote extensively not only from the Babylonian Talmud but from other Agadic collections and especially the author of the one on Numbers was already acquainted with the poems of Eliezer Kalir (Sec. 116), later mystic teachings, and the later books of Kabbala, all of which prove the late date of its compilation.

83. THE TANḤUMA CYCLE ON THE PENTATEUCH

Besides the cycle of Rabba, i. e. Large Midrashim on the Pentateuch, there exists another Midrashic cycle on these books, known as the *Tanḥuma-Yelamdenu-Midrashim*. The first name given to it is because of the numerous homiletic interpretations of verses quoted in the name of Tanḥuma, the son of Abba, a famous Palestinian Agadist who lived towards the end of the fourth century. The second name of this cycle arises from the fact that a very large number of homilies open with the formula *Yelamdénu Rabénu,* i. e. may our master teach us. It begins with a question in Halakah, and while the Halakic matter is dispensed with in a few words, the discussion turns to Agada and homiletic interpretation.

Of this kind of Midrashim, we have several versions: (*1*) An older Midrash which was known to the early scholars of Italy and France by the name of *Yelamdénu,* but which is now practically lost except for a few fragments; (*2*) the printed *Tanḥuma;* (*3*) the manuscript *Tanḥuma* which was edited and published in 1883 by the late Solomon Buber. All three belong to one Midrashic cycle, and the *Yelamdénu* seems to have been the earliest, as collections of such homilies where the Halakah was joined to the Agada, inasmuch as the preacher was a teacher of both, existed in large numbers. It is these collections which served as the background and source books for the later Midrashim, the compilers of which drew upon them in abundance. For this reason, we find the homilies beginning with the formula, "May our master teach us," scattered through all Midrashic cycles such as the *Tanhuma, Pesikta* (Sec. 84) and in the books of the *Rabba* (Sec. 82). The date of the *Yelamdénu* collection is, therefore, an early one and is probably contemporaneous with the *Genesis Rabba,* about the beginning of the sixth century c. e., and the place of origin, Palestine.

Of the other two versions, namely, the *Tanhumas,* the printed one seems to have been the earlier, but it could not have been the work of the author whose name it bears, as there are evidences which show definitely that the compiler was acquainted with the Karaite movement, with the works of Geonim written in the eighth century and other late events. The date of compilation is, therefore, placed by most scholars to be the second half of the ninth century. As for the place where the author lived, there exists amongst scholars a difference of opinion. Some assert it to be Babylonia, while some take it to be Southern Italy. But as their proofs for such assumptions are not conclusive, it is not impossible to assume that the home of the *Tanhuma* is likewise Palestine. The manuscript *Tanhuma* is not much younger than the printed one. It dates most likely from the end of the ninth century and is an incomplete version, as it contains new material only on the first three books of Moses; the other two are alike in both. It was compiled in Palestine.

84. THE PESIKTA CYCLE

Besides the sets of the Midrashim which follow the books of the Pentateuch, section after section, in a more or less order of sequence, there is found another cycle of homilies which are known as the *Pesikta,* derived from the root *Pasek,* i. e. to divide, to cut. The meaning of the word is section, inasmuch as these homilies deal only with selected passages of the Bible, as well as that of the Prophets. These passages constitute the readings from the Torah on the holidays and special festive Sabbaths, such as the Sabbaths during Hanukkah, or the four Sabbaths preceding Passover. It also contains twelve homilies on the readings from the prophetic books (Haftorot) of the twelve Sabbaths preceding Succoth, beginning with the three weeks of mourning before the ninth of Ab, and followed by the seven weeks of rejoicing from

"Sabbath Naḥamu," i. e. comfort, and the two Sabbaths of penitence. All these readings, both those from the Pentateuch, as well as the prophetic portions, have special significance, and were made the subjects of discourse. These discourses were collected and because of their discursiveness were named *Pesiḳtot,* i. e. homiletic sections.

Of the *Pesiḳta,* there are two versions: (*1*) *Pesiḳta di-Rab Kahana* and (*2*) *Pesiḳta Rabbatai,* i. e. the large one. The first one is the older, and though it is not compiled by Kahanah, a Babylonian-Palestinian *Amora* of the second generation to whom it is ascribed, it belongs to the older Midrashim and its date of compilation cannot be later than the end of the seventh century, the place of the compiler, Palestine. Some scholars, however, consider Babylonia to be the place of compilation, yet the material employed, the names of the Agadists, and the large number of Greek words used point undoubtedly to Palestine. It contains thirty-one *Piskot,* i. e. homilies.

The second one is a much later collection; the date of its compilation is stated in the book itself to be 845 c. e. It bears the impress of the younger Agada and is distinguished especially by the use of Hebrew words and expressions instead of Aramaic employed by the earlier Midrashim, by its poetic style, and by snatches of rhymed poetry which shows an acquaintance with the school of neo-Hebrew poetry which began to flourish in Palestine in the seventh century. The large *Pesiḳta* is not compiled in an orderly manner, as it contains many duplicate homilies on the same passages and other signs of confusion. On the whole, it is a careless collection of statements drawn from previous compilations, such as the *Tanḥuma* and the *Yelamdénu* collections. On that account, it contains many homilies beginning with the well-known formula, "May our master teach us," and most of its material can be traced to their sources. It contains in all forty-six sections.

85. NATURE AND CHARACTER OF MIDRASHIC LITERATURE

The Agada contained in all these collections belongs primarily to homiletic Agada. It was, as pointed out previously, an outgrowth of the activity of the preachers and its moti was the interpretation of the Bible in all ways and manners possible. Sometimes the commentary method was used and sometimes the pure preaching method, where a verse, merely used as a text, was employed. It is for this reason that the books included in these collections bear various characters. Some approach that of a commentary and some that of a collection of short sermons. Of the *Rabba* cycle, those resembling more the character of a homiletic commentary are the *Genesis Rabba* and most of the Midrashim on the Scrolls. In *Genesis Rabba,* each verse is taken up and interpreted. But in order not to make the book unwieldy, it was divided into chapters, the number of which is one hundred. This division is more or less an arbitrary one, as it does not correspond to any of the several divisions of the book itself, but they are merely devised to break up the entire subject into smaller sections to facilitate study and reading. The same method is followed to a large degree in *Exodus Rabba* and the Midrashim on the Scrolls.

The homily or sermon method is the one used by two other cycles, the *Tanḥuma* and *Pesiḳta* cycles and also by Leviticus, Numbers, and *Deuteronomy Rabba.* The last two contain in general much borrowed material from the *Tanḥuma* or from the *Pesiḳta,* and follow, of course, their method. Where the sermon method is followed, the verses of the Bible are not taken in consecutive order, but one or two verses of a section, usually the opening verses, are selected and are made the subject of a number of short homilies, quoted in the names of various preachers or Agadists. When the subject is exhausted, the next section is taken up. In dealing with the sections, the Palestinian order of sections is followed.[1] To make the sermon more interesting, Halakic questions were propounded at the beginning with the usual formula of "May our master teach us," to which an answer was given; hence the prevalence of that formula in Midrashim based on the sermon method.

Yet, though homiletic Agada is the background of these Midrashic collections, it by no means forms the entire substance of these collections for as explained above (Ch. III, Sec. 53) the homiletic element absorbed all the other elements of the Agada, the historical, ethical, and poetic. In order to illustrace their teachings, the preachers were forced to draw upon all sources of the Agada, historical facts, legendary biography, fables and folk stories, maxims and parables. Hence, it came about that while the Midrashic Agada is primarily homiletic, it contains all forms of literary expressions, and is thus encyclopaedic in character, and forms the storehouse of the many-colored Jewish lore.

[1] In the reading of the Law on the Sabbaths, there was a difference between the Babylonian and the Palestinian. The former finished the Pentateuch in one year, and divided the Torah into fifty-four or fifty-three different sections, usually called *Parshot,* the weekly portion, while the latter finished the Torah in three years, and divided the Pentateuch into one hundred and fifty-five sections called *Sedorim,* orders. It is this division which is usually followed in the Midrashic cycles based on the sermonic method, where the subject contained in the beginning of the sections is taken as the theme.

The method used by these Agadists, either in expounding a Biblical verse, or in delivering a homily was an indirect one, namely, the verse was not immediately explained nor the subject of the sermon treated at once but always prefaced by one, two, or three, or more introductions. These introductions or *Petihot,* as they are technically called, are as a rule based on a verse from the Hagiographic writings, as the Psalms, Proverbs, Ecclesiastes, etc., or from the Prophets, and are in themselves short sermons imparting a certain teaching, thought or moral. Then by comparison, the same idea or moral is extracted from the verse of the Pentateuch. At times, these introductions present to the reader a kaleidoscopic panorama of various thoughts, ethical maxims, and parables, so that the particular interpretation of the text of the day is lost in the maze, but the reader is not the worse for that, as he is amply compensated by the wealth of instruction contained in the introductions proper. At times, the introduction is of a simpler nature, as it may only be a story or a legend, or more usually a Halakic question which supplies the keynote to the sermon. For example, if the Sabbath is the subject of discussion it opens with a practical question bearing on a point of its observance, the answer to which as a rule is given briefly, then a discourse on the Sabbath, its sanctity, and the merit of its observance, and the reward in store for the observer follows. Other subjects were similarly treated.

As remarked, the question method of introduction is prevalent in the *Tanhuma* cycle. The complex homily form of introduction belongs primarily to the *Rabba* and *Pesikta* cycles. But as all those books were more or less compilations, and the various kinds of material were not really separated from one another, the compilers of one cycle did not hesitate to borrow whole sections, chapters, and sometimes even the greater parts of books from another cycle. It thus came about that the compilers of the various versions of the *Tanhuma* borrowed extensively from the older *Pesikta,* while the compiler of the larger *Pesikta,* the later compilation, borrowed in turn from the *Tanhuma.* The compilers of the later *Rabba Midrashim,* such as those on Exodus, Numbers, and Deuteronomy, borrowed both from the *Pesikta* and the *Tanhuma* cycles. Thus, the *Rabba Midrash* on Numbers contains a large part taken from the *Tanhuma-Yelamdénu* cycle. *Deuteronomy Rabba* is almost ninety percent *Tanhuma* matter, and all its introductions are of the question type, while the Midrash on Numbers contains such introductions only to a limited extent. There is likewise borrowing from other sources, from earlier *Rabba Midrashim,* from the Talmud versions, and other books.

On the whole, it would be in vain to search for strictness of division and arrangement both in the books in general, and in each sermon or homily in particular. The Agada was not produced in accordance with logical rules and scientific precision. The preacher or the scholarly Agadist turned whither the spirit moved him, and took hold of whatever material which was appropriate to inculcate his message in the hearts of the hearers. This Agada represents a gushing fountain which continues to spurt forth its waters in all directions without system or regulation, but merely from a superabundance of energy which forces it to flow incessantly. Thus, the Agada flowed for half a millennium with the force of emotion out of the depths of Jewish life through the mouths of the sages and scholars, and its living waters quenched thirsty souls and once again fostered new life and vigor in the Jewish people.

86. MIDRASHIC COLLECTIONS ON OTHER BIBLICAL BOOKS

There existed, undoubtedly, in older times, many Midrashic collections on all prophetic and Hagiographic books, but most of them were lost. We have only a few such books. The first is a Midrash on Psalms, a favored Biblical book which is also called *Shoḥer Tob,* on account of its beginning with the verse *"Shoḥer Tob Yebaḳesh Roẓon"* (Prov. XI, 27). "He that diligently seeketh good, produceth favor." It contains interpretations and short homilies on one hundred and forty-three Psalms. It is, of course, a compilation of sayings bearing on the verses of the Psalms scattered throughout the Agada, but contains also some original material. The Midrash on Psalms belongs to the younger Midrashim, but not to the youngest as it was already well known in the eleventh century. It was most likely composed towards the end of the tenth century, and the place of origin probably was Southern Italy. The second is a Midrash on Proverbs which is of a more original nature than the one on the Psalms. It is more in the form of an Agadic commentary on the book, and contains sayings, parables, proverbs, and short homiletic interpretations on each chapter. The author undoubtedly borrowed a good deal of his material, but he fashioned it in his own way. Its date of composition is approximately the same as that of the Midrash on Psalms. The third one is an Agadic compilation on the Book of Samuel. It contains thirty-two chapters twenty-four of which deal with I Samuel and eight with II Samuel. It is not a commentary but a collection of sermons, bearing on subjects which are ultimately connected with the contents of a verse or two in a chapter on Samuel. It usually begins in the manner of the older Midrashim, with the interpretation of a verse from other books which serves as an introduction to the theme. It is of later date, most likely an eleventh century production.

Older authorities mention and even quote short excerpts from Midrashim on Job, Ezra, Chronicles, and Isaiah, but they seem to have been lost.

87. ETHICAL AGADIC BOOKS

Besides all the Agadic collections which are primarily homiletic we have two books the aim of which is to inculcate to a greater or lesser extent certain ethical teachings and ways of conduct. The first of these is a book known as "The Chapters of Rabbi Eliezer." It is one of the Apocryphal Agadic books which are ascribed to sages of earlier generations. This one is ascribed to Eliezer, the son of Hyrcanus, the disciple of Johanan ben Zakkai, a scholar of the generation succeeding the destruction of the Temple. But, in reality, it is a production of the eighth century c. e. All signs point to that time. The author is acquainted with the names of the wife and daughters of Mohammed, with the Arabic rule in Palestine, with the building of the Mosque of Omar, and similar matters. The book is of a peculiar character; it cannot be said to be a strictly ethical book as it contains a good deal of extraneous matters, such as chapters on astronomy, the calculation of the calendar, and many exotic legends. It is best characterized by calling it an ethical narrative book. The author's aim was to show the people the great moral value of many episodes of the Bible, their beauty and their meaning in daily life, and this he succeeded in doing by relating them in a quite orderly fashion embellished with many legends and stories, and pointing out the ethical teachings to be deduced from the events.

The book is divided into fifty-four chapters, of which the first two are introductory, telling the story of Rabbi Eliezer, the supposed author of the book; nine chapters are devoted to creation, including several chapters on astronomy and the calendar which contain also a description of the luminaries and planets, and ten chapters to Adam and his sons. He then turns to Noah and the flood, Abraham, Isaac, Jacob, Joseph, Moses, the giving of the Law, and the attack of Amalek, and breaks off abruptly with the story of the punishment of Miriam, the sister of Moses.

The ethical lessons are skilfully interwoven with the events; thus in connection with creation, the institution of the Sabbath is exalted and its observance enforced; while discussing the banishment of Adam and Eve from Paradise, an excursus on Hell and Paradise and the reward of the just and charitable is introduced; when telling of the punishment of Miriam for speaking against her brother, remarks pointing out the great sin of slander are inserted, and so on in numerous cases. The author has a love for numbers; topics are discussed in numerical groups of seven and ten. The book abounds with legends and stories, and although of later date, the material is old. Parallels to the stories and even to some of its cosmological notions are found in the Apocalyptic books of Jubilees and Enoch. It resembles also the former in an attempt to trace the observance of certain laws and customs to the Patriarchs.

It is written almost in pure Hebrew, and at times, its style waxes poetic, especially when it deals with the coming of the Messiah, to which subject many passages are devoted. It has of late been made accessible to the English by an accurate English rendering.

The second book is a work known under the name of *Seder Eliyahu,* or *Tanna de-be Eliyahu,* i. e. the Agadic order of Eliyahu or "The Studies of Elijah," an ethical-religious work par excellence, a veritable jewel of ethical literature. The name of the author, Elijah, aroused in some pious souls the notion that he is no other than the eternal prophet Elijah, and verily, the sentiments expressed in that book are deserving of Elijah who is known in Jewish story as the typical lover of Israel, the harbinger of good tidings, and the miraculous saviour in time of need. Yet, with the best of intentions, we are compelled to rob the beloved prophet of the glory of writing this excellent work, and assign it to a pious mortal who bore the same name and whose age is definitely known. The book was written, according to the testimony of the author himself, towards the end of the tenth century, as he himself tells us that more than nine hundred years have passed since the destruction of the Temple. As for the place where the author lived, there exists a division of opinion among earlier scholars; some were inclined to assume Babylonia as the place of his residence, and some Southern Italy. But recent research has established definitely that Elijah or as he is called in the book, Abba Elijah, was a native of Palestine. He did, however, travel through the Orient and visited Babylonia quite frequently.

The book is divided into two parts, one which is known as "The Large Order of Elijah," and the other the smaller (Eliyahu Rabba and Eliyahu Zuta), the first consisting of thirty-one chapters, and the second of twenty-five. Its nature and character differs from all other Agadic productions, as it does not center around any book or part of a book of the Bible. It is merely a series of moral discourses on the value of certain virtues and the need of their cultivation. In the course of the discourse, verses are expounded in an Agadic manner, and at times, chapters are interpreted. The three great themes of the book are Torah, Israel, or rather the love of Israel, and righteous social life. The love of the author for the Torah knows no bounds. He does not tire of the subject; he turns to it again and again, extolling its worth and recounting its virtues. The study of the Torah alone gives man the desired light. "All precepts which a man can observe," says Elijah, "give only as much light as the flame of a candle, but the Torah lights from one end of the world to the other." [2] Man may have many deficiencies, but none is as grave as ignorance of the Torah, for he who is ignorant of the words of the Torah is blind, and deaf, and lame. [3] In such and similar sayings did this great preacher inculcate in the hearts of his hearers the passion for study.

But as great as was his love for the Torah, still greater was his love for Israel. In one place he says, "Some say the Torah precedes everything, but I say Israel takes precedence." [4] His favorite expressions were, "I am the dust under the feet of the children of Israel," or "Master of the world, may I be the atoning sacrifice for Israel (Kapparaton Shel Yisrael) wherever they may dwell." He, therefore, taught continuously the love for a fellow-Jew and right dealing with each other, emphasizing the great value of moral social conduct. In a characteristic passage, he remarks, "Said God to Israel, what do I require of you? Only that you should love each other, honor and revere one another, and there shall not be found among you any transgression or violence, or any ugly acts so that you shall be without blemish." [5] But his love was not limited to Israel; it extended to all men, and with great zeal, he admonishes to act justly towards Gentiles as towards Jews. "It is the duty of every Jew," he says, "to sanctify the name of God, for it was for this

[2] *Eliyahu Rabba* Ch. III.
[3] *Ibid*. Ch. XXV.
[4] *Ibid*. Ch. XIV.
[5] *Ibid*. Ch. XXVIII.

purpose that the Torah was given." Hence, every Jew must be pure from any taint of dishonesty whether towards a Jew or a Gentile. Furthermore, if one steals from a Gentile, in the end he will also steal from a Jew. Any injustice done to Gentiles is a profanation of the sacred name of God." [6] This is the kind of moral teaching imparted by Abba Elijah and the breadth of spirit pervading the book.

With all his piety, Elijah was no ascetic, and he teaches the joy of life and severely reproves rigorism, saying, "If one despises good and joyful living in this world, it spells bad for him." [7] The virtues inculcated are numerous, and the ethical maxims scattered throughout the book are so many that one would have to reproduce the greater part of the book in quoting them. The author, however, gave us a valuable aid towards the appreciation of the book by giving the gist of the spirit permeating it in a short epigram which reads as follows, "I revere God, Israel, and the Torah through great joy; I rejoice through my reverence, but my love exceeds all." [8] Thus, reverence, joy, and love, these are the characteristics of the high ethical work of the otherwise unknown sage Elijah.

The style of the book is like that of the "Chapters of Rabbi Eliezer," pure Hebrew, and is replete with poetic expressions. It is amply provided with parables and stories which impart to it vividness and a popular air.

88. HISTORICAL AND LEGENDARY AGADIC BOOKS

In addition to all these books, there are quite a number of small books which belong to the class of Agada known as historical, though the name historical is used rather by courtesy. They are, in reality, groups of legends and stories concerning Biblical personages as well as post-Biblical sages, embellishments of their lives and deeds. They are all narrative in character, and though of late date, contain older fragments of material. Many parallels of these legends and stories are found in the Apocalyptic and Apocryphal books as well as in the historical narratives of the Alexandrian writers. Some may be even Hebrew translations of such books, all of which goes to prove the ancient origin of a part of their material. It is needless to say that they bear the stamp of the time of their collection, the early Mediæval Ages, and as most

[6] loc. cit.
[7] Ibid. Ch. XIII.
[8] Ibid. Ch. III.

of these books were compiled either in Palestine or Babylonia, they evince influence of Arabic legendary literature, while many additions to the ancient legends were culled also from other sources, often non-Jewish.

Of such books, there are several versions of the life of Moses, known as *Dibré ha-Yomim Shel Moshe* (The History of Moses), a small booklet; *Ptirat Moshe* (On the Death of Moses); *Ma'asé de Abraham Abinu* (The Story of our Father Abraham); "Parables of Solomon," stories about his wisdom; "Jacob and the Wars of his Children"; and "Midrash Jonah," a poetical description of his stay in the belly of the fish and his exit from there, and many more. At times, episodes in history are taken as the subject and are embellished, such as the crossing of the Red Sea which is the theme of a little Midrashic book called *Wa-Yosha* (He helped), so named after the first word in Ex. XIV, 30, and likewise are similar events treated.

89. MISCELLANEOUS AGADIC BOOKS

Besides all these books enumerated above, there is quite a considerable number of small Midrashim which as far as content is concerned, defy all form of classification. They deal with various subjects; some devote themselves to the description of Messianic times, the tribulations preceding the coming of the Messiah, the miracles occurring at the time, the wars of the first Messiah from the House of Ephraim (Moshiah ben Yoseph)[9] with the typical arch-enemy of Israel, Armilus, and the final coming of the Messiah from the House of David, and other matters connected with this great event. Most of these Messianic Midrashim are Apocryphal, and bear names of persons of Biblical or Talmudic fame as their authors. Thus we have an Agadic story book ascribed to Daniel, and one ascribed to Zerubbabel which tells of Messianic events. A book by the name of "Chapters on the Messiah" goes into these matters with great detail.

Other books deal with different subjects and use different devices. A favorite one is the number device. The authors selected a certain

---

[9] According to the Messianic traditions found in Midrashim and also occasionally referred to in the Talmud, there will first arise a man from the tribe of Ephraim, some name him Nehemiah, the son of Amiel, who will bring back a part of the Jews into Palestine. This is the Messiah of the House of Joseph. Against him and the kingdom he will establish, the nations will rise, the leader of which will be a certain Armilus, a one-eyed monster and of peculiar wickedness. In the wars that will ensue, this early Messiah will be killed, and only then the real Messiah will appear and gather all the Jews to Palestine.

number of things which they take as their subject for homilies. Thus we have books known as the "Ten Exiles," the "Ten Commandments," the "Ten Kings." In these, subjects relating to the various exiles of Israel, to the commandments and to the ten great kings who ruled and will rule over the world, the last one being the Messiah, are discussed and interpreted. The numbers seven, three, and four are employed. We have booklets known as "Three and Four," "Seven Canopies" (also known as The Canopy of Elijah), referring to the canopies of honor which God will spread over the heads of the righteous. Some, on the other hand, take a single subject of the Bible for their theme. As an instance, we have a *Midrash Temurah*, i. e. vicissitude, taking for its text verses 1–10 of Ecclesiastes III where it says, "There is an appointed time for everything," and discussing the vicissitudes of time enumerated therein. Some take the description of Hell and Paradise for their subject. We have a *Maseket Gan Eden* and a *Maseket Gehenom*, i. e. tractates on Paradise and Hell. Others again deal with the letters of the alphabet discussing their meaning and significance. There is a small Midrash called the *Aleph-Bet di Rabbi Akiba*, which this great sage is supposed to have composed (see below Sec. 178). It is difficult to determine the age and land of all these productions; a number of them belong to the early Mediæval Ages, the seventh, eighth, and ninth centuries, and some were written later. But these differences really affect their content and character little except in small details, as most of the material dates from older sources and it was only a matter of shifting and arrangement.

We cannot, however, close our review of the collections of the Agada without mentioning several large collections, which though of a later period, yet, as the authors followed in the footsteps of the former compilers and also manipulated with the same material, they belong here. The first is a large Midrash on Genesis, and probably on other books by Moses ha-Darshan, i. e. the preacher of Narbonne, a scholar who lived in the second half of the eleventh century. This Midrash is quoted by earlier Jewish scholars and even by Mediæval Christian savants, but the book itself seems to have been lost. From the nature of the quotations, it seems to have been more in the nature of a Midrashic commentary compiled from older sources with a modicum of original interpretation. Another one is a Midrash on the whole of the Pentateuch and some of the Scrolls by Rabbi Tubia, the son of Eliezer, who hailed from Germany, but towards the end of the eleventh century settled in Greece. This Midrash is often quoted as *Lekah Tob,*

(Good Instruction), or the smaller *Pesikta*. The first name is applied to it because the author manages to preface each section with a verse which contains the word *Tob,* i. e. good; the second, on account of his method as he interprets the Pentateuch in a sectional and paragraphic way, quoting excerpts to each verse. He drew both on Agadic and Halakic sources, giving both interpretations at the same time. Not all of the *Lekah Tob,* however, was preserved for we possess only the part on the last three books of the Pentateuch and a short Midrash on Ruth.

Finally, we have, what may be termed the largest Agadic compendium to the Bible. This is the *Yalkut,* compiled by Simon Karo, a thirteenth century man. It is a compendium of Agadic statements and interpretation on all the twenty-four books of the Bible. It is a great work, for the compiler had to arrange thousands of sayings scattered in the entire literature, both versions of the Talmud, numerous Midrashim, and many more sources, each in its own place in the Bible, so that as a result it appears as if each book in the Bible has its own Midrash. Rabbi Simon drew upon numerous sources, and as some of the works quoted by him are now entirely lost, he thus performed an additional service for Jewish literature. Karo's work closes the great literary activity known as the Agadic which lasted for a period close to fifteen hundred years.

Book II

MEDIÆVAL PERIOD

DIVISION I

From 600 c. e. to 1200 c. e.

MEDIÆVAL PERIOD

DIVISION I.

90. GENERAL CHARACTERISTICS

The period of literary activity which forms the subject of the following chapters represents the heyday of Jewish literature. During the six centuries dealt with, Jewish literature bloomed and flourished, increased both in quantity, and deepened, varied, and ramified in quality. If the literature of the first period can be compared to a tree divided into several trunks shooting directly forth from common roots—the life of the nation, the literature of the second period, pursuing the simile, may be likened to a mighty tree whose roots have spread in all directions, drawing moisture from all sources and whose many branches extend far and wide to the four sides of the world, covering a great area. And as the sources of its nurture vary, so vary its fruits, for though they all resemble the common tree, they often differ in color, shape, and taste.

It is this heterogeneity and complexity which form the primal characteristic of the literature. The literature of the first period is comparatively homogeneous, of one color, though of several hues. It is primarily religious and the Bible is the central axis around which everything turns; its application to life, its interpretation, its reconciliation with foreign ideas are both the motives and the problems of the literary expression. In the second period, it is true, the same problems are still there, and the Bible is still of great importance, but the situation is changed. In the domain of practical religion, the Talmud takes the place of the Bible and other literary currents flow beside the religious one. The secular element is in great evidence, the world of nature claims its attention and science takes its place beside religion. Nor does beauty both of nature and of man lack a place of prominence in this literature. Poetry expressing the appreciation of beauty in both realms is also cultivated, and many more emotions of the human soul find their expression. Even the problem of reconciling religion to current ideas assumes a different aspect; a deeper and more earnest tone pervades it, and as a result, we have a genuine religious philosophy which is not separated from science but is grounded upon its principles. Thus, the kaleidoscopic panorama widens and broadens.

The cause of heterogeneity and complexity in this literature is, of course, its geographic extent which follows from the extension of the Jewish Diaspora. The bulk of literature of the former period arose on the native soil of Palestine where the Jews, even when subjected to the rule of the conqueror, nevertheless led almost a complete national life, and even in the land of the second literary center, Babylonia, that life was, on the whole, quite as complete nationally as in Palestine. In addition, Palestine then held the spiritual hegemony and exercised its influence over it. But the literature of this period is primarily one of the Diaspora. As the centuries pass, Palestine recedes from view, and new centers emerge. At first, Babylonia takes the place of Palestine and for a time exercises sway over the newer Jewish settlements in Southern Europe. Soon, however, its hour strikes and like Palestine, it disappears from the view of history, and other centers appear, each claiming a prominent place in Jewish life and history, though none ever took the place of Palestine or Babylonia. There is Northern Africa, Spain, Italy, France, Germany, and later Poland and Lithuania in Eastern Europe. Each of these contributed its quota to Jewish literature and brought forth its current to swell that great spiritual ocean.

The currents, though, were different in the same measure that the modes of Jewish life in those centers which engendered them were different. No more did one center possess spiritual hegemony; each one led its own life. There was, of course, harmony and coördination among them but no subordination. As a result, Jewish life in each center varied from that in the other, being subjected to the influence of the general life of the country and modified by it, and this influence is reflected in the literary productions, changing their nature and character. The fact that Jewish literature, in the Mediæval period, had the world for its stage, imparted to it a peculiar character, the like of which is not found in any other literature. The constant interaction between Judaism and the cultures it came in contact with, in the course of its history, gave to its literature that checkered appearance which not only affected the medium of its expression, namely, that it used many languages instead of one, but its very substance and character.

Yet there was unity in Jewish life in the Diaspora as well as diversity. Mediæval life in general was of a cosmopolitan character and was impressed with a certain unity of type. Nationalism, the great dividing factor of humanity was unknown and life bore the unity of religion—one religion, one type of life. In Christian Europe, life in France, for instance, differed but little in many aspects from that in England or Germany, and as far as the upper stratum of the population was concerned, its life differed only in a small degree even from that in distant Poland. And as for literature, it had a universal language—Latin—which in turn helped to unify life. A similar situation reigned in all Mohammedan countries; life there was also cosmopolitan, one religion and one language—Arabic. The only line of division that did bar one people from another was the political rule or government, and as these were not constant, and countries frequently changed hands, the unity of life was intensified by these frequent vicissitudes.

Under such circumstances, it was also possible for Jewish life in various countries to maintain a unity of type and in spite of the slight diversity that existed in the types of the life of the various Jewries, it presents on the whole a uniform character. As a result, the literary activity going on in different countries was conducted on similar lines. There was, however, one line of cleavage in the Jewish life in the Mediæval period which corresponded with the same line in general life and that is the difference in the types of culture of Mediæval Christianity, on the one hand, and that of Islam on the other. This line of cleavage which was marked enough in the general world, inasmuch as the Mohammedan countries were at the time the seat of enlightened culture, was still more accentuated in the Jewish world. For, in addition to the influence of general culture upon Jewish life, there enters also another factor into consideration, and that is the treatment the Jews were accorded by the respective Christian and Mohammedan governments.

As it is well known, the Jews fared well in Mohammedan countries, where they were not only unmolested, but even attained prominence and wealth, while in Christian countries, their life was a bitter struggle for existence and a continuous agony. This great difference in the daily life of the two groups of Jewries, was, of course, reflected in their literary productions. And if we were to draw a line across Europe touching the foothills of the Pyrenees on the one hand, and that of the Apennines on the other, it would represent the line of division between the two types of Jewish literary activity. The literature produced in all countries south and east of that line bears a brighter color and a broader and more ramified aspect, while that produced to the north and the west is of narrower dimension, of sterner character, and gloomier aspect, though at times more intensely Jewish. In the former, grammar, Bible Exegesis, philosophy, and other subjects of a more secular nature take their place by the side of Halakah and other religious subjects. In the latter, Halakah and its further development, i. e. the study of the Talmud, interpretation, and application of the law to daily life, to- gether with the cultivation of pious ethical literature as well as liturgical poetry constitute the chief literary productions.

Of course, the lines are not fast drawn. There were many Talmudic scholars, whose works in Halakah became the standard guide to stu- dents of succeeding ages, who lived and acted in Mohammedan coun- tries, while there were great commentators of the Bible and even grammarians in Christian countries. The unity of Jewish life helped to obliterate the lines of demarcation. Literary activity in one part of world Jewry in a certain direction stirred up similar activity in the other part. There was much interchange of ideas and mutual influence, but on the whole the general distinction between the two types of the literary productivity in the two geographical areas holds true.

There is also a distinction of language in these two types. The Jews of the Mohammedan countries employed to a great extent the language of the country in their writings, and a large part of Jewish literature in those lands was written in Arabic, while the Jews of Christian coun- tries wrote as a rule in Hebrew. As a result, many of the writings of the former were lost, while those of the latter were preserved almost in entirety.

Besides the heterogeneity and complexity of this mass of literature of the period, there is to be noted another important characteristic and that is its individuality. The literature of the first period is, as indicated, of a national character, and is as a whole, a mass production. That of this period is entirely individual with few exceptions, such as the *Massorah* and other works which belong largely to the first period. In it, each production bears the stamp and the impress of its author, and thus we possess more variety of type and character.

A third characteristic of the literature is, at least as far as the first division is concerned, its closeness to life and its influence on life. In no other period of Jewish history were life and literature so closely harmo- nious as in the epoch of the Golden Age in Spain. There, we meet with writers who wrote with one hand heavy treatises on Halakah discussing the minutiæ of law, and with the other, works on philosophy or even poems on beauty of nature and men. Life in all currents and phases pulsates in that literature, with only slight traces of the isolation of religion from life so marked in the later days. It is no wonder then, that in turn literature influenced life. Even in Western Europe there was proximity between the Jewish literature and the type of life prevailing there in the first half of the Mediæval period, and its influence on life was exceedingly great, even to a degree that it actually molded and shaped it in its impress and form. That exceptions and digressions abound goes without saying.

It is impossible to describe in a minute and accurate manner the character of a literature of such a varied nature. We have only endeavored to give some of its leading characteristics. As for the rest, we will have to deduce them from the unfolding picture of its history.

Chapter VII

GRAMMAR AND LEXICOGRAPHY

91. THE MASSORAH

The first remarkable phenomenon, which we note at the opening of this period of literary activity, is the revival of Hebrew as the medium of literature, and an increased interest in the language which ultimately led to the scientific study of its structure, the development of its grammar, and systematic lexicographical activity. This revival opened up a path for literature, for poetic expression, for fine and elegant writing, and raised Hebrew to a first-class literary language. The phenomenon is more remarkable because of its appearance in Palestine at a time when Jewish life there was at an ebb, and the glory was about to depart from the motherland for a long time, and further, because it reached its climax in the lands of the Galut, Diaspora.

For centuries, from the close of the Mishnah on, Hebrew ceased to be a medium of literary expression, and the mixed Aramaic took its place. The Talmuds, both the Palestinian and the Babylonian, are written in its different dialects, and the earlier Midrashic collections employ this language. But suddenly, there is revealed before us the use of a beautiful Hebrew style in many literary works. The later Midrashim, such as the *Tanḥuma* and others, use a good deal of Hebrew, and even go to the trouble of translating Aramaic proverbs into Hebrew. The later Agadic productions, such as "The Chapters of Rabbi Eliezer" and others are written in pure Hebrew. This is followed by the first outbursts of Hebrew religious poetry in Palestine. Together with the change of style, we note a deep interest in the Bible, resulting in the standardization of its text; accents and vowel points are invented, and, occasionally, books begin to appear where grammatical rules are mentioned, and the movement continued to grow until Hebrew broke into real bloom, reaching its height in the literature of the Golden Age in Spain.

A veil of darkness is spread over the beginnings of this revival. It may be surmised that an impetus was given to it, as to many other movements, by the contact of the Jews with the Arabic culture, though that may not be the only cause.

The conquest of Palestine by the Arabs in 638 and of Babylonia in 642 brought the Jews of the two centers in contact with the young rising nation which was soon destined to become an important factor in the history of civilization and culture. The Arab was a great lover of poetry and fine writing from time immemorial and poetry had been his chief spiritual staple for many centuries. This poetry was usually handed down by word of mouth from generation to generation, but when the Arabs after Mohammed became a literary people, written poetry began to flourish. Closely associated with poetry was the science of language which developed along with it. Many grammarians arose who displayed great skill in their work and wrote grammars and dictionaries.

This cultural movement among the masters and neighbors of the Jews evoked a similar movement among them and rekindled the love for their ancient language and called forth a desire to sound its depths and to ransack its treasures. But before such work could be carried on in a systematic way, before any structure of rules could be erected, some preliminary work had to be done. The Hebrew language is embodied in the Bible and any work which tends to develop that language must begin with that Book itself. It was, therefore, necessary first of all, to have a standard text of that Book, a proper division of its verses, a correct reading of all its words, and many more things connected with a book which embodies the treasures of a language. In order to standardize the reading of all the words of the Bible a system of vowels was necessary, and in addition, accents and signs of punctuation which should mark the division of the verses were needed. This stupendous work was done by schools of scholars known as Massorites, and their chief work known as Massorah, i. e. tradition.

The Massorah is really not a work of one generation or one school. It is only the standardization and canonization of this work which belongs to this period, but the work itself went on for generations previous to that. The Bible, as we know, was the center of Jewish life through the ages; it is evident, therefore, that the guarding of its text, the preserving of the form of the correct reading of the words, or the divisions of chapters and verses was also the concern of some scholars who specialized in this particular branch. These scholars were known as *Soferim,* in the literal sense, scribes, who wrote the books of the

Bible. The Talmud states, however, that this appellation was given to them, because they actually counted the number of letters in the Bible. These same scholars were also readers of the Torah in the synagogues and were called readers (Kara). As such, the correct pronunciation was their special task. It is almost definitely established that vowels and accents were not known during the Talmudic period, and the art of reading was a matter of tradition. Likewise was the Bible written without division into chapters and verses, the stopping at the proper places was considered an art and was taught by special men. There were also a number of differences between the written text and the traditional reading. These differences are known as *Ketib* and *Keri,* i. e. the way the word is written and the way it is to be read. These differences were again made a subject of study, for the text was not changed and the words continued to be written one way and read another way. Changes were also introduced, a limited number, eighteen in all, in the text to avoid improper expressions concerning God. These are called the corrections of the Soferim (Tikkune Soferim). New words were also at times substituted in reading for the obsolete words. All these changes were noted and memorized and transmitted orally by one generation of scribes to the other.

But memory, even at the best, is an unreliable guide and it must ultimately be replaced by the written word. When the age of great compilations arrived, that of the redaction of the Talmuds and the collection of Agada, the time also came for all these traditions about the text of the Bible to be standardized and definitely fixed and written down. Then, the real work of the Massorites began.

We cannot definitely determine the year of its beginning, but it most likely began during the sixth century, and was carried on both in Palestine, mainly at Tiberias, and Babylonia. Both academies there, Sura and Pumbedita, had their Massoretic schools. The first work of the Massorites was to purify the text of the Bible from all possible errors which crept in by copyists and hand down to posterity an authentic and absolutely correct text. This text is known as the Massoretic text which is the text of the Hebrew Bible as it is known through the centuries. In order to accomplish this purpose and to guard against further possible errors by scribes, lists were compiled of all the differences between words written one way and read another (Ketib and Keri); both forms were given there; other lists, noting how many times certain words are written plena, i. e. with *Waw* or *Yod* where these letters are only signs for vowels, and how many times they are written without *Waw* or *Yod* were also prepared. Likewise lists were compiled noting how many times certain words take the *Waw* conjunctive or the *Waw* conversive, and how many times they do not. In this way and many others, the text was standardized. The work of the Massorah seemed to have been carried on in two different ways, by notes on the margins of copies of the Bible, and by separate treatises containing such lists of words and their mode of writing arranged in alphabetical order. In making their notes, the Massorites gave references to the verses where the words were found, and in order that the references might easily be remembered they used mnemonic signs in the form of sentences, each word of which was taken from the various verses referred to. Of such separate treatises, we have one named *Okhlah we-Okhlah,* so named because it begins with a short list of the number of times the word *Okhlah* occurs in the Bible without *Waw* conjunctive and with one. The work contains a large number of lists of words found in the Bible with prefixes and without prefixes.

In general, the work of the Massorah while it is more of a mechanical nature and does not presuppose grammatical rules, does presuppose division of verses, and these in turn, in written work, must have some signs for separation. These had to be invented. Nor could the purpose of the Massorah be carried out without vowels, signs, or accents for pause and joining, for otherwise the correct reading would have remained a matter of memory and ultimately the text would have been again corrupted. The Massorites could, therefore, not have completed their work without attending to all these matters. And this brings us to vowels and accents.

92. VOWELS AND ACCENTS

History is silent regarding the date when our vowel signs were invented and introduced into use. But as said it seems to be the work of the Massorites in their effort to standardize the Hebrew text. It seems, however, that there was a gradual evolution in the establishing of that system. At first, some accents and marks of punctuation were invented. These were necessary, as without them no division of verses could be indicated and the traditional division could not have been handed down to posterity. In fact, reference to the punctuation signs known as *Sof Posuk* and *Etnahto* corresponding to period and colon is found in a small treatise *Soferim,* dealing with the writing of the Torah, appended to the Talmud.

Together with the first simple punctuation marks there were used undoubtedly other marks for reading of a very simple nature, such as points above or below the letters and a point within the letter known as *Dagesh,* indicating the doubling of certain letters. These preceded the more involved vowel system.

Later, during the middle of the seventh century when the influence of the Arabic language began to be felt, the system was completed, probably following the fashion of the Arabic and the Syriac both of which use three vowel signs. Yet it served only as an impetus for there is no direct borrowing. The Hebrew vowel system is more developed than either the Arabic or the Syriac, as it contains more sounds.

The work of the Massorah, as said, was going on simultaneously in Palestine and Babylonia. We, therefore, find that two vowel systems were likewise invented and used. One is the Babylonian called the Assyrian, and the other the Palestinian, or the Tiberian, the one now in use. The Babylonian vowel system seemed to be the older one. In it, contrary to the Tiberian, the vowel signs are placed above the letters and the signs are simpler. It is probable that the Babylonian system was brought over to Tiberias where there was a great Massoretic school, and there it was changed to the form we use. In time, the authority of the Tiberian Massorites prevailed and their system was adopted while the other was entirely forgotten, and was only discovered in the nineteenth century in certain old manuscripts.[1]

In the Tiberian system, the vowels as known are placed under the letters with the exception of the "oi" and the "oo," which are placed above and in the middle of the letter respectively. It contains seven vowel sounds, o, ä, ā, ĕ, ĭ, oi, oo, and the signs are more elaborate than in the Babylonian.[2] The Babylonian vowels contain only six sounds; no provision is made for the ĕ sound. The present system which distinguishes three more vowel sounds, adding the shorter ĭ, the short ŏ, and the short ŭ, is of later origin and dates from the grammarian Joseph Kimḥi (twelfth century).

Along with the perfection of the vowel system, there went on the

---

[1] On this subject see S. Pinsker: *Introduction to Assyrian Vowel System.*

[2] The vowel sounds given in the text represents the German or Ashkenazic pronunciation which is the more prevalent one among the Jews. The Sephardic pronunciation, which is considered the scientific one, is represented by the following vowel sounds, ā (long), ä (short), ē (long), ĕ (short), ĭ, o, oo.

perfection of the punctuation or accent system. There is quite an elaborate system of punctuation marks. In the adopted system, the Tiberian, there are twenty-six signs, eighteen of which serve as signs of pause (Mafsikkim), and eight as signs of conjunction, namely, they join words together. Because of their function, namely, to join the previous word to the word which bears the sign of a pause, they were called by grammarians *servants,* as they serve the sign of the pause. The eighteen pause signs are further divided into classes according to the degree of pause they indicate and were given fanciful names, such as kings, viceroys, adjutants, and officers. The three Biblical books, Psalms, Proverbs, and Job, were for some reason provided with a different system of accents. These signs also serve as notes in reading the Bible. The Bible in olden times was read with a certain chant, and this chant has been preserved by tradition and embodied by the Massorites in these signs. Each sign has also a peculiar tone inflection and note, hence, they were called accents as well as punctuation signs. In accentuation as well as in the introduction of vowel marks, there is a double system; the second one is the Babylonian which, like the vowel system, was slowly forgotten when the Tiberian became the adopted one. In that system, there is the same simplicity as in the vowels inasmuch as the accents are fewer.

The value of the accent system for the development of the Hebrew language cannot be overestimated, for not only did it facilitate the reading and stabilize the whole vowel system and its possible changes, but it contributed greatly to the exegesis of the Bible, inasmuch as it supplied the proper connection as well as the separation of the words in the verses of the Bible, and thus elucidated the meaning of the content. The Massorites who introduced the system of accents were great Biblical scholars and by their work, they laid the very foundation of Biblical exegesis, as it really forms a running commentary.

After the vowel signs and accents were introduced, the Massorah notes were revised to include remarks on vowel pointing and accentuation of words, especially on exceptional accentuations of vocalized letters in certain words. In the special Massoretic treatises, there were added new lists in alphabetical arrangement enumerating peculiarly pointed and accented words, or those that take a certain accent and all other deviations. In general, we note in the Massorah certain strata in regard to the vowel points. Some parts of it mention only the names of two vowel signs, i. e. the Kamez (O) and Patah (A); the others are designated by placing the points above or below the letters *Aleph, Waw,* and *Yod*. In other parts, especially in the separate treatises, the names of all the vowel signs are stated. This only supports the view often propounded that the standardization of the vowel system as well as the Massorah itself took some considerable time.

93. PERIOD OF MASSORETIC WORK

As stated, we cannot determine with accuracy the beginning of the period of activity in the field of the Massorah, and likewise we cannot determine with any definiteness the close of that period. All that we can assert about the extent of that period is that it lasted several centuries, and that by the beginning of the tenth century, it was considered an accomplished work.

Of course, this rather indefinite time limit refers only to the standardization, namely, to the written Massorah, but as far as the oral Massorah work is concerned, it goes back to early Talmudic times. Some traditions speak of a certain Nakki, a contemporary of Simon Ben Yoḥai, a *Tanna* of the second century, that he came to Babylonia and established a Massoretic school. The same tradition quotes also a few more Massorites who continued their work there during the Talmudic period. It is interesting, however, that while tradition knows of a few names of the early Massorites in Babylonia, it did not preserve any names of Palestinian Massorites in the early days. Yet, it was the Tiberian school that really put its impress on the Massorah, for in spite of the fact that intense activity was going on in the Massoretic schools in Babylonia, both in the earlier and later period, the Palestinian system was adopted and Palestine even in its less glorious days conquered the Diaspora.

Of the later school of the Massorites in Palestine, we have the names of a few of its leaders. First, Phineas, the head of the Academy (Pinḥas Rosh Yeshibah), who lived in the middle of the eighth century in Palestine, who is often referred to in Massoretic literature. Towards the close of that century, there flourished in Tiberias, Asher the elder, who was the founder of the Asher family which devoted itself to Massoretic work through six generations. The last member of this family was Aaron ben Asher who lived at the beginning of the tenth century and who seemed to have closed the Massoretic work, as the Bible which he provided with vowel points, accents, and Massoretic notes was preserved by generations and was the very one which Maimonides took as the authoritative model in formulating the rules in his code about vowel pointing and accentuation of Biblical books. This Aaron ben Asher also wrote a book on the accents.

Of the later Babylonian Massorites, only one name is preserved and that is ben Naftali, whose Massoretic notes differ considerably from those of ben Asher. They especially differ in the *Keri* and *Ketib,* as well as in the writing of words plena or defectiva, namely with a *Waw* or a *Yod* or without them. The difference between these two men represents the Massoretic difference between the two schools, Babylonian and Palestinian, otherwise known as the Easterners and the Westerners respectively.

The printed Bible was first provided with Massoretic notes in the Venice edition published by Bomberg in 1525. The work was done by Jacob ben Ḥayyim, an Italian scholar who copied these notes from various manuscripts. There are two kinds of notes, one known as the *Massora parva* (Small Massorah) and the other as *Massora magna* (Large Massorah). The first is printed on the outside margin of the text, the second, above or below, or on the inner margin of the text. The smaller one gives only the number of times the word with its peculiar spelling or punctuation is found in the Bible. The larger one gives the references with mnemonic devices for remembering them. In addition, there is also a *Massora finalis,* namely, at the end of the book alphabetical lists of words are given where these peculiarities are noted. In our time, several editions of the large Massorah were published in a separate book from manuscripts.

GRAMMAR AND LEXICOGRAPHY

94. EARLY EFFORTS IN THE FIELD OF GRAMMAR AND LEX- ICOGRAPHY

After the groundwork in the field in Hebrew philology was laid by the activity of the Massorites, the very building began slowly to rise. Many were those who contributed to the edifice of grammar and lexicography which was constructed through several centuries. The first workers in the field only contributed some stones to the structure, those who followed them did more and actually laid layer upon layer. The first attempt to formulate some grammatical rules was made by the anonymous author of the mystical book known as *Sefer Yeẓirah* (The Book of Creation). The book itself is primarily a treatise upon the mystic powers of the letters of the Hebrew alphabet, and is one of the early Kabbalistic works (Sec. 180), but indirectly, we find there the first classification of the letters according to the organs of speech from which they issue. This classification was adopted by all the succeeding grammarians. The author was most likely a Palestinian who lived in the middle of the seventh century.

A more definite attempt at formulating rules of grammar was made by the last Massorite, Aaron ben Asher. He was the author of a book on accents in Hebrew (Dikdukē ha-Teomim) where he also deals with grammar. As a Massorite and as one interested primarily in vowel pointing, he deals primarily with the grammatical part of the vowels and the placing of the *Dagesh,* i. e. the stronger and the weaker pronunciation of letters. But he also attempted to classify the parts of speech into nouns, numerals, verbs, pronouns, and adjectives. He foresaw the distinction of the prefixes and suffixes from the letters of the roots, but he did not enunciate it clearly. This was left for some one else. Ben Asher, was, of course, influenced by the Arabic grammarians. His work seems to have been the last contribution of Palestine towards the study of the Hebrew language, as conditions made work in this field impossible. The foremost place in Jewish literature belongs henceforth to Babylonia.

There the Arabic culture, which, during its heyday in the East, from the seventh to the eleventh centuries, made great strides in all branches of knowledge, strongly influenced the Jews, and called forth similar activities in their own literature. An additional impetus toward the study of the Hebrew language was the Karaite schism (Ch. XIII). This sect, which renounced all oral tradition and the authority of the Talmud, reverted to the Bible only. They thus fell back upon an intensive study of the Bible and its language in order to refute the Rabbinic interpretation and deduce their own. This forced the Rabbinic scholars to do likewise and devote themselves to similar studies in order to defend the Talmudic interpretation of the Bible. In time, these studies, which at first might have been a means for something else, became an end in themselves. Thus began a period of flourishing literary activity, the exponent of which was the Gaon, Saadia.

95. SAADIA

Saadia ben Joseph Al-Fayyumi, who left an indelible impress upon Jewish literature in all its branches and whom we will meet again and again in the course of our story, was born in the year 892 in the village of Dilaz in the district of Fayyum in Egypt. His father was of an humble vocation, but that did not prevent him from giving his son an excellent education. We know very little of his youth, for when he is revealed to us, he is already a full-fledged scholar. But Egypt must have been, at the time, a center of learning and young Saadia must have had great teachers both in Rabbinics and other studies. We, though, know only of one, a certain Abu-Kathir of Tiberias, a grammarian and philosopher. However, Saadia's study under him really belongs to a later period in his life. While yet a young man, he began to write books in the field of Hebrew lexicography and grammar. In 915 c. e., at the age of twenty-three, Saadia left Egypt and went on his journeys. He lived for a time in Palestine, from there went to Babylonia, then to Aleppo in Syria and back to Babylonia. All the while he kept on writing and his fame grew daily. He especially distinguished himself in a controversy with a Palestinian scholar, ben Meir, about the Jewish calendar in which he defended the position of the Babylonian Geonim.

In 928, at the age of thirty-six, he was appointed by the Exilarch David, son of Zakkai, to the Gaonate of Sura, i. e. head of the famous Academy, a great distinction conferred upon a young man who was a foreigner. But there his troubles began; Saadia's honest nature could not tolerate many of the deeds of the Exilarch and a quarrel broke out between the two. The struggle between these two powerful men was a bitter one and caused much anxiety to both parties. During the strife, Saadia was deposed and suffered greatly. Finally, a reconciliation was effected and Saadia spent his last few years in peace. He died in 942 at the age of fifty.

Saadia's life, though short, was but one long chain of continuous literary activity, and it is almost miraculous for one man to have accomplished so much in such a short span of life. There is not a branch of Jewish study where he did not take the leading part, grammar and lexicography not excepted.

His first work in that field was the *Agron,* a Hebrew dictionary in two parts. In the first part, the words were arranged in alphabetical order according to their initials, in the second, according to the final letters. The book was primarily intended to help the poets in their rhyming. It was further provided with a Hebrew introduction where the history of the Hebrew language was given. The first edition was written by him at the age of twenty; later he issued a second and enlarged edition with an Arabic translation of the words and an Arabic introduction. Only the introductions and a portion of the dictionary remained, the rest is lost.

As no dictionary can be composed on scientific principles without recognizing the fact that words have roots and suffixes, Saadia enunciates clearly this fundamental principle in his introduction, and divides the letters of the alphabet into two classes, eleven which can be used both as roots and suffix or prefix letters, and the other eleven which are root letters only. He elaborates there also other grammatical rules.

He was, however, not satisfied with these remarks, but wrote a large book in twelve parts under the name of *Sefer ha-Lashon* (The Book of the Language). The book was written in Arabic, and constitutes the first grammar of the Hebrew language. Each part deals with a special phase, as for instance, part one deals with the combination of letters into words and roots; part two with the letters; other parts treat of the assimilation and interchange of letters and suffixes where the above theory is discussed in detail. He also deals with the conjugation of the verb, and seems to have elaborated the first schematic table of a conjugation though it is far from complete. Saadia, thus, practically erected the walls of the Hebrew grammar.

He also wrote a third work in lexicography which comprises a list of ninety words which are found in the Bible either once or seldom. He not only gives the references where the words are found, but also explains them according to the meaning of kindred words in the Mishnah and Talmud. He thus showed the close relation between Biblical Hebrew and the language of the Mishnah and the Talmud as well as Aramaic. This little work is preserved in its entirety. Besides the special books, many grammatical and lexicographical materials are scattered in his commentary on *Sefer Yezirah* (The Book of Creation) and his commentaries on the Bible (Ch. VIII).

96. JUDAH IBN KOREISH AND DUNASH BEN TAMIN

The contact of the Jews with Arabic culture aroused literary activity in all Jewish centers and Northern Africa, a rising center at the time, was not excepted. From there hails one of the early grammarians and lexicographers by the name of Judah Ibn Koreish (about 900). His great contribution to Hebrew philology is not so much in the field of grammar as in the study of Hebrew words in comparison with the other Semitic languages, namely, the Aramaic and the Arabic. He was the first one to initiate comparative philology. His work *Sefer ha-Yaḥas* (The Book of Relationship) to which is appended his letter to the community of Fez urging them to study the *Targum,* for the purpose of a better understanding of Hebrew, was divided into three parts, the first two containing lists of Hebrew words which have Aramaic affinities, while the third was devoted to those words which are related to the Arabic. It seems that he also wrote a larger dictionary which was lost, and only a half of the first book is preserved. Many grammatical rules are given in his work on relationships and also references from the Mishnah and Talmud where the Biblical words are used in similar meanings. The references show an extensive acquaintance with Rabbinic literature, a fact which explodes the theory that Ibn Koreish was a Karaite.

Dunash ben Tamin (900–960) of Kairawan was another North African worker in the field of comparative study of languages. He was a physician by profession, a pupil of the famous Isaac Israeli (Sec. 108), but like all Jewish scholars of his day also devoted himself to the study of Hebrew. He wrote a book in Arabic where he endeavored to demonstrate the close relationship between Hebrew and Arabic, and even maintained that Hebrew is only a purer form of Arabic.

97. MENAḤEM BEN SARUK

Spain, which about the middle of the tenth century became a center of Jewish learning, soon rose to a prominent position as a seat of Jewish literature, and for a long time it held that position compared with which other countries dwindle into insignificance. There, as well as in other centers, the Golden Age of Jewish literature began with the study of the Hebrew language, and the first worker in that field was Menaḥem ben Saruk. Menaḥem was born in the year 910 at Tortosa, Southern Spain, and distinguished himself as a master of Hebrew. His fame reached the ears of Ḥasdai Ibn Shaprut, the Vizier of the Caliph Abd-ar Rahman at Cordova, who being a patron of learning took him into his house and made him his secretary. During the years that Menaḥem enjoyed the patronage of Ḥasdai he produced his literary work which entitles him to a place in the history of Jewish literature. But his peaceful days did not last long; through the intrigues of his contemporary, Dunash ben Labrat, poet and grammarian (Sec. 98), he fell into disfavor with Ḥasdai and the latter not only ceased supporting him, but even arrested him on some charge. Menaḥem then wrote a letter in masterful Hebrew to Ḥasdai where he reproaches him for persecuting him. He was released, but it seems that he was never restored to his former position. He died in 970.

Menaḥem's great work in the field of grammar and lexicography is his Hebrew dictionary called *Maḥberet* (literally a joining of words). This dictionary is the first lexicographical work in Hebrew which covered the entire field of the Biblical language. Previous attempts were not as exhaustive and were incomplete. The dictionary is prefaced with a long introduction where he states his views on Hebrew grammar. He, like Saadia, whose works he saw and used, divides the alphabet into two classes, one including the letters which are used as root letters only, and the other those which are used both as root letters and as prefixes and suffixes, and devotes considerable discussion to the distinction between roots and added letters. He believed that the number of letters in the roots of words is variable, from one to five. There are roots of five letters, of four, three, two, and even of one. Menaḥem contributed greatly towards the theory of the derivation of nouns from verbs, and explained it quite extensively. He also enriched the Hebrew grammatical terminology by a few terms, among which is the term *Medaḳdeḳ,* i.e. grammarian which implies the term Dikduk, to denote grammar. The dictionary proper contributed much towards the root fixation of words as well as to their explanation. In his explanation of words he made use of the Aramaic and Mishnaic Hebrew. The book has also great exegetic value, but of that later. Menaḥem's work, because it was written in Hebrew, exerted great influence upon Jewish literature, for it was the only book that was accessible to the scholars of France and Germany and they made extensive use of it for centuries.

98. DUNASH BEN LABRAT

The other renowned grammarian of the day was Rabbi Adomin ha-Levy or Dunash ben Labrat (920–970). He was born in Bagdad where he sat in his youth at the feet of Saadia. Later, he lived for a time in Fez, Northern Africa, but ultimately settled in Cordova where, like Menaḥem, he was the recipient of many favors from Ḥasdai Ibn Shaprut.

His grammatical views are contained in his polemical works against Menaḥem and Saadia. His review of Menaḥem's dictionary, called the *Teshubot* (Responsa of Dunash), is the most important one and is written in the form of a long metrical poem, the first grammatical, lexicographical poem in Hebrew literature. In it, besides correcting one hundred and sixty errors of Menaḥem in the explanation of words as well as their derivation, he made an important contribution both to the theory of grammar and to its terminology. He was the first to distinguish between transitive and intransitive verbs, to call the letters of the roots by the names of the letters of the word *Poal,* (to do), namely, the first letter *Pe,* the second *Aen,* the third *Lamed.* He further divided the verb forms into lighter and heavier ones, or weaker and stronger, and distinguished the *Piel* form, whereas Saadia did not know of it; he also enunciated the three parts of speech, i. e. noun, verb and other words including adverbs and prepositions. In his criticism of Saadia, he makes the important contribution of distinguishing between strong and weak verbs, namely, those that have three consonants for their root which are called Shelemim (complete), and those which have as one of their root letters, either an *Aleph, He, Waw,* or *Yod,* which drop out at times in conjugation. Dunash intended to write a complete Hebrew grammar for which he drew up an elaborate program, but he never carried out his intention. His activity was not, however, limited to the field of grammar and lexicography, and we will have occasion later to speak of his great services to the cause of Hebrew poetry.

99. THE DISCIPLES OF MENAḤEM AND DUNASH AND THEIR CONTROVERSY

The attack of Dunash on Menaḥem's dictionary aroused deep interest in learned circles. They were soon divided into two camps, but Menaḥem's camp seemed to be the more numerous. Three of his pupils, Isaac Ibn Gikatilia, Ibn Kapron, and Judah Ibn Daud Ḥayyuj, published a rejoinder against Dunash's criticism under the name *Teshubot,* i. e. rejoinder. Though all three participated in the writing of the book, only one speaks and the form is singular. The book is prefaced by a poetical introduction, one part of which is a dedication to Ḥasdai Ibn Shaprut, and the other a general critique of Dunash. This is followed by an introduction in prose and an attack on Dunash for an attempt to apply the Arabic meter to Hebrew verse. After these preliminary remarks the writer or the writers discuss the particular articles of Menaḥem's dictionary to which Dunash took exception. They refute his criticism and vindicate Menaḥem. In the course of their vindication, they make many interesting grammatical remarks which contributed to the elucidation of grammatical theory. Judah Ibn Sheshet, a disciple of

Dunash, wrote a rejoinder to the rejoinder in the name of the disciples of Dunash, where he, in a biting satire written partly in metrical rhymed poetry, refutes the disciples of Menaḥem.

100. JUDAH ḤAYYUJ

Of the above-mentioned disciples of Menaḥem, only the last one attained prominence and greatness; this was Judah Ibn Daud Ḥayyuj (end of tenth and beginning of the eleventh century). The details of his life are unknown. He was born in Fez, North Africa, and later emigrated to Cordova where he had many pupils among whom was also the famous Samuel Ibn Nagdila.

His fame rests mainly on his writings and he is proclaimed by later grammarians as the founder of scientific study of Hebrew grammar. He wrote in Arabic three grammatical works, "On Weak Verbs," "On Doubled Verbs" and Sefer ha-Niḳud (The Book of Punctuation). In the first one, after speaking generally on the pronounced letters (he called them letters in motion) and the silent and weak or quiescent letters, he devotes himself to a systematic elaboration of the weak verbs and their conjugation. In the course of the discussion, he establishes definitely the law of triliterality of Hebrew roots, namely, that every root must have at least three letters as its root, and overthrew completely the theory previously held that there may be roots of two letters and even one. He divides his treatise into three parts, one on the verbs beginning with a weak letter Aleph or Yod (Pē Aleph and Pē Yod), the other on the verbs having the second radical Waw or Yod (Aen Waw, Aen Yod), and the last on verbs whose third radical is Hē or Aleph (Lamed Hē, Lamed Aleph). Not only is there in the book a systematic delineation of the rules of all these conjugations, but there is a list of all such verbs given, with complete reference to their use in the Bible in various forms and all peculiarities noted. The same thoroughness is seen in his work on the doubled verbs (Kefulim) where all laws of their conjugations are clearly treated. In both works, the various derivations of nouns from verbs are discussed and elucidated.

In his work on punctuation, he discusses the Sheva, (i. e. semivowel), the Dagesh, and the vowel pointing of nouns and their various changes. Considerable space is given to the law governing the placing of accents and the changes accruing in the vowel pointing from that. His works were later translated into Hebrew by Moses Ibn Gikatilia.

101. IBN JANNAH

Ḥayyuj was succeeded by one still greater than he, one whose labors in that field practically completed the structure of Hebrew grammar, and that was Jonah Ibn Jannaḥ, also known as Abulwalid Mervan (990–1050). He lived at first in Cordova, but also spent some time in Lucena, where he was instructed by Isaac Gikatilia, the pupil of Saruk, in the science of grammar. In the year 1012, when Cordova was destroyed by the Berbers, he together with many other Jews among whom was also Samuel Ibn Nagdila, fled and settled in Saragossa. Ibn Jannaḥ was a physician by profession and even wrote a number of books on medicine, but his real interest lay in the Bible. It is only because of his great desire to understand the Holy Writ that he devoted himself to the study of the Hebrew language and its structure.

His first book in this field, written in Cordova, was one which was intended to complete the theories of Ḥayyuj on the weak and doubled verbs, and he named it in Arabic *Mustabila*, i. e. the complement. There, he not only completed what Ḥayyuj had omitted on this subject, but also criticized him on a number of points and refuted some of his views. This called forth rejoinders from Hayyuj's pupils, especially Samuel Ibn Nagdila, who wrote a polemic against Ibn Jannah's book. The latter wrote another book replying to Nagdila's objections. He also wrote two other books on the same subject, one called "The Reconciliation," where criticisms are refuted, and one a commentary upon Hayyuj's works. In all these works, he elaborated his own theory of the construction of the larger part of the verbs.

His Magnum Opus is his grammar which he called "The Book of Critique," namely, critical studies of the Hebrew language (Arabic, Al-Tankikh). This book was supposed to comprise the entire science of the language, embracing both its grammatical construction and the vocabulary. It is divided into two parts, one devoted to grammar named *Rikmah* (Many-Colored Web) and the second one, "Book of the Roots," a lexicon. The first part contains forty-six chapters, half of which are devoted to grammar proper, and the other half to syntax and exegesis. In the grammatical section, he discusses the parts of speech, phonetics, the use of the prefixes and the changing of their pointing, the structure of verb forms, and especially noun formation. To this subject, he devoted many chapters and gave a complete outline of the declensions of all nouns. The subject of verbs he treats rather briefly, inasmuch as he dealt with it in his previous writings. Of especial value is the section devoted to syntax. He is considered by many the founder of the Hebrew syntax, and indeed he was hardly surpassed in that field by his successors. In the elaboration of his theories of syntax, he fixed numerous rules for the exegesis of the Bible and also explained hundreds of difficult passages, but this service of Ibn Jannaḥ will be discussed in the proper place. The second part also contains valuable grammatical remarks but is of especial lexicographical importance, inasmuch as Ibn Jannaḥ endeavors to give the various shades of meaning which each root has and elucidates it by examples. Besides, he made greater use than his predecessors of the comparison with Arabic and thus succeeded in elucidating the meaning of many words hitherto unknown. Ibn Jannaḥ's books were written in Arabic, but his "Critique," the Magnum Opus, both parts, the *Riḳmah* and "Book of Roots," were translated into Hebrew by Judah Ibn Tibbon.

102. THE SPANISH SCHOOL OF GRAMMARIANS AND LEXICOG-RAPHERS

The works of Ḥayyuj and Ibn Jannaḥ aroused great interest for further study in the science of language, and a number of greater and lesser scholars continued to labor in this field, and by their works enriched Hebrew literature and the knowledge of the sacred language. The foremost among them was Samuel Ibn Nagdila (993–1055), the leader of the Jews in Andalusia known as ha-Nagid, i. e. the prince. He was a pupil of Ḥayyuj, and, according to the testimony of Ibn Ezra in one place, he wrote twenty-two books on grammar, but these must have been small treatises and were most likely combined in the larger book, *Sefer ha-Osher,* (The Book of Riches), i. e. on the rich treasures of Hebrew. It was, however, lost and we have only a few citations. The poet, Solomon Ibn Gabirol (1021–1070), also wrote a long grammatical poem containing an outline of grammar.

Of greater value is the work of Moses Ibn Gikatilia, who like Ibn Jannaḥ hailed from Cordova and later settled in Saragossa. He translated Ḥayyuj's works into Hebrew and wrote a book on the gender in Hebrew under the name *Zeḳorim u-Neḳebot* (Male and Female). Ibn Ezra cites many of his views on a number of grammatical points. His contemporary, Judah Ibn Balaam (d. 1100), born in Toledo and a resident of Seville, wrote a number of treatises on grammar and lexicography. These are, "A Book of Homonyms," i. e. explanation of words which are used in different meanings (Tajanis), a "Book of Particles," namely, prepositions and conjunctions, on "Derived Verbs," and finally, a very valuable book on accents and vowels known as *Horoyat ha-Koré* "A Guide for Bible Readers." All these books were written in Arabic but were translated into Hebrew.

Of some importance are also the works of Isaac Ibn Yashush of Toledo who lived about this time and who wrote a book of conjugations and Levi Ibn Al Taban whose work *Mafteah* (The Key) is often cited by later writers. To the number of workers in this field may also be added the name of the famous poet Judah ha-Levi (Ch. 9) whose passages in the Kuzari on the nature of Hebrew and on the characters of the vowels and accents elucidate a number of points in grammar and phonetics.

103. ABRAHAM IBN EZRA

The great interest which was manifested in Spain and in other Mohammedan countries in the Hebrew language and its grammar and lexicography did not at first spread to the Jewish communities in Christian Europe. The scholars there were primarily interested in the study of the Talmud and its commentaries. But gradually, an awakening of interest in the Bible and its language took place also there. The Hebrew writings of Menahem and Dunash and others on the subjects of grammar, exegesis, and lexicography spread to all parts of Jewry and were great factors in calling forth this awakening. The more they were studied by the scholars of France, Italy, and Germany, the deeper became the interest. It is true, that for a long time only the theories of Menahem and Dunash held sway among the French and German Jews, even at the time when they were already abandoned in Spain, for the writings of Ḥayyuj Ibn Jannah, and others were unknown to them as they were written in Arabic. Thus, the famous Bible commentator, Solomon Izhaki (Rashi, Ch. 8) still follows Menahem and Dunash, though his fine sense of language discerned many a flaw in their theories and he often deviated from them. Likewise, Rashi's famous grandson, the Talmudist, Jacob ben Meir, known as Rabbi Tam, i. e. the innocent and perfect, wrote a book by the name of *ha-Hakraot* (The Decisions) to decide between Menahem and Dunash, where he often also criticizes both of them. But as a whole, the grammatical views of the early Spanish scholars prevailed.

The interest aroused in Hebrew studies by such spiritual leaders as the above-mentioned gradually increased, and it did not take long before Italy and France, especially Southern France became important centers of Jewish literature in all its branches. A great factor in bringing about this phenomenon, practically the mediator between Spain and the other countries, was the well-known Abraham Ibn Ezra.

Ibn Ezra, after long wanderings (for his life see Ch. VII) settled for a time in Rome (1140) and there he began his literary activity in the field of Hebrew philology. His works are first, the *Moznaim* (The Scales) which is the earliest. In it he deals primarily with the explanation of the grammatical terminology. But it is not a mere dictionary of the terminology of grammar, but almost a complete grammar in a brief form. It is something like an introduction to the study of Hebrew grammar. The second one, *Sefat Yeter* (The Preferred Language), is primarily devoted to a defense of Saadia Gaon against the strictures of Dunash but contains also some of his own grammatical views. The third work is his *Yesodé Dikduk* (The Elements of Grammar), where a complete set of rules of Hebrew grammar is given dealing with all its parts. And finally, he wrote the *Zahot,* i. e. purity or clarity, meaning by it the purity of the Hebrew language. This books deals, like his "Elements" with the entire field of Hebrew grammar but in a more intensive and extensive way. It contains also several chapters on prosody and the theory of the Hebrew meter. He wrote also another book under the name of *Safah Berurah* (The Pure Language), where he discusses certain problems in grammar but, in spite of the name, not in a very clear manner. In the introduction to the book, Ibn Ezra discusses certain phases of Bible exegesis and language study, especially the relation of Hebrew to Arabic and Aramaic.

Ibn Ezra's contribution to Hebrew philology consists not so much in the novelty of his theories as in the fact that his were the first systematic grammatical works which were written in Hebrew, and which embodied the fruits of the labors in that field by the great Spanish grammarians and lexicographers. He thus made this accumulated knowledge accessible to the Jews of Western Europe to whom Arabic was a sealed book. Yet, Ibn Ezra was no mere compiler. Everything he wrote he stamped with his personality. Not only is there originality in his recasting of the grammatical knowledge in a systematic and methodical way, but also in his concise, vivacious, and witty style which imparts a peculiar charm even to dry rules of grammar.

The activity of Ibn Ezra gave impetus to other scholars to continue his work. His disciple, Solomon Ibn Parḥon, followed his example. He emigrated from Spain and settled in Salerno, Italy, where he composed a dictionary under the name of *Maḥberet ha-Aruk,* a name borrowed from Menaḥem's work on the one hand and from the Talmudical lexicon of Nathan ben Yehiel (Ch. X, Sec. C), the *Aruk,* on the other hand. It is modeled primarily after Ibn Jannaḥ's "Book of Roots," but with many additions from Ḥayyuj and his own. He drew on both Mishnaic Hebrew and Aramaic for his explanations of Hebrew words and explains many Biblical passages. There are also contained in this work a number of historical data bearing upon the development of the scientific and literary study of Hebrew.

104. THE KIMḤI FAMILY

The sojourn of Ibn Ezra in France and Italy left more than a passing impression. It practically helped towards the establishment of a new center of learning and great literary activity, namely, the above-mentioned center of Southern France. The Provence, as that part of France was then called, was in the twelfth century, next to Spain, a haven of rest for the Jews. The liberal policy of its counts and dukes enabled the Jewish communities to prosper and increase in numbers, and on account of its proximity to Mohammedan Spain, the center of culture at that time, it also became a seat of learning. For the same reason, the Jews of the Provence were influenced by their brethren across the Pyrenees, and, likewise, began to develop a considerable literary productivity. An important factor in this development was the influx of immigrant scholars from Spain, who settled in various cities of the Provence. These were, practically, the mediators between the cultures of the East and the West. Being proficient in Arabic and also masters of Hebrew, they laid open to their brethren the treasures of Jewish knowledge contained in Arabic works by translating the latter into Hebrew. We will have a good deal more to say about this service of theirs, but for the present, we may remark that it was through them that the Provence became, in the succeeding centuries, the center of Jewish literature which ultimately took over the leadership from Spain. The twelfth century saw the rise of that center.

As in Spain, so in the Provence, study of Hebrew and exegesis of the Bible preceded the other phases of literary activity. Work in this field began simultaneously in two different places. Judah Ibn Tibbon, born in Granada, Spain, and settled in Lunel, translated there Ibn Jannaḥ's

Magnum Opus, the *Rikmah,* and the "Book of Roots" into Hebrew and thus introduced him and his works to the Hebrew-reading Jews of Western Europe. In Narbonne, another city of the Provence, an entire family devoted its energy and great ability for two generations to the work of searching the mysteries of the sacred tongue and to the exploration of the treasures of the Bible. This was the Kimḥi family, consisting of Joseph and his two sons, Moses and David. Joseph Kimḥi emigrated from Spain in his youth and settled in Narbonne. There for a period of twenty years (1150–1170), he carried on his literary activity, writing poems, translating books from the Arabic, and writing a commentary on the Bible as well as other works. But his real contribution was in the field of grammar. His first work is *Sefer ha-Zikaron* (The Book of Remembrance). It was intended as a textbook and covers the entire field. He made two important contributions to Hebrew grammar, as he was the first one to introduce the division of the vowels into long and short, and thus increased their number from the adopted seven to ten. As he followed the Sephardic pronunciation, he arranged them thus: long: A, O, I, E, (EI) U, and correspondingly short: A (Pataḥ) O, I, E, U. He gained three vowels, short O (Kamez Katan), the short I (Ḥirik Katan) which is not followed by *Yod,* and Kubuẓ, short U, represented by three dots. His innovation was accepted by all grammarians, and even by the German though it does not exactly tally with their pronunciation, but it produced good results as it facilitated the promulgation of a number of rules. His second contribution is the introducing of two verb forms, the passives of *Piel* and *Hifhil.* They were already mentioned by Ibn Ezra, but not sufficiently elaborated.

His other work is of less importance and is called *Sefer ha-Galu* (The Document) and deals with lexicographical and exegetical questions and is primarily a criticism of the book of Jacob Tam (above, The Decisions), where he attempts to decide between Menaḥem and Dunash. Joseph Kimḥi's books were for a long time forgotten and only recently brought to light and published, but his theories were given wide publicity by the writings of his sons.

His son, Moses Kimḥi (1170–1190) followed in the footsteps of his father and wrote a grammatical textbook by the name of *Shebilé ha-Da'at* (The Paths of Knowledge). Its merit consists in its brevity, and on this account it was long used in the schools and was even translated into Latin and used by Sebastian Münster, a Christian Hebraist of the sixteenth century.

The greatest of this family was the younger son, David (b. 1160 d. 1235), of whom we will have much to say later. He was distinguished in many fields, and likewise in that of Hebrew philology. His chief work is the *Mikhlol* (Compendium) which, following Ibn Jannaḥ, he divided into two parts, a grammar, and a dictionary of roots of Biblical words. This part bears the name *Sefer ha-Sherashim* (The Book of Roots). His grammar differs from those of his predecessors by his comprehensive dealing with the verb, to which he devotes more space. He covers all the rules governing the conjugations of verbs, changes of punctuation, and accents. The *Mikhlol* contains also complete tables of conjugations, and is distinguished by the clarity of its style and conciseness. On account of all these qualities, it overshadowed all previous works and for centuries was considered the leading grammar.

His "Book of Roots" enjoyed similar popularity. It is not merely a recast copy of Ibn Jannaḥ's book, but an original work. In each article, all forms of the verb are given as well as its derivatives, nouns, and adjectives. Wherever he found it necessary, he added brief exegetical remarks upon Biblical passages wherein the forms of the root are found.

Besides the *Mikhlol* in two parts, David wrote also the *Et Sofer* (The Pen of the Scribe), a manual of punctuation where the rules of punctuation together with the rules of the accents are discussed. In the writings of David Kimḥi, Hebrew grammar and lexicography reached its zenith, at least as far as the entire Mediæval Ages are concerned. Those that came after were only gatherers of grain after the reapers.

Chapter VIII

BIBLE EXEGESIS

A. The Gaonic Period

105. INTRODUCTORY

As we have seen in the previous chapter, the intensive study of the Hebrew language, its grammar, and vocabulary which began in the East, i. e. Babylonia, was practically only a means to a better understanding of the Bible. It followed, therefore, that the very same people who devoted a great deal of their energy to the exploration of the secrets of Hebrew, should have devoted still more energy to the exploration of the Holy Writ. And thus it was that simultaneously with the activity in the field of grammar and lexicography, there flourished great literary activity in the field of Bible exegesis.

But this field was a wide one and the number of its workers greater than in other fields. They hailed from different lands and different parts of the world, as almost every Jewish center contributed its quota of Bible exegetes. The Bible was the deep concern of every Jew, and wherever they were, it was studied and commented upon. Yet, this period of Biblical exegesis differs greatly from the earlier period of Midrashic exegesis. It is primarily a period of *Peshat,* i. e. an endeavor to understand the plain meaning of the words and to present the sense of the contents in as lucid a manner as possible. It, of course, intended to extract all the moral and religious teachings of the Bible, but on the whole, it kept aloof from homiletics, though it was not wanting in many commentaries. The studies and investigations in Hebrew grammar and lexicography prepared the way for this kind of exegesis and made it possible.

This kind of exegesis, like the study of language, received in its birthplace, Babylonia, a strong impetus from the Karaite movement. They who fell back upon the Bible were the first to delve into the explanations of the sacred writings, either in order to disprove Talmudic interpretations, or to deduce new ones. The Rabbanites, on their part, had to do likewise in order to show that Talmudic interpretation is not forced and that it agrees with the actual sense of the word rightly understood. In time, the explanation of the Bible became an end in itself. At the time when philosophic thought began to occupy the minds of Jewish scholars and a need for the reconciliation of the principles of philosophy with the ideas of the Bible began to be felt, philosophic exegesis arose where an attempt at reconciliation similar to that of Philo (Ch. V) was made. But the later philosophic exegesis differed from the Philonian as it avoided excessive allegorizing and was based on a deeper knowledge of the language. Thus, Bible exegesis during this period exhibits many phases and forms an important branch of the literary activity of the period.

106. EXEGETIC WORK OF SAADIA

The great Saadia, the founder and the pioneer in many branches of study, was also the first great commentator of the Bible. Yet in his early youth, he undertook to defend Jewish tradition against the Karaites, as well as against all who either misinterpreted the Bible, or attacked it from various points of view. Among the many enemies of traditional Judaism at that time, the ninth and tenth centuries, there was one by the name of Ḥivi Al-Balkhi (fl. in the middle of the ninth century) who was extremely rabid in his attacks on Judaism. This Ḥivi wrote a book wherein he propounded two hundred arguments against the teachings of the Pentateuch. This radical book which pointed out many contradictions in the sacred writings was widely spread in many circles for two generations, and its ideas found many adherents. Saadia, therefore, wrote a book entitled "A Refutation of Ḥivi Al-Balkhi," wherein he refutes his questions one by one with great skill. The book was written in Hebrew in rhymed prose, though the title was in Arabic; a large part of it is still preserved.[1]

In this book as well as in several others which he wrote against the Karaites, Saadia made many contributions to the exegesis of the Bible. But these polemic controversies were only preliminary to his work in the field of Bible explanation. He became convinced that what the Jews needed at the time, was a complete translation of the entire Bible into Arabic, as well as a commentary on it in the same language,

---

[1] A considerable fragment of it found in the Cairo Genizah was edited and published with English introduction and notes by Prof. Israel Davidson in 1915.

both of which should definitely vindicate the traditional view of the Bible. And he undertook this task single-handed.

Saadia's translation of the Bible into Arabic is an epoch-making work. It not only became the standard Arabic translation for all Arabic speaking Jews for centuries, but it exerted great influence on the Mohammedan world. It is a masterpiece from both the point of view of style and manner of interpretation, as it is not merely a translation, but a commentary as well. Saadia himself was conscious of it and called it *Tafsir,* i. e. commentary. Yet it is not a paraphrase. On the whole, he translated every word of the Bible, though wherever necessary, for the sake of elucidation and clarity, he added a word or even a phrase here and there. He seemed to have taken the *Targum Onkelos* as his model. Like it, Saadia removed all anthropomorphisms, but he went further than the author of the *Targum.* He also translated proper names, especially of tribes, nations, countries, and cities. In this, of course, he had to analyze them etymologically or adopt some suggestions. Saadia seemed to have prepared two versions of his translation of a large number of the Biblical books, one with an extensive commentary intended for scholars and one without commentary, a popular edition.

But great as he was in his Bible translation, he appears still greater in his commentaries. In them not only the deep student of the Hebrew language is evident but the philosopher as well. His general point of view is, first that the Bible is compatible with all principles of reason; second, that it is as a whole a revealed book; and thirdly, that tradition has great validity in interpretation. On this triple basis his commentaries are founded, namely, reason, revelation, and tradition. He, however, lays great emphasis on the element of reason, and he endeavors to make the Bible so clear that nothing obscure shall remain.

In his endeavor to maintain the unified point of view in the explanation of the Bible, he, as a rule, prefixed to each book an introduction wherein he propounded the basic principles from which the book as a whole should be viewed. He also briefly summarized its contents, pointing out its divisions and their relation to each other. Especially interesting are his introductions to the Pentateuch and the Book of Proverbs. In the first, he dwells on the educational value of the Five Books of Moses, how they are intended to train the Jewish people in the path of religion and righteousness. He then tells of their unique value and authority, showing how the teachings agree with the principles of reason, which agreement in itself serves as a proof for the validity of the Torah. He also adduces another proof for the validity and applicability of its laws, from the way the prophets applied them to all exigencies of life. In the introduction to the Book of Proverbs, he discusses extensively the opposition between the sensual nature of man and his reason, and shows how the book intends to teach the path of life by recording this antagonism. This psychological discussion is followed by remarks on the content and form of the book, its divisions and their logical connections.

In the commentaries proper, Saadia follows a strictly scientific path. He evinces deep insight into the meaning of the words, elucidates each word by numerous references to other passages where the words are used, and although he uses tradition as his authority, he keeps aloof from homiletic interpretation. He was the real founder of the *Peshat* exegesis, i. e. a rational explanation and one built on the understanding of the language. With great zeal, Saadia reconciles in his commentary all apparent contradictions of the Bible. In such passages where contradictions to their contents may be quoted from other passages, reference is made to the contradictions and the difficulties straightened out.

It is to be regretted that a large part of the translation of the Bible, and especially of the commentary, is lost. We have only the Pentateuch without commentary and some fragments of the commentary on Exodus. Of the other books of the Bible, only the translations of Isaiah, Psalms, Proverbs, Job, and Daniel are preserved together with their commentaries.[2] There are also some translations of several of the Scrolls and fragments of commentaries on them. From what is left as well as from the hundreds of quotations in the works of the later commentators, we can estimate the importance of Saadia as an exegete of the Bible.

107. OTHER BABYLONIAN COMMENTATORS

Saadia showed the Babylonian Geonim, heads of academies, how important it is to study the Bible and understand it. Some of them followed in his footsteps. Thus, Aaron ben Sarjadah, Saadia's opponent at the time of his conflict with the Exilarch David ben Zakkai, who later became Gaon of Pumbedita, also wrote a commentary on the Pentateuch (about 960). We know little about it except that it bore a philosophic character.

[2] These were edited and supplied with a French translation by the late scholar, J. Derenbourg.

A commentator of greater importance was the last Gaon of Sura, the father-in-law of the famous Rab Hai, Samuel ben Ḥofni (d. 1034). He translated the Pentateuch and commented upon it. He followed Saadia in the translation but was more literal. His commentary was an extensive one, and contained excursuses on various questions. Ibn Ezra tells us that Samuel in his commentary on Genesis XXVIII, 10–22 had two long discussions in connection with the journey and the dream of Jacob, one on journeys in the Bible and the other on dreams in general. Samuel was a rationalist and he tried to rationalize many events in the Bible. Thus, he says that Jacob's wrestling with the angel as well as the speaking of Balaam's ass occurred in dreams. From some recovered fragments of the commentary, we can see that where he does not digress, it is a very excellent one. It is analytic, and the meaning of every word is given and ascertained by comparison with references to the usage of the word in other passages.

His son-in-law, Rab Hai, the last Gaon who was a student of the Hebrew language, also wrote a commentary on the Book of Job. He was very exact in his search for the true meaning of words, and even inquired once of the Syrian Katholicos, head of the Christian Church, how to explain a certain passage in the Psalms.

108. BIBLE EXEGESIS IN OTHER COUNTRIES

Just as we have seen in the case of the literary activity in the field of language study, that it rapidly spread from Babylonia to North Africa, another Jewish center under Mohammedan rule, so likewise in the case of Bible exegesis, Kairawan came upon the heels of Babylon and produced commentators of note. The contemporary of Saadia, the physician and philosopher Isaac Israeli (845–940), wrote an extensive commentary on the first two chapters of Genesis which dealt at length with the problem of creation from a philosophic point of view. The grammarian, Judah Ibn Koreish (Ch. VII), besides explaining many Biblical passages in his dictionary, wrote a commentary on the Book of Chronicles, for he is quoted repeatedly in an anonymous commentary on that book, the author of which seemed to have been a pupil of Saadia.

A generation later, we meet in Kairawan a great commentator in the person of Rabbi Ḥanannel (1000–1050), the famous North African Talmudist. Though his main activity was the Talmud (Ch. X) he did not neglect the Bible and wrote a commentary, in Hebrew, on the Pentateuch. The entire commentary was lost, but from the copious quotations found in later commentaries, it is evident that it exerted great influence upon the generations. The fragments show a tendency towards Midrashic explanation, yet on the whole there is noted in the commentary a keenness of understanding of the Bible. At times, when it concerns a matter of oral tradition which the Karaites denied, Hanannel launches a lengthy polemic against them though he does not mention them by name. Thus, in his excursus to Exodus XII, 2, he deals at length with the question of the calendar and tries to prove that it was always fixed by mathematical calculation, and that the fixing of the first of the month by testimony of witnesses who saw the birth of the moon was only a formal act. All this was intended against the Karaites who rejected the Rabbanite calendar and reverted to the testimony of eye-witnesses. Hanannel also knew Arabic and explained many words by comparison with similar Arabic words. His style is light and easy, and at times, he breaks into rhymed prose. His colleague, Rabbi Nissim (Ch. X), also wrote a commentary on the Pentateuch, of which a few quotations are found in later exegetical works.

109. THE SPANISH SCHOOL OF COMMENTATORS

With the rise of Jewish learning in Spain and along with the flourishing of the school of Hebrew grammarians and lexicographers, there began also activity in the field of exegesis, for as said, the study of language was only a means for understanding the Bible. As early as the second half of the tenth century, we hear of a commentator, Joseph Ibn Abitur, who wrote a Hebrew commentary on the Psalms of which some fragments are preserved. It follows the Midrashic method of interpretation, but its style offers some interesting points, inasmuch as Ibn Abitur attempts to coin a number of new Hebrew words.

Menahem ben Saruk's Mahberet (Ch. VII), while it was intended as a dictionary, is an important contribution to exegesis for many difficult Biblical passages are explained there. He is constantly quoted by the great exegete Rashi. He also deserves credit for first discovering the basic form of Biblical poetry, parallelism, namely, that each verse is divided into two halves, the second one repeating the same thought only in different language. His assumption has been verified by all modern commentators and followed in all explanations. Dunash's strictures on Menaḥem as well as the polemics between him and Menaḥem's pupils also added to the exegesis of the Bible.

Very great was the contribution to exegesis of Ibn Jannaḥ (Ch. VII). Not only did he explain in his grammar, *Riḳmah,* and in "The Book of Roots" hundreds of Biblical passages but he really laid down principles of exegesis. He demonstrated the theory of frequent interchange of letters, and made the observation that words in passages were often omitted for some reason or other and are, therefore, to be understood. All these remarks facilitated the explanation of difficult passages and many emendations suggested by modern commentators can be traced back to Ibn Jannaḥ.

Yet, he was no Bible critic in the modern sense; on the contrary, he believed not only in its divine character, but also accepted the interpretations of the Talmud and Midrash as truth. He believed, however, that his own interpretations based on the signs of language are also true for the words of the Bible have more than one meaning.

Moses Ibn Gikatilia (Ch. VII), the grammarian who followed Ibn Jannaḥ, wrote commentaries on the Books of Isaiah, the Minor Prophets, Psalms, and Job. He is copiously quoted by Ibn Ezra in his commentaries on these books from which it is evident that his commentaries were widely read. From the quotations, it is to be seen that Ibn Gikatilia belonged to the liberal school of commentators. He is especially distinguished by his keen historical sense which he utilized in assigning certain chapters of the Prophets and the Psalms to different periods. Thus, he was the first one to assume that there are chapters in the Book of Psalms which were written at a later date. According to him, some Psalms were written in Babylon. He even indicated his belief in a later origin of the chapters XL–LXVI of Isaiah. He also endeavored to explain the miracles of the Bible in a rational way. In addition to his commentaries, he translated the Book of Job into Arabic, which translation is still preserved while the commentaries are lost.

His contemporary, both colleague and opponent, the grammarian Judah Ibn Balaam (Ch. VII), also wrote commentaries on the Pentateuch, Joshua, Isaiah, and Psalms. His commentary on Isaiah is preserved and from it we can see that he followed the method of Saadia. He is quoted also by Ibn Ezra in his commentary on Psalms, which quotations testify to his fine understanding of the book. Ibn Balaam is more orthodox in his exegesis, and often takes Ibn Gikatalia to task for his rational views on miracles. His commentary on the Pentateuch, he named "The Book of Decisions," which can only be explained by the assumption that he endeavored there to decide between different views and select the right one, and from the few fragments preserved, we see that he really did follow this method for he quotes copiously from Saadia and other commentators and compares their views.

The period (the end of the eleventh century) produced also an exegete who was rather a radical Bible critic by the name of Isaac Ibn Yashush who is also known as a grammarian. This Isaac ventured to suggest that certain passages in the Pentateuch, such as Genesis XXXVI, 31–43, were not written by Moses. He also made an excessive number of emendations in the Bible. Ibn Ezra quotes him by the name of Yizḥaki (as his name was Yizḥak) and censures him severely, applying to him a number of unkind epithets.

The philosopher and poet, Solomon Ibn Gabirol (Ch. IX), also seemed to have written some commentaries on at least part of the Pentateuch and perhaps even on the Psalms. But nothing is known of their nature except one quotation by Ibn Ezra in his comment on Genesis II, 8–12 from which we can see that it was of an allegoric mystic character. In the quotation we read that Gabirol said: Eden symbolizes the upper world; the garden, the lower world; the stream which flows from the garden, universal matter; Adam, Eve, and the serpent symbolize the rational, animal, and vegetative (desiring) souls respectively, and so forth.

In conclusion, we must also mention the chapter by the poet Moses Ibn Ezra (Ch. IX) in his book on poetry [3] dealing with the rhetoric of the Bible. It is not directly exegesis but in his careful and detailed explanation of the Biblical figures of speech, their nature and usage, he contributed to a better understanding of many chapters in the Bible, especially in the prophetic and poetic books.

B. THE FRENCH SCHOOL OF EXEGETES

110. GENERAL CHARACTERISTICS

Simultaneously with the flourishing of Biblical exegesis in Spain and other lands where Arabic culture was dominant, there arose also in Northern France a school of Bible commentators whose works

---

[3] It has been recently translated into Hebrew by the late Dr. Benzion Halper under the name *Shirat Yisrael*, (Poetry of Israel).

left a lasting impression upon Jewish literature, probably even greater than that of the first.

The difference between these two schools is as great as the difference between these two types of Jewries and the difference in their general cultural status. The Jews of Spain, as we know, participated freely in the general culture of the land and were saturated with it, and this mastery of secular knowledge is reflected in all their literary work. The Jews of France and Germany, on the other hand, confined their activity almost entirely to the study of the Talmud, and were as a rule but little influenced by the culture of their neighbors. Besides, their neighbors hardly had any culture or literature that could exert any influence on the Jews. And whatever culture there was in these lands, was entirely in the hands of the representatives of the Church with whom the Jews could scarcely fraternize. Jewish life thus flowed on in its own channel undisturbed by external currents, and it is no wonder then that it developed in a somewhat one-sided manner.

Yet what it lost in variety, it gained in depth and intensity. Its world view was thoroughly Jewish, and this view is reflected in all forms of literature produced by the Jews of France or Germany, in the study of the Talmud and its application to life, in the religious poetry (Ch. IX), and Bible exegesis. The center of spiritual interest in these countries was the Talmud and all that belongs to it, but at no time did the Jews anywhere forsake the Bible, and side by side with the mighty stream of Talmudic study, there flowed a lesser stream of Biblical study. In this Biblical study of the French Jews, there are to be discerned two currents, one, the *Derash,* i. e. the homiletic-Midrashic, and the other the one of *Peshat,* i. e. the plain explanation of the Bible based on understanding of the words and their connected meaning. These two currents were never totally separated. At times the first prevailed, and at times the other, but very often they were united. This happy combination of *Derash* and *Peshat* is the peculiar characteristic of the French school of exegesis, and is typified in its greatest exponents, as will be evident.

The beginnings of Biblical exegesis in France are very difficult to trace. It seems that French and German Jewries were in their earlier development greatly influenced by Palestine, which, even in its low state during the ninth and tenth centuries, never ceased to influence the Jewries of the Diaspora. As historical documents are constantly being brought to light, we begin to see the effects of that influence. There was a continual stream of Jewish travelers to Palestine from West-European countries and vice versa. Inquiries were sent from Germany and France to Jerusalem as late as the eleventh century. On the other hand, teachers from Palestine, especially Agadists and Massorites, and Biblical scholars, visited these countries.

It was in this way that both Palestinian specialties, the homiletic-Agadic and the Massoretic-linguistic, were transplanted to these countries. The fact that conditions in France and Germany were not unlike those which existed in Palestine under Christian rule when Agada was fostered (Ch. VI) explains the deep interest of the Jews there in that form of Biblical explanation. Here, like there, the Jew suffered deeply and his soul thirsted for comfort and alleviation from misery. And this, the mild and colorful Agada supplied him. There were also traveling preachers who delivered their homilies on the Sabbath in the crowded synagogues. There developed then a kind of later Midrashic school of exegetes. The greatest of these was Moses ha-Darshan, i. e. the homiletist or preacher, of Narbonne. Another was Eliezer ben Tubia who, though he produced his work in Greece, hailed from Mayence, Germany. The compiled Midrashic commentaries were discussed above (Sec. 88). It may be added that these works though called Midrashim were not all compilations of earlier Agada but contain the explanations of the authors themselves which are of exegetic value. These two homiletic exegetes found followers, such as Menaḥem ben Solomon of Rome who in the year 1139 compiled a similar commentary under the name of *Seḳel Tob* (Good Reason), and others. But the works of Moses exerted great influence upon his countrymen and he is constantly quoted by the later exegetes.

From Palestine was transplanted to France also the knowledge of the *Massorah* and as much grammar and linguistics as were known there, and in early times the great Talmudic scholars occupied themselves likewise with *Massorah* and Bible study. We hear of Rabbi Gershom, the son of Judah, known as the Light of the Exile (Ch. X), copying Massoretic lists and transmitting correct readings to posterity. Joseph Bonfils, known as *Tob Elem* (the Hebrew translation of the French cognomen), also copied Massoretic books, and according to the testimony of some, also wrote a commentary on the Pentateuch. And thus interest in the Bible grew and spread among scholars.

Soon, however, Biblical scholars formed a class for themselves. There were some people who specialized in writing, punctuating, and reading the Bible in the synagogue. They were called by various names, either scribes, punctators (Nakdonim), or readers (Karaim). These people also became interested in exegesis and some of them began to compile commentaries. The purpose of these commentators was to explain the Bible in the way of *Peshat*. The earliest of this class of exegetes was Rabbi Menahem, the son of Helbo, in the middle of the eleventh century, who was also given the title of *Kara*. He must either have written a commentary on the entire Bible, or at least notes to the same, for he is quoted frequently by Rashi and by his nephew, Joseph Karo (Sec. 111). From these quotations we can see that Menahem possessed a keen understanding of the Bible and that he was also well grounded in the rudiments of Hebrew grammar and was able to discern the shades of meaning in words.

But Bible study in France could never remain the share of the few or of a class. The great Talmudists again found time also for the Bible and it seems that these two studies really went hand in hand during that time. The heads of the Talmudic academies (Yeshibot) expounded the Bible to their students along with the Talmud. It is no wonder then that it did not take long and these academies produced from their midst one of the greatest commentators of the ages.

111. SOLOMON BEN ISAAC (Rashi)

This man was Solomon Izhaki, son of Isaac, or as he is commonly known, Rashi, initials of Rabbi Solomon Izhaki. Rashi was born in the year 1040, in the city of Troyes, France. He received his education first at home, but later went, as was customary in those days, to study at the academy of Worms under Jacob ben Yakar, disciple of the great Rabbi Gershom, and later under Isaac ha-Levi, another disciple of Gershom. After staying there for some time, he proceeded to the academy at Mayence, presided over by Isaac, son of Judah, to complete his studies. At the age of twenty-five, he returned to Troyes and being a married man, he engaged, like most of his countrymen, in the wine industry.

His real occupation, however, was the study of the Torah, for though he was not an official rabbi, he was considered one of the greatest scholars of the day, and from all sides Rabbis turned to him for decisions on all questions bearing upon religious matters. As most scholars of the day, he founded an academy, and due to his fame it was frequented by hundreds of students from all parts of Europe including the Slavonic countries. For a period of forty years, Rashi taught Torah to his students, both Talmud and Bible, and as a result his commentaries on these two great collections of Jewish literature were produced. His old age was embittered by the suffering of the Jews during the first Crusade (1096) and also by his own sickness. He died in 1105 at the age of sixty-five, mourned by all Jewry.

Many were the qualities which fitted Rashi to be the commentator par excellence, and probably the greatest of them was his character. He is the typical example of the Jewish scholar, the *Talmid Ḥaham,* and his outstanding trait was his simplicity of soul. He was simple in all ways of life; he practically lived in his own daily life the Torah which he taught for forty years to his students. And along with his simplicity went his modesty; he was never conscious of his greatness and was always willing to receive instruction as well as to impart it. His love for his people was unbounded and it included every member of his people, even those who had gone astray. But still greater was his love for the Torah. This was the essence of his life, hence his deep knowledge of it. There was not a branch of Jewish literature in which he was not master. He did not draw any lines, everything—law, Agada, history, and grammar, or even secular sciences, as much as he could derive from Hebrew books, were all open to him. His all-absorbing mind drank in thirstily any information he could possibly lay hold of. Yet with all his piety and absorption in learning, Rashi knew life. He informed himself on matters of business, trade, industry, and even government affairs, as is evidenced from his commentaries.

All these qualities are reflected in his exegetic work and made his commentary what it became. His commentary is an ideal example of the French school of exegetes. In it, there is a harmony between the two methods, the *Derash* and the *Peshat.* The French commentators lacked the deep knowledge of grammar and language, and all the scientific apparatus for exegesis that the Spanish Jewish scholars possessed. But they were led by a simple sense which was close to the spirit of the Bible and were thus enabled to penetrate the depth of its meaning, at times, even better than their more learned brethren. The Spanish scholars often tried to read into the words of the Bible their own ideas, while the French commentators only endeavored to draw out from the Bible whatever they could.[4] This tendency is best exemplified in Rashi. He absorbed the Bible, in the degree it was possible for

[4] On this, see A. Geiger, *Parshandata,* German Part p. 10.

him, and through this absorption, he often penetrated to the very depth of the meaning of the verse. He was saturated with the spirit of the Agada and its world view. He looked upon the Bible through its own glasses, but he understood also the great value of the words and verses. He used, therefore, many Agadic interpretations, but also gave the *Peshat* interpretation. The simplicity of his soul demanded simplicity of meaning, and when he did use a Midrashic interpretation he chose the one which harmonized with the meaning of the words.

As a great commentator, he knew the importance, for the understanding of the verse, of the meaning of single words; he therefore endeavored to explain wherever necessary each word, giving its grammatical derivation. For this purpose, he utilized the works of Menaḥem ben Saruk and Dunash to their fullest extent and often added his own suggestions. He utilized fully the Aramaic *Targumim,* both Onkelos and Jonathan, and followed them quite frequently, and likewise made use of all previous commentators and all explanations he read or heard from his teachers, quoting every remark in the name of its author.

As a teacher, he knew the pedagogic value of similes and examples which bring out the meaning more clearly to the average reader, and used them profusely; and his illustrations and similes are so well known and simple that they bring the unfolded thought of the verse into clear relief. Likewise, are his illustrations and explanations of technical matters clear and numerous. Being endowed with a fund of practical knowledge relating to various trades, agriculture, commerce and other pursuits, he drew upon them for illustration and explanation.

But the greatest merit of his commentary is its style. The style of Rashi reflects his soul; it is simple and natural, for there is hardly an unnecessary phrase in it, and it is as pure and clear as was his noble heart. It is very close to the style of the Agada in its poetic touch. Rashi embodied many Midrashic remarks in his commentary with slight changes, but they are hardly distinguishable from his own words. Many are the quotations of Talmudic proverbs and *bon mots* which Jews quote in the improved and changed form that Rashi has given them, and many are the quotations from Rashi that go under the name of Talmudic sayings, though they are never found there, so close is the harmony between the style of Rashi and that of the Agada. Great is also the spirit of his commentary, for not only does it reflect his own soul but the soul of the people. His love for the Jewish people, for tradition and Torah shines forth from every page. He did not teach ethics, but his words are saturated with an ethical glow which the reader absorbs unconsciously.

It was all these qualities which made his commentary, notwithstanding its shortcomings, the outstanding commentary of the ages. Generations and generations of Jewish children were trained upon it, and Rashi was their constant companion during childhood. *Humesh,* i. e. the Pentateuch, and Rashi became inseparable and even the most uneducated had a smattering of it. Not to have learned Rashi meant to the Jew during the centuries, even to the one of only a generation ago, a sign of degradation and one who was actually so unfortunate was considered beyond the pale of Jewish civilization. Quotations from Rashi were current in the mouth of almost every Jew, even the ignorant, and many of its expressions are even current in the Yiddish dialect spoken by the Jews of Eastern Europe. Thus, Rashi's commentary became part and parcel of Jewish folk-life for centuries.

The commentary made also a great impression upon the non-Jewish world. The Christian commentator of the Bible, Nicolaus de Lyra (1265–1349), utilized it to a great extent, and through his influence and other Christian scholars, many of Rashi's interpretations were embodied in the later Latin translations of the Bible as well as in the Standard English Version (King James).

Rashi wrote his commentary on the whole Bible except on Chronicles. The commentary on that book bearing his name does not belong to him, but emanated from the school of a German exegete by the name of Saadia, and was given the name of Rashi to gain popularity. Part of the commentary on Joel was also completed by his pupils.

112. OTHER FRENCH COMMENTATORS

Rashi left after him a number of disciples to whom he taught the Bible and who continued his work in the field of Biblical exegesis. One of these who attained prominence in this branch is Joseph ben Simon Kara (1080–1160). He was the nephew of the commentator, Menaḥem ben Ḥelbo, and like him, was surnamed Kara on account of his occupation as a Bible reader. At first, he studied with his uncle, and after his death, came to Rashi. He coöperated with him in his commentary, reciting before him explanations of verses in the name of Menaḥem, also making his own suggestions here and there. Rashi quotes both the remarks of Menaḥem which he heard from Joseph and also Joseph himself.

Joseph wrote commentaries on all the prophetic books, on Job, and the Five Scrolls, but as for the Pentateuch, he only added notes to Rashi's commentary. Besides, he seems to have been the editor of Rashi's commentary on the Bible, and many of his remarks are included there, sometimes under his name and many times anonymously. In his own commentary, he followed Rashi's method, in combining *Peshat* with *Derash,* but he surpassed his master, at times, by his inclination towards the simpler explanation of the Bible. He is especially painstaking to elucidate the connection of the successive verses and endeavors to present to the reader the ideas implicit in the chapter as a whole. He is careful to ascertain the grammatical meaning of words, their derivation and changes. Kara also possessed critical acumen and was not afraid to express his opinions. In his commentary on Samuel, IX, 9, he concludes from the verse that it was not written by the prophet himself but later, contrary to the Talmudic opinion on the matter.

The other noted commentator is Samuel ben Meir (1085–1160), the colleague of Joseph and the grandson of Rashi. He is usually known by the abbreviation of *Rashbam,* i. e. Rabbi Samuel ben Meir, and also wrote commentaries on several Talmudic tractates, and was one of the leading Tosafists (Ch. X). Samuel studied the Bible together with Joseph under Rashi, and also made a number of suggestions to his grandfather who accepted them and quoted them in his name. His main exegetic work is his commentary on the Pentateuch. He deviated greatly from his grandfather by following mainly the method of the *Peshat.* His commentary is permeated with a liberal spirit, and in his explanation, he follows strictly the meaning of the words, and though his grammatical knowledge was limited, he was able by his fine linguistic sense to discover independently many grammatical rules established by Ḥayyuj and other Spanish grammarians. He, at times, makes statements which are contrary to accepted traditional opinion; thus, he says in his explanation of Genesis I, 5 that the days of creation terminated with dawn making the night a part of the preceding day. But Samuel was not conscious of any contradiction between tradition and the plain meaning of the Torah, for he believed whole-heartedly in the principle of double interpretation of the Bible. Samuel wrote also commentaries on other books of the Bible, but they were evidently lost and only some quotations in later commentaries were preserved. It is, however, assumed by many Jewish scholars, that the commentary on the last two chapters of Job, namely, XLI and XLII, was written by him, though it goes under the name of Rashi.

The last important French commentator was Joseph Bekhor Shor (fl. about 1130), literally the firstling of the bullock, so named from the title given to Joseph in the Blessing of Moses, Deut. XXXIII, 17. The metaphorical meaning of this title is, productive, for the ox is the symbol of productivity as he is the tiller of the soil, as it is said in Prov. XIV, 4, "Much produce is by the strength of the ox." He was a pupil of the famous Tosafist, Jacob Tam, and himself a profound Talmudic scholar and Tosafist. He wrote a commentary on the Pentateuch. His commentary is distinguished by a fine sense for straightening out difficulties and apparent contradictions. Though not acquainted with the Spanish school of Jewish philosophy, he independently explained many passages in a philosophic theological way and made a number of suggestions regarding the proper place of certain verses, displaying a fine critical sense.

Besides those enumerated there were many Talmudic scholars who busied themselves with the Bible and wrote commentaries on various books. There is even a collective commentary on the Pentateuch in the name of the Tosafists (Ch. X) by the name of *Hadar Zekenim,* (The Glory of the Elders). We thus see that the study of the Bible went hand and hand with the study of the Talmud in France for a long time until the glory of that Jewry began to depart.

C. The Spanish Provence School

113. ABRAHAM IBN EZRA

About the time when the French school of exegesis began to decline, there appeared a man who, through his great knowledge and vast erudition and the brilliant way in which he disseminated that knowledge, gave a great impetus to Jewish learning in France, especially in the southern part, the Provence. That man was the above-mentioned Abraham Ibn Ezra (Ch. VI), grammarian, Bible commentator, poet, philosopher, and astronomer.

But while he was rich in knowledge, a king in the realm of the spirit, he was, on the other hand, poor in the goods of this world, a wanderer on the face of the earth. His life was full of struggle and suffering, and we are often amazed at the remarkable strength of his spirit that could produce such valuable works under trying conditions.

Ibn Ezra was born in the year 1093 in the city of Tudela, Spain. Yet in early youth, he made a name for himself as a Hebrew poet and as a master of that language in many ways. His thirst for knowledge was unbounded and he became proficient in all branches of knowledge of his day. With all this, he suffered greatly and was exceedingly poor. He bewailed his poverty and persistent lucklessness in a brilliant epigram which reads, "Were candles my merchandise, the sun would never set, were I trader in shrouds, men would live forever." He seemed to have spent a great part of his life in Spain, most likely wandering from place to place. However, his impetuous spirit did not permit him to remain in his native land, and he ultimately started on his journeys, partly in search for knowledge and partly from a desire for wandering. He went to Egypt first where he stayed for some time, then to Babylonia, Persia, and probably even to India. After leaving his only son, Isaac, who accompanied him, in Bagdad, he returned to Spain via North Africa. There he made the acquaintance of a generous man, Joseph ben Aruran, who acted for a time as his Mæcenas. Soon, however, his benefactor died, and he remained as poor as ever. He again departed on his journeys and in the year 1140 he stayed for a short time in Rome being honored by the Jews of the city. There he began his literary activity, wrote his commentaries on Job and Ecclesiastes, grammatical books, and poems. With his usual inclination for wandering, he soon left Rome and visited many cities in Italy where he was welcomed by the leaders of the communities. He dazzled them with his versatile knowledge, writing books for them, composing poems, epigrams, and puzzles, and they repaid him with honor. In 1145, we meet him in Lucca where he completed his commentaries on Isaiah, the other Four Scrolls, the Books of Joshua, Judges, and Samuel, and began his shorter commentary on the Pentateuch.

From Italy, Ibn Ezra went to France visiting various cities. Thus, we find him in 1155 in Rhodez where he composed many books on mathematics and astronomy. A year later, we find him in Dreux, Northern France, and there he completed his commentaries on Daniel, Psalms, and the Minor Prophets and also began to compose his longer commentary on the Pentateuch. From Dreux he went to England, making on the way the acquaintance of the famous Talmudic scholar, Jacob Tam. An exchange of scintillating short poems between these two intellectual giants shows the respect they entertained for each other. During these years of wandering in France, Ibn Ezra learned of the death of his only son, Isaac, in distant Bagdad, and he mourned over him deeply. But depressed as he was, he never for a moment ceased writing, ever composing new books. The years 1158–60 he spent in London, where he wrote several books among which is the *Iggeret ha-Shabbat* (the Letter on the Sabbath) against the interpretation of Samuel ben Meir (Sec. 110) of the first verses of Genesis according to which the day begins with the morning and not with the preceding evening. Ibn Ezra feared the danger of such a theory, which may induce people to reckon the beginning of the Sabbath from Saturday morning and not from sunset on Friday. He retraced his steps to the Continent, again visiting France, staying for a time at Narbonne in the Provence and ultimately went back to Rhodez where he lived for a few years, finishing his second recension of the Pentateuch commentary. From there he intended to return to his native land, but on reaching Calahorra on the boundary of Spain he died at the age of seventy-five, in the year 1167, satiated with wandering and suffering.

The industry and literary productivity of Ibn Ezra were remarkable. He is said to have written one hundred and eight books covering almost all fields of knowledge known in his day, and some of his books, especially his commentaries, were written in several recensions. However, great as he was in other fields, his fame rests on his exegesis, and he is primarily known in the Jewish world as a commentator though his laurels as a poet (Ch. X) are by no means faded as yet.

He seemed to have written commentaries on all the books of the Bible but we have only his commentaries on the Pentateuch, including two recensions on the Book of Exodus, Isaiah, the Minor Prophets, Psalms, Job, Daniel, and the Five Scrolls. The commentaries on the other books were lost.

Ibn Ezra's commentaries, though composed far from Spain, represent the very height of Spanish exegesis, for not only did he make use of all earlier Spanish commentators, drawing even upon Karaite exegetes whom he quotes by name, but he brought to bear all the accumulated knowledge in the fields of grammar, language study, and exegesis of the Jews of Spain upon the task in hand. In his Hebrew written commentaries, the works of the great masters of the Hebrew language, who themselves wrote in Arabic, found their redemption and became known to the great Jewish world. But we must not by any means consider Ibn Ezra a mere mediator and transmitter of the ideas of those who had gone before him. On the other hand, it is his own fine sense of exegesis and keen understanding of the nature and character of the Hebrew language which make his commentaries so valuable, though he utilized to a very great extent the works of his predecessors. In his two introductions to the commentary on the Pentateuch, he defines his method of exegesis by contrasting it with other previous methods. He says that the truth is like the central point in a circle but that the commentators of the Bible have all gone astray, some in a line far flung from it, some in a line approaching it, yet seldom touching the very point. The ways the commentators followed are four. The first, is that of the Geonim, who in their eagerness to find in the Bible all philosophic ideas went far afield and brought in all kinds of unnecessary digressions on irrelevant matters. The second, is the way of the Karaites who forsook tradition and wandered far away from the truth. The third, is the way of the allegorists—by that he meant the Christian commentators—and the fourth way, that of the Darshanim, homiletists and Agadists, which though close to the truth, yet is not satisfactory. Against these, he outlines his own method which is that of pure *Peshat*. He proposes to first explain the single words, elucidating their derivation and grammatical structure, and then give the connected meaning of the verse independent of any Midrashic interpretation with the exception of verses containing precepts where the Talmudic tradition of the Halakah is to be followed.

This program he carried out to a great extent though not fully. In a number of commentaries, he does give the meaning of the words first and then the meaning of the verse. In others, he disregards the method. In spite of his denunciation of the Gaonic method of digressions, he himself has a number of lengthy digressions which at times amount to whole essays on certain subjects. Here and there, he also uses mystic allegory and a good deal of polemics, especially against the Karaites. But on the whole, he lived up to his standard. His grammatical remarks are elucidating, the explanation brief and penetrating, and with the exception of a few points, he does not deviate from the traditional interpretation as far as Halakah is concerned.

Otherwise, his commentary is permeated by a very fine spirit, and he displays great critical acumen. He thought Job a translated book and intimates that the Chapters XL–LXVI of Isaiah were written during the Babylonian exile, and also that some Psalms are of later origin. His free spirit is especially evident in the hints he dropped concerning the later origin of some chapters or passages even in the Pentateuch to which remarks Spinoza called attention. But all such remarks were veiled by him in mystical language so that we can hardly be sure of their exact meaning. Notwithstanding his free remarks and veiled allusions, Ibn Ezra was a conservative and defended vigorously the sanctity of the Torah against all its attackers, championed the integrity of the text and attacked Ibn Jannaḥ vehemently for his proposed assumption, that other words should be substituted instead of those written in the text of certain difficult passages.

Though Ibn Ezra was a master of Hebrew as evidenced in his poetry, his style in the commentary is not lucid. It is witty, often scintillating, but not clear. He leaves many things unsaid, and very often uses the formula, "There is a mystery involved here." Under this cloak, he smuggled in many of his freer thoughts, but as they are not explicit, we cannot guess at their real meaning, in spite of the super-commentaries. Ibn Ezra, though a rationalist, had a mystic vein and was a great believer in astrology and in astral influence on human life. These beliefs are even injected in his commentaries.

Yet, with all the defects, his commentary was held in esteem next to Rashi's, except that it was studied by the intellectuals. An acquaintance with Ibn Ezra was considered a mark of intellectual aristocracy, and the prying into his secrets (Sodot) and mysteries was a favorite diversion with Jewish scholars. As a result, we possess a number of super-commentaries on his works, which prove their popularity in learned circles.

114. THE KIMḤI COMMENTATORS

Just as the Kimḥi family in the Provence took the lead in grammar and language study (Ch. VII), they likewise led in Bible exegesis. The father, Joseph, wrote commentaries on Proverbs and Job. His commentary on Proverbs is of the nature of a moral treatise, as he endeavors, besides explaining the meaning, to derive a moral from each proverb, and for this purpose, he cites parallels from Arabic literature which make his explanations interesting. He also wrote commentaries on the Pentateuch and other books of the Bible but they were lost. However, from the quotations mentioned by his son, David, in his own commentary, we can conclude that they were of great exegetic value. His remarks are very keen and a good number of them are adopted by modern scholars and incorporated in their Bible translations. Of Moses Kimḥi's commentaries, we possess those on Job, Proverbs, Ezra, and Nehemiah. The last three, however, are printed under the name of Ibn Ezra, which shows us how closely he followed the method of the former that they could be interchanged. The one on Proverbs is an excellent commentary and is deserving of the name of the assumed author.

The leading exegete of the family, like the leading grammarian, was David (1160–1235). He lived in Narbonne all his life and was a teacher of Talmud and Bible. Besides his linguistic and exegetic studies, he was deeply interested in philosophy and was a devoted follower of Maimonides whom he defended vigorously in the controversy about his books (Ch. X).

He commented upon all the prophetic books and in addition, on Psalms, Chronicles, and the Book of Genesis. David took his exegetic work very seriously, and in his introduction, he speaks of it as a religious duty, and considers it as the second class of good deeds (Ma'asim Tobim). His method, like that of his father and brother, approaches that of Ibn Ezra, following the *Peshat*. But he also often accepts the *Derash* utilizing Agadic interpretations to a great extent. Like Rashi, he made extensive use of the *Targum*. His grammatical knowledge helped him greatly in his exegesis, and much of it is embodied in the commentary. As a follower of Maimonides, he introduces some philosophic views in his commentaries and explains some events as visions. In his commentary on Ezekiel, Ch. I, he offers a long philosophic explanation of the Theophany (Visions of the Merkabah). His commentary on Psalms contains many controversial passages against Christianity which passages were later collected and published separately under the title of *Teshubot la-Noẓerim* (Answers to the Christians).

His style is lucid and brief. David's commentaries, both on account of their intrinsic value as well as on account of the spirit of piety permeating them, were ranked very highly, and the *Radak* (abbreviation of Rabbi David Kimḥi), as it is usually called, was placed next to Rashi and Ibn Ezra. As a matter of fact, Kimḥi's commentary at times took precedence over that of the latter, for in the early printed Hebrew Bibles with commentaries, Rashi and *Radak* were the only two commentaries.

Chapter IX

POETRY

115. GENERAL CHARACTERISTICS

The origin of Mediæval Hebrew poetry, like many other literary productions, goes back to the Bible. The Psalms, Canticles, parts of the Book of Job, of Ecclesiastes, and numerous passages in the prophetic and historical books, and even in the Pentateuch itself are all of a highly poetic caliber, though they do not possess the usual earmarks of poetry, rhyme and meter. In the Psalms, the individual pours out his heart before his Maker, or the poet, overcome by the grandeur and beauty of the universe, sings the praises of the great Artificer, or again, the singer, stirred to the depths of his soul by the suffering of his nation, cries out to God on their behalf calling for protection from the enemies, or pleading for the mighty hand of the Lord to appear once more as in the days of yore—all these are specimens of noble lyrics and in time served as prototypes for later Jewish poetry.

The whole range of Mediæval Hebrew poetry can be divided into two main divisions, sacred and secular, and although the division is not of equal proportions, the sacred predominating, yet the secular element is well represented. It is, of course, the sacred poetry which has the Bible as its antecedent; the secular, on the other hand, is almost purely a product of this period, a result of contact with the Arabic culture and changed conditions of life, though not wholly so.

Still, even the sacred poetry of this period is not the direct descendant of Biblical poetry; there were many more factors in its production. Between the rise of Mediæval sacred poetic productions and the Bible there lay a period of one thousand years and a vast multifarious literature. There is the Jewish liturgy which gradually began to assume shape and form during the centuries, there is the great production of Agada in its ramified branches, and finally, there is the renewed interest in the Bible and its language, all this vast literature of philology and exegesis which brought about the revival of Hebrew. These factors combined made the appearance of sacred poetry possible.

First as to liturgy. It is almost an impossibility to give a connected story of the Jewish liturgy, many of its links being hidden in the dimness of the ages. It is only a bare outline of its growth that we can possibly hope to draw. During the period of the First Commonwealth, prayer was left entirely to the individual; it was a spontaneous affair on his part. Whenever one desired, he offered a prayer according to the needs of the moment. Such individual prayers were offered by Hannah (I Samuel, Ch. II, 1-11), by David (2 Samuel, Ch. XXII, I Chronicles, Ch. XXIX, 10-20), by Solomon (1 Kings, Ch. VIII, 22-64), and many more. Likewise, many of the Psalms are in reality prayers. There are only two short obligatory prayers mentioned in the Pentateuch which had a fixed form, and these are the prayer recited by those who brought their first fruits to the Temple and the one pronounced by each Jew at the end of the third year of each seven-year cycle when all separations of tithes were completed (Deut. XXVI, 5-15).

It is with the period of the Second Temple that the liturgy began to assume a definite shape and form. It was then that the religious feeling of every individual Jew clamored for daily expression. We are therefore told that the men of the Great Synagogue instituted the three daily services, but we are not informed exactly of the nature of the prayers recited at these services. From indications in the Talmud, we learn that the reading of the *Shema* (Deut. VI, 4-10; XI, 13-22, and Numbers XV, 37-41) and six more benedictions, formed the nucleus of the liturgy. These passages and a few more Biblical passages, such as the Ten Commandments were originally recited, in early times, at the Temple. But as time went on, the religious feeling clamored for more expression, and more prayers and benedictions were added before and after the *Shema,* thanking God for the creation of light and describing His greatness. By the end of the period of the Second Temple, the liturgy was much enlarged and the Mishnah tells of a number of prayers that were offered on special days, such as the Sabbath, and especially on the Day of Atonement and other fast days. Of the prayers recited on the Day of Atonement we have a few transmitted to us, such as the confessions of the High Priest and his prayer on behalf of the Jewish people, enumerating their various needs. It is a fine vigorous prayer remarkable for its brevity. There are also a number of benedictions given which were recited on that day as well as on the other fast days. In these benedictions, pleas for forgiveness of sins and for help in need are expressed.

With the destruction of the Temple and the concentration of the Jewish spirit within the study of the Torah and observation of religion, the liturgy begins to develop more extensively. It becomes not only a substitute for the sacrificial service, but the expression of the soul of the nation, and the national character of prayer begins to be asserted. The sufferings of the Jews in exile begin to be heard, and the cry for redemption reverberates through it. Immediately after the destruction of the Temple, at the Sanhedrin in Jabne, the eighteen benedictions (Shemoneh Esré)—next to the *Shema* the most important prayer in our prayer book—are instituted and standardized by the order of Raban Gamaliel, the president of the Academy. In this prayer, the national needs take precedence over the individual, though the latter are by no means neglected. Though the name of the organizer of this prayer is given as Simon ha-Pakuli, it is by no means an individual composition. His work consisted more in incorporating older prayers and standardizing their style and form than in composing new ones. Not only were the six benedictions recited in the Temple incorporated, but the majority of the benedictions were adaptations from current prayers for various occasions. Only one benediction directed against heretics and informers (Birkat ha-Minim) was composed by an individual, Samuel the Younger (Shemuel ha-Katan). From that time on the liturgy developed rapidly.

In the Talmudic period, many additions were made. Especially fertile in this field was Babylonia. There the great scholars, the founders of the Talmud, busied themselves with composing hymns and prayers. Rab (Ch. V), the founder of the Jewish center of learning in Babylon, indited the series of beautiful prayers for the Musaf service of the New Year's Day, where such hymns as *Alenu* and "Therefore we hope to Thee" are found. In these hymns pure conception of God and fervent hope for His Kingdom are expressed. Many more anonymous prayers were composed there and in Palestine, such as the series of liturgical pieces prefacing the beginning of the *Shemoneh Esré* for New Year and the Day of Atonement, the first of which is "Lord impose Thine awe" where a plea for unity of mankind and the abolition of evil from the world is entered. These are only a few of the prayers that were composed during that period. There are many individual prayers that scholars used to recite daily before they began their study, which on account of their loftiness of spirit became the property of the nation and were later incorporated in the liturgy. Thus we have such prayers by Rabbi Johanan (Ch. V), by Rab, and other scholars.

The spirit of this growing liturgy is of a multifarious nature. It not only expresses the needs of the individual on every occasion, on the one hand, and the state of mind of the nation, on the other hand, but also the innermost religious feelings of those who were God-intoxicated. It recites the praise of God in hymns, it tells of His glory in doxologies, and dwells on the littleness of man as compared with the Author of all being. The prayers are as a rule written in Hebrew and are tinged with poetic touches. They thus constitute real literary productions, and the ideas and spirit permeating them were the basis for the later sacred poetry.

The second source is the Agada. That great production of the Jewish spirit, the forms of which were described above, contains, whether in description of historic events, or in depicting the miseries of the Jewish people, or in painting the glories of the future, many poetic elements expressed in delicate and fine language, and very often also liturgical pieces. These prayers are distinguished by their form, as they often paraphrase the Bible or use Biblical lines in an interwoven way. All these poetic attempts influenced directly the liturgy and later the sacred poetry. Not only were some of these prayers or parts of prayers incorporated in the regular liturgy, but they evoked a desire for imitation and even for improvement. Many of the prayers of the liturgy are also distinguished by the tenderness of language borrowed from the Agada.

The Gaonic period produced a number of liturgical pieces which were either incorporated in the older parts of the liturgy or constituted mere additions. These pieces are composed in the older poetical form already found in the Bible, namely, the alphabetical order of words or sentences. They stand then midway between the liturgy and the sacred poetry. Of such nature are the beautiful hymns *El Adon* in the Sabbath prayer, *El Baruch* in the week-day morning prayer and many more.

But still greater was the influence of the content of the Agada. The historical Agada the purpose of which was to embellish the lives of the heroes, or events of the past, or the glories of the future, supplied the epic elements for the later sacred poetry. The love for the Jewish people, the yearning for redemption, the glorification of God and the Torah, which formed the very substratum of Agada, were later elaborated in poetry. And even the very method, the simile, the Mashal, the parable were all borrowed and elaborated upon.

Finally, the third factor, the revival of Hebrew and the intensive study of the language and its construction, supplied the matter for poetry and brought it to its highest bloom, especially in Spain.

The sacred poetry of the period represents many shades, which how-- ever are included under one name, that of *Piyyut,* the writers of which are called *Paitanim;* both names come directly from the Greek, *poietria* and *poietes.* These names were already used in the early Midrashim to designate that particular art and its producers. In general, we may distinguish in that great mass of *Piyyutim* two main types: the Palestinian-West-European, including the Italian, French and German productions, on the one hand, and the Babylonian-Spanish on the other. The former type is not only the earlier, but the more primitive, the more intense, and the more national. The second one is the more developed, the more refined, and we may even say the more individual. Rapoport aptly characterized in one sentence the difference between these two types by saying: "The Sephardic sacred poetry is the medium of expression for the soul of the individual Jew, the go-between, between it and its Maker, while the Italian Franco-German *Piyyut* is the go-between, between Israel and God." This applies, of course, in a general way; exceptions in both cases abound.

The springs which fed this stream of poetry during the ages were two: first, the deep religious emotion which broke all bounds, and second, the suffering of the nation. It arose as an expression of an overflowing soul which is desperately struggling to articulate its emotions towards God and not finding sufficiency in the established prayers, each gifted man wanted to add something of his own, hence the hymns, poems, and the doxologies, and many more forms of *Piyyut.*

But in spite of the religious emotions of the writers and their desires to express it, these are not individual vagaries. On the contrary, like the Psalms, they express the spirit of the nation. And this spirit, as said, was two-sided. At times, it broke forth in pæans of praise, singing the glory of God, and at times, it was a turbulent spirit, one tortured in the very fires of Hell. Sacred poetry then represents the voice of a nation which sees itself hemmed in on all sides, living in constant terror of oppression, and in its anguish, it cries to the only protector—its Father in Heaven. The synagogue was the only place of safety for the Jew. There, he expressed his bitter protest against his oppressors, and also voiced the hope for redemption. Suffering and the cry for redemption, these are the two notes running through the entire mass of sacred poetry.

Suffering is practically the very woof of the life of the Jews during the entire Mediæval period, and without understanding even partially its extent and intensity, we can hardly appreciate that life. The words of Zunz give us an inkling of the depth of that suffering. Says Zunz, "Were there a ladder of suffering, then Israel would have reached the highest rung on it. If burning pain and the patience to suffer can ennoble a people, then the palm of nobility goes to the Jews. If a literature is said to be rich, when it possesses a few tragic classical plays, what place shall we assign then to a tragedy which has lasted for fifteen hundred years and which is composed and acted by the very heroes of the tragedy itself?"[1] The echo of this tragedy reverberates through Mediæval Hebrew poetry.

Yet, as stated, the Jew did not always cry and protest; he never lost faith in his God, and expressed his exaltation and love for Him in noble poems. Sacred poetry is therefore divided into two classes: (*a*) *Piyyutim* in a narrower sense, such as hymns of praise, doxologies wherein God is glorified in philosophical terms, and otherwise religious lyrics where man pours forth his heart before his Maker, as well as historical epics eulogizing God's miraculous wonders in Jewish history; (*b*) *Selihot,* penitential prayers which include all kinds of poems of a plaintive as well as of a devotional nature. Together with it go also the *Kinot,* elegies for the day of the commemoration of the destruction of the Temple, the ninth of Ab, or other black-letter days in Jewish History.

116. THE FORMS OF HEBREW POETRY

The basic and the oldest form of Hebrew poetry that we find is the parallelism of thought according to which each verse is divided into two halves the thought of the second half running parallel to the first except that it is expressed in different words. It is really a kind of rhyme, but not of words, only of thought. This form is used in several modifications and is the most frequent in the Bible. The Psalms, Proverbs, Job, and large parts of the prophetic books are written in this manner. Of actual word rhymes we find little in the Bible. But by the side of the parallelism, we find the use of a more artificial poetic form

---

[1] L. Zunz: *Die synogogale Poesie des Mittelalters,* p. 9.

affecting the construction of the words proper, and this is the alphabetical or the acrostic.

(a) The alphabetical form is then the first or the earliest form of Jewish poetry. We find, as said, its use in the Bible. Many chapters in Psalms are arranged according to the Hebrew alphabet, each verse beginning with a letter of the alphabet. At times, the alphabet is doubled or tripled and even used eight times, namely, instead of one verse beginning with a particular letter, two or three or eight begin with the same letter, and so on successively until the alphabet is repeated several times. Thus, we have the third chapter of Lamentations where the triple alphabet is used, and the famous Psalm CXIX where the alphabet is used eight times.

It is no wonder then that the early liturgical poetry seized first upon this form and exploited it to its fullest extent. Not only was the alphabet repeated a number of times, but various combinations were used. At times, the reverse order of the alphabet is used, namely, instead of beginning with the *Aleph*, the *Taw* is placed first. The form is named in Hebrew *Tashrak*, i. e. *Taw, Shin, Resh, Kuf,* the successive order of the reversed alphabet. This form, both the straight alphabet and the reverse is used extensively in early poetical liturgy incorporated in the prayer-book as well as in many early *Piyyutim*. In fact, it is the most frequent one, and persisted through the ages even when rhyme and meter were introduced. Later, more artificial combinations were added, the alphabet was divided into two groups, eleven letters each, and the verses or the words alternate, the first beginning with a letter of the first, and the second with the last of the second group. Thus, the first with *Aleph*, the second with Taw, and so on (At-Bash, i. e. Aleph, Taw, Bet, Shin, etc.). There are other fancy combinations of letters which are too many and too complicated to enumerate.

(b) Another frequent poetic form is that of name acrostics. About the middle of the seventh century, poems appear which are arranged according to the letters of the names of the authors, so that the initials of the verses or words spell out the names of the poets. In longer poems the names of the fathers as well as titles were added. Later, the patronymics were added, such as Cohen, Levi, and still later, even the occupation or social status, such as *Rofe,* i. e. physician, *Hazan,* cantor, or *Parnas,* community leader, and all of these titles and many others were spelled out in poems. Of this, as of the previous form, many odd uses were made; sometimes names of relatives were introduced in addition to the names of the author and his father; at times, the name of the child of the author is used, with an additional blessing such as, "May he live," or "May he increase in the study of the Torah and performance of precepts" (Yigdal be-Torah u-we-Miẓwah). That these additions prolonged the poems goes without saying.

(c) As poetry kept on developing, the need of a stronger form was felt, which need was satisfied by the use of the rhyme. The Bible uses rhymes occasionally, and a still more extensive use of rhymes is found in Talmudic literature, in many Agadic passages, and early prayers. When poetry developed, especially in the Gaonic period, the employment of rhyme became frequent and almost universal. The influence of Arabic poetry contributed much towards its extensive use. The Arabs delighted in rhymes, and they used them even in prose. The Jews followed them, and the Hebrew language which is rich in like-sounding suffixes, gave them ample opportunity to develop the art of rhyming to its extreme. But here we note the division between the two main currents of Hebrew poetry, the Palestinian-West-European, and the Babylonian-Spanish. The former employed mostly a single monotonous rhyme which was repeated continually. The latter not only used different rhymes, but introduced many various forms and combinations in rhyming. In general, there are three kinds of rhymes: (1) When only the last syllables in the two lines rhyme, the lowest form; (2) the two-syllable rhyme which was considered more worthy, and finally, (3) the three-syllable rhyme called the praised or the aristocratic one. At times, they developed a more artistic form where not only all the syllables of the last words of the lines rhymed but the very same final word was repeated in each line and often was continued through hundreds of lines. It was, of course, a monotonous rhyme but it was considered an art to prolong it, and poets vied with each other in prolonging that form. Variations were introduced in the placing of the rhyme. The simplest form was the successive rhyme where every two lines rhymed; the more complicated had the alternating rhyme, namely, the first line rhymed with the third and the second with the fourth, and there were many more combinations.

There was also some ornate rhyming where one rhyme is repeated at the end of each strophe, consisting of seven rhymed verses. This was borrowed from the Arabs and at times, this type was called in Hebrew *Anak,* i. e. a necklace, for the rhyming was compared to the stringing together of pearls, and the rhyme was named *Haruz* which means a string of pearls. Hence, an artistic poem was called a necklace, where fine workmanship was displayed, and very often one large pearl was set among smaller pearls. Thus we have the name *Anak* applied to the large poem of Ibn Gabirol on grammar, to similar poems of Moses Ibn Ezra and others. There are also other forms of this general mosaic style. At times, a Biblical verse is taken apart, and a word from it is placed in the rhyme at the end of a strophe; at other times, it is a sentence from a prayer which is placed in a similar manner. In addition, there are poems which have a peculiar rhyme inasmuch as each two lines end with the same word, but with different meanings. Such poems are called Tajanis in Arabic and were composed by great master poets who had the entire Hebrew language at their command. In the later period, double rhymes were used, namely, each line was divided into halves and these also rhymed with each other, but this was a later development which came only after the introduction of the meter.

(*d*) The meter was introduced in Hebrew poetry in the tenth century by the grammarian Dunash ben Labrat in Spain. He borrowed it from Arabic poetry, but only the idea and not the form. The Hebrew meter is very simple and consists of two basic forms, (*1*) measured vowels, namely, an equal number of vowels in each line, and (2) vowels to which a consonant is prefixed, namely, the *Sheva mobile* (Sheva N'a). The first one corresponds to the spondaic and the second one to the iambic. The second is called *Yated,* i. e. a peg, on account of the *Sheva* being joined to the following vowel as the peg is joined to the wall. The *Sheva quiescent* (Shevah Naḥ) was considered as part of a plain vowel. The plain vowel is considered long, and the *Yated* with the following vowel short-long. It happened very seldom that poems consisted either entirely of voweled letters (Tenuot) or entirely of *Yatedim,* i. e. *Sheva mobile* and voweled letters. When either form was used it was called a simple poem. Usually, it was a compound or a mixed one, namely, *Yated* and *Tenuah,* or several *Tenuot,* or several *Yatedim* and many more *Tenuot.* From this simple meter, there arose a large number of combinations, so that we have as a result nineteen different meters, and some even count as many as fifty-two.

The poem is divided into strophes named *Bayit,* i. e. a house as each strophe expresses a certain thought and is supposed to be complete. The line is divided into two halves, the first half called *Delet,* i. e. door, meaning by it that it opens the door to the verse, the second half was called *Soger,* namely, the closing half. The two halves sometimes run their own rhyme, and thus the two halves of the line also rhyme. The strophes are at times longer, and at times shorter; some poems contain strophes of four lines and some of six or more. At times the first strophe is used as a refrain. Such poems are called by a technical name *Pismon,* which is variously derived from the Greek and from Aramaic and Arabic, but the meaning is clear—response. This kind of poem is mostly used in sacred poetry as the congregation was expected to chant the refrain.

The metrical measures and their various combinations were used by the Spanish school both in their secular poems as well as in the sacred. The West-European poets, or those whom we would call the *Paitanim* (in contradistinction to the Spanish who deserve the name poets) employed the meter but little. As a rule, they followed the older forms, acrostics of name and of alphabet, though they used rhyme to a great extent.

We have thus far viewed the origin of the Mediæval Hebrew poetry, the factors that brought it about, and the external forms it assumed. We will now turn to the poetry itself and follow its development in the various centers of Jewish literature.

A. Palestinian Sacred Poets

117. EARLY PALESTINIAN POETRY

As in other literary productions, such as in Agada and *Massorah,* Palestine took the lead even in the days of its decline, so it was in the field of sacred poetry. As the veil of mystery which hung over Palestine in the early Mediæval centuries is gradually being lifted by the patient labors of many Jewish scholars, its literary activity is being revealed to us. There, the national Jewish spirit, though bowed down by oppression, was still at work. And if the mind weighed down by tribulation could not devote itself to the difficult Halakah, then the heart gave vent to its feelings; the accumulated bitterness and agony had to find expression, the deep religious emotion which increased in intensity with every new persecution had to become articulate; when the way of Agada was exploited to its fullest extent, the prayer-book became the next vehicle for these feelings and emotions.

We have already indicated the first shoots of sacred poetry which found their way into the prayer-book itself (Sec. 113) and became a part of the liturgy proper. But these were soon followed by others which on account of their number as well as their forms were not incorporated in the prayer-book, but were considered as additions. We cannot determine with accuracy when these *Piyyutim* began to be composed, but somewhere in the dim sixth and seventh centuries when the revival of Hebrew (Ch. VII) took place, they began to make their appearance.

These first attempts at sacred poetry are as a rule anonymous, and are written in alphabetical acrostics, either in a single alphabet or double or triple. Little or no rhyme is employed. But what they lack in form, they make up in purity of style and beauty of content. The style is pure Hebrew, and the content is of a philosophic-poetic character. There might have been many such pieces, but only a few have come down to us, and these few are distinguished by their nobility of spirit. The poem, "Thou Understandest the Thoughts of the Heart," which is an admonition (Tokeḥah) to man to remember the shortness of life and his ultimate destination, gives a very graphic description of the shortcomings of the life of man from his earliest days to the last. It is of a high moral tone, and it calls upon man to utilize the few days allotted him for justice, charity, and communion with God. A translation of the noble poem, "All the World Shall Come to Serve Thee," is here given.

> All the world shall come to serve thee
>   And bless Thy glorious Name,
> And Thy righteousness triumphant
>   The islands shall acclaim.
> And the peoples shall go seeking
>   Who knew Thee not before,
> And the ends of the earth shall praise Thee,
>   And tell Thy greatness o'er.
>
> They shall build for Thee their altars,
>   Their idols overthrown,
> And their graven gods shall shame them,
>   As they turn to Thee alone.
> They shall worship Thee at sunrise,
>   And feel Thy kingdom's might,
> And impart their understanding
>   To those astray in night.
>
> They shall testify Thy greatness,
>   And of Thy power speak
> And extol Thee, shrined, uplifted
>   Beyond man's highest peak.

And with reverential homage,
Of love and wonder born,
With the ruler's crown of beauty
Thy head they shall adorn.

With the coming of Thy kingdom
The hills shall break into song,
And the islands laugh exultant
That they to God belong.
And all their congregations
So loud Thy praise shall sing,
That the uttermost peoples, hearing,
Shall hail Thee crowned King.

This poem which is used in *Musaf* service on the Day of Atonement, is a veritable gem in religious literature, as it expresses a passionate desire for the Kingdom of God to be realized not in any mystic way but in the spread of knowledge of pure religious belief throughout the world. There is a universal ring to it.

118. JOSÉ BEN JOSÉ HA-YATOM

But the period of anonymity did not last for a long time. Soon there arose poets who left the impress of their personality on their productions and their names were left to posterity. The earliest of these is José ben José ha-Yatom i. e. the orphan (ca. 600–640); he was therefore named after his father. José ben José's style is still a pure Hebrew, and his poems are as yet without rhyme, except occasionally. He uses, however, the alphabetical acrostic in a multiple way, six and seven times, and also other artful devices, such as alliteration and the repetition at the end of each strophe of one or two words which epitomize the subject, as the word *Kingship* in his poem included in the New Year's, *Malkuyot* prayers of the Musaf service, or *Remembrance* in his poem, included in the *Zikronot* prayers in the same service. His poems are distinguished by the epic spirit. Not only God alone is his subject, but God and His manifestations in Jewish history. He, therefore, recites in his pieces the outstanding episodes in Jewish history. Especially beautiful is his epic poem known as the *Abodah* which is recited in the *Musaf* service of the Day of Atonement. The main theme is the High Priest's service in the Temple on that day (Abodah), but it is prefixed with a long introduction telling of the main events that had transpired in this world, beginning with creation and ending with the consecration of Aaron as

High Priest. In stately lines we are told of the wonders of creation, the story of Adam and Eve, Cain and Abel, the Deluge, Tower of Babel, the deeds of the Patriarchs, and of Moses and Aaron. He then goes on with his main theme. The religious and poetic spirit of José ben José can be seen from the following lines taken from his poem, *Abodah:*

> His creatures break forth in a song divine;
>   His praises resound from deep to sky;
>   One God on earth, All-Holy on High.
> The waters proclaim: "All glory is Thine."

> From below, the abyss pealeth forth with might;
>   The luminaries, all join in His laud;
>   The days declare the glory of God
> And sweet melodies arise from the night.

José was the first to interweave Agadic interpretations and embellishments in his poems, though to a slight degree. We have beside the *Abodah* also the poems in the *Musaf* service of New Year's day referred to above, and a few more.

119. JANAI

José ben José was followed by Janai (about 640). He was the first to use the rhyme in addition to the alphabetic acrostic. He also introduced the name acrostic and left a few poems with his name indicated in the beginning of the strophes. For a long time his poems were lost, with the exception of two, one for the *Shemoneh Esré* on the Great Sabbath before Passover, and the song "And thus it happened at midnight" which is recited on Passover night at the Seder. Recently, Dr. Israel Davidson discovered a whole cycle (*Mahzor*) of his poems for the Sabbaths of the entire year. From these it is seen that Janai broke a new path by interweaving Halakic and Agadic matters into poems. It showed skill but detracted from the poetic spirit, and besides the multitude of the thoughts expressed required an expansion of the language. He, therefore, took to coining new verbal forms and new words. This process undoubtedly enriched the language, but since he hardly observed any rules in his coinage, the purity of the language suffered.

120. ELIEZER BEN KALIR

The greatest of all these Palestinian poets was Eliezer ben Kalir, or as he is usually known, The Kalir. He was not only one of the most prolific *Paitanim,* but he really left his impress upon the entire Italian-Franco-German school which followed in his footsteps and imitated him. He wrote poems for all festival services, for the special Sabbath services, for Purim and Ḥanukkah services, as well as elegies for the Ninth of Ab, and in general there is hardly an important service to which he did not add his poems. On account of his importance, legends clustered around his name. The earlier scholars placed him in different lands; some in Babylonia, and some in Southern Italy, taking the name Kalir to be a mispronunciation of Caligiari, a city in Southern Italy. Others, on the other hand, considered him a Palestinian but elevated him to the rank of a *Tanna.* The truth is that he was a Palestinian, but lived much later than the *Tannaim,* about the end of the seventh or the beginning of the eighth century.

Kalir was one of the first *Paitanim* who, in the impetuosity of spirit and in his eagerness to express all that he had to say, deviated from the purity of the Hebrew language and intermixed with it not only a large number of Aramaic words but also coined a multitude of new words, and used new forms which are not in accordance with the rules of Hebrew grammar. He also drew much upon the Agada, interweaving its stories, interpretations, and parables into his poems. At times, he merely referred to an Agadic statement or interpretation leaving the reader to guess for himself. It is this characteristic which makes many of his poems obstruse and difficult to understand. He used rhyme, alphabetic and name acrostics, and paid much attention to alliteration. He evinced great skill in bending the language to his will and purpose, and at times wrote poems consisting of a jingle of rhymes, namely, rhyming every pair of words in the entire strophe.

The Kalir was much berated by the Spanish poets who could not forgive the barbarism of his style and his breaking of all rules of grammar. His severe critic is Ibn Ezra. Yet, he cannot be denied strength of poetic spirit. Like José ben José, he possesses ability for epic poetry, and several of his poems are fine epic productions, of which the one before *Kedushah* (Sec. 130) in the New Year's second day morning service, where the life of Abraham is especially described, can serve as a fair example. He also had a fine observing eye for the beauties of nature. In his poem to the *Geshem* (rain) service of the *Shemini Azeret,* eighth day of the Feast of Tabernacles when prayers for rain are offered, a sublime poetic description of the descending rain is given, the swift flight of the clouds, the movement of the wind, the eagerness of the thirsty earth to receive the blessings of rain are graphically depicted. But, of course, Kalir is not chiefly a nature poet, his theme is primarily God, His justice and wonders in both nature and history, especially Jewish history. He does not tire of singing of God and His glory, and is longing for the great day when the Kingdom of God is to come. He also dwells upon His justice and righteousness, and begs God to proclaim the Day of Judgment when the universal court will be held. Of this court, Kalir gives a fine description in his *Kedushah* poem on the first day of the New Year, how the earth will tremble and the wicked quake when God comes to judge, and how when the court will adjourn and justice will be proclaimed, jubilation and shouting will break forth. The inseparable unity of God and Israel, the bitter fate of the Jewish people, their future and destiny find their full expression in the poems of Kalir. Kalir is the first of a line of poets who submerge their own individuality and speak on behalf of their nation.

B. BABYLONIAN AND SPANISH SCHOOLS OF POETRY

121. POETRY IN BABYLONIA

Just as in other literary productions, Babylonia followed Palestine and often even surpassed her, so it happened in the field of poetry with the exception that this time it hardly equaled the former. As we have seen, the schools in Babylonia contributed much towards the development of the liturgy and that interest in this branch of literature was very high there. We must, therefore, assume that a number of anonymous sacred poems were composed in Babylonia. In fact, we find the Geonim referring to a number of *Piyyutim* that are also known to us, which were recited there in the services in early times. With the rise of interest in the study of the Hebrew language and exegesis which came as a result of the contact with Arabic culture, poetry received a strong impetus for development. Yet, the contribution of Babylonia to Hebrew poetry is not great. Only a few poets of note arose there. The first was Saadia Gaon. He, whose labors contributed so much to every branch of literature, also planted a few vines in the vast vineyard of Jewish poetry. We have a number of his *Piyyutim* and one lengthy "Admonition" poem (Tokheha) where the life of man from infancy to the grave is reviewed, its shortcomings pointed out and contrasted with the greatness of God. The language is pure Hebrew and the poem is written in alphabetical acrostics, but the poetic spirit does not rise above the mediocre. Evidently, it is not given to one man to excel in everything. Another Gaon who also distinguished himself as a poet, was Hai, the last of the line, who in many ways resembled his illustrious predecessor. He left us a long didactic poem by the name of *Musar Haskel* (Wise Instruction), where he develops in measured verse his system of Ethics. The content will be discussed in the proper place. For the present, we will only note the new trend in Hebrew poetry which broke the liturgical bounds and began to spread in other directions. This was only the beginning, for its complete development and ramification, another place was destined and that was—Spain.

122. EARLY JEWISH POETRY IN SPAIN

The three centuries, from the ninth to the end of the twelfth, represent, as we know, the golden period of Jewish literature in Spain, and it is also of course, the period of bloom for Jewish poetry there. During this period, there arose poet after poet, one more exquisite than the other; yet the bloom and flourishing of Jewish poetry in Spain does not lie entirely in the greatness of the poets, but in its completeness and in its all-encompassing nature. It is a perfect expression of life in all its phases and shades. There is hardly a form of life which is not reflected in that poetry; it speaks with many tongues and touches the very heart-strings; all emotions, the yearning for God, love, the feeling for beauty in nature, mirth, anger and wrath, pain and sorrow, all find an outlet in it. In brief, it is completely secular as well as completely sacred.

Still the first steps of Jewish poetry in Spain were not rapid, they were rather slow. Poetry arose together with language study and exegesis, and the first two grammarians there, Menahem ben Saruk and Dunash ben Labrat, were also the pioneers in Hebrew poetry. Menahem was a master of Hebrew, but his style is heavy and he was not blessed with a poetic spirit. His poetry, from the little that is left to us, was of a more secular nature. Like the Arabs of his day, he wrote eulogies of great men, especially of his patron, Hasdai Ibn Shaprut, elegies on the death of his friends, and other poems of a similar nature. He also wrote rhymed prose; as samples of this kind of prose we have his letters of reproach to Hasdai which he sent from the prison, where he was placed by his former patron, and the letter to the King of the Khazars sent by Hasdai but written by Menahem. Both are excellent examples of fine writing. To Dunash belongs the honor of introducing the meter in Hebrew poetry. In sacred poetry, it was not used as often. Yet Dunash, though using rhyme and meter and perfect language, is hardly a poet as far as the content of his poems is concerned. He wrote a long grammatical poem as a refutation of Menaḥem's dictionary, the *Maḥberet,* and a number of eulogies. He is also said to have written some sacred poems, but little is left of them.

The followers of Menaḥem and Dunash continued to write poetry on various subjects, on grammar, eulogies, epigrams, and dedicatory poems and even some sacred poetry. Thus, we have long grammatical poems by the pupils of Menaḥem (Ch. VII) who wrote Responsa in verse to Dunash's refutations of the teachings of their master. These Responsa contain also dedicatory poems to Ḥasdai Ibn Shaprut. Likewise, the disciple of Dunash, Judah Ibn Sheshet, wrote a refutation of the Responsa in verse. Joseph Ibn Abitur (about 992), who contended with Ḥanokh for the Rabbinate in Cordova, wrote a number of sacred poems the style of which is pure and are permeated with a noble religious feeling. There were also a number of others who followed the muses with more or less success.

123. SAMUEL IBN NAGDILA

The first poet who deserves that name was Samuel Ibn Nagdila, also known as the prince (Nagid). He was born in 993 in Cordova, but was forced to leave his native city along with other Jews in the time of the civil war (1013) and settled in Malaga, a city in the kingdom of Granada, occupying himself there as a storekeeper. His great learning attracted the attention of his neighbor, the Grand Vizier of the kingdom, and he engaged Samuel as his secretary and confidant. Shortly thereafter the Vizier died, and before his death he recommended Samuel to the king as the most suitable candidate for his place. The king listened to his advice and, contrary to all precedents, he appointed the Jew, Samuel, as Grand Vizier of a Mohammedan kingdom. For twenty-eight years, Samuel piloted the ship of state of Granada under two kings with great skill and ability and won praise even from the Mohammedans. He became the leader of the Spanish Jewry, hence his name *ha-Nagid* (the prince) and he utilized his exalted position also to promote learning, inasmuch as he was a patron of learning and supported poets and writers in an exceedingly liberal way. He died in 1055.

Samuel, however, was not only a patron but was himself a man of talent who contributed to Jewish literature in all its branches. We spoke (Ch. VII) of his contribution to Hebrew grammar, and we will meet him again. As a poet, he ranks high. He wrote on various subjects, friendship poems, elegies, love and wine poems and sacred poetry. He also wrote three works imitating three Biblical books, Psalms, Proverbs, and Ecclesiastes under the names of *Ben Thilim* (Son of Psalms), *Ben Mishlé* (Son of Proverbs), and *Ben Koheleth* (Son of Ecclesiastes). The first contains prayers, the second, proverbs and didactic pieces, and the third, poems of a philosophical ring. Samuel uses both rhyme and meter, and his style is pure and strong. He possesses considerable wit in his epigrams and mirth in his wine poems. His poems bristle with fine thoughts, elegant expressions, and wise sayings, but his style, though strong, is not elastic, and at times is even obstruse.

Samuel, in the variety of his subjects and the richness of thought expressed in his poems as well as in the skillful use of language, was considered by the later poets as one who began a new period in Jewish poetry. The historian, Abraham Ibn Daud (Sec. 191) says of Jewish poets that "they began to chirp in the days of Ḥasdai Ibn Shaprut, but in the time of Samuel, their voices rang loud," meaning that the poetic voice of Samuel reverberates in the history of Jewish poetry.

124. SOLOMON IBN GABIROL

The herald of the Golden Age of Hebrew poetry was Solomon Ibn Gabirol who rises in depth of poetic feeling, in mastery of style, and loftiness of thought, not only above the mediocre poets of his generation, but also above many generations of his successors, and probably has no equal in the entire range of Jewish poetry. His was one of those rare souls wherein depth of feeling, sense of beauty, and all-encompassing thought combine into one delicate mosaic, and in whose light the world with all its beauties and the power beyond it are reflected. Unfortunately, the delicate fibres of this wonderful soul were too strained and twisted by the sad events of his tragic life, and this straining, at times, marred the harmonious tunes of the song which this soul emitted, so that we occasionally get a false note in the otherwise perfect song.

His life was not only tragic but short. Ibn Gabirol was born in Malaga about the year 1021, and seemed to have lost his parents very early in life, and having neither brother nor sister, he remained a little waif in a strange world. This fact impressed his soul with sadness from his early youth. Added to this, he was attacked by a malignant illness which pursued him through life. It is no wonder then that notes of stinging bitterness and pessimism pervade some of his poems. Being thus deprived by force of circumstances from life's joys, he threw himself with all the energy of his great mind into the acquisition of knowledge. When he was a mere youth, he was already master of all branches of learning of his time. When a mere boy, he moved to Saragossa which was then a center of Jewish learning, and there he began to write and compose his poetry. At sixteen, he was already a full-fledged poet of the first rank. Being morose, he had very few friends and led a lonely life. For a time, he found a friend and patron in Yekutiel Ibn Al-Hasan, but unfortunately the friend was soon snatched away from him, having been killed in an uprising. This second loss embittered Gabirol still more, and the sadness of his nature took on a darker hue. Samuel ha-Nagid befriended him for a few years but through the poet's impetuosity, the friendship terminated and he remained alone in the world again, and was even attacked by his enemies who were envious of his greatness. The constant strain of his tragic life ultimately broke his fragile body and he died at Valencia in the year 1052 at the age of thirty. Legend surrounds his death with a halo. It tells that he was killed by a Moorish noble who was envious of his great fame as a poet. He buried Gabirol's body under a fig tree in his garden which immediately broke forth in most exquisite bloom, an event which ultimately led to the arrest of the murderer.

The literary output of Gabirol is immense for such a short life, for besides hundreds of poems, he wrote a number of philosophical works which are of exceptional value (Ch. XI). It is almost incomprehensible to grasp how a mind so young and a body so fragile could stand the strain of such labor. But his was a master mind which rose above circumstances and conditions.

Gabirol was both a secular and a sacred poet, but he excelled in the latter capacity. It is there where he really attained the highest pinnacle of poetry. The range of his secular poetry is, however, limited in its extent by his peculiar tragic life. It embraces only the following divisions: (a) On himself where his own soul and bitter life is the object; (b) friendship poems in praise of famous persons; (c) elegies on the death of friends; (d) didactic poems including a long masterful poem on the rules of grammar by the name of *Anak,* a necklace (Sec. 114). There is only one love poem, and that to an imaginary beloved, most likely his muse, one wine poem, and two or more nature poems. Gabirol's personality as reflected in his poems presents a sharp dualism. In his secular poems, he is self-centered and exceedingly proud. He was conscious of his great genius and makes one of his friends say:

> Know that you are unique in your generation
> And thy poems are like pearly necklaces.[2]

In another place he says:

> I am the master and song is a slave to me;
> The harp of all poets and minstrels am I.
> My song is a crown to all kings of the earth,
> And a mitre on th' heads of the noble and high.
> Though my body but treads on the earth, here below,
> My spirit yet soars to the clouds in the sky.
> Sixteen though I am, yet my wisdom excels
> The wisdom of one who is eighty well-nigh.[3]

This aging before his time, this being a man of another world, a denizen of heaven who is perforce confined to earthly existence, left an impression on his secular poems. In the poems where he himself is the subject, he is constantly complaining of his bitter fate, and as if by way of apology why he does not taste of the joys of life which seem so sweet and attractive, he speaks of the fleeting of life, of the vanity of the world. He finds refuge in wisdom which is to him all joy and desire. These notes, though extremely pessimistic, are expressed in such beautiful style, in such exquisite rhymes and meter, that they make pleasant reading in spite of their sad note. Gabirol practically ransacked the treasures of the Hebrew language and used them lavishly in his poems. He employed all kinds of devices to make his songs more attractive. His boast that the song is his "slave" was not a vain boast; even his poem on grammar reads like a hymn. Gabirol was endowed with all the qualities of a poet, chief of which was a strong sense of beauty, and though it was not always fully expressed except in form, it was in him. In the few nature poems we have, we see not only an observing eye, but a feeling heart for the changing beauties of nature. In his description of spring, in the poem "May Winter Keep his Vow," [4] we have one of the finest gems of nature poetry where the delicate tints of the fresh plants covering the earth, the joy of the creatures in spring, and the flight of the birds in the sunlight, and its

[2] *Songs of Solomon Ibn Gabirol,* ed. Bialik and Ravnitzki, Vol. I, No. 41.
[3] *Ibid.* No. 110.
[4] *Ibid.* No. 44.

reflection in their gay feathers are artfully reproduced. From a gloomy soul like Gabirol's, mirth is hardly expected, but when it broke forth it rang clear and true. His wine song testifies to that. It runs as follows:

Chorus: Of wine, alas! there's not a drop,
    Our host has filled our goblets to the top
        With water.

    When monarch wine lies prone,
    By water overthrown,
    How can a merry song be sung?
    For naught is to wet our tongue
        But water.

Chorus: Of wine, etc.

    No sweetmeats can delight
    My dainty appetite
    For I, alas! must learn to drink,
    However I may writhe and shrink,
        Pure water.

Chorus: Of wine, etc.

    To toads I feel allied,
    To frogs by kinship tied;
    For water drinking is no joke,
    Ere long you all will hear me croak
        Quack water.

Chorus. Of wine, etc.* [5]

He also possessed considerable wit as is evident from his epigrams, but due to the bitterness of his soul, it is as a rule biting.

In the sacred poems, we see before us a different Gabirol. His personality seems to shrink before the infinite power of the Almighty; his pride is gone and he is at a total loss how to approach the "Endless-All" (En Sof).

Thus he sings:

    And in Thy presence to myself appear
    As a little earth-worm.
    O, Thou, who fillest the earth and whose greatness

* Translation taken from *Jewish Literature and other Essays* by Gustave Karpeles.
[5] *Ibid.* No. 83.

Is endless,
Shall one like me laud Thee,
And how shall he honor Thee? * [6]

But this lowering of himself does not come from fear but from penetrating knowledge into the great mystery of God. Gabirol was a mystic and strove with all his heart to unite with God even to merge in Him, as he says:

My thoughts astounded asked me why
Towards the whirling wheels on high
In ecstasy I rush and fly.

The living God is my desire,
It carries me on wings of fire,
Body and soul to Him aspire.

God is at once my joy and fate,
This yearning me He did create,
At thought of Him I palpitate.

Shall song with all its loveliness
Submerge my soul with happiness
Before the God of Gods it bless? [7]

It is no wonder that he found no words to express his love and longing for God, and therefore sings:

At the dawn I seek Thee,
Rock and refuge tried,
In due service speak Thee
Morn and eventide.

Little to thy glory
Heart or tongue can do;
Small remains the story,
Add we spirit too.

Yet since man's praise ringing
May seem good to Thee,
I will praise Thee singing
While Thy breath is in me.[7a]

* All translations of pieces from sacred poems are taken from the volume in the *Jewish Classic Series*, issued by the Jewish Publication Society of America, entitled, *Selected Religious Poems of Solomon Ibn Gabirol*, ed. by Israel Davidson and translated into English verse by Israel Zangwill.

[6] *Vol. of Selections*, No. 14.
[7] *Ibid.* No. 12.
[7a] *Ibid.* No. 1.

Strong as was Gabirol's desire, love, and longing for God, equally
strong was his love for his people. He imbibed its suffering and gave it
tongue and expression. He complains bitterly on behalf of his people.

> Six years were decreed for a slave to wait
> When his freedom he sought at his master's
>   hand;
> But the years of my bondage lack term or date,
> It is hard, O my Master, to understand.[8]

This is not a plea but a demand upon God for redemption. This demand
is expressed sometimes in plaintive tones and sometimes in tones of
love and longing. A plea to God to redeem His people is expressed in
such terms:

> Come up to me at early dawn,
> Come up to me, for I am drawn,
> Beloved, by my spirit's spell,
> To see the sons of Israel.

And ends:

> The joy in Thee, I will evince
> With which a people greets its prince.
> O son of Jesse, holy stem,
> God's servant, born of Bethlehem.[9]

Such love poems abound in large numbers. Gabirol wrote profusely
all kinds of sacred poetry for all festivals and holy days, devotional and
penitential, national and individual. In the individual penitential poems,
his pessimistic inclination takes hold of him and he chants of the misery
of human life in striking words like these:

> Life is a vine branch,
> A vintager—death;
> He threatens and lowers
> More near with each breath.

Gabirol, who was as Heine says of him, "The poet among philosophers and the philosopher among poets," wrote a number of philosophical poems where the lofty thoughts match the height of poetry,

[8] *Ibid.* No. 9.
[9] *Ibid.* No. 4.

and the crown of these poems is "The Royal Crown," a long poem of remarkable beauty and sublime thought. In this poem Gabirol poured forth all the richness of his heart and the treasures of his mind. It is an exalted ode to God, and an all-encompassing epic of the universe. In it, the poet, philosopher, and scientist join hands, for all the knowledge of the time is interwoven there, and all that the poet gathered during his life in the fields of wisdom is laid before the reader. The poem is logically divided into five parts with a prologue and an epilogue. The prologue is a short ode to God where His ineffable name, His might and potence, the two worlds, existence and all are described briefly. Then follows part one where each of His attributes, oneness, existing, living, source of light, and wisdom are described. Part two describes the universe, the handiwork of God; in it the seven planets, their size, orbit, time of revolution and their peculiar influence over human life are accurately depicted. He then gives a description of the other three spheres, namely, that of the constellations, the first sphere, and that of the Active Reason. Part three speaks of the soul, its nature, migration to the earth and influence on the body. Part four deals with the life of man, his struggles with the desires and passions, his suffering from life's vicissitudes, and the shortness of his sojourn on earth. Part five is a confession of sin and a plea for mercy, and the epilogue ends with a passionate prayer to God whose greatness cannot be described. The style of "The Crown" bristles with literary gems culled from every nook of Hebrew literature; it is as pure as crystal and flows as lightly as a forest brook. It is not bound by meter but has rhyme and each strophe ends with a Biblical verse. This poem alone honestly earned for Gabirol the exquisite line of Heine, "Gabirol, the nightingale of piety whose rose was God."

125. THE SUCCESSORS OF GABIROL (Baḥya, Isaac Ibn Giat, Moses Ibn Ezra)

The great Ibn Gabirol was followed by a host of other poets and singers. They came from all ranks, from the lay professions as well as from the ranks of Talmudists and Rabbis. All vied with each other in the esteemed art of poetry. We will turn to the few outstanding figures. Baḥya ben Joseph Ibn Pakuda, the judge, a man of great learning and deep piety, possessed of a keen philosophic sense (Sec. 165), whose exact time and place are not definitely known though it has been surmised that he was born in 1040 and died 1110, has left us a number of sacred poems which are distinguished by their depth of thought and beauty of expression. The best of them is a dialogue with his soul where he admonishes her to reflect upon the state of human life and its ultimate destiny and purpose. In it he also expresses a few reflections on life in general which possess a deep pathos though somewhat gloomy. He sings thus:

> Death is life's brother,
> They keep fast to one another
> United by ends of a frail bridge
> Over which all creatures pass.
> Life is the entrance—death the exit;
> Life builds—death demolishes;
> Life sows—death reaps;
> Life plants—death uproots;
> Life joins together—death separates;
> Life links together—death scatters.

A poet of note was also the Talmudic scholar, Rabbi Isaac Ibn Giat (b. 1030 d. 1089), who wrote numerous poems, sacred as well as secular, but his distinction lies in the sacred poetry which bears a national character where he represents the relation between God and Israel as between a lover and his beloved. He sings of the beloved in exile complaining to her lover of his forsaking her and begging him to return to her bower.

Soon a great star arose upon the horizon of Hebrew poetry. He was Moses ben Jacob Ibn Ezra of Granada. He was born 1070 and died 1150. His life was embittered by an unfortunate love affair. In his youth, he fell madly in love with his niece, the daughter of his older brother, Isaac. She requited his love, but her father interfered and she was forced to marry his younger brother. This stinging disappointment embittered him against his brothers and he left his native town and wandered about for the rest of his life in strange countries. His wound was never healed and he attempted to assuage it by pouring out his soul in burning love songs, and in complaints against the treachery of friends and brothers. The love songs were intended for his quondam love, who, though married, always seemed to entertain a deep affection for him. In his poetry, he rises to great heights. He was a master of Hebrew, and under his skilled pen it emitted wondrous sounds. He devoted himself to secular poetry, songs of friendship, love, nature, and life, and at times, he overcame his gloom and sang on wine and the joy of life. Here is one of his epigrams, "A pretty maiden, a cup of wine, a beautiful garden, the song of a bird, and the murmur of the brook are the cure of the lover, the joy of the lonely, the wealth of the poor, and the medicine of the sick"; or he sings of age and youth as follows: "Tell me, gazelle, why do you hate an old man from the depth of thy heart?" "Why," she replied, "do you love a youthful maiden better than an old woman?" These, however, were only fleeting moments in the flight of his poetic spirit. On the whole, he is dominated by the spirit of gloom and he reflects upon life and its vicissitudes morosely thus, "The years of man are dreams and death is the interpreter." "Man travels to his end daily but he thinks he is resting, like a man on a boat imagines rest while he floats on the wings of the wind."

His masterpiece is "The Necklace," also known as the *Tarshish,* a collection of twelve hundred and ten verses, all arranged in a peculiar way, each couplet ending with the same word, but with a different meaning in each line. But great as he was in his secular poetry, he was still greater as a sacred poet. Moses Ibn Ezra's suffering soul found in religion a refuge and he poured forth his heart to his God in hundreds of hymns and songs of praise. He devoted himself especially to penitential poetry (Selihot) and on account of this he was called *Moshe ha-Salah* (Moses the writer of Selihot). In his penitential poems, we hear the cry of a contrite spirit calling upon his Maker for forgiveness for possible aberrations which, though, they might not have been consummated in action yet existed in thought and desire. In them, the longing and yearning for God is expressed with deep pathos. He heard the cry of his people and felt their suffering, and he gives strong expression to the nation's plaint against God for allowing them to remain so long in captivity, but on the whole, he is the typical individual religious poet, the interpreter of his soul; yet, his religious individuality is of a universal nature, so that his poems became the medium of religious expression for every Jew. Moses also wrote a poetic paraphrase of the Book of Jonah for the Day of Atonement which was adopted in the Avignon *Mahzor* (sacred poetry cycle). It is a fine example of a Biblical epic. He also wrote a book in Arabic on the art of poetry where he discusses its various forms and gives a review of the development of Jewish poetry. All these poets were great and sweet singers in Israel, but soon there arose one who excelled his predecessors both in the poetic art and in depth of feeling, and whose poems represent the very acme of poetry in that period.

126. JUDAH HA-LEVI

Judah ben Samuel ha-Levi was born about 1080 in Toledo, at that time the capital of Christian Spain, and died in the Orient about the year 1140. His soul was one of the noblest and purest that ever descended on earth and is wonderfully characterized by Heinrich Heine who said of him as follows: "When God created the soul of ha-Levi, He was so enraptured by its beauty and exquisiteness that He could not restrain Himself and kissed it." It is this divine kiss which reverberates in all his creations, both poetic and philosophic. This soul possessed also serenity and harmony, a boon which was denied to his two great predecessors, Gabirol and Moses Ibn Ezra. His life was not marred by suffering or by disappointment but flowed peacefully and quietly, and hence his poetry reflects that nature.

In his youth, he attended the Academy of Isaac Al-Fasi in Lucena where he acquired many friends. After completing his course there, he returned to Toledo where he practiced medicine with great success. He married there and had an only daughter. Later, he removed to Cordova, Mohammedan Spain, but was soon seized with longing for Palestine, which longing became a passion, as he says,

> O, city of the world most chastely fair
> In the far West, behold, I sigh for thee,
> Oh, had I eagle's wings, I'd fly to thee,
> And with my falling tears make moist thine earth.*

At last, deciding to carry out his wish, he left home, wife, daughter, and his beloved grandson and sailed for the Orient. He visited Egypt. We meet him later in Tyre and Damascus, but then he suddenly disappears. Jewish legend has it that he was killed by an Arab while kneeling at the gates of Jerusalem and singing his famous ode to Zion.

His poetry may at times lack the depth of Gabirol's all-penetrating spirit, but it is, as said, more harmonious; it does not break forth in wrath and anger but flows bubblingly like water from an inexhaustible well. In general it may be divided into three classes, secular, religious, and national. In his secular poetry, we have before us a poet with a cheerful view of life who knew life's pleasures and rejoiced in them. In short, in ha-Levi, we have the perfect harmony of man and Jew. He sang on friendship, love, and wine, and on the joy of life as well as on its reverses. His love songs are noble and show a keen sense for beauty, both of nature and the human form. Thus he sings:

* Translation taken from Lady Magnus: *Jewish Portraits*.

Through the veil are seen two serpent-eyes.
A snake coils o'er your cheek—your hair;
It stings the hearts of many from afar, my fair.

Or

O beautiful of sight,
And sweet of voice;
In you I sight
A beauty choice,
In which there mingle
The rising of the light
And coming of the night.
Upon your cheek and the hair of your head,
I bless Him, who darkness made,
And "Let there be light" said.[10]

Even in his old age when on his way to Palestine, on passing through Egypt and being asked what he saw in the land of the Pharaohs, he replied:

Wondrous is this land to see,
With perfume its meadows laden,
But none, fairer than all to me is yon gentle maiden.
Ah, time's swift flight I fain would stay
Forgetting that my locks are grey.*

Ha-Levi was more interested in life but he also had an observing eye for the beauty of nature. His song on "The Roses of Spring" is a gem of nature poetry. Says he,

Yestreen the earth, like a suckling babe, drained the breasts of the wintry
    clouds;
Or, like a bride with soul shut up, yearning for the time of love;
Yearned for the summer of its love when its weary heart is healed;
Or, like a dainty girl, blushing in her new-donned robes,
In garments all of golden flowers and broidered work of lilies,
The earth each day its robes renews and wins fresh beauty,
Changing here from lily white to rosy red, and there to emerald green,
Now turns pale, and now it blushes like a bride kissing her lover.
The beauty of the flowers was surely stolen from the starry skies.* [11]

[10] *Anthology of Hebrew Poetry*, ed. Brody, p. 176.
* Translation taken from *The Jew. Enc.* Vol. VII, p. 347.
* Translated by Joseph Jacobs in *Jewish Ideals*, etc., p. 110.
[11] Judah ha-Levi, *Collected Poems*, Hebrew, ed. Harkavy, V. 2, p. 58.

Likewise is his description of a storm at sea:

> The billows roar
> As the wheels roll o'er;
> They fall and soar
>   On the face of the sea.
> The heavens grow black,
> And each wave as a stack
> Rises up, then rears back
>   Till the depths you can see.
> The cauldron boils o'er
> With a hiss and a roar,
> And none can restore
>   Its tranquillity.
> And mighty waves hide
> As the waters divide
> And a mountain with pride
>   Rises near a valley.* [12]

Only a short time did ha-Levi play with the secular muse. Soon he felt the years passing, and a religious spirit took hold of him and he calls to his soul:

> Asleep in the bosom of youth, how long wilt thou lie?
> Know that boyhood is like shaken tow.
> Shake thyself from the lure of time—like birds
> Shake themselves from the dewdrops of the night. [13]

And verily did his soul fulfill his call—his deep thirst for God knew no bounds; with all the might of his soul, he strives towards Him. He is filled with thoughts of Him; he rises from bed at night to praise Him and feels His nearness. He says,

> O Lord, where shall I find Thee?
>   All-hidden and exalted is Thy place;
> And where shall I not find Thee?
>   Full of Thy glory is the infinite space.

Without Him his soul would wither away, and he sums up his feelings in the words,

---

* (Taken with alterations from Joseph Jacobs' *Jewish Ideals*, pp. 129–130.)
[12] *Ibid.* Vol. I, p. 35.
[13] *Selected Poems of Judah ha-Levi, Jewish Classic Series*, tr. by Nina Salaman, No. 45.

> Longing I sought Thy presence;
> Lord, with my whole heart did I call and pray,
> And going out toward Thee,
> I found Thee coming to me on the way.* [14]

But at times his heart contracts from pain of doubt. Why should the God of justice whose ways are just and merciful, the God of goodness be unjust to his people? Why should the selected people cleaving to the Torah be martyred and tortured? And to this problem, he endeavors to find an answer.

The problem and the search for its solution is the keynote of his national poetry. Ha-Levi is the poet par excellence of the Jewish nation and most of the sacred poems are of a national character. He is the interpreter of the heart of the nation to its God. Like Gabirol, he sings at times love poems to the God of Israel and calls:

> Come beloved, come Thou to me;
> In the bower of the lilac woo me.
> Stay the fiend that would pursue me.
> Harps and chimes and cups all golden
> To the joy of old embolden
> 'Neath the radiant glory olden.*

But at times he demands the justification of his people. He tells of their suffering for His sake, of their clinging to Him, and asks:

> Thou turnest thy right hand,
> And the enemy has stretched forth his right hand.
> Hast Thou forsaken us, or is Thy hand short? [15]

The solution to the problem is redemption. Redemption is to ha-Levi the central idea. It is not, like with other poets, a refuge from suffering but an aim in itself. He negates the present and lives entirely in the future, and hence his burning love for Zion. Zion is the central point in his desires and as long as he is not there, he feels that his very life is defective and incomplete. He therefore sings,

> My heart is in the East,
> But I am in the ends of the West.
> How then can I taste what I eat,
> And how can food to me be sweet? [16]

---

* Translated by Nina Salaman, *Selected Poems of Judah ha-Levi*, pp. 168–169.
[14] *Collected Poems*, ed. Harkavy, Vol. II, p. 131–2.
* Taken from *The Jew Enc.*, Vol. VII, p. 348.
[15] *Collected Poems*, Vol. I, p. 61.
[16] *Ibid.* p. 7.

But it is not his life alone which is defective, but the life of the nation as well. Here in the Galut, in exile, that life can never be complete. It is only in Zion that God is near to man, there Israel will find his youth and will fulfill his great mission to be the light of nations. In his serenade to Zion entitled "Zion Dost Thou Ask for the Peace of thy Exiles," his love for his people and land, the story of their great past, their miserable present, the hope and vision of a glorious future are glowingly set forth by ha-Levi.

And well did he characterize in that very song his own national poetry:

> I am like a jackal to bewail thy woe,
> But when I dream of thy restoration
> I am a harp for thy songs.

A silver harp with many strings which emitted wonderful melodies was indeed the soul of ha-Levi.

127. ABRAHAM IBN EZRA

A poet of great note was the famous commentator of the Bible, grammarian, and astronomer, Abraham Ibn Ezra. This remarkable man whose intellect was all-encompassing brought to his poetry besides a feeling heart also a keen penetrating mind. He can well be compared to Browning in the tone of his poetry which raises man to an intellectual height from which he surveys the world and life. His is a lyrical genius which draws inspiration from a complete understanding of nature and man. He observes the nature of God, His power and creation, and the relation of God to the world. He also penetrates into the intricacies of the human soul, the constant struggle between flesh and spirit, and all these observations he expresses in his poems. Some of them are of a didactic nature and help man to understand both the forces of nature and the soul of man, but many of them raise man to an ethical height. Ibn Ezra, in spite of the fact that his life was spent in wandering and suffering, does not complain like Moses Ibn Ezra, nor does he rise above existence and soar in heavenly spheres like Gabirol, but expresses in his poems a quietude of soul which arises from a true understanding of the world and its vicissitudes, and brings us to a conception of their necessity, which in turn brings one to a restful state of the soul.

Ibn Ezra's range of poetry is very wide and covers every subject under the sun. He is the master par excellence of the Hebrew language, and in his hands it was so elastic that it served all purposes. He wrote sacred poetry, poems of friendship, poems of love, wine ditties, and didactic poems on nature, astronomy, the seasons, and the calendar. He has even a long poem on the chess game, where he relates in a punctilious manner in fine verse and meter all the intricate rules of the game. Another fine poem of this kind is one on hygiene and dietetics, where he gives in meter and rhyme sound advice to man how to care for his body and how to choose his diet according to each month of the year. Each month is given two strophes and in addition there is an epilogue of two strophes, twenty-six strophes in all.

Ibn Ezra possessed a keen and biting sense of humor and this he turned to good account in a number of satiric poems. He did not even disdain to write puzzles and queer poems remarkable for their peculiar construction in fantastic shapes. Such is the poem, "The Tree," written in honor of Jacob Tam, the great Talmudic scholar of France. The construction of the poem is as follows: In the center there runs a line which is the trunk, saying, "Pene Rab Yakob Oru ke-Ḥamah beno Meir u-Meir la-Adamah" (The face of Rabbi Jacob is like the sun, he is the son of Meir, i.e. light, and lights the world). Out of this trunk, there run branch lines to the right and left, each beginning with a word of the trunk. Thus each word in the trunk is made to serve three purposes as a part of the trunk line and as parts of the two branch lines. He was, it seems, very proud of his great skill in mastering the language and delighted in it. We have, therefore, a number of short poems where the lines read both ways, a wonderful little poem which consists almost entirely of alliteration. It is a sacred *Piyyut* to the *Geulah* prayer before *Shemoneh Esrē* (eighteen benedictions) and its beginning is as follows:

> Four stood by the sea
> Ẓur, Ẓir, Ẓon, and Ẓor.

Ẓur, i.e. Creator, God; Ẓir, i.e. Messenger, Moses; Ẓon, i.e. Sheep, Israel; Ẓor, i.e. Enemy. A play is then made upon these four words.

In his sacred poems, we note in spite of his otherwise known skepticism an expression of a deep religious soul. He longs for God and emphasizes especially the infinite distance between Him and man. Here is one where a play is made upon contrary emotions and sensations:

When I hunger to praise Thee, I'm sated;
  When to worship I thirst, I am drunk.
Then my heart is secure, when I fear Thee
  When in terror and awe I am sunk.
When I bow to Thee low, I am lifted;
  When I fall in Thy presence, I rise.
I am free when I serve, for Thy name's sake,
  My oppressors who Thy name despise.
All suffering is sweet to my heart,
  When I know that my God Thou art.[17]

or,

In Thee, my God, is my desire;
  In Thee my passionate love and fire.
To Thee my reins,[18] to Thee my heart;
  To Thee my soul and spirit dart.
To Thee my hands, to Thee my feet;
  From Thee doth come my form complete.
My blood, my bones, they all are Thine,
  My body and image divine.
To Thee belong my eyes and thought,
  The form and pattern Thou hast wrought.
To Thee my soul, to Thee my might;
  Thou art my trust and my delight.
To Thee, to whom there is no peer,
  I give my soul, to me so dear.[19]

This is the kind of religious spirit which animated Ibn Ezra. The poem aside from its elevated religious feeling is in itself a masterful example of style, as half of its lines begin with the *Lamed* and the other half with *Waw,* and there is a monorhyme for its eighty-five lines. Ibn Ezra wrote also a long philosophical poem, like Gabirol's "Royal Crown." It runs along the same lines and contains also an expression of his philosophy and science. Like Gabirol, he describes first, God and His attributes, then, the world depicting the planets and constellations, and dwells at length on the sub-lunar world, i. e. the earth, describing its parts and elements. From the world, he comes down to man and gives a minute description of his anatomy, followed by that of the soul and its struggles with the desires of the body. Finally, a brief review of the vicissitudes of human life is given, its purpose, destination,

---

[17] *Anthology,* ed. Brody, p. 195.
[18] The kidneys were thought to be a secondary seat of thought and emotion. Cf. the Biblical expressions: My reins instruct me (Ps. XVII, 8), or God searcheth the heart and tries the reins, Jeremiah XVII, 8.
[19] Abraham Ibn Ezra, *Collected Poems,* ed. Kahana, No. 133.

and the impending judgment. The poem closes with a confession and plea for forgiveness.

In his national poems, he feels deeply the pangs of pain and suffering of his people, and at times breaks out in vehement protest against such a state and argues with God thus:

> The God of Israel Thou wast called of yore—
>   Thou wast their Father
> And they were Thy children—but are they no more?
> Then why didst Thou for thousand years forget them?
> And enemies from all around beset them.
> Dost Thou not see, or is Thy hand so weak,
> That Thou canst not save those who help do seek?
> Redeemer there is none as near as Thou;
>   Thy name from ever was Redeemer.
> So hasten, our God, redeem us now.[20]

His wandering life, where he met all vicissitudes and underwent all kinds of experiences, some pleasant and some unpleasant, afforded him ample opportunity for his biting wit, and as a result we have a number of delightful poems interspersed with bits of remarkable satire. He once came to a place where he was not treated well. He wrote thus:

> Emptied of wine is the cask;
> To swallow the cheese is a task.
> Blind on both eyes is the dame
> Withered, crippled, and lame,
> And yet does she strut without shame.
> Each person in the town
> Is perfectly a clown.
> In this place man and beast
> Are not unlike in the least.

Or his plaint against hard fate:

> I come in the morn
> To the house of the nobly born.
> They say he rode away.
> I come again at the end of day,
> But he is not at his best, and needs rest.
> He is either sleeping or riding afar—
> Woe to the man who was born without a star.

[20] S. D. Luzzatto, *Collected Letters*, p. 374.

His complaint against the flies is a delightful piece of humor:

> To whom shall I cry in my anguish?
> And where shall I flee from the flies?
> No breathing-space do they allow me;
> They treat me as would enemies.
> They buzz in my ears all their love-songs,
> And creep on my brow and my eyes.
> I try to partake of my breakfast—
> They swarm on the coveted prize.
> They drink of my wine from the goblets,
> Considering me in no wise; [21]

In addition to his poems, Ibn Ezra wrote many semi-poetic works in what we call rhymed prose. Some of these works are masterpieces and are written either in the form of letters or separate books. The best of these semi-poetic writings is "The Letter of Hai ben Mekiz." It is partly modeled after Avicennas' "Letter of Hai, the Son of Yaktan." The letter is a description of a journey through three worlds: (1) the sublunar world, i. e. the earth; (2) the world of the seven planets where the nature of each planet is described in accordance with the astrologic notions of the time; (3) and finally, the divine world where God and the angels dwell. The letter is an allegory. *Hai ben Mēkiz* means the man who is living and awake, i. e. the Active Reason which penetrates all creation and endeavors to conceive the Creator.

128. JUDAH BEN SOLOMON AL-HARISI

With Ibn Ezra, there closes the Golden Period of Spanish poetry. The succeeding age can be called the silver one, which was in turn followed by an age of brass and copper. To this age belong a few names of note, such as that of the philosopher Joseph Ibn Zaddik (b. 1081—d. 1149), David Ibn Bakudah (d. 1150) who wrote sacred and secular poems, as well as a number of others. But the greatest of this age is Judah ben Solomon Al-Harisi. He was born in Spain in 1165, somewhere near the city of Barcelona. His education he received in that city which was at the time a center of learning and literature, and while still a youth, he mastered both the Hebrew and Arabic languages. Being of a restless nature, he left his native land early in life and traveled in the Provence, where at the time Jewish learning and literature began to flourish. The Jewish communities there were eager for knowledge and

[21] *Collected Poems,* ed. Kahana, pp. 10, 13, 21.

many patrons were found who were willing to pay well for translations
of Jewish books from the Arabic into the Hebrew. Ḥarisi seemed to
have been the first Hebrew writer who made literature a profession
from which he derived his livelihood. Thus, he was commissioned by the
Jewish community of Marseilles to translate the commentary of Maimonides on the Mishnah from Arabic into Hebrew. He had executed a
part of the work—the commentary on the first order, *Zeraim*—with
great skill, and this gave him prestige and his name as translator became known. Soon he was commissioned to make a new Hebrew translation of Maimonides' "Guide of the Perplexed," which task he
ably carried out. His translation is clear, and his style light and
popular, but it is hardly as accurate as that of Ibn Tibbon (Ch. XII).

In 1205, he returned to Spain, and we find him then in Toledo where
he was urged to translate the poetic satire of Hariri (1054–1121) from
Arabic into Hebrew. He accomplished this difficult task, but seemed
not to have found satisfaction in this work. He then started on his long
journey through the Orient, visited Palestine, Babylon and stayed for
a time in Egypt. On his journey, he visited the most important Jewish
communities, and came in contact with all famous Jewish leaders. He
was received favorably everywhere and found many patrons during
his travels who paid him liberally for his verses of praise and also encouraged him in his work. It was on these journeys that he conceived
and executed his Magnum Opus, the *Taḥkemoni* (place or book of
wisdom), a kaleidoscopic satire like Hariri's, but of purely Jewish character (see for characterization Ch. XVI, Sec. 204). This book which is
divided into fifty portals or chapters is interwoven with a number of
poems of diverse character, and it is on these poems that his fame as a
poet rests. He returned from his travels to Spain where he died in the
year 1225. In addition to the *Taḥkemoni* and the above-mentioned translations, he made a number of translations of several ethical books which
will be discussed in the proper place (Ch. XVI).

Ḥarisi is primarily to be classed as a secular poet. He wrote love
poems, wine songs, many songs of praise to his patrons, and a number
of diverse poems of a moral didactic nature. One of his love poems runs
thus:

> Gazelle who hath drawn my heart like with a string and burnt
>   it on the coals of her love,
> Pity upon a lover whom his soul has sold and whose eye put
>   him in a prison of love.

O, pity him and turn with grace to him, lest they say a
woman killed him.[22]

He also wrote several devotional and national poems. Of his devotional poems there is one on the plaint of the soul (Taḥkemoni, Ch.
XIII) where the soul complains bitterly of her exile from the heavenly dwelling place and her enforced stay in the body, and expresses a
longing for the return to her source. He has also several fine poems on
Zion where genuine feeling is expressed and an unconscious imitation of
ha-Levi is noticeable. But he lacks the pathos and depth of the earlier
poets. Ḥarisi's style is light and delightful and his greatness lies in his
skill in manipulating the language and his fine delicate humor. His
poetic versatility only testifies to his mastery of style. He wrote short
poems on the industry of the ant, on the fly, probably imitating Ibn
Ezra's poem on the flies, on the plaint of the rooster, in which he complains bitterly of the ingratitude of man who repays him for his services with evil, on the eight virtues, where each virtue, such as humility,
industry, courage, faith, wisdom, instruction, good heart, and generosity is extolled in a short masterly strophe. A very keen observation
of life is seen in his poem on the strife which goes on in life. In a
short strophe of eight double lines, he gives a striking picture of the
strife of creatures going on in the world, saying very pointedly, "Creatures of the world, their very life depends on death for some are the food
of others. The strong pursue and devour the weak, but then comes the
great equalizer and gathers them all alike, for in death both the devourer and the devoured are equalled upon the earth." Thus Ḥarisi
could be serious at certain moments in life, but most of the time, he
sang and laughed, and probably in this consists his uniqueness and his
greatness.

C. Sacred Poetry of the Italian and Franco-German Schools

29. GENERAL OBSERVATIONS

The sacred poetry written by Italian, French, and German authors
is a direct descendant of the Palestinian liturgical poetry. It is in fact
a continuation of the work of José ben José, Janai, and Kalir with occasional variations. The field of sacred poetry in these countries was a
very fertile one and the productivity lasted for centuries and the mass of

[22] *Taḥkemoni,* ed. Kaminka, Ch. XX.

Piyyutim (sacred poetry), *Seliḥot* (devotional and penitential prayers), and other kindred forms of poetic religious expressions is so enormous that a complete survey is almost impossible. Almost every scholar of note in the countries mentioned, every master of Hebrew during the three centuries from the ninth to the thirteenth, the heyday period of Paitanic activity, found it necessary to add a hymn or a prayer of his own to the constantly increasing literature of religious poetry.

Yet, with all these numerous writers hailing from different lands and living in different centuries, there is hardly any fundamental variety noticeable either in the content or in the form of the different layers of the literature, as was noted above (Sec. 113). The sacred poetry of the Palestinian-West-European schools is not stamped with the individuality of the authors. It is the mediator between the nation and God and it is the voice of the people which speaks through it. We see, therefore, that the same topics, namely, the greatness of God, suffering of Israel, hope of redemption, historical events of the past, which formed the subjects of poetic embellishment to the poets of the Palestinian school, are also employed by the *Paitanim* of the West-European countries.

If there is a change in the content it is in the depth and intensity of feeling. The suffering which the Franco-German Jews had undergone in the eleventh and twelfth centuries, the depth of misery, the incessant persecutions, the massacres of the Crusades all left their indelible mark upon the character of the Jew. Of course, the religious feeling was not lessened, but on the contrary was strengthened through these persecutions. The frequent martyrdom of whole communities and numerous individuals who sanctified the name of God and accepted death willingly for His sake, only intensified the love of God and the devotion to the Torah, and this intensified feeling found expression in the sacred liturgy. But at the same time, there is a strong note of protest pervading the poems, a cry of anguish of the *Kenesset Yisrael* (the Community of Israel) to its God against all these persecutions and suffering. A mighty question rises from the lips of these singers, "Why does God allow His only one, His chosen nation, to be the prey of merciless enemies?" This cry of anguish is accompanied by a deep yearning for redemption. It is not an ideal yearning or merely a longing for Zion, it becomes a soul-stirring feeling for immediate delivery from the burden of oppression, and again a question arises, "Why does God delay His salvation, why does the Messiah tarry? Does not the promise of God hold good? or is the cup of bitterness not yet full?"

Direct solutions to these problems were not offered by the poets but hope did not forsake them and by visions of the future and pictures of the glorious past they attempt to assuage the burning pain of the present. It is an old trodden way, the way of the masters of the Agada who bequeathed their spirit to the *Paitanim*.

And just as the content did not change, so was there barely any change in form. The meter which was introduced by the Spanish Jewish poets was hardly utilized by these *Paitanim*. They still followed the way of rhymed meterless poems, alphabetically arranged. Most of them used their name acrostics. Those who were ambitious used various combinations of rhyme and alliteration producing fine examples of style. Their language though is hardly pure. In their struggle to express their overflowing feelings, they were short of words and borrowed wherever they could, from the treasures of Halakah and Agada, and often even coined new ones. This maltreatment of the Hebrew language evoked severe criticism from purists like Ibn Ezra, but with all the barbarisms of their style the *Paitanim* contributed to the richness of the language, and gave it flexibility and elasticity.

130. CLASSES OF PIYYUTIM

As noted above, the main divisions of sacred poetry are two, *Piyyut* and *Selihah*. *Piyyut* includes all poetry intended for the festival days and certain Sabbaths; *Selihah*, all devotional prayers for days of penitence, fast days, and Day of Atonement. Besides, there are smaller classes, such as *Hoshannahs,* especially intended for the seventh day of Succoth, Feast of Tabernacles. They are named thus, because they begin with the words *Hoshiah No,* (Help, O, God). Another class are the *Kinot,* elegies intended for the Ninth of Ab, where as a rule the destruction of Zion and the exile of the Jews are the subjects, but they treat also of persecutions of their own times.

The *Piyyut* is directly connected with the standard liturgy, and as a rule embellishes the content of the service. The *Selihah*, on the other hand, is a free expression of religious feeling and is not related to the service, though on certain occasions, as on the Day of Atonement, it is included in it. The *Piyyut* is subdivided into certain groups arranged according to the groups of prayers. Most of the *Piyyutim* center around the morning service (Shaharit) and they follow along its lines. We have then (*a*) *Yozer,* coming after the benediction of creation of light; (*b*) *Ofan,* after or before the praise of the spheres (Ofanim); (*c*) *Me-*

orah, before the close of the benediction of light; (*d*) *Ahabah,* before benediction of *Ahabah Raba;* (*e*) *Zulat,* following the prayer after reading of *Shema;* (*f*) *Geulah,* preceding the last benediction of redemption. The *Piyyutim* to the Eighteen Benedictions (Shemoneh Esré) are called *Kerobot,* derived from an old root used in Midrashic literature for that purpose which means to plead (originally from Korab, to draw near, hence to conciliate) as their content is usually a plea to God to remember the deeds of the Patriarchs. As a rule, they cover only the first three benedictions and usually conclude with a long poem before *Kedushah* which is called *Siluk,* the final hymn. Most of the festivals have no hymns for the Musaf, additional service, with the exception of the first day of Passover and the last day of Tabernacles, when special poems are recited on behalf of Palestine, namely, that God grant it copious dew (Passover) and rainfall (Tabernacles); New Year and the Day of Atonement have *Piyyutim* for every service. Many hymns were also composed for the evening service of the festivals; these are known as *Ma'arobot,* i. e. to the *Ma'arib* service.

The *Piyyutim* of the group mentioned deal both with the subject of the prayer, as well as with that of the particular day, as for instance, the *Yoẓer Piyyutim* speak of the creation of the world or light, and together with these basic ideas is interwoven the subject of the day, if it is New Year, Judgment; if Shebuot (Feast of Weeks), the Torah, and so on. *Ofan* is always a doxology to God which sings of His greatness. In *Ahabah,* the love of God for Israel is dwelt upon, and in *Geulah,* redemption is the theme. Thus, for Passover, there is a special hymn of redemption for every day composed by various authors, by the name of *Braḥ Dodi* (Flee, My Beloved). The name is taken from Canticles, VIII, 14. In these *Geulah* poems, the purest love of a martyred people for its God and Maker is expressed, and a noble plea is entered that He redeem His chosen bride. Some of the stanzas run thus:

> Flee, my beloved, till the day be breaking,
> Beyond end of vision—then arise
> And chase these shadows—him Thou wast forsaking,
> Despised, shall be exalted, high and wise
> And with his wisdom sprinkling the nations.
> Bare Thine arm, Lord, when we cry
> "The voice of my beloved sounded high." [23]

or

[23] *Geulah* to first day Passover.

Beloved, hasten to our shrine, all-holy,
And though sin claims us almost for its own
Behold how bound in chains we cower lowly.
Thou art the sacred Saviour, Thou alone,
To Thee we give ourselves in prayer wholly
O, grant redemption from Thy holy throne.[24]

The *Kerobah* deals with the subject of the day. If it is New Year, the Day of Judgment is portrayed; if Passover, the Exodus; if the Feast of Weeks, the Torah, or the process of bringing the first fruits, and so on. In all these, and especially in the final poem, *Siluk,* there is always an epic element involving certain episodes in Jewish history, such as the Exodus, and others which greatly embellished by the Agada, furnished excellent material for the poets. They borrowed the Agadic stories and wove them into the fabric of their poetry. Thus, we find a number of final poems of the *Kerobah* dealing either with the Exodus or with the crossing of the Red Sea. The struggle of the Maccabees together with the suffering of the martyrs, as the famous mother and the seven sons (Ch. I, Sec. 6) formed the subject for the Hanukkah poems. The story of Judith was also utilized. In this way, every historical episode of importance became the subject of poetical production. The heroes in the Purim story, the various incidents of the destruction of the Temple, Elijah, the hero of Jewish legend, all found their proper place in sacred poetry. The Purim poems centered around the first, the *Kinot* for the Ninth of Ab around the second, and the *Habdalah* (Saturday evening service) poems around the third. The New Year and Day of Atonement furnished material for meditative poems. There, the Day of Judgment, littleness of man, the soul and its struggles, vanity of life form the themes of the poems. Thus, the *Piyyut* embraces all phases of the life of the Jew, both the individual and the national.

131. THE SELIḤAH

The *Seliḥah* poems, or *Seliḥot,* which as said, are of a devotional nature and are not, as a rule, attached to a particular service, are free expressions of an overflowing religious spirit. They are, primarily, of a lyric character. In the *Seliḥot* the most individual side of the Jew is expressed. Yet, as most of the *Seliḥot* were composed in times of national distress, the national pain became articulate here, and it is in the *Seliḥot* that we often hear expressed the strongest protest to God. In

---

[24] *Geulah* to the Sabbath service during Passover week.

Jewish life, we can hardly separate the individual from the community and the wishes and the desires of the community as a whole merge together with that of the individual.

When *Selihot* were destined for special days, such as the Day of Atonement, they sometimes dealt with subjects similar to that of the *Kerobah Piyyutim*. But on the whole, the subjects of the *Selihot* can be divided into five types: (*a*) The admonition type (Tokhohah) which is of a meditative nature like the meditative poems, where the call is issued to the soul to consider its destiny and purpose. In this type, the shortness and vanity of life, the value of penitence, the Day of Judgment, the strife between reason and passion, between spirit and body are the themes. These subjects are dealt with in various ways and forms, and some of the *Selihot* strike a deep lyrical chord. (*b*) The *Akedah* (Sacrifice of Isaac). This stirring story of patriarchal life forms the subject of many a *Selihah*. In most cases, it is only a pretext for relating the martyrdom of the hundreds of Jews who sanctified the name of God in all the massacres. They, likewise, are considered *Akedot,* and their merit is invoked as a plea to God to forgive the sins of His people for the sake of the martyrs. (*c*) In a similar manner, the persecutions, the massacres form the theme of many *Selihot* and *Kinot*. Both classes afford many soul-stirring examples of lyric poetry. (*d*) The story of the ten martyrs of old, the great scholars—among whom is included also Akiba—who were killed in the Hadrianic persecutions and their martyrdom is a frequently used theme in a number of variations. (*e*) The last class contains a plea to God (Tehinah and Bakashah). In this class, the relations between God and Israel are touched upon. It is not the individual who pleads but the nation. Very often, intercession is called for—the Angel of Mercy, the Torah, the Throne of God are called upon to intercede on behalf of Israel. The *Selihot* of this type vary in character and nature, but the basic idea is the same.

132. SACRED POETRY IN ITALY

As Jewish history is gradually becoming more and more an open book through the patient labors of a large number of scholars, the role of Italy as the mediator between Palestine and Europe becomes evident. The Jews of Italy were the channel through which Palestinian influence flowed to the communities of the West. It is, of course, natural that the Paitanic activity, modeled after the Palestinian sacred poetry, should first have begun in Italy. The earliest *Paitanim* hail from

Southern Italy. There, in the city of Oria, which, in the ninth century belonged to the Byzantine Empire, was a great Jewish community where intensive literary activity was going on. This community produced a few *Paitanim,* and it seems that the poetic ability ran in a certain family, and father transmitted it to son. The first of this family of *Paitanim* was Rabbi Shefatyah (died 887) who was the leader of the Jewish communities in Southern Italy, and was greatly honored by the Emperor Basilius to whom he remained loyal even during the invasion of the Saracenes. Several of the poems and the *Selihot* of Rabbi Shefatyah are incorporated in the *Selihot* collections of the German ritual. They are written in pure Hebrew style, and in monorhyme and with the name acrostic, but not in alphabetical order. His son, Rabbi Amitai (about 900), surpassed his father in poetic ability and several of his poems express the deep longing of the Jews for Palestine, and his plaint has become the plaint of the people. Here is one of his stanzas:

> Lord, I remember and am sore amazed
> To see each city standing in her state,
> And God's own city to the low grave razed,
> Yet all time we look to Thee and wait.

Another poet of Southern Italy was Zebadiah from whom we possess a number of *Selihot,* written in varying rhyme and alphabetic acrostic with great skill.

From Southern Italy, the Paitanic activity spread to Rome and Northern Italy. Towards the end of the tenth century, we hear of a great *Paitan* in Rome, Rabbi Solomon, the son of Judah (c. 980), who for some reason or other was named the Babylonian. He wrote many *Piyyutim* and *Selihot* which were incorporated in the various *Mahzorim* (poem cycles). His style is rather heavy, and he follows the Kalirean method, coining words and using the alphabetic acrostic, both in straight and reverse order, namely, beginning with the *Taw* instead of the *Aleph.* In Northern Italy, in Lucca, there was at that time, a learned family, the head of which was a certain Rabbi Meshulam (ca. 780). One of the descendants of the family, either Kalonymos or Yekutiel was, according to the story, transferred by Charles the Bald * to Mayence in order to establish an academy there. But it seems that a branch of this family remained for a time in Italy, and only later

* See note on p. 254.

towards the end of the tenth century moved to Germany. This family produced a great number of *Paitanim*. The first of them was Meshulam, the son of Kalonymos (c. 976), who resided at Lucca, and who moved to Mayence in his old age. Meshulam was a very prolific poet, and wrote poems for almost every festival. Especially noted is his *Abodah* for the Day of Atonement which the German ritual had incorporated. There, like Josē ben Josē (Sec. 116), he reviews the events from the creation to the establishment of the priesthood and then relates the events of the service of the Day in the Temple. Meshulam uses a varying rhyme in each strophe, and very often employs the device of ending each strophe with a Biblical verse. His style is mixed, employing many Aramaic words, borrowed from the Agada.

133. FRANCO-GERMAN PAITANIM

From Italy, the Paitanic activity was transferred to Franco-German soil, especially to the Rhine provinces. There, where towards the end of the tenth century, a great center of Jewish learning began to develop, all the best minds of that Jewry gathered and a great literary activity in all fields was undertaken. Along with the intensive study of Halakah there went on a feverish Piyyutic activity. The number of *Paitanim* during the two centuries, the eleventh and twelfth, probably reached several hundred. The fact is that in this composition of sacred poems, we really find a parallel to the double activity of the first period, namely, that of Halakah and Agada. The first expressed the legal and intellectual aspects of Judaism, the second, the emotional and the inner religious feeling. Likewise, in the Mediæval period, sacred poetry took the place of Agada expressing the inner aspect of Judaism. The same great scholars, masters of Halakah, the great commentators of the Talmud, the codifiers of the Law, in their spare moments gave vent to their inner feelings and expressed the emotions of the martyred Franco-German Jewries in their *Piyyutim* and *Seliḥot*. They complained to God, protested against suffering and also instilled hope and comfort in the hearts of their brethren.

One of the first of these scholars and Paitanim is Rabbi Gershom ben Jehudah (960–1028), known as the "Light of the Exile" (Meor ha-Golah), the founder of the Mayence Academy of Talmud commentators. He, whose own son was killed in one of the massacres, felt bitterly the pang of suffering and he constantly complains to God in stern tones. Thus he asks:

> Lord of Hosts! Where are Thy wonders,
> The mighty and awesome deeds of yore
> Of which our fathers told us?

In another place he wails:

> My throat is parched from crying—violence!
> At seeing the wicked trample the place holy.
> I cried for help—for the day of vengeance is hidden
> Wherefore my bowels tremble and my heart melts.

Or

> Long are the days and lost is the vision,
> The Holy City and strong place have grown
> To be reproached, despised;
> Sunken and hidden are the things of the prized
> And naught remained but the Torah alone.

The eleventh century was especially productive in sacred poetry. Simultaneously with Gershom, another great *Paitan,* Kalonymos, the son of Meshulam (ca. 1000), poured forth his soul in stirring poems. One of his poems which goes under the name of another man, Rabbi Amnon, and around whom the halo of legend shines,[25] describes in exalted language and with great pathos the Heavenly Court on New Year's day. It reads thus:

> The great trumpet is sounded;
> The still small voice is heard;
> The angels are dismayed;
> Fear and trembling seize them as they proclaim,
> Behold the Day of Judgment!
> As a shepherd seeketh out his flock,
> And causeth them to pass beneath his crook,
> So dost Thou cause to pass, and number,
> Tell and visit every living soul,
> Appointing the measure of every creature's life
> And decreeing their destiny.[26]

[25] It is told that Rabbi Amnon of Mayence was repeatedly urged by the Archbishop to change his faith. Finally exasperated by his refusals the latter ordered Amnon's hands and feet to be amputated. The festival of the New Year was at hand, and the Rabbi requested that he be carried to the synagogue. When the cantor was about to recite the *Kedushah,* sanctification, in the Musaf service, Rabbi Amnon rose and recited the poem *u-Netane Tokef,* at the conclusion of which he expired.

[26] Part of the famous poem *u-Netane Tokef,* in the Musaf service of New Year and Day of Atonement.

Of this family, there arose *Paitan* after *Paitan,* the son of Kalonymos, Moses (1020), his sons, Kalonymos and Yekutiel (1050), and their sons —all held important places in liturgical poetry. The art of composing sacred poetry became a hereditary trait in this family and for over a century and a half, they were the mouthpieces of the Jewries of France and Germany voicing their grief and hope.

Simon, the son of Isaac (1020), the uncle of Solomon ben Isaac (Rashi), both the colleague and the disciple of Rabbi Gershom, was a prolific *Paitan.* He wrote *Kerobot* for many festivals and many *Selihot* where he implores the Torah to intercede on behalf of Israel. In this century, there were writers of *Piyyutim,* such as Isaac ha-Levi (1050), the teacher of Rashi, Benjamin, the son of Samuel (d. 1040) of Normandy, a prolific composer of *Selihot,* Elijah ben Mordecai, and Rashi himself. A *Paitan* of note was Meir ben Isaac, the cantor of Worms (d. 1060). He wrote poems both in Hebrew and Aramaic. One of his Aramaic poems is known as *Akdomot* (Prologue). It is read on the first day of the Feast of Weeks before the reading of the Law. This poem is written in a monorhyme of one hundred lines, a double alphabetic acrostic and a long name acrostic. The first half is a hymn to God and the Torah, the second half, a picture of redemption and days of the Messiah. It was intended to comfort Israel in tribulation and encourage them in their suffering for the sake of God. The second half is introduced by a dialogue between Israel and the nations which reads as follows:

> They came in multitudes (the nations) like the waves of the sea,
> And in mock astonishment asked about His miraculous deeds.
> Who is He thy resplendent lover
> For whose sake thou hast thrown thyself into a den of lions?
> Worthier and fairer wilt thou be, if thou yield to our command;
> All thy desires wherever thou be will be gratified.

To this call of the nations, Israel makes a reply which pictures the great day of redemption in bright colors.

Over the twelfth century, there hangs the pall of the Crusades. The fearful massacres which the Jewish communities of the Rhine province had undergone, find expression in the *Piyyutim* and *Selihot* of the period. It is practically one prolonged wail which a martyred nation raises to its God. At times, they sound very bitter, calling upon God to avenge the innocent blood mercilessly shed, and at other times, sharp invectives are uttered even against God Himself. One poet, in his bitterness says,

> O God, there is no one like you among the dumb;
> Thou art silent when the enemies ask, Where is your king?
> But no answer comes forth.

Another one cries out to God,

> Why art Thou silent?
> Is not speech better than silence?

Many are the *Paitanim* who thus poured forth their soul in fiery speech, in rhymes and acrostics. Among the leading are: Isaac ben Meir of Narbonne, France (ca. 1000); Kalonymos ben Judah, who described the massacres of the First Crusade in a soul-stirring *Kinah;* Isaac ben Shalom (d. 1147) who wrote plaintive and protesting *Piyyutim;* Elijah ben Shemayah (d. 1150), a prolific writer of *Seliḥot;* Ephraim of Regensburg (1175); and Ephraim of Bonn, a witness of the massacres of the Second Crusade who bewailed the tribulations of his brethren in a number of stirring poems, one of which is written in Aramaic and begins with, "Come and hear, Master of the World," where he invites God to incline His ear to the cry of the martyrs.

However, not all sacred poetry of the century is plaintive. Here and there, we catch a note of pure religious emotion, where the poet forgets the present and exults in his praise of God. The outstanding work of this kind is the *Shir ha-Yiḥud* (Hymn of Unity), written towards the end of the century by Samuel ben Kalonymos. In this hymn, God, His attributes, His relation to the world and Israel are described philosophically and poetically. It is written in a varying half-line rhyme, namely, the two halves of the line rhyme, and on the whole its style is pure Hebrew. From the point of view of the noble and exalted contents, it holds a place next to Gabirol's "Royal Crown," though it falls far below it in style, richness of language, and poetic flight.

CHAPTER X

RABBINIC LITERATURE

COMMENTARIES, CODES, AND RESPONSA

134. NATURE OF THIS LITERATURE

We have thus far surveyed the literary efforts made by Jewish scholars and writers during the first half of the Mediæval period, which centered around the Bible and its language, namely, that of Biblical exegesis, Hebrew grammar, and lexicography, and the cultivation of Hebrew poetry. We will now turn to other literary endeavors which deal primarily with the practical side of Jewish life and the central point of which is the Talmud or to call it by its older name, Halakah.

Jewish life in the Middle Ages in its spiritual aspect divides itself, according to the great historian of Jewish literature, L. Zunz, in three main currents, practice, divine worship or synagogue ritual, and religious knowledge or contemplation.[1] By practice, we are to understand the daily religious and moral life of the Jew, namely, all phenomena pertaining to a life in accordance with Jewish law and ethical conception— for as we know in Judaism, law and practical ethics are not differentiated. By ritual is understood all details relating to the synagogue service. By religious knowledge, we mean all such spiritual phenomena which brought about the saturation of Jewish individual and public life with the divine spirit. In literature, these currents are respectively reflected in Halakah, liturgy, both prayers and religious poetry, and theology, Biblical exegesis, philosophy, ethics and homiletics, all forms of literature which aim at inculcating the religious spirit. Of these three literary reflections of life, that of Halakah occupies a very prominent position, inasmuch as it covers the greater part of Jewish life. In bulk, legal, or Halakic literature probably exceeds either of the other two divisions, for no matter how important a role the Bible or other Jewish knowledge played in Jewish life, it was by the Talmud and its decisions that the Jew measured his daily routine of life. The best minds

[1] *Zur Geschichte und Literatur*, p. 159.

of Jewry have occupied themselves with the study, analysis of the contents and deductions of practical decisions of the Talmud for over twelve centuries, and it is no wonder then that the literary results are so voluminous and extensive.

Halakic literature has developed along three lines, which though different in form, are yet one in nature and purpose. These are: (1) Talmudic exegesis and commentaries; (2) Codes and collections of legal decisions; (3) Responsa and *novellae,* i. e. analytical discussions and comments. The lines between these classes of literature are not fast drawn and they often overlap each other, for the early Responsa contained a great many explanations of Talmudic passages, and most Responsa certainly deal with legal decisions, yet on the whole, each class bears a distinct character of its own as will be evident. ·

Besides the general unity noted, namely, that of contiguity of subjects, it displays also a unity of character. Halakic study was not as greatly affected by geographic division as the previously mentioned forms of literature, namely, poetry, linguistics, and Biblical exegesis, were. In it, the line dividing the literary productions of the Sephardic Jewry from that of the West-European Jewries is not as deeply marked as in the former kinds of literature The Talmud being the same for all Jewries and the purpose sought the same, the results of the study were closely similar. I said closely similar and not identical, for differences in intellectual work there are bound to be, and even Halakic work could not have escaped the effects of a different environment, mental habits and training of the various Jewries. Not entering for the present into details, we may remark in general that the Halakic literature of the Jewries under Mohammedan rule is generally distinguished by its simplicity, clearness, and systematization. That of the West-European Jewries, on the other hand, is distinguished by mental acumen and scholastic analysis but lacks the above-named qualities. It is for this reason that the Halakic activity of the former Jewries was developed more along the line of code making and Responsa, giving plain decisions on legal matters, while that of the latter Jewries followed more in the line of commentaries and *novellæ* where mental acumen could be displayed. That there were scholars in both Jewries who engaged in all lines of Halakic literature is needless to say.

We will now turn to these various branches of the extensive field of Halakic literature. We will begin with Talmudic exegesis, for though, as will be seen, some early codes precede the earliest commentaries, yet, it is Talmudic exegesis which constitutes the *nervus vivendi* of the entire Talmudic study, as without a correct understanding of the meaning of the Talmud, no practical decision can be reached. And for this very reason, the early codes contain a great deal of exegesis.

A. COMMENTARIES

135. EARLY COMMENTARIES

As the study of the Talmud as a textbook was, during the period immediately succeeding its redaction, almost principally confined to Babylonia for it took some time until written copies of the Talmud began to circulate among the Jews in other lands, there was, therefore, no need for a commentary on the Talmud. The two academies, Sura and Pumbedita, the very workshops, in an earlier generation, of the Talmud itself, still maintained the methods of study, traditions, and customs of that generation. The students there were thoroughly acquainted with the language, idioms and modes of speech of the Talmud, as they employed them themselves, and as a result little commenting was done during that period. The main task of study consisted in remembering by heart the content of the Talmud, to obtain correct readings, to amend the Talmud, and sometimes to interpret a difficult passage. But the interpretation was mostly oral, from teacher to pupil. Thus, we see that for a period of one hundred and seventy years from the close of the Talmud in 500 to the time of Shishné Gaon, 670 (term of office 670–689), there is not a written word left from the work of the *Saburaim* and Geonim. It is only after that period when the Talmud gradually spread among Jewries of other countries, who were not acquainted as thoroughly with the language and meaning of the Talmud, nor could they easily abstract from it the practical decisions, that inquiries were addressed to the Geonim, heads of the academies, for explanations and decisions. The said Shishné is the first Gaon from whom we possess Responsa where he gives practical decisions, and here and there offers to the inquirers explanations of passages in the Talmud. As time went on, such inquiries increased, and the number of Responsa multiplied accordingly.

We see then that the early attempts at commenting upon the Talmud were contained in the Gaonic Responsa where they were given sporadically and disjointedly, elucidating single passages according to the needs of the inquirers. Many were also the explanations offered in the various codes collected during that period (Sec. B). But it seems that no systematic attempt was made to write down either a commentary on the whole or a part of the Talmud which should afford some assistance to the reader or student. If such commentaries were written at an early period they were lost. The first book, which is partly of a lexicographical nature and partly a commentary, was written towards the close of the ninth century by the Gaon Ẓemaḥ, the son of Paltoi of Pumbedita. This was called the *Aruk,* meaning a prepared system. It was a dictionary of Talmudic words, phrases, and expressions alphabetically arranged. But it was more than a mere dictionary as it contained explanations of many passages. It seems that the Gaon felt that the book was a necessity for the students of his day, as they already found difficulty in understanding the words and phrases of the Talmud, for they were no more conversant with the language. The Gaon was well equipped for his task, as besides the Talmud, he also knew Persian, which helped him explain the large number of Persian words found in the Talmud. The book was lost, but it was known as late as the fifteenth century, for Abraham Zacuta, the author of the *Yuḥasin* (Vol. II, Ch. IX), quotes a number of articles from it. The author of the later *Aruk,* Nathan of Rome (Sec. 145), incorporated many of Ẓemaḥ's explanations.

The honor of being the first to write more or less connected commentaries on parts of the Talmud, that is, a number of tractates, falls to Saadia. This all-embracive intellect saw the necessity of such work and set out to do it. These commentaries were lost, but references to them are made by many authors. Likewise, Saadia's son speaks of his father's commentaries. Of late, fragments of Saadia's Arabic commentary on *Berakot,* the first tractate of the Talmud, were recently discovered in the Cairo Genizah[2] and were published. These fragments, though containing later additions, are parts of a larger commentary. It is also certain that he wrote commentaries on four other tractates, namely, *Pesaḥim, Sotah, Baba Meẓ'ia, Baba Batra* and on the order *Taharot* of the Mishnah. The nature and character of the Arabic commentary as far as can be determined from the few fragments was, that it was

---

[2] Genizah literally means storehouse. The Cairo Genizah is the exceptionally large collection of discarded books and parts of books which were kept in rooms adjoining the Synagogue of Elijah in Cairo. The late Dr. S. Schechter explored this storehouse of Jewish writings in 1897 and, finding it of exceptional value, transported the larger part of its contents to Cambridge University. It is in this Genizah, which has since become the hunting ground of scholars, that so many discoveries were made and from which many valuable documents shedding light on Jewish history and literature were brought forth.

merely confined to the explanation of words and phrases with occasional brief explanations of the meaning of certain passages. Saadia was too close to the Talmud to go into lengthy analytical explanations.

The next Gaonic commentators were the last two in the line of Geonim, Sherira (920–1000) and his son Hai (969–1038). Nothing is left of the father's commentaries except a few quotations of his explanation of certain words in the works of later authors. But of Hai's, we have a complete commentary on the sixth order of the Mishnah, *Taharot,* and a large number of fragments of commentaries on various tractates of the Talmud, such as *Berakot, Shabbat,* and *Ketubot.* The large number of quotations of Hai's explanations of passages in the *Aruk* of R. Nathan and later commentaries, prove that Hai must have written commentaries, if not on the entire Talmud, at least on a large part of it. Hai used two different methods in his commentaries. In his commentary on the Mishnah, he, as a rule, explains principally words and expressions, either by their derivation from roots in various languages or by comparison with other passages in the Mishnah or Talmud where they are used. In his endeavor to explain the meaning of words, he draws upon Talmudic sources and also upon the *Targumim.* Hai, who possessed great linguistic skill and seemed to have an acquaintance also with Greek, traces very often Mishnaic expressions to their source in other languages. He also often introduces more correct readings, which remove difficulties in the understanding of the meaning of the *Mishnayot* (sections). In the commentaries on Talmudic tractates, he employs more the method of explaining the content of the Talmud. But he still uses the Gaonic method which is paraphrasing the words of the Talmud and giving the contents of the passages in his own words and thus elucidating the meaning. When explaining an Agadic passage which contains some strange assertion, he attempts to rationalize it. He is especially careful to remove anthropomorphic conceptions of God which the figurative Agadic words convey. He is also said to have written a commentary on the first order of the Mishnah, *Zeraim,* but no trace is left of it.

136. THE ESTABLISHMENT OF NEW CENTERS OF LEARNING

With the death of Hai, Babylonia ceased to be a center of spiritual influence in world Jewry, and its place was gradually taken by other centers. The process of spiritual development must have been a slow one, and at first, these Jewries depended upon Babylonia for guidance and instruction, but as the Babylonian Gaonate declined, they became more and more independent, and ultimately by the end of the tenth century emancipated themselves entirely from the influence of Babylonia. Thus, by the year 1000, there are revealed to us a number of centers of literary activity throughout Europe and part of Africa. We have Northern Africa, Spain, Italy, Northern France, and Germany in Europe. In each of these countries, there are in this period well-developed centers of study with men of great intellectual ability and wide erudition, which fact goes to prove that the intellectual development in these various Jewish settlements went on for centuries previous to that point.

As stated, the gradual process of that development is veiled in mystery. But on the whole, we can discern two factors which aided in this intellectual development of these Jewries, one is the well-known influence of the Babylonian academies, and the other, the less known but none the less potent influence of Palestine scholarship. The influence of the Babylonian Gaonate extended mostly to the Mohammedan countries, and that of Palestine to the Christian countries. It is by this time certain that the Jewries of Italy, France, and Germany received their Talmudic knowledge, ritual, religious regulations, and decisions from Palestine, Italy serving as the medium of influence, as it alone probably had direct connection with Palestine. It may also be surmised that the contact with Palestine by the Jews in European Christian countries was closer than the contact of the Jews of the Mohammedan countries with their center of influence, Babylon. From a number of evidences, we may deduce that there were constant pilgrimages by Jews from Italy to Jerusalem, and most likely, there were a large number of travelers from Palestine to European countries. For the frequent visits of Palestinian scholars to Northern France, we have the testimony of Rashi. There was thus the personal touch between Palestine and the European Diaspora. The Jews of the Mohammedan countries, on the other hand, communicated with Babylon only through correspondence, namely, by interchange of inquiries and Responsa. At least it is true as far as Northern Africa and Spain are concerned. Other Eastern countries, such as Syria and Egypt most likely also sent students to the Babylonian academies.

It thus came about that Italy became in the eighth and the ninth centuries a center of learning, especially of Talmudic study, which sent out great men to other countries. There is a tradition that Charlemagne, or Charles the Bald, desiring to improve the education of the Jews transported in the year 787 or 876 respectively a family of scholars, headed by Rabbi Kalonymos from Lucca, Italy, to Mayence in Germany where they established an academy.* It is true that there is another tradition that the same Charlemagne ten years later, 797, made a request through an embassy to the Caliph, Harun-Al-Rashid, that the latter send him a Jewish scholar from Babylon who should propagate knowledge among his Jewish subjects. The Caliph sent him one by the name of Rabbi Makir who settled in Narbonne, Southern France, and opened an academy there. But the influence of the latter was much smaller than that of the former. Another tradition relates of an event which took place about two centuries later and which places Italy again in the role of a disseminator of knowledge to Jewries of the world, and which was the immediate cause of the total emancipation of Spain, North Africa, and perhaps even Egypt from the sphere of influence of Babylonia. The story runs as follows. In the year 960, four great men, namely, Rabbi Ḥushiel, Rabbi Shemaryah, Rabbi Moses, and one whose name is unknown, set out from Bari, Southern Italy, in order to collect money for a charitable purpose. On the way, their vessel was captured by Ibn Rumahis, the Admiral of the Caliph of Cordova, Abd-Ar-Rahman. He sold Rabbi Moses and his son Ḥanokh to Cordova, Rabbi Ḥushiel to Kairawan, North Africa, and Rabbi Shemaryah to Alexandria, Egypt. These men established academies at the respective places, and thus severed the last spiritual bond between these Jewries and Babylon. That these scholars were Italians and not emissaries from the Academy at Sura, as former historians assumed,[3] is proved from the fact that immediately upon their arrival the Palestinian Talmud became known in these new centers of learning, while in Babylon it was almost unknown. In Italy, however, which derived its influence from Palestine, it was studied for centuries.

* There is a difference of opinion among scholars whether the tradition refers to Charlemagne or Charles the Bald. I am personally inclined in favor of the opinion that it was Charles the Bald who did the transporting. But as the other opinion has the support of the famous historian Graetz, I mention them both in the text.

[3] Earlier historians, including Graetz, basing themselves on an erroneous interpretation of a few words in the narrative of the four captives in the history of Abraham Ibn Daud (Sefer ha-Kabbala, i. e. tradition), propounded a different theory of the origin of these four scholars. They asserted that they all hailed from Babylon and were sent by the Academy of Sura as emissaries to the Jews of Europe to raise money for the support of the school. But the source mentioned above, which is the only source for the story, does not bear out the theory, while the place of debarkation of the scholars, their destination, and the method of their teaching all speak for Italy as their native place.

These scholars brought with them not only the Palestinian Talmud, but a great store of knowledge of the Babylonian Talmud which was studied for centuries in both Palestine and Italy, and later also in France and Germany. This knowledge seemed to have been of a deep and intense nature, and consisted in penetrating the very meaning of the Talmud. In other words, they prepared the way for real commentaries on this great work.

137. THE KAIRAWAN (North Africa) COMMENTATORS

The intellectual center of North African Jews was the city of Kairawan. Even before the advent of Hushiel, there were Jewish scholars there who devoted considerable time to the study of the Talmud. The Responsa of the Geonim during the tenth century and even earlier contain many inquiries from Kairawan scholars. The famous letter of Sherira Gaon, containing the history of Talmudic tradition, was written as a Responsum to a Kairawan scholar by the name of Jacob. The arrival of Hushiel gave great impetus to study, and soon his labors bore fruit. Hushiel himself left no literary work, but his work was undoubtedly incorporated in that of his son, Hanannel.

Rabbi Hanannel (period of activity 1015–1055), surnamed by later generations, Gaon, is a prominent commentator of the Talmud. It is possible that he wrote a commentary on the entire Talmud, but we have with us only the complete commentary on three orders of the Talmud, Moed, Nashim, and Nezikin, with the exception of the tractate Baba Batra in the last order, of which only fragments exist. Quotations from his commentary on other tractates are given by many later authors.

The method of Hanannel in explaining the Talmud shows improvement upon those of the Gaonic predecessors. He still summarizes the contents of Talmudic passages, but wherever the meaning is difficult, he is more elaborate in his explanation. Especially noteworthy is his use of the Palestinian Talmud for purposes of elucidating difficult subjects. He often compares what was said on a certain subject in the Babylonian with the discussion of the same subject in the Palestinian Talmud, and the comparison helps towards the understanding of the contents of the passage. He makes, in general, extensive use of comparison and seldom neglects to quote what was said about a certain Halakah in other places of the Talmud. Like Hai Gaon, whose explanations he quotes frequently, Hanannel endeavors to rationalize exotic Agadic statements. Other features of his commentary are his interest in history and the endeavor to abstract the practical decision from the flowing discussion of the Talmud. The commentary is strewn with historical notes, and Ḥanannel invariably quotes the *Pesaḳ,* i. e. decision at the end of each discussion. Yet with all its qualities, it is not an all-sufficing commentary. It seems that it was not intended to be such, at least not for beginners. It was meant as an aid to scholars who already possessed considerable knowledge of the Talmud, and one of its chief purposes was the decision of the practical Halakah, i. e. rule of actual conduct. However, with all its shortcomings, Ḥanannel's work proved to be of great help to Talmudic students of his generation. His explanations were extensively quoted by succeeding commentators. He deserves also great credit for his endeavor to obtain the correct readings. In that, he followed to a great extent the traditions of his father who most likely brought with him correct copies of the Talmud from Italy.

The second Talmud commentator of Kairawan was Rabbi Nissim ben Jacob (period of activity 1015–1055), a colleague of Ḥanannel, and like him, a disciple of Ḥushiel. He was likewise given the title Gaon by later writers. It is possible that he wrote commentaries on a large number of tractates as there are a few quotations of his comments on other tractates, such as a lengthy comment quoted in a fragment of a later commentary on tractate *Ḥulin* in the order of *Kadashim.* But we possess only his commentary on the three tractates, *Beraḳot, Shabbat,* and *Erubin.* He named this commentary *Sefer ha-Mafteaḥ* i. e. the Key, and the name is indicative of his method. He primarily elucidates the meaning by comparison with passages from the Palestinian Talmud and other sources, such as the Tannaitic Midrashim, *Sifra, Sifre,* the *Tosefta* (Ch. III). He does this to a greater extent than Ḥanannel, and shows special inclination towards the Palestinian Talmud, often even accepting its opinions against the Babylonian, which indicates a departure from the way of his predecessors. Rabbi Nissim mastered Arabic and used that language to a considerable extent in his commentary.

138. SPANISH COMMENTATORS

The scholastic bloom of North Africa was of short duration. With the passing of Ḥanannel and Nissim, the period of its greatness is closed. Most of the scholars left Northern Africa, and immigrated into neighboring Spain, as was the case with the great Isaac Al-Fasi about whom we will hear later. It is to Spain that we must now turn for the fruits of extensive and intensive Talmudic study.

Moses, one of the four captives, established in Cordova a Talmudic academy which was continued under the presidency of his son, Ḥanokh, and soon other academies were opened in other cities. The eleventh and twelfth centuries which practically mark the Golden Period of Spain in other branches of Jewish literature as we have seen, were also productive in the field of Talmudic study. Many of the great men whose names were mentioned previously as Bible exegetes, grammarians, and poets were also Talmudic scholars, and besides, there were others who specialized in that field alone.

The Talmudic literary activity went on in many directions, codifying, writing Responsa, and commenting on the Talmud, but it seems that the greatest amount of energy was devoted to the first two branches, and only a small share was given to the last one. Of the writings of Rabbi Moses very little was left, only a few Responsa. Of Rabbi Ḥanokh, a later source asserts that he wrote an Arabic commentary on the Talmud, but no trace is left of it to prove the assertion. Some Responsa, however, bearing his name are extant. A great Talmudic scholar was Rabbi Joseph Ibn Abitur, the disciple of Rabbi Moses and competitor of Ḥanokh (Ch. IX). Of him, it is also said that he commentated the entire Talmud in Arabic, but the historical source [4] where the assertion is made does not make it clear whether a commentary or a translation is meant. As the chronicler tells us distinctly that the work was done for the Sultan, we may safely surmise that it was a translation, either of the Mishnah or a part of the Talmud. Ibn Abitur is thus the first translator of the Talmud in another tongue, and also indirectly a commentator, for every translation is also a commentary. Unfortunately, nothing is extant of this work.

The following generation produced a large number of scholars. Rabbi Samuel ha-Levi called ha-Nagid, statesman, grammarian and poet, was also a great Talmudic scholar, and although he did not write any systematic commentary on any of the tractates of the Talmud, he explained many difficult passages in his collection of Halakic decisions which are quoted by later writers.

Of the five distinguished scholars of this generation all bearing the name of Isaac, who flourished in Spain in the eleventh century, each contributed his share towards the explaining of the Talmud. Isaac Ibn

---

[4] *Sefer ha-Kabbala*, i. e. The Book of Tradition, by Abraham Ibn Daud.

Giat (Ch. IX), poet and codifier (Sec. B), is said by Abraham, the son of Moses ben Maimon, to have written a commentary on the Talmud, but nothing is extant of that commentary except a few quotations quoted by Maimonides in his commentary on the Mishnah. Isaac, the son of Baruch Ibn Albalia (1035–1094), astronomer and scientist and also Talmudist, wrote a commentary under the name of *Kupat ha-Roklim,* i. e. the treasure box of the collector, wherein he comments upon especially difficult discussions of the Talmud.[5] The book came down to us in an incomplete state. But even the part we possess, shows the departure of the author in his method of commenting from those who preceded him. It is a real commentary and not merely a collection of notes on difficult words or passages. It displays a penetrating insight into the Talmudic discussion and a tendency to analyze completely the intricate subject matter. Ibn Albalia's method resembles more the Franco-German way of Talmudic study than that of the Spanish scholars, and this. is due to the fact that one of his teachers was a French scholar by the name of Perigora, who immigrated into Cordova. His colleague and contemporary, Isaac ben Reuben, the Barcelonian, is also credited with the writing of a commentary on the tractate *Ketubot,* and possibly on *Erubin.*

The greatest of these five scholars was Isaac ben Jacob Al-Fasi. He was born 1013 in a town near Fez, North Africa, and spent the greater part of his life in that country. Al-Fasi specialized only in Talmudic study and attained eminence in that field. He mastered the Arabic tongue, and wrote a part of his work in that language. In the year 1088, at the age of seventy-five, he was forced to flee his native country and settled in Alisana, Spain, where he opened an academy which was visited by large numbers of students, among them also the poet, Judah ha-Levi. He died in 1103. His great work is the compendium of the Talmud which often bears his name Al-Fasi. This work, though primarily a code as will be evident (Sec. B), contains numerous explanations of difficult passages in the Talmud. Many comments on certain sections of the Talmud are also found in his Responsa and other trea-

[5] As to the peculiar name of the books, it is to be noted that Mediæval authors in all branches of literature very often use euphimistic titles for their works which are at times based on some allusions to Talmudic dicta. The book in question literally means the basket of the peddler, and is derived from the use of the name as a title applied by an Amoraic scholar, in tractate *Gittin* 67a, to a Tanna Johanan ben Nuri. He describes him as a *Kupat ha-Roklim,* i. e. a basket of the peddler which contains all kinds of merchandise to signify that he possesses various kinds of knowledge. In a similar sense did Albalia use the title of his book meaning that it contains knowledge on different subjects. My rendering of it in the text is a rather free one.

tises. Thus Al-Fasi contributed much towards the exegesis of the Talmud, even though he did not write a systematic commentary.

His most distinguished disciple, who impressed his contemporaries with his vast knowledge, was Joseph ha-Levi Ibn Migash (1077–1141). As a youth of twelve, he entered the Yeshibah of Al-Fasi, and for fourteen years, he sat at the feet of the great master whom he succeeded in 1103. His master wrote of him that his knowledge was not exceeded by any scholar of the generation and that even in the time of Moses there was no one like him. Maimonides later writes of him that his erudition was astounding. He wrote commentaries on many tractates of the Talmud, but only two are extant, on *Baba Batra* and *Shebuot*. From these we can see that his method differs but little from that of Rabbi Ḥanannel, namely, that he does not explain the meaning of each paragraph and sentence but paraphrases the contents of the Talmud and thus elucidates the general meaning.

139. MAIMONIDES AS A COMMENTATOR

The greatest commentator that the Spanish school produced was Moses ben Maimon (Biography, Sec. B). He himself tells us that he wrote a commentary on three orders of the Talmud, *Moed, Nashim Nezikin,* and also on *Ḥulin,*[6] but these were either not completed or lost, only one commentary on the tractate *Rosh ha-Shanah* is extant, and it is doubtful whether even that is genuine. On the other hand, we have a complete commentary of his on all the six orders of the Mishnah, and on this work rests his fame as a commentator. He began this work at the age of twenty-three in Spain and completed it ten years later in Egypt working on it through all his wanderings.

In this commentary, as in all his other works, there is seen the systematizing skill of Maimonides, his correct reasoning and logical ability to classify things and subsume subordinate subjects under their general heads. He prefixed the commentary with a general introduction where he treats in a scientific manner the principles of oral law, classifies the *Halaḳot* contained in the Mishnah and explains their division. He then endeavors to find logical reasons for the order of the Mishnah, why the various tractates follow each other in the adopted succession. Finally, he gives a historical survey of the order of tradition, how it was transmitted from generation to generation, and enumerates the successive orders of the *Tannaim* up to Judah ha-Nasi. Maimonides perhaps

[6] Introduction to the commentary on the Mishnah.

lacked a critical historical sense, but he knew well how to systematize all the knowledge he possessed, and because of that his introduction to the Mishnah is a valuable contribution towards its understanding.

There was a fourfold purpose to his commentary: (*1*) To explain to the reader the meaning of each Mishnah, i. e. section, without having recourse to the lengthy discussion of the Talmud. (*2*) To give the Halakic decision in each Mishnah. (*3*) To act as an introduction to the science of the Talmud so that the reader will be prepared by the commentary to understand the Talmud proper. (*4*) To serve as a sort of brief compendium of the subjects discussed in both the Mishnah and the *Gemarah*. He executed all these tasks with remarkable skill. With great agility, he selected from the mass of discussion of the *Gemarah* the very plausible explanations of the Mishnah and incorporated them briefly in his commentary, adding many others both of his predecessors and of his own. At times, he even explains the Mishnah according to its natural meaning, that is, the sense the words convey, without taking into consideration the explanation of the *Gemarah*. As a rule, he does so where the explanation will not change the accepted decision of the Halakah, but there are exceptions to this rule. He also explains the words and expressions grammatically showing their derivation from Hebrew and Aramaic roots. Needless to say that in explaining such subjects where a knowledge of mathematics, astronomy, physics, and medicine is required he drew upon his great fund of knowledge in those sciences, and that in such cases he is the clearest of all commentators.

He renders the decision of the Halakah, namely, whose opinion is accepted, at the end of each Mishnah, wherever such is necessary. Wherever the Mishnah contains a *Setam,* i. e. an anonymous opinion, which as we know is by itself an indication of decision, he is silent. He prefixes, as a rule, an introduction to every tractate, giving the underlying principles of the subjects discussed, and classifies and analyzes them. His introduction to the order of *Taharot* is especially extensive and lucid. There he systematizes all that has been said in Talmudic literature, in the Mishnah, the *Gemarah* and other books, on the subject, namely, of classes, rules and regulations of purity and impurity (Taharah and Tumah). It is a veritable aid to the student of these subjects throughout the Talmud. Maimonides does not neglect the Agada. Whenever he explains an Agadic Mishnah, or in his commentary on *Aboth,* he displays his philosophic skill in drawing out the moral of the statements and systematizing the rules of conduct. His fourth purpose is obtained by the brevity of his style and conciseness and clearness of statements. Maimonides drew in his commentary upon the comments of his predecessors, both Gaonic and non-Gaonic, and often mentions them by name. In his introduction, he mentions that he incorporated many of the explanations of his father, which he, in turn received from Joseph Ibn Migash whose disciple he was.

As the commentary was intended for the ordinary student and reader, it was written in Arabic, and only later, successive parts of it were translated by various scholars, one of whom was the poet, Judah Al Ḥarizi, who translated, at the request of the scholars of Marseilles, the introduction·and the commentary on the order of *Zeraim*.

140. THE ITALIAN AND FRANCO-GERMAN SCHOOLS OF COMMENTATORS (Early Efforts)

As we have seen, an intensive Talmudic study was going on among the West-European Jewries, and generation after generation of scholars sunk their energy in the exploration of the mazes of that literary labyrinth. It is no wonder then that the art of explaining and commenting upon the Talmud reached its highest degree of perfection in these countries, especially in the Franco-German center. We will, therefore, turn our attention to it first, though in point of time, Italy might take precedence.

The early efforts, however, must be surmised at, as very few written records were left. The first commentaries, as in Babylonia, were mostly oral; the teachers explained the Talmud to their pupils in the academies, and these transmitted them in turn to their own pupils. Some time had to elapse before these oral commentaries were put into writing, and in time, even the names of the teachers were forgotten.

The first Talmudic scholar whose comments and decisions are mentioned by the later scholars was Judah ben Meir ha-Kohen, who is more generally known by the name of Leontin (fl. 950–1000). He was the teacher of Rabbi Gershom, and the latter speaks of him with the greatest reverence. He left no written works, but many of his explanations and probably the very method of interpretation were adopted by his great disciple, Gershom. Of this period, we have one attempt in the field of Talmudic commentaries, and even that is more in the field of lexicography than actual commentary. This is the *Aleph-Bet* of Rabbi Makir, the brother of Rabbi Gershom. The book itself is lost, but excerpts are quoted by Rashi and others. From this we can see that it was a dictionary where subjects were alphabetically arranged, hence its name. It explained words and expressions in the way of the *Aruk* of the Gaon, Zemah, and was thus intended as a manual for students.

141. GERSHOM BEN JEHUDAH AND HIS CONTEMPORARIES

The founder of the school of the Franco-German commentators and Talmudic scholars was Gershom ben Jehudah (960–1028), surnamed "The Light of the Exile" (Maor ha-Golah). He was born in France, but later emigrated and settled in Mayence. There he opened an academy which was frequented by hundreds of students, and thus the study of Torah spread to all parts. The influence of Gershom on his generation was exceedingly great as evidenced by his surname. His decrees (Takanot) in matters religious and social were accepted by all European Jewries as irrevocable and perpetual. Of these, the most famous is the prohibition of bigamy among Jews. His institutions were usually strengthened by a ban (Herem), namely, that the one who transgresses them shall be under penalty of ban and excommunication. They are therefore known as the bans of Rabbi Gershom (Herem de Rabenu Gershom).

And great as was his personality, so great was his literary activity. He occupied himself with all fields of Jewish knowledge cultivated in his time, that is Bible, Talmud, and decision of laws. As stated above (Sec. 108), he copied Massoretic lists and endeavored to obtain Bibles that contained correct readings. This same service, and in a greater measure, he rendered for the Talmud. He spent a lifetime in clarifying and establishing the right readings in the Talmud, sparing no efforts in obtaining the most authentic copies from all parts of the world until he succeeded in producing a correct text of the Talmud.

He was not alone in this work in that generation. We know of another scholar in France, Rabbi Joseph Tob Elem (Bonfils) in Limoges, who specialized in preparing Halakic texts. This work was preparatory to the great work of teaching, expounding, and commenting upon the Talmud. Rabbi Gershom taught at the academy for many years, and the result of his teaching was a commentary on the entire Talmud. Parts of it, though, were lost, and we have only the part covering nine tractates. This is published in editions of the Talmud under the name of "Commentary of Rabbi Gershom."

However, this commentary which bears the name of Gershom is really not an individual production, but a work of two generations of scholars. It emanated from his school, and his method, explanations, and comments predominate there, but it is in reality a product of the work of students who frequented academies and in turn became teachers, and passed on their knowledge to their students, and the successive efforts were all incorporated in that commentary. Its proper name should be the "Mayence Commentary." Its history deserves to be briefly told.

When study of the Talmud became intense in the academies of France and Germany, the student, whose whole soul was enwrapped in this fascinating study, began to take notes of the explanations offered by the teacher. These notes were circulated in little booklets called "Cuntres," in plural "Cuntresim," a mispronunciation of the Latin word *commentarius,* a notebook and also commentary. These Cuntresim were individual ones, each student having his own. But as most of them copied what they heard from the teacher or teachers, they bore a similar character, but also possessed a good deal of variation. Students very often added comments which they heard from others, or even wrote down their own remarks. Sometimes, they copied from the notes of their friends and thus added another layer to their Cuntresim. In this way, each academy had its own general adopted "Cuntres," or at the close of Rabbi Gershom's activity, there was most likely a note-commentary on the whole Talmud in the Academy of Mayence which went by the name of "Mayence Cuntres." This "Cuntres" continued to grow during the time of the successors of Gershom, Eliezer the Great (fl. 1050), Isaac ben Judah (fl. 1060) at Mayence, and Jacob ben Yakar and Isaac ha-Levi at Worms. These men were all disciples of Rabbi Gershom and continued to expound the Talmud in his way and manner. They had undoubtedly written their own "Cuntresim" which were incorporated in the one of the academy. As there were several academies, there were undoubtedly several "Cuntresim," but the one of Mayence was the principal one. It became more or less the standardized one. After going through many vicissitudes, it was completed by Eliyakim ben Meshullam, who presided at the Academy of Speyer at the beginning of the twelfth century. It is this "Cuntres of Mayence" which bears now the name of the commentary of Rabbi Gershom, but is really a work of generations. However, inasmuch as Rabbi Gershom was the fount and source from which all this work of commentating emanated, his stamp is impressed upon it and his spirit permeates it. The name it bears is therefore not unfitting.

142. CHARACTERISTICS OF FRANCO-GERMAN METHOD OF TALMUD INTERPRETATION

The French method of commenting upon the Talmud not only strikes a new note in that branch of study, but differs radically from the Spanish method. The latter was distinguished by its systematization and by its tendency to arrive at a practical decision of the Halakah. That method which reached its perfection in the commentary on the Mishnah by Maimonides aimed, as we have seen, at fixing general concepts, and subsuming the particulars under these concepts, and thus arrive at the meaning of the Mishnah or Talmudic passage. Rabbi Ḥanannel, another great representative of the school, recounts briefly the content of the passage, thus bringing closer to the readers the Talmudic discussion, summarizing it for them. The former method, i. e. Franco-German, did not systematize but clung to the text, and busied itself with the particulars, with the explanation of words, expressions, and individual parts of the section. It ran close to becoming a commentary in the narrower sense of the word in its natural form.

The Spanish scholars intended their commentaries for people who study the Talmud occasionally and want to get its general drift without actually penetrating into its mazes. They were written or composed individually. The Franco-German commentaries, on the other hand, were intended for students to whom the study of the Torah was part of life. They grew out of actual teaching in the academy where the pupils sat at the feet of the masters and listened to the expounding of every part of the passage. They were intended as a guide to the student, to encourage him in original study, to call forth in his mind by his own efforts the concept of the entire section or subject discussed. They, thus, acted as an incentive for further penetration into the depths of the Talmud. Moreover, the Franco-German method aimed at bringing the student into the world of the Talmud, to identify him with its spirit, to acquaint him with its intricacies, and then let him become a denizen in its strange world. It did so by leading him step by step, by giving him details, but not the entire content, leaving the student to find that for himself. And the students at these academies to whom the Talmud was the very part and parcel of their lives, did really dive into the great sea and explored all its mysteries, and in turn became guides to future generations. It was thus that the most perfect of the Franco-German commentaries became an inseparable part of the Talmud.

143. SOLOMON BEN ISAAC (Yizhaki, Rashi)

Solomon ben Isaac of Troyes (for life see Sec. 109) was, as we have seen above, destined by Providence itself to be the great commentator of the ages. But while as a commentator of the Bible, his work, in spite of its greatness, lacks perfection, and is here and there surpassed by others, as a Talmud commentator, he stands supreme and unexcelled. The world of the Talmud was his world, and he felt perfectly at home there, and that is the reason that he succeeded in interpreting it to others. Rashi did not aspire to be considered a great authority in rendering Halakic decisions. If he gave them, it was only under compulsion, and he concentrated his whole soul on his commentary. He began his work as a student. Coming to Worms to study under Jacob ben Yakar, the disciple of Rabbi Gershom, he began to prepare his own "Cuntres." There, he not only noted down what he heard from his teacher, but also copied from many other sources. He continued this work at Mayence, whither he went after he left Worms, to study under Isaac ben Judah and there he completed his first draft of his commentary. Although in this draft there is extensive copying from the current "Cuntresim" of the day, and especially from the one of Mayence, yet the originality of Rashi is already evident in his choice of material and brevity and lucidity of style.

On completing his first draft, the inexhaustible toiler set forth to revise his entire work, and the revision began in Mayence and was completed at home in Troyes. There he added all new explanations that occurred to him and also introduced the corrected readings which he found in improved manuscripts, filled out the gaps, extended the short remarks into lengthy ones, and brought the whole work up to the standard of a commentary.

When Rashi became a teacher himself and for many years expounded the Talmud to hundreds of students, it was then that the third and final edition was undertaken and almost brought to completion. This edition grew gradually from the daily study in the academy and was brought forth through the needs of the students. Every passage was scrutinized, every expression tested and weighed, doubtful readings examined and better ones substituted, the style improved, and thus it became an ideal commentary.

It is this third edition of the commentary which was largely left to the succeeding generations and appended to the Talmud editions. Rashi's commentary extends on the whole Talmud with the exception of a large part of the tractate *Baba Batra* and of a small part of *Makot*. On most of the tractates it is the third edition which is extant but on several tractates we have only the first draft, such as Rashi's commentaries on *Ta'anit* and *Moed Katan,* and the commentary on the tenth chapter of *Pesahim.* Two tractates contain Rashi's commentaries. in the edition of his disciples, and lack the perfection of the hand of the master; such are those on *Nedarim* and *Nazir.* With these exceptions, and it is almost certain that these leaks were due only to the negligence of the copyists, for quotations prove that the improved editions of Rashi's commentaries extended also on these tractates, Rashi's work embraced the entire Talmud.

The unique character of Rashi's commentary on the Talmud is due not only to the fact that he carried the French method of commentation to its highest degree, but primarily to his own personality and originality. Of course, he borrowed material extensively from his predecessors, but even the borrowed material is stamped with his genius. A great commentator must possess, first of all, as we noted, spiritual affinity with the subject and the author, second, great knowledge, and third, pedagogic ability.

Rashi possessed all these and more, and that is an intuitive sense for divining the true meaning of the subject or passage. As for his Talmudic affinity, he possessed it in a remarkable degree, and it was this that made him divine the sense of a complicated subject at a glance. And equally wonderful was his knowledge; it embraced the entire Talmudic literature, all that was written in that field, both Talmuds, the Tannaitic Midrashim, Gaonic commentaries, and all other books. All that could have been gotten in his time out of books, bearing directly and indirectly on the Talmud, was stored up in his mind, and when a passage came up for consideration, all repetitions of that passage in other places in the Talmud or elsewhere, the changes occurring there in reading or expression, various explanations offered, were unrolled before his mental eye and difficulties vanished by themselves. He drew extensively upon his knowledge in all fields. Greater than all was his pedagogic ability displayed in his method. In his method, there is an harmonious blending of induction and deduction. He explains every word, every expression, slowly by degrees, and thus busies himself with the particular, but at the same time, he explains also the meaning of the entire passage which is interwoven in the explanation of the parts. He varies his method according to the needs; at times he explains the entire expression first, and then each word, and at times the reverse. Rashi utilized all pedagogic means; he employed considerably the method of apperception, explaining the unknown by the known, very often using similies, comparisons, and other devices. He carefully selects the key expression or concept in a complicated subject, and as soon as this key is found and made known, the other dependent thoughts are clarified by themselves. When certain thoughts or ideas cannot be rendered understandable without lengthy analyses and explanations, he substitutes instead other representations which are only hints or symbols but contain briefly the entire order of thoughts. These symbols are further clarified. He is very careful to guide the student in his studies. The Talmud contains no punctuation system, no question marks, and wherever a doubtful remark occurs, he points out whether it should be read as a question or not. When the discussion is very complicated and the repartee between the scholars confusing, one asks and the other answers, Rashi informs the reader as to who is the inquirer and who replies. He thus supplies to the inexperienced student the thread which guides him in the mazes of the labyrinth of the Talmud. In explaining the meaning of a passage Rashi is very concise and limits himself to the subject in hand, without encumbering the reader with unnecessary repetition of what has gone before or information on what is to follow. Only when a knowledge of what follows is required for the understanding of the passage does he give a succinct account of it.

Whenever necessary, Rashi explains the rules of Talmudic hermeneutics, i. e. the regulations by which laws were deduced as well as that of the discussion. He supplies historical data in a sufficient measure necessary for the understanding of the subjects discussed. He also endeavors to describe the customs of the times, determines the location of geographic places with as much accuracy as he could, according to the state of knowledge at the time. In short, he did not neglect any point in the Talmud which required explanation.

His great and deep knowledge of the Bible and his linguistic sense helped him to explain the verses quoted in the Talmud and their interpretation. It stood him especially in good stead when he came to explain the Agadic passages. In the explanation of the Agada, he was also greatly helped by his knowledge of the Midrashim, and he often explained difficult passages in the Talmud by parallels in the many Midrashic collections.

A few words should also be said about his wonderful style. Rashi had not only brevity and conciseness, but the happy quality of proportion. In spite of his unlimited knowledge, he was careful not to burden the student with details, nor on the other hand, was he sparing of words when it was required. He always managed to crystallize his thoughts and centralize his ideas into few central and important concepts which included them all. In this, he was a veritable master. No wonder then, that with all the qualities the commentary possessed, it became *The Commentary* of the Talmud.

The greater part of the commentary or the "Cuntres" of Rashi was left by him in almost a completed state, namely, in the third edition. His disciples, however, prepared a kind of fourth edition. They copied his manuscripts carefully, with great love, correcting technical errors, obtaining the best copies and comparing notes. In such tractates where the commentary was left in the stage of the first or the second draft with a multitude of notes at the bottom, they recast it and included the notes in the text. Thus, after a few years, the "Cuntres" or commentary of Rashi received its final stamp of completion and has thus come down the ages.

144. COMMENTATORS OF THE SCHOOL OF RASHI

With the death of Rashi and the completion of his commentary, the Talmud was considered no more a closed book, and the need for its explanation greatly diminished. The intellectual energy of the great scholars was, therefore turned in a different direction. But still, here and there, some disciples were found who continued the work of the master, and their chief interest lay in filling the few gaps left open by the teacher. Thus, we see Judah ben Nathan (end of the eleventh and beginning of twelfth centuries), the son-in-law of Rashi, complete the commentary on the tractate *Makot* of which five folios were left unfinished by Rashi. He also wrote or edited the commentary on the tractate *Nazir* which bears the name of Rashi. But he showed little originality in his work as he was more of a compiler than a real commentator.

Of greater originality as a commentator was another disciple of Rashi, his grandson, Samuel ben Meir, known briefly as *Rashbam,* initials of

Rabbi Samuel ben Meir. He, as we have seen above (Sec. 110), possessed great ability as a commentator, for his commentary on the Pentateuch is of high character, and he likewise employed his ability in explaining such portions of the Talmud as were uncommentated. He completed the commentary on the greater part of the tractate *Baba Batra* left unfinished by Rashi (about 150 folios) and also on the tenth chapter of *Pesahim* where Rashi is very brief. Samuel ben Meir utilized the notes of Rashi, but added many ingenious explanations of his own. He adopted the method of his grandfather and is very lucid and clear but he could not imitate his wonderful style. He is verbose and confuses the reader with an excessive number of details. It seems, though, that besides completing the commentary of his grandfather, he also wrote commentaries on other tractates, but only fragments are left. Another disciple of Rashi, Rabbi Shemayah, filled the last gap in his master's work, and wrote a commentary on the tractate *Midot*, i. e. measurements, dealing with the measurements of various buildings and parts of the Temple. This tractate contains only *Mishnayot*, but no *Gemarah*. He quotes him often and seems to have utilized his notes.

145. THE TOSAFISTS

As was noted, the completion of the commentary of Rashi freed a great quantity of intellectual energy, which was hitherto spent in ascertaining the meaning of the Talmud, and this energy had to be employed by the scholars in another, though allied, field. And it did not take long and the field was found. It is that of the *Tosofot,* which literally means additions. The *Tosofot,* the writers of which were called Tosafists, continued to be the chief literary productions of the Franco-German academies for a period of over one hundred and fifty years. They began to appear even in the lifetime of Rashi and continued to the middle of the fourteenth century. The name is a generic one, and includes a number of things, comments, supercomments on commentaries, discussion and analysis, as well as decisions on points of law. But the *Tosofot,* like the commentaries, centered around the Talmud, and hence can be classed as a form of commentaries, though they are really not so in content.

The principal characteristic of these hundreds of additions and glosses, is really implied in the very name, *Tosofot,* which was already used in early times, such as the *Tosefta* (Sec. 50) which was intended to complete the Mishnah. Likewise, these *Tosofot* were meant to broaden and complete the Talmudic discussions contained in the *Gemarah,* and to clarify and explain them.

The writing of the *Tosofot* was really an attempt to revive the very spirit of the Talmud, the vivacity, depth, and brilliancy of its discussion. That unique kind of discussion which we find in the *Gemarah* had been slumbering for centuries, and was reborn in Northern France, Lorraine, and other Rhine provinces. Hitherto, the Talmud was considered a closed book, and all that was left was either to systematize its content, or to establish rules and explain its passages. But now when the work of mere commenting was done, the keen-minded French and German scholars decided that the Talmud, as a text, may be closed, but the science of the Talmud and its methods were not closed.

The methods of the Tosafists were very similar to the method of the *Gemarah* in relation to the Mishnah. The *Gemarah* is indeed a commentary on the Mishnah, but not a mere commentary; it is a new creation where analysis is employed to the fullest extent, discussion widens to include a multitude of new subjects and the peacefully flowing stream of the Mishnah turns into a roaring sea of the Talmud. In the same way, can the *Tosofot* be called a commentary on the Talmud.

The work started with criticism of the commentaries. In its very beginning, the older "Cuntresim" were taken as the basis of criticism, their explanations were scrutinized and tested, refuted or corrected. But soon Rashi's "Cuntres" was substituted—the Tosafists always refer to his commentary as "The Cuntres"—and it became the basis for addition and discussion. However, this forms only a small part of the *Tosofot.* The main purpose was to delve into the Talmudic discussion itself, to analyze every part of it, to remove all possible difficulties, to straighten out all contradictions, and to draw sharp distinctions between concepts. These scholars were not satisfied with merely understanding the difficult passages of the Talmud, but raised difficulties themselves by pointing out those arising from contrasting one passage with another, and then set out to remove the contradictions.

This method which is often called *pilpul,* i. e. peppery (pilpal, in Talmudic language means a pepper), and is the Hebrew equivalent for scholasticism, is frequently severely criticized and is considered useless effort, but it has great advantage if used properly. In fact, it was the very method of the Talmudists, the *Amoraim,* and the same method was developed by the Tosafists to its fullest extent. It brought fruitful results, it opened limitless fields for the exercise of the intellect of the scholars, it deepened and broadened the understanding of the Talmud, and finally, it brought forth new decisions in Halakah, inasmuch as the clearer, deeper understanding of the intricacies of the Talmud greatly facilitated the arrival at a decision.

The *Tosofot* also resemble the Talmud in their arrangement and order. Like the latter, it is a work of generations and is a composite of many parts. A large number of scholars contributed towards its composition, and finally it was arranged as a unified composition, covering the entire Talmud. It was the work of editors and compilers who pieced together the various parts into one whole. Originally, each scholar wrote *Tosofot* on one or more tractates or even on parts of them. These contained comments, objections (Kushiot), and answers to the objections, logical distinctions and many similar matters. The students who copied the additions of the master often carried these notes to other academies where they were seen by other masters and students, and these refuted the objections of the others, solved their problems and offered explanations. Thus, there was a constant interchange of opinion, and the objections or difficulties raised by the scholars in one academy were known in the other, and the whole mass of discussion became the common property of the scholarly world. It was, therefore, possible, like in the time of the Talmud, that a scholar in one city should answer an objection to a Talmudic statement raised by a scholar in another city, and the other in turn offer a refutation of the answer. Most of the *Tosofot* were composed, like Rashi's commentaries, in the academies, in the course of teaching and bear the character of public discussion, one asking and the other answering, and the third endeavoring to reconcile the opinions of both. There were, therefore, many editions of the *Tosofot* bearing different names. The later compilers selected various parts from the great mass of *Tosofot* notebooks, and arranged them in order on each page of the Talmud, dividing it in sections. The sections are also composed of parts, a question or objection of one scholar and an answer from another scholar, very often the answer being given by a scholar of another generation. On the whole, there is not much anonymity in the *Tosofot,* both the names of the ones who raise the objections, and those who remove the difficulties are frequently given. But that there are anonymous statements issuing from the compilers or from other scholars, is needless to say.

The *Tosofot* in their last form as appended to the Talmud are, as said, arranged in sections. Each section bears as a heading a short quotation from the Talmud, indicating the beginning of the passage to be discussed. In most cases, the discussion begins with an objection, pointing out a difficulty, and then a solution is offered, sometimes several. At times a refutation to the answer is given, and another answer offered. There are technical terms for the questions and answers. The first is introduced by *Tema,* i. e. "it is to be wondered at," or by *We-'Im Tomar,* i. e. "in case you say so," namely, in case you anticipate a difficulty, I am ready with an answer. Often the plainer form *We-Koshe,* i. e. "it is difficult," is used. The second is introduced by *We-Yesh Lomar,* "it may be said or answered." Quite frequently, the *Tosofot* begin with a statement from Rashi whose opinion is criticized, refuted, and another explanation offered; on another occasion, a plain explanation of the Talmudic passage is offered, then analyzed and critically tested. At times, the correctness of a reading (Girsa) is discussed, and either it is retained or a better one substituted, for as said, critical commentation was an important function of the Tosafists. In conclusion, we may say, that the *Tosofot* are permeated with a spirit of logical acumen, brilliancy of intellect and vivacity which calls for the deepest interest of the student. And not in vain did they exercise a magnetic power over generations of students, and for centuries, in all published editions of the Talmud and in hundreds of manuscripts, the *Tosofot* occupy the same page with the *Gemarah* itself, opposite Rashi's commentary.

146. COMPOSERS OF TOSOFOT

The leaders of the *Tosofot* activity were all of the family of Rashi. The very first one to write *Tosofot* was Rabbi Meir of Rameru, the son-in-law of Rashi. He is quoted by his son, Rabbi Jacob, a number of times. He was surpassed by his three sons, Samuel (1080–1140), Jacob (1096–1171), and Isaac (fl. 1150). These three impressed their personality upon this literature. In the printed *Tosofot* on the Talmud, they are mentioned frequently, the first by the name of *Rashbam,* Rabbi Samuel ben Meir; the second, by the name of *Rabénu Tam,* i. e. the innocent, or the perfect one, a surname given him on account of his piety and exceptional erudition; the third by the name of *Ribom,* i. e. Rabbi Isaac ben Meir.

The greatest of the three was Rabbi Tam. He can be said to represent in his own personality the essence of the *Tosofot* spirit and was the very soul of it. Born at Rameru where he received his education from his father and older brother Samuel, he also studied for a time in

Limoges at the academy of Joseph Tob Elem the second. He later opened an academy in his native town whence his fame spread throughout Jewry, so that he was considered the leading authority in his age. His word was law, and his decrees (Takanot) were accepted without murmur. In 1147, on the first day of the Feast of Weeks, Crusaders broke into his house and dragged him out with the intention to kill him or force him into conversion. A knight of his acquaintance who happened to pass by saved him from their hands by taking him into custody. Rabénu Tam shortly afterwards moved to Troyes where he died on the ninth of June, 1171.

His chief work is the *Sefer ha-Yashar,* namely, "The Book of the Righteous," which contains his *Tosofot* on thirty tractates as well as legal decisions. But this was not all; his comments and critical remarks on the entire Talmud were spread by word of mouth among the thousands of Talmudic students in the academies, and close to a thousand were incorporated in our *Tosofot.* His greatness lies in the keenness of his mind. He typifies in his "Additions," the *Tosofot* method which, as was remarked, is a return to the method of the *Amoraim* themselves. He penetrated to the very depths of the Halakah, no thread of that intricate web escaped his mind. His method is purely analytical; every statement was tested whether its difficulties could be removed. If the statement, hypothesis, or opinion stood the test it was pronounced correct. Raising objections and answering them was therefore his favorite method of study. His motto was, there must be no difficulty in the Talmud, no contradiction—the words of the Rabbis are faultless. If contradictions occurred, they must be removed. His purpose was not mere mental casuistry, but to elicit by this method the real truth. We, therefore, see him very often turn mere commentator and explain whole pages of *Gemarah.* He also endeavored to ascertain the proper readings, and was very severe with those who carelessly emended books without first ascertaining whether the reading was really faulty. He himself made many corrections in the Talmud, relying mostly upon the Spanish copies, but with great deliberation. Taking into consideration all his accomplishments in the field of scholarship, it is no wonder then that he is quoted in the *Tosofot* almost on every page, and often several times, and that his name is inherently connected with the study of the Talmud.

Another great Tosafist, whose name is likewise mentioned almost on every page of the printed *Tosofot,* is Rabbi Isaac ben Samuel of Dampierre, France (fl. 1175). He can be considered the second influential personality after Rabénu Tam in the Tosafist activity. Besides the large number of comments, he is also distinguished by the keenness of his mind which expresses itself in the happy ability to solve difficulties and straighten out contradictions. He was the nephew of Tam, being his sister's son, and undoubtedly was greatly influenced by him. He is usually quoted under the name *Ri,* i. e. Rabbi Isaac, and very often *Ri ha-Zoken,* i. e. Isaac the elder, to distinguish him from other scholars who bore the name Isaac. He wrote *Tosofot* on a number of tractates, which are quoted by later authors. The comments quoted in our *Tosofot* are largely taken from these, plus the hundreds of oral remarks incorporated in the final *Tosofot* compilation.

The other outstanding Tosafists are: Isaac ben Asher ha-Levi (fl. 1150) of Speyer, quoted by his initials *Riba,* i. e. Rabbi Isaac ben Asher, who wrote and compiled *Tosofot* on many tractates; Rabbi Eliezer ben Nathan of Mayence, quoted by the name of *Reban;* Isaac ben Mordecai of Regensburg (fl. 1175); Eliezer ben Samuel of Metz (1195); Isaac ha-Laban, the white one, of Prague (1175), quoted frequently in our *Tosofot* under the name of *Ri ha-Laban,* who also wrote *Tosofot* of his own and a commentary on the tractate of *Ketubot;* Judah ben Isaac of Paris (b. 1166–d. 1224) named Sir Leon; and Baruch ben Isaac of Regensburg. The last is said to be the compiler of our *Tosofot* on tractate *Zebaḥim,* dealing with the rites of sacrifices, and also wrote *Tosofot* on other tractates. Finally, at the end of the twelfth century, we have Isaac ben Abraham of Rameru, France, who is quoted under the name of Rizba, i. e. Rabbi Isaac ben Abraham (d. 1205).

The prominent Tosafists of the thirteenth century—the activity is prolonged to that century, and no dividing line can be drawn—are: Simon ben Abraham of Sens (d. 1235 in Acco, Palestine), the compiler of our *Tosofot* on tractates *Shabbat* and *Menaḥot,* besides a special collection known as *Sens Tosofot;* Moses of Coucy (d. 1245) compiler of *Tosofot* known as *Old Tosofot;* Samuel of Evreux (1245), compiler of the printed *Tosofot* on tractate *Sotah,* besides a collection of his own; Isaac of Corbeil (fl. 1270), quoted frequently in our *Tosofot;* Eliezer of Toucques, author of a collection under the name of *Tosofot Tuk* from which our *Tosofot* on tractates *Ḥulin* and *Gittin* are taken; Meir ben Baruch of Rothenburg (fl. 1270–1293) (Sect. B); and Rabbi Perez ben Elijah of Corbeil. This Rabbi Perez is one of the last compilers of the printed *Tosofot*. The edition of *Tosofot* on six tractates: *Bezah, Nadarim, Nazir, Sanhedrin, Makot,* and *Meila* came from his collection. Besides those enumerated, there were many more scholars who contributed to the *Tosofot* and whose works were incorporated in their various versions.

The *Tosofot* printed in our Talmud edition cover thirty-eight tractates of the Talmud and were compiled by various men. We know only the names of the compilers on sixteen tractates. To the list of authors named above, we may add Moses of Evreux, brother of Samuel (1245), who compiled the *Tosofot* on Berakot, and Samuel of Falaise (1245) who compiled the same on tractate *Abodah Zarah*. The rest bear an anonymous character. Besides those printed in the Talmud edition, there are several collections of *Tosofot* in manuscripts under different names. They are (a) *Old Tosofot,* including the Sens collection compiled by Simon ben Abraham, and separate treatises by various men; (b) *Tuk Tosofot* collection, compiled as stated above by Eliezer of Toucques; (c) *External Tosofot,* a later collection, and (d) *Marginal Tosofot,* glosses and additions to the standard collection. These are the principal collections, but there are also a large number of smaller ones, individual glosses on one or more tractates. These belong mostly to the last period of the Tosafist activity, namely, the beginning of the fourteenth century, when it dwindled down to mere individual efforts and lost its intensity and vigor.

147. TALMUD COMMENTATORS IN ITALY AND THE PROVENCE

The study of the Talmud in Italy was very intense for centuries, and in the dim centuries of the early Middle Ages, Italy was the source of Torah for almost all the countries of Western Europe, as we saw above. But, unfortunately, the names of the scholars were forgotten. Only in the early part of the tenth century, we hear of one Jacob Gaon, the head of an academy at Rome. Later in that century, a few more scholars are mentioned, one of whom is Rabbi Mazliah Albazek of Sicily. He is said to have had communication with Hai Gaon of Babylonia, but none of his books are left, except some stray comments on Talmudic passages which are quoted by his successors. Other scholars of this age were Moses Halfo of Bari, and Yehiel of Rome whose comments were also incorporated in the works of their successors.

148. NATHAN BEN YEHIEL OF ROME

At the end of the tenth century, there arose in Italy a man whose contribution both to the lexicography and the exegesis of the Talmud is of great and lasting value. This man was Nathan ben Yehiel (1020–1106) of Rome. He was remarkably equipped for his great task, as hardly anyone in his generation surpassed him in knowledge of Talmudic literature. No passage or statement in any of the books of this mass of literature escaped his attention, whether Halakic or Agadic. Besides he was a linguist who mastered a number of languages, Hebrew, Aramaic, Arabic, Latin, and even some Greek. His teachers in Talmud and Agada were Rabbi Mazliah of Sicily, Rabbi Moses ha-Darshan (the preacher) of Narbonne (Ch. VIII), and Rabbi Gershom, the Light of the Exile. Nathan's great work is the *Aruk,* a lexicon and dictionary of all the words of Talmudic literature, alphabetically arranged.

It is really not a mere dictionary, but a veritable encyclopedia, as not only does Rabbi Nathan quote, as examples, passages from the entire Talmudic and Midrashic literature including the Targumic where such words and expressions are found, but he also explains the passages. It is thus an alphabetical commentary. In his explanations, he quotes comments from all great men of his time, and also from many Geonim. He, therefore, preserved for us hundreds of documents from scholars which would otherwise have been lost, as the works from which they are excerpted are lost. Great value is also attached to his quotations from many Talmudic and Agadic books, for besides that they contain correct readings in many places where our editions are erroneous, there are numerous quotations from books, especially Agadic ones which are lost, and their existence can be traced only through these quotations. Likewise valuable are his lexicographic remarks, as he gives the origin of hundreds of words and expressions in Talmudic literature, and traces their sources to various Semitic languages, to the various *Targumim,* some of which are lost, and also offers Latin and Greek parallels. In addition he supplies many data of historical importance, comments on customs and ways of Jewish life in his own and former times.

In his arrangements, he follows the biliteral system of Hebrew roots, the one adopted by the French and German scholars, and followed by Rashi, and most of his words are arranged in accordance with the biliteral view, but he also believes that there are a number of roots of one letter only. There are many more services performed by this work, but that would require giving many details. In general, it may be said that the *Aruk* is the basis of all modern lexicographical works on the Talmud, for without his comments, and especially without the vast material of examples from the entire Talmudic, Targumic and Agadic literature collected there, no modern scholar could have undertaken the writing of a dictionary of the Talmud.

The *Aruk* was published in many editions, and later with additions and improvements. The most noted editions are the ones published at Amsterdam in 1655, which contains the additions by Benjamin Musfia, a physician at Hamburg, where all words derived from Greek and Latin are lucidly explained, and their derivation traced, and that of Dr. Alexander Kohut bearing the name of *Aruch Completum,* in eight volumes, where the *Aruk* is much enlarged by many additions and the meaning of the words given in German.

A younger contemporary of Rabbi Nathan was a commentator of the Mishnah, Rabbi Isaac, son of Malki Zedek, or as he is called Rabbi Isaac of Simponto. He wrote commentaries on the first and last orders of the Mishnah, i. e. *Zeraim* and *Taharot.* His commentaries are brief and intended only to explain the meaning of the passages, and his method is similar to that of Rashi. It is not known whether he had seen Rashi's commentary or not, as we know very little about him and cannot determine his time accurately. But from the quotations by other scholars, we can safely assume that he lived not later than the first half of the twelfth century.

The Tosafist activity also found an echo in Italy. It seems that the twelfth century was a period of intensive Talmudic study there, and at the end of the century, the results became evident. A large number of scholars arose, and the greatest of them was Rabbi Isaiah di Trani (1180–1260). He hailed from the city of Trani in the province of Bari, an old center of Jewish learning, but lived most of his life at Venice. He distinguished himself both as commentator and Tosafist of the Talmud. He wrote *Tosofot* on a large number of tractates under the name of *Tosofot Rid,* i. e. Rabbi Isaiah di Trani. A large portion of his *Tosofot* is still extant in manuscript; those on two tractates, *Kidushin* and *Ketubot,* are published. In his additions he adopted both methods, that of Rashi and that of the Tosafists. They contain a large number of plain and lucid explanations, but also much analytic and pilpulistic remarks, in the way of the French Tosafists. Whenever he turns commentator, he uses a clear style and displays great ability in explaining knotted passages. He also utilized secular sciences in clarifying Talmudic subjects and was not ashamed to consult specialists in those sciences on difficult points. He was a great lover of truth, and expressed his opinion without bowing to authority. Isaiah di Trani was the outstanding Talmudic scholar in Italy during the thirteenth century and his authority was recognized by all, even outside the bounds of Italy. He also wrote codes and decisions, but of those later.

149. THE PROVENCE SCHOOL OF COMMENTATION—ZERAHYAH HA-LEVI.

That part of Southern France, which in Mediæval Ages was known as the Provence, was slowly developing during the eleventh and twelfth centuries into a great center of Jewish learning and literature. Being situated between the three great intellectual centers, Spain, Italy, and Franco-Germany, it was destined to be a meeting point for the different views and systems of various literary currents, and fortunately its scholars knew how to utilize the opportunity and blend those currents into an harmonious stream. We have noted already (Chas. VII, VIII), the contribution of the Provence to grammar, lexicography, and Biblical exegesis, and we will now survey briefly its contribution to Talmudic study. Like their brethren in the north of France, the Jews of the Provence considered the study of the Talmud the highest degree of perfection, and its study was intense. There were many academies in a number of cities—at Narbonne an old center of learning (see above), Lunel, and other places, as well as great scholars, of whom a very prominent one was Zerahyah ha-Levi of Lunel.

Rabbi Zerahyah (b. 1125 d. 1186) was born in Spain, but his family having immigrated to Girondi in the Provence, he followed them there, studied at Narbonne, and ultimately settled at Lunel, which was also the residence of the Tibbon family, the famous translators, and many more scholars. Zerahyah was considered a great authority in his generation, and his erudition was profound.

He can be considered a commentator of the Talmud indirectly. His chief work is the Sefer ha-Maor, i. e. the book of light or luminary.[7] It is primarily a critical commentary containing additions to the Com-

---

[7] We already noted that the euphuistic names of the books written by Mediæval authors contain some hidden meaning. In the case of Zerahyah, the name of ha-Maor refers both to his own name which in Hebrew means shining and to the name of his city, i. e. Lunel meaning the moon. This city is very often quoted by authors as Yoreah, Hebrew for moon, which is a Hebrew translation of the French name. His book has two parts ha-Maor ha-Katan, smaller luminary, i. e. moon, and ha-Maor ha-Godol, i. e. sun, referring to his own name, Zerahyah.

pendium of the Talmud by Isaac Al-Fasi (Sec. B.). But as this Compendium contains a large part of the Talmud, his commentary and remarks explain whole sections of the Talmud. Zerahyah displays keen mental acumen in his commentary. He analyzes sharply the views and decisions of former scholars, especially those of Al-Fasi, Rashi, and other authorities. His love for truth was unbounded, and he takes as his motto in his introduction to his book *ha-Maor* the maxim of the ancients, "I love Plato, I love Aristotle, but love the truth more than both of them." This motto expresses his attitude towards his predecessors. He speaks of them with reverence but criticizes their opinions and views with remarkable openness and frankness. Rabbi Zerahyah was also a noted religious poet and wrote many poems in meter and rhyme, and a number of them are included in the Maḥzor of the Sephardic Jews.

150. ABRAHAM BEN DAVID OF POSQUIERS

The other distinguished Provence scholar of this generation was Abraham ben David of Posquiers (1125–1198). His erudition was great and equally great his piety. Unlike other Provence scholars, he devoted very little time to other studies but concentrated all his energy on the study of the Talmud and law. Being a rich man, he utilized his wealth in the spreading of the knowledge of the Torah as he practically supported all the students of the academy who were in need of aid. His name spread far and wide, and his authority was recognized by scholars of many lands.

His work expressed itself primarily in criticism of the methods and views of the commentators and codifiers. He wrote critical remarks to the Compendium of Al-Fasi, refutations of the *ha-Maor* of Zeraḥyah ha-Levi, and is especially famous for his refutation of the Code of Maimonides. On account of this tendency, and especially of his belligerent style in his refutations, he was named *Rabad* (Rabbi Abraham ben David), "Master of Refutation." But he was also a good and productive commentator. He wrote commentaries on a number of tractates of the Mishnah. His commentaries on *Eduyyot, Kinim,* and *Tamid* are published. His method as a commentator is close to the pilpulistic one, as he not only explains the *Mishnayot,* but also offers a number of explanations to a passage and tests each by attempting to refute them until he finds the one which cannot be refuted. He displays wide knowledge of Talmudic literature in all its phases and draws upon all sources for elucidation of a passage. In general, it seems that he did not intend his commentary for students but for scholars, and is therefore at times very deep and difficult. But the scholar who is already versed in the ways of the Talmud will find great joy in his penetrating and all-embracive method. He was also the first man who turned his attention to commentate other Halakic books besides the Talmud. He wrote a commentary on the *Sifra,* the Tannaitic Halakic Midrash on Leviticus. His commentary on that book is a very clear and lucid one and made the book accessible to students. There he also included an extensive commentary on the Baraita (Sec. 57) of the Thirteen *Midot,* i. e. rules or norms of the interpretation of the Bible (Pt. I, Ch. III) where he discusses the application of these rules in the formation of the Halakah.

B. Codes

151. EARLY ATTEMPTS

The Mishnah, as we have seen (Ch. V), was not only a textbook of Halakic study, but also indirectly a code. The Talmud, however, or more specifically the *Gemarah,* was not a code. It analyzed and commented the Mishnah and added many things to it, but left no definite decisions, only occasionally indicating the decision. With the close of the Talmud there was still a want for a clear-cut practical code. But the need was not felt, for the *Saburaim,* the successors of the *Amoraim,* were too close to the Talmud, and they could orientate themsèlves in it, and arrive at practical decisions in the Talmud proper. The only thing that these *Saburaim* did was to compile certain rules for decision, namely, indicating who of the *Amoraim* is more reliable and whose opinion is to be preferred. These rules are incorporated in the Talmud itself and are ascribed to these very *Saburaim.* Thus, we see that very little was done in the way of code making during the first two centuries after the close of the Talmud.

Yet, some attempts were made at codification even in these early times. Of these there should be considered the seven small tractates which were added after the close of the Talmud during the time of the Saburaim or early Gaonic period. These are: (1) *Sefer Torah* (rules for writing of the Scrolls; (2) *Mezuzah;* (3) *Tefilin* (phylacteries); (4) *Zizit* (fringes); (5) *'Abadim* (on slaves); (6) *Kutim* (Samaritans); (7) *Gérim* (proselytes). As can be seen, they all deal with practical questions, and to a great extent with ritual, for with the exception of the tractate on the Samaritans which is most likely of Palestinian origin, they are all of a practical nature, as even the questions of treatment of slaves and the acceptance of proselytes were of daily concern. To these should be added the tractate of *Soferim* dealing with the rules of writing the Holy Scroll, as well as phylacteries and other sacred writings, and also with the synagogue ritual. All these small tractates are really attempts at partial codification, for the matters dealt with there are given in the form of decisions, and no differences of opinion are quoted. As a rule, the opinions are given anonymously, but even if quoted in the name of a *Tanna* or *Amora,* only the statement is given.

There are also several books of decisions of Gaonic origin; one of them is called *Shimusha Rabba,* i. e. the "Large Book of Practice." A considerable fragment of it is contained in the writings of the early codifiers. It deals with the laws of phylacteries and most likely with other subjects.

152. BABYLONIAN CODES

As years passed, the need for a code or codes was felt more and more. From distant places, where the study of the Talmud was just in its beginning, there came constant inquiries to the Geonim in Babylonia concerning practical decisions. The inquirers asked for rules of action. The first Responsa (Sect. C) gave short answers to the correspondents and tendered decisions. These Responsa too belong partly to the code literature. But soon in Babylonia proper, the need arose in equal measure, for no more did people live in the atmosphere of the Talmud. It thus happened that during the second half of the eighth century, three codes were produced by men who were practically contemporaries.

The first of these is the *Sheiltot,* (Problems), by Rabbi Aḥai Gaon (fl. 748–760). Rabbi Aḥai, though a leading scholar in the Academy of Pumbedita, was not, for some political reason, appointed as the head of the Academy at the death of Rab Samuel in 756. His disciple, Rab Natrui, was appointed instead. This slight on the part of the Exilarch (Resh Galuta) angered the master, and Rab Aḥai left Babylonia and settled in Palestine. It is not, however, definitely known where he wrote the *Sheiltot* whether in Babylonia in his younger years, or in Palestine. The form of the *Sheiltot* points to the time of residence of Rabbi Aḥai in Babylonia, as it is a compilation of Halakic discourses actually delivered at the Academy.

The *Sheiltot* contains one hundred and ninety-one discourses which are intended as answers to questions stated in the beginning of each discourse. They are arranged according to the sections of the Pentateuch which are read in the synagogue and are also based on the order of the precepts (Miẓwot) as they are presented in the Pentateuch. It might be a collection of actual oral discourses held on the Sabbaths, either by Rabbi Aḥai himself, or even by former Geonim. We know that such discourses were held, as we find in the *Midrash Yelamdénu* (Ch. VI) that the Agadic discourses open with an Halakic question.

The purpose of the book was to explain the precepts in accordance with the views of the Talmud and other Halakic books. The author therefore abstracted the essence of Talmudić opinion concerning each precept discussed and placed it in the Biblical section where such precept is either directly stated or implied. The gist of Talmudic opinion is given in the very words of the Talmud by selecting the important passages scattered both in the Babylonian and Palestinian Talmuds as well as in other sources dealing with the subject. The passages selected contain important statements embodying the results of the discussion, minus the discussion itself. For instance, in the discourse on the first section of Genesis, where the Sabbath is mentioned for the first time the question of the Sabbath is discussed, and all passages bearing on its enjoyment (Oneg Shabbat) are given and decisions rendered. The discourses on the section Noah deal (*1*) with the precept to marry and beget children, and passages concerning this duty are adduced; (2) with the prohibition against eating a limb torn from a living animal, as these two precepts are referred to in this section of the Bible saying: "And God blessed Noah and his children and He said to them, 'Be fruitful and multiply, and fill up the earth' (Gen. IX, 1), and also, 'But flesh with the life thereof which is the blood thereof, ye shall not eat.'" (Ibid. 4.) The first half of the last verse is interpreted by the Talmud as an injunction against eating any limb from a living animal, hence the discourses of Aḥai. In the section of Lek-Leka [8] where the pre-

---

[8] The Hebrew Bible is divided not only into chapters, but also into larger sections or portions, each portion being the reading assigned for each week of the year in the Babylonian reading cycle which covers the entire Pentateuch in one year. These weekly portions or sections were named after the opening word of the first sentence, or those succeeding the opening words. Thus the first section is named *Bereshit*, i. e. in the beginning, the first word; the second, Noah, which occurs in the opening sentence, the third, *Lek-Leka*—being the fifth and sixth words in the sentence: And God said unto Abraham *Lek-Leka,* Get thee forth, these words forming the burden of the entire sentence, etc.

cept of circumcision is stated, namely, God commanding Abraham to circumcise himself and his household, a discourse on the laws and regulations of circumcision is given, stating all practical decisions, and thus the entire Pentateuch is covered. In most cases, the decision is directly stated by the words, "And thus is the law"; at times, the selected passages speak for themselves.

The discourses consist mostly of two parts, one which begins with the word *Sheilta*, i. e. question, which states briefly the subject or the law, and then the passages showing its origin and derivation follow. The second part begins usually with the words, "But it is necessary to deduce." This part is intended to solve an additional problem, or remove some doubt concerning a certain law, or rule, or custom. The relation of the discourse on the Pentateuch portion is not always direct. Very often Halakic discourses are given on a certain portion where the laws discussed are not stated explicitly, but are only remotely implied. Thus, in the portion of *wa-Yigash* (Gen. XLIV, 18; XLVII, 31) where it is stated (XLIV, 22) that Judah guaranteed Jacob the safety of Benjamin, a discourse on the laws of surety and guaranty is given. At times, the subject discussed bears no relation at all to the content of the portion. Due to the fact that the author follows the order of the Pentateuch, subjects are repeated and scattered, for example, the laws of the Sabbath which are mentioned a number of times in the Bible are scattered through various portions where the observance of the Sabbath is mentioned, and some laws are repeated.

The book has come down to us in an incomplete form, for the discourses touch only on one hundred and forty-five precepts, sixty-eight positive commandments (Miẓwot Asé) and seventy-seven prohibitions (Miẓwot lo-Ta'asé) and also forty-six Rabbinical precepts or customs. It must have originally contained all the six hundred and thirteen precepts. As the purpose of the book was to be a practical one, the author pays due attention to ethical precepts, and quotes a considerable number of ethical Agadic passages. The *Sheiltot* served also as a compendium of the Talmud on all subjects discussed there, and was used as a textbook by those who did not want to study the intricate discussions of the Talmud proper and preferred to have the gist of it on certain subjects. It was thus a forerunner of the great compendia which followed.

The *Sheiltot* was the first definite attempt at compiling a code. It did not take long and other authors began to do likewise. The second code was the work of Judai Gaon (756–770). It is what is known as

Halaḳot Pesuḳot, or *Halaḳot Ketuot,* i. e. either Halakic decisions, or cut-off *Halaḳot.* They are at times called *Halaḳot Keẓubot,* namely, measured ones. All these peculiar names were given them for the reason that the collections initiated a new way in codifying the law, and that is merely quoting the decision without quoting the source. This is practically the way of a real code. But Jewish opinion never favored such methods, for there was always the lurking fear that the adoption of such a method would jeopardize the study of the Talmud. We see, therefore, two tendencies henceforth in the codification of the law, one that of giving the law without the source, and another stating the source and then the deductions. The former is best exemplified in the Code of Maimonides, the other in that of Al-Fasi. The period under discussion gave rise to both methods, the *Sheiltot* to the second, and the *Halaḳot Pesuḳot* to the first.

Of the code of Judai Gaon only fragments remain. Most likely, a large part of it was incorporated in the later codes, and in various collections of Gaonic Responsa of later origin which also bear that name.[9] The third code is the *Halaḳot Gedolot,* i. e. the large collection of *Halaḳot.* About the authorship of this book, there is divergence of opinion among earlier authorities. Some believe the author to be the same Judai Gaon who wrote the *Halaḳot Pesuḳot,* others, among whom is the great Jewish historian of the Mediæval Ages, Abraham Ibn Daud (Ch. XIV), assert that the author of the book is Simon Kaira who originally hailed from Cairo, Egypt, but later settled in Babylonia. This opinion seems to be the right one. This Simon Kaira flourished in the second half of the eighth century, and although he was a great scholar, as evidenced by his book, he, like Rabbi Aḥai, never received an official appointment as Gaon. The author must undoubtedly have seen the brief code of Rabbi Judai, for the name the "Large Halakot" indicates that the new code is distinguished from an earlier smaller one.

The *Halaḳot Gedolot* follow partly the *Sheiltot* in method, inasmuch as it is likewise a compendium of the sources of Talmudic law, and what is more a real compendium of the Talmud. The book is arranged according to the tractates of the Talmud, but with important changes. The author was the first one to give a detailed list of the six hundred and thirteen precepts (Miẓwot) which are said to be con-

---

[9] One such collection, also called *Halaḳot Pesuḳot,* was published in Constantinople in 1693 and republished by Joel Miller in 1893. It contains decisions on various laws by a number of Geonim.

tained in the Pentateuch, thus affording a basis for the entire Jewish law. Yet he did not follow that method in his compendium, but as said, he took the order of the Talmud. His important contribution, however, is his systematic grouping of the Talmudic law. In the Talmud, the order is loose, one tractate contains several subjects, and one subject may be scattered through several tractates. The author of this Code grouped all laws concerning one subject under one head. For instance, the first tractate of the Talmud, *Berakot,* deals with all forms of prayer and benedictions, but the benedictions of the sanctification of the Sabbath (Kiddush) and that on the departure of the Sabbath (Habdalah) which are pronounced over a cup of wine and are important ceremonies, are hardly dealt with in that tractate. They are treated in the tenth chapter of the tractate *Pesaḥim.* Our author therefore abstracted the laws discussed in that chapter concerning these benedictions and placed them immediately after his compendium of the tractate *Berakot* so as to have the entire subject of prayers and benedictions complete. He likewise follows a logical system in other places. At the end of his abstract of the Talmudic order, *Moed,* which deals with the Sabbath and holidays and all their regulations, he placed several small collections of law concerning mourning, the reading of the law, the putting on of phylacteries, and the wearing of *Ẓiẓit.* These subjects are scattered in a number of tractates. But our author followed a more logical and consecutive order. The last tractate of the order of *Moed, Moed Katan,* deals with the laws of the semi-holidays, i. e. *Ḥol ha-Moed,* the intervening days between the first and last days of Passover and the Feast of Tabernacles, but it likewise treats of some laws of mourning, as certain injunctions concerning cessation of work apply to both the semi-holiday and period of mourning. Our author, therefore, thought it logical to collect at this place all laws of mourning, and on completing these, he brought together also all laws concerning priests, for the injunction that they should not defile themselves by touching a dead body makes that subject contiguous to the preceding one. On the other hand, the laws concerning priests contain also regulations regarding priestly benediction in the synagogue which is a part of the ritual, hence, the other laws of the synagogue ritual follow, such as the reading of the law. These, in turn have similarities with the laws of phylacteries and the others, so they are grouped together. Our author introduced changes of grouping in all other departments of Jewish law, and at times, when one Talmudic tractate contains several subjects of law, he breaks it up into the various subjects, and treats each separately. The tractate of *Baba Batra* treats of the laws of buying and selling, partnership, of inheritance, and other matters. These subjects are scattered throughout the tractate, parts in one chapter and parts in another. Our author separates the subjects and groups the passages under the various heads.

The grouping system is, however, not carried out to perfection, for the author, in following also the order of the Talmudic tractates and giving an abstract of their discussion, is at times forced to treat of several subjects at once, but on the whole, he endeavors to maintain a logical consecutiveness.

The method of codification consists, as stated, in giving the gist of the Talmudic discussion. The *Halakot Gedolot* gives more extensive extracts than the *Sheiltot,* and quotes different opinions but is careful to indicate the decision. The author quotes also decisions of individual Geonim and their comments. Quite often, he states the law briefly at the beginning of the subjects, and then the abstract of the sources follow. He, of course, utilized other sources besides the Babylonian Talmud and quotes at times the Palestinian Talmud and the *Tosefta,* as well as the Tannaitic Midrashim, but not to a great extent.

As the purpose of the book was a practical one, the author left out all such groups of laws which after the destruction of the Temple became inoperative, such as the laws of sacrifice, all that relate to the Temple service, laws of purity and impurity (Tumah we-Taharah). He therefore omitted the abstraction of all such tractates or parts of tractates dealing with such subjects, with few exceptions. He does have abstracts of several tractates of the order of *Kadashim,* but only of such parts dealing with laws practiced at all times.

The *Halakot Gedolot,* thus, by his grouping system afforded a basis for later codifiers who followed in his footsteps. The book as we have it today seems to have been edited by later hands who made a number of additions. We find there also quotations from the *Sheiltot* which cannot be determined whether they were incorporated by the author himself or by the later editors, as most likely Simon Kaira, the author of the book, was a contemporary of Rab Ahai, and we do not know whether he had seen the *Sheiltot* or not.

During the following one hundred and fifty years, there were hardly any codes composed with the exception of a practical code containing laws and regulations of the liturgy. This is the *Seder,* i. e. order of the prayers, of Amram Gaon (term of office 846-864). This *Seder* gives a detailed order of the prayers and their text for the whole year, besides all the laws affecting the liturgy as well as all regulations concerning ceremonial observances of the Sabbath and holidays. This order of Rab Amram was accepted as the basic order of the standard prayer-book almost by all Jewry, though there are in both the later Sephardic (Nusaḥ Sefard) and the German (Nusaḥ Ashkenaz) prayer-books a great number of variations in the texts of the individual prayers, as well as additional prayers. On the whole, though, the Sephardic prayer-book is very close to that of Rab Amram, as his *Seder* was compiled at the request of a community in Spain and sent to them. It was used there for centuries and the modifications were introduced later.

The last codifiers of the Gaonic period were Saadia, Samuel ben Ḥofni, and Hai. The first wrote a number of small codes on various groups of laws such as (*1*) "On Inheritance," (*2*) "On Pledges," (*3*) "On Testimony and Contracts," (*4*) "On Unity," (*5*) "On Gifts." All these are part of a code in civil law. Several small codes on other subjects are attributed to him, among which are those on "Prohibited Marriages," on "Defilement and Purity," on "Gifts due to Priests," and on "Meat Prohibited for Food" (Terefa). Most of these are known to us by quotation, but the book on "Inheritance" is preserved to us in its entirety. It is written in Arabic and was the first code of Jewish laws written in another language, besides the Hebrew and Aramaic.

Saadia adopted the method of Judai Gaon giving merely legal statements, without reference to the sources, but he made great improvement upon the first crude attempt. He brought to the work of codification his knowledge of logic and systematization employed by him in his other studies. He lays down at first general principles then deduces the laws which follow from the application of these principles. He also divides the laws embraced in a subject into certain classes and subdivisions, thus facilitating the matter of decisions for the student. His codes served as a model to the successive codifiers who followed in his way and adopted his method.

Rab Hai Gaon, the last Gaon of Pumbedita, also wrote a number of codices on civil law. They are on "Buying and Selling" (Mekaḥ u-Memkar), on "Pledges," on "Loans," on "Conditions in Transactions," and on "The Oath" (Sha'arē Shebuot). All these books were written in Arabic and were translated into Hebrew. The first and the last were translated by Isaac Albarceloni in the year 1078, the others by an anonymous translator. The first book which is the largest contains sixty chapters or portals dealing with all forms of buying and selling transactions. It is logically arranged and follows the pure code method, though not entirely, for not only are the laws stated but their derivation from the sources is given briefly. At times, even a comment is offered on some of the passages quoted. The same method is followed in the book on the oath and the other codices.

The father-in-law of Hai, Samuel ben Ḥofni, the last Gaon of Sura, also wrote a number of small codes, both on subjects of civil and ritual law but most of them were lost as they were written in Arabic, with the exception of one on "Benedictions" (Berakot) which was translated into Hebrew.

Besides these special codes, we have from the Gaonic period thousands of Responsa which contain decisions in law in all its phases, and collectively, they make a complete code though not expressed in an orderly manner.

153. THE NORTH-AFRICAN AND SPANISH SCHOOLS OF CODIFIERS

The work of the scholars of North Africa and that of Spain was, as we have already seen, really a continuation of that of the Geonim of Babylonia, as they were the real heirs of the latter, being close to the Gaonic view of things and followers of their method. It is, therefore, expected that the codification work of these schools should resemble in character that of the Gaonic, and the expectation is amply justified. Both methods of codification described above, which were used by the early codifiers attained their perfection at the hands of various representatives of these schools. The early codifiers of North Africa were the abovementioned scholars, Rab Ḥanannel and Rab Nissim. The first wrote a code under the name of *Mikzo'ot,* (Special Subjects). The book, as evident from the copious quotations in later codes, was a collection of decisions by Geonim and also his own decisions on a number of legal subjects. But they seem to have been arranged according to a certain order, most likely the Talmudic order. They covered a large part of religious and civil law, as the quotations refer to various subjects, such as to the laws of prayer and synagogue ritual, and the like, on the one hand, and to laws of commercial documents, oaths, pledges, and property on the other hand. The book seems to have been lost, only a few fragments are extant in a manuscript.

To Rab Nissim is ascribed a partial code by the name of *Megillat*

Setorim, i. e. a "Secret Scroll." We know, however, very little of its nature and character. The book seems to have contained also comments on Talmudic passages besides some decisions.

Turning to the Spanish school, we meet in quite early times, probably in the middle of the tenth century, a work of codification of importance, quoted under various names, such as *Hefez* and *Sefer ha-Mizwot.* The book is ascribed to Rab Hefez ben Yazliah, whose age and residence are not definitely known. He is mentioned by different titles, as *Aluf,* prince or leader, *Rosh Kalah,* head of a group of scholars, and Gaon. All these titles were used in the Babylonian academies, and bestowed by them at times on scholars of other countries. It has been suggested by some that he was a resident of Babylonia, by others of Palestine, still others placed him in Kairawan, and others in Spain. The last assertion seems to be the more probable. The book itself is a code arranged according to the various precepts, and decisions of previous codifiers are quoted. The book was written in Arabic and is well preserved, and was recently published in this country by the late Dr. B. Halper.

Of the work of the first scholars, at the rise of Jewish learning in Spain, almost nothing is left in the field of law codification except a few Responsa. It is only with Samuel ha-Nagid (Ch. VII) that the code literature begins to develop. The *Nagid* is said to have written a code named *Hilkata Gibbarata,* i. e. Decisive *Halakot.* No part of it is extant except quotations by later authors. From these we can see that the book contained a collection of laws on various subjects, arranged on the order of the tractates of the Talmud, but it was probably more like a code without lengthy source quotations.

His contemporary, Isaac Ibn Giat (Chas. IX and X, Sec. A) also compiled a code which was preserved under the name of *Sha'arē Simḥa* (Portals of Joy), inasmuch as it deals with laws relating to the holidays. It follows the usual method of collecting the various decisions in the Talmud, plus the added decisions of the Geonim. The order was not the Talmudic one but the subject system, namely, that all decisions both Talmudic and Gaonic are collected under the heading of the subject.

154. ISAAC AL-FASI

All the afore-described works of codifying pale in worth and value as compared with the Magnum Opus of Isaac Al-Fasi (Sec. A of this

Ch.). His work was originally named *Halakot,* but is more popularly known after his own name, *Al-Fasi.* In his work, the source method of codifying reached its height. It surpasses in value and bulk all previous compendia of the Talmud, such as the *Halakot Gedolot* and others, for this is the real compendium of the Talmud. The work can best be characterized by calling it an abridgment of the larger part of the Talmud. He did not try to collect the sources of a certain group of laws and arrange them under the heading of that group, but took tractate after tractate and abridged it, omitting from the Talmudic discussion all he considered unnecessary leaving only such passages which bear directly on the subject of the law discussed in the Mishnah. The decision then becomes evident. When a difference of opinion is quoted a statement is added that the law is according to this or that opinion. At times, the decision becomes evident by inclusion and exclusion, namely, that since one opinion is given by Al-Fasi while the other is omitted, it follows that the one included is the right one. Where there has been a later Gaonic interpretation of a certain Talmudic law altering it, or some regulation has been added by Geonim or a new law enacted, they are all mentioned. Though as a rule, he abridges the discussion of the Talmud in the proper order, yet when the case requires, he quotes passages from other places bearing on the subject in hand, and also utilizes the Palestinian Talmud when it does not differ with the Babylonian.

However, the *Halakot* of Al-Fasi is not a mere work of abridgment, but a work executed with skill and remarkable erudition for it required great ability to exercise the right judgment in selecting the proper opinion. Rabbi Isaac is quite independent in his judgment, and he differs frequently with the opinions of the Geonim. He usually lets the Talmud speak for itself, but when the case requires, he extends a passage and analyzes it deeply, deducing from the discussion all possible phases of the law. He is then very systematic, using logical divisions of the subject. That for his purpose, he not only had to select the passages and decide between opinions, but also to comment and explain hundreds of Talmudic passages goes without saying. Al-Fasi also established a number of methodological and interpretative rules of the Talmud. In his explanations and additions to the actual passages of the Talmud, Al-Fasi often employed the Arabic tongue. Not only are certain words explained in Arabic, but whole subjects are commented upon in Arabic. These commentaries come usually at the end of the tractates as separate sections. The purpose of Al-Fasi in making his abridgment of the Talmud was to obviate the danger of minimized study of the Talmud and lack of knowledge of sources. At this time, many of the rabbis neglected the study of the Talmud and rendered decisions according to Gaonic Responsa and compilations of decisions, and he feared that the interest in the Talmud proper would wane altogether. To remedy this, he supplied a code which not only gave the decisions, but the most essential parts of the Talmud itself. He believed that the study of his abridgment would arouse the students to study also the unabridged edition of the Talmud.

Having a practical purpose in mind, he abridged only those tractates which bear on the laws practiced even after the destruction of the Temple and omitted such tractates which deal with sacrifices and other matters not in practice today. Such matters of law which are not dealt with in separate tractates but are scattered in a number of them, he grouped together under their respective subjects. Thus, he has a group known as *Halakot Ketanot,* (Minor Halakot) dealing with the laws of phylacteries (Tefilin), fringes (*Zizit*), and scroll writing.

The compendium of Al-Fasi became not only a subject of study but also an object of commentaries and a center of literary activity. Zerahyah ha-Levi wrote additions to and refutations of the *Al-Fasi* (Sec. A above). Likewise, Abraham ben David of Posquiers wrote comments and *novellae* on the book. Many wrote commentaries; Jonathan ben David of Lunel (twelfth century) was the first one to write a commentary on one of the tractates abridged by Al-Fasi. Rabbi Nissim ben Reuben (fourteenth century) wrote a commentary on the greater part of the *Al-Fasi,* and thus through the ages, scholar after scholar added his *novellæ,* comments, and remarks on the work of Al-Fasi.

155. THE CODE OF MAIMONIDES

The work of Al-Fasi was accepted by all scholars as a basis for decisions of all religious and legal questions in practical life, but only as a basis, for it merely indicated the way and with all its great value there was a need felt for a more clear-cut and orderly code where the law shall be given briefly and decisively. The few codifiers in Spain in the generation after Al-Fasi did not fulfill the need. The most important of them, Rabbi Judah ben Barzilai-Albarceloni (fl. end of eleventh century), who wrote *Sefer ha-I'tim* ('The Book of the Times), only followed Al-Fasi. The book is a code covering the laws relating to the observance of the Sabbath and Holy Days, hence, its name, and is principally a digest of Al-Fasi's *Halaḳot* with additions of Gaonic decisions which were overlooked by Al-Fasi. Fragments of it are still extant and were published.

But soon there arose a man whose knowledge was unbounded and skill unsurpassed, and he it was who prepared the complete code of Jewish law which is both authoritative and scientific. That man was Moses ben Maimon.

Moses ben Maimon was born on the Sabbath, the fourteenth of Nisan, 1135, at one o'clock in the afternoon, in the city of Cordova. His father, Maimon, a judge, *Dayan,* of the community and a great Talmudic scholar, the pupil of Joseph Ibn Migash (Sec. A) was his first teacher. When Moses reached the age of fifteen, his father together with the other Jews were forced to flee from their native city on account of the persecution of the fanatical Almohades, who then became masters of Cordova, and the Maimon family settled for a time in Almeria. Soon, however, they left that city too, and several years were spent in wandering from city to city. In spite of that, the young Moses kept up his studies which covered Talmud, philosophy, mathematics, astronomy, and medicine. During these wanderings, he made the acquaintance of many scholars among whom were also the son of the astronomer, Ibn Alpha, and another, a student of the philosopher Avempace. At the age of twenty-three Maimonides turned author, and his first work was a treatise on the calendar (Ḥeshbon ha-'Ibur) which was soon followed by one on logic, later translated into Hebrew by Moses Ibn Tibbon under the name of *Milot ha-Higayon,* (Terms of Logic). He then turned his attention to the Talmud and wrote commentaries on some tractates and began his famous commentary on the Mishnah discussed above. In 1160, the Maimon family left Spain and settled in Fez, North Africa. Here the same fanatical sect held sway, and Maimon and his family were forced to conceal their adherence to Judaism. But an epistle which Moses wrote to his Marrano brethren under the name *Iggeret ha-Shmad,* i. e. "Epistle Concerning Conversion," where he encouraged them to remain loyal to Judaism, though officially Mohammedan, aroused the wrath of the authorities, and the Maimons were forced to flee again. In 1165, they set sail for Palestine where they spent some time, and finally settled in Egypt at Fostat where Moses became the court physician. Shortly after that Maimon died, and David, the brother of Moses, was drowned in the Indian Ocean, yet through all these vicissitudes, Moses kept up his literary work, and in 1168, he completed his commentary on the Mishnah and soon began his code. This he completed in 1180 after assiduous work of twelve years. Ten years later, 1190, he finished his "Guide of the Perplexed." Maimonides was revered by the entire world Jewry in his lifetime, and his authority was unquestioned even by the greatest scholars of his age. He died in 1204 at the age of sixty-nine.

The Code of Maimonides represents the greatest attempt ever made to arrange the entire mass of what we call the Oral Law, scattered and complex as it is, in a clear, orderly, logically coherent manner. In it, the method of pure codification without reference to the sources reached its highest point and was never surpassed. In reality, it is more than a code; it is in a way a digest of the entire Oral Law contained in the entire Halakic literature. A code is usually composed for practical purposes and is intended for judges and lawyers, or in case of purely religious law, for all such persons who possess authority to decide questions of law. The earlier Jewish codifiers had this purpose in view, and have therefore omitted to include in their collections or compilations all such groups of laws which ceased to be operative with the destruction of the Temple. Not so Maimonides; he included not only such laws, as that of the sacrifices, or those of purity and impurity, but also laws of ethics, and even principles of theology, for he had a different purpose in mind.

Thus, he says in his introduction, "At this time when the tribulations of our people have increased, and wisdom has diminished, all the Responsa, comments, and *Halakot* of the Geonim are becoming difficult for a great part of our people to understand, not to speak of the Talmudim proper, the Babylonian and the Palestinian, which are very difficult and complex so that only men of broad minds can penetrate their depths and select the decisions. And therefore, I, Moses ben Maimon, the Sephardi, girded my loins and relying on the help of God devoted myself to all these books and wrote this treatise, where I have given the results of all matters pertaining to what is permitted (Mutor) and what is prohibited (Osur), what is clean (Tohor) and what is unclean (Tome), and all other laws, so that the entire Oral Law shall be clearly ordered for everyone without question and answer, without differences of opinion. Briefly, this treatise purposes to obviate the necessity for any other book, on any matter of Jewish law. In it is collected the entire Oral Law together with the institutes, customs, and decrees that were made from the time of Moses, our teacher, to the close of the Talmud, and also including the comments of the Geonim and their decrees. Therefore, I called this treatise *Mishnah Torah* (The Second Law to the Torah) for a man should read first the written law, i. e. the Pentateuch, and then read this book and he will know the Oral Law, and will not need any other book."

From this is to be seen that he did not write a code for rabbis and judges, but a digest of the entire Oral Law in his own style and order. To the uninitiated, the stupendity of the work may not be evident, for only the one who knows the enormous mass of the entire Halakic literature which runs into thousands of pages, the nature of that literature where opinions differ and no definite decision is given, where matters relating to a single law are scattered in various tractates, where there are innumerable other difficulties in the way of arriving at a decision, will appreciate the task of Maimonides. He not only had to remember practically the entire literature so that no statement could be hidden from him, but he had to coördinate and piece together various statements from different places which bear on a certain point. In addition, he had to weigh the opinions of his predecessors, the Geonim and other scholars, to accept them or refute them, and very often to break a new path in the labyrinth of Talmudic interpretation. As the code lies before us, it flows smoothly like a clear brook, and is easily read and understood, but beneath it lie depths of knowledge and eddies of mental keenness.

Thus far as regards the content of the *Mishnah Torah;* but the form, namely, the order and arrangement, is likewise a masterly piece of work. In it is displayed all the logical skill and systematizing ability of Maimonides. As a basis for his work, he took, like the author of the *Halakot Gedolot* (Sec. 149), the enumeration of the six hundred and thirteen precepts making some changes in the list of the former. In his grouping of the laws of the Code, he indicates which precepts, whether positive or prohibitive, are included in the group. The grouping itself does not follow the order of the precepts, as they are given in the Pentateuch nor as they are treated in the Talmud, but according to a logical system of his own. He divided the entire sum of written and oral laws into four divisions: (*1*) Those bearing on the relation between God and man. (*2*) Those concerning the life of the individual in its several phases. (*3*) Those laws the operation of which depend on the possession of Palestine. (*4*) Laws relating to the life of society, namely, civil and criminal law. He divided the code in accordance with this arrangement into fourteen books each containing a number of closely-knit groups of laws. To the first division he devoted two books, (*1*) The *Sefer ha-Madah* (Book of Knowledge) and (*2*) *Sefer Ahabah* (Book of Love). The first book deals with the principles of theology, the primary duties of man to God, and ethics. It contains five groups of laws: The first is the fundamentals of the Torah, dealing with such precepts, as the duty to know that there is a God, to love Him, fear Him, consecrate His name, etc., as well as all prohibitory precepts, namely, not to think of any other gods, not to desecrate His name and others. The second group deals with ethics (Dēot), describing minutely all laws and regulations of human conduct. The third, fourth and fifth groups embrace the laws of the study of the Torah, idolatry, and penitence (Teshubah), respectively. The laws of idolatry are included here, for they refer to the primary transgressions against the Godhead. In the first book are also included the laws of blasphemy and those referring to prohibited practices of idolators, such as sorcery, witchcraft, and others. The second book, designated *Ahabah* (Love), covers all such laws of the ritual which express the love and admiration of God, such as that of prayer, benedictions, phylacteries, fringes, circumcision, and others. In all the precepts relating to this group of laws is expressed either the love of Israel for God, or that of God for Israel whom He selected as His people by special covenant, and gave them certain laws as a sign of this covenant.

The second division contains four books, the first of which is called *Zemanim* (Times), dealing with the laws of all Holy Days, both with the Biblical, such as Passover, Feast of Weeks, Tabernacles, and the rabbinically instituted ones, as Hanukkah and Purim. In these books, there are ten groups of laws. The second book called *Nashim* (Women) covers the subject of family law, dealing with laws of marriage and divorce, levirate marriage (Yebum), and some other laws, such as the laws relating to the woman suspected of adultery (Sotah). The book contains five groups of laws. The third book is called *Kedu-shah* (Holiness) and deals with laws mostly prohibitive, relating to incestuous relations and to prohibited foods. The name of this book is derived from the fact that the passages regarding these laws in the Bible always close with the pronouncement "And ye shall be holy, for I, your God, am holy." And it was always taken to mean, that these prohibitions inculcating that one shall not defile himself, neither by promiscuous sexual relations, nor by unclean food, were given for the purpose of making human life more distinct and more noble, which means sanctification of life. The book contains three groups of laws. The section on prohibited foods is a very extensive one and includes all prohibitions relating to food or drink even when the food is only temporarily forbidden, such as not to eat grain before the tithes are separated and the like. The laws relating to the mode of slaughtering the animals (Sheḥitah) form a separate section, as they are merely preparatory conditions without which the food cannot be eaten. The fourth book is called *Haflaha* (The Book of Separation) and deals with vows, oaths, laws of Nazirites, and the like, all such laws arising from an oath, a vow, or promise made by a man which places upon him a special obligation. The name is derived from the Biblical expression (Numbers VI, 2) used in regard to the vow of a Nazirite, which he takes to abstain from the use of wine.

The third division likewise contains four books, all dealing with laws directly connected with Palestine and Temple worship, which ceased with the destruction of the Temple and the exile. The first, *Zeraim* (Seeds) covers all laws relating to tithes, first fruit offering (Bikkurim), the first born, both of man and animals, the Sabbatical and Jubilee years, and the like. The second is named *Abodah* (Worship) and describes the order of worship in the Temple, the regulations concerning the holy vessels and ordinances concerning priests, as well as the general laws of fixed types of sacrifices. It contains nine groups of laws. The third book is called *Korbonot* (Sacrifices) and deals with special kinds of sacrifices, such as the Paschal Lamb, sacrifices brought when a sin is committed involuntarily (Shogeg), and others. The fourth book is designated *Taharah* (Purity), dealing with all laws of uncleanness, giving a detailed description of the classes of defilement, their prescribed purification and other things.

Four books are also devoted to the fourth division. The first one called *Nezikin* (Damages) covers all cases of direct damages and injuries which one man can inflict upon another, including the greatest injury, that of murder. It contains five groups of laws, dealing with general damages, stealing in all its phases whether direct or indirect, such as giving false weight and measures, robbery, assault, and battery, and murder in all its aspects. The second book denominated *Kinyon* (Acquisition of Property) covers the subject in its entirety. It describes all modes of transfer of property, such as buying and selling, giving of gifts, laws concerning buying of slaves as well as their treatment, laws of agency and partnership, and similar matters. The third book named *Mishpatim* (Judgments) deals with general laws affecting commerce, trade, and other similar relations, such as trusts and bailments, loans, relations between employee and employer, and laws of inheritance, its sequence and order. The fourth book, *Shoftim* (Judges) is devoted to procedure, and covers all the laws relating to the establishment of courts, especially the High Court, or the Sanhedrin, its jurisdiction and method of punishment. Under this head come also the kinds of capital punishment formerly practiced by Jewish courts, and all modes of procedure. The book also includes groups of laws concerning evidence, the qualification of witnesses and their examination, laws concerning those who rebel against authority, both against authority of court and authority of the parents, namely, such crimes against parents as striking or cursing, both of which are punishable by death. Finally, the laws of the state are dealt with, namely, those affecting the king and his administration, laws of war and peace, and such public matters arising from administration. To this book there is appended all such regulations which we may call *jus gentium,* namely, all laws obligatory on the Gentiles residing in the Jewish state, who though they do not fall under the Jewish law are yet obliged to observe certain fundamental laws necessary for the welfare of humanity. Technically, these laws are called the "Precepts of the Children of Noah," namely, laws affecting non-Jews who are not of the descent of Abraham. At the very end of the book, a few chapters are devoted to the description of the Messianic age and the rule of the Messiah. Maimonides is here, as elsewhere, true to his rationalism, and excludes from his conception of the Messianic rule all mystical and miraculous elements, but pictures his administration as one based on the old state laws of Israel guaranteeing justice to all, and conducive to peace, both of the nation and of the individual. "The prophets and the sages," says Maimonides, "desired the arrival of the Messianic days, not for the purpose that the Jews may rule the world, neither that they have dominion over the Gentiles, nor that the latter exalt them, nor in order to eat and drink and enjoy pleasures, but that the Jews shall not be oppressed and shall have leisure to occupy themselves with the study of the Torah and wisdom, so that they may be deserving of the life in the world to come. At that time, i. e. the Messianic, there will be neither hunger nor war, nor jealousy and competition, and the main business of the whole world will be to know God.

And therefore, the Israelites will be great in wisdom who will conceive their Creator in the highest degree possible for men as it is written, (Isaiah XI, 9) 'For the earth shall be full of the knowledge of God as the waters cover the sea.' " These words are undoubtedly a fitting ending to this great code which began with "The Book of Knowledge."

On account of the division of the Code of Maimonides into fourteen books, it received a second name beside that of *Mishnah Torah,* namely, *Yad ha-Ḥazaḳah* (The Mighty Hand, as Yod and Dalet in Hebrew signify numerically fourteen, Yod—10, Daleth—4).

The order of the Code is, as we have seen, based on a logical scheme, and on the whole, the various groups of laws follow in connected sequence. There are, however, some deficiencies in the arrangement, and at times a forced grouping. But these are not due to Maimonides' lack of system, but to the nature of Jewish law. Jewish law does not draw any distinction between a religious sin and social crime. All laws emanate from one source—God, and the one who worships idols in the presence of witnesses, after being warned by them, is punished by death, like one who commits murder, and there are quite a number of purely religious sins punishable by death. No grouping could, therefore, be logically carried out, the respective laws, the transgressions of which entails capital punishment, had to be scattered according to the general classes where they belong, and could not be subsumed under one aspect of criminal law. Some laws could not be classified at all and had to be forcibly joined to some groups; thus, the laws of mourning are included by Maimonides in the division of civil and criminal laws. The reason for it is that nowhere in the Bible are there given any laws regarding mourning; but there is a precept that those executed by court should be interred on the day of their execution, hence Maimonides joined the laws of mourning, which are conceptually connected with interment, to the laws dealing with the execution of criminals by court. Maimonides was very careful of his logical arrangement and whenever an apparent interruption of the order occurred, he stated his reason for the forced grouping.

Strict logical sequence is followed in the statement of the laws proper in the treatment of the subject. Each group of laws dealing with a subject is carefully analyzed into its component parts; the criterion for this analysis is the concept of the precept under which the part can be subsumed, for as a rule, each group contains a number of Biblical precepts whether positive or negative (i. e. prohibitory). If a group of laws contains four or five precepts it is divided into four or ... order of Halakic statements follows the order of the ... given at the head of the section. The most general and ... laws are usually stated first, the particular and detailed later. ... Biblical laws precede those deduced by Talmudic method of inte... tion, rabbinical laws, institutes, and decrees come last. The Code, ... whole, shows the stamp of a master mind, who planned every detail with skill and in accordance with a well-defined logical system.

Formally, the Code is modeled after the Mishnah; each book is divided into groups of *Halakots,* each group into chapters, and each chapter into statements of single *Halakot.*

The style of the *Mishnah Torah* also deserves special attention. It is in itself a classic creation, and a contribution to the development of the Hebrew language during the Middle Ages. Rabbi Moses himself says in the preface to his "Book of Precepts" concerning the style of the Code, "I have chosen not to compose it (i. e. the Code) in the style of the prophetical books, for that language is not sufficient to express all the details of the laws, nor will I use the style and language of the Talmud, for only few will understand it on account of its construction and difficult words, but I will adopt the style and the language of the Mishnah so that the majority of our people may understand it." But in reality, the style of the *Mishnah Torah* is only modeled after that of the Mishnah and is not the same style. It is distinguished by its harmony, both that of syntax and of diction. On the whole, it is a pure Hebrew with a slight admixture of Aramaic words. Maimonides exploited the Hebrew language to its fullest extent, and used a much larger number of Biblical words than the Mishnah does. Besides, he also employed a great number of Biblical phrases in order to beautify the style, and thus the dry language of a Code is softened and adorned. In addition, Maimonides uses a number of Mishnaic words in new meanings and at times even new and different forms of Mishnaic verbs. He also coined new verbal forms and words to express new meanings or shades of meaning. All these changes impart to the style both elasticity and preciseness, richness, and even a kind of beauty. His Code is, therefore, a great work not only from the point of view of content but also from that of form and style, and its influence on Hebrew literature is inestimable.

The Code of Maimonides aroused great admiration and was widely circulated and accepted in all parts of Jewry. Later, it became a subject of commentaries. Many scholars wrote lengthy commentaries not so

explain the text, for this needed no explanation as it is very
it to explain the reasons which guided Maimonides in his de-
, and also to supply the sources whence he derived his *Halaḳot*.
n the other hand, it also aroused opposition. Some well-meaning
nolars saw a great danger in his attempt. They feared that his Code
which is a digest of the entire Oral Law would supplant the study of
the Talmud and thus bring about a standstill in the study of the Law.
Their fears were not entirely unjustified for in some places in the East,
such as in South Arabia where the Code of Maimonides was considered
the last word in Oral Law, Talmudic study dwindled to a minimum.
They, therefore, opposed the complete acceptance of the Code as the
final authority on all matters of legal and religious decisions and urged
the continued study of the sources. The greatest of these opponents was
Abraham ben David of Posquiers (Sec. 150) who immediately upon
the appearance of the Code wrote refutations of some of the decisions,
quoting different customs, and pointing out errors. These refutations
were appended to the Code and were later printed together with it.
Yet, the opposition did not weaken the respect for the Code. It took its
respective place in the Halakic literature and became the model and
basis for later codes. Nor on the other hand, did the Code in most
Jewries diminish the study of the Talmud. Halakah was still the subject of study in all European Jewries and its literature kept on growing, and even codifying in various ways continued to a great extent.

156. THE FRANCO-GERMAN SCHOOL OF CODIFIERS

As stated, the appearance of the Code of Maimonides did not affect
the codifying activities in other countries. The Franco-German scholars
kept up their intensive study of the Talmud and Law, and as a result,
there was always something new in the field. Besides, customs as well
as opinions differed, and not all the decisions of Maimonides were accepted, so that there was ample room for new complete or partial codes.
Simultaneous with the appearance of the Code of Maimonides, we have
several partial codes which appeared in the Provence. The opponent of
Maimonides, Abraham ben David, wrote partial codes on the law of
family purity, under the name of *Ba'al ha-Nefesh* (Master of the Soul),
also on food laws, i. e. on prohibited kinds of food, and on certain
ritual and holiday laws. These sections are parts of his larger work,
Temim Deim (Perfect Knowledge).

His opponent, Zeraḥyah ha-Levi (Sec. 146), likewise wrote some partial codes on the laws of slaughtering and *terefa,* also on family purity. A partial code of greater importance was the one written by Isaac ben Abba Mari of Marseilles (b. 1122—d. about 1200) under the name of *Ittur Seforim* (The Crowning of the Scholars). The code deals primarily with civil law, especially devoted to the question of documents, and also with laws of marriage and divorce. There are appended to it several sections dealing with food laws. It follows the source method, quoting the Talmudic passages on each subject or subdivision and then giving the Gaonic decisions as well as those of Isaac Al-Fasi wherever necessary, and finally drawing his own conclusions. The arrangement of the subjects is a very peculiar one. They are arranged in accordance with the letters of a certain phrase which reads in Hebrew *Tashkef be-Geza Hokmah* (Look at the Trunk of Wisdom), and each subject comes under a letter of the three words, namely, subjects beginning with *Taw* are treated first, with *Shin* next and so on.

The Tosafist school in France and Germany produced many codifiers. The first of this school was Eliezer ben Nathan (b. 1080—d. 1165), one of the older Tosafists. His book, *Eben ha-Ezer* (Rock of Salvation), is a kind of compendium of the important three orders of the Talmud, *Moed, Nashim, Nezikin,* containing the laws practiced after the destruction of the Temple. It contains, besides comments on the Talmud proper, the gist of the legal decisions, together with a number of customs and opinions of the older Franco-German scholars.

A more important code, though not a complete one, is the book *ha-Terumah* (The Selection) by Rabbi Baruch ben Isaac, a pupil of Isaac ben Samuel, leading Tosafist. The book is so named for it is a selected offering of the best of scholarship of his generation, especially of the teachings of his great master. It deals with all laws concerning food, such as slaughtering, terefa, and other such matters, laws of the Sabbath, marriage, and divorce, family purity, and ritual. In fact, it covers with certain omissions almost the entire field of religious law, including even family relations, but does not touch upon civil law. The method is more of a code than a source method, as it gives a quite accurate description of the practical laws, though the sources are copiously quoted and commented upon. To make his book still more practical and code-like, the author prefaced it with a detailed digest of all decisions contained in the book.

Of the school of Rashi, we have a number of partial codes, the most important of which are the *Mahzor Vitry,* and the *ha-Pardes* (The

Garden). The first was compiled at the beginning of the twelfth century by a pupil of Rashi, Rabbi Simḥa of Vitry. Its name is derived from the fact that it was primarily devoted to the cycle of religious laws which embraces the life of the Jew daily throughout the year, especially those that relate to the liturgy and synagogue service. It also contains a complete text of the prayers for the entire year plus the selections of sacred poetry (Piyyutim). This fact is another reason for its name, for the name Maḥzor was given to such liturgical compilations, but in reality it contains more than that, as it includes all laws which are incumbent upon a pious Jew to perform. It is found in two versions, a shorter one, which is probably the original one, and a longer one which includes many additions, and a number of large extracts of laws from other codes, especially that of the *ha-Terumah*. In its larger recension, it is an exceptionally valuable book, for it is encyclopaedic in character. It contains a valuable collection of *Piyyutim* by various poets for Sabbaths and holidays, which are not found anywhere else, a treatise on the calendar with directions for its calculation, large extracts of certain Midrashic books now lost, numerous Gaonic Responsa, an excellent commentary on Aboth, the ethical tractate of the Mishnah, and texts of other smaller tractates, and similar matters.

Its order is as follows: It begins first with the order of the week day, giving briefly the laws and regulations concerning the daily obligatory prayers and benedictions and then the text of the prayers is given together with explanations of various customs as well as the order of prayers, their origin and source. This is followed by the treatment of the Sabbath in the same manner, first the description of all customs, order of worship, and then the texts of the prayers and poems for every service, as well as the songs recited at the table (Zemirot). Then the holidays are dealt with similarly until the entire year is completed. To make the Maḥzor a real manual of religious laws, a guide for every Jew in the performance of his duties, selections of Rashi's decisions on other subjects besides liturgy and prayers are given, such as the laws and regulations concerning marriage, especially the ceremonial part, concerning circumcision, and family purity (concerning menstruation). There are also short digests of general laws of the Sabbath, of Passover, of phylacteries, of writing the Scroll of the Law, and even of the slaughtering of animals and food laws, excerpted from the code *ha-Terumah*. The Maḥzor is, as stated, a great contribution to Paitainic literature and has been used as a source book by all scholars writing on the history of liturgy and sacred poetry. Finally, it is also valuable as a source for folk customs during the Middle Ages, as its encyclopaedic character affords us a glimpse into Jewish daily life during that period.

The second book, the *ha-Pardes,* was compiled by another pupil of Rashi, Shemayah, about the same time. It is more in the nature of a code and is closely related to Rashi, as it contains to a large extent his decisions. It deals likewise with the entire field of religious law with only a few remarks on certain phases of civil law. Its order is not very systematic; each subject is dealt with separately, but the arrangement of the subjects is at random. This book, like the Maḥzor, contains to a certain extent selections from Gaonic Responsa and other codes, and also some texts of Midrashic treatises, and that of the tractate *Beraḵot* of the Palestinian Talmud. The inclusion of such matters in a code can only be explained by the fact that copies of such texts were rare, and the author who possessed them thought it worth while to preserve them for future generations.

We have several more codes which were produced by the Tosafist school, two of which are important. The first one is the *Sefer Yeréim* (The Book of the Pious) by Rabbi Eliezer of Metz. Rabbi Eliezer was a disciple of Rabbi Jacob Tam and was one of the leading Tosafists of the second generation. His book shows the influence of the Maimonidean Code, inasmuch as it is an attempt to give a complete code of the entire Oral Law. He also adopted, like Maimonides, the number of precepts as the basis of the arrangement of the material, and it contains four hundred sixty-four sections which include, according to him, all the six hundred and thirteen precepts, as he at times included two or more precepts in one section. The number, however, is not complete, as several subjects of civil law are missing.

He adopted, however, an original scheme in the division of his book. He divided his book into seven parts which he calls pillars (Amudim) and each part into subdivisions. Each main division and subdivision contains the practical legal interpretations of a number of precepts, both affirmative (Asé) and prohibitive (Lo-Ta'asé). The precepts themselves, he classified according to their content. Thus, he has six parts—the first one is missing: (*a*) All laws relating to prohibited foods, prohibitions of all kinds whether they still operate or have ceased to operate on account of the destruction of the Temple. (*b*) Those laws relating to things which even the use or any enjoyment of is prohibited, e. g. idols and their appurtenances, etc. (*c*) Laws the infringement or performance of which involves a monetary consideration, such as civil laws and others. (*d*) All laws, the infringement or non-performance of which involves both disobedience of God's command and harmful results to man, such as criminal laws and the like. The last two classes concern only purely religious laws and include: (*e*) Religious laws depending merely on speech which involve disobedience towards God in a positive or a negative way, such as blasphemy on the one hand, or failure to pray on the other hand. (*f*) Religious laws of the same class which relate to an action. The first part most likely related to the principles of religion and ethics.

His method is more code-like, but sources are quoted verbatim, and to a great extent earlier codes are utilized and quoted by name, and short discussions of the authenticity of their decisions are given.

The second one is the *Rokeah* [10] (a Compound of Spices) by Rabbi Eleazar of Worms (b. 1160—d. 1238). The book was most likely intended to be a complete code, but only a part of it remained. It contains four hundred and ninety-seven sections, and deals with the entire set of religious laws, such as the laws of the Sabbath and all the holidays, the ritual in all its details, laws observed in the home, such as mourning, marriage ceremony, slaughtering and prohibited foods, and other practical religious laws. The book, however, opens, like the Code of Maimonides, with a number of chapters on the principles and ideals of the Jewish religion, such as the love of God, unity of God, duty of piety and penitence. Over all these chapters, there rests the spirit of sincere, deep Mediæval piety. These principles are not discussed from their theoretical side but from the practical one. In his chapter on penitence, he does not emphasize the psychological side as Maimonides does, but the practical, and he actually prescribes certain kinds of penances and self-torture for various sins.

The method is pure code method, giving the decisions without quoting the sources, only here and there, are sources referred to. He also includes customs to which he devotes special sections, indicating their nature. In these customs we already note the influence of the Kabbala or mystic teaching upon practical religious life, as many of them cannot be explained except from the point of view of that teaching.

The arrangement of subjects seems to be an arbitrary one, though the yearly cycle of festivals seems to be the central point in the work.

[10] The name of the book was chosen by the author because the numerical value of the three Hebrew letters *Resh, Kuf,* and *Het* equals 308, the same value of the letters of Eleazar, his own name.

C. Responsa

157. *CHARACTER OF RESPONSA LITERATURE*

It was already observed in previous sections that both the commentaries and the codes had their origin in the Responsa of the Geonim. Yet, it would be incorrect to speak of the large number of complete and incomplete collections of Responsa which we possess, both from the Geonim and from the generations of succeeding scholars, merely as disjointed commentaries or dissected parts of codes. It is true that many of the earlier Responsa can be freely considered as the raw material for both the later commentaries and codes, yet this extensive literature of Responsa which kept on growing for a period of fifteen hundred years has a soul and character of its own. Its prime quality is its constant touch with changing life. No legal system, and still less a way of life as Judaism is, can be encompassed in a code. A code is a fixed and stationary thing; life is flowing and changing, and new cases are constantly coming up which have to be decided by interpretation, analogy, and other logical rules of deduction. Roman law has its set of Responsa; modern legal systems, especially the American one, have their constantly growing sets of decisions and cases, and Judaism its Responsa.

The Responsa were not written hypothetically or fictitiously but, as their name indicates, were actual replies by authoritative persons to queries addressed to them. As such, they reflect Jewish life in all its various phases, both the inner and the external life. In them, we hear the echo of Jewish suffering, as well as the rejoicing at escape from threatening disasters. In the many volumes of Responsa, we can trace the political, social, economic, and industrial conditions of the Jews in various lands and ages. There we can follow the origin and development of customs, forms of conduct, methods of education, and many more expressions of life during the centuries. This literature, therefore, is a most valuable source for Jewish history and serves as a depository of first documents. But Judaism, as stated, is not merely a set of practical injunctions, as it also comprises thoughts, ideas, feelings, and sentiments; hence the Responsa reflect also all these and serve as an index of the thoughts, ideas, and sentiments of the people, inasmuch as many of them were written as answers to queries upon matters of ethics, theology, religious philosophy, and even history and chronology.

As the Responsa were written singly and only collected later, very seldom by the writer himself, but by disciples of the writers, or by students of literature centuries later, it could hardly be expected that they should have been arranged systematically. Most of these collections are put together without any plan or division of the subject-matter. Exceptions, of course, abound. The only guiding line is often the numeration of the Responsa. In reality, however, this should not surprise us. Taking into consideration the exceedingly difficult conditions under which Jewish literature was produced, the extent of the Jewish Diaspora, the persecutions, and the exiles which the Jew underwent, the lack of libraries and other facilities, the imperfect state of manuscript copying and preserving, we are rather surprised that these Responsa could have been preserved at all. It is only the excessive zeal and deep love of a people for knowledge which enabled the accomplishment of that feat, to preserve such a mass of literature consisting of single decisions and comments, and extending over a period of fifteen hundred years, even if not in an entirely perfect state.

The Responsa literature is conveniently divided into five periods which begin with the end of the seventh century, and run into the nineteenth century. For the present we will cast a glance over the first two periods, namely, the Gaonic and the one following it.

158. THE GAONIC RESPONSA

The Gaonic Responsa begin, as stated, at the end of the seventh century about fifty years after the establishment of the Gaonate. The first Gaon from whom we have a few Responsa was Rab Shishna, Gaon of Sura, who lived in that period. From that time on until the close of the Gaonate in 1038, we have an unbroken line of successive layers of Responsa in which almost all Geonim participated. These Responsa were the cords which bound the scattered Jewries of the Diaspora to the great spiritual intellectual center at Babylonia, the nerves through which the spiritual influence was carried to distant parts of the world.

The Responsa were not as a rule preserved by the Geonim themselves as to them it was merely the discharging of a daily function. Fortunately for us, the inquirers, however, did preserve copies of the answers, as to them these answers contained rules of action and information on important matters, and served as texts which could be consulted on future occasions. That a great part of these Responsa was lost is evident, but the part that was preserved, both in separate collections and in innumerable books by later authors, if it could be collected in one edition would fill many volumes.

Of the separate collections of Gaonic Responsa, we have about twelve, some of which had already been published several centuries ago, but most of them only during the nineteenth century by various scholars from manuscripts which came to light. The most important are: (1) *Halakot Pesukot* (Gaoʒic Decisions) published in Constantinople in 1516 and republished in 1893 by Joel Miller with explanatory notes. This collection contains one hundred and ninety-five briefly written decisions given by various Geonim to inquirers concerning all matters of religious laws. (2) *Sheolot u-Teshubot me-ha-Geonim* (Inquiries and Responsa of the Geonim) published first at Constantinople in 1575, which contains three hundred and fifty Responsa by Geonim on all matters of Jewish law, religious and civil, as well as comments and explanations of Talmudic passages. In this collection, most of the Responsa are anonymous nor are the names of the inquirers given. (3) *Sha'aré Zedek* (The Portals of Justice), published at Salonika in 1792 contains four hundred and thirty-three Responsa, mostly signed. This collection originally contained four parts but the first two were lost. Of the last part, the third is devoted to matters of purely religious law and the fourth to civil law. This collection has the best arrangement as the Responsa are grouped according to the subject-matter they deal with. (4)*Sha'aré Teshubah* [11] (The Portals of Responsa) published in Salonika in 1802 contains three hundred and fifty-two Responsa without any particular arrangement, which deal mostly with religious laws. (5) "Responsa of Early Geonim" published by David Cassel in 1848 with an introduction by Solomon Rapoport. This collection contains one hundred and fifty-two Responsa and comments, and is really a larger edition of original smaller collections consisting of various groups of Responsa or comments on certain tractates written by individual Geonim. (6) "Gaonic Responsa" published by Abraham Harkavy from a manuscript in St. Petersburg in 1887. This seems to be the most authentic collection as the Responsa are given in the original form in which they were issued from the hands of the Geonim, and many of them are written in Arabic.

The other six collections resemble these six. On the whole, all collections as they were made by copyists centuries later contain many repetitions and variants. Sometimes individual Responsa are repeated five or six times. Each of these collections, not excepting that of Harkavy, con-

[11] In this name there is a play on the word *Teshubah* which means both repentance and response. The phrase "Portals of Repentance" occurs frequently in Agadic literature.

tains also Responsa from later scholars who succeeded the Geonim, especially from the first Spanish and Franco-German scholars. In most of them, the Responsa are abbreviated, longer ones divided up and otherwise changed from the original form.

Besides these collections, there are hundreds and perhaps thousands of Responsa of the Geonim quoted in the codes and other books of the scholars of later ages, especially of those who lived in the first four centuries after the close of the Gaonic period. In addition, the bringing to light of hordes of Jewish manuscripts in the Genizah of Cairo and other cities of the East has added hundreds of single Responsa of the Geonim, so that the total number reaches many thousands.

With all the imperfections which the fragmentary nature of these collections represents, the value of these Responsa is inestimable not only from the legal point of view but from many other angles. They reveal to us the state of the minds of the inquirers in many parts of the world, their perplexities and doubts on many subjects. As the inquirers were not only individuals, but frequently whole communities, we can see at a glance the inner and external life of the communities. The legal side reveals commercial and industrial relations. These inquiries were written at a time when the Talmud was not as yet spread, when customs in ritual and other ways were not yet established, when questions of religious principles were agitating people's minds, in short, when all that we call today the mass of Jewish tradition was not as yet solidified, but was still somewhat flexible. They, therefore, reflect a free spirit of inquiry, a desire to know the origin of things and the reasons why certain things are to be performed. The legal side is well represented, but there are hundreds of inquiries dealing with passages in Mishnah and Talmud, how they are to be read and explained, hundreds dealing with strange and curious Agadic passages, asking for their interpretation. Others ask for guidance in religious conceptions, still others for the reason of certain customs, in ritual or life, others again inquire concerning the origin of the Mishnah or Talmud and other historical questions. The Responsa, therefore, present a kaleidoscopic aspect wherein all students of law, of history, of theology, of literature, and all other phases of Jewish life can find interest.

As the Responsa bear an individual character, namely, each Gaon answered the inquirer according to what he believed to be true, it is no wonder then that contradictions are frequently found in them and a decision of one Gaon on a certain legal matter, or other subject, is at times overruled by another. They could, therefore, not be taken even collectively as a code. Later scholars in citing them have often reserved their opinion on a certain decision and changed it, if they found sufficient reason or authority for doing so. In general, where there is no difference of opinion between the Geonim themselves, the decision of a Gaon was considered authoritative. It was thus that the Responsa supplied the bases of many sections and parts in later codes. The Responsa are, as a rule, motivated, namely, reasons are given for the decision or opinion, and sources are quoted and interpreted. These motivations are important not only for the outcome of the decision, but for the understanding of the Talmud, as the passages referred to are explained and interpreted. There are, however, many unmotivated Responsa. On the whole, the Gaonic Responsa are brief and distinguished by simplicity, far from the later dialectic spirit.

159. RESPONSA LITERATURE IN THE ELEVENTH AND TWELFTH CENTURIES

The Responsa of the second period bear both a more orderly and more individual character. The period which is the flourishing epoch of Jewish literature in many fields is distinguished by the individuality of the producers of literature. Each author attached his name to his work and endeavored to preserve his writings in their integrity. The Responsa of the great Talmudic scholars are, on the whole, no exception though the nature of such work requires that there should likewise be found a number of single and isolated Responsa. We possess, therefore, many collections containing Responsa of various scholars. This is especially true of the Responsa of the early part of that period. The scholars then still conducted themselves in the manner of the Geonim and decided the questions propounded by the inquirers and troubled themselves little about their collections. Their Responsa were, therefore, included by later collectors among the Gaonic Responsa, but the aspect soon changed.

Turning to North Africa and Spain, we notice that almost every noted scholar wrote Responsa, but that those of the earlier ones were not collected and are found scattered in later books, while we possess whole collections of Responsa from the later ones. Thus, we have a number of single Responsa of Rab Ḥanannel and Rab Nissim of Kairawan quoted by later authors. Likewise, there are included, in Gaonic and other collections, Responsa from Rabbi Moses (ca. 960), one of the four captives, his son Rabbi Ḥanokh, Samuel Ibn Nagdila, Isaac Ibn Giat, and other scholars of that generation.

On the other hand, there exist large books of Responsa by Isaac Al-Fasi and his pupil, Joseph Ibn Migash, and later collections by Moses ben Maimon and others. That of the former is named *Sheolot u-Teshubot le-Morona Izḥak Al-Fasi* (Responsa of our Master, Isaac Al-Fasi). It consists of three hundred and twenty Responsa on various subjects. Many of them were written in Arabic and were later translated into Hebrew by Abraham ha-Levi. Likewise, the large collection of Responsa by Joseph Ibn Migash who followed Al-Fasi contains many, especially of a practical import, written in Arabic. In addition, many more Responsa of both these scholars are found in collections of later authors. Of the Responsa of Maimonides, we possess a considerable collection which was published, under the title of *Kobez Teshubot ha-Rambam* (A Collection of the Responsa of the Rambam), at Leipzig in 1859. Besides, we also possess a long Responsum written in Arabic to the Jews of South Arabia in regard to the question of the Messiah under the title *Iggeret Teman* (A Letter of Yemen). Most of his other Responsa were written in Arabic and only later translated into Hebrew. They are, on the whole, very brief and concise, and bear the character of decisions.

The sphere of inquiries is still a wide one and is not narrowed down to mere legal cases. The inquirers, though to a lesser extent than in Gaonic times, ask for explanations of difficult Talmudic passages, meaning of curious Agadic statements, and even touch on theology and philosophy. The spirit prevailing in the Responsa is a liberal and free one. Not only Maimonides, who was a philosopher, but also Al-Fasi and Ibn Migash endeavor in their answers to rationalize many of the difficult Agadic statements, and introduce a spirit of research based on sound reason.

There is also a large number of Responsa both scattered and in collections by the Franco-German scholars, including those of the Provence. We meet here with the same phenomenon as in the African and Spanish schools. The earlier scholars did not collect their Responsa, and they are therefore scattered in the collections of later scholars who quote them extensively. Thus we have Responsa by Rabbi Kalonymos (10th century), his son, Rabbi Meshulam (11th century), which are included in the collections of Gaonic Responsa. Likewise, Responsa of Rabbi Gershom ben Judah (Sec. 138) are preserved by later authors in large numbers. Rashi's Responsa, which are quite numerous, were not collected by his pupils in one book, but were included in the several codes bearing the name of Rashi which were compiled by his pupils, especially in the *Pardes* (Sec. 154). It is only when we come to the twelfth century that definite collections of Responsa begin to appear. Rabbi Jacob Tam (Sec. 143) devoted a large part of his book, *Sefer ha-Yashar,* containing glosses (Tosofot) and decisions, also to Responsa. Likewise, Eliezer ben Nathan collected his Responsa in his book *Eben ha-Ezer* (Rock of Salvation), the other parts of which are a code. There are also Responsa of the Provence scholars, Abraham Ab Bet Din (Dean of the Court, 12th century) and Abraham ben David of Posquiers, collected in a book named *Temim Deim* (Perfect of Knowledge). This book compiled by the latter contains, besides his own Responsa and that of his father-in-law, also Responsa of many others.

The Responsa of the Franco-German schools are more limited in their extent. They deal almost exclusively with legal cases, and only here and there, inquiries of a different nature occur. On the whole, they are more lengthy, and are rather in the nature of dialectic discussions than brief decisions. The decision is usually reached only after a long criticism of the opinions of previous authorities, and very often a reinterpretation of the sources. In this criticism and reinterpretation, great mental agility and logical acumen are displayed, and the Responsa thus constitute not only a contribution to legal decisions, but to the understanding of the Talmud. The inquiries reflect not only the inner religious life of the West-European Jewries but also their sufferings and tribulations. We hear there the echo of the persecutions of the Crusade, the relations of the Jews to the Church, nobles and other potentates of the Mediæval World. We meet with inquiries concerning the ransoming of captives, paying of fines by communities and distribution of taxes and all such matters arising from the peculiar political position of the Jews. In brief, the Jewish world is reflected there.

D. Methodology

160. BOOKS ON METHODOLOGY OF THE TALMUD

In addition to all these various phases of Halakic activity, there is still one more phase to be considered, which in spite of its rather meager quantity is of literary importance, and that is the small number of books dealing with the methodology of the Talmud. The Talmud, in the form in which it has been transmitted to us, verily justifies the epithet often applied to it, "The Sea of the Talmud," for like the sea it represents an uncharted expanse, and the one who undertakes to navigate it must have some guiding lines, a set of rules by means of which he can find his way, especially if he wants to arrive at some definite practical decisions. Such rules undoubtedly were in vogue at the Babylonian academies with the early teachers, such as the *Saburaim* (Sec. 151) and first generations of the Geonim. At first, they were, like the commentaries, taught orally, but as time went on, a need for writing them down grew, and it was at last fulfilled.

The earliest book on Methodology is the *Seder Tannaim we-Amoraim* (The order of Tannaim and Amoraim) hailing from Gaonic times. It was variously ascribed to Rab Nahshon Gaon (ca. 888) and to Rab Zemah ben Paltoi Gaon (term of office 864–873), but it seems that the author was not a Gaon, only one of the leading scholars of the academy at that time. The time of composition given by the author himself is the year 884. The book serves two purposes, historical and methodological. The author gives at first a list of the important *Tannaim* and *Amoraim,* classifying them according to generations together with the necessary dates, and then devotes himself to the methodological part. He first explains very briefly certain terms of the Mishnah, gives rules for determining the decisive value of the opinions of the important *Tannaim,* namely, whose opinions are authoritative and determines the relation between the Mishnah and the *Baraita* as well as other Halakic books such as the Tannaitic Midrashim. He then takes up the *Gemarah,* defines its terms, and gives a set of rules for deriving decisions from its discussion. The work, though a small one, is of great value in understanding the Talmud and its method, and it was utilized to its fullest extent by later writers on the subject.

The great Saadia, whose love for system in all phases of Jewish study is well known to us, is said to have paid attention also to this field and is reported to have written a *Seder Tannaim we-Amoraim* of his own, but nothing is known of the content of that book. The next book on that subject is from the pen of another scientific Talmudic scholar, Samuel Ibn Nagdila, the *Nagid.* It is called *Mebo ha-Talmud* (Introduction to the Talmud). It is entirely devoted to methodology, and is systematically arranged. He at first defines the terms, Mishnah, *Tosefta, Baraita, Gemarah;* then, the terms used by the *Gemarah,* both for purposes of discussion and decision of Halakah; finally he devotes a brief chapter to rules of decision between various opinions of *Tannaim* as well as of the *Amoraim*. The introduction of Maimonides to his commentary on the Mishnah contains many valuable remarks on the methodology of the Talmud, though it is primarily historical, as he gives a full list of all the *Tannaim* mentioned in the Mishnah and other Tannaitic books and classifies them according to generations. It is reported though that the introduction contained originally a few more chapters dealing with rules of the Talmud and definition of its terms, but though the report emanates from such an authority as Hayyim Joseph David Azulai, the eminent Hebrew bibliographer who claims to have seen them himself, yet, we cannot be certain about these chapters as they were never published.

A more systematic and more extensive introduction to the Talmud was written by Rabbi Joseph ben Judah Ibn Aknin of North Africa. It seems that in spite of likeness of names and places of residence, this Ibn Aknin is not the favorite pupil of Maimonides, but another scholar of the same period. The book was written about the end of the twelfth century and contains twelve short chapters systematically arranged. The first chapter gives the various epithets by which a number of scholars, both *Tannaim* and *Amoraim,* are quoted in the Talmud, in addition to their own names. The second, points out who of the *Tannaim* are meant by the Mishnah when their names without their patronymics are given, as there were usually several who bore the same name. Chapters III–IX are devoted to rules of decision in general, and decisions between opinions in particular, both the opinions of the *Tannaim* and those of the *Amoraim*. The ninth chapter gives an alphabetical list of *Tannaim*. The tenth and eleventh chapters tabulate the successive generations of *Tannaim* and *Amoraim*. The twelfth chapter closes with a discussion about the differences between the schools of Shammai and Hillel. The influence of Maimonides is evident in this book, but its comparative extensive treatment of certain parts of the methods and terms of the Talmud imparts to it considerable value.

Chapter XI

PHILOSOPHY AND THEOLOGY

161. INTRODUCTORY REMARKS

All philosophy starts in doubt. And what is true of the origin of philosophy, in general, is especially true of the rise of religious philosophy in particular. But while general philosophic thought is frequently a production of the mind of the individual and its rise can therefore be attributed to doubts of the intellect of an individual, religious philosophy which is, as a rule, a mental phenomenon of the group, inevitably rises through contact of group cultures and exchange of ideas.

In times of national seclusion, when tradition and ancient customs hold sway, there is hardly any need for a philosophy. The religion as such is the philosophy of the group. It is only when the nation or the group emerges from its seclusion and comes in contact with other nations and the respective cultures meet, that the religious ideas of one group begin to be tested, analyzed and explained in the light of the ideas of the other group. First, as a result of the testing and analysis, doubts as to the exact meaning of the religious principles arise, and secondly, there arises on the part of the adherents of the attacked religion a desire for defending it, for reinterpreting its principles in the light of the stronger or prevailing culture, and very often to prove its identity with the most elevated principles of that culture, and thus a philosophy arises.

It was thus with Judaism when it first came in contact with Hellenic culture in the Diaspora, especially in Egypt, that a religious philosophy was born, the greatest representative of which was Philo (Ch. V). With the disappearance of that Diaspora, its philosophy fell likewise into desuetude, and the very name of the great Philo was almost forgotten in Jewish literature.

Yet, its ideas were not entirely obliterated and the need for a religious philosophy did not cease altogether. Even hedged in and secluded as the Jews were in the first six centuries after the dispersion by the Halakah and the Agada, ideas from the outside did penetrate into the

Jewish world, and there was a necessity to counteract their influence. This was undertaken by the Agada, where many philosophic ideas of the Alexandrian school (Ch. V) are taken up and new ones developed. But in the Agada, things are not arranged systematically and they become mixed up with a multitude of other matters. The need, therefore, for a systematic Jewish philosophy arose in the early Middle Ages, when once more the Jew met a strong and vigorous culture with which he had to contend—this was the culture of the young Arabic nation.

The Arabic culture, as we have seen, influenced Jewish life and literature in many ways. It gave rise to Hebrew poetry, to philological study of the Hebrew language. But still greater was its influence on the development of Jewish thought. In fact, it can almost be said that Jewish philosophy was a child of the current Arabic philosophy. Yet, that should not be taken to mean that the successive development of Jewish thought was a simple imitation. It only signifies that the needs and the conditions which called forth the process of philosophizing in the Jewish world were not only similar to those of the Arabic world, but were impelled by the thought movement in the larger sphere within which the Jewish world moved.

The seventh and eighth centuries were centuries of great intellectual fermentation in the East. This fermentation arose, like all such movements, from the contact of the Arabs with Greek speculation which continued in the East after it was driven out from the West by Justinian in 529 c. e. These ideas of the ancients dressed now in Arabic garb, through the many translations of the works of Aristotle, Plato, and a few others, created a disturbance in the minds of the devotees of the Koran, who testing its principles by the light of the newly acquired wisdom found them often wanting. Added to this there were also theologic differences among the various interpreters of the Koran. As a result, sects in Islam were springing up in great profusion, and various currents of thought were set in motion. Chief among these was the more or less orthodox philosophy, the aim of which was both to defend the doctrines of religion against heresies, as well as to reconcile them with the principles of reason. This philosophy was, of course, not of one color. It soon divided itself into a number of wings, some inclining to the right, and some possessing a more radical tendency. Some philosophers went so far as to break with religion, or at least with some of its principal tenets altogether. These, however, were the exceptions; the original tendency of reconciling religion with reason remained the predominating one. It is usually called the Kalamitic philosophy, from the Arabic word *Kalam*, i. e. word, and also reason.

The intellectual fermentation and division of opinion current in the larger Arabic sphere were soon reflected in the Jewish world. Here too sects arose, the most important of which was the Karaite (Ch. XII); here too doubt of principles and forms of tradition began to be voiced, and free thought made its appearance. Not only was the Talmud bitterly assailed by the Karaites and kindred sects, but even the Bible, the very foundation of the Jewish religion, found severe critics. One of these by the name of Ḥivi Al-Balkhi wrote a book containing two hundred questions which, in their pertinence and severity of attack on the Bible, hardly fall behind those of a modern rabid Bible critic. All these necessitated, of course, a systematic, scientific and organized defense of the doctrines and forms of tradition that should prove not only their validity, but also their compatibility with the principles of reason and science as taught and understood then. This defense had to use the very same weapons employed by the doubters and skeptics, namely, the material borrowed from general philosophy. It is thus that Jewish philosophy began. We do not really know when it began, nor can we determine accurately who was the very first Jewish philosopher. It satisfied a great need, and as such it most likely had several beginnings in different places. But we do know that by the beginning of the tenth century, it was already a developed current of thought and was given complete expression by Saadia Gaon, though attempts at philosophizing were made much earlier.

162. NATURE AND CHARACTER OF JEWISH PHILOSOPHY

The character of Jewish philosophy is determined by the conditions of its birth as well as by the general trend of thought characteristic of that era. It is primarily a theologic philosophy, as its main purpose was to defend the principles of Jewish religion from all attacks which might emanate from philosophic thought. But it had also another aim, which though a result of the former, yet is of no less importance, and that was to rationalize religion, and to found the principles of belief on a speculative basis. As such, the theologic element in this mass of philosophic literature occupies as much space, if not more, than the purely philosophic one. It is as much its business to enunciate as clearly as possible the dogmas of Jewish religion, as to prove their validity and rationality. The majority of the great Jewish philosophers not only devoted considerable space in their writings to the classification and fixation of the dogmas of Judaism, but even arranged the plan of their books in accordance with the dogmatic scheme.

From the fundamental traits of the nature and character of this literature, there follow the general lines of its division. Roughly speaking, Jewish philosophic literature is divided into two great divisions, metaphysics and ethics, namely, books which deal primarily with problems of a metaphysical nature, or where the principles of religion are discussed in the light of metaphysics, and books where the center of gravity is the delineation of human conduct. But as both the principles of Jewish religion and ethics are grounded in the Bible, intelligent discussion of any of these problems could not be carried on without recurring to the necessity of a reinterpretation of the Bible along philosophical lines. And in course of time, a considerable branch of philosophical exegesis and ultimately also homiletics came into being.

Again, no philosophy or rational theology or any process of thought could be carried on without devoting some attention to the principles of logic as preparatory to all thought. So as a result, logic occupies an important place in that literature, and books devoted to its elucidation increased with the development of that literature. Likewise, certain metaphysical-religious problems as well as ethical, such as that of the soul and human conduct, cannot be understood without a knowledge of psychology, and of course, even this study had to be included in the scope of this literature. Nor can the question of God which, as will be seen, is the kernel of this philosophy, be understood without a knowledge of the physical world and its laws. And thus the circle widened, and as the interest in study grew, it became more ramified and included more and more branches.

For our purpose, however, we will divide this literature into its three main branches. (a) Philosophy, dealing primarily with problems of metaphysical theology, the enunciation of dogmas, and also including logic, psychology and physical sciences; (b) Ethics; and finally (c) Philosophical Exegesis. On the whole, the last two divisions consist primarily of original books written by Jewish scholars either in Arabic or Hebrew. Of the first division, only those relating to metaphysics and theology are mostly original, while those relating to logic, psychology, and physical sciences are to a greater extent translations, which, in view of the fact that they served as the channel through which the wisdom and science of the East flowed to the Christian West, assume exceptional importance and deserve special consideration.

163. PROBLEMS OF JEWISH PHILOSOPHY

From all that has been said, the nature of the problems which are dealt with in Jewish philosophy and theology can easily be inferred. God, of course, occupies the central place around which the discussion turns. This central problem really comprises a group of problems. In general, there are to be discerned in it two phases, the concept of God as such, and God and the world. The first comprises discussions of the following subjects: proofs for the existence of God, conception of His essence and unity, and the problem of attributes.

The second, embracing the relation of God to the world, includes the problems of creation, providence, and human freedom. Together with these problems there are inherently connected a number of theological questions, as for instance reward and punishment of man for good and bad actions, which is only a species of providence. But we cannot speak of good and bad actions unless we deal with God's commandments which are embodied in the Torah and the Bible. Hence, the authority of the Bible, its purpose, and eternity are brought in, which again involves the conception of prophecy in general, and that of Moses, the Law-giver in particular. Thus, the circle widens, and the chain of problems extends until it covers the entire field of religion.

The other important problem is the problem of the soul, its nature, divisions, and mainly its immortality, and finally the problem of ethics. This last one occupies an exceptionally important place in Jewish philosophic literature, for is not all Judaism a way of life?

Yet, the lines between these problems can only be formally drawn, for in reality, they all intertwine with one another. We can hardly speak of an ethical personality without attributing to man freedom of action, but this can hardly be understood without a clear conception of the relation of God to man, namely, does God know beforehand human action, or does He not? If He does not know, then His providence is impaired. If He does know, how can man act otherwise than what God in His wisdom ordained for him? And how can he be said to be free? The solution of this problem has occupied the best minds in Jewry. But no solution is here intended, merely an endeavor to show the interconnection of the problems. Again, no Jewish ethics can be spoken of without understanding the nature, character, and authority of the Torah, the very source of Jewish ethics, and thus again, ethics is linked to the other problems. In general, it can be said that God and the Bible are the two poles of the axis around which this philosophic-theologic literature revolves.

It is of course true, that not all these problems were really solved by Jewish philosophy. It is, in general, very doubtful whether philosophy as a whole has ever solved its problems with certainty. But that this great attempt to rationalize the principles and doctrines of Judaism, which has occupied so many brilliant minds for centuries, has contributed to the elevation of Judaism, and that the literature wherein it is embodied is of a lasting value, of this there is no doubt.

A. PHILOSOPHY

164. LOGIC

As no philosophical thinking can be carried on without a knowledge of logic which supplies the very basis for such processes of thought, it is understood that logic occupied an important place in Jewish philosophic literature, as well as in philosophy of the Middle Ages in general.

As a matter of fact, the logic of Aristotle, which during that period comprised the entire science of logic, was the basis of all Mediæval philosophy, constituting the most important subject of education in those days. His "Organon," consisting of eight books, which includes also his "Rhetoric" and "Poetics," was translated into Arabic several times and a number of digests and compendia were made of it by various philosophers. Likewise, numerous commentaries were written on these books.

All this literature, or at least a large part of it, was destined to be translated into Hebrew later, after the interest in philosophy among Hebrew reading people increased. But in the very period of bloom of Jewish philosophy, in the period from Saadia to Maimonides, which may be called the classical period, few books on logic were written or even translated by Jewish scholars. The reason for it can readily be seen. The Jewish philosophers of the classical period wrote their books, almost without exception, in Arabic for an intelligent reading public which was acquainted with the current Arabic philosophy, and they took the acquaintance of the readers with the principles of logic for granted. They, therefore, did not think it necessary to write special treatises on logic.

Only two men, one in the beginning of the period and one at the end, thought it necessary to deal with that subject. These were Isaac Israeli and Maimonides. Isaac ben Suleiman Israeli (845–945) was born in Egypt, and later migrated to Kairawan, North Africa, where he served for a long time as court physician to the Caliph Ubaid-Allah, the founder of the Fatimide Dynasty. He was famous as a physician, and his works were translated into Latin, and for a long time used as textbooks. He was also a Jewish philosopher, probably the earliest one, and wrote a number of works. He wrote a book on logic which is mentioned by Arabic writers under the name of the "Garden of Wisdom." The book, however, is lost. Another work of his also written in Arabic and entitled "On Definitions and Description," is preserved in a Latin translation, and a part also in a Hebrew translation by Nissim ben Moses. The book is primarily a collection of excerpts of philosophical statements on definitions of certain concepts from the writings of philosophers. Of the concepts defined, the most important are: the essence, or the whatness (quidditas) of things, quality, and causality. The book was well known in his time and is even referred to by Maimonides.

Maimonides' contribution to logic is a little book written in Arabic called "Logical Terms." It was one of his early works written about 1160 and was later translated into Hebrew by Moses Ibn Tibbon under the name *Milot ha-Higayon*. It can really be termed a brief intro-duction to philosophy, inasmuch as it covers all philosophical terms and also describes briefly the division of the sciences. It contains fourteen chapters, where, with the usual Maimonidean clearness, all philosophical terms are defined. The first chapter defines the terms: subject, predicate, and judgment; Chapters II–V define the various kinds of judgment, positive, negative, contrary, and contradictory. The following two chapters deal with the syllogism, and Chapter VIII with concepts. Chapters IX–XIV describe the four causes—material, formal, active and final, genus and species, the categories, substance and accident and sundry rhetorical terms such as synonyms, homonyms, and figures of speech. The last chapter describes briefly the various sciences, the parts of philosophy, namely, metaphysics, ethics, and politics.

165. THE EARLY JEWISH PHILOSOPHERS

As stated above, we can hardly determine with accuracy the begin-ning of Jewish philosophy. Undoubtedly, attempts were made by vari-ous men to philosophize much earlier than the beginning of the tenth century, the time when the first philosophical treatises began to appear. The need came not only from without, that is, through the influence of Arabic thought, but also from within. The leaders of the Karaites often boasted of their superiority in interpreting the Bible in a rational way, so as to remove all anthropomorphic expressions, and accused the Rabbanites, i. e. the Jews who accepted the Talmud of holding grosser conceptions of God, and to substantiate their claim they pointed to anthropomorphic Agadic passages. To refute the claims of the Karaites, leading Jewish scholars began early to delve into philosophy and show not only the purity of Rabbinic theology, but also the rationality of that tradition. However, if there were any philosophical treatises before the century indicated, they were lost.

The early Jewish philosophers whose treatises are wholly or partly preserved were David Ibn Merwan Al-Mukamis of Rakka in Mesopotamia, and the above-mentioned Isaac Israeli of Kairawan. David Al-Mukamis is quoted a number of times by Arabic and later Jewish scholars, but little is known of his biography. It is, however, almost certain that he was a younger contemporary of Saadia and died before the year 937, for in that year, he is spoken of by a Karaite author as dead. He must have had a checkered career for it is told that he was converted to Christianity and then returned to Judaism.

His philosophic treatise was called the "Book of the Twenty Tractates," and was written in Arabic but it must have been later translated into Hebrew, as fragments of a Hebrew version were preserved. The book deals primarily with the proofs for the existence of God and His attributes. From what was preserved, we can see that he resembles Saadia in his philosophic method. As a matter of fact, one of his proofs for the incorporeality of God, which is based on the assumption that a body, being composed of matter and form, must have a creator, and this is contrary to the concept of God as the Creator of all, is almost identically stated by Saadia. It was even said that Saadia was influenced by Al-Mukamis, but it does not necessarily follow, for both employed the methods of the current philosophy—the Kalam (Sec. 160). The book treated also of the Jewish law, and besides contained a history of Jewish sects. Karaite authors quote extracts from it on this subject.

Isaac Israeli wrote, besides his works on logic, also a number of treatises dealing with metaphysical problems of the day, such as the existence of God, creation, the soul, and other kindred questions. The most important of his treatises is "The Book of the Elements" written in

Arabic which was translated in 1210, at the request of the great scholar David Kimḥi, into Hebrew by Abraham ben Ḥisdai. The bc k is divided into three parts. In the first one he explains the Aristotelian theory of elements, in the second, that of Galen and Hippocrates, and in the third, he discusses the nature and characteristics of the elements. The book shows Israeli's extensive knowledge of the philosophy and science of his day. As a great physician, he was a master of physics and medicine, and the book appears more as a treatise on these two sciences, but the purpose was a metaphysical one. Its aim was to prove the most important contention for religious philosophers of that period, namely, the creation of the world from nothing, which involves, of course, the refutation of the accepted Aristotelian doctrine of the eternity of the world. It is, in reality, a reconciliation of the Aristotelian principles of metaphysics and physics with the Jewish principle of creation. He shows, therefore, by an interpretation of these very principles, especially the conceptions of being and becoming of things, that we must arrive at the notion of creation, and not at the eternity of the world as Aristotle did. This is his main thesis, for with the exception of this defect in Aristotle's theory, Israeli, like so many Jewish philosophers, is in perfect accord with Aristotle and is quite satisfied with the latter's proofs for the existence of God. For this reason, he does not touch upon this problem. His thesis is proved at length with many arguments drawn from the entire field of science, especially from medicine, his own specialty.

Besides this book, he wrote another treatise on the spirit and the soul where psychological problems were discussed, but only a fragment of the Hebrew translation is preserved. He also wrote commentaries on the first chapters of Genesis, and the famous mystic work, "Book of Creation" (Ch. XII), but of these later.

166. SAADIA

These previous attempts were only partial efforts to elucidate one or more of the problems of Jewish philosophy. But soon there arose a man who knitted all these strands of philosophical thought into one system and gave us a complete statement of Jewish religious philosophy as bearing on all phases of theology. That man was the Gaon Saadia (for life, see Ch. VIII). His book, called in Arabic *Kitab Al-Amanat Wal-I'tiḳadât*, better known by its Hebrew name *Emunot we-Deot*,

(Doctrines and Religious Beliefs), was the first systematic treatise in philosophic literature.

In his elucidating introduction, Saadia states the purpose of his book, saying, that having observed how so many Jews are engulfed in matters of belief by doubts and buffeted by waves of error, he took pity upon them and undertook to write this book to guide them in their search for the right path. That such a thing is possible, Saadia was convinced, for error he believed, together with Aristotle, arises not from the sense perceptions but from an inability to operate with the instruments of knowledge which is logical reasoning. At times, it may be due to the impatience of men to go through the entire process of reasoning. He, therefore, advises both patience and skillful use of reasoning in order to arrive at pure belief which is in harmony with reason. It is only little and hasty knowledge that leads to heresy. Heresy may also arise when men possess only simple belief without any foundation of reason. It is, therefore, the duty of the great man to show to all intelligent men, that all that we received through revelation and the prophets can be understood by us through reason. This purpose or rather double purpose, namely, to show that the principles of Judaism are compatible with reason and are not to be doubted, and also to interpret them in such a way that their rationality be evident, first outlined clearly by Saadia, became the purpose of all succeeding Jewish philosophers. Saadia bases his contentions, in the introduction, on an elaborate theory of knowledge which is skilfully though briefly stated. After that he proceeds to the main body of the book.

The book is divided into ten sections each of which is subdivided into chapters. The first nine sections establish philosophically the ten fundamental articles of faith—which were almost unnecessarily expanded by Maimonides into thirteen; the tenth is devoted to ethics. The first two are devoted to the problem of the existence of God and the pure conception of the Godhead, namely, His attributes. Saadia gives these sections a theologic turn by naming the former *Hidush,* i. e. creation, and the latter *Ahdut,* i. e. unity, for in the first, he proves not only the existence of God, but also the creation of the world, thus establishing two dogmas at once. In this, he was influenced by the philosophers of the *Kalam* who always proved the existence of God by the indirect method of creation from nothing. It would be too abstruse to enter into the details of the proofs here. Suffice it to say, that they are primarily based on Aristotelian principles which were all dominant then but with certain deviations, which deviations, of course, led to the overthrow of the Aristotelian conclusion that the world is eternal. These principles are two, the finitude of the world and the composite nature of all matter. There is added a third non-Aristotelian principle, and that is the finitude of time. The logical manipulation of these principles proves that the world is created, and *eo ipso* that there is a Creator, i. e. God. This last, however, needs further proof, for one may argue that the world created itself. After the theory of chance creation is refuted, Saadia proceeds to prove the third link, the creation from nothing, and not from some primal matter, a theory which was advocated by Plato and his followers. This problem of all problems in Mediæval religious philosophy, namely, that of creation, which has quite some importance even today, was handled by Saadia with great skill, and his method was frequently imitated by later philosophers.

The establishment of the existence of God and His being the Creator of the world leads directly to a pure conception of Him, for the very proofs involve such a conception of God, namely, that He is incorporeal and immutable, and above all establish His unity. Unity of God is the most important of them, for its pure conception involves also incorporeality and immutability, as it does not mean only that God is one numerically, but also that He is absolutely simple and pure spirit. Hence, the whole second section is denominated Unity, for on its right conception depend all other attributes. The attributes are, according to Saadia, four: one, living, potent, and wise. The first relates to the concept God, the other three to God as creator of the world. The main problem consists first, in showing that we can describe God by these attributes and yet not impair His absolute unity and imply no change in His essence, and secondly, in reconciling the pure conception of these few attributes with so many passages in the Bible where God is described in human terms. Both phases are dealt with by Saadia in a detailed way, explaining how all attributes are really one in essence, and we only speak of them as several because of the inadequacy of language. Likewise, other attributes which we apply to God, such as loving or hating are to be understood in a figurative way. Similarly all Biblical passages which deviate from the high conception of God only speak figuratively but do not imply anything which may impugn that pure conception. In this fine and elaborate explanation, Saadia enunciates a great principle of philosophical exegesis, which reads thus, "Know the rule that wherever an expression in the Bible or anywhere else concerning God and His deeds differs from the way of true philosophy, it is undoubtedly to be explained figuratively." [1] This principle had far-reaching consequences.

After establishing the three fundamental dogmas, the existence of God, the purity of His conception, and His creation of the world, Saadia turns to the relation of God and the world. The third section is devoted to the authority and value of the Torah. God commanded people to observe His teaching, but wherefore? In answer to this question, Saadia explains first the reason for the creation of the world and man. Creation came as an act of His infinite goodness, for existence is good in itself. And since creation is a result of God's goodness, it follows that He should endow the creatures with means to make their existence still better, and hence He gave them the Torah, which is a means for a good life. He did not create men naturally good, for there is a higher degree of good obtained when man struggles for its attainment. This Torah is divided into two parts, one containing precepts which are fully substantiated by reason, and the other such precepts which are to be obeyed merely because God commanded them, although we cannot comprehend their reason. Yet, he says, there was need for a revelation even as regards the rational part, for the details of the precepts needed such a revelation; reason may recognize the general validity of such precepts but not their extent and mode of operation. As for the precepts which merely require obedience, even they have a reasonable basis, although it is not always evident.

This revelation was given through the prophets, and he discusses therefore the question of prophecy, its authenticity and its necessity for the people. He makes the point that the real authority for the prophetic teaching is not the miracles by which it was demonstrated, but its inner worth. The same is applied to the Torah; its value is intrinsic, and hence its immutability. This last doctrine is proved at great length, in the course of which Saadia raises a point which deserves special attention. He proves the eternity of the Torah from the promised eternity of the Jewish people. "Our people," he says, "is a distinct people only by its teachings, and if it is eternal in its uniqueness, it follows that its Torah must also remain eternally unchanged." [2]

[1] *Emunot,* Sec. 2, Ch. III.
[2] *Ibid,* Sec. 3, Ch. VII.

From this discussion of the character of the Torah as a means to human happiness, Saadia proceeds to prove, in the fourth section, the freedom of man, which is a necessary assumption for his previous contention of the Bible as a means of happiness. Here, he stumbles on the difficult problem of free will and its compatibility with divine prescience of human actions. He grapples with the problem and solves it by saying that God knows the ultimate decision of man, but His knowledge does not determinate the latter's choice of action.

If man is a free agent, then it follows that he deserves both reward and punishment for his good and bad deeds. To the elucidation of this question and the problem it entails, the fifth section on "Merits and Demerits" is devoted. Saadia endeavors to demonstrate the Biblical teachings on this subject in the light of reason. He is especially interested in the old problem of Job, why the wicked prosper and the righteous suffer. He offers various solutions, but the subject is not really exhausted here, as the main solution, namely, that the real reward and punishment come in the hereafter, needs as its basis the assumption of the immortality of the soul. To the soul, then, the sixth section is devoted. It contains really Saadia's psychology. Briefly it is thus: The soul is created by God and it is of a fine spiritual substance. As to its manifestation in the body, it appears under three aspects or parts, the *appetite,* i. e. those desires which crave to satisfy the elemental needs of man, such as food, procreation, and others; emotion or spirit, and cognition or reason. This primarily Platonic-Aristotelian division corresponds to the three appellations of the soul in Hebrew, *Nefesh, Ruah,* and *Neshamah,* respectively. The immortality of the soul is partly proved here from its very nature, and partly later in the ninth chapter.

The three succeeding sections are all devoted to the problem of reward and punishment under different aspects. The first is that of resurrection (Sec. 7). It is intimately connected with the nature of the soul and also with the question of divine justice, especially justice to the Jewish people which suffered so much. Resurrection is to be part of the reward. He discusses its possibility from a natural point of view and endeavors to prove it. Intimately connected with this question of divine justice to the Jew, is the coming of the Messiah to which the eighth section is devoted. He shows that the prophecies must be fulfilled, for otherwise the suffering of Israel cannot be explained, and he even attempts to determine the time of the coming of the Messiah.

As usual, he devotes a good deal of space to criticism of theories which deny this doctrine or interpret it in a figurative way. Finally, he comes to the point of his problem, picking up here the trend of his thought in the previous sections, namely, that of the immortality of the soul and its reward and punishment after death. The first is proved again from the fact that life is too short, and therefore God's scheme of justice cannot be carried out in the earthly life, and must be prolonged till after death; hence the soul is immortal. The nature of that reward and punishment is discussed together with the conception of the world to come. As always Saadia tries to give a more rational aspect to some of these conceptions expressed in the Bible and the Agada.

With this chapter, the book properly comes to an end, but he added a tenth chapter on ethics, where after a detailed criticism of various theories and ways of life, he offers his own which is, that the best way to follow is the one which aims at a coördination and harmony of the various forces of human nature, where each force is given sway but in a limited and controlled way. He refers to the harmony in nature and music, and advises us to follow it in life. Even from this rather brief glimpse of the contents of Saadia's work, we can glean the completeness of his system and the masterly way in which it was executed. He can really be called the Father of Jewish Philosophy.

167. SOLOMON IBN GABIROL

With Saadia there closes the school of Jewish philosophy in Babylonia, and like all other phases of Jewish literature of the period, also that of Jewish philosophy found its great center in Spain. The first Jewish philosopher in that country was the poet, Solomon Ibn Gabirol (Ch. IX). His great philosophical work is the *Fons Vitæ,* (Heb. Mekor Ḥayyim), which was originally written in Arabic but for one reason or another, was not translated into Hebrew in its entirety, only selections of it were made by Shem-Tob Ibn Falaquera (1224–1290). It was, however, translated into Spanish as early as the beginning of the twelfth century by Johannes Hispalensis and soon into Latin about 1150 by Dominic Gundisalvi. In the Latin translation, it made a great impression upon the Christian world, and for centuries it influenced Western scholastic thought. But the name of its author, Gabirol, was forgotten. It assumed a number of variations, Avicebron, Avicebrol, and others. The author was thought to be an Arab, and some believed him even to be a Christian. Only in the middle of the nineteenth cen-

tury, the great Jewish scholar, Solomon Munk at Paris, made the discovery that the famous Avicebron is no other but Solomon Ibn Gabirol.
He then published the Hebrew selection of Falaquera. In our own
day, a complete Hebrew translation of the book from the Latin was
made and published in Palestine.

And just as the career of his book was so different from those of the
works of the other Jewish philosophers, so is his philosophy different
from that of all his predecessors and those who follow him, except the
few who were, to a small degree, influenced by his teachings. Gabirol
swerved in his teachings from the beaten track of Jewish philosophy
which is in nature both theologic and Aristotelian. His book is purely
a philosophic one, and does not attempt to reconcile Jewish teaching
with philosophy. He could not, of course, escape the religious kernel in
philosophy, for that was the very essence of philosophic thought from
the time of Plotinus (d. 270) and even of the earlier thinkers. Nor
did he escape the influence of Aristotle, for both things were an impossibility in those days. Gabirol is, therefore, a religious philosopher,
not a theologic one, and that par excellence, for his was a deeply
religious soul as we have seen in his poetry. He is also more of a neo-
Platonist than an Aristotelian though he differed from both. We do not
really know how he could have been so deeply influenced by neo-
Platonic teachings, as little of the works of the founder of the school,
Plotinus, and his followers were translated into Arabic, yet he seemed
to have mastered their teachings.

His main problem is that of personal salvation, namely, to define the
purpose of the life of man. This he finds to be the communion of the
soul with the upper world or with its source. The next question which
presents itself is, by what means can this communion be effected? and
the answer is given, by knowledge and action. But though both are
mentioned, the emphasis is placed on knowledge or contemplation,
and to the elucidation of this answer the whole book is devoted. It is
supposed to answer the questions, what there is to know as well as
what the content of the knowledge is. The answer to the first states
briefly that there are three things to know: (a) God, the first existent,
(b) matter and form, and (c) the great divine power, the will. The
second question, namely, what is the content of this knowledge, is
treated in detail. As we can see from the subjects of knowledge, the
problems are three, God, the world (matter and form), and creation.
Yet Gabirol deals very little with the subject of God, he offers no proofs

for His existence, nor does he dwell on His attributes except in his philosophic poem, "The Royal Crown" (Ch. IX), where he speaks of them more in a figurative way. His main theme is the world and its becoming and the five sections or portals of the book are primarily devoted to it.

There are seven substances: (1) God, pure spiritual substance; (2) the will which is an all-embracive power in God, conceived both as something of the essence of God and as something separate; (3) universal matter; (4) universal form, which in their combination produce the universal reason; (5) universal soul; (6) universal nature; (7) the substance of the nine categories. This last one forms the boundary between the world of Intelligences and the sensible world. Of these substances, God, the first one is practically the unknown. He is above all conceptions, hence Gabirol refrains from discussing His attributes. All that we know of Him is His existence. He is also denominated the first agent. But how has this universe arisen? To this Gabirol attempts to give an answer; it arose through the mediacy of the other three substances, the will, matter, and form. The will which is a kind of emanation flashes through the universal matter and unites it with the universal form and henceforth becoming gradually descends. The whole universe is one grand ladder where there are many rungs, but it is all one; the various higher substances serve as causes and places for the lower, until we reach this sensible world which is expressed by space and body in space. In all this gradual series of emanation of substances, the further a substance is from the first source, the more material and corporeal it becomes. But through all this series, the Divine Will flashes and lights it up, and thus unifies it into one.

The human soul is an emanation and a part of the world-soul, and is of course eternal. In uniting with the body, it acquires sensibility and thus is really lowered from its pristine purity. But it retains the desire to return to its source, which return can be accomplished by reason, by striving to unite with the world reason and through it with the source of all sources—God.

In all this, there is much neo-Platonism, but Gabirol differs from it in two important points. First, he introduces the will of God as the leaven of all these emanations, while in that system the gradual emanations are performed in a kind of mechanical way. Gabirol has thus saved the Jewish idea of creation. The second is the acceptance of the Aristotelian doctrine of the dualism of matter and form, but he deviates from it as he raises matter above form, in making the universal matter one of the first substances—and thus one of the first emanations. This subject is not entirely clear in Gabirol, and lent itself to various interpretations, some making universal matter an emanation, and some believing it to be an uncreated thing. It still needs investigation.

Gabirol's philosophy, though original and deep, did not influence the course of Jewish philosophy to a great extent, and only some of his theories found followers. On the whole, his ignoring of Jewish matters and his neo-Platonic bent subjected him to severe criticism on the part of his immediate followers. He was thus severely criticized by Abraham Ibn Daud (Sec. 169), but later entirely neglected. Only the much later mystics again picked up the trend of his thought, but even then seldom mentioned his name, though utilizing his ideas to a great extent.

168. BAHYA BEN JOSEPH IBN PAKUDAH

Bahya ben Joseph Ibn Pakudah (ca. 1050), surnamed the judge, was another Jewish philosopher of that period and probably lived in the same town with the poet-philosopher, Gabirol. He was primarily interested in ethics, but also dealt with the fundamental philosophic problems of the day, namely, God, His attributes, and the creation of the world which involved, of course, that of matter and form. His main work is the *Hobot ha-Lebabot*, (Duties of the Heart). The book was written in Arabic, but later translated into Hebrew by the master translator, Judah Ibn Tibbon. There is also another translation of that book by Joseph Kimhi, grammarian and commentator, but that of Tibbon is the accepted one.

The purpose of the book, as stated, is an ethical one. The author says in the introduction, "The Torah is divided into two parts, one is *the duties of the organs,* i. e. all such precepts the performance of which depends upon the external organs of the body, and the other is *the duties of the heart,* namely, those belonging to the human conscience. But while," says Bahya, "so many books were written on the first part, such as the codes, few have dealt with the other." Hence he undertook to write this book. But, *the duties of the heart* which include the love of God, His worship, and trust in Him cannot be understood without a clear conception of the Godhead. He, therefore, devoted the first portal or section to this very conception. The book contains in all ten portals, where phases of ethics and piety are discussed, such as service of God, trust in Him, humility, temperance of human conduct, and finally the love of God.

The first portal is called "The Portal of Unity." In it, Bahya proves the existence of God and defines His attributes. His method is similar to that of Saadia whose book he read and even mentions in his introduction, inasmuch as he also proves the existence of God indirectly through the fact that the world needs a creator, and adduces a number of philosophical proofs. On the whole, they are less complicated. He was the first to employ, in Jewish philosophy, the famous "Argument from Design," namely, that the world in its complicated aspect and its harmonious arrangement testifies that it was created by the design of a creator.

As his main interest lies in forming a pure conception of God, he devotes considerable space to the unity of God for which he quotes seven proofs, one of which is that the world testifies not only to a creator but to one, for it is so beautifully harmonious that we must involuntarily conclude that it is a manifestation of the plan of one creator. In his theory of attributes, he differs greatly from Saadia. He makes a distinct division of the attributes into two classes, essential and active. The first are those which belong to God, independently of the fact that He is the creator of the world; the second are those we bestow on Him by observing His actions. The former are: existent, one, and eternal. These are, of course, sublime, pure, and abstract, and can by no means be understood positively, but negatively. For example, when we say God is existent, we do not mean to imply that we have any positive knowledge of the nature of His existence, but we merely mean to deny the assertion that He does not exist, and thus with the others. He was the first one to introduce the term negative meaning, as applied to the attributes, and was followed by many.

There is also ascribed to Bahya another book called, *Torat ha-Nefesh,* (The Doctrine of the Soul), which was only lately translated into Hebrew. But while in his "Duties of the Heart," he follows the rationalistic philosophy of the day, i. e. the Aristotelian, tempered by the Arabic *Kalam,* in the other, he is influenced by the neo-Platonic strain which came to him as well as to others through the mystic philosophy of the "Society of the Pure Brothers," a philosophic mystic brotherhood of the East which flourished in the tenth century, and which left an encyclopaedia where its ideas are expressed. He discusses there primarily the nature of the soul and its conduct, but this problem brings him to other problems, such as the emanation of the soul from higher spheres, the different worlds, and ultimately the nature of the creation of the world which, as always, involves a discussion of matter and form. On the whole, there is resemblance in this book to some of the doctrines of Gabirol, and an air of mysticism and asceticism pervades it.

169. ABRAHAM BAR ḤIYYA, MOSES IBN EZRA, AND JOSEPH IBN ẒADDIK

Besides these leading men, the age produced a number of philosophers of minor importance, yet who nevertheless made some important contributions to philosophic teaching. The first one is Abraham bar Ḥiyya, the Prince (1065–1136). He was primarily a scientist and wrote many books on astronomy and mathematics (Ch. XV), but also several books on philosophy, the most important of which is "Reflections of the Soul." It was written originally in Hebrew and was probably the first of its kind written in that language. It is primarily an ethical book (Sec. B) divided into four sections, or as he calls them, pillars, three of which are devoted to defining the best way of life, to repentance, and to the destiny of man. The first deals with the beginning and nature of the world. It is here where he develops philosophical ideas on the nature of things and matter and form. He also makes the assertion, which was already made by Philo, that the world was first created potentially and later called forth into actuality by the Word, and this is the creation which is described in the first chapter of Genesis.

The poet, Moses Ibn Ezra (Ch. IX), also wrote a book on philosophy under the euphonious name *Arugat ha-Bosem* (Bed of Spices), where he deals with problems of creation, the triple nature or three souls of man, on truth, and other philosophical theological questions. There is little originality in the book, as it is mostly eclectic, and it seems that he was greatly influenced by Gabirol in his views.

The most important of these thinkers was Joseph Ibn Ẓaddik, judge at Cordova (b. 1080—d. 1149). His main philosophic work is *Olam Katan* (The Microcosm) which was written in Arabic and later translated into Hebrew. By the microcosm man is meant, who in his body and soul resembles the great world. This analogy was well known in Jewish literature. Ibn Ẓaddik makes man the starting point of his inquiry. It is, he believes, through knowing himself that man can arrive at a perfect knowledge of the world and its creator, God. The first section of the book is therefore devoted to an analysis of man and his soul, and deals with the inevitable problem of matter and form of which all things and man are composed. In this discussion, as well as in the conception of the soul, the influence of Gabirol can be detected.

After he analyzed the microcosm and its two elements, the finite and infinite—body and soul—he comes to the main purpose, the knowledge of God. He believes that such knowledge, pure theology, is the root of all religion, for the fruit of philosophy and its practical value is to imitate the actions of God as much as possible. He launches then a criticism against the current conception of the attributes of God, of the *Kalam,* which, according to him, is not pure. He then begins to develop his own theory which is, that the essence of God as such cannot be conceived except through His actions. All that we can know is that He exists. He offers a few proofs for the existence of God, then goes on to define His unity and makes the point that it is really uniqueness, for God is unlike all His creatures and is therefore undefinable. He finds difficulty in explaining how creation in time, by the will of God, was effected, but he overcomes it. He then comes to the theory of attributes. As he proves the existence of God through the creation of the world, so His attributes can only be deduced from that concept. God, in essence is really inconceivable, but on observing His activity, we may conclude that He is existent, potent, wise and also good. We may add also truthful, for truth and reality are one, whatever is real is true, and since God is reality, it follows that truthfulness is an attribute. But all these attributes are only human attempts to understand God, and are in no wise to be understood as possessing a positive description of Him.

Ibn Ẓaddik's contribution consists mainly in his critical efforts to show that we cannot really conceive the essence of God, a task which he performed with thoroughness, and thus ennobled the conception of the Divine.

170. JUDAH HA-LEVI

Judah Ha-Levi, who, as we have seen (Ch. IX), was one of the outstanding poets of this period, also made a mark as a Jewish philosopher. His philosophy is expressed in the book *Al-Kuzari* which was originally written in Arabic, and later translated into Hebrew by Judah Ibn Tibbon.

The purpose of this book is not so much to reconcile the principles of Judaism with that of the current philosophy, as to show practically the insufficiency of philosophy and the superiority of the truths revealed by religion over those arrived at by mere logical reasoning. Yet, in spite of this intention, he made important contributions to Jewish philosophic thought, and developed what we would call a philosophy of history. Besides, he did not really reject philosophic tenets and incorporated many of them in his system so that in a general way he is in accord with the other Jewish philosophers. He only aimed to combat extreme rationalism, which not only claims sufficiency for reason, but makes contemplation the highest good.

The *Kuzari* is unique not only by its content but also by its form. It is practically the only book in Jewish philosophy, at least in the classic period, written in the form of a dialogue. Ha-Levi utilized the story of the conversion of the Khazars—a Tartar tribe on the Volga—to Judaism as the basis of his discourse. The story, which was related in the letter of the Khazar king, Joseph, to the Jewish leader, Ḥasdai Ibn Shaprut (920–970) of Cordova, tells of a dramatic episode how a Khazar King, Bulan by name (ca. 740), was in search of the true religion, for an angel had appeared to him in a dream admonishing him to do so. He thereupon summoned the representatives of Christianity, Mohammedanism, and Judaism to hear their arguments and finally became convinced of the superiority of the last named which he shortly afterwards embraced, inviting a Jewish scholar to teach him the principles of Judaism. Ha-Levi embellished the story somewhat and cast his discourse in the form of a dialogue between the Khazar king and the Jewish scholar, where in the course of inquiry and response, his ideas on all important phases of Judaism are unfolded.

The fundamental principle underlying ha-Levi's philosophy is, that God cannot be found or conceived by reason, and hence all proofs for the existence of God produced by philosophers are insufficient. He is to be conceived by intuition, or as he calls it by the "inward eye of the soul." However, curiously enough ha-Levi does not enunciate the principle in the opening of his discussion but much later. It is, though, tacitly assumed at the very beginning but given more a historical, rather than a philosophical, form. Two incidents in the story of the king's conversion, contained in the opening paragraphs of the first section, give the key to his philosophy. First, ha-Levi makes the angel say, in a dream, to the Khazar king, "Thy intention is satisfactory but thy deeds are not satisfactory," by which phrase he wants to tell us that the strength of religion in general, and Judaism in particular, does not lie in speculation, as philosophical theologians would have us believe, but in actual practice of the precepts. The second incident is that when the king interviewed privately the representatives of Christianity and Islam and asked each one of the relative merits of Judaism, Christianity, and Islam, each replied that except for his religion, Judaism is the highest. This mutual agreement on the verity of Judaism is the basis of the discourse. When the dialogue begins, the Jewish scholar, in answer to the query of the king regarding his religion, tells him that he believes in God as He is revealed in Jewish history. When the king is astonished at such a statement, for he expected a more theological description of God, namely, as the Creator and Guide of the universe, the scholar points to the general agreement of all people on the truth of the Jewish revelation. This general agreement, or "consensus omnium," on the truth of a thing, was considered sufficient proof for its actual veracity. Philosophically, the idea of general agreement is connected with that principle of intuition stated above, for since all people agree on a belief, it must arise from an intuition.

Ha-Levi then does not attempt to prove the existence of God logically from manifestation of His power in the world of nature, but from such manifestation in Jewish history. But such a proof involves a limitation, and the king rightly objects that Judaism is not a universal religion but belongs only to the Jews. This is partly admitted by the scholar. Everybody can embrace Judaism, he says, but the Jewish people have an innate spiritual superiority. To substantiate his claim, he points to the gradation we see in nature. We have there, minerals, plants, living beings, and finally man, who is a distinct class by himself. Similarly there is a gradation among men, some are at the very top, and some are lower and the highest type of man is the prophet, not the philosopher. He is of a unique type, distinct from other people, as man is distinct from animals. As regards the Jews, they all have potentially prophetic ability. The inward light, the divine influence (*'Inyan Elohi*), the intuition which makes for the highest religious attainment, was at first, in the history of humanity, only the share of the individual. It was given by God to Adam, he transmitted it to his son, Seth, and so on until it reached Jacob. From Jacob on, it became the biologic share of the group, i. e. his twelve sons, and hence the entire Jewish people became endowed with it. It is an hereditary trait, which though it may not be developed in every Jew, the potentiality is there.

The Jewish people thus became the kernel of spirituality in the world, or to use another phrase of his, Israel is the heart of all nations, which purifies and distributes spiritual life blood. At times, ha-Levi waxes enthusiastic and calls Israel the intermediary between God and the world, the very proof for the existence of God. From this fundamental teaching, there follows the high value of the Torah since it is an expression of the Will of God. It was given to the Jews as a way of life by means of which their potential spiritual ability rises to actuality.

Ha-Levi meets also the many objections raised by the king to his rather chauvinistic theory, the principal one being the very low state of the Jews which is a glaring contradiction to their claim of superiority. To this, the scholar answers first, that suffering is no disgrace, and secondly, since the Jews could really liberate themselves from that suffering by merely pronouncing a formula of conversion to another religion, and yet they do not employ this means of escape, their suffering then is a voluntary discipline which will ultimately lead to glory.

It is this line of reasoning that distinguishes ha-Levi from the other Jewish philosophers and which is largely stated in the first section of the book. The other sections are devoted to the elaboration of a complete philosophy of Judaism and its problems. In them is given a detailed exposition of the various parts of Judaism. The second section really completes the teachings of the first, taking up each in detail. Here, the questions stated in the first come in for a scrutiny. To these questions belong first of all that of the attributes, which expressed succinctly is as follows: Granted the truth of the existence of God and the revelation of His will, but how shall we conceive Him? What attributes shall we ascribe to Him? And as far as the answer to this question is concerned, ha-Levi is no less philosophical than his predecessors and followers. His theory of attributes is one of the purest in Jewish thought.

He divides the attributes into three kinds, active, relative, and negative. The active are those which are supposed to describe God's actions. The relative are such as men bestow upon Him out of gratitude, like holy, praised, sublime, etc. They arise entirely from the subjective state of the human mind. The negative ones are the really important attributes as they are supposed to give us a conception of His essence. These are: living, one, eternal, and willing. They are really negative in meaning, for all that the attribute living, for instance, connotes is that God is not not-living, and no more. Nothing positive is meant by the attribute living, for we cannot conceive the kind of life we attribute to God, and in the same manner, the other attributes are to be understood.

He was the first one to introduce in Jewish philosophy the term negative for attributes, though the fact that their meaning is negative was already pointed out by Baḥya. He includes will as an attribute, for he says the wonderful harmony of the world shows that not only is there a creator but also a willful one.

From this high conception of God, it follows that revelation on Sinai as well as so many Biblical anthropomorphisms have to be explained. To the latter problem, a great part of the second section is devoted, the various metaphors are analyzed and clarified including the symbolic meaning of the sacrifices. As for the first problem ha-Levi explains it by adopting partly the theory of Saadia, that a voice especially created by God vibrated the air so that the Jews heard words—and thus revelation was accomplished.

In this section, ha-Levi completes also his view of the philosophy of Jewish history. Not only does the Jewish people possess a distinct function in the scheme of things, namely, the realization of the religious-moral ideal in the world, but Palestine also possesses a distinction. It is the only land where the Jew is able to develop to perfection the divine spiritual kernel in him. Outside of Palestine, it is impossible, for in the Diaspora, the divine spark in the Jew does not operate. When the king points out that he has not observed any particular advantage in Palestine, the scholar replies that the influence of environment is very great even in the sphere of nature, as we see that certain fruits grow only in certain localities; and what is true in the physical world, he concludes, holds true also in the domain of humanity and spirit. In short, ha-Levi negates the Diaspora, and considers it only a temporary evil, hoping for the day of restoration when the Jews will be able to discharge their great function as the spiritual heart of humanity.

The third section is devoted to the development of his other principle, namely, that Judaism is a religion of action. Here, its practices are described in detail, the values of the important institutions, such as the Sabbath, the festivals, and the like, are explained and classified. Very interesting is his ideal of the pious and ethical man. It is modeled after the Platonic ideal as described in the Republic. In fact, he calls him a ruler, one who rules his soul and body with justice, namely, that none of their parts is prevented from exercising its legitimate function. The ideal man is neither ascetic nor devoted to appetite, but enjoys life in moderation, and of course, strives to attain the highest degree of perfection, which is divine spirituality, not philosophic contemplation. In this, however, ha-Levi parts company not only with Plato but with all Jewish philosophers who make rationalism the highest attainment. In this section, a vigorous defense of the Rabbinic tradition against the Karaites is made.

The fourth section is devoted to a discussion of the names of God which is really an attempt to explain His relation to the world, and contains observations on nature, creation, and the manifestation of divine powers in nature. A more detailed exposition of these problems would lead us beyond the limits of this work. In the fifth section, a skillful résumé of the philosophical ideas of the day is given, both of the Aristotelian theory and the Jewish philosophers. In this résumé, the proofs of Saadia and Baḥya for the creation of the world and ha-Levi's own theory of attributes are restated and proofs offered for each attribute. Finally, the problem of free will and Providence is taken up, and our author offers an interesting solution. There are, he says, two kinds of divine causality, direct and indirect. As examples of the first kind may serve such things as the order of the universe, the fixation of genera in the kingdoms of plants and animals and all such phenomena which testify to the plan of a wise maker. As an instance of the second kind, we may cite the burning of a log of wood by fire. The immediate cause of this phenomenon is easily explained, but this cause has another cause and so on until we finally reach the first cause, hence this kind of causality—although ultimately emanating from God—is indirect. We have then a fourfold division of events, divine, natural, chance-wise, and elective. The divine are those phenomena, mentioned above, which are immediately referred to Divine attention. The natural arise through mediate causes with an end in view; the chance-wise without order and design. The elective are those of which the human will is the cause. It is true that we can trace the action of the will through a chain of causes back to God, but the connection is a loose one, no force is exerted and man is therefore free to choose. This solution, as well as all other solutions of this difficult problem, may be found wanting, but it introduces a new element of the double kind of causality, making human will a cause in itself. To the other feature of this problem, namely, the compatibility of the foreknowledge of God with freedom, ha-Levi did not contribute anything new, but, with Saadia and others, he asserts that God's foreknowledge of the happening of an event is not the cause of the realization of that event. With a few remarks on the departure of the scholar for Palestine—who is none other than ha-Levi himself—this remarkable book closes.

171. ABRAHAM IBN EZRA

Abraham Ibn Ezra, the poet, grammarian, and exegete was also a deep thinker and wrote several books on philosophy. They are (*1*) *The Sepher ha-Shem* (The Book on the Name of God), where certain theories regarding the conception of God as far as His names convey are expounded; (*2*) *Yesod Mora* (literally, Foundation of Reverence, but in Ibn Ezra's terminology, it means the Foundation of the Knowledge of God); (*3*) *Shaar ha-Shamayyim* (The Gate to Heaven), which was supposed to be an introduction to Genesis, but only the first chapter is preserved, while the rest is lost; (*4*) *Arugat ha-Ḥokmah u-Pardes ha-Mezimah* (Flower Bed of Wisdom and the Garden of Thought), a short pamphlet with a long, rather popular name, on the proof of the existence of God and His attributes. But Ibn Ezra's philosophy is not contained entirely in these few small books. It is rather scattered in all his numerous writings, especially in his various commentaries on the Bible, and even in his grammatical works there are many deep philosophical passages. The fact that Ibn Ezra did not collect the various parts of his philosophical speculations into one place, and in addition, the jerky and unsystematic manner in which he stated his thoughts as well as his rather cryptic and mystic style, make an orderly exposition of his philosophy extremely difficult. We can only gain glimpses of his thought process here and there.

In general, it can be said that Ibn Ezra did not deal with all the problems of Jewish philosophy, as his psychology and ethics are very imperfectly stated. Only scattered remarks can be found on these subjects in his writings. He devoted himself, like Gabirol, primarily to the problem of the world, namely, the right conception of the universe, its forces, the manner of its becoming and its relation to God. In his theories, he was greatly influenced by Plato, Aristotle, neo-Platonism and Gabirol. Knowledge, according to him, consists mainly in reason, not in sense experience. True, experience supplies the material, but it is reason which gives us knowledge by giving form to this raw matter and thus obtains the general concept. Therefore, higher knowledge consists only of the general concepts. These concepts are eternal, and likewise, the very essence of all things is eternal, so is also the human soul, which is the essence of man, eternal. In general, there are not in this world any pure material things entirely devoid of spirituality, except, that in some the spiritual force is more in evidence and in others it is hidden. Pure bodies, such as minerals also possess a spiritual side, namely, the forces and the laws according to which they operate. In plants, there is a higher manifestation of spirituality inasmuch as its activity is more complex and so on. The higher we ascend in the scale the more spiritual things become, until we come to the existence of pure spiritual forces—and above all to God.

All things, says Ibn Ezra, have substance and form. That substance, abstracted from all material properties which are only accidents, is also a kind of spiritual force, but the real form determines it and gives it a more definite shape. Like Gabirol, he believes in the prior existence of that substance—substratum to the form. We cannot really determine what Ibn Ezra thought on the subject of the general or, as he calls it, the hidden substance whether it existed eternally, or whether it is a kind of emanation from God. But creation he supposes in this way: God through His will—this also is of great importance with him—implanted the form, which is the active dynamic force in this hidden substratum, and hence all activity began through a series of worlds.

There are, teaches Ibn Ezra, three worlds—the upper world which contains the forces, pure spiritual forces, the middle world where there are nine spheres which are bodies but of a higher type, namely, imperishable bodies, then the lower world—the earth—where the laws of operation are more mechanical. Of this complicated system of worlds, God only is the staying power, and it is His power or will which flashes through all the worlds.

Ibn Ezra did not elaborate his system and we know little about other problems which troubled the Jewish mind. He only endeavored to save the doctrine of the creation of the world from nothing by saying that the hidden substratum-matter was really nothing until form was given to it. In his popular treatise mentioned above, he proves the creation of the world and the existence of God in the manner of Saadia and Baḥya. He states the attributes to be: one, eternal, and wise. This treatise is written in fine rhymed prose.

On the whole, Ibn Ezra appears as a man of a dual nature. He has been considered a radical and a rationalist, yet there is a mystic strain in all his writings, and especially in his philosophy. Many of his expressions and assertions remind us of the Kabbalists and his particular style lends itself to a mystic interpretation. We can see in him a man who in his inner personality strives after communion with God and thirsts for Him, but in his external personality appears often in a lighter mood. He lacked the completeness and harmony of soul of Gabirol and ha-Levi and was therefore unable to give us a complete system of thought. But what he gave us helped to deepen the current of Jewish thought.

172. ABRAHAM IBN DAUD

Abraham Ibn Daud (b. 1110–d. 1180) of Toledo, was one of the outstanding men in Spanish Jewry, in the first half of the twelfth century, and he made important contributions to Jewish literature. Unfortunately, very little is known about his life. All that we know of it is that he belonged to a noble family, which traced its descent to the exiles from Jerusalem who came to Spain, in early times, and that he studied, under Rabbi Baruch Ibn Albalia, the famous Talmudic scholar and astronomer, until the sixteenth year of his life. His education must have been many-sided for he was a physician by profession and wrote works on philosophy, astronomy, and Jewish history. Of the rest of his life, practically nothing is known, except its end which was very tragic, as he died a martyr's death.

As a philosopher, Ibn Daud holds an important place in the history of Jewish philosophy, and his book entitled *Emunah Ramah* (Exalted Belief) is a meritorious attempt at reconciliation between religion and philosophy. It was, as all books of this kind, originally written in Arabic under the name *Akida Rafia* (the same meaning as the Hebrew) and later translated into Hebrew several times, the first time by Samuel Motot in 1392. It is his translation which was ultimately printed, but the title was slightly changed.

The book was written at the request of a friend, who asked Ibn Daud to enlighten him on the problem of free will and determinism. The author felt that the problem could not be treated properly, unless the entire subject of Jewish religious philosophy be taken up, for this problem is only a link in a chain. And as the previous books on the subject were not sufficient for the purpose, he found it necessary to compose one of his own. He mentions only two previous books on philosophy, Saadia's *Emunot* and Gabirol's "Fountain of Life." The first he praises highly, but says that it is too brief and does not deal clearly and sufficiently with the problem of freedom. The second he criticizes exceedingly, both for the erroneousness of the theory and for its failing to deal with Jewish matters.

His own book he divides into three parts, the first, dealing with the principles of philosophy, including both physics and metaphysics, the second, with the principles of religion as they are based upon and compatible with philosophy, the third, with the cure of the soul, or with ethics. Ibn Daud is the first Jewish philosopher who can be called a close follower of Aristotle and his arguments bear the philosophic stamp in both content and form. His method is clear and lucid except for the difficult Hebrew style of the translator. And while he is anxious, as the other Jewish thinkers, to base his arguments on the verses of the Bible, he does not mix them as they did, but first states his view, and then in a separate section to each chapter, he quotes the Biblical verses which in his interpretation substantiates his view.

The first part contains eight chapters. The first is devoted to a definition of substance and accident where substance is defined in the usual Mediæval way, as that which needs no other subject for its existence, and accident as that which is found in something else. The nine categories embracing all kinds of accidents are then given and explained. The second chapter is devoted to the elucidation of substance. Substance is composed of matter and form. But in these we must also discern different stages, namely, the primal matter, called the hylic which is mere potentiality to assume any form, and matter in general which already possesses a definite form, the primal form, namely, extension. This general matter, or rather, corporeality, is the fundamental matter of the four elements which undergoes numerous changes assuming different forms. He believes that God first created the primal matter, the hylic, and then endowed it with the primal form of general matter, and then with other forms. But he turns round and says in good Aristotelian manner, that after all what really exists is the individual thing composed of matter and form, and that these distinctions are only in the mind, namely, in the mind we discern, hylic, general matter, and forms, but in reality, in time, they are all one, and creation was also in like manner, namely, of individual things. Creation, then becomes, of course, a more complicated matter which he promises to elucidate in the second part, but he is not very clear on this matter even then. He further posits the existence of pure spiritual substances, pure forms.

The third chapter defines motion in its various forms, and here again, Aristotle is followed, inasmuch as motion is defined as a change from the potential to the actual, and any kind of change, even growth, is included under motion. The impossibility of the existence of an infinite in any form is then proved in the fourth chapter. In the following chapter motion is taken up again, and the proposition is proved that all movement ends at the First Mover (a synonym for God) who, though being the cause of all movement and change in the universe, is Himself not moved. This is made clear by what was proved in the previous chapter, that no infinite of any kind, not even an infinite chain of causes exists. If the case is so, we must assume that movement stops with the First Mover, for otherwise were He likewise moved, we would have then another mover, and so on up to an infinite number, but this is impossible as there is no infinite number of causes. Ibn Daud, in fact, already proved the existence of God in this way, but he does not dwell on this matter now as he relegates the subject to the second part.

The sixth and the seventh chapters are devoted to the principles of psychology. The purpose of this psychology is to prove the existence of angels, or mediate forces between God and the world. He begins with a definition of the soul in general and describes it to be the perfection of the natural body, but not of all kinds of bodies, only of such that are organic. He then tries to prove that the soul, though having its seat in a body, is yet a substance and not an accident. He thus gains his point that there are incorporeal substances, in other words, pure forms without matter, and thus we may assume the existence of angels and mediate spiritual forces. This is followed by a description of the parts of the soul or rather kinds of souls, which is the usual one, namely, the lower or vegetative soul, the animal soul, and the human soul or reason. Ibn Daud gives a detailed description of the functions of each part, discussing at length the senses, and the faculties of memory and perception, displaying great skill in the mastery of the principles of science. The main problem, however, is the nature of the peculiarly human soul, that is, the highest element of the soul, reason. For a man like Ibn Daud who wanted to hold the rope at both ends, to follow Aristotle and yet preserve every principle of the Torah, the question of the soul presented great difficulty. He could not well accept the Platonic doctrine of pre-existent souls to which his definition of the soul as a substance is leading to, for the Bible speaks of the creation of a soul.

He therefore propounds a complicated theory, which is that the soul has existence prior to the body, but only potentially. This means that the angels or mediate beings who move the world pour their influence upon the body, or endow it with form, and thus the soul begins its course of development during life. The more it develops, the more power and perfection it acquires. This acquisition is called the acquired reason. And it is this acquired reason which, on becoming perfected becomes a more complete substance and, being directly connected with the Active Reason of the world, remains immortal. Ibn Daud recognizes degrees in the perfection of the soul, for there are different classes of men, the highest of which is the prophet, yet he does not deny immortality to any man.

With an exposition of the theory of the spheres, which says, that they are a higher kind of bodies and have souls, and that they influence the events in this world, the first part closes.

The second part is devoted to the principles of religion. It is divided into sections arranged according to six expositions, or six principles of religion, or dogmas, which expositions are again subdivided into chapters. The principles or dogmas are: (*1*) existence of God, (*2*) His unity, (*3*) His attributes, (*4*) His actions, or the inherent relation between Him and the order of the universe, (*5*) belief in prophecy and tradition, (*6*) providence and free will.

In the introduction to this part, Ibn Daud emphasizes the importance of theology, that this is the highest science and is the perfection of man. He then proceeds to prove and expound the principles. As for the first, i. e. the existence of God, he proves it from the premises already established by him in the first part. There must be a First Mover which is not moved, for otherwise there would be an infinite number of movers and this is impossible. There is also another proof along the same line, but too complicated to reproduce. His proofs are presented in very logical and lucid form.

The exposition of unity comprises three chapters. The first proves His simplicity, that is there is no composition in His essence for He is incorporeal, and therefore not composed. The second proves the numerical unity, i. e. one God, in the manner of Saadia, for were there two Gods they would have to be somewhat alike and somewhat different. Hence they would be composite, namely, of an element of likeness and an element of difference which is contrary to the conception of God.

The third chapter emphasizes the uniqueness of God, that His unity can only be conceived in a negative sense, namely, that He is unlike all other beings.

The third exposition is devoted to the attributes of God. He enumerates eight attributes which are: one, existent, true, external, living, knowing, willing, and potent. He realizes that some are superfluous, for living is included in knowing and willing, as one who knows and wills lives, but he says that it is best to be popular, and not strictly logical. But he devotes much space to their explanation and says that whatever these attributes may mean in themselves, to us they have only a negative meaning.

The fourth exposition contains three chapters. The first proves the existence of angels from the conception of the human souls, which is that the soul is not a corporeal substance. It follows, then, that since the soul is constantly influenced by some powers that these powers should be simple incorporeal substances, and these are the angels, or Intelligences in the terminology of the philosophers. The second proves the same hypothesis from the movement of the spheres. The third gives a résumé of the arising of the universe according to philosophers. It is rather a long exposition of the theory of the world of the Arabic philosophers—with a good deal of neo-Platonic coloring. The gist of it is that from the *One,* there emanated first a force, which, he says, the philosophers call reason, but which we will call angel; from this first angel there emanated another, from whom in turn emanated a third, and so on. The last Intelligence is called Active Reason. These constitute the world of the Intelligences or angels; next comes the world of the spheres, and finally the lower world where things rise and perish. Ibn Daud is a bit doubtful about the theory of emanation, but he believes in the existence of the three worlds, and the mediacy of the Intelligences and their constant influence in life.

Prophecy and the Torah are the themes of the fifth exposition. He defines the first as the rise of the soul to a higher plane where it communicates with the Intelligences and then indirectly with God. There are various degrees to it, visions in dreams and visions in a wakeful state. He also emphasizes the necessity of the prophet possessing the highest ethical qualities. Moses was perfect in this regard, hence he is the father of prophecy. In the second chapter, he takes up the immutability of the Torah and the verity of the oral tradition. There he defends the Bible and the tradition both from the attacks of the Christians and the Karaites. In his defense, he makes use of the argument of general agreement which we have noted in ha-Levi.

In the sixth exposition, he reaches the aim of his book, namely, the problem of Providence, freedom, and God's foreknowledge of things. His theory of mediate forces facilitated much. The great events, such as creation and others, were caused directly by God, the other things which are renewed in this world, i. e. all happenings, come through mediates—called angels or Intelligences. Of the new things in this world is also prophecy. As for God's knowledge of things he confesses that it is a mystery how He can know things and yet remain simple without adding something to His essence. Man is free and has the power to overcome evil inclination. The struggle to overcome it determines the value of the good act. He also produces the theory of fourfold kind of causality, i. e. divine, natural, chance-wise, and elective, which was noticed in ha-Levi—whether he borrowed it from him or not is a moot question. As to the foreknowledge of God, he says that He knows only that certain actions will be presented to the human choice, but not which way he will choose. Ibn Daud is especially helped by the theory of mediates, saying that so many things happen and are accomplished in the world, not directly by God, but through the agency of the Intelligences. He also introduced a scale of Providence, saying that the one who strives more in the knowledge of God and the principles of reason is especially looked after, a theory which Maimonides later developed.

The third part deals, as said, with Ethics. It is rather brief. Practical philosophy aims at happiness. This can be obtained (*1*) by personal morality, (*2*) family conduct, (*3*) political or social laws. As for the principle of personal morality, he finds it—being influenced by Plato and Aristotle—in the equal and proportionate exercise of the functions of the soul. He finds this principle as well as the principles of the other means of happiness, i. e. right conduct of family and state, embodied in the Torah. The Torah consists of five parts, (*1*) precepts concerning theology; (*2*) ethics; (*3*) conduct of family; (*4*) conduct of society; (*5*) and precepts for which we have no reason. The first four parts agree with reason and philosophy and are of prime importance. The fifth part, though we do not understand it, still claims our duty in no less degree. With special emphasis on the value of belief and a picture of the pious man, the book which gave an impetus to Jewish philosophy in the Aristotelian direction, closes.

173. MOSES BEN MAIMON

Moses ben Maimon, or as he is commonly known, Maimonides, can be quite safely spoken of as the Jewish philosopher. From the time of the appearance of his philosophic Magnum Opus, *More Nebukim* (Guide of the Perplexed), he has dominated Jewish thought, and no subsequent Jewish thinker can be properly estimated without relating him somewhat to Maimonides. But he is even more than that; his philosophy is practically the complete systematic résumé of the entire philosophic process, which was going on in Jewry from the time of Saadia to his day. And not only in the Jewish world was Maimonides known as the great philosopher, but also in the non-Jewish world he passed as the representative of Jewish thought.

The work was originally written (1190) in Arabic under the title *Dalälat Al-Haïrin,* but was soon translated into Hebrew in the year 1200, only ten years after its appearance, by Samuel Ibn Tibbon of Lunel under the title, *More Nebukim,* the one chosen by Maimonides himself with whom Samuel corresponded. It was immediately translated again by the famous poet, Judah Al-Harisi (Ch. IX). Harisi's translation, though surpassing Ibn Tibbon's in clearness and beauty of style, yet falls behind it in exactness, and hence it receded in the background, and the former became the adopted version and was printed many times. At the beginning of the last century, a Hebrew scholar, Mendel Levin, retranslated the first part of Ibn Tibbon's version into Mishnaic Hebrew.

The "Guide of the Perplexed" made its entry in the non-Jewish world almost simultaneously with that in the Jewish world. Yet in the lifetime of Maimonides, parts of the book were transcribed into Arabic characters and studied by Mohammedan theologians. The Christian world did not lag behind and, as early as the first quarter of the thirteenth century, a Latin translation of "The Guide" was circulated and since then several other Latin translations were made, one of which was by the famous scholar, Johannes Buxtorf Junior, which appeared in print in 1629. Peter of Toledo translated the book into Spanish in 1419, and a Jewish scholar Amades (Yedidyah Jededia) ben Moses into Italian in 1581. During the nineteenth century, it was translated into almost all European languages, the most distinguished translations being those of Solomon Munk into French and of Michael Friedlander into English.

The *More Nebukim* was assiduously studied by the thinkers of the ages, both Jews and non-Jews, and was consequently the object of numerous commentaries. There are more than thirty commentaries on it in Hebrew by known authors, and a large number of anonymous ones, the latest Hebrew commentaries being that of the philosopher Solomon Maimon (1791) on Part I, and that of Isaac Satanow on Parts II and III. Of commentaries by non-Jewish writers we know of one on the first chapters of the second part by an Arabic scholar, Abu Bekr Al-Tabrizi (13th century), and scattered comments and notes by the famous German philosopher, Leibnitz. Quotations from the book are found in the works of almost all scholastics, especially in those of the two greatest of them, Albertus Magnus and Thomas Aquinas.

The *More Nebukim* was composed at the request of the favorite disciple of Maimonides, Joseph Ibn Aknin, who begged his master to explain the *Sodot,* or esoteric ideas of the Bible, to treat of metaphysical problems and to expound the theories of the *Kalam,* i. e. the Arabic orthodox philosophy. Maimonides undertook to do all this and added another subject, the explanation of the anthropomorphisms of the Bible, namely, all terms applied to God in the Bible which speak of Him in human terms. Logically, then, the book contains four parts: (*1*) On the removal of anthropomorphisms from God, including the theory of attributes; (2) the theory of the *Kalam;* (*3*) God and His relation to the universe; (*4*) esoteric ideas of the Bible, namely, prophecy, *Ma'asé Bereshit,* i. e. the history of creation (Gen. Chas. I–IV) and *Ma'asé Merkabah,* description of the Divine Chariot (Ezekiel Chas. I, X). Technically, the book is divided into three parts. Part I treats of the first two subjects, Part II and seven chapters of Part III of the other two. The last forty-seven chapters of the third part can be considered as an appendix to the original plan but they contain discussions of important problems, such as the existence of evil in the world, omnipresence of God and providence, freedom of the will, purpose of nature, the rationality of the precepts of the Torah, and finally the true way of worshipping God. All these discussions complete the theories of Maimonides and weld them into a system of Jewish religious philosophy.

The *More Nebukim,* as Maimonides himself asserts several times, in his letters to his disciple, Joseph Ibn Aknin, and in the book itself (I, 68), was written neither for accomplished philosophers nor for those who never studied philosophy, but for a limited circle of students who did study philosophy and were acquainted with its principles, but were baffled by certain problems which seemed to indicate a contradiction between religion and philosophy. Chief of these problems was the difficulty presented by the language of the Bible in speaking of God. They also wanted to know more about the religious philosophy itself and the deeper problems of metaphysics. It was for the purpose of removing the difficulties of these perplexed students, as well as to give them further instruction, that the book was written.

It is this purpose underlying the book which determined its character and arrangement and which explains many aberrations from a thoroughly systematic order, one which we might have expected from a great systematizer like Maimonides. Thus, for instance, we might have expected him to begin, like most previous Jewish philosophers, with the proofs for the existence of God, follow it up with the theory of attributes and then explain briefly the anthropomorphisms of the Bible. But he does not do so. He devotes almost the entire first part to the last two subjects and produces the proofs for the existence of God only in the second part. It is also for this reason that Maimonides does not discuss the theory of knowledge, nor busy himself with other psychological data which should have been included in a complete philosophic system, for Maimonides was speaking to a circle who were acquainted with all these data, who were philosophically trained believers, but who had difficulties in the conception of God.

The first object therefore was to clear these difficulties and elicit a pure conception of God. It was only then that he could proceed to the treatment of the philosophical problems.

The great contribution of Maimonides consists not so much in the originality of his ideas, though there is much to that, but in the thoroughness with which he treated his problems, and the criticism of the ideas of other people. The circle to which he spoke were well aware of the fact that the Bible uses metaphors and similes, but they wanted to have a detailed exposition of the application of the principles to the various terms and a complete theory. Maimonides certainly gratified their wish, for in forty-seven chapters of the first part, he discusses every conceivable term applied to God in the Bible, whether a noun denoting an acquisition, or a verb signifying an action or an affection, and explains it thoroughly and completely. The chapters on the anthropo-morphisms are therefore a masterly exposition of the entire subject. We can not, however, follow him in the winding course of his system and will have to be satisfied with a brief exposition of his philosophy.

In his proofs for the existence of God, Maimonides differs in method from that of all Jewish philosophers before him, with the exception of Ibn Daud. They all proved the existence of God from the fact that the world is created and hence there is a creator. He, on the other hand, asserts vigorously that the existence of God is not dependent on the question whether the world is eternal or created. Creation is a question by itself which has to stand on its own merits. He therefore proves the existence of God as one who is the principle of all being and its ground, and in this he follows Aristotle entirely. He produces his proofs at great length by positing twenty-six propositions taken from Aristotle's physics and metaphysics. With the help of these propositions, he proves that there exists a Prime Mover, one who is a necessary existent. In this proof the idea of an impossibility of an infinite series of causes forms the main element. He also produces three more proofs for the existence of God. The oneness and incorporeality follow from the conception of the Prime Mover, or the Being who is a necessary existent. Were He corporeal, He would be moved while moving the world, for this is the law of bodies as demonstrated in one of the propositions (9), and then He would require a cause for His being, and so on to infinity, but this is impossible. He is One for a number of reasons; one of them has been quoted by us before, and that is that there could not be two Gods, for then they would have both difference and likeness, a supposition which would imply that they are composite and hence no Gods. He also points to the harmony of the universe as bearing evidence of one God.

As for the attributes of God, Maimonides dealt with them, as pointed out, in the first part of the book at length (Chas. LI-LXI) and in a most thorough manner. After criticizing the theories of some of his predecessors who asserted the possibility of ascribing positive essential attributes of God, namely, that we can speak of God in attributes which express His essence, he says that it is true that we have to accept four attributes, living, potent, wise, and willing, but they are entirely nega-tive. The only positive knowledge we have of God is that He exists. The attributes mentioned merely mean that we assert that the opposite of the quality signified by each one is denied of Him, such as potent means that He has no impotence, etc. In this question as in all others, it is the thoroughness and clearness of conception which are his chief contribution.

The problem which occupies the mind of Maimonides next to the existence of God and the purity of His conception, is the creation of the world. He subjects first Aristotle's theory of the eternity of the world, as well as the Platonic opinion of the existence of chaos, and the neo-Platonic theories of emanation, to a strict criticism, but while he is mild regarding the last two theories, he is more severe against the former, for it is the Aristotelian philosophy which appeals to him. The gist of his criticism against the eternity of the world is, that it was never fully and satisfactorily established by Aristotle, for his arguments for it are drawn from the order of the existing world and its laws, and it cannot be shown that these laws also hold good for a world which is only coming into being. And if the case is so, as long as the theory of eternity of the world possesses no certainty, he will rather accept the Biblical theory of creation from nothing, although he admits that he cannot solve the difficulties connected with it.

The creation of the world involves a number of problems. First of all, the problem of the world order itself. He accepts the existence of Intelligences as mediators between God and the world which he, like Ibn Daud calls angels, but he differs from the former in a number of points. As usual, he takes the matter up in detail and interprets the verses connected with such matters. The second problem is how to explain the process of creation as expressed in the Bible. This is one of the *Sodot*, estoteric doctrines, an explanation of which was asked by Ibn Aknin. The explanation of *Ma'asé Bereshit* completes the question of the creation of the world. But this, in turn, leads to the question of the truth and veracity of the Torah, for creation has been assumed on the strength of it, and not because of any philosophic proof. Hence, Maimonides takes up the problem of prophecy, the means of revelation of the Torah and truth.

Maimonides treats prophecy with a deep psychological insight and in a thorough manner (Part II, Chas. XXXII–XLII). There are, he says, two opinions of prophecy, one a popular one which claims it to be entirely dependent upon the will of God, namely, that even the most common man can become a prophet if God wills so. The other, a more philosophical one, which makes prophecy entirely dependent upon the disposition of the soul of man, and asserts it to be an expression of the highest perfection of a man properly prepared by his ethical conduct and intellectual attainment. Both of these theories, says he, are not true. Prophecy combines both conditions, proper preparation of man and the influence of the Divine Spirit. The would-be prophet must possess great intellectual ability, a rich phantasy, and perfect ethical conduct. But even then he may not become a prophet if God does not pour over him His spirit. He cites the example of Baruch ben Neriah, the disciple of Jeremiah, who in spite of all his strivings for the coveted gift never attained it. The influence of the Divine Spirit affects the reasoning powers of the prophet and through these his imagination, and thus the prophecy is visualized and uttered. He enumerates the various degrees of prophecy, eleven in all, and says that they are indicated in the Bible by the various forms in which the prophets received their messages, such as dreams, visions, voices, appearances of angels, the voice of God, and other forms.

But above all these kinds of prophecy stands the prophecy of Moses which is of a *sui generis* nature. Moses, who differed from all men in his wonderful deeds, differed also in his attainments. He was the acme of perfection, subdued all earthly and corporeal inclinations and rose to the very height of spirit. His prophetic inspiration is therefore different from that of the other prophets in kind, not only in degree. He reached direct communion with the Divine, and the immediate truth revealed to him is embodied in the Torah which he gave to Israel. Maimonides asserts that only the first two commandments were heard by the Jews at Sinai from God alone through the mediacy of a created voice, but the rest of the commandments and the entire Torah were communicated by Moses. The Torah therefore is a revelation and direct influence of the Divine Spirit. It is the expression of both the highest truth and divine wisdom. It is, therefore, immutable and its laws hold good for all time.

After completing his exposition of prophecy, proving thereby the verity of revelation and enhancing the validity of the Torah, he fulfills his promise to his pupil and takes up another phase of the *Sodot,* esoteric teachings of the Bible, namely, the *Ma'asé Merkabah,* the chariot vision of Ezekiel. This occupies the first seven chapters of the third part. The original plan of his book is thus completed, but his system involves the discussion of more problems to which he devotes the rest of Part III.

The first problem which presents itself as relating to the order of the world is the question of evil. If the world is a creation of the All-

Good and Wise, how comes it that there is so much evil on this earth? This age-old problem Maimonides tries to solve by saying that evil is really not a positive thing but a negative, namely, a lack of good. If the case is so, evil is not a divine creation. It really arises from the deficiency of matter which is unable to receive all the divine good, and is by nature changeable and destructible. Hence, death, sickness, suffering, and even passion, and foolishness all arise as consequences of the mutability of matter of which the body is composed. The world, however, could not be created otherwise, for the generation of one individual necessitates the decay of another. In this way it can be said, the mutability of matter is good in itself, but mutability presupposes decay and death, so that these very things are conditions of existence, which in its totality is good.

But one may ask, "Is not evil more predominant in the world than good? How then could a good God create such a world where there is more evil than good?" To this, our philosopher answers, that the case is not so. There are three kinds of evil, says he, one arising from natural phenomena which are due to the very nature of matter, such as earthquakes, storms, lightning, etc. But these, he says, happen so seldom, and were we to draw a balance of the good and evil that is found in the order of nature, we would find that the good exceeds evil. The other two are those that are caused to men by their fellow-men, such as by war and other means of violence, and those that happen to men through their own conduct. Both evils can be remedied by men themselves and cannot be attributed to God. Maimonides was thus able to save God from being the direct author of evil, but the problem as a whole is not solved. We still have to consider the course of events in this world. Is it all chance, or is there divine providence ordering them? And this brings him to the problems of Providence and the order of nature, and God's foreknowledge of things and freedom.

To these problems, nine chapters are devoted (Part III, Chas. XVII–XXV). Maimonides first states four different theories regarding Providence, all of which are insufficient, and then offers his own, which he believes is that of Judaism. Man is free in his actions, otherwise all religion and ethics would be unthinkable. It is true that some men may be, by nature and temperament, more inclined towards doing good than others, but all have the possibility to overcome their inclinations by training themselves to follow in the right direction. Man is therefore judged according to his actions.

The world is conducted by God's providence, but there is a great distinction between other living things and the human genus. As far as the other things are concerned, Providence extends only to the preservation of the genera, but the individuals are left to natural law and chance. But as for man, each individual of the genus is under divine providence. Yet, there is a distinction even there, Providence in the human genus is also graded. The one who is intellectually developed, and who is more able to suppress his corporeal passions is in closer touch with the divine influence, and is the recipient of a greater degree of Providence.

The problem of God's foreknowledge is solved by Maimonides more in a mystic way and is connected with his theory of attributes which says that we cannot really know them. His knowledge is so different from ours that the laws applying to our knowledge do not apply to His. Hence, He knows everything from eternity, and His essence is not increased by this knowledge, nor does His knowledge of the human way of acting affect in any way the freedom of man. A similar mystic strain is also noted in his treatment of the problem of injustice, namely, why do the righteous suffer and the wicked prosper?—in other words the problem of Job. He at first attempts to adopt some of the more common theories propounded in the Book of Job, namely, that the righteous is only apparently righteous but in reality he sinned or that punishment befalls a man as a trial and then his reward is increased, or that the good and evil befalling men are also apparent and not real. Finally, he confesses that the real answer is, that we do not know the nature of Divine Providence. It is totally different from our own conception of it. He adds, however, one more point and that is that real happiness of man consists in his perfection, namely, the knowledge of God, and the higher the degree a man reaches, the more happy he is, so that material benefits dwindle into insignificance. And it is to this high point that Job ultimately reached after he heard the speech of God.

In direct relation with his theory of graded Providence stand his theories of immortality and the purpose of man's life. The soul, according to him, is not originally a substance but a potential power given to man. When through effort and diligence man develops this potential power, it acquires separate existence; it becomes the acquired reason. This acquired reason is immortal. The power which brings about this realization from the potential reason to the actual is the influence of the Active Reason of the universe, one of the Intelligences. By his moral and intellectual perfection, man shows his relation to the Active Reason and transforms his soul into an immaterial immortal substance. This then is the purpose of man's existence, to rise to intellectual heights.

From the discussion of the purpose of man's life, Maimonides proceeds to a detailed exposition of the reasons and principles underlying the Torah and its precepts. He believes that the Torah is the very means for the attainment of that aim to which man strives. Its purpose is a double one, that is, to improve the body of the individual as well as the body politic, and to improve the soul. He divides the precepts of the Torah into fourteen classes and shows the reasonable purpose underlying most of them except some classes for which no human reason can be found. He believes, however, that even these laws were arranged by divine wisdom.

This great work closes with a picture of the true life ideal of the religious man. That ideal consists in attaining intellectual truth, or in other words, to know God in the fullest sense of the word. Ethical perfection is a necessary means for this attainment, but the aim is divine contemplation.

B. ETHICS

174. IBN GABIROL

In view of the fact that one of the principal aims of Jewish philosophy is the evolving of an ethical way of life, the line of demarcation between it and ethics proper is not distinctly drawn. Hence, we have in reality few books which deal wholly with ethics from a philosophical point of view. Most of the Jewish philosophers have included their ethics in their metaphysical and theological writings, and what is left for the historian to do is to disentangle the ethical teaching from the other elements with which it is intertwined.

Yet, there are several books which deal primarily with ethics. The first of these is, *Tikkun Midot ha-Nefesh* (The Improvement of the Moral Qualities), by Solomon Ibn Gabirol. It was originally written in Arabic and was later translated into Hebrew by Judah Ibn Tibbon. It is the only ethical book written by a Jewish philosopher, where an attempt is made to systematize the principles of ethics independently of religious belief, but merely on psychological and physiological principles. It was intended to be a popular manual to guide people in the conduct of their everyday life. It seems, however, that it was not completed in the way the author meant to expound his principles.

The book consists of an introduction and five sections, each containing four chapters. In the introduction the author lays down the following principles: The soul consists of two elements, a higher and a lower one. The higher one is an emanation from God and strives for reunion with its source. The lower one, connected with the physical senses, is the seat of the moral qualities which we employ in our daily life. This part of the soul can be cultivated, and it is the degree of cultivation which constitutes the difference between man and man. The purpose of the book then is to teach the cultivation of the soul.

The qualities of the soul, says Gabirol, are manifested through the five senses, and to each sense he ascribes four qualities, which, he says, correspond to the four elements in nature, namely, air, fire, water, and earth. All together he finds twenty qualities in the human soul which he classifies in the following table:

Sense of:

sight	hearing	smell	taste	touch
pride	love	anger	joy	parsimony
meekness	hatred	will	grief	generosity
pudency	mercy	jealousy	peace	courage
impudence	cruelty	diligence	remorse	cowardice

Gabirol promises in the introduction to explain in detail his scheme of division of the qualities and why he subsumed them under the respective senses. But he fails to carry out his promise, and we really lack the psychological and physiological reasons. We are, therefore, often at a loss to understand why such and such a quality should be assigned to this sense and to no other. In the twenty chapters that follow the introduction, where each quality is discussed, some explanations are offered for this classification, but few are satisfactory. The connection of the qualities with the senses are often based on a verse in the Bible, and often on general assumption. Thus, the qualities subsumed under the sense of sight, are ranged so, first because the eye indicates the attitude of the man, whether he is proud or meek, or bashful, or impudent, and secondly, because the Bible often expresses pride by the phrase "One who has his eyes on high" (Gebah 'Enayyim., Ps. CI, 5). As for grouping love, hatred, mercy and cruelty under the sense of hearing, it seems to be based on the verses of the Bible (Deut. Ch. VI, 4-5) where it is said: "Hear, O Israel: God our Lord is one God. And thou shalt love the

Lord thy God with all thy heart, and with all thy soul and with all thy substance." In this we see that love, the fundamental quality of the group, is intimately connected with the sense of hearing. The other qualities are merely either opposites of love or modifications of it. We must also note that the love spoken of by Gabirol here, is primarily love for fellow man, which is really connected more with hearing than with sight, for when we hear one praised and spoken well of, we may come to love him. The same can be said about the other qualities of the group. Of the four qualities subsumed under the sense of smell only two, those of anger and jealousy, can be explained by the Biblical expression which often represents anger as a kindling of the nostrils. The very word for anger, *af,* means both anger and nose. Jealousy is only a species of anger. It is difficult, however, to see how will and diligence can be connected with that sense.

Those qualities which, according to Gabirol, belong to the sense of taste, are placed by him thus only because taste seems to him to be synonymous with pleasure, and pleasure, or the denial of it, is the fundamental trait of all these qualities. It is, at the first glance, difficult to see how remorse or penitence can be related to taste, but considering that each of these qualities brings about a diminishing of pleasure, its relation becomes clear. The classifying of liberality, parsimony, valor and cowardice under the sense of touch is based on symbolism. The hand, the main organ of touch, symbolizes both giving and striking, both external expressions of liberality and valor, while the other two qualities are merely the opposites of the former.

The scheme of classification of the qualities, on the whole, can be pronounced as unsatisfactory, but as an attempt to reduce the virtues to physiological and psychological elements, it is important. More important, however, is the discussion of each quality contained in the twenty chapters, where keen analysis of their nature and character is displayed. In general, moderation in the use of each quality is counseled, and insistence on the values of training and control of the senses is repeatedly made. Here and there, deep psychological insight is shown. One such remark deserves to be quoted. Grief, says Gabirol, arises from the fact that a man fails to realize his wishes and desires. He therefore counsels man to desire less and consequently the disappointment will be less keen. Moreover, let the man, he says, imagine beforehand that he may fail in his ambitions, and when that really occurs the failure will be less grievous. This advice has the background of psychology and experience, and does by no means undermine self-reliance. It merely supplies a safety valve for disappointment by imagining its possibility beforehand.

Gabirol uses copious quotations for his ethical teachings from the Bible and from the rich Arabic proverb literature.

175. BAḤYA

The second great ethical work, which really exceeds by far that of Gabirol, is the one of Baḥya—"The Duties of the Heart." We already discussed its first section dealing with metaphysics. But the book is primarily an ethical one, as nine tenths of it are devoted to the teaching of the conduct of life and to the inculcation of piety and fear of God. It teaches pure ethics, based on the principles of Jewish religion.

The principal thesis underlying Baḥya's system of ethics is, that thankfulness to God for his creating this wonderful world, in His infinite wisdom, is the source of all ethical duties. He therefore devotes his second section or portal, as he calls it, to a description and examination of the manifestation of divine wisdom in the various kinds of creation, in the universe as a whole, and in the kinds of creatures. "Divine wisdom," says Baḥya, "is one, but it is differently manifested, like the sun which is one but its rays are reflected in different colors, when they pass through white, red, or black panes of glass." He then describes in detail the order of the inanimate world, the various kinds of animals, the body of man and finally the soul and its activities. This examination proves not only the greatness of God but His infinite goodness. Hence, Baḥya shows in the third section, which he calls, "The Worship of God," how grateful man should feel towards God and how it devolves upon him to submit willingly to His worship and follow the divine precepts which are the hygiene of the soul. Baḥya examines the various forms of thankfulness, which man may feel towards his benefactors, and finds that the one we feel towards God is the purest, for His goodness is without blemish, as He cannot have any possible ulterior motive. One point in this analysis is worth while quoting. In speaking of the kindness shown by the charitable man towards the unfortunate recipient, Baḥya remarks that it contains an egoistic element, for the man who gives the charity desires to assuage his own pain which he experiences at the sight of suffering. This analysis of sympathy is very keen, and closely resembles the one made, centuries later, by the Scottish philosopher and economist, Adam Smith, in his book on "The Moral Sentiment." Bahya carries his rationalism into his ethics, and in describing the nature and character of the worship of God, he insists that it shall be based not on the expectation of reward, but on reason, namely, it shall be such a worship which emanates from a deep contemplation of the sublimity of God, and which fills the soul with awe and with a desire to unite with Him. The section on "The Worship of God" is concluded with a chapter on the various qualities of the soul which can be employed in the worship of God, and the list of these qualities is almost identical, both in number and kind, to those contained in the table of Gabirol.

The next section deals with the trust in God (Sha'ar ha-Bitahon). Bahya analyzes, in a keen and detailed manner, the subjective and objective aspects of trust, and describes the proper conduct of man in regard to this trust in God, namely, that it must not lead to neglect of occupation, but that he must endeavor to do all that he can in order to earn his livelihood, and then leave the rest to God. Real trust in God brings man to a happy state of mind, accepting all vicissitudes of life in a cheerful mood. This is followed by a section, on "Devoting Human Actions to the Name of God," its principal thesis being, that whatever man does in worshipping God must be only for the sake of doing His will and for no other motive. He then launches upon a lengthy discussion of how such attitude can be attained. He describes the obstacles in the way of its attainment, the chief of which is the allurement of the desire of worldly things. This brings him to a classification of virtues and evil inclinations. He finds that of all such inclinations pride is the most harmful, while meekness is the most desirable virtue.

To the description of meekness (Anawah) the next section (the sixth) is devoted. In it, this virtue is described in all its details, especially in relation to God. As in all other portions in the book, Bahya here too introduces his rational element and explains that meekness must not be a mere slavish humility, but is to be based on knowledge of self and God. This meekness must be manifested in all ways of life, in dealings with all kinds of men, and in relation to God. Meekness leads to penitence, and hence the section on penitence follows, wherein penitence, its nature, character and requirements are described. Penitence in turn leads to self-examination (Heshbon ha-Nefesh) which is the subject of the eighth section. Bahya goes into this subject at length, and gives a minute description of the various forms of examination to which a man should subject his soul. Their number is thirty. He finally gives us a beautiful illustration of the use of this scrutiny. Suppose, he says, you are in a place where there is a beautiful picture hanging behind you, and for some reason you cannot see it with your eyes, even if you turn around. You then take an iron tablet, burnish it and polish it with oils until it is bright, and place it opposite the wall on which the picture hangs. The image of the picture will of course be reflected in that tablet. Likewise, he says, divine wisdom is the picture, the soul is the tablet, but the reflection of the former can be seen in the latter only after it has been burnished by moral conduct and polished by the examinations and investigations which were mentioned.

As one of the forms of examination of the soul was the practicing of a certain kind of asceticism, Baḥya takes up this question in the next section (ninth). In no way does he advise forsaking the interests of this world; on the contrary, he urges the people to participate in all activities of life. He only asks for the control of reason over the passions. This is the kind of self-restraint that he preaches for the average man. For the more pious ones, he advises a mental separation from the allurements of the world, though they too should participate in all matters of life. Finally, he comes (tenth section) to the crown of virtues, the love of God. This love he defines as the longing of the soul for the Creator and the striving to unite with the higher light. This love is to be unlimited, and man must be ready to sacrifice, for His sake, wealth, limb and life. He believes, however, that only very few are able to reach the highest degree, i. e. the ability to sacrifice life for His sake, but almost everyone is able to sacrifice wealth and limb, if he is only properly trained. And the way to attain that love of God is to pass all the preliminary steps enumerated by our author, namely, to understand His unity, His wisdom, worship Him, be meek and penitent, examine the soul and practice self-restraint. Only after going through all these steps, can man reach the highest point—love of God, which will fill his soul and permeate his whole being.

176. THE BOOK OF THE PIOUS

The ethical literature heretofore discussed was the product of the Spanish Jewry where philosophy was dominant, and all literary endeavor outside of Halakah was tinged with its spirit. But the great Franco-German Jewry, where Jewish life was carried on with a unique intensity, and piety was the goal and ideal of life, also produced its ethical books, which, though they may lack the philosophical background and the logical sequence, nevertheless display deep ethical sentiment and reach a high moral altitude seldom equaled by ethical literature. The typical and classical book of this literature is *Sefer Hassidim* (The Book of the Pious) ascribed to Judah ben Samuel of Regensburg (ca. 1200).

The book, as we possess it, seems to be a composite work, consisting of several books which originally bore the same title, "Book of the Pious," or a similar one. The first 162 sections comprise most likely the original book composed by Judah the Pious (Hassid); sections 163-468 were incorporated from another book by the same name. The sections 469-1028 are additions by the same compiler. Sections 1029-1173 constitute the third part and bear the inscription "transcribed from another book of the pious." All these things show us that there were many manuals of ethics and piety current in the twelfth century, which often bore the name, "Book of the Pious," but the most important of them was the one by Judah. A later ethical compiler took the book of Judah and added parts from the others, and in this enlarged form, the book was handed down to the generations.

The book, as a whole, is of a practical nature; no ethical theories are taught there. Theorizing was unnecessary, as it is all based on the ethical teachings of the Talmud and Agadic literature, and permeated with the deep religiosity of life. What it does contain is detailed instruction of the conduct of daily life covering practically every part of it. It embraces a multitude of subjects; first of all the conduct of man in relation to God, namely, rules about worship, prayer, penitence, Sabbath observance and other things; then the conduct of man in business, marital life, treatment of servants and animals, relations between Jew and Gentile, rules of education, writing and copying of books, even the minutiæ of table manners and other modes of personal conduct are not overlooked.

The book which, as said, contains collections of rules and statements of conduct does not admit of a regular system, but it seems that at least the first part, the one originated by Judah, followed a fairly well laid-out plan. It originally contained three sections, the first, dealing with piety, the second, with meekness (Anawah) including kindred subjects, such as penitence, prayer, abstinence and similar matters, the third, dealing with the fear of God. In the subsequent compilation the sectional headings were removed but the original plan was followed. Yet the plan is merely a broad outline, there is really no logical sequence and many subjects are treated in the same sections. The second part, which occupies the bulk of the book from sections 163–1029, is put together without any order or plan, but contains merely rules and statements. The third part is devoted primarily to the events which happen to the soul after death.

The book, as a whole, reflects very faithfully Jewish life in the Franco-German Jewry, during the thirteenth century, with all its virtues and defects. In it is mirrored the deep piety that permeated all strata of Jews, the great love for Judaism, the longing for the Torah and the sanctity of conduct on the one hand, the gross superstition and crude belief in the supernatural, on the other hand. The book is full of stories telling of meetings with dead men who wander around in the world as a punishment for their sins, of demons who prowl around at night on their wayward missions, of the attempts of sorcerers and sorceresses to injure men in various ways, and also of advice how to counteract their actions. Yet, with all this the moral value of the book is not impaired, for it truly deserves the name the "Book of the Pious." We find there not only religious piety but piety of life in general, in the highest degree. It is, as one Jewish scholar remarked,[2] a noble commentary on the verse "Love thy neighbor as thyself" (Lev. XIX, 18), and a call to realize it in all ways of life. Some of its dicta equal the best moral utterings of all ages.

Here are some of them:

Speaking of the injunction not to shame your fellow-man, our author tells us, "In case men sit in company and one of them is accused of having committed a wrong act, but the name of the culprit is not given, each one of the company should confess to that sin in order that the real transgressor shall not be ashamed when he is compelled to confess" (Sec. 22). Similarly, he admonishes us not to enter with our guests into a learned discussion, unless we are certain of their ability to do so, for otherwise they may be brought to shame (p. 312).

He is especially insistent that men restrain themselves with all their might from causing the least grievance to their fellow-men. As a general injunction he says: "One who caused grievance to another man we consider as if he caused grievance to a whole world, for man

---

[2] Dr. M. Guedemann in his book: *Geschichte des Erzihungswesens und Cultur der abendländischen Juden,* Heb. translation, Part I, p. 141.

is a microcosm" (Sec. 411). In another place he tells us not to praise a man before his enemy, as it will annoy the latter.

Regarding the general conduct of man in relation to his equals and subordinates, he says: "Man in conversation must always use his friend's name first, namely, he must say you and I, and not I and you" for such manner of speaking inculcates modesty (Sec. 13). Again, "a man should rather make friends with an ignorant man, who is liberal in money matters and is of a pleasant disposition, than with a scholar who is irascible and parsimonious" (Sec. 369). He further advises, "Give the right counsel to everyone even to thy enemy, and by no means attempt to mislead him." Here our author displays keen psychology, for he adds: "By giving the right counsel to thine enemy you will really revenge yourself on him. He most likely will think that you, being an enemy, advised him the wrong way and at once will do the opposite" (Sec. 134). Of subordinates he says: "Do not insult your servant whether man or maid; if they did what you wanted, do not deny them praise, for ingratitude is the worst quality." "If a man employs several Gentile maid servants, he shall not cause any quarrel among them, for that will bring about slander in his house" (Sec. 941). "Do not be ungrateful even to a beast, and the riders who stick their spurs in the horses will be punished" (Sec. 44).

Love of man in general, whether Jew or Gentile, is reflected in the following dicta: "If you see two men whisper do not ask them what they are talking about, as you will cause them to tell you a lie, for were they satisfied that you know of it, they would have told you beforehand" (Sec. 1062). "If you have to hire a laborer to do a certain kind of work and there are two candidates and one is skilled only in this work and the other is able to do also other kinds of work, hire the former" (Sec. 1065). He repeatedly emphasizes that a man must deal honestly with Jews and Gentiles alike. "If the Gentile cheats himself in accounts, the Jew must return the additional amount, and if a Jew is poor, it is better for him that he beg than cheat a Gentile" (Sec. 661). Again, "If a Jew who is kind-hearted marries a kind-hearted proselyte woman, it is better for other Jews to marry their descendants rather than the descendants of pure Jews who lack their virtue" (Sec. 377). Such dicta were inculcated and taught, at a time, when the Gentile world considered every Jew an outcast, when the Jew was not safe with life and limb, when the Church declared every Jew a perpetual enemy. And the Jew on his part retaliated by treating them as equals before the law and morality. Such sayings reflecting pure love of humanity, and sanctity of life and conduct could be multiplied by the hundreds. But even the few that were quoted are sufficient to show the height of morality to which German Jewry reached during an age which, on the whole, was not distinguished by its moral tone.

177. MINOR ETHICAL WORKS

The number of small treatises dealing, wholly or partly, with ethics, written during this period is considerable, but few advance new theories or make contributions to the science of ethics. Several of them, though, deserve to be mentioned, either on account of their intrinsic worth, or because of their author who made himself otherwise famous.

The earliest of such small treatises is *Hegyon ha-Nefesh* (The Reflection of the Soul) by Abraham bar Ḥiyya, spoken of above (Sec. 169). The three last sections of the book deal with ethics. The subjects discussed are the right way of action, penitence, and the changes in life and the world. On the whole, it contributes little to the ethical theory, and belongs more to homiletics, as it is primarily a collection of several homilies on the prophetical portions (Haftorot) read on the Day of Atonement, namely, Isaiah, Ch. LVIII, and the Book of Jonah. But here and there are found brilliant ethical and philosophical remarks. One of them is his statement that the Ten Commandments really contain all the 613 precepts contained in the Pentateuch. He explains it in the following way. All human activity in the world can be divided into three classes: things which bear on the relation between man and God, between man and his family, and between man and his fellow-men. These three kinds of activities are further expressed in three ways, either by mere thought, or by speech, or by action through the various organs. We have then nine modes which cover all phases of human life.

Turning to the Ten Commandments, we see that after the first commandment which pronounces the existence of God, there follow nine others which fall into three groups corresponding to three classes of human activity. The first group covers all relations between man and God, inasmuch as the second commandment treats of the belief of the mind and heart, the third one of such relations with God which are dependent on speech, and the fourth one, enjoining the observance of the Sabbath, deals with divine worship by action. The second group covers the three kinds of relation between a man and his family, the fifth speaks of honor to parents, which honor is rooted in the thoughts of man; the sixth—thou shalt not murder—refers, according to our author, not merely to actual murder, but also to pronouncing such command to the family which may cause them injury; and the seventh deals with immoral action within the family circle. In the last group the order is reversed, the eighth commandment refers to stealing, an evil act affecting relations between man and man, the ninth, concerning false witness, warns against activity expressed by speech, and the tenth, prohibiting covetousness, refers to evil thoughts and desires. Taking in consideration that the Commandments include all kinds of precepts which can be arranged under that tripartite classification, we have then the inclusion of all the precepts contained in the Pentateuch. This observation of our author is rather an ingenious one.[3]

A more important ethical work is that of Maimonides called, "The Eight Chapters," which serves as an introduction to his commentary on Pirķé Aboth, (The Sayings of the Fathers). In this small work, Maimonides develops his ethical theory, though in a succinct but complete manner. The first chapter is devoted to psychology which is the basis of ethics. In it, the author asserts the unity of the soul, and takes exception to the current theory that there are several souls, such as the vegetative, animal and rational. It is all one but, of course, it possesses several faculties. These faculties or parts are, according to him, five: the nutritive, sensory and emotional, imaginative, conative (will) and rational. He insists also on the uniqueness of the human soul, for though some faculties, such as the nutritive and sensory resemble the same faculties in plants and animals, they are not the same. These faculties in man are distinct and of an entirely different order than those in the plants or animals, and man is nourished by means of the nutritive faculty which is a part of the human soul, while the donkey is nourished by the nutritive faculty of the asinine soul which is different in kind from that of man. All this is stated, in order that we may be able to understand better the ways of human conduct; for, says Maimonides, the improvement of the qualities of man is the medicine of the soul, and like in the cure of the body, the physician must know its anatomy in order to locate the disease, so in the cure of the soul, its physician must have a knowledge of its parts and make-up for the very same purpose.

After giving a detailed division of the faculties of the soul, the author

<hr />

[3] The classification of the 613 precepts under the heads of the Ten Commandments was not new. It had already been done by Philo, and also by Saadia. It was a favorite exegetic method with the Karaites. The originality of Abraham bar Ḥiyya consists in his explanation how the classification is to be made.

endeavors in the second chapter to determine those faculties where the virtues and the vices are located. He finds that these have their seat in the faculties of sensation and feeling and that of will, while the other three faculties have little effect on conduct.

The third chapter is devoted to defining the disease of the soul. The soul, says Maimonides, is healthy when it is so disposed as to perform good deeds, and is sick when it has a contrary disposition. This unhealthy state arises mostly from lack of discernment, namely, the people do not know what is right conduct and often think evil conduct good. It is therefore the duty of the physicians of the soul, i. e. the wise, to cure them and train them to discern between good and evil.

The art of curing the soul is discussed in the fourth chapter which is the most important of the book. In it, Maimonides adopts the Aristotelian criterion for good and bad. It is the famous *Via Media,* middle way. All actions can be performed in three ways, two extreme ones and one which holds the equilibrium between the two. The last is the right and good one. For instance, the art of spending money can be discharged in three ways, one, by spending very sparingly; this is the lower extreme—stinginess; the other by spending very recklessly —prodigality, which is the higher extreme; and finally, spending in a generous manner. Generosity, then, is a virtue while stinginess and prodigality, both extremes, are vices. The same applies to all other actions. However, the acts are only external expressions of the qualities in the soul proper which are the virtues, and the acquirement of the virtues is the most important thing. This, says Maimonides, can be accomplished by constant repetition of good acts. It is then that it becomes a habit of the soul, and hence the importance of moral training. When, however, bad habits are contracted, the physician is to cure the patient by inclining him towards the opposite way. As an instance, let us take a man who is inclined towards stinginess. His cure is, that he be forced to spend, for a time, his money lavishly until the inclination for stinginess will be weakened. Then he should be trained to generosity. It must, however, be done carefully, for sometimes the patient may cling to the new vice which is given him as an antidote. With this chapter the practical ethics of Maimonides is closed.

The other chapters deal with the higher aim of human life. That aim is briefly defined by our author, in the fifth chapter, to be the conceiving of God in the highest possible manner. This is in accordance with Maimonides' rationalism which emphasizes philosophic thought as the goal of life. In order to reach that aim man must concentrate all the powers of his soul for that purpose. He must make his daily conduct both physically and morally subservient to this aim. This idea is strengthened by his theory (Ch. VI) that the truly pious is one who has overcome all inclination to evil and has trained his soul so that it desires only the good. He is higher than the one who struggles with evil desires and overcomes them. It is to the acquisition of such a state of the soul that a man is to strive.

After discussing in chapter seven the obstacles that lie in the way of one who endeavors to reach the goal, namely, the contemplation of God, he launches in the final chapter upon a long discussion of the problem of human freedom. He first shows that man is free from predisposition—he does not recognize the influence of heredity—and when born his soul is a *Tabula rasa,* i. e. a blank tablet, on which education can impress either good or bad qualities. He does recognize a certain propensity on the part of man to certain qualities which comes from his physical endowments, but, on the whole, man is free to mold his soul. Next, comes the more difficult problem of compatibility of human freedom with God's ordaining human affairs and his fore-knowledge of man's actions. Our author champions freedom in all its phases, and attempts to solve a number of theological problems with more or less success.

The important point in this ethical work is the constant insistence on moral education and on acquiring the habit of right conduct, and especially the training of the moral will.

To the minor ethical works belong also the ethical portions of the codes of Rabbi Eleazar of Worms, *Sefer Rokeah* and of Eliezer of Metz, *Sefer Yereim,* and a small work by Joseph Ibn Aknin, written in Arabic, under the name *Tab-Al Nafus,* (The Medicine of the Soul.)

178. ETHICAL TESTAMENTS AND WILLS

Another species of ethical literature is the ethical testaments and moral wills which pious scholars wrote for their children, when they felt that their end was approaching. This form of imparting in-struction in the conduct of life is of ancient origin. We have traces of it in the Bible, such as the advice of David to his son Solomon (1 Kings, Ch. II, 1–10), the instructions of Jonadab, son of Rechab (Jeremiah, Ch. XXXV, 6–8), to his children, and others. In Apocry-phal literature we have a whole book of ethical testaments, "The Testaments of the Twelve Patriarchs" (Ch. I, Sec. 24). In the Talmud we have a number of such short testaments left by *Tannaim* or *Amoraim* either to their children or disciples.

As ethical literature begins to develop during the first epoch of the Mediæval period, these wills begin to reappear, this time in a more elaborate and complete form.

The earliest of these wills we possess is one entitled *Orḥot Ḥayyim* (The Ways of Life) by Eliezer ben Isaac of Worms (ca. 1050), surnamed the Great, the disciple of Rabbi Gershom, written to his son, who is surmised to be Tubia, the compiler of a Midrash on the Pentateuch (Ch. VI, Sec. 89). The testament reflects the noble piety and high morality of the writer and enchants us with its simplicity and ethical beauty. It covers all relations of life and inculcates love of God, family, and fellow-men. The author opens with a short admonition to honor God who is the creator of man, and points out human frailty and the uncertainty of life, saying, "Remember how many have lain down on their beds at night never to rise again, or have risen in pain and sickness." He then enjoins his son to honor scholars and observe the prayers and the morning benedictions, for all such actions display our gratitude to God who preserves us in life. A number of paragraphs are then devoted to the honor and respect due to fellow-men. Quoting the saying contained in *Aboth* (Ch. III, 3) "Despise no man," he adds, "for many pearls are found in the poor man's tunic," referring of course to learning and moral qualities. He then enjoins the son to visit the sick and advises him to enter the sick chamber in a cheerful mood— for the sick person watches the faces of the visitors—to attend funerals and comfort the mourners. Eliezer emphasizes also the duties to gladden the hearts of the bride and groom, to treat the poor kindly and to honor them. Regarding charity he says, "Give it secretly and not in the presence of other people, nor shalt thou look at the poor guest when he is seated at your table, for he may be hungry and swoop on the food ravenously." He further says concerning charity, "My son, prepare provision for thy soul and kindle a lamp to give light before thee. Leave it not to those who come after thee, lest they be unable to kindle it and it be left forever unlit." After speaking of the sanctity of the Sabbath, Eliezer takes up matters of personal conduct, enjoins modesty in all ways of life, prescribes table manners and gives a few rules of hygiene, such as to eat vegetables, not to eat food cooked in a pot which was not used for thirty days, and other things. He then advises not to pursue honor, to keep a secret and not reveal it even to one's wife, not to display anger, and be gentle to friends. He says, "Be not as a fly over thy fellow-man's sore, but cover up thy neighbor's disease and reveal it not to the world." He winds up his instruction by laying down the rule of the golden mean, quoting Ecclesiastes (Ch. V, 16, 17), "Be not righteous overmuch, neither overwicked." He adds, "Nor too shamefaced and yielding, but balance your actions, and often over-balance for the good."

The second work of this character is *Musar Ab* (A Father's Ad-monition) by Judah Ibn Tibbon. It was written to his son, the famous translator, Samuel, about 1190, while Judah went on a journey, and being an old man and fearing his end was near, he sent this parting epistle. This testament reflects the character both of the writer and of the recipient. It is written by a man of high culture, a physician of noble spirit, and the wide reading and extensive knowledge of the writer are traceable in every line. The son, on the other hand, is pictured there as of an impetuous nature and as one not too prone to learning. Yet, taking into consideration the literary accomplishments of Samuel in later years, we must assume, either that the father underestimated him, or that his parting words bore fruit. The work bears a personal character, but the nobility of its teachings and the charm of its style make it a valuable ethical document. On the whole, it is more of a secular nature, though it is permeated by pious sentiments.

Judah begins by extolling the value of the commandment con-cerning honoring a father, and gently reproaches his son for his errors in the past, tells him of his endeavors to educate him, of the great library he provided for him and all other means of learning. He there-fore exhorts Samuel to continue his studies, both of the Torah and the sciences, especially medicine, and not to neglect them while he is still young before he reaches old age, for "old age is the mother of for-getfulness." He also advises him to acquire the habit of virtue and choose his friends wisely. He then gives rules for literary excellence. He should make his books his gardens, and pick their flowers, should write every day at least a page, and read his manuscript twice, should write in a beautiful handwriting and observe the rules of grammar; when compos-ing poetry he should use the easiest words and light meter. This is fol-lowed by professional advice, namely, to be pleasant to patients—both were physicians—not to take money from poor patients, to inspect the medicines every week, and not to use an herb or medicine of which he has not full knowledge, and finally to take care of his own health. This is followed by admonition for personal conduct, to respect his wife and pay her full honor, for as the Arabic proverb says of women, "None but the honorable honors them, none but the despicable despises them." He further urges the son to be economical, take care of the education of his children, continue to study with his teacher and to teach others, to inspect his Hebrew books once a month, and the Arabic once in two months and keep them in good order. He should also lend willingly of his books to others. He concludes with an admonition to honor his teachers and his friends, and finally to read the testament once a day. The work is interspersed with beautiful maxims and proverbs and short poems, making it not only useful but also pleasant reading.

The third work of this class is "The Portals of Instruction," an ethical testament, ascribed to Maimonides. Its authenticity has been somewhat doubted, but the teachings imparted there bear the stamp of his thought. The work, as a whole, is inferior to the other testaments from the point of view of style and charm, but there are flashes of deep thought here and there. The author begins with an admonition to serve God, both from fear and love, for fear brings to abstinence from sin, and love to diligence in performing the divine precepts, so that both elements are necessary. He then exhorts his children to acquire the habit of virtue, for good deeds depend upon habit. This is followed by rules for study, namely, to love wisdom, to concentrate attention upon the studies while in the study hall, otherwise the confinement in the room will only injure the body, while the mind will not profit by it. As for success in life, truth and justice will lead to true happiness, for happiness acquired through falsehood and injustice "is built on sand." These two are the best remedy for timidity and no shield is of more protection than truth and justice. He further enjoins his children to deal honestly in business and pride themselves on their virtues for "There is," he says, "no pedigree as noble as virtue and no heritage equal to honor." Maimonides then extols the virtues of a peaceful disposition and forbearance, and especially meekness which is "the ladder to the heights of morality." As a physician he counsels moderation in food and drink, for overfeeding is the cause of many a disease. He also recommends economy and makes the following fine remark: Expenditure is divisible into four categories, profit, loss, aversion and honor. Profit is expenditure on loans to the needy, for we enjoy the interest, while the capital remains (reference to reward in heaven, Mishnah

Peah 1, 1); loss is money spent in gambling; aversion is that spent on food, for it is consumed; honor is the money spent on clothes. Therefore, he says, loathe gambling, eat less than your means allow, clothe yourself in accordance with your means, and devote the greater portion of your wealth to charity. With an admonition to the children to honor their wives and serve their friends with their bodies and wealth, but not with their souls, as this belongs to God alone, the testament ends.

C. PHILOSOPHIC EXEGESIS

179. EXEGETICAL WORKS OF ISRAELI AND GABIROL

Since Jewish philosophy was primarily an attempt to harmonize the teachings of the Bible with the current philosophic thought, it might have been expected, that there should develop a particular species of exegesis which can be called philosophic. This kind of exegesis attempts to solve the problem in connection with the text it undertook to explain. Its real development, however, belongs to the post-Maimonidean period. In the period we are discussing, we have only its beginnings. Only a few have attempted to follow this kind of exegesis, and little was preserved of such commentaries. Isaac Israeli (Sec. 162) wrote an extensive commentary on the first two chapters of Genesis, under the name "An Essay on 'Let the Waters Bring Forth'" (Gen. I, 20) where he discusses theories of creation. Gabirol must have also written some commentaries in a philosophic and allegoric manner, as some of his explanations to passages are quoted by Ibn Ezra in his commentaries. And finally Ibn Ezra himself, though he disparages such methods in the introduction to his commentary, yet he made extensive use of them. A considerable part of his commentary is devoted to such philosophic exegesis, and many are the excursuses that he makes in the field of philosophy, in various parts of his commentary.

There are also beginnings of philosophic homiletics in this period, but very little has been preserved. The only booklet of this nature which came down to us is the one mentioned above (Sec. 177), "The Reflections of the Soul" by Abraham bar Hiyya, which is both a work on ethics and a collection of homilies.

Chapter XII

MYSTICISM

180. GENERAL REMARKS

Mysticism, like philosophy, arises from the elemental human desire to search and investigate both natural and spiritual phenomena, and to understand their manifestations more thoroughly. But, while philosophy relies mainly on human reason and accepts it as the standard, mysticism, which is permeated with the emotional religious feeling inherent in man, is, in addition to reason, actuated by revelation and inspiration. It is thus a third current in the history of human spiritual development, standing midway between dogmatic religion and philosophy.[1] It is bound to rise in the life and literature of every religious people whose religion is revealed, and which revelation finds expression in sacred writings. These writings or scriptures in their literal meaning, can never satisfy the searching mind nor the thirsting spirit, who want both more of religious warmth and depth of meaning. Hence, bold religious people begin to believe that there must be more in these writings than the literal meaning of the words convey, and that they undoubtedly contain some hidden mysteries, and therefore efforts are put forth to unfold these mysteries from the words of the Scriptures, to probe their depth and bring out the truths they contain.

The method used is the old famous method of allegory and symbol. Passages are taken to contain allegories; words and stories are supposed to stand not for their simple connotation, nor for the facts they relate, but are understood as symbols of great ideas, or of past and future events. Once the current of mysticism starts, it swells like a mighty stream, for imagination is one of its elements and there are no bounds to human imagination. Fancy and poetry become its forms of expression, and it often happens that the element of reason, which it originally contained, is lost in the manifold manifestations and forms of imagination and fancy.

And what was said about mysticism in general can be applied with

[1] On this see A. Franck, *La Cabbale,* German trans., p. 29.

greater justice to Jewish mysticism in particular. Jewish mysticism, even in its most exotic form, later known as Kabbala, concerning which so much has been written, is not a foreign importation into Jewish life and literature, as many have maintained, but of indigenous growth. Undoubtedly in the course of its development and its different permutations, it absorbed foreign elements and was certainly subjected to external influence, but its roots lie deep in Jewish antiquity, and in its older form— pre-Zoharite, or pre-Kabbalistic—is closely allied to Agada. When after the Babylonian exile, the expanded religious life demanded a wider interpretation and an unfolding of the Pentateuch for the purpose of finding the way how to live in accordance with the law, the more intensified religious feeling demanded a similar broader interpretation of the moral narratives and poetic portions of the Bible, to satisfy the growing inner religious needs; and the results of all these interpretations were Halakah and Agada. At that time, there arose also a demand, on the part of a few very deep religious souls, to interpret and explain such portions of the Bible, which deal with the very root of things, namely, with God and His primal relation to the world, i. e. its creation.

It is possible that Babylonian influence had somewhat to do with the rise of the urge for understanding the very fundamentals of existence, but be that as it may, the fact remains that the portions of Genesis dealing with creation, and the Visions of Ezekiel (Ezek. Chas. I, X) containing the Theophany, or the description of the *Merkabah,* i. e. Divine Chariot, formed the nuclei around which the first mystic speculations centered. There are even references to such speculations about the *Merkabah* in the Book of Chronicles,[2] which is included in the very Canon of the Bible and was composed in the fourth century B. C. E.; Ben Sira, who wrote at the beginning of the second century B. C. E., warns his readers not to occupy themselves with the mysteries of creation.[3] All this goes to show that as early as the fourth and the third centuries before the common era, there already were in evidence mystic speculations in Israel. In fact the Bible itself gave the impetus for such speculations. The very contradiction between the anthropomorphic descriptions of God used by the Prophets themselves, on the one hand, and the high and lofty conception of Him embodied in such expressions, "I am that I am" (Ex. Ch. III, 15), and many other places, on the other hand, spurred on thinking minds to speculation. Moreover, it

---

[2] Chr., Ch. XXVIII, 18, see L. Zunz, *Die gottesdienstlichen Fortträge,* p. 162.
[3] *Ecclesiasticus,* Ch. III, 21.

even supplied the very method, for were not the *Merkabah* and similar visions symbolic expressions of the revelation and manifestations of God? It is no wonder, therefore, that people endeavored to unravel these mysteries and understand what these symbols really meant. Again as to creation, does not the Book of Proverbs speak of wisdom in such terms as, "When He prepared the heavens I was there" or, "I was by Him as one brought up with Him, and I was daily His delight" (Prov. VIII, 27, 30)? What do these expressions mean if not that "Wisdom" played an important role in the creation of the world? But how? Was it an instrument of creation or something else? And what is that "Wisdom"? Here is food for thought and the germs of later mystic teachings even of the Kabbala itself.

It was not, however, until the rise of the Alexandrian School of Jewish thought, that such teachings began to take shape in a more systematized form. In Alexandria where Oriental wisdom, Greek philosophy, and Jewish speculation mingled, teachings with a decided mystic trend became prevalent. We have already seen above (Ch. I) the traces of such theories in the Apocryphal books, such as the extreme hypostasization, i. e. personification, of "Wisdom" in the book, "Wisdom of Solomon" (Sec. 18), the allegories and the excessive use of symbols in the Books of Enoch and Jubilees, which, though of Palestinian origin, were yet greatly influenced by the Jewish Alexandrian School. Similar movements were going on in Palestine proper. We find in the later chapters of Daniel, which were most likely added after the close of the Canon, mystic appellations of God such as "The Ancient of Days" (Dan. VII, 9) and there is there also an attempt to describe His garment "Which was white as snow" and the hair of His head which was "like pure wool." Clearly, these are symbols, for God is not meant here, but a revelation or a manifestation of His presence. Such expressions show evidently the trend of thought going on in certain Jewish circles.

During the centuries, different elements were added to the mystic current. Undoubtedly the Essenes had their peculiar teachings, but almost nothing was left of their writings if they ever had any. Again the teachings of Philo (Ch. IV, Sec. 68), especially his theory of the Logos, found their way into Palestine and even into the schools of the early *Tannaim*. A greatly modified form of the Logos, which was named *Memra,* i. e. word, or expression, was used in the authorized Targum as a substitute for many anthropomorphic expressions in the Bible (Ch. IV). But it is really difficult to follow the development of the current of mysticism, as it seems that the teaching was imparted orally. We only know that at the beginning of the period of the *Tannaim,* two different forms of mystic teachings were imparted to especially deserving students, one named *Ma'asé Bereshit* (relating to creation) and the other *Ma'asé Merkabah* (relating to the Merkabah, i. e. Divine Chariot).

An old Mishnah states: "We are not allowed to disclose the *Ma'asé Bereshit* to two people together, nor the *Ma'asé Merkabah* to one, unless he is wise and possesses exceptional understanding."[4] This shows us the great secrecy in which the teachings were held. In the Talmud a number of *Tannaim* are named who busied themselves with these mysteries. Among them Johanan ben Zakkai, the founder of the school at Jabne, his disciple Joshua ben Hanania and others. Four others are mentioned as those who entered the "Garden" (Pardes)—a name used by many mystics to denote the secret teachings—Akiba, ben Zoma, ben Azai, and Elisha ben Abuya. Ben Zoma became insane, ben Azai died young, Elisha became a heretic. Only Akiba entered in peace and left in peace.[5] This story proves again not only the mysteriousness of the teachings, but the peculiarity of their character and the danger connected with their study, which shows their deviation from the beaten path of Judaism.

Yet, though there are many references to these studies in the Talmud, we are nowhere actually told what these teachings contained, and we have to rely on scanty gleanings that are to be gathered from different passages. Many are the theories advanced by different scholars concerning the nature of these studies. The most plausible, however, is that the *Ma'asé Bereshit* centered around the question whether the world was created from nothing or that there was a primordial element, i. e. primitive matter, out of which this world was created. The idea of eternity of matter, in one form or another, was common property in Greek philosophy. Plato taught it, Aristotle went further and taught the eternity of the world (Ch. XI), so that the question of creation was the most important in the thought of the day. The Church fathers and the various mystic currents of pagan and Christian philosophy of the first centuries, known as Gnosticism, all deal with it. These ideas also penetrated into Jewish circles, and the Jewish scholars were bound to deal with them, to combat the current notions and guard monotheism.

[4] Mishnah tractate *Hagigah,* Ch. II, 1.
[5] Babylonian Talmud, *Hagigah* 14b.

But, at times, certain elements remained, as we notice certain pro-
clivities towards a more modified form of creation than the usual
conception, namely, that God, who is all spirit, created the extremely
material earth. Water is often mentioned in the Agada as being the
primitive element out of which the earth was created.

The same question, but under a different aspect, was most likely dealt
with in the *Ma'asé Merkabah*. Here, there were more delicate subjects,
such as, God, His attributes, revelation and manifestation to man, and
above all His relation to the world, to be explained and clarified. Again,
the question arose: how could the most high God, stripped of all
qualities, the Pure Spirit, have any relation with matter, or how did
matter come into being altogether? A theory of emanation was proposed, namely, that out of the Godhead there emanated a series of
forces, and these forces, the further they descended in the scale, the
more material they became, and in this way matter was emanated
through a long series from God. All these questions were included
in some way in the *Ma'asé Merkabah*.

However, we have only pointed out the philosophic kernel in these
speculations. In reality it was not that way. This kernel was surrounded
by a thick crust of symbolism and figures. Close to the *Ma'asé Merkabah*
there is the whole hierarchy, so to say, of angels. Angels are mentioned
by name in the Bible, such as Michael (Daniel X, 13. 21; XII, 1) who
is called "The great prince who standeth over the children of thy
people" and Gabriel (Ibid VIII, 16). They are also mentioned before
(e. g. in Ezekiel, Zechariah) but not by name. These angels are the
ministers of God, and in the later mystic teachings they were identified
with the "Divine powers" taught by Philo. All these powers or angels
are the mediators between God, the world and man.

Sometimes, in an effort to grasp the attributes of God more tangibly
even they, i. e. the attributes, were likewise hypostatized, i. e. personified,
and were spoken of as if they were separate things, such as we have in
Agadic literature *Midat ha-Din*, i. e. attribute of justice, and *Midat
ha-Rahmim*, i. e. attribute of mercy, spoken of in a quasi-personified
way. And at times these attributes were often given names and called
angels and assigned different functions. Their names were as a rule
compounded with the name of God especially *El*, such as the Biblical
names of Michael (Heb. Mi-Ko- El, i. e. who is like God) and the later
Talmudic names as Raphael (Heb. Rpha-El) and Suriel, which signify
the healer of God and the Prince of God, respectively, inasmuch as the

first was supposed to be the angel of healing and the second the chief
of the angels. When under the influence of ideas current in the outer
world, which dealt with similar problems, God was constantly exalted
above the world, and the scope of the mediators, or powers, or angels
increased, the various functions of the angels were also increased, and
their names were often borrowed from the Greek or Latin in order
to define their function more precisely and correctly. Thus, the name
of the angel *Metatron*, who plays an exceptionally important role in the
mystic teachings, is borrowed from the Latin in a Grecized form. His
importance is indicated in the name, for *Metator* means, in a borrowed
meaning (original meaning surveyor), overseer. He is variously designated in the mystic passages of the Agada, at times as chief of the
angels, and at other times, prince of the world (Sar ha-Olam) which
shows that he is entrusted with the conduct and overseeing of the
world. In later mystical books he assumes still greater importance and
is almost considered second to God. In this conception there are the influence and echo of the Philonian teachings of the Logos (Ch. IV)
and other mystic teachings current in the first centuries. The source of all
this conglomeration of ideas is that God Himself, who is often denominated, by the mystics of all religions at that time, as the Unknown, is so high and elevated that He can have nothing to do with
the world, and only the powers or mediators take care of it. Hence
the importance of the greatest of mediators, *Metatron*.

In these mixed teachings, where Jewish mystic ideas absorbed some
ideas of the mystics of other nations, especially of the Eastern esoteric
teachings, there was involved great danger, for the Gnostic sects who
were both pagan and Christian also emphasized the importance of
the mediators and taught a well-ramified system of angels. In fact,
Christianity made use of this theory and identified Jesus with the
Prince of the Angels, and with the Logos. It is also stated in the Talmud
that one of the four who entered the "Garden," i. e. Elisha ben Abuya,
who became a heretic, mistook *Metatron* as a second God, and that
this was the cause of his heresy.[6]

To avert this danger, the great sages and especially Akiba, who was
also a student of mysticism, began to emphasize once more pure
monotheism, that God himself conducts and guides the world, and that
the angels are only created beings who are subservient to the will of
God, and furthermore, it was officially taught that angels do not exist

[6] *Ḥagigah* 15a.

forever but rise and pass away; and still more that every day a new group of angels are created and as soon as they sing the praise of God they pass away.

Thus, a check was put in official Agada on the spread and development of dangerous tendencies in mysticism. But that the old teachings still remained and were taught and even developed, especially along the lines of angelology, is certain. As will be evident later, we note, in mystic literature, that the number of angels is increased, and the forms of their names multiplied.

Even more, this same Akiba who was such a great defender of traditional teachings but who was also a student of mysticism, himself supplied some of the important factors for the development of mysticism, which also became a cardinal point in the teachings of the Kabbala. He, whether to combat the dangerous teachings of the Logos and the mediator ideas, or from his unbounded love for the Torah, taught that the Torah was the instrument of God in creating the world.[7] That it, of course, preceded the world for countless ages seemed self-evident. Apparently, it seems that there was nothing new in this doctrine, for that wisdom existed before the creation of the world is already spoken of in the Book of Proverbs, and that it was the instrument of creation is often repeated in the Hellenistic Apocrypha. But there is a great difference between the abstract wisdom and the Torah. The Torah is a concrete thing and what is more, it is expressed in language and through letters. When the Torah assumes such an office, every word and letter in it becomes important and is endowed not only with sanctity but with a supernatural power. Hence, we see that Akiba in his Halakah, derived laws from every letter, and even from the ornamentations of the letters. This theory of the power of the letters, though not exploited fully by Akiba himself, was destined to play an important role in the successive development of the phases of mysticism.

Another element of mysticism which is of great importance is the exceptional value attached to the name of God, to the very letters composing it. In the East, in general, the name of a person means really a part of the essence and personality of the one who bears it, and the same idea is expressed in the Bible continually by concealing the name of God, and giving it various appellations. The Tetragramaton (i. e. the four letters JHVH) is very often substituted by the name Lord (Adonai) though the punctuation is borrowed from the Divine Name.

---

[7] *Aboth*, Ch. III, 14.

Later, the name was considered ineffable, and only very select priests were allowed to pronounce it, and as a result various appellations were substituted. Hence the use of the name was considered a very mysterious means for performing supernatural deeds. By the use of the Ineffable Name (Heb. Shem ha-Meforosh) wonders were performed, and only very pious people versed in mystic lore could use it.

Again, on account of the sanctity attached to the name of God, an intense study of the meaning of the name, the significance of each letter, as well as the numerical value of each of these, sprung up. New names were mystically evolved from the initials of certain words in certain verses of the Bible, and thus we have the Divine Name of twelve letters, of forty-two letters and even of seventy-two letters. Besides, by a mystic method which utilized the permutations of the letters of the alphabet, new names were evolved, and consequently we have later mystical books speak of seventy names of God.[8] Each of these names of course, has not only a special significance, inasmuch as it indicates a power or attribute, but also a certain mystical power.

Furthermore, power was also attached to the names of the angels, who also discharge certain functions, and appellations were given them, so that consequently their names were multiplied and increased, especially those of the great mediator *Metatron*. It is mentioned in the same mystic writing, that *Metatron* also has seventy names and a list of them is given. Thus, an extensive teaching arose concerning the names of God and those of angels, their permutations and changes which ramified into various directions and became the woof of many a mystic book.

To sum up, there are three main elements in the mystic teachings of Judaism, in its earlier phase, which should be called plain mysticism (Torat ha-Nestor or Nisteret) as well as in the later phase, that of Kabbala. There are, first of all, those teachings clustering around the questions of the *Merkabah* i. e. the manifestations of God, His attributes and His relation to the world on the one hand, and around the question of creation on the other hand. The second is the hypostatization of the Torah making it together with its letters an eternal, or the earliest, being as well as an instrument in creating the world. The third is the power attached to the names of God and the angels. Together with these teachings, we must also take into consideration the development of the belief in angels, and the theory that they are powers of God and

[8] The *Alpha-Bet di Rabbi Akiba*, p. 9.

mediators between Him and the world which theory may be considered in a certain way a fourth element, though it is really a result of the teachings themselves which endeavored to explain the manifestations of God and His relation to the visible world.

We must, however, note, that although there were originally two currents, which were distinguished by the early *Tannaim* by two different names, *Ma'asé Bereshit* and *Ma'asé Merkabah,* they soon were joined into one current of mysticism which swelled into a mighty river. Furthermore, the earlier philosophic kernels they contained not only were amalgamated with the excessive symbolism used and the theories of angelology, but were overwhelmed by them, and at times, in certain books became indiscernible. On the whole, though, especially in a part of the later Kabbala they are quite distinguished. In general we note here a phenomenon common to other attempts at symbolism. All symbols are meant to be a bridge between the limited human mind and the high abstract conceptions. They are supposed to stand for great ideas which cannot be expressed in their entirety and cannot be encompassed by human language. But it often happens that the symbols become not means of expression but an end in themselves. All the sanctity and reverence for the higher things of which they are supposed to be an index are ultimately given to the symbols themselves, and thus the very purpose of the use of the symbols is defeated. The same happened in Jewish mysticism. While originally names of God and angels as well as the figures employed otherwise were intended as symbols of attributes of God, of high conceptions, they ultimately became objects in themselves, and thus, we see teachings which were intended to impart an exalted conception of God, employ a most anthropomorphic language, and devote much space to description of measurements of the Glory of God, which they hypostatitized, and also of the bodies of angels, and even, which is almost impossible to say, of the "limbs" of God Himself. A very strange phenomenon indeed, yet such are the facts, though we cannot exactly say whether these descriptions should be taken literally, or whether they contain some hidden meanings.

After we have had a short glimpse into the elements and genesis of the mystic teachings we may have a survey of the literature thereof.

181. THE EARLY MYSTIC LITERATURE

All these teachings, the essence of which we outlined, are referred to here and there in the Talmud. We find quite a number of passages, both in the Talmudic Agada and in the special Agadic collections, the Midrashim, which express these ideas, both of the nature of the creation and of the *Merkabah*. We find there references to the names of angels, and even quotations of dicta of angels, which were communicated by them to a few of the *Tannaim*. Especially prominent among the recipients of those direct angelic teachings is Rabbi Ishmael, the son of Elisha, a contemporary of Akiba and his generation, who was supposed to have ascended to heaven, and thus communicated with the chief angel of the Presence, Suriel (Sar ha-Ponim). These mystic teachings are not limited to the earlier generations of the *Tannaim;* later scholars such as the *Amoraim* also busied themselves with these studies, and a certain "Book of Creation" is mentioned in the Talmud, which was the subject of study by a few scholars of the third generation of *Amoraim*.

Yet, throughout Talmudic times, and even a century or two after the close of the Talmud, there hardly existed any special written literature of this kind. It is only in the middle of the Gaonic period that such books begin to appear. The books bear a pseudepigraphic character, as they are ascribed to early *Tannaim,* especially to those whose names are known from the Talmud to have occupied themselves with mystic teachings, such as Rabbi Ishmael and Rabbi Akiba. The form of these books is either the Mishnaic, namely, given in the form of single statements, or the Agadic, i. e. the form of Midrash. In this earlier literature, the mystic teaching is mostly given in the form of Agada, i. e. interpretations of verses by means of which the teachings are supposed to be evolved.

Thus, we have the *Aleph-Bet di Rabbi Akiba,* a Midrash on the letters of the alphabet, and a group of small books, or parts of books, bearing the name of *Hekalot* (Palaces). There is a larger one (Hekalot Rabbati) and a smaller one (Hekalot Zutrata), both of which are ascribed to Rabbi Ishmael ben Elisha. They also bear other names, such as *Pirké Merkabah* (Chapters of the Merkabah), *Ma'asé Merkabah* and several more. There is also another group of works ascribed to Rabbi Ishmael, several small books which bear the name of *Ma'asé Bereshit,* and a larger work known as the Book of Enoch, which contains the communication of Enoch or *Metatron* (Ch. I, Sec. 22) to Rabbi Ishmael when he ascended to heaven. Besides these, there are a number of anonymous mystic Midrashim, such as the *Midrash Konen,* so called after the first word of the verse in Proverbs III, 19, which forms the motto of the book, another alphabet Midrash, and finally the famous booklet *Shiur Komah* (The Extent of the Height) which is supposed to give the proportion of the height of the Godhead. This book, on account of its gross anthropomorphism, formed a point of attack by many writers against mysticism, especially by the Karaites, and called forth attempts of defense in various ways by several of the Geonim.

In attempting to delineate the character of these books, one finds himself in great difficulty, inasmuch as they contain much repetition, and are in most cases a collection of fragmentary sayings. In general, they can be divided into two classes, one primarily Agadic and only partly mystical, and the other primarily mystical. The latter is divided into those dealing with creation and description of the world, namely, *Ma'asé Bereshit,* and those devoted to description of the heavens and the *Merkabah,* i. e. the number of angels, their size and names, as well as other particulars of the Theophany. The lines, however, are not fast drawn, as there are a number of descriptions of angels even in the first division.

As we have noticed, the supposed authors of most of the books are as a rule two, Akiba and Ishmael. The reason for this is that Rabbi Akiba is known as one of those who entered the "Garden" (Pardes) and was deeply interested in mystic study. It was he who emphasized the theory that the Torah was the instrument of God in creating the world. Rabbi Ishmael again is referred to several times in the Talmud and Midrashim, as the one who ascended to heaven, primarily to protest against the order issued by the Roman proconsul in Judea, during the Hadrianic persecutions, decreeing a death of martyrdom to ten great Jewish scholars, of which number he was one.[9] There, according to the story, he was told that the decree was confirmed by the heavenly court, so that the Jews might expiate their sins by the death of these martyrs. It was therefore natural that all mystic teachings should be ascribed to these two outstanding figures. Rabbi Ishmael was especially favored, for he was supposed to have surveyed the heavens and to have had secrets communicated to him during his visit there by the angels, especially *Metatron*.

The several versions of the alphabet Midrash ascribed to Rabbi Akiba contain mainly Agadic homilies on each of the letters of the

[9] The ten Martyrs, or as they are known, *'Asara Harugé Malkut,* are referred to in the Talmud, and are the subject of special Midrashim, describing their death, and also of several *Piyyutim,* sacred poems. Their names are variously given in different lists, but Akiba and Ishmael are contained in all of them.

alphabet tinged with mystic interpretations. The source of all these queer interpretations is the conception that the letters have a kind of existence and power. The names of the letters are interpreted in various ways, every letter of the name signifying a word, and thus moral teachings are derived, e. g. the name of the first letter *Aleph,* means: "Teach thy mouth the truth" (i. e. Emet Lamed Pikha, representing the three letters of the name respectively). Besides these simple significances of the letters, they are hypostatized and given functions in the *Merkabah,* in the creation of the world. A great deal is made of the combination of letters and especially of the letters composing the names of God. In this book there is also, probably for the first time, an attempt to raise *Metatron* to an exceptionally high position as the greatest mediator between God and the world. He, like God, has seventy names, and is, on the whole, placed almost in a secondary position to God. This kind of teaching is really in direct opposition to the teachings of Akiba and other scholars of his age, who on the contrary, endeavored to minimize the importance of the angels, and made *Metatron* a created being like other angels. And yet, strangely enough, such teachings were ascribed to him. In the book there are also several passages which speak of the measurements of the angels and even of the Divine Presence (Shekinah) in fabulous numbers. Thus, though the bulk of it is of an Agadic moral nature, it contains all the elements of mystic teachings expounded at greater length in the other books and even in later Kabbala. Similarly, it can be said about the other anonymous alphabet Midrash.

Of the two groups of writings ascribed to Rabbi Ishmael, the first one which we called, in our classification, *Ma'asé Bereshit* and which contains several small booklets under that name, deals with a general description of the extent and measurements of the entire universe and its component parts, as the earth, the abyss (Tehom), the heavens, and so on. These writings also tell of the creation of the world, or rather worlds, for there are many of them—according to a strange calculation of the numerical value of the letters of a certain word—one hundred ninety-six thousand. There are according to these books, seven earths and seven heavens, and the abyss extends below all these earths. All these booklets are full of fabulous numbers into which these measurements run. There are also mentioned the seven heavens and a long list of the names of the various angels stationed at the gates of the sides of each one is given. The sun and the moon are not forgotten and strange notions regarding their nature are stated. Likewise, the names of the angels taking charge of the luminaries are given. On the whole, these writings represent a curious trend of mysticism with peculiar cosmogonic notions. Parallels to the cosmogony found here, we find in the ancient Apocalyptic Book of Enoch, which proves the antiquity of the ideas.

Very similar to the *Ma'asé Bereshit* group of booklets is the *Midrash Konen*. It is divided into three parts. The first deals with the creation of the world, speaks of the Torah as the instrument of creation, but in a modified way, namely, that since the Torah contains seventy-three names of God (the numerical value of the Hebrew letters of Hokmah = 73) it is by means of these names that the world was created. It also speaks of three primal elements: water, fire, and light which preceded the creation of the earth. We shall soon see how all these disjointed elements were later united into a system by the author of the "Book of Creation." The second part deals with the description and measurements of the world. In the center is the habitable earth. It is surrounded on the four sides as follows: by paradise on the east, by the ocean and desert beyond it on the west, by the Gehenna or hell, on the north, and by the chambers of the winds and storms on the south. A description of paradise and hell is also given, describing their various parts, and of course giving their measurements in fabulous numbers. The unit of measurement is the number of miles a man can walk in a year, and is simply called a "year." It is in these years that the measurement is given. Just to have a conception of the peculiar magnitudes our author is dealing in, suffice it to mention that the extent of paradise is eight hundred thousand years, and that of hell is a million and seven hundred and five years. Yet even these pale beside the thousands of light years our astronomers are dealing in.

The third part is devoted to the wisdom reflected in life and how things are balanced in it. There is always a protection for the weak against the strong. This is especially applied to the people of Israel who are protected by their guardian angels, Michael and Gabriel, against the onslaughts of the nations of the world and their angel princes—for every nation has a prince in heaven. The motto of the book is the passage in Proverbs (III, 19, 20): "God has founded the earth with wisdom and established the heavens with understanding." The passage is variously interpreted in order to derive the different teachings from it, and wisdom is identified with the Torah.

Of the other group ascribed to Rabbi Ishmael, the Book of Enoch is the most orderly arranged. It consists of five chapters. In the first one Rabbi Ishmael tells of his ascending to heaven and meeting with *Metatron,* who took him under his protection and acted as his guide there. *Metatron* then relates to Rabbi Ishmael the story of his translation and transformation from the man Enoch into the angel he is now. The rebellion of the angels is referred to. The story is similar to the one contained in the Apocalyptic Book of Enoch. The following chapters describe systematically a trip by Rabbi Ishmael through heaven under the guidance of *Metatron.* The second chapter gives an account of the functions of certain angels who hold a high and important place in the heavenly hierarchy, such as the cherubim and seraphim. An attempt is made to give the measurements of the greatest of them. The third and fourth chapters are devoted to a description of the process of judgment, the former telling of the *Irin,* special angels who act as members of the heavenly court, and the latter of the process of judgment itself and its execution. In the last chapter, Ishmael relates what he saw in the various parts of heaven, the groups of angels stationed in different places, the chambers where the souls of the righteous dwell, both those that are yet unborn, and those that had already returned from a life in this world, and also describes the chambers where the deeds of men of past and future generations are stored, and other wonderful things. In this book, we meet with peculiar forms of personification and hypostatization. The theory of the power of the letters as a means of creation is also made much of. Ishmael, led by *Metatron,* sees the letters by means of which heaven and earth, the constellations, and even the very angels, and the holy throne were created. It is evident that by the letters here is meant the first emanations of divine powers.

In the books of *Hekalot* various descriptions of the seventh heaven are given. In the smaller *Hekalot* book a chart is drawn of that heaven which is named *'Arabot* (the name is mentioned already in the Talmud). It is told that it contains twenty-eight palaces in four groups of seven each, and a heavy wall separates each group, then the number of angels in each palace, and finally measurements of the Throne of Glory, are given. The larger book of *Hekalot* contains thirty chapters and is written in Mishnaic form and style. Its purpose is to describe the process of ascension to heaven, or as the book calls it, "peering into the *Merkabah.*" It is in the form of a narrative by Rabbi Ishmael, who tells sometimes of his own experience, sometimes in the name of Nehunia ben ha-Kanah [10] the various tribulations which a gazer into the *Merkabah* has to undergo, until the highest vision is revealed to him. He has to pass through seven palaces until he reaches the throne. At each palace he is examined by angels whether he is worthy to enter, and is permitted to pass only after proving his worth. The book contains many hymns and songs of praise, also some extracts from a Midrash on the Ten Martyrs, as well as much extraneous matter. It is interesting that Rabbi Ishmael, though he is the principal narrator, associates with him Akiba as his companion on his ascension to heaven and refers to him for verification. Akiba, unlike Ishmael, is not spoken of in the Talmud as one who ascended to heaven, but the writer of the book, wanting to strengthen the verity of its content, included him in the heavenly expedition.

The last one of the group, *Shiur Komah* (Measure of Height) is the most anthropomorphic of all these books. It is likewise ascribed to Rabbi Ishmael, and it undertakes to give an account of the limbs of the Godhead; that they are measured in fabulous numbers, goes without saying, but as it is, it is appalling. Not only is the measure of every limb given, but every organ is given a name. And as if to strengthen this strange description, the testimony of Ishmael and Akiba is appended at the end of the book.

All these booklets are written in pure Hebrew and little of Aramaic is employed. This fact testifies to the time of their origin, as the middle of the Gaonic period, the eighth century, for it is then that a Hebrew revival took place (Ch. VII, Sec. 90). But, that they contain older material in the form of extracts and fragments of older books, especially Apocalyptic books, is beyond doubt.

The question arises: What was the purpose of these writers in their gross descriptions of heaven and its inhabitants? Did they intend us to believe that all these descriptions really gave an account of existing realities, or did they merely use a kind of tangible and gross symbolism for more subtle ideas, which these figures are intended to convey? It is almost impossible to answer this question conclusively. The fragmentary nature of these writings prevents us from tracing the symbolism in all its degrees, namely, from the more subtle ones to the grosser ones. We know, though, that these writings formed a point of attack. In later Gaonic times the Karaite scholar, Salmon ben Yeruham

[10] Rabbi Neḥunia is not mentioned in Talmudic sources as one who delved in mysticism, yet the mystics refer to him as one of their sages, and later the Kabbalists ascribed to him a special book in Kabbala.

(Ch. 13), a contemporary of Saadia Gaon, made considerable references to the anthropomorphic expressions contained in the *Shiur Komah* and other similar books, and thus blames the Rabbanites for conceding to such books a measure of authority. Saadia, in reply to his strictures, attempts to rationalize many strange Agadic passages by saying that they do not refer to God, but to visions of created light, in which God appears to the prophets. As for the *Shiur Komah,* he says, it is not authoritative and it is most likely a spurious work for which Judaism cannot assume responsibility. He adds, though, that even if it were true that the book emanated from the school of Rabbi Ishmael, we could interpret it to mean that these measurements refer to the visions of created lights, reflection of Divine Glory. Another Gaon, Rabbi Hai, says distinctly that these expressions, "Ascension to heaven," should not be taken literally by any means, but that they mean the inward gazing of the soul at the divine attributes, and the gazers, in passing various degrees of contemplation, speak of it as passing from palace to palace.[11] We see then attempts to interpret, to allegorize and symbolize these writings. My own view is, that these mystic writings represent the strange phenomenon, often observed in similar mystic movements, that opposites meet in a strange way. Jewish mysticism started out to evolve an elevated and subtle conception of God, His relation to the world and the process of creation. In the course of development it evolved the theory of emanation of forces from the Godhead, but was forced to use the prevalent theory of angels, and other kindred beliefs. To make its teachings more understandable and tangible it employed symbolic expressions borrowed from these very beliefs. In time these symbols became more prominent than the ideas they intended to convey. And ultimately, the angels and the letters and their various combinations began to assume an independent existence, hence the content of the books described. I believe that the *Shiur Komah* is only a crude and inadequate attempt to express the greatness of God in human terms. The ordinary human mind cannot conceive the Infinite, but has a conception of fabulous figures of measurement, though they be millions or even billions of miles, hence, the use of such figures. We cannot, however, endorse this method as it did not bring the desired results. Mystics, in the subsequent generations, took the descriptions of these books as literal and the angels and the "palaces" and their various names became the cornerstone of a peculiarly constructed edifice known later as

[11] Responsum of Hai quoted in *Aruk,* Art. *Eben.*

Kabbala Ma'asit (Practical Kabbala), which claimed to be able to perform wonders and miracles by the various uses of these names.

All mysticism, however, did not degenerate to mere descriptions of the heavens and their hierarchy. There still flowed another current, a more spiritual one, which kept on developing and assuming the definite shape of a system, where the elements indicated above were joined in a more or less unified way. This attempt was made by an unknown author in a book which likewise became current in the middle of the Gaonic period, at the close of the eighth century, and bears the title of an older book mentioned in the Talmud, namely, "The Book of Creation."

182. THE BOOK OF CREATION (*Sefer Yezirah*)

"The Book of Creation" consists of six chapters, each one divided into statements, which modeled after the Mishnah, are called *Mishnayot*. The first chapter contains thirteen such *Mishnayot,* the second six, the third eight, the fourth twelve, and the fifth and sixth four each. The style is pure Hebrew. On account of the symbolism of its language and the curious meaning of many of the terms, it is very difficult to summarize its content, but a mere outline may be given.

Its main problem is, as Judah ha-Levi had well seen,[12] the old problem of explaining how the manifold has evolved from the One, namely, how this world with its creatures and their vicissitudes have come forth from the one God. It is the mystic *Ma'asé Bereshit* of the ancients, spoken of above, in a new form, poetic and symbolic. It must have adopted also the theory of emanation from the old teachings of the *Merkabah*. Accordingly, there are two moments in the progress of the evolving of the manifold from the One, emanation of primal materials, and actual creation, forming and combining of elements into tangible and visible things. The first is not explained, the second, i. e. creation (Beriah), is described to some extent. The author of this book adopted the already prevalent theory, which as we have seen, was repeated constantly in the other mystic books, namely, that the letters of the alphabet, as well as those composing the ineffable name of God, are symbols of divine wisdom and possess power, and by the combination of these powers, things are created. It is in this way that he cryptically intends to explain or rather to indicate the process of creation. Most likely, the meaning is, that by the combination of the powers which the letters stand for, all things were brought forth, but the mystic who uses external

[12] *Kuzari,* Sec. 4., v. 25.

symbols always speaks in a language which emphasized the external manifestation of the spirit and the inner meaning is thus hidden.

The first two *Mishnayot* or statements are in a way introductory and give us a clue to the book. The first reads: "By means of thirty-two wonderful paths of wisdom had God, Sebaot, the God of Israel, living God, Eternal Being, etc., (here follow other attributes) engraved or established His name and created His world." There follows another sentence, which some consider an addition, but whose few words, and especially the last three, *Sfor, Sefer, Sippur,* puzzled commentators and called forth numerous explanations. The clear-sighted ha-Levi also saw the right meaning. He takes these enigmatic words (derived from the Heb. root Safor, to count, and also to tell) in their simplest meaning, namely, *Sfor,* numbering, measuring, *Sefer,* script, and *Sippur,* speech. But he interprets them later in a philosophic manner. To my mind they only contain the symbolic signs for the process of creation which the author wants to develop. The sentence is to be understood as follows. Continuing the previous thought, it says, "And He created His world by three signs" (Heb. Sforim), by *Sfor,* numbering or measure, by which is meant the emanation of a number of primitive materials, by *Sefer,* script, the letters which constitute the means of creation, i. e. further combinations of elements, and by *Sippur,* i. e. speech or pronouncement of these letters—the actualizing of these combinations. The creation of the world by the voice of God is mentioned in the Bible and in the Mishnah.

The second statement explains the thirty-two paths of divine wisdom and reads: "Ten *Sefirot,* intangible, and twenty-two letters, of which three are fundamental, seven double, and twelve plain." Here, we meet in mystic literature, for the first time, the name "Ten Sefirot," a term which was destined to become the very cornerstone of the later Kabbala. The very name *Sefirot* has been a subject of much discussion. Some wanted to connect it with the word sphere (derived from the Greek) and some otherwise. But it is evident, that they really mean here numbered powers. The number ten in relation to certain powers by which the world was created, is already mentioned in the Talmud. Here this number stands for the emanated elements, or categories of being, and is meant to indicate their all-inclusiveness, for numeration contains only ten degrees. After ten all goes back to one, e. g. ten and one eleven, etc. A group of *Mishnayot* (11) is then devoted to defining, though cryptically, the nature of these *Sefirot.* They are ten, divided into two groups, like the ten fingers, five opposite five, but in the center is the covenant of unity. It means to tell us that these manifold manifestations, which presage a kind of dualism, active and passive, later symbolized by masculine and feminine, are permeated by a unity, or are united by God (M. 3). We are further told of the all-importance of the *Sefirot,* namely, they are ten and not nine, ten and not eleven, i. e. neither more nor less, and one must use all his wisdom to conceive them, and then the Creator will be understood (M. 4). They are infinite in all phases, in the future or in the past, in goodness or in badness, in height or depth or in the extent to the east, west, south and north (M. 5). Enigmatic language, indeed, but the meaning is that they are endless in all phases. After a few more remarks are made about their infinity and relation to the throne of God, their interrelation with each other and to the great Unity—God, is described in a beautiful poetic phrase—namely, their relation is like the flame and the coal which are inseparable (M. 7).

After these remarks intending to describe the *Sefirot* as the highest principles of being, the numeration of the *Sefirot* begins. But here a certain change occurs. Instead of the ten abstract powers or categories, which we might have expected after the preceding descriptions of their nature and character, only one corresponds to that character; the others are of a more material nature. Thus the Mishnah (9) states: "The first *Sefirah* is the spirit of God, blessed be His name—Voice, Spirit and Word; this is the holy spirit." It is evident that by the first *Sefirah* is meant the first emanation which is infinite and is the basis of all other succeeding emanations and using older expressions, the author calls it Voice and Word (Logos). The second *Sefirah* is, according to our author, "Air from Spirit" (M. 10). By means of primal air the twenty-two letters were engraved. The third, is primal water, wherein void, chaos and slime were established (M. 11). The fourth, is fire which comes from water, and by means of it the holy throne, the Serafim, and the angels were created. The other six are the six points of space —four points of the compass and height and depth. These points of space are also connected mystically with the six permutations of the first three letters of the name of God, namely, *Yod, He, Waw,* each point having been sealed with a certain arrangement of this name. This particular remark is also oft repeated in the other mystic books previously mentioned. This theory of the *Sefirot* is to a certain degree baffling, for why should space be turned into six *Sefirot,* counting each of its points separately? Yet we can see here an attempt at forming a theory of emanation. The spirit is the first emanation and the further the emanations go, the more material they become—then primal air, water, and fire are the elements of all material beings. Earth is not mentioned, for it is only a last combination. It is also evident that these elements are, as said, primal elements and not the ultimate elements of this world, but prototypes of a higher spiritual nature. With this ends the first chapter devoted to the *Sefirot,* i. e. to the emanation of fundamental elements.

The rest of the chapters are devoted to the actual creation of the world, by means of combination of the letters. Here a peculiar system is developed. The letters are divided, as stated, into three classes, fundamentals or mothers (Imot), namely, the letters, *Aleph, Mem* and *Shin;* seven doubles, those that take a *Dagesh* (i. e. a point which gives them a double pronunciation hard and soft), i. e. *Bet, Gimmel, Dalat, Kaf, Pé, Resh, Taw,* and the twelve simple, those that have only one sound. He then says that by combinations of pairs of letters, that is, when each letter is paired with every other, there are 231 such pairs. And these can be reversed so that there are numerous other combinations. With this the second chapter is concluded.

The third chapter gives more details. Here the author adopts a three-fold system in the universe: the world, time, and man; each of the classes of letters express creations in all these three divisions. The three fundamentals signify the three elements, air, water and fire in the world (Aleph stands for Awir—air; Mem for Mayyim—water; Shin for Esh—fire, Shin being the last letter of the word), to which correspond heat, cold, and moisture in the year, i. e. time, each being related to each of the elements—heat to fire, cold to water, moisture to air.[18] Likewise is the relation of the three principal parts of the body, head, belly and the chest in man, traced to the elements. Emphasis is also laid here on the division between the masculine and feminine. All elements and principles in the world, time and man are thus divided.

The fourth chapter then takes up the symbols of the seven double-sounded letters. They represent by their two sounds, the hard and soft, such things in this world, which serve opposite purposes. By their means, seven planets were created in the world which sometimes exert

---

[18] The year spoken of here is the Oriental year where heat stands for the summer, cold for the winter, i. e. the rainy season, hence watery, and moisture for the middle season, i. e. spring and fall, when it is somewhat moist, neither dry nor wet.

a good influence upon affairs of man, sometimes a bad influence. These correspond to seven days of the week which is a part of the year, and to seven apertures or gates in the human body, namely, two eyes, ears, nostrils, and the mouth. The seven letters correspond also, in human life, to seven pairs of events of an opposite character, such as life and death, peace and war, wisdom and foolishness, riches and poverty, grace and ugliness, settlement and desolation, mastery and slavery.

The symbolic functioning of the twelve monosound letters is taken up in the following chapter. These twelve reflect the creation of twelve constellations in the world, twelve months in the year and twelve important organs of the human body, as well as the twelve functions of the body, such as seeing, hearing, smelling, eating, sleeping, thinking and others. As we see, the twenty-two letters of the alphabet reflect in their hidden power all the forms of entire existence which is divided into three systems, i. e. nature, time, and man. Our author is, however, anxious to show the unity in this manifold and he states that each system is dominated by a center. The center of the external world is the *Teli*, which is the axis of the world, sometimes called the line of the *Drakon*, the center of the year is the revolution of the sphere of constellations, and that of man, the heart. Each one of these is like unto a king, in different positions; the first is like a king sitting on a throne, namely, performing the highest and most exalted functions; the second, the revolution of the sphere, is like a king among his subjects, for the year is an aggregate of weeks, weeks of days, and all these are caused by that revolution; the heart is like a king in war, for among the human organs, there are some organs that nourish love, others hatred, others increase life, bring constant accretion to the body, while others cause changes in the body, and ultimately bring death, and the heart regulates all these functions of the organs which are at war with each other. It is, of course, not to be forgotten that the heart was, during the early Middle Ages, thought to be the seat of the soul. The author, wanting to emphasize the unity in this great manifold, concludes by a remark saying: "Thus, here is one above three, the three above seven, and the seven above twelve," referring to his hierarchy in the universe—three elements, seven planets, twelve signs of the zodiac in nature, and correspondingly in time and man.

At the very end there is appended a statement that Abraham, when he conceived all these mysteries, rejoiced very much and then God was revealed to him and blessed him. This was undoubtedly inserted in order to give authenticity to its teachings. But we indicated already the time of the composition of the book. We may add that certain other signs show definitely its date. The author is the first source for the division of the letters of the alphabet into five groups according to the five organs of speech, the throat, the tongue, the palate, lips and teeth. This division makes its appearance only in the first grammatical investigations which appeared about the eighth century. The fact that the author speaks of the letter *Resh* taking a *Dagesh* and having double pronunciation is taken by a number of scholars to indicate the Palestinian origin of the book, for it is only there that such a distinction was made in the pronunciation of the letter *Resh*. The Babylonian and the later grammarians know of no such distinction. But besides this, the whole trend of thought, as well as its borrowing of a number of passages from other mystic books which are distinctly Palestinian, indicate unmistakably its place of composition.

The book, as a whole, is an attempt to bring the various elements of mystic teachings into a system, to present a view of creation, and system and order into the world. The unity and the manifold are shown to be interrelated, the latter flowing out of the former. God is infinite and so, to a certain degree, are his manifestations, which are denominated *Sefirot*. The whole scheme of the letter combinations may be a kind of symbolism of the combination of divine thoughts, which are the creative forces of the universe and its various divisions. But in spite of the underlying philosophic thought of the book, the language and expressions introduced a different element, namely, that of too tangible symbolism and in time it formed the basis for the later Kabbala. We find here all its elements, the theory of emanation of the *Sefirot*, the importance of letter combination and the power of the names of God. There is also the dualism running through the entire universe, between active and passive, or masculine and feminine elements, and the conflict between opposites and the ultimate reconciliation which are permanent elements in existence. All these teachings, which here are only casually mentioned, are later enlarged upon, exaggerated and make up the very woof of the Kabbala.

Chapter XIII

KARAITE LITERATURE

183. GENERAL REMARKS

The second half of the eighth century witnessed the rise of a schism in Jewry and the creation of a new sect which later became known as Karaites. The supposed founder of that sect was, as we know, Anan ben David (period of activity 754–775), a nephew of the Exilarch Solomon ben Ḥisdai. The cause of his secession is supposed to have been a personal grudge against the Geonim who refused to appoint him Exilarch in the place of his uncle, as they suspected him of heresy, and gave the office to his brother. Anan then attacked the authority of the Talmud and, allying himself with a number of people who entertained similar ideas, proclaimed a secession from the Oral Law as taught by the Talmud and interpreted by the scholars of the academies.

The followers of Anan were numerous, for in a very short time the schism assumed the character of a well-organized sect and its teachings began to spread also in other countries. It seems probable, though not definitely established, that Anan was forced by the government to leave Babylon and therefore settled in Jerusalem, which served, during the first period of the development of Karaism, as the capital of that movement. But besides the two centers, Babylon and Palestine, it gradually spread to other countries, such as Egypt, Spain, the Byzantine empire, and Crimea. The Karaite sect managed to survive through the ages, and created a considerable literature, but, after having passed its zenith in the twelfth century, it began to decline and only remnants of the sect are now scattered in various parts of the world, and its end is already in sight.

In order to be able to survey the literary productions of the creative period of the Karaite sect, namely, from the end of the eighth century to the thirteenth, we must first understand the nature and character of the movement itself. Karaism, in spite of the fact that Anan is reputed to be its founder, was not a one-man movement. There were many, at the time, who were dissatisfied with the authority of the Talmud, and refused to submit to the interpretation of the Oral Law by the representative of Talmudic Judaism. Whether these people were secret adherents of the remnants of the Sadducean sect, as some scholars maintain,[1] or mere imitators of similar movements in the Islamic world, as others maintain,[2] the fact is that there were such people who entertained ideas contrary to the standard view of Judaism. Anan, therefore, became their mouthpiece, and they rallied around him to form a separate sect. He was the one who gave articulation to the formless and shapeless dissenting opinions and casting them into a mold he pronounced a fairly coherent doctrine which served as a basis for further development. In fact, the first sectarians were called *Ananites* and not Karaites. That name was assumed later, though the exact time of its origin cannot be determined. It is derived, according to most scholars, from the Hebrew root, *Karo*, i. e. to read, as well as to study, namely, those who read and accept the authority of the Bible (usually called Mikrah) only. The name bears a special significance for its use meant to indicate, on the part of those who bore it, a further digression from the ways of the Talmud than that of Anan. Anan and the *Ananites* still clung to a good number of Talmudic interpretations and ordinances. The later followers who designated themselves *Karaim,* abandoned, to a great extent, even these ordinances.

But no one must assume that the primary motive in the Karaite schism was the desire to lighten the burden of oral tradition, namely, to do away with the mass of laws and institutes which had accumulated, during the ages, around the written law. On the contrary, the Karaite teachers from Anan on, are distinguished by a rigorousness which imparted to their religion a gloomy aspect. In all their innovations there are very few attempts to lighten the burden of ceremonial practice of the Rabbanites (the name the Karaites gave the great mass of Jews following the Talmud), but there are many additions of a rigorous character. The real difference was a theoretical one. Anan and his followers believed that the written law alone is the source of authority and that the Mishnah and the Talmud have no authority, but that each one has a right to initiate his own interpretation of the Bible. Anan's motto was, "Search the Bible thoroughly" (Ḥafisu be-Oraito Shapir). By the term Torah, Anan understood not only the Pentateuch, as the scribes and the *Tannaim* who considered the Pentateuch only as the legal authority, but

---

[1] On this point see Pinsker's classic work *Likkuté Kadmoniot,* pp. 15, 16.
[2] Rapoport in *Kerem Ḥemed,* Vol. V, p. 205.

the entire Bible. He applied legal interpretation to all the twenty-four books and derived laws from prophetic and Hagiographic passages as well.

But the way of Anan was a dangerous one, for being torn from the moorings of a well-established and well-organized tradition, the Karaite leaders were left adrift on a sea of individual interpretations of the Bible. As is well known, the written law (Torah She-bi-Ketab) cannot be well applied to a later developed life without interpretation. And if interpretation is left to the individual scholars, confusion and conflict are bound to result and, of course, did result, and the first teachers of the Karaites were quite perplexed at these contradictions. Besides, there were a number of practices which the Karaites could not possibly abrogate, though they were not explicitly expressed in the Bible; they had therefore to borrow a large number of such practices from the Rabbanites. But not wanting to appear as borrowers, they invented a tradition of their own, and claimed not only antiquity for their sect, but even originality, asserting that they observed Judaism as it was observed by the prophets, during the First Commonwealth, and also by Ezra and his followers until Simon ben Shataḥ (Ch. I, Sec. 34), who first deviated from the true tradition and established the Oral Law of the Rabbanites. Some even claimed that Jeroboam ben Nabat was the first to lead the Jews astray in the way of the Rabbanites, while the people of Judah and Benjamin who remained loyal to the house of David kept the pure type of Judaism which they, the Karaites, were endeavoring to preserve.[3] In all events, they were careful not to be identified with the Sadducees, whom they really resemble, for the latter denied resurrection and immortality, which the Karaites professed.

All these things brought about a formulation of some principles of interpretation and practice which served as a guide to the teachers and their followers. These principles are: (1) The Writing, i.e. the Bible, namely, all laws and practices that are expressly stated, or even implied indirectly, in the entire Bible whether in the Pentateuch or in later books; (2) Analogy, namely, all laws which can be deduced by the method of analogy. It was a mighty weapon, wielded but too unscrupulously by the teachers in their method of interpretation, and the result

---

[3] On this point see the Karaite writer in his book *The Division between the Karaites and the Rabbanites,* quoted by Pinsker in above cited work: Addenda, p. 99 seq., also Posnanski in his introduction to *Zeker Zaddikim.*

was a multitude of rigorous practices based on faulty analogies applied by different scholars. (3) Tradition, but the Karaites did not want to use the Rabbinic name Kabbala, so they called it by various names, as Agreement (Haskamah), or Translation (Hatakah), or more commonly, The Burden of Inheritance (Sebel ha-Yerushah). These terms are supposed to denote all laws and practices which, though not expressed in the Bible, were accepted by the entire Jewish nation for ages. These principles introduced a semblance of harmony and unity in Karaism, yet, having no definitely established code, confusion continued. Each scholar kept on interpreting the writings in his own way, applying analogy, according to his standard, and hence differences were very frequent. Almost every Karaite scholar felt it necessary to write a *Sefer Miẓwot* (Book of Precepts) of his own, as well as his own commentaries on the Bible. In these books of precepts, we often note that one writer prohibits what his predecessors allowed, and vice versa.

This character of Karaism determined in a way the character of Karaite literature. The slogan of Anan, "Search the Bible thoroughly," and the constant need for interpretation of the Bible, gave great impetus to the study of the Bible, which of course, involved an intense interest in the grammar and lexicography of Hebrew. Every exegesis must pay great attention to the grammar of the language, in which the text is written, especially an exegesis which was mostly polemic, which intended to show that the Rabbinic and Talmudic interpretation of the Bible was erroneous because it did not follow the plain sense of the verses. We have, therefore, an extensive literary production along the lines of the science of language and Biblical exegesis. Yet, between the two, the works on exegesis exceed by far those on grammar and language, in both quantity and quality. The Karaite contribution to Hebrew philology, notwithstanding the opinions of earlier Jewish scholars, is not great. It is the Rabbanites who have largely built the great edifice of Hebrew grammar and lexicography. As for exegesis, almost every Karaite scholar found it necessary to write a commentary, at least, on the Pentateuch, and very often on the other books, where his interpretation of the precepts was given. Frequently, these commentaries were written especially on the Ten Commandments, where attempts were made to group all *Miẓwot* under these ten heads.

Again, the lack of an adopted code or textbook like the Mishnah or Talmud, necessitated the writing of "Books of Precepts" and almost every outstanding scholar wrote, as stated, either a whole book of this kind, namely, where all the precepts were included, or a partial one, where only a part of the precepts were treated.

The Karaites, in repudiating the Talmud, very often reproached it for strange Agadic passages found therein where anthropomorphic expressions of God are given, and accordingly prided themselves on the purity of their conception of God. This gave rise to a philosophic literature among the Karaites. But even in this field there is little originality, and the Karaite philosophy falls behind that of the Rabbanite. In the classic period, it follows mostly the Arabic Mutazilite system and in the post-classic, Maimonides.

The interest in Hebrew and exegesis also produced some poetic productions, mostly sacred. And here as in philosophy, in spite of their avowed love of Hebrew, the Karaite poets hardly surpass the mediocre standard. Even the greatest among them, Moses Darai, cannot measure up to an ha-Levi or a Gabirol, or even to a Moses, or Abraham Ibn Ezra. Their books were written, to a great extent, in Hebrew but a considerable part of their literature was also written in Arabic and later translated into Hebrew. Yet, in spite of their zeal for Hebrew, the style of the Karaite writers is hard and heavy. In their passion for purism and in their endeavor to avoid the Aramaisms of the Talmud, they lost all elasticity and flexibility of style and very often it is difficult to find clearness in their writings. In order to satisfy the need for expression, they were forced to coin many new words out of the meager material of the Biblical language, but there is little grace in these newly coined words and their use only encumbers the style. Thus, Karaite literature, like Karaism, paid the price for separating itself from the bubbling well of life of a nation flowing for many centuries, and was cut off from advantages which an ever-flowing fountain, like that of the genius of Israel, can supply.

184. THE EARLY PERIOD OF KARAITE LITERATURE

The Karaite literature of the first four centuries can be conveniently divided into several periods, the first period from the rise of Karaism to the beginning of the tenth century, the second embracing the tenth and eleventh centuries, and finally that of the twelfth century. During the first period, the literary productions are mostly written either in Rabbinic Aramaic or Hebrew, and they deal mainly with Halakic matter. As such, they consist primarily of books of precepts, or commentaries on the Bible, the purpose of which is to interpret the Bible in such a way as to deduce from it new Halakahs and practices. Little attention is given to other fields, and only here and there we meet with a grammarian, or lexicographer, or a pure exegete. The centers of literary activity are Babylon and Palestine.

i. Of the outstanding writers of this period, the first one is Anan, the founder of the sect. Of Anan we know definitely that he composed a "Book of Precepts" of which a large part is extant, and of the rest we have numerous quotations by later writers. This book is written in the current Talmudic style, namely, Aramaic mixed with some Hebrew. There seems to be no particular method adopted in grouping the laws and precepts. Groups of laws are chosen at random. The method of interpretation of the verses quoted and the deduction of the practices is essentially the old Midrashic one, but it differs greatly from the Rabbinic, inasmuch as special efforts were made to deviate from the Talmudic interpretation of the same verses and arrive at different results. On the whole, it can be said that comparing the interpretations of Anan with those of the *Tannaim,* or even the later *Amoraim,* the former are more forced and really bear little relation to the plain meaning of the verse. Since Anan repudiated the rules of interpretation established by Hillel (Ch. III, Sec. 37) and the later ones added to by Rabbi Ishmael, he practically remained without any other means of operation except the analogy (Hekesh) and was forced to fall back upon the twisting of the words of the verses in many a strange and peculiar manner. These writings brought strange results and the laws assumed a gloomy aspect. The matters are too technical to go into detail, but it is sufficient to point to the stern aspect that the Sabbath assumed with the Karaites, which arose either from taking some of the verses literally, or interpreting them in a forced way. Due to this, the burning of any light on the Sabbath, even if it were kindled before sundown, is prohibited. Likewise, free movement on that day is greatly restricted, and a number of other pleasures considered legitimate under the Rabbinic law, are rigorously prohibited by Anan.

A typical example of forced and peculiar interpretation on the part of Anan can serve us the extremely complicated system of prohibited or incestuous marriages (Arayot), originally instituted by him and primarily based on a peculiar interpretation of a verse in Genesis. The verse in Genesis II, 24, which reads "And therefore shall a man leave his father and his mother and shall cleave unto his wife and they shall be one flesh," which the Talmudic authorities merely took as expressing the sanctity of marriage and derived from it some ethical teachings, became to Anan a source for deducing numerous new prohibited marriages. The words "And they shall be one flesh" mean, according to him, that husband and wife are to be considered as one always. The tie is never severed, either by divorce, or even by death, and consequently all relatives of the wife acquired by new marriages after divorce or vice versa, the new relatives of the husband, acquired by a marriage, are prohibited for them as well as for their children from their own union or from former or later unions. Similarly, the prohibited relatives of the wife remain prohibited for the husband even after she dies, e. g. the wife's sister is prohibited to the husband even after the wife dies. Other verses in the Bible regarding prohibited marriages were interpreted accordingly. Consequently the very complicated system of incestuous marriages ensued as a result. This system is known as *Rikkub* (from the verb Rakeb, to compound or join) and it weighed heavily upon the Karaites, for it happened often that whole communities were prohibited to intermarry with each other. It was though later modified.

Such and other things can serve us as examples of Anan's interpretation, which was aggravated by his successors. When the Pentateuch was not sufficient the other books were drawn upon, and even passages of historical narrative or poetic ones were often made to yield a legal prohibition. Anan himself, however, followed to a great extent Talmudic interpretation; his successors digressed more in this strange method.

Some Karaite writers have also ascribed to Anan a commentary on the Pentateuch and an Arabic book by the name of *Fadilikah,* i.e. a *summa.* But we are not certain about them, as no trace is left of these writings. It is also possible that the last name was only an Arabic summary of "The Book of Precepts."

ii. Benjamin Nahawandi (i.e. of the city of Nahawand), who flourished about forty or fifty years after Anan (ca. 830), is considered by the Karaites as the second founder of the sect. He evinced a more rigorous tendency and in some cases he is more antagonistic to the Talmudic law, but in other practices he deviated from Anan and adopted again the Talmudic law and practice. He wrote, likewise, a book of precepts by the name of *Masat Biniamin* (The Present of Benjamin). This book was written in Hebrew and is primarily a book on civil law, including that of family law. As said, he was very rigorous and he was the one who gave a great impetus to the development of the complicated system of prohibited marriages. But he also mentioned in his book the Rabbinic practices and at the close of his book, copies of which he sent to all Karaite communities, he appended a letter calling attention to the fact that he included Rabbinic practices in civil matters, and that those who desire can follow them and judge according to them. Benjamin was also the first Karaite philosopher. He followed the Mutazilites in removing all anthropomorphism from God, but went to extremes in that direction, inasmuch as he propounded a theory that God first created the angels, especially the primate angel, whom He commissioned to create the world and be the mediator between Him and this world. According to this, then, wherever it is written in the Bible "and God appeared, or descended, etc.," this angel is referred to. Likewise, the revelation on Sinai will have to be relegated to him. We have here a modified theory of the Philonian Logos (Ch. IV, Sec. 68) with this difference though, that with Philo the Logos is an emanation, while with Benjamin the angel is a created thing. He entertained also a peculiar notion regarding punishment after death which, he says, falls entirely on the skeleton and not on the soul, to the refutation of which Saadia devoted a few paragraphs in his *Emunot we-Deot*. From all this, it must be evident that Benjamin wrote a whole book on philosophy, but his successors who quote his opinions never mention the source.

Benjamin wrote commentaries in Arabic on several books of the Bible. Thus, we have lengthy quotations from, and references to, a commentary of his on the Five Scrolls. There are also quoted several of his comments on verses in Isaiah and Daniel, from which we may possibly conclude that he commented on these books too. From the quotations we can see that Benjamin was really a good exegete and endeavored to explain the text, in accordance with the plain meaning (Peshat) and principles of grammar. He displays a fine sense of the language and keen understanding of the text.

iii. A third outstanding scholar of this period is Daniel ben Moses Al-Kumisi (fl. at the end of the ninth century), who hailed from the city of Kumis, the capital of a province in Persia. Daniel wrote, like all the Karaite scholars, a "Book of Precepts" in Hebrew, where he displays a very rigorous attitude towards the observance of ceremonies. Especially strict was his teaching regarding the Sabbath, as he even forbade the cleaning of the hands when not absolutely necessary. He was equally strict in regard to prohibited foods and included among them also eggs, as he considered the egg an unfinished thing. We find in his "Book of Precepts" also other peculiarities, such as that the New Year begins with the Day of Atonement. He also wrote a commentary on the Pentateuch where he followed closely the plain meaning of the words and was especially averse to speculative interpretation.

iv. David ben Boaz, surnamed by later writers the prince (ha-Nasi) (fl. ca. 910), is frequently quoted by various authors. He wrote a commentary on the Pentateuch, which was lost, but from the excerpts found in other writings, we can conclude that his commentary was widely read and quoted and he acquired a great reputation as an exegete. Besides his exegetic work, he also composed a book on the fundamental doctrines of religion or as he called it a *Kitab Al-Uṣūl* (Book of Dogmas).

v. Of this period we know one grammarian and Massorite, Judah ben Elon of Tiberias (d. 1032), who settled at Jerusalem and was the head of the academy at that city. He wrote a book on the Hebrew grammar by the name of *Meor Ennayim* (The Light of the Eyes). This book, as we can see from a quotation by a later encyclopaedist,[4] dealt primarily with the derivation and classification of the nouns. He is also known to have composed some sacred poems.

185. THE ARABIC PERIOD

The tenth and eleventh centuries which form the great classic period in Jewish literature in general, can also be denominated the classic period of the Karaite division. During these two centuries, the Karaite sect brought forth its best literary productions. And like the Rabbanite literature of this time, the Karaite used Arabic to a very great extent as the medium of expression. Most of the great writers wrote their works in that language, of which a considerable number were translated into Hebrew, while many books remained in the original and were thus lost to posterity and are only known to us by quotations.

i. The first distinguished writer who opens this period is Jacob Al-Kirkisani (fl. first half of the 10th century). He is usually known as Abu Yusuf by later writers, and was also, at times, called Joseph, which fact brought a good deal of confusion among scholars as to the identification of this Karaite savant. Kirkisani composed his great work in Arabic in the year 937. The work is divided into two parts, the first being called by a euphuistic name, "Flower beds and Gardens." It is pri-

---

[4] Judah Hadasi in his encyclopaedia *Eshkol ha-Kofer*, p. 69a.

marily a commentary on the Bible. The second part is called grandiloquently "The Book of Beacon Lights" and is mainly a book of precepts, but it also treats of other subjects, especially of history and theology. The first four sections of the book are devoted to these subjects. Of especially great value is the first section which is the introduction to the whole book. It deals with the history of religious sects, and is divided into eighteen chapters discussing the origin and history of all then existing sects. He tells first of the older sects, the Samaritans and the Sadducees. He believes that the latter were nearer to the path of true religion than the Pharisees. It is interesting to note that he speaks of Sadducean books which were still extant in his time. The other chapters are devoted to the description of a dozen Jewish sects, some of them bearing strange names, such as one named the Megarians, i. e. cave men, for their sacred books were supposed to have been found in caves, and other sects similar to them. These sects led an ascetic life and were somehow akin to the Essenes in Temple times. He also discusses the Christians, quoting the opinions of the Rabbanite and Karaite scholars about them, and treats also the various divisions of the Karaites themselves. In these matters he supplied valuable data about Anan, his teachings, and about Benjamin Nahawandi and his philosophy. This section does not, of course, lack polemic matter. Kirkisani devotes several chapters to an attack on the Agada of the Talmud and the mystic books where anthropomorphic expressions are used, thus vindicating the purity of the Karaite conception of God. The second section is devoted to showing the necessity for investigation and interpretation of the Torah, the third, to a refutation of the erroneous conceptions of the various sects, and the fourth, to the discussion of the right path of knowledge of the law. The body of the book is the usual Karaite book of precepts with a good deal of polemics against Saadia, his contemporary, in particular, and the Rabbanite interpretation of the law in general. To him is also ascribed a book on dogmas, but little is known of it, and it is probably a section of his Magnum Opus.

ii. Abu'l Surri ben Zuta, usually referred to as Ben Zuta, was a Karaite exegete, who lived in Egypt during the first half of the tenth century, and was a contemporary of Saadia Gaon, as well as his opponent. Ibn Ezra, in his commentary on the Pentateuch, quotes Ben Zuta's interpretations of certain verses several times, as well as Saadia's refutations to some of these interpretations. From the few quotations by Ibn Ezra, it is evident that Ben Zuta's commentary was greatly distorted by the polemic spirit against the Rabbanite interpretation of the Bible, as he very often deviates from the plain meaning of the verse in order to offer a different explanation than the Rabbinical one. The polemic between him and Saadia must have been an oral one, as we find no trace of a book or pamphlet by Saadia against Ben Zuta.

iii. Another contemporary of Saadia, and a violent polemic writer against Rabbinism and Rabbinic law, was Ibn Sakuya. His main literary work seemed to have been a book written in Arabic under the name of *Kitab Al-Fadaih* (The Book of Shameful Things) by which term he meant to characterize the Rabbinic interpretations of the Bible. The book was divided into ten sections, each one taking a certain phase of Rabbinic law. He especially accused the Rabbanites of describing God in anthropomorphic terms, of misinterpreting the Bible and falsifying the calendar. His book must have exerted, at the time, considerable influence, for Saadia thought it necessary to reply to it in a special book called "The Refutation of Ibn Sakuya," where he refutes his arguments and does not spare his person. Saadia says satirically, that the name "Shameful Things" given by Ibn Sakuya to his book is a very appropriate one, for it is really full of shameful things uttered by the author.

iv. An important figure in Karaite literature of this period was Salmon ben Yeruham (910). He was a younger contemporary of Saadia but he seems to have begun his polemical activities against him after the latter's death. Salmon was born in Egypt and settled later in Jerusalem, but he made frequent trips to Egypt and Babylonia. He wrote both in Hebrew and Arabic. His Hebrew work is a polemical book against Saadia under the name of *Milhamot Adonai* (The Battles of the Lord). The book takes up mainly the question of the calendar and the fixation of the holidays, but also deals with the observation of the Sabbath and other legal matters, and, as other Karaite scholars, Salmon does not fail to attack the Talmud for the strange Agadic passages wherein God is represented in gross anthropomorphic terms. Salmon is vehement against Saadia and makes reproaches against his personal conduct, which are very unbecoming a dignified opponent.

Besides this polemical work he wrote a voluminous commentary on Psalms, commentaries on the Five Scrolls, on Daniel, and Job, and Proverbs and possibly on the Pentateuch. His commentaries were written in Arabic. Salmon was of a fanatical trend of mind, and in his commentary on Psalms, he attacks those who do not devote themselves to the study of the Torah. On the other hand, he was permeated by a deep religious and ethical zeal, and in his commentaries on the Hagiographa, he inculcates ethical teachings in his explanations of the verses.

v. Another polemical writer as well as exegete and scholar of the tenth century, was Sahal ben Mazliah (second half of the tenth century). He also lived in Jerusalem but, prompted by the zeal of a propagandist, he went to Babylon after Saadia's death, and there carried on a sharp polemic against the Rabbanites at first in Arabic. His activity called forth a reply from Jacob ben Samuel, a pupil of Saadia, for the refutation of which Sahal wrote a work called *Tokhahat Megulah* (Open Letter of Reproach) in Hebrew. In that book, he attacks the Rabbanites for their apparent laxity in observance of the Sabbath, laws of purity, and other matters. He further questions their source of authority, namely, the Talmud, and points to the many different opinions found in the Mishnah. The style is incomparably superior to the usual Karaite Hebrew style, inasmuch as it is simple and flowing and no attempt is made at rhyme. He wrote also a commentary on the Pentateuch and Isaiah, a book of precepts, and one of laws. According to a later Karaite encyclopaedist, he also composed a Hebrew grammar. Sahal, though an exegete and grammarian, was a rigorist and in his codes he is very severe and champions the complicated marriage system.

vi. Jephet ben Ali ha-Levi (end of tenth century), surnamed Al-Busari, was the great Karaite exegete. He performed for the Karaites the same service in Biblical exegesis which Saadia did for the Rabbanites. He translated the entire Bible into Arabic and wrote in the same language an extensive commentary on it. His commentary was voluminous, for the part on the Pentateuch alone occupied twenty volumes. A large part of it is still preserved in manuscript. Jephet possessed a keen linguistic sense and great insight into the plain meaning of the Bible and his commentaries possessed great authority for the exegetes who followed him. With the Karaites he was considered *the* commentator and almost every successive exegete followed him and quoted extensively from his works. But even Rabbanite commentators drew considerably upon him. Abraham Ibn Ezra quotes him copiously. He also wrote a Hebrew grammar under the name of *Safah Berurah* (The Plain Language), but little is known of it.

Besides his exegetic works, he also composed two polemical writings, one against Saadia himself and one against Jacob ben Samuel, his disciple mentioned above. The latter is in rhymed prose. In addition, he also wrote a book of precepts. His son, Levi ben Jephet ha-Levi, was also known as a scholar and composed in the year 1007 his "Book of Precepts" which is frequently cited by later writers as authoritative. This book, written in Arabic, was later translated into Hebrew. In addition, he also wrote some exegetic pieces to several chapters of Deuteronomy.

vii. The constant interest of the Karaites in the Bible and its interpretation at last brought forth an outstanding grammarian and lexicographer, David ben Abraham Al-Fasi (second half of the tenth century), who hailed, as the surname indicates, from Fas, North Africa. His principal work is a dictionary (Agron) covering all words in the Bible alphabetically arranged according to the roots. David ben Abraham still believed, like his countryman, Judah Ibn Koraish, in the biliteral or even monoliteral theory of Hebrew roots (Ch. VII) and his arrangement follows accordingly. The dictionary is written in Arabic, the greater part of which is still preserved and is really a valuable contribution to the knowledge of Hebrew as well as Biblical exegesis, for like the dictionaries of Saruk and Ibn Jannaḥ (Ch. VII), that of Al-Fasi's also contains a good deal of Biblical exegesis. His method is as follows. At the beginning of each section he gives a list of all the verses of the Bible containing the words which are given in this section, and while explaining the words, he is also explaining the difficult verses. The book is also replete with rules of grammar and remarks on the proper punctuation of Biblical words. He uses the comparative method in deriving the meaning and origin of Hebrew words. Most of his comparisons are with the Arabic, but here and there also with other languages, especially with the Aramaic. David also wrote a book on punctuation and commentaries on Psalms and Canticles. His dictionary was considered authoritative with the Karaites and his successors repeatedly issued abridged editions of it.

viii. Another grammarian of this period was Abu Al-Faraj Harun, or Aaron ben Yeshuah of Jerusalem (fl. ca. 1002). However, little remained of his grammatical works, except some quotations by later writers who all call him by the surname, the great grammarian. He also wrote in Arabic a commentary on the Pentateuch of which a number of quotations survive.

ix. The eleventh century was a very productive one for the Karaite literature. At its very beginning, we meet with a writer who distinguished himself both in the field of law as well as in exegesis. This writer is Nisi ben Noah (fl. first half of the 11th century). The age of this writer was long disputed. The earlier historians of Karaism, such as Pinsker and those that followed him, including Graetz, considered him an immediate follower of Anan and placed him early in the ninth century. But this has been rejected by later scholars and it is now accepted that he lived in the eleventh century, somewhere in Persia.

Nisi was one of the Karaites who reverted to the use of Hebrew and his works are written in that language. He was a widely traveled man and well educated. He tells of himself that he knew four languages, Hebrew, Aramaic, Greek, and Latin, besides, of course, Arabic. Yet he chose to write in Hebrew, since it is the sacred language. His works consist of an extensive commentary on the Decalogue, where the method so often employed by the Karaites—though employed also by Rabbanites—of deriving all the 613 precepts from the Ten Commandments, is not only followed but the derivation and classification of the precepts logically carried out.[5] This commentary is really an introduction to a book on laws and precepts which he called by a euphuistic name *Bitan ha-Maskilim* (The Garden of the Enlightened Ones). The book itself is lost but the opening remarks are preserved. In these remarks an outline of the divisions of the book is given, from which we can see that the book, at least in its systematic arrangement, excelled many such books by earlier and later Karaites. Nisi was, on the whole, a rigorous Karaite, yet, he urges his followers to study the Mishnah and Talmud and other Halakic books of the Rabbanites. Nisi displays a fair acquaintance with the philosophic notions of his time, refers often to syllogistic forms, and is also acquainted with the division of studies, or sciences. Thus, he speaks in one place of the cycle of studies known throughout the Middle Ages as the quadrivivium. This consists of geometry, arithmetic, astronomy and music. From all this it is evident that he studied philosophy and though he did not write any special book on it, his commentary on the Decalogue is tinged with its spirit. The later Karaite scholars quote him frequently as a great authority on law.

[5] The question of who was the first one to introduce the method of grouping the 613 precepts under the Ten Commandments is quite an interesting one. Pinsker, who considers Nisi ben Noah to have lived in the ninth century, makes him the originator and believes that the Gaon Saadia who used this method in his liturgical poem *Azharot*, only imitated Nisi. But in view of the fact that Nisi really lived at least a century later than Saadia, the preference will have to be given to the latter. It is worth while, however, to point out that this method was originally employed by Philo Judaeus. In this case Saadia utilized a method which was most likely known in his time. See also Ch. XI, note 2.

x. Joseph Al-Basir (d. 1040) is the outstanding Karaite author of the century. He is usually quoted as Joseph ha-Roeh (same as Basir), i. e. the seer, which is supposed to be a reverse name for blind, as the usual Talmudic title, Sagé Nahor, of great light, is applied to blind scholars. Of his life we know very little, except that he traveled much and learned much. Besides Arabic, in which he wrote his books, and Hebrew, he also knew some Greek and uses a number of Greek philosophical terms in his books.

Joseph holds the distinction of being the only Karaite philosopher of importance during the classical period. He composed three works of a philosophical nature: (a) "Thirteen Questions," addressed to Jewish and Gentile scholars, (b) The Neimot (Pleasing Discussion, but in Arabic the name is an entirely different one, Al-Muchtavi fi El-Asl El-Din, which means a Survey of the Dogmas of Religion), (c) Mahkimat Peti (Enlightening the Fool). The first work is of little value as it consists of a long list of Biblical verses proving the unity of God. Of the other two, the Neimot contains thirty-five portals and is supposed to be a book on dogmatics, but the purpose is, however, not carried out completely, as it deals primarily with the conception of God, His attributes, and His relation to the world. It contains also polemical matter against erroneous philosophical opinions of various Arabic philosophic sects. The Mahkimat deals with the same problems in a briefer and more systematic way and contains thirty-three portals.

Joseph in his philosophy follows the system of the Kalamite Mutazilites of the Arabs completely and evinces on the whole little originality. His proofs for the existence of God are those of the Kalamite philosophers who proved the existence of God through the creation of things, namely, that all things are created, hence there must be a creator. He believes also, following the Kalam, that God created the world by His will which in turn was also created, a theory which was objected to by later Jewish philosophers, as Joseph Ibn Zaddik (Ch. XI, Sec. 166) and others. He taught that God possesses essential attributes, which are: living, knowing, potent, and existing. He vigorously defended the justice of God, and, of course, the freedom of man. He was extreme in his defense, so that he even implied that animals, which are slaughtered by men with the permission of God, will get some reward in exchange for their suffering, a view which was greatly influenced by a notion current in Kalam, that even the souls of animals possess immortality of a kind. Yet, with the exception of these peculiarities, he succeeded in giving, on the whole, a rationalistic view of the most important religious conceptions and his books exerted considerable influence upon the successive religious philosophers. The later Karaite philosophers borrowed extensively from them and the Rabbanite, Joseph Ibn Zaddik, devoted a great part of his book, "The Microcosm," to combat Al-Basir's views. Besides his philosophical works, Joseph wrote a number of other books, several of them on law. These are *Sefer ha-Maor* (The Book of Light) where various groups of laws are treated, such as circumcision, the fringes, some marriage laws and others; and a "Book of Precepts," where the laws are treated in the usual manner of Karaite books of this kind. The ninth section of the book was usually considered a separate treatise on prohibited marriages (Arayot). To Joseph Al-Basir belongs the credit of initiating a reaction against the extremely cumbersome and complicated prohibited marriage system (Rikkub) of the Karaites. His disciples carried on the struggle for reforms in this direction with much zeal and vigor. He also wrote a book on festivals and on the calendar (Heb. Abib, i. e. spring), where he polemizes against Saadia. His books were mostly written in Arabic, but were later translated into Hebrew, and a number of them are preserved. Al-Basir's opinions on all matters were considered authoritative and are frequently quoted by later writers on all subjects and he was by them styled, the great teacher.

xi. The last important writer of the eleventh century was Yeshuah ben Judah (fl. 1050–1100), known as Abu Al-Faraj Furkan Ibn Asad, which is the Arabic translation of the Hebrew name (Furkan being Arabic for Yeshuah, Asad, lion, for Judah). His literary activity resembles that of Joseph Al-Basir, inasmuch as he was an exegete, a writer on law and a philosopher. Yeshuah lived almost all his life in Jerusalem, but in spite of that he exerted great influence on all Karaitic communities. He was an ardent propagandist, and he succeeded in drawing pupils from all parts of the world. Among his pupils there were Tubia from Constantinople, and Ibn Teras from Spain. The latter carried on a vigorous propaganda on behalf of Karaism in Spain.

Yeshuah translated the Pentateuch into Arabic and wrote a commentary on it in two recensions, a longer and a shorter one. The shorter commentary on Exodus and Leviticus was translated into Hebrew and is still preserved. Yeshuah evinced great skill as an exegete and together with Jephet ben Ali was extensively quoted by later commentators, even by the Rabbanites. Ibn Ezra quotes him twenty times in his own commentary on the Pentateuch. From the quotations it is evident, that Yeshuah endeavored in his commentary to explain the Bible in a logical manner, and in accordance with the rules of grammar and the sense of the language.

In the field of law, his great contribution is the *Sefer ha-Yashar* (Book of Righteousness), a treatise on prohibited marriages (Arayot) written in Arabic but later translated into Hebrew by his disciple, Jacob ben Samson. This book is one of the important ones on this subject, inasmuch as Yeshuah continued the struggle of Joseph ha-Roeh against the rigorousness of the complicated system (Rikkub) and advocated reforms in that matter. The question is gone into in detail, and the opinions of leading scholars, from Anan on, are quoted and analyzed. He also wrote a few philosophical works, a philosophical commentary on Genesis, known as *Bereshit Rabba,* and a book on God and His attributes, by the name of *Marpé le-Ezem* (Healing of the Bones, referring to Proverbs VI, 22 and other places, where words of wisdom are spoken of as a medicine for the soul and body).

186. THE TWELFTH CENTURY

The twelfth century, which was the heyday period of Jewish literature among the Rabbanites, and during which there arose such literary giants as ha-Levi, Ibn Ezra, and Maimonides, to name but a few, was with the Karaites already a period of decline. Yet, though it cannot compare with the preceding century, it still retained some of the comparative productivity of the former. It can boast of a few outstanding literary figures whose works were preserved during the generations and which are quoted by later writers. It is to be noted, though, that the center of literary activity was removed to Byzantium, and Constantinople became the literary capital of Karaism instead of Jerusalem, or Babylonian cities. This can be explained by the fact that the Karaite settlement in Palestine dispersed, with the beginning of that century, during the persecutions of the Crusaders who held the country at that time, while the Babylonian Karaite centers suffered from the effects of the general decline of that Jewry.

i. Among the leading literary figures of this new center was Tubia ben Moses, surnamed ha-'Obed, i. e. the God-fearing man, a title which he acquired on account of his great piety. Tubia lived in Constantinople at the beginning of the twelfth century. We know little of his life except that in his youth he studied at Jerusalem under Yeshuah ben Judah. He distinguished himself especially as a translator of his teacher's books, as well as those of Joseph Al-Basir, to whose philosophical works he also made some additions. He himself wrote a commentary on the Pentateuch in Hebrew under the title, *Zot ha-Torah* (This Torah). Some scholars ascribe to him also a book of precepts under the name, *Yehi Meorot* (Let there be Light), which is in the form of legal discussions on selected verses of the Pentateuch which contain precepts and commandments, but there is doubt whether Tubia is really the author of this book.

ii. Another writer of this new literary center is one by the name of Elijah ben Abraham, who, as it seems from his writings, also lived somewhere in Byzantium in the middle of the twelfth century. Of his works we have one left, which is entitled: *Hiluk ha-Karaim we-ha-Rabanim* (The Division between the Karaites and the Rabbanites). It is a small work of a historical nature, and purports to establish the antiquity of the Karaites. He repeats the assertion already advanced by Kirkisani (Sec. 183) that the division between the Rabbanites and the Karaites dates from the time of Jeroboam and that the Rabbanites are his followers. He adds, however, a new note, by saying that a part of the followers of the true religion left Palestine, at that early date, and went to Ethiopia in order to be able to observe Judaism in its purity, while another part remained in Jerusalem and clung tenaciously to the Torah in its pristine state. It goes, of course, without saying that the Karaites are the descendants of these selected few. He is, though, not very certain of his rather bold assertions, and in several places, he concedes that it is possible that the Karaitic schism is of later origin, and it may be even assumed that Anan was its founder. He insists, however, that this origin in no way impairs the authenticity of their beliefs, for he claims that divisions were always going on among the Rabbanites, such as the division between the Pharisees and Sadducees, between Bet Shammai and Bet Hillel and others. In general, the whole work bears an apologetic character and displays a feeling of weakness and inferiority. Its main importance consists in a list of Karaite scholars and leaders from the time of Anan to his own day. The list is not above reproach, yet it contains valuable information.

iii. The greatest writer of this period and one of the leading authors of the entire Karaite literature was Judah ben Elijah Hadasi, surnamed ha-Abel (i. e. the mourner, a title often assumed by Karaite savants on account of their mourning for the destruction of Jerusalem). Of his life we know little except that he lived during the middle of the twelfth century in Constantinople. His education was a most complete one. Besides Hebrew he also had a fair knowledge of Greek, inasmuch as Greek words and phrases abound in his book. He was versed in the entire Karaitic literature up to his day and also studied the Talmud and the Rabbinic literature; besides, he studied philosophy and all other sciences of the day. His was an encyclopaedic mind and he absorbed all knowledge of the generation. All this knowledge he poured forth in his Magnum Opus, *Eshkol ha-Kofer* (A Cluster of Camphor, a phrase found in Canticles I, 13, and it is probably applied to the book on account of its encyclopaedic character, for *Eshkol* was used in the Talmudic literature in such wise), which was composed in 1148.

The book is a veritable encyclopaedia and, as said, contains all knowledge, law, dogmatics, philosophy, exegesis, grammar, and even astronomy, zoölogy and other sciences. It is, of course, superfluous to say that it contains a good deal of polemics and intends to defend the correctness of the Karaitic theory and views on all subjects against the Rabbanites. Its arrangement and order is a peculiar one, but more unique is its form. It is written entirely in rhyme and each section is arranged according to the alphabet, namely, each verse begins with a letter of the alphabet. For the sake of variety, the alphabet is frequently reversed, namely, that instead of the first verse beginning with *Aleph* and the last one ending with *Taw,* the former begins with *Taw* and the latter ends with *Aleph*. This arrangement is usually known as *Tashrak* (i. e. Taw, Shin, Resh, Kuf). To complicate the matter, some sections have instead of the alphabetic acrostic, an acrostic of the author's name as well as his father's. Each few verses have a monotonous rhyme of *kho* (i. e. the final kaf) which forces Hadasi to add the suffix to words that do not require it, and thus adds another difficulty to the reader. Bound by such complications, it is really to be wondered at how Hadasi was able to execute such a voluminous work, inasmuch as the book contains 379 long sections. It, of course, testifies to his skill in Hebrew, but it makes his style, though on the whole pure Hebrew, difficult and hard to understand on account of the twistings and turnings, and artificial ornamentations with which it is adorned.

Yet, in spite of the fact that the form of the book is rather peculiar, its content is of exceptional value. As said, it covers almost every subject ever touched upon in Jewish literature. The method employed is the one already referred to, which was used by a former Karaite writer,

Nisi ben Noah (Sec. 183), that of grouping all precepts and all religious knowledge under the Ten Commandments. The book, therefore, is really divided into ten unequal parts. But Hadasi is not strict; he interprets each commandment in the widest possible sense, and often includes such subjects which apparently have no relation to the commandment at all, but are included only by resemblance to other subjects which do fall under that commandment.

Thus, he opens his book with the laws relating to the praise of God, namely, all laws of prayer as well as the order of prayer and benedictions on various occasions, such as benedictions pronounced on food, on drinks, those pronounced at marriage ceremonies and others. This subject is treated first, for the first commandment, "I am the Lord thy God," implies, first of all, the duty of man to praise God. But Hadasi knows no limitation, and while speaking of the benedictions of betrothal and marriage he begins to discuss the forms of betrothal and marriage. These subjects are treated again, *in extenso,* under the proper commandment, and thus there is a good deal of duplication. But the knowledge of God involved in this commandment includes much more than prayer and benedictions. It involves a conception of God, His attributes, His actions, His conduct of the world, relation to man and man's relation to Him, so Hadasi launches upon a wide sweep of subjects. In a number of sections he unfolds an entire religious philosophy, discusses the attributes of God, the anthropomorphic expressions of the Bible, revelation at Sinai, prophecy, God's justice, reward and punishment, and penitence and its conditions. Since God is primarily the creator of the world, he deemed it necessary to include a number of sections on the world and its wonders, touching on astronomy and physics, and from the inanimate world, he passes over to the animate, and gives an epitome of his zoölogical knowledge, incorporating all the absurdities current in the Middle Ages regarding some strange animals. Hadasi is also a great antagonist of the Rabbanites, and does not forget to include, while discussing the purity of the God conception, all the anthropomorphic passages of the Talmud and the mystical books and tabulates them, in order to show the errors of the antagonists. Thus, the chain lengthens and the first commandment alone swells into a fairsized book.

In this way he continues until he practically exhausts all law and all religious knowledge. It would be useless to follow him in his constantly swelling discussions. We shall only cite a few more examples illustrat-

ing his peculiar encyclopaedic method. Under the second commandment: "Thou shalt have no other Gods before me," he includes besides
discussion on laws of idolatry, a history of all sects in Judaism that have
arisen from early times to his day. Here, too, he finds space to discuss
all kinds of sorcery, as well as forms of superstitions, and naturally
attacks the Rabbanites for their forsaking the path of true Torah, and
again gives a long list of Talmudic passages which he turns into rhyme,
and claims that they defamed the prophets and other Biblical heroes,
ascribing to them imaginary sins. These charges are again repeated
under the ninth commandment: "Thou shalt not bear false witness
against thy friend."

In his treatment of the fourth commandment, that of the Sabbath,
under which are included the discussions of all laws of the Sabbath and
festivals, he enters into controversy with the Rabbanites for their interpretations of these laws. But this controversy brings him to a long discussion of the laws of interpretation of the Torah. He increases the
hermenutic rules to eighty and is involved in the question of punctuation. This makes him give a complete treatise on grammar and punctuation.

Again, while subsuming all laws of inheritance, mourning and kindred subjects under the fifth commandment, "Honor thy father and
mother," he also includes discussions of human conduct in general, how
one should conduct himself towards society, the poor, elders, officers,
teachers and all other social relations. Similarly, under the sixth commandment, "Thou shalt not murder," all criminal laws and those of
damages are discussed; under the seventh, all family laws and kindred
subjects. Thus, his discussions constantly swell and include all tribu-
taries of knowledge. It is no wonder that Hadasi's book was held in
great esteem by later generations, as it was an inexhaustible source of
information, and was supplied by a later scholar, Kaleb Apopondopolo,
with a detailed table of contents.

Of the characteristics of Hadasi's philosophical teachings, these are
to be noted: First, that he is practically the only Karaite philosopher in
this period who accepted the four elements as the basis of the physical
world. All previous philosophers followed the Kalam in accepting the
atomic theory, namely, that the physical world consists of innumerable
small particles moving in the void, which are constantly being created
by God and destroyed. Secondly, that he followed Nahawandi in teaching that the angels were created first, and that they performed many of

the functions often ascribed, in the Bible, to God. In general, wherever it is said, God descended, saw etc., it refers to an angel. Even the very descent on Sinai was performed by an angel, except that the voice was God's. Thirdly, that among the ten articles of faith or principles of religion he counts also the duty to know Hebrew, the language of the Torah, as well as its exegesis.

Returning once more to the book, it is to be noted that besides its varied content, it possesses invaluable importance for the hundreds of quotations from Karaitic writers. Hadasi drew on the entire Karaitic literature, and he quotes many books which are now lost, and the only source of information we have about them is the *Eshkol ha-Kofer*. It thus serves us as a guide to Karaite literature and its teachings. With this encyclopaedia, the classic period of Karaite literature is closed.

Chapter XIV

HISTORY, GEOGRAPHY, AND TRAVEL

187. GENERAL CHARACTERISTICS

The historical literature of the Jews, during the earlier period of the Middle Ages, can very often be called historical only by courtesy. As is well known, the science of history in the modern sense was entirely unknown during the first half of the Middle Ages. Not only was the critical faculty absent among the writers of history in those days, but they even lacked the ability of telling a connected story wherein the concatenation of events is pointed out and demonstrated. Most of the "histories" of the period are merely chronicles of events, or lists of kings and other outstanding personalities in a more or less consecutive order, interspersed with stories of miracles and curious happenings. There is very seldom an attempt to sift the facts or doubt the narratives. Credulity, which was a fundamental characteristic of Mediæval life, reigns supreme in these histories. All that the narrators of former generations related was respectfully incorporated in these chronicles or histories. And the same can be said about the Jewish historical books of the period that they display, with few exceptions, the same characteristics in a marked degree. The Jewish people in exile, lacking a united national life, could not well produce a real history. Its memories clustered around the lives of its outstanding personalities who, for a long time, were either the scholars, or the chiefs of exile and patriarchs. Hence a large number of these histories contain merely the lists of generations of scholars and especially the leaders of these generations. Only in such cases where the historian turns to the earlier period of Jewish life, namely, the one before the destruction of the Temple, do we get a more or less connected history. Yet this is not the rule, these books are not always dry. We have also a few small works dealing with phases of life in certain periods, and thus giving us a reflection of that life. As the ages speed on and suffering becomes the very woof of Jewish life in exile, the histories or chronicles assume a more somber aspect; they become gloomy narratives of martyrdom and persecutions, or lists of martyrs and massacres.

The books which deserve the name of histories deal mainly with Jewish life, but inasmuch as that life was inherently interwoven with the general life, we catch glimpses occasionally of that life too. Certain events of the peoples among whom the Jews lived are narrated, kings are mentioned and data given. At times we have even a book dealing entirely with the history of other nations. We must also note, that the line drawn between history and geography is really an arbitrary one, for many of these books classed as geographical can be just as well denoted historical. The travelers, who supply us with the geographical data, really dwell more on the life of the people in the Jewish communities they visited and describe it in a detailed manner. Their books are thus excellent sources for Jewish history of the periods in which they were written. We have therefore drawn the line, in many cases, only for the sake of convenience and it does not represent a real distinction. To say that these geographical books, and especially the tales of travel, suffer from the same defects as those on history, is almost superfluous, for credulity and lack of exactitude were just as much common vices of the travelers and geographers as of the historians.

Yet, with all their shortcomings, these books are of great value, inasmuch as they serve as the sources of Jewish history and often are the only means through which we can get a glimpse at the past life of the people. As historical material they do not fall behind other "historical documents" which are the bases of the histories of other nations, and it is left for the historian to sift out the truth by the usual methods. On the whole, these chronicles and histories possess a common virtue, for with few exceptions, they are written from a more or less objective point of view, inasmuch as Jewish historians had no courts or nobles to flatter. Yet there is, of course, personal bias, and as stated, there are exceptions.

A. HISTORY

188. ANONYMOUS WORKS

i. The first of these kinds of works is a small chronicle called *Seder Olam Zuta* (The Brief Order of the World). It is named so, because it follows in method and form the older chronicle by that name composed by a *Tanna* of the second century, José ben Ḥalafta (Ch. IV, Sec. 72), except that it is much briefer. The author seemed to have a special aim, namely, to prove the direct descendancy of the Exilarchs in Babylon, until a certain time, from David. For this purpose, he gives a list of generations from Adam to that time, mentioning chiefly the outstanding personalities in each generation. He pays little attention to events, only stating a few. According to him, the office of the Exilarch in Babylon began with Zerubbabel, the grandson of King Jehoiachin, who returned thither after he built the Temple at Jerusalem. He gives a complete list of the Exilarchs from Zerubbabel down to about the eighth century, from which it is to be concluded that the book was written about the end of that century. As to his chief contribution, namely, the names of the Exilarchs in that long list, it is doubtful whether a large number of them are really historical. It is believed that the names of the Exilarchs from Zerubbabel down to Huna, who died about the end of the second century c. e., are purely fictitious. First, we do not know whether the Jews in Babylon had any such officer during the first six centuries of their settlement there. The first reference to an Exilarch in the Talmud is in the time of Simon ben Gamaliel, during the second half of the second century, while Huna who is mentioned by name there, died about the end of that century.

There seems to be more historical value to the names of Exilarchs from Huna down, and the events of the later period and the names of the later generations of Exilarchs possess real value. The author closes the list of Exilarchs in office with Mar Zutra the Second about 420 c. e. who left Babylon and settled in Palestine on account of persecution. He gives, however, the names of eight more descendants of the Davidic house, but these seemed not to have held that office, as they lived in Palestine. The office of the Exilarch continued in Babylon to the middle of the ninth century, and really began its more glorious period with Bustanai who rose to the office, at the time of the conquest of Persia by Ali in 641, but of all these later Exilarchs there is no mention in our book. It is therefore concluded that the author was dominated by the tendency to show that the Bustanai line of Exilarchs was not descended from David, inasmuch as the original dynasty terminated in Palestine by the flight of Mar Zutra II. It will thus prove to be one of the exceptions, namely, a historical book written with a certain tendency.

ii. Another small work of this kind is the *Seder Tannaim we-Amoraim* (i. e. The Order of the Tannaim and Amoraim) referred to above (Ch. X, Sec. 157). The book was composed about the end of the ninth century and emanates from a Gaonic school. It contains, besides the methodological part discussed above, also a historical part, as it gives lists of all the patriarchs in Palestine from Hillel to the abolition of the patriarchate, of the generations of *Tannaim* of the Mishnah and the heads of each generation of the *Amoraim* and the scholars immediately succeeding them, the *Saburaim*. It is to be noted that the list of the Palestinian *Amoraim* is very incomplete—only a few of them are mentioned. The book is found in several versions, and was used as a source book by subsequent historians.

iii. The most important work of this class is the one known as *Yosippon* (i. e. the smaller Josephus). The book purports to be a condensed account of Josephus' historical works written by Josephus himself. It is strange, however, that he is not called here the son of Mattathias as in his books, but the son of Gorion, the name of one of the Jewish generals and governors of Jerusalem in the early stage of the war. The book is thus a historical pseudepigraphic work. It was compiled, as is evident, from a number of sources among which was, most likely, a Latin translation of Josephus' works. It may also be possible that the compiler did not use Josephus' work itself but only the book of Hegessipus, an abridgment of that work composed in the fourth century. Besides the work of Josephus, or Hegessipus, the author drew upon Roman historians, especially Titus Livius, for items of Roman history, upon the life of Alexander the Great written by Archpresbyter Leo, in the middle of the tenth century, and other works.

The facts that the author of *Yosippon* was already acquainted with books written about the middle of the tenth century, as well as his mention of such European nations as the Danes, Irish, Burgundians, and other geographical data, which could only be known by one who lived in the last century of the first millennium of the common era, determine approximately the date of the composition of the book. It is placed around the year 960.

As to the place of its composition all evidences point to Southern Italy. The author's acquaintance with European geography, with Latin books, the number of Latin words as well as the Latinized forms of names and places, show that he lived in a European country. On the other hand, he shows also an acquaintance with Arabic literature and culture, and such a wide knowledge of both the Occidental and Oriental cultures could only be acquired by a man who lived in Southern Italy, in the tenth century, where both cultures were known.

The book is not a chronicle but a regular, well-connected history. In the fashion of the day, it begins with Adam, gives a brief genealogy of the children of Noah and then deals extensively with the table of na-

tions in Genesis, Ch. X, giving a geographical description of the distribution of the nations mentioned in the table. In this geographical
description he shows a wide knowledge. He knows of the Germans but
calls them peculiarly enough by their French name, Allemand, of the
Russians who dwell on the Dnieper, of the Slavs, Danes, and other
nations. While he identifies the *Kitim* of the Table of Nations with the
Romans, he starts with early Roman history and brings that down to
the time of the fall of Jerusalem. This leads, of course, to his main
purpose, the narrative of Jewish history.

There follows, then, the story of Cyrus, much embellished, of
Cambyses, of Daniel and his exploits, taken from the Additions to
Daniel (Ch. I, Sec. 4), the story of Zerubbabel and the building of the
Temple, and the story of Esther. All of these episodes of early Jewish
history are greatly embellished by the Apocryphal tales. From Darius a
jump is made to Alexander and his relation to the Jews. Alexander must
have been a favorite of our author, as he was generally the favorite in
the Middle Ages. He devotes to his life a considerable number of pages
giving it in great detail, incorporating the well-known romance of
Alexander. His successors, however, he treats briefly but does give a
short chronicle of Roman history up to Augustus.

From then on he devotes himself to Jewish history. Beginning with
the reigns of Seleucus in Syria and Ptolemy in Egypt, he gives first the
story of the Septuagint translations, and continues in detailed manner
up to the destruction of the Temple. In this last part, the author interrupts his narrative of Jewish history at times to tell of a few outstanding
episodes in Roman history. These are the stories of Hannibal, of Cæsar,
that of the ravishing of Paulina, illustrating the moral corruption of
Rome in the time of Tiberius, and the coronation of the king.

The book, on the whole, contains a good deal of genuine historical
material, but much of it is mixed with legends and tales common to
that period. The author, like all writers of the period, identifies Biblical
personages with the heroes of Roman history. Thus he makes Zepho, a
grandson of Esau, one of the founders of Rome. The style of the book
is pure Hebrew and only here and there, it is interspersed with expressions of Midrashic language. On the whole, it is a fair specimen of
historical prose. It is flowing, elastic and smooth. In some places it
betrays attempts at translating Latin phrases into Hebrew.

Yosippon was well received and became popular. The first reference
in Hebrew literature to the book is by Dunash ben Tamim (Ch. VIII,

Sec. 94), a tenth century man. It must have been translated into Arabic early, for an Arabic writer, Ibn Hazam, who died in 1063, already quotes a long excerpt from it. From the eleventh century on, it is quoted and referred to by almost every important author, such as Rashi, Ibn Ezra, Kimḥi, and many others. During the ages it was the favorite book of the Jewish youth who drew their historical knowledge from it.

iv. To this class of anonymous historical works belongs also one more book, though it hardly deserves that name, as it is primarily one of historical legends or Agada. This is the *Sefer ha-Yashar* (Book of the Righteous), an embellished story of the early part of Biblical history, namely, from Adam to Joshua. The author collected all legends, tales and stories connected with Biblical events or persons of that period and intertwined them with the narrative. It seems that his purpose was to compose a popular story book which should attract the readers and thus acquaint them with a part of the Bible. He drew upon all sources, Apocryphal books, Talmud, and Midrash—in fact, all kinds of Midrashim, some that are lost today—*Yosippon,* the letters of the Khazar king (see below B) and even Arabic sources. He was anxious, however, to give it the authenticity of antiquity and hence the name *Sefer ha-Yashar,* as a book by that name is mentioned in Joshua X, 13 and 2 Samuel I, 18 as a book of history. In fact the first editor who printed the book in 1625 at Naples, Joseph ben Samuel of Fez, tells a legendary story about the origin of the book, that it was found at Jerusalem, at the time of the destruction of the Temple and later brought to Seville. It is called there also by another name, *Toldot Adam* (History of Adam).

The book was most likely composed in Spain in the twelfth century. The first is proved, besides the notice in the introduction, also from the fact that the author is well acquainted with Arabic, as he uses a large number of Arabic names to denominate the children of Ishmael and also from other evidence. He also uses philosophical terms current in Spanish Jewish literature. The second, namely, the date, is determined by the fact that the eleventh and first half of the twelfth century scholars have no reference to it. It is only from the thirteenth century on that it is referred to.

The author is very detailed in his narrative and is painstakingly careful to supply the names of all the children of the persons mentioned in the Bible as well as the names of their wives. He even does not forget to give the names of the witnesses to the deed of Abraham to the cave of

Machpelah. He is likewise careful in supplying dates to events of the period, though such are not mentioned in the Bible. He must have drawn on the "Book of Jubilees" (Ch. I, Sec. 23) in such matters. This book, like *Yosippon,* was very popular and is preserved in many versions. Since its first edition in 1625, it was reprinted many times. Its style is likewise pure Hebrew with a slight admixture of Aramaic words. It is an exceptionally fine specimen of Hebrew prose, possessing beauty and charm.

189. CHRONICLES OF RABBI NATHAN

The first historical book which bears the name of its author is one by a scholar, Nathan the Babylonian, called "The Order of the Academies." Rabbi Nathan was a contemporary of Saadia Gaon, and he found it necessary to record the events of his time and depict the cultural life of the age. The book is logically divided into two parts, one dealing with a description of the important institutions of the day, namely, the two academies, Sura and Pumbedita, their manner of study, the office of the Gaonate and its functions. Next comes a description of the office of the Exilarchate, its functions and privileges. We have also a detailed record of the sources of income of each of the academies, and of the Exilarch, together with a description of the ceremony of induction of the Exilarch in office.

The second part records the important historical events of the period, the first being a quarrel between the Gaon Cohen Ẓedek and the Exilarch Ukba, the second, the strife between the Exilarch David ben Zakkai and the Gaon Saadia. The historical value of the book is great, for besides giving an authentic account of a contemporary of an important episode in the life of Saadia, it gives a real picture of the intellectual and political life of the Jews of Babylonia. Nathan's description of the academies and of the judicial and communal affairs of the Babylonian Jewry holds good not only for his time but for the entire Gaonic period. We thus really gain an insight into the inner life of these two great workshops of Jewish learning of that period.

The book was preserved in Hebrew and for a long time it was thought that Rabbi Nathan wrote his work in Hebrew. Of late, however, an Arabic fragment of Nathan's records was discovered, and it is now thought that Nathan wrote his work in Arabic and that the Hebrew is a translation.

There has been recently discovered also another fragment in Arabic containing the story of the leader of the Bagdad Jewish community, Natira, and his sons, telling of their high position at court during the reign of the Abbaside Caliphs, Almutadhid and Al-Muktadir (892–932), their conduct, and their generosity. This story is also ascribed to Nathan and it is suggested that it was a part of a larger work.

190. THE LETTER OF SHERIRA GAON

A more important historical work, since it is more complete, is the famous "Letter of Sherira Gaon" (920–1000). This work was written in answer to a query addressed to the famous Gaon by Jacob ben Nissim of Kairawan, in the year 986, consisting of a number of questions affecting the authenticity of the Mishnah and Talmud and the sequence of tradition. The questions were as follows: First, how was the Mishnah written? namely, was the Mishnah written down little by little from the time of the Great Assembly (Kenesset ha-Gedolah) until Judah the Prince finally closed it (as Saadia maintained), or did Judah write it altogether? In this case, the question arises, why did the earlier scholars leave the task to the later ones? Second, is there any reason for the arrangement of the tractates in each order? Third, what is the purpose of the *Tosefta* (additional collection), why did Judah himself not incorporate it in the Mishnah, and how were the *Baraitot* (Ch. V, Sec. 59) written? Fourth, how was the Talmud written down? Fifth, what is the sequence of scholars, namely, the *Saburaim* and Geonim, to Sherira's time?

The people of Kairawan were motivated to ask this series of questions because of their constant argumentation with the Karaites, who questioned the authenticity of the Mishnah and Talmud and claimed to possess versions of *Baraitot,* or even whole collections of them which differed in a number of matters from the teachings imparted in the Mishnah and Talmud. The people of Kairawan were therefore very anxious to know all about the Mishnah and Talmud, the manner of Halakic tradition, the nature of the composition of these books, as well as about the scholars who continued the chain of tradition after the close of the Talmud.

To all these comprehensive questions, Sherira wrote an equally comprehensive answer. His epistle falls, therefore, into two parts, the first dealing with the four questions affecting the manner of composition and order of the Talmudic literature, and the second dealing with the fifth question, the chronological sequence of the post-Talmudic scholars.

He deals with the questions *seriatim*. First, he takes up the authenticity of tradition, explains that there was an uninterrupted chain of tradition from the men of the Great Assembly and that each generation handed down the principal Halakahs to the other. At first, he says, there was little necessity to write anything down, for there was little difference of opinion and they could well continue their study orally. It was only after the destruction of the Temple, when times were turbulent, that differences began, and as time went on the differences multiplied, so that it became necessary to collect *Halakot,* arrange them and write them down. This is the gist of his answer to the question why the Mishnah was not ordered and arranged and written down until the time of Judah the Prince, though its main material is old. He then goes on to explain the nature of the Mishnah, the relation of Judah's work to earlier collections, especially Rabbi Meir's, the order of the tractates and the nature of the *Tosefta.* He also describes the work of the *Amoraim,* the meaning of the concept Talmud and its method, for which he claims great antiquity. In the discussion of all these questions, Sherira also deals with the order of succession of the *Tannaim* and *Amoraim,* and gives a large number of methodological data which help us to understand the mechanism of the Talmud.

The second part, which deals with the last question regarding the order and sequence of the generation of leading scholars from the close of the Talmud to his own day, is of great importance. Here Sherira becomes the only source for the history of intellectual life in Babylon from the year 500 to 1000. He introduces his real subject, however, by giving a list of all patriarchs from Hillel to Judah, as well as a detailed chronological list of the leading Babylonian *Amoraim,* noting their time of office, to the close of the Talmud. From there on he becomes more detailed and chronicles in regular succession all the *Saburaim* and Geonim, who served as heads of the academies. He is careful to tabulate the heads of each academy separately, namely, he enumerates the Geonim of Pumbedita, for a certain period, and then takes up those of Sura for the same period, and so on.

His chronicle is not dry, for he records the important events of the time, the institutions and legal reforms of the Geonim, and all other matters of historical value. The sources employed by Sherira were the archives of the Academy of Pumbedita, as well as oral reports that were current in his time regarding the lives and deeds of earlier Geonim. He possessed a keen historical sense in selecting materials, and his epistle thus has great validity and authenticity. The style of the letter is the usual mixed Aramaic employed in the Talmud and all Gaonic Responsa.

Of the "Epistle of Sherira" we possess two versions, one emanating from the Spanish school and one from the French school. The versions differ in a number of things but their chief difference centers about the passages that refer to the writing down of the Mishnah by Judah, as well as the Talmud by Rabbi Ashi. The Spanish version states explicitly, in a number of places, that Judah not only edited and compiled the Mishnah, but actually wrote it down. All these passages are so changed in the French version, as to leave no reference to the writing down of the Mishnah by Judah. They state only that he arranged and placed its material in order but pass over in silence the writing down. It is believed by scholars that the Spanish version is the correct one, as the Spanish scholars were in close touch with the Geonim, and they undoubtedly received the letter directly either from Babylonia, or from the people of Kairawan to whom the epistle was sent and with whom the early Spanish scholars, such as Samuel Ibn Nagdila (Ch. VIII), were in close touch. Thus, Nissim, the son of Jacob, the one who addressed the inquiry to Sherira was the father-in-law of Joseph, the son of Samuel, and most likely, Samuel had an authentic copy of the original letter. On the other hand, we know that the French scholars abhorred the idea that such an important part of the Oral Law as the Mishnah should have been written down as early as Judah the Prince. They preferred to have the writing down of the Oral Law deferred as late as possible, for the Talmud states distinctly that the Oral Law is not allowed to be written down. It is, therefore, surmised that copyists of the French school consciously or unconsciously changed the passages in Sherira's letter so that they might conform with their views on the matter.

191. THE CHRONICLE OF AHIMA'AZ

Among the various discoveries made by Jewish scholars in the last few decades in the field of Jewish literature, there is also a historical chronicle which sheds light upon the life and history of the Jews of Southern Italy during the ninth and tenth centuries. This chronicle, known as "The Chronicle of Ahima'az," the name of the writer, was published by Adolph Neubauer, in 1895, from a unique manuscript in the library of the cathedral at Toledo, Spain. The chronicle was writ-

HISTORY OF JEWISH LITERATURE

ten in the year 1054 by Aḥima'aẓ, a descendant of a family of great Jewish leaders, scholars, and famous sacred poets (Paitanim). It is really more of a family chronicle, aiming to tell of the vicissitudes of the fortunes of the various members of the family, for two hundred years. But the author, in telling the fortunes of that family, relates also the history of the Jews in Southern Italy, for the members of that family were their leaders. The founders of the family were Rabbi Amitai, and his son, Rabbi Shephatyah, both of whom were renowned *Paitanim,* whose sacred poems were incorporated in the prayer-books of the Italian and German Jews. Another member of the family was Rabbi Paltiel, who, through his acquaintance with the Mohammedan governor of Sicily, entered the service of the Fatimide Caliphs in Northern Africa and rose to be the counselor of several caliphs. Under Al Mo'izz he moved, together with him, to Egypt and became also the prince of all the Jews in the empire including that of Palestine. From that chronicle, we learn many events of Jewish life in Southern Italy during the two centuries. There is a record of the persecution of Jews in that province under Basilius, emperor of Byzantium, who ruled at that time also over Southern Italy, of the kindness shown to the Jews by his successor, Leo VI, and of the invasion of Calabria by the Saracens. There are also many glimpses of the inner Jewish life. From it we learn of the judicial autonomy of the Jews of that province, and several cases are recorded where Jewish courts condemned criminals to death, in accordance with Jewish law. We also learn that Southern Italy was a great center of Jewish learning, that sacred poetry was highly developed there, and that mysticism was held in high esteem and that many scholars devoted themselves to the practical application of mystic teachings. There are a number of legends told about various men who performed miracles aplenty, and the stories are told, as a matter of fact, as usual occurrences. The chronicle also reveals to us the close communication between the Jews of Italy and Palestine. It seems that Jews of Southern Italy used to make frequent pilgrimages to Jerusalem, and these served as the channel of influence of Palestine on the lands of the Diaspora. They also kept in touch with Babylonia. There is mention also of a Babylonian scholar, Rabbi Aaron, who arrived in Oria, a town in that province, and established an academy there. This Aaron was also a great mystic as well as a composer of sacred poetry. He figures, in later writings, as the one who taught the art of *Piyyut* to the Jews of Italy, and he most likely also introduced the teaching of mysticism to the

Jews of Europe. The chronicle is written in rhymed prose and is a fine example of Paitanic style.

192. CRUSADE CHRONICLES

Of the terrible persecutions that the Jews of Germany suffered during the Crusades, we have several records and chronicles. There are five of them. Three relate the events of the First Crusade, the fourth one, of the second, and the fifth of the persecution in Mayence in the years 1187–88.

The first one is the chronicle of Solomon ben Simon of Mayence. Of the life of the author we know little, save that, as he tells us himself, he lived in that city and that he wrote his chronicle in the year 1140. He tells in detail of the massacres perpetrated by the crusaders at Worms, Mayence, Speyer, Cologne and a few other cities. He gives the names of the martyrs and the story of their martyrdom, how men, women and children gladly and willingly sacrificed themselves for the sanctification of the name of God. He is bitter against the murderers and constantly invokes God to avenge the innocent blood. He, therefore, tells, rather gleefully, the story of the defeat of certain armies of crusaders in Hungary and how they were cut down by the Byzantians. To this original document there is a later addition telling of the massacre at Blois, France, as a result of the first blood accusation in the year 1171.

The second one is a shorter record of the same events by Eliezer ben Nathan, a famous Talmudic scholar and codifier (Ch. X, Sec. 153), also of Mayence. He must have been an eye-witness of these horrors, but records them in a more general way, giving fewer names of the martyrs. There is no date given, yet it is certain that Eliezer wrote before 1146 when the Second Crusade took place. The chronicle contains also a few elegiac poems over the fates of these martyrs, of his own composition.

The third one is an anonymous record of the events of the First Crusade and adds but little new. In general, there is much resemblance among these three sources, and much speculation was aroused as to which one is the earlier. But it is assumed that all three probably wrote independently, most likely using common sources, either oral or written. These three records often differ in the names of the martyrs and one document at times contains certain data missing in the others, so that they complement each other.

The fourth one, written by Ephraim of Bonn (1132-1200), is divided into two parts, the first one called *Sefer Zihronot* (Book of Records or Memorials) contains the records of the persecution during the Second Crusade. He is very general and does not limit himself to Germany but tells also of events in France and England. He records also the story how the great Tosafist, Jacob of Rameru, (Tam) was saved from death by a knight of his acquaintance. This part was written in the sixties of the twelfth century. In the second part Ephraim records a series of persecutions and attacks which happened subsequent to the Second Crusade, at various times and places. He mentions the Blois accusation of 1171, the massacre of the Jews in London at the time of the coronation of Richard Cœur de Lion in 1190, and other events. The latest events he reports are the scattered attacks on Jews which came as after-effects of the Third Crusade in 1196.

The fifth report is written by Eliezer ben Judah of Worms, the famous scholar, codifier and mystic (Ch. XI, Sec. 173). It is a mere fragment describing an attack on the Jews at Mayence in the years 1187-88 which occurred at the beginning of the Third Crusade.

All these reports are of great historical value as they were written either by eye-witnesses or contemporaries of the events, or at least by those who lived immediately after their occurrence. They are our sources for these gloomy episodes in Jewish history.

193. THE HISTORICAL BOOKS OF ABRAHAM IBN DAUD

In Abraham Ibn Daud, the well-known philosopher (Ch. XI, Sec. 172), we have likewise a great historian, taking in consideration that his shortcomings are principally due to the peculiar conception of history which prevailed in the Mediæval Ages in general. He left us three works, the first being the *Seder*, or *Sefer ha-Kabbalah* (Order or Book of Tradition), the second, "The History of the Jewish Kings in the Second Commonwealth," the third, *Zikaron Divré Romi* (The History of Rome).

"The Book of Tradition" written in the year 1160-61 is his principal work as it is the largest, most complete, and most original. It was written, as he himself states, for the purpose of combating the erroneous opinion of the Karaites who deny the authenticity of tradition. He, therefore, proposes to give in brief an account of the chain of tradition, namely, the history of the leading scholars from the time of the Great Assembly to his own days. He is, therefore, not interested, as far as this book is concerned, in political history, and supplemented it by his second book. The first parts of this book up to the close of the Talmud are very brief, and with the exception of a few digressions, he gives only the names and dates of the transmitters of the law and a few biographical data. For the periods of *Saburaim,* Geonim and that of the Spanish scholars, he grows more eloquent and gives a good many details of Jewish life in general.

The book opens by way of introduction with a short chronological and genealogical list from Adam to Judah the Prince. In this list he gives also the names of the princes of the exile (Exilarchs), during the Second Commonwealth up to Hillel, following the lists of the short *Seder Olam* (Sec. 186). He then begins the order of tradition with Moses and comes immediately to the men of the Great Assembly, following the order given in *Aboth* (Sayings of the Fathers). The mention of the Great Assembly leads him into a digression wherein he discusses chronological questions of the length of the first exile, the period of the Second Temple and relates these questions to the prophecy of Daniel (Ch. IX). He then begins with Simon the Just and follows up the chain of tradition to the generation succeeding Judah the Prince, counting a total of fourteen generations of scholars, nine before the destruction of the Temple and five generations of *Tannaim.* He begins the period of *Tannaim* with Raban Gamaliel the Second of Jammia, and ends with Hanina ben Hama, who followed Judah as head of the academy. In giving the leaders of the generations of transmitters he, as a rule, gives the names of their important fellow-scholars. He also digresses often in discussions of certain questions. Thus, when telling of Simon the Great he tells of his meeting with Alexander the Great as embellished in the Talmud; speaking of Antigonus, the follower of Simon, he tells about the rise of the Sadducean and Bethusian sects, which according to a notice in Abot di R. Nathan, were founded by Zadok and Baithus, disciples of Antigonus. While mentioning Joshua ben Perahyah, he mentions the Talmudic tradition that he was the teacher of Jesus, and is greatly perplexed how to reconcile this tradition, which antedates the birth of Jesus 110 years, with the real date. He proposes that there were two Joshuas, one at the time of Hillel.

The next period, that of the *Amoraim,* is dealt with more in detail. On the whole, with the exception of Rabbi Johanan of Palestine, to whom he devotes a few lines mentioning that he compiled the Palestinian Talmud, the section is devoted to the Babylonian scholars. Of these *Amoraim* he counts seven generations. While telling of the persecution of the Jews in Babylon in the fifth century, he gives a brief sketch of the history of the Persians and correlates certain events with dates and episodes in Roman history. The history of the *Saburaim* follows next. He counts five generations of these scholars and differs thus from Sherira, who shortens the period of the *Saburaim* and begins the Gaonic period earlier.

The Gaonic period which, according to him, consists of eight generations of heads of academies is described fully, even the biography of each Gaon, especially of the important ones, is given at length. At all events, no important episode in Jewish life is omitted.

The last part is devoted to the intellectual life in Spain. Ibn Daud is the only authority for the story of the four captives (Ch. X, Sec. 133) who founded spiritual centers in Spain, North Africa, and Egypt. Here in describing the first three generations of, what he calls, the Rabbinic period, he waxes eloquent and eulogizes his favorite heroes, Samuel the Prince, Isaac Al-Fasi, and his pupil Joseph Ibn Migash. After carrying out his purpose and giving the uninterrupted chain of tradition from the last prophets, Haggai, Zechariah and Malachai to Joseph Ibn Migash, —said chain consisting of thirty-six generations of sages,—he turns his attention to the Karaites. He delivers a virulent attack against them, charges that they never composed any important book on any subject, and did not contribute to science and poetry. Here, he has a chance to supply some deficiency in his book, for thus far he has spoken only of the transmitters of the law and has not mentioned the great men in other fields. Now he gives a list of Jewish grammarians, exegetes, poets, philosophers, mentioning all the luminaries of the Golden Age, in order to show the spiritual wealth of the Rabbanites as against the poverty of the Karaites. Of the Karaites he mentions only Anan, Jacob Al-Kirkisani and Yeshuah Al-Faraj, against whom he is virulent.

It is also worth noting that he hardly mentions the famous scholars of France and Germany; Jacob Tam, the great Tosafist is the exception. However, in an addition to the book, found in some manuscripts, he gives a short sketch of the rise of learning in the Provence, tells of Rabbi Makhir who was brought by Charlemagne from Babylon to Narbonne, and subsequent scholars. He also mentions Rabbi Gershom and Samuel ben Meir (Rashbam).

Ibn Daud, who was a lover of the sciences, does not neglect to give data about the composition of books in all sciences, even though they have little to do with his subject. Thus, he records, while writing about the disciples of Akiba, that in their days there lived Ptolemy the astronomer, and the Almagest, the great book on astronomy was then written by him. When writing on Judah the Prince he remarks that Galen's medical treatises were then written, while Hippocrates' books were written much earlier.

The influence of this book was very great. For generations it was considered an authentic source book on Jewish history. Almost all subsequent historians throughout the ages, up to modern times, have made it their principal source and even modern historians used it to a great extent, though with a more critical attitude.

"The History of the Jewish Kings in the Second Commonwealth," deals with the political history of the Jews of that period. It is, as stated, a supplement to his main work. The book begins with the death of Alexander, tells of the translation of the Septuagint and goes over to the story of persecution under Antiochus. It relates of the struggle of the Maccabees, but only the character of Judah is delineated extensively, the reign of the other brothers is passed over briefly. John Hyrcanus and Alexander Jannaus are treated at greater length, especially the war of the former with the Samarians and the break of the latter with the Pharisees. Likewise, all the wars of the brothers, Hyrcanus and Aristobolus, and the reign of Herod are given in detail and a special description of the beauty of the Temple built by the latter is included. Before the author goes over to the siege of Jerusalem, he describes the various parties of the Jews and then the story of the last revolt is told. The book closes with a quotation from a Midrash bearing the name, "Ten Exiles," where the various exiles of the Jews are enumerated, and is wound up by a symbolic interpretation of Zechariah Ch. XI, showing that all the events told in the book were foreshadowed in that prophecy.

"The History of Rome" is a short tractate telling briefly, and in a rather dry manner, the succession of the Roman rulers up to the time of Mohammed. He begins with the foundation of the city, gives a list of the Roman kings up to the foundation of the Republic and then goes over to Cæsar and follows up with a list of emperors up to Honorius. Then he tells of the invasion of Spain by the Visigoths and their subsequent affairs. After this he resumes the enumeration of the Roman emperors up to the time of Mohammed.

We cannot ascertain exactly the sources used by Ibn Daud. We can only surmise that for "The Book of Tradition" he used the letter of

Sherira, records of Nathan the Babylonian, and besides these also some chronicles of the Academy at Sura and other sources. For the history of the Second Commonwealth he used mostly *Yossipon*. In fact, according to later testimony, he is supposed to have compiled an abstract of *Yossipon* and probably this book is referred to, though there are certain differences between the work of Ibn Daud and *Yosippon*. For the Roman history, he must have used the chronicle of Isidore of Seville, composed in 615 which concludes with the seventh century. The style of Ibn Daud is only second to *Yosippon*. It is a pure Hebrew, concise and flowing. At times, it possesses even poetic beauty and it is on the whole Biblical.

B. Geography

194. EARLY GEOGRAPHICAL WRITINGS

Jewish geographical literature in the classical period consists mostly of tales of travel. Of geography proper there are only several books and these deal with a few data connected with astronomy and belong properly to mathematical geography, which will be discussed in the chapter on science. These tales of travel, however, contain many important descriptions of the countries visited, as well as the customs and manners of the people inhabiting them. They are thus contributions to geographic knowledge. That they also contain many historical data goes without saying, and their proper name would then be historical geographic narratives.

i. The earliest of such books is "The Tales of Eldad the Danite." These stories, were, as it seems, not written by Eldad himself but by others who heard him tell the stories. Eldad appeared in Kairawan, North Africa, about the year 890 and told the Jews strange stories about the lost tribes. He himself claimed to belong to the tribe of Dan and described in glowing colors the mode of life of the tribes, their independence and their government. These stories, together with his peculiar use of Hebrew and somewhat different versions of legal tradition which he quoted, aroused not only the curiosity of the Jews of Kairawan but also their suspicion. They then dispatched an inquiry to the Gaon Zemah ben Hayyim at Sura. This inquiry contains the gist of his stories. The Gaon told them that he had also heard of this Eldad who visited Babylon some years previously and that, on the whole, he believes his stories to be correct, namely, that the exiles of the ten tribes really do live in the parts of the world indicated by Eldad, in a free and independent manner under their own kings, and that the changes in legal tradition are mostly due to Eldad's travails sustained by him in his travels which caused him to make some mistakes in his statements.

Besides the text of the stories contained in this inquiry, there are a number of other versions which differ somewhat from one another, but agree in the main parts. The content of the stories is as follows: Eldad, who hailed as it seems, either from Arabia or East Africa, where in those times there were some independent Jewish tribes, left his country and went on a journey in a boat. On the way, he was shipwrecked, but he and another Jew from the tribe of Asher were saved by clinging to a board of the ship. They were seized by a Negro cannibal tribe who devoured his companion, but Eldad managed to escape that fate. This tribe was meanwhile attacked by another tribe from a distance, who took him with them to their country. There he was ransomed by a Jew from the tribe of Issachar who brought him to his country. Then he began his travels.

As for the location of the ten tribes, Eldad distributes them over the whole of the known globe. Four tribes, namely, Dan, Naphtali, Gad and Asher, live in Eastern Africa; Issachar, Zebulun and Reuben on the mountains near Persia, Ephraim and half the tribe of Menasseh in Arabia, and Simeon and the other half of Menasseh in Khazaria. Since he himself comes from Dan he is very loquacious about that tribe, tells us that it left Palestine previous to the exile by the Assyrians (722 B. C. E.), namely, at the time of the division of the kingdom under Jeroboam, as they did not want to fight against Judah. They passed through Egypt on their way to Eastern Africa, where later, the other three tribes joined them. They are under the leadership of a king of a tribe of Dan and lead a warlike life, each tribe going out on a raid for three months during the year. Their land is very fruitful and abounds in precious metals, yet they lead a nomadic life and live in tents. Of the other tribes he only gives their habitat and a few details of their life. On the other hand, he tells at length of the children of Moses who live on the other side of the wonderful river, Sambatyon, a river mentioned in the Talmud and Agada as one which is very stormy the whole week and casts forth stones but is quiet on the Sabbath. These children of Moses were carried thither by a cloud at the time of the destruction of the Temple, and are protected by the River Sambatyon. Eldad gives their location also in Africa, further than the place where the other tribes live. The land beyond the Sambatyon is a wonderful one. It contains no dangerous animals, and plants grow there twice a year. The people are very rich, live long, possess a Talmud in Hebrew, which traces legal tradition directly to Moses. Their communication with the other tribes is by means of carrier pigeons, and thus he continues to relate of their exceptionally happy life.

The kernel of truth in all these mixtures of story and legend is, that Eldad himself most likely hailed from among the Jews who inhabited the shores of the Gulf of Aden and who lived an independent tribal life. When he began his travels he found it necessary to tell the dispersed Jews, whether with the purpose of encouraging them, or some other aim, the stories about the ten tribes. He collected all tales about independent Jewish kingdoms and wove them into one. He most likely heard about the conversion of the Khazars and mistook them for Jews.

The style of his Hebrew is peculiar and contains many Arabisms and strange words which, for one reason or another, were in vogue in his native country where Hebrew in a more primitive form was spoken. His legal tradition is also that of the native Jews, who, not being acquainted with the Talmud and later Rabbinic traditions, conducted themselves according to the traditions they brought with them. These traditions agree in a number of things with those of the Talmud and the deviations are to be explained by ignorance.

Eldad's stories made a great impression upon the Jews of his time and even upon those of the succeeding generations. The Jews rejoiced hearing of the existence of Jewish kingdoms somewhere on the globe. In fact, many of his stories were known to them. The legends about the River Sambatyon and the children of Moses are found in Agadic literature, yet his words seemed to them a corroboration of these tales, as he imparted to them the strength of the testimony of an eye-witness.

ii. A more important historical-geographical document is the series of letters exchanged between Ḥasdai Ibn Shaprut (915–970), diplomat and Nagid, i. e. prince of Spanish Jewry, and Joseph, King of the Khazars, a Tartar tribe, who embraced Judaism.

Ḥasdai, having heard through the various ambassadors from the kings of Germany and the Slavs who used to come to the court of his master, Abd ar Raḥman, of the existence of a Jewish kingdom in Khazaria, was anxious to communicate with the king. His interest was especially aroused since he was misled by the tales of Eldad, who placed some of the Ten Tribes in that country, to believe that the Khazars were really a part of these Jewish tribes. After several unsuccessful attempts, he finally managed to send a letter to that king which was received by him.

In that letter, Ḥasdai gives the king a number of geographical data about the kingdom of Andalusia, its distance from the equator, from the sea, its boundaries, extent of the land and natural resources. He also describes the exact position of the capital, Cordova, its distance from the sea and its area. While he determines the distance of Andalusia from the equator, he makes general remarks about the degrees and the equator, and also determines the distance of Constantinople from the equator as well as that of Khazaria. It is interesting to note that Ḥasdai is very close in his calculations of geographical locations of the countries he mentions to those we know them to be today.

He then asks the king a series of questions regarding the extent of his kingdom, its nature and character, the form of his government, the routes of commerce, his relations with the kingdoms of Armenia, Persia, and the Byzantine colonies on the Black Sea. Also, believing him to be a Jewish king ruling over part of the Ten Tribes, Ḥasdai asks him to tell him of their traditions and whether they possess more definite information about the coming of the Messiah.

The letter is written in a pure, flowing Hebrew style, and as it seems, its writer was the famous grammarian and exegete, Menaḥem ben Saruk (Ch. VII, Sec. 95).

To this letter the Khazar king, Joseph, answered in a lengthy epistle. After expressing his joy over Ḥasdai's letter, he disillusions him and tells of the Tartaric descent of the tribe, of course relating it, in the manner of the times to *Tugarma,* one of the grandchildren of Japheth, mentioned in the Table of Nations, Genesis Ch. X. He then tells him of the story of conversion, referred to above (Ch. XI, Sec. 167), and finally gives him the geographic data desired. From these we learn that the Khazar kingdom occupied the area between the Volga, Caspian Sea (called Gargan by Joseph in the letter, which is the same as Jarjan used by Arabic geographers, the Gimel pronounced as J), and the river Don. At times, though, the boundaries extended to the Dnieper (Uzg, in the letter which is the Tartaric name Eski for that river). He also tells him of the three capitals, Semender towards Caucasia, Sarkal on the Don, and Itil on the Volga—Itil being also the name of the river in Tartaric. There are several versions of that letter, and a fragment of one, published by the late **Dr.** Schechter from the collection of manuscripts in Cairo, gives a more rational version of the conversion of the Khazar king or Kagan, omitting the appearance of the angel to the Kagan Bulan (Ch. XI, Sec. 167), but ascribing it to the influence of the constantly increasing number of Jewish settlers. The gist of the matter is, that though these letters have undoubtedly received in the course of time some embellishments, they contain historical truth about the conversion of the Khazars. The geographical data are corroborated by contemporary Arabic geographers. The letter is likewise written in a fine flowing Hebrew, employing here and there some expressions modeled after the Arabic.

195. THE TRAVELS OF BENJAMIN OF TUDELA

An exceptionally important historical geographical document is the record of the travels of Benjamin of Tudela. The book possesses great value for Jewish history, for general history, for geographical knowledge and especially for the history and geography of commerce. We know little about the life of the author except his name and birthplace, the city of Tudela in Navarre, Spain, and the date of his travels. Though he is often called Rabbi Benjamin, it is doubtful whether he was a professional scholar. On the contrary, from the tone of the description and from the very accurate information he gives regarding trade and commerce, it can be concluded that he was a merchant.

It is difficult to ascertain the purpose of his travels, but it may be surmised, that he was actuated by two motives, to visit the holy places of the Jews, and to get acquainted with the totality of Jewish life all over the world. Possessing a keen observing eye and a practical sense of conditions of life, he left us a record stocked with information about the state of world Jewry in the second half of the twelfth century in all its phases, spiritual and economic. But he does not limit himself to the Jews alone, he gives also the geographical data of the places he visited, quotes facts regarding general life of the peoples, their governments, trade, wars, and religious beliefs. Hence, the itinerary of Benjamin is of interest to the general historian and geographer as well.

The period of his travels extends for about thirteen or fourteen years, approximately between the years 1159 to 1173. The lands and places described by him practically cover the entire habitable part of the globe at that time. But we must admit that he did not visit all the countries he describes. A number of them, such as parts of Persia, India, Ceylon,

Arabia in Asia, and France, Germany and the Slavic lands, such as Poland and Russia, were not visited by him, but he collected data about them and records the reports he heard. In general, the itinerary of Benjamin is to be divided into two parts, what he saw and what he heard. In the first part his account is fuller and more detailed, and as a rule, he always names the leaders and elders of the Jewish communities and gives many more details about their life. In the second part, the description is general and brief.

Benjamin started his journeys from Saragossa in Aragon, proceeded along to Barcelona, from there to the Provence, visiting almost all important cities, such as Narbonne, Beziers, and Lunel, until he reached Marseilles. From Marseilles, he went by boat to Genoa, then to Pisa, Lucca, and Rome. In all these visits, he describes not only the number of Jews living in each place, giving the names of the leading scholars and heads of the communities, but also the centers of trade and mode of government. Thus he tells us of the Republics of Genoa and Pisa, the constant warfare between them and the exact distance of Pisa from the sea and other things. To the description of Rome, Benjamin devotes considerable space. He has an eye for beauty and describes the palaces, even telling us the names of their builders, with some legendary embellishments, of course. That he gives a clear account of the Jewish community of Rome is self-evident. From there he proceeded to travel to Brindisi through the cities of Southern Italy, and noted everything on the way, not neglecting to tell of the great Medical University at Salerno, of the petroleum wells near Sorrento, and of Trani, the port of embarkation for the Crusaders.

From Brindisi he went to Otranto and embarked for Corfu and thence through European Byzantium to Constantinople, visiting all important cities, marking their natural resources and the trade and the nature of the people inhabiting them. Benjamin gives an accurate description of the Wallachians, their mode of life, and their constant raids upon Greek settlements. This description is corroborated by contemporary Byzantine writers. Constantinople is described at length, the palaces, churches, especially the one of St. Sophia, the Hippodrome, the revenues of the government, the leading officers of the empire and the geographic location of the city on the Sea of Marmora and the Bay of Bosphorus are all portrayed. Benjamin's description of Constantinople evoked the approval of a historian like Gibbon who quotes him on this point.

From Constantinople Benjamin went, by way of Rodosto, to Galipoli and thence through the Ægean Archipelago, visiting the Islands of Mytilene, Chios, Samos, Cyprus, to the coast of Asia Minor, disembarking at the port of Corycus. Thence he proceeded along the Syrian coast to Acre, or Acca, in Palestine. Benjamin noted all things worth while noting. Thus he tells us of the cultivation of the mastic tree, which exudes a kind of resin formerly used in medicine, describes the waterworks of Antioch, gives the name of the Christian Prince, Bohemund Poetivin, and even his nickname, Le Baube (the baby), which he received on account of his imperfect speech. He also describes, being the first European to do so, the Mohammedan sect of Assassins, a sect of the Shiites, supporters of the claims of the descendants of Ali, son-in-law of Mohammed, to the Caliphate. This sect, which during the twelfth century spread throughout Western Asia, was a great political factor in those days and its members were notorious for their implicit obedience to their chief and also for employing all means, especially murder, in order to gain their aim. The name assassin, though, does not mean murder, but is derived from a plant, *Hashishim*, which they used as an opiate during their services. Benjamin's description of them is very accurate, though brief. Equally true is his description of the sect of the Druses.

To his description of Palestine, Benjamin devotes a number of chapters. He visited every important city and states the number of Jews, their occupations, leaders, and scholars. He also gives the location of the graves of the great men in Israel and a few legends, as well as a description of the Samaritans. As Palestine was then in the hands of the Crusaders, Benjamin gives the Latin and French names of certain localities.

From Palestine, the traveler went back to Syria, visited Damascus, which he describes extensively, and then through Baalbek and Mesopotamia to Bagdad. This city, which was at the time not only the capital of the Caliphate, but the center of a large Jewish population, attracted the attention of Benjamin. He gives all details of the Mohammedan government, the conduct of the Caliph and that of the Jewish community, the office of the Exilarch, which was still in existence in a lesser form, and finally describes the city itself.

After Bagdad there follows a description of a large number of countries, such as Persia, Yemen, the Island of Kish in the Indian Ocean, the coast of Malabar, and the Island of Ceylon. It is almost certain, though, that Benjamin did not visit all these countries and he only reports on what he heard about them. This is proved by the fact that with very few exceptions he does not mention any names of leaders of all the numerous Jewish communities he writes about. Nevertheless, though Benjamin, most likely, did not visit these countries, his report of them is comparatively a detailed one. As might be expected, this report, which is gathered from others, contains a good deal of exaggeration, yet it also contains a good deal of true information. There are a number of legends, such as the one about the wonderful coffin of Daniel, which hangs suspended in midriver at Susa, or Shushan of the Bible.

In his description of Persia and Media, there are exaggerations about the number of Jews residing there as well as about their strength and military prowess. Influenced by unfounded reports and by the tales of Eldad, he speaks of the four tribes residing in the mountainous part of Persia. He describes them as free and independent, engaged in warfare and as the allies of powerful Turkish tribes. While writing on Persia, he tells of the false Messiah who arose there in the twelfth century, David Alroy, which story became the subject of a novel by that name, written by Benjamin Disraeli. Benjamin is the only authority for that event.

In his report of the countries lying beyond Persia, he becomes more practical and accurate. He was the first European to report of the Island of Kish in the Indian Ocean, which was in his time a great emporium of exchange between the merchants of India, Persia, and Arabia. Benjamin does not neglect to give an account of the products bartered and also the number of Jews living there. He then describes the coast of Malabar, gives the customs of the natives, the climate, and mentions that pepper, ginger, and cinnamon grow there. He tells us that the people are fire worshippers, which would mean that a large number of the ancient Parsis found refuge there after the conquest of the Mohammedans, and even describes their mode of burial which is, placing the dead in the open air until the flesh is dried and only the skeleton remains which is then interred. He also knows of the black Jews of Malabar.

He then describes the Island of Ceylon and with his usual carefulness gives an account of the inhabitants of the country and their customs. He also tells of the remarkable sea between that island and China, where, at times, on account of severe storms, all vessels are wrecked, and adds a strange tale regarding the way people save themselves from being drowned. They wrap themselves up in the skins of cattle and throw themselves into the ocean. A big bird, called the griffin, then comes and picks them up and carries them to land with the intention of devouring them, but there the men kill the bird with knives prepared beforehand and thus escape. All that Benjamin relates about these distant places is more or less corroborated by later travelers and even the strange tales are repeated by Marco Polo, who visited India and China about two decades after Benjamin.

Benjamin seemed to have returned by way of the Indian Ocean from the vicinity of Bagdad or some port in Persia through Arabia to Egypt. However, his description of Yemen and Abyssinia is scanty and brief, and contains only a general statement about the free Jews dwelling in the mountains around Aden, a place in Assyria, which he confuses with Eden of the Bible (2 Kings, XIX, 12). He resumes his trend of detailed narrative of Egypt. Of this country he gives a full description, treating of its government, its agricultural products, the Nile, its course, division into arms, and cause of its rise. He pays, of course, special attention to the Jews living in Egypt, telling of their customs and divisions. To Alexandria, he devotes an entire chapter describing the beauty of its buildings, and especially the port and the wonderful lighthouse. As one who had a special eye for business, Benjamin gives a list of all the nations who came to trade at this port. From Egypt our traveler went by boat to Messina, Sicily, and thence through Italy back to Spain where shortly after his return he must have died. This then constitutes the circle of his travels. But in order to give a complete picture of the Jews the world over, Benjamin adds a brief chapter on the Jews of Germany, France, and the Slavic countries, mentioning the names of the important cities including that of Kiev in distant Russia.

The style of the book is the usual Rabbinic Hebrew, a very plain prosaic narrative, with no pretension to fine writing, in other words, the style of a learned merchant. The book as we possess it, must have been abridged by its editors whoever they were. From some indications, it is evident that Benjamin's account was longer. That the names of the countries and places were wrongly transcribed by the later copyists goes without saying. The best edition of the itinerary is that of A. Asher published with an English translation and copious notes in 1840.

Benjamin's account was held in great esteem by subsequent writers on history and geography, both Jewish and Gentile. It was translated into almost all European languages beginning with Latin. The main sober facts in his story were corroborated by subsequent travelers. As for the exaggerated numbers and fables, they must be charged, as Zunz says, to the spirit of his time. The itinerary of Benjamin was a favorite book with the Jews as the many printed editions testify.

196. ITINERARY OF PETAHYAH

Only a few years after Benjamin completed his circle of travels, another Jewish traveler took his wandering staff and made a similar circuit, of which we also have a record, though a more fragmentary one. This time it was a German Jew, Petaḥyah of Regensburg. He was the brother of one of the famous Tosafists, Rabbi Isaac ha-Laban of Prague. Two recorded events determine the period of his travels. While describing Damascus he mentions the fact that the King of Egypt rules over this city. This could not have been before November, 1174, when Saladin, the ruler of Egypt, conquered Damascus. On the other hand, he visited Jerusalem when the Christians still held it, and this must have been before 1187, for in that year it was conquered by Saladin. Consequently, his travels must have taken place between 1175–1185.

The purpose of his travels is unknown. He was, probably, motivated by a desire similar to the one of Benjamin, namely, to visit the holy places and observe Jewish life. He lacked, however, Benjamin's keen eye and practical sense, and his information is rather scanty. With few exceptions, he limits himself to Jewish life. Besides, he did not write the record himself, but gave his notes to his friend, Rabbi Judah the pious, at Regensburg, who again turned it over to a writer to compose the itinerary. It thus assumed a fragmentary character, for the editor omitted many things, especially geographic data. The records speak of Petaḥyah in the third person. As a result, this itinerary is of much less value than that of Benjamin. Yet it has some value, for this traveler covered some countries which Benjamin did not visit; besides, his notes of the countries visited by both serve as a check upon Benjamin's information, and thus they complete each other.

Petaḥyah took a different route from that of Benjamin. Starting from Prague in Bohemia, he proceeded East to Poland, from there to Kiev in Russia, and crossed the Dnieper into Crimea. While he gives few details about the geographical position of the country, he tells us of the peculiar mode employed by the inhabitants in crossing the river, namely, placing the wagons on skins tied to horses which swim in the waters. He also makes some remarks about the life of the Tartars. More important is his information about the large number of Karaites who lived, at the time, in Crimea. According to him there were hardly any Rabbanites there.

From Crimea he proceeded through little Tartary, parts of Caucasia and Armenia, until he arrived at Nisibis, and ultimately at Mosul. From this point his notes become fuller. He gives more details about the Jewish communities in Babylon, also mentioning the names of the leaders and scholars. To Bagdad he devotes considerable space, but primarily to the state of Jewry. He mentions the head of the academy to be Rabbi Samuel ben Ali, the very one mentioned by Benjamin, who is otherwise known to us as an opponent of Maimonides. The Exilarch, Daniel, spoken of by Benjamin, Petaḥyah states that he died a year before he arrived. All these data are important for Jewish history.

From Bagdad he went to Susa, but very little is given us about the cities he visited. He devotes his notes to exaggerated and fabulous tales about the graves of Ezekiel, Ezra, and Daniel, repeating the stories of Benjamin and adding more. It seems that he had compiled a list of the locations of the graves of the *Amoraim* but forgot it in Bohemia. On the whole, he was more credulous and less observant than Benjamin.

From Susa, he came back to Bagdad and turned West, passed Nesibis again and then through to Aleppi to Damascus. He gives a few important data about Damascus, including that it belongs to the Sultan of Egypt, the number of Jews there, and the name of the head of the academy, which was Ezra. From Damascus, he came to Tiberias and passed through Galilee to Jerusalem. In Jerusalem he found only one Jew instead of the two hundred mentioned by Benjamin. It seems that the constant wars between the Christians and Mohammedans, centering around the city, reduced the number of inhabitants. He also visited Hebron and the vicinity of the Dead Sea. The notes of Petaḥyah on Palestine are very meager and are mainly limited to descriptions of sepulchers, such as the Cave of Machpelah and the grave of Rachel, in Hebron and Bethlehem, those of Joshua, the prophet Obadiah, and Hillel and Shammai in Galilee, and many others. He does not mention any names of leaders and scholars in Palestine with the exception of one man at Tiberias, Rabbi Nehorbi, who was both a physician and spice vender. His distinction was that he claimed to be a descendant of Judah the Prince, the compiler of the Mishnah and thus of Davidic descent.

With Palestine, the itinerary of Petaḥyah ends. There are only a few lines devoted to Greece, saying that there are many Jews there, and that a number of young men among them are practicing necromancy. He must have then returned to his home city, Prague, through Greece and the Balkans, but no record is found. It is possible that much of his itinerary was lost. On the whole, his record pales in comparison with that of Benjamin's, yet it is not entirely his fault. It is partly the fault of the editor who says distinctly that the names of the cities and the distances between them given by Petaḥyah were omitted by him as of no significance.

"The Itinerary of Petaḥyah" was printed several times and was translated into Latin by Wagenseil and later into English, German, and French.

CHAPTER XV

SCIENCE

197. GENERAL FEATURES

The contact with the Arabic culture which acted as a stimulus to Jewish literature and opened up new vistas of literary activity, such as poetry, philosophy, philology and all other manifestations that we have chronicled heretofore, likewise aroused the interest of Jewish savants in science. True, scientific knowledge was not entirely strange to the scholars of the Talmudic period. There are many fragments of science scattered in the vast Talmudic literature. There are numerous passages there touching on mathematical, astronomical, and medical matters. These prove conclusively that a great number of scholars were well acquainted at least with the principles of these sciences. But this knowledge was only used as a by-product, as means to illustrate certain points in legal discussion, as was the case with mathematics and astronomy, or in the case of medicine, more in matters of Agada in order to inculcate a moral or teach the conduct of life.

Throughout the whole Talmudic and Agadic literature composed of so many books and treatises, we do not find even one treatise devoted especially to a systematic exposition of the principles of one of these sciences. There may be, however, some exception in regard to astronomy. This science which plays an important role in the fixation of the calendar which determines and regulates observation of the festivals, was especially cultivated by the doctors of the law. It is quite possible that some treatises on this science were composed early, but they were not preserved. It is true that several astronomical treatises which we do possess bear the name of *Baraita* (i. e. an Apocryphal Mishnah) and one of them is ascribed to Samuel of the first generation of *Amoraim* (Ch. V, Sec. 75). But careful analysis shows that it is of later date (see below). There are also several astronomical chapters included in the late Midrash, *Pirḳé di Rabbi Eliezer* (Chapters of Rabbi Eliezer) (Ch. VI, Sec. 86). This Midrash, however, is a product of the Gaonic period. Yet it is possible that it includes material

from earlier treatises of Talmudic times, for we find distinct reference
to a treatise on calendar calculation in the Talmud which is called,
Sod ha-'Ibur (Secret of Intercalation). The fact that such matters were
not discussed openly in the schools but were considered a secret teaching, relegated only to scholars, may account for the non-preservation of
the treatises.

With the entry of the Arabic period when the Jews participated freely
in the culture of the age, there begins the production of a real scientific
literature. There arose Jewish scholars who were interested in the
sciences as such. The role that the Jews played in transmitting scientific
knowledge from the East to the West was very great, and is well
known. The list of Jewish scientists from the eighth century, the beginning of the bloom of culture in the East down through the Middle
Ages, is very long. But a detailed exposition of this role belongs more
to a history of science. Here we are concerned only with the literary
productions of importance in Hebrew, and accordingly we will survey
them briefly.

Astronomy

198. CALENDAR CALCULATIONS

As we have seen, the science of astronomy was cultivated by the
Jews as an important element in calendar fixation. We have, therefore,
a considerable number of treatises bearing on that subject, which begin
to make their appearance in the eighth century. To that period belong
the three astronomical chapters in the "Chapters of Rabbi Eliezer,"
where the questions of the length of the solar and lunar years and that
of the solar and lunar time cycles are discussed.

A more important astronomical work is the one called, *Baraita di
Shemuel,* which was composed, according to the statement of its author,
in the year 776. This deals only slightly with calendar fixation but primarily with the position and the movements of the planets and the
luminaries. It describes the position of the constellations, the distance
between them and the time of the solar and lunar eclipses. He gives
also rules for calculating the solar solstices and other matters. As
astronomy in those days was inherently connected with astrology, the
author adds a chapter on the special influence of the stars on human
destiny.

The style of the book is difficult. It lacks clearness and is very
cryptic. It is made more difficult by the fact that the author was de-

sirous to give the treatise a Midrashic form and intertwines many verses of the Bible as proof that certain astronomical data were already referred to there.

Other calendar treatises are: "The Cycle of Naḥshon," ascribed to Naḥshon Gaon (877–885), where the nineteen-year cycle is discussed;[1] Saadia's works on the calendar were written with a controversial purpose against the Karaites who denied the validity of the calendar system, and also against a Palestinian Gaon, Ben Meir, who wanted to introduce some changes in it. Of these writings, the more important are *Sod ha-'Ibur* (The Secret of Intercalation) and *Sefer ha-Moadim* (The Book of the Holidays). These, most likely, were written in Hebrew, but of the first nothing was preserved, except that it is frequently referred to by later writers, and of the second, a few fragments came to light from the *Genizah* in recent years.

The same work was taken up by scholars in other countries. Hanan, a judge at Cordova (970), wrote extensive works on the subject, which were, however, lost, but are quoted by later authors including Isaac Israeli, the philosopher and physician in North Africa. A very important work on the subject was written by the astronomer, Abraham bar Hiyya (Ch. XI, Sec. 166), under the name *Sod ha-'Ibur* (Secret of the Intercalation). This was a complete treatise on the subject, in Hebrew, and served as an authority to later writers. In it rules and regulations for calculation of various festival dates and calendar making are given. A book under a similar name was also written by Abraham Ibn Ezra. It is called *Sefer ha-'Ibur* (The Book of Intercalation). It was recently discovered and published by S. Halberstamm.

Maimonides also wrote extensively on the subject, both in his code, where he devotes a special section to it, and in a special book, a treatise on intercalation. In the code, besides dealing with the calendar proper, he devotes also a few chapters to astronomy in general, giving a description of the spheres and their movement in their orbits and especially of the various movements of the sun and the moon.

Even the French and German scholars, who were not well versed in astronomy, wrote treatises on the calendar. Thus we have chapters

---

[1] The nineteen-year cycle is the cycle in which there are seven intercalated years, i. e. seven years having thirteen months and twelve plain lunar years. The seven months thus added make up the difference between the lunar year of 354 days and the solar 365¼. In this way the Jews are able to equalize their lunar calendar with the solar, and maintain the fixity of the festivals, preventing their circling throughout the year, as is the case with the Mohammedan festivals.

on the calendar by Simḥa' of Vitry, disciple of Rashi, in his code, *Maḥzor Vitry* (Ch. X) and a book by Jacob ben Samson (1123) on the subject.

199. GENERAL ASTRONOMY

With the bloom of the Arabic culture in the East and the rise of the science of astronomy, Jews began to participate in the development of these sciences. They were active both as translators from the Greek and as writers of books on the subject. One of the earliest of Jewish astronomers was one by the name of Messahla (754–813), who hailed from Egypt, but resided at the court of the Caliph, Al-Mansur. He wrote a number of treatises on astronomy and astrology. The most important are, a "Treatise on the Astrolabe," [2] "On Rain and Wind" and "On the Conjunction of the Stars." The first two are of astronomical importance, the last belongs to astrology. The two last ones were also translated into Hebrew under the names of *ha-Geshem* and *Sepher ha-Hiburim*. He was primarily known, though, as an astrologer and his works in this field are numerous.

Sahae, called Raban Al-Batir, was another scientist of that century (800). He seemed to have translated the Almagest of the celebrated Ptolemy of Alexandria, the bible of astronomers during the ages, into Arabic. He also wrote numerous works on astrology. An astronomical work was also written by the physician, Isaac Israeli.

The Spanish school of scholars made important contributions in science as well as in other literary fields. Hebrew scientific literature really begins with them. Abraham bar Hiyya, mentioned above, was the first one to write a complete textbook on astronomy in Hebrew. It is called *Ẓurat ha-Arez* (i. e. The Form of the Earth). But the full name is much longer and it tells us that it treats of all the heavenly bodies and the course of the stars. In the introduction he divides astronomy, which he calls *Ḥokmat ha-Ḥizayon* (The Science of Vision), namely, the observation of the heavens, into two parts, (a) the description of the forms of the heavenly bodies, i. e. astrography, (b) the theoretical part by means of which we calculate the position of the stars at any time. The book is devoted to the first part, the other part he promises to deal with elsewhere. He, most likely, refers to the book on the calendar, mentioned above. He also speaks of astrology, which he calls

[2] The astrolabe is an instrument used for more than fifteen centuries by astronomers and mariners to determine the altitude of the stars, sun, and moon. The modern instruments are only improved astrolabes and are operated on the same principle.

the practical science but he does not value it as highly as astronomy. Still he promises to treat it in a separate book.

The book is divided into ten portals, or sections, which are subdivided into chapters. The first one deals with the general description of the heavens as well as of the earth. He devotes a few chapters to prove the sphericity of the world in general, and the earth in particular. He then discusses its position in the center of the world, the division of the heavens into 360 degrees, the celestial plane, the equator and the division of the earth into seven climes or weather zones, and other things. The second portal is devoted to the description of the planets and their forms and the course of the sun. The third describes the moon, its course and orbit, the fourth the eclipses and their causes. The fifth and sixth portals deal with the various courses of the planets, except the sun and moon; the seventh discusses the position of the stars in reference to the sphere of constellations, and the eighth deals with the effect of the light of the sun upon the visibility of the stars. The ninth discusses the area of the earth and its measurement, and the tenth gives the various opinions regarding the fixed stars.

Abraham Ibn Ezra wrote several books on astronomy and astrology. To the first belongs his book on the astrolabe, by the name of *Kli ha-Nehoshet* (A Copper Instrument), and his translation of the commentary of the Arabic astronomer, Al-Matani on The Tables of Al-Kwarizmi, into Hebrew. To the second belong *Sefer ha-Moladot* (The Book of Nativity) and *Sefer ha-Goralot* (The Book of Destiny) where rules are given how to forecast the events that will happen to men, by the coursing of the stars.

Books on astronomy and astrology were also written by the physician, Sabbatai Donolo of Aures, Italy (913–970). He describes himself as an assiduous student of these sciences. But his special books on these subjects were lost and only a considerable number of his astronomical and astrological observations are incorporated in his commentary on "The Book of Creation" (Ch. XII, Sec. 180).

200. MATHEMATICS

Mathematics was of great interest even to scholars in Talmudic times. Certain measurements and calculations affect the discussion of certain laws. We find, therefore, in the Talmud a number of mathematical discussions and rules for measurements which show, that both the *Tannaim* and *Amoraim* possessed considerable mathematical knowledge. But we have no books on that subject left to us from these times. There is, though, mention of a treatise by the name *Baraita di Mem Tet Midot* (Treatise of the Forty-nine Measurements of Rules), ascribed to Rabbi Nathan, a *Tanna* of the last generation. But as the book is lost and it is not certain whether the title refers to measurements or rules in general—as the word *Midot* may mean both—we cannot conclude anything about its character.

In the Arabic and Gaonic period Jews became greatly interested in this science, for astronomy and mathematics are intimately connected. Ibn Ezra claims that a Jew was instrumental in introducing the Indian decimal numeral system to the Arabic world. It is from that period that the first mathematical books hail.

The earliest treatise on that subject is an anonymous one by the name of *Mishnat ha-Midot* (The Mishnah of Measurements). It is undoubtedly from Gaonic times, as it is written in Mishnaic form. The language, though, is pure Hebrew. It contains five chapters. The first gives the definitions of a square, a triangle, a circle, a semicircle, and an arc. The second states the rules for computing the areas of squares, triangles, cylinders, parallepoids and pyramids, the third is devoted to the properties of polygons, the fourth to triangles, and the fifth states rules for calculating the area of circles. Of great interest is the terminology used in the book, which differs somewhat from the one adopted later by Hebrew mathematicians.

Other works on these subjects were written by Abraham bar Hiyya and Abraham Ibn Ezra. The first wrote a geometry in Hebrew called *Ḥibur ha-Meshihah we-ha-Tishboret* (A Treatise on Areas and Measurement). The book was considered of great importance in its day and Plato of Tivoli, a celebrated mathematician of the twelfth century, translated it into Latin. Ibn Ezra wrote several books on mathematics. These are: *Sefer ha-Mispar* (The Book of Numbers), an arithmetic, *ha-Eḥod* (The One), on the properties of the first ten numbers, and *Ḥibur Ḥokmat ha-Tishboret,* (Treatise on the Science of Measurements), a geometry.

201. MEDICINE AND PHYSICS

The close association of the Jews with the science and profession of medicine, during the Mediæval Ages, is well known. The list of Jewish physicians during that period runs into the hundreds. But as their contributions to that science, in this period, were mostly written in

Arabic and the period of translation into Hebrew had not yet begun (for it begins with the thirteenth century), they were mixed up with the Arabic medical writings and it is difficult to disentangle them from the mass of literature. Only a few of the writings on medicine, during the period ending with the twelfth century, were translated into Hebrew and thus escaped oblivion. The great mass of translated medical works belong, as said, to the following period.

Of the Jewish contributions to medicine in this period, the works of the following writers are worth noting. In the tenth century, the otherwise celebrated Hasdai Ibn Shaprut (915–970), in Spain, helped to translate the medical book of Discorides from the Greek into the Arabic. He also perfected a certain medicine, well known in the Middle Ages under the name of *Teriak*. At the same time, Sabbatai Donolo in Italy, who preferred to write in Hebrew, wrote in that language an original book on medicine by the name of *Sefer ha-Yakar* (The Precious Treatise). It dealt, as its subtitle indicates, with the concoction of medicines, salves, making of bandages and other matters. Fragments of the book were only recently discovered and were published by Steinschneider in "The Journal for Scientific Anatomy," in Germany. Donolo, on the whole, can be given the credit of being the first medical writer in Hebrew.

Isaac Israeli of Kairawan, North Africa, was a famous physician of his time. He wrote a number of books on medicine, all in Arabic, which were considered important enough to be translated into Latin by Constantinus Afer, of the University of Salerno. His books were used as textbooks at that university and the author was known as Ysacus. Three of his works were translated into Hebrew several times, both directly from the Arabic and from the Latin of Constantinus. They are: (*1*) *Be-Teba ha-Mezonot* (On Dietetics). There are also two more translations of the same book, evidently from the Latin, under the titles *Sefer ha-Misodim* and *Sefer ha-Makholim*. (*2*) *Marot ha-Sheten* (Colors of Urine). (*3*) *Sefer be-Kadahat* (The Book of the Fever), the most celebrated of his works.

To this century belongs also a medical book in Hebrew, called *Sefer Refuot* (Book of Medicine), ascribed to Asaph. It is a compilation of medical matters from many books and contains also other data. It is entirely doubtful whether such a man existed, and the book is most likely a translation from the Arabic.

The eleventh century offers us little of medical literature in Hebrew and there are even few translations. All the great physicians that arose during this century wrote in Arabic, and little is known of them. There is, however, a reference by Rashi (Ch. X, Sec. 111) to a *Sefer Refuot,* current in his time, but nothing is known of it.

Maimonides, who was also a celebrated physician, wrote a number of books in Arabic on medical subjects. Most of them were translated into Hebrew. The most important of these are (*1*) *Ma'amar be-Refuat ha-Tehorim* (A Treatise on the Cure of Hemorrhoids); (*2*) "On Poisons," which he wrote at the request of the Vizier Al-Fadhl. It was translated into Hebrew by Moses Ibn Tibbon, under the name of *Ma'amar ha-Nikhbod be-Samim* (The Worthy Treatise on Poisons); (*3*) "On Hygiene," one of the most important of his works, translated by the same Moses under the name of *Hanhogat ha-Briut* (Regimen of Health); (*4*) *Pirké-Moshe* (Chapters of Moses), medical aphorisms. They are culled from Galen's writings, but he added many of his own. The book was considered very valuable and was translated into Latin.

Another medical writer in this century, Shesheth the Prince, wrote a treatise in Hebrew on laxative medicines *Sefer Refuot Menakot* (Purifying Medicines).

Chapter XVI

PROSE LITERATURE

202. *TALES AND FABLES*

In the development of literature, the prose phase as a rule makes its appearance comparatively late. The earlier stages are devoted to poetry and instruction. It is only after the craving for knowledge and expression of the deep soul-stirring emotions have been satisfied, that some attention is paid to the lighter phases of life, and a literature is created, the purpose of which is not so much to teach as to entertain and amuse. Jewish literature, especially, being the product of an exceptionally serious-minded people, which was constantly engaged in a bitter struggle for existence, did not encourage this particular kind of literary production. True, the Agada, in its wide range, contains many stories, fables and parables, but these came there, as a rule, by way of illustration of certain teachings. On the whole, we possess no books of this kind from that period. Even the great classic period, the progress of which we have been delineating in these pages, cannot boast of many books of this kind.

It is only towards the end of that period that such books begin to appear in larger numbers and keep on increasing during the succeeding centuries.

The nature and character of this literature is similar to the prose literature of Mediæval Europe in general. On the whole, it is Oriental in character. As many phases of Jewish literature, these productions were greatly influenced by the Arabic models, or some are even direct translations from Arabic works. It is many-faced and multi-colored. It contains folk tales, collections of fables, proverbs, and apothegms, for it is not emancipated as yet from the desire to teach, and while it aims to entertain, it simultaneously wants to instruct. As in all Oriental literature of that kind, its tales are grotesque and fanciful and the fables are animal fables, the proverbs pithy and always contain a moral. The style of most of the books is not only flowery but semi-poetic. The Arabs were great lovers of rhyme and they even used it in prose. This is the well-known rhymed prose of Arabic literature. It was imitated by the Jewish writers and rhymed prose became an elegant mode of expression. In this form, lengthy letters and treatises on various subjects were written. However, the extensive use of that style, as well as the literature itself, reached its height in the post-classic period. In the one we are dealing with, the number of rhymed prose books is not large. Only a few can be named. To these as well as to the few other prose books we will devote our survey.

The earliest book of this kind written with the purpose to entertain and instruct the people is *Sefer ha-Ma'asiyot* (The Book of Stories) by Rabbi Nissim of Kairawan (Ch. X, Sec. 134), who wrote it for his father-in-law at a time when the latter was mourning for his son, in order that he might be occupied by the reading of pious and moral stories and thus assuage his pain.

It contains a large number of stories, mostly drawn from Jewish sources, from the Agada of the two Talmuds and Midrashim, and also from such collections which we do not possess any more. It contains, however, a number of stories taken from Arabic sources, but Nissim as a rule tinged them with Jewish color, changing in several instances the names of Arabic kings, who figured as the heroes of the stories to that of Solomon. In general, Nissim was not a mere compiler, but re-worked the stories in an artistic fashion. When we compare the versions of the stories found both in his collection and in the Agadic books we possess, his version is on the whole the more excellent of the two.

The book was written in Arabic but it was early translated into Hebrew and for a long time it was thought that it was the original language in which it was written. Only when the late Dr. Harkavy discovered the Arabic original of "The Book of Stories," the question of the original language of the book was definitely determined. The storybook was widely read in the Mediæval Ages, and some of the tales found there even served as themes for poets in their songs. Thus, one of the stories about the goodness of Elijah found in Nissim's story-book, to which we find no parallel anywhere, is as follows: There was a very pious man, who devoted himself to the service of God with all his heart, to the neglect of all affairs of this life. His family suffered greatly from want until it could bear it no longer. His wife then insisted that he go to the market-place in search of business, but he did not have the necessary clothing to go out among people. She borrowed the clothing and sent him out to the market-place while the entire family prayed for his success.

In the market-place the pious man met Elijah who told him to sell him (Elijah) as a slave to the first bidder. The man followed his advice and proclaimed the sale of an exceptionally wise and skillful slave. One man bought the slave for a large sum and offered him his freedom, on the condition that he complete for him certain palaces which were under construction. Elijah prayed to God and angels completed the building in the period of one night. He was, of course, freed and the pious man enriched. This story was elaborated by a later poet into a sacred song to be sung Saturday night, after the *Habdalah* (parting benediction pronounced on a cup of wine at the exit of the Sabbath) is recited, and hence its great popularity.

There are paraphrases of the story in later Agadic collections, but no trace of it is found in the main Agadic source. To my mind, it is a Jewish version of a part of the Aladdin story in the "Thousand and One Nights" where the genii are said to have built for Aladdin a great palace in one night.

This book is, however, the only one dating from the early part of the classic period. The twelfth century is the one during which, as said, books of popular tales and legends begin to appear, both original and translated. To the translated books belong first of all the Hebrew translations of the Hindu Bidpai fables, under the Arabic name, *Kalilah we-Dimnah*. These fables and animal stories, for the heroes of the stories are two jackals by these respective names, were famous in the Middle Ages and were translated into all languages. The Arabs, especially, valued them very highly, and in the Arabic editions, a special chapter is devoted to telling of the pains taken by a wisdom-loving king in order to procure the translation of the book, which was guarded as a great secret. The first Hebrew version was made by Eliezer ben Jacob (1170–1233) at the end of the twelfth century. Of this version we possess a fragment. A little later another translation was made by Rabbi Joel, which was later retranslated into Latin and thus introduced to Europe.

An original book of moral fables and legendary stories was written in Hebrew some time in the twelfth century under the name of *Sefer ha-Musar* (The Book of Instruction) by Isaac Krispon. Part of it was later translated into Arabic. But it was not preserved in Hebrew and is only mentioned by Al-Ḥarisi.

The outstanding book of this period containing tales, fables, and proverbs, which makes both pleasant reading and also supplies instruction, is the one written by Joseph Ibn Zabara under the name of *Sefer Shashuim* (The Book of Delight).

Joseph ben Meir Ibn Zabara was born about 1140 in Barcelona. There he received his education in all Jewish subjects from his father and also studied medicine, probably at the Jewish School for Medicine at Narbonne, where he met many famous Jewish scholars. It seems that he returned to Barcelona and practiced medicine there the rest of his days until about the year 1200.

Zabara had an extensive education, was a good Talmudic scholar, mastered several languages, Arabic, Spanish and knew some Greek, but above all he was a master of Hebrew. He was well versed in the art of medicine but knew also other sciences, such as astronomy, especially calendar calculation, mathematics, and physics. During some part of his life, he was persuaded by a stranger to undertake a journey and visit together with him foreign lands and cities. It seems, that he did it with some hesitation and only after much persuasion by his companion and must have always regretted it. It is this journey which serves as the frame for his book. From the fact that his companion is pictured there as a descendant of Satan, and from the uncomplimentary way in which he is spoken of, it is evident that the journey was not to Zabara's liking. On the other hand, all scholars agree that the journey and the companion are not fictitious, but a grossly exaggerated record of events.

"The Book of Delight" because of its varied content baffles exact description, for it is a veritable little encyclopaedia of the knowledge of the day. It has a large number of folk tales and fables, an exceedingly large number of chosen proverbs and epigrams, a good deal of anatomy, and other branches of medicine and bits of other sciences, and above all, a healthy and sound humor.

Its summary is as follows: In the first chapter or portal, the author tells us how one night he dreamt that somebody was waking him and inviting him to eat and drink. He awakes and actually sees a stranger standing before him with food and drink in his hand. Before inquiring who he is, he plunges into a monologue proving that one should pray before he eats. In the monologue the Rabbis and Aristotle are quoted on the value of prayer, the latter being quoted as saying that prayer makes for the life of the soul, while food only for the life of the body. As he sits down to eat, a battle of wits ensues between Zabara and the stranger regarding the drinking of wine, the former deprecating wine and the latter praising it. Proverbs and aphorisms fly from both sides, Galen, Hippocrates, and Aristotle are invoked by both, and the result is that both agree that moderate drinking of wine is beneficial.

The second chapter opens with the invitation of the stranger to join him in his travels. Zabara then looks at him and noting his strange and gigantic appearance, hesitates. He is especially reluctant after hearing the stranger's name, which is Enan ha-Natash, the son of Arnon the Dosh (Natash and Dosh, when reversed read Satan and Shed, i.e. devil), a name full of terror. An argument on the merits and demerits of travel is then started, and when finally pressed for the reason of the refusal, Zabara delivers himself of a discourse on physiognomy, supposed to be taken from a book ascribed to Plato, in which he indicates his aversion to the appearance of Enan. The latter takes umbrage at the insinuation. Zabara then tells him a long tale of the fox and the leopard. This tale, which is of Hindu origin and very elaborate, serves as a frame for five other tales.

The gist of it is as follows: A fox who is afraid of the nearness of the leopard in the vicinity attempts to persuade him to change his residence. He points out a swampy place which in dry season looks glorious, but dangerous when flooded by the rains, as a suitable place of residence. The leopard is captivated by the place but tells the fox that he must consult his wife. The fox makes some uncomplimentary remarks about women and tries to prevent the leopard from consulting his wife. Nevertheless, he does ask her and she casts suspicion on the sincerity of the fox and tells him a story about the fox and the lion where the former proved perfidious. The leopard tells the fox of his wife's remarks. The fox then grows eloquent and tells the leopard four stories about women where the woman is pictured as perfidious and unfaithful to her husband. The moral is that no one should listen to his wife. The leopard is then convinced and moves to the new place, with the result that when the rains come, he is drowned and is, of course, made to remark that woe to the one who does not listen to the advice of his wife.

In this story, the general moral is that a man should listen to the advice of his wife, while the four other stories speak to the contrary. So we cannot decide whether Zabara loved or hated women. The stories have parallels in Jewish and world literature; among them is also the story of the widow of Ephesus, who is said to have exhumed the body of her recently dead husband in order to save the life of her more recently acquired lover.

The purpose for which the long tale was quoted by Zabara, is to prove that no man should allow himself to be persuaded to leave his birthplace. Enan resents the epithet of fox and redoubles his persuasions until finally Zabara yields. The chapter contains also a number of sharp proverbs against women. Most of them are found in Arabic and Hebrew collections but many are not. One in particular deserves to be quoted. Socrates, whose wife Xantippa, was not only evil-tongued but evil-looking, being short and thin, was asked why he chose such a wife. The answer was, "I chose as little of evil as possible."

In the third chapter, after they started on their journey, Enan tells Zabara a tale about a king who saw in a strange dream a monkey jumping on the necks of the wives in his harem. He is anxious to know its meaning and after long search a peasant's daughter tells him the secret that a man dressed in woman's clothing is hiding in his harem. He is discovered and all the wives are killed and the peasant girl marries the king. This story which is of Hindu origin, for we have a close parallel to it in Hindu folk stories, is as usual complicated and includes another one.

The fourth chapter proves that Zabara's fears of Enan were not unfounded, for he treats him badly on the way, supplying him with poor fare and no wine. The former protests and the latter quotes book and proverbs that the less food one eats the better off he is.

In the fifth chapter, while the travelers pass through a city, Enan tells of the wisdom of the judge who resides there, and illustrates this by several stories. The stories include one about a prince who bought a necklace from a Jew and denied the purchase, but the judge, who took cognizance of the fact that the defendants take off their shoes in Mohammedan courts, recovered it by sending his bailiff with the shoe of the nobleman to his house for the necklace, showing the shoe as a proof of the noble's command. This as well as the other stories are of Arabic origin and are found in the "Thousand and One Nights" in a somewhat changed version. As one of the stories mentions a cantor who was a thief, a diatribe against cantors is launched and Zabara asks Enan why do people say that cantors are fools? Enan offers several answers to this grave question. In general, cantors are very unpopular in Jewish literature, and almost all satirists have made them their butt.

In the sixth chapter it is told how they travel on and while stopping in one city at the house of an old man, he entertains them with stories. One of these stories is the story of Tobit. This Apocryphal story is told by Zabara a little differently than it is told in the Apocryphal book, and most likely he had a Hebrew version before him or an Arabic one.

The seventh chapter contains one hundred proverbs, very pointy, and they are wittily told by another host, in another city, by the name of Judah. The proverbs are culled from various Arabic sources. We will, however, quote one or two. A nobleman reproached a wise man on account of his low descent. Replied the wise man, "My nobility begins with me but yours ends with you." An Arab was asked, "What was the cause of your brother's death?" and he answered, "His life."

In the eighth chapter, Enan entertains Zabara at his own house, and being stingy, he dissuades him from eating much. Here begins the great battle of wits. All authorities are invoked, Plato, Aristotle, Galen, Hippocrates and a host of others, medical rules are cited mostly by Enan in order to prevent Zabara from eating too much. Zabara, here and there, quotes an authority on his side, but is not convinced by his opponent and does justice to the food, consuming practically all of it.

The ninth chapter contains thirty-two questions on medicine and physics asked of Zabara as a punishment for his excessive eating. He, however, stands the test and answers them all. But when in the next chapter (X) Zabara turns upon Enan and asks him diverse questions in medicine, physics, astronomy and mathematics, he answers to all of them, "I do not know." When Zabara chides him for his ignorance and reminds him that he said beforehand that he knows of all sciences half, Enan gives a very clever answer, "Aristotle said," he says, "that the one who says I do not know, has thus stated half of the knowledge." This saying is quoted several times in proverb literature.

In the last three chapters (XI–XIII) Zabara tells us that he found that Enan is of the genus of demons, but the latter assures him that no evil will befall him. He then spends some time with him in his city, and advises Enan not to marry a certain girl, the daughter of a man of evil repute. During their discourse a discussion on women develops. Zabara disparages low descent and praises a woman of scholarly lineage. Finally, Enan agrees with him and he himself tells a story of a woman who performed the mission of a devil working mischief, and ultimately marries a woman of Zabara's choosing. Zabara finally returns home to Barcelona, the city wherein dwelt the Prince, Rabbi Shesheth, the great physician and benefactor. The book ends, like the preface, with a panegyric to Rabbi Shesheth, and it is also dedicated to him.

The style of the book is delightful. It is written in rhymed prose, Zabara being the first to write a whole book in that style. It is flowing and lucid, and if we add the sparkling wit and the wisdom expressed in many sayings, we can say it deserves its name—The Book of Delight.

203. PROVERBS AND APOTHEGMS

The Jews, like the Arabs and all people of the East, loved the pointy proverb, the apothegm, which is the best vehicle of wisdom, and not only delights but instructs as well. "The Proverbs of Solomon," and the other wisdom books are the best examples of such predilection for this form of literature. The Talmudic and Agadic literature contains hundreds of proverbs and aphorisms scattered throughout its various books dealing with all phases of life and conduct. In the later period, when the Jews came in contact with the Arabs, the vast collection of Arab and Oriental proverb literature was frequently drawn upon by Jewish writers in their books for purposes of illustration. Almost every book on ethics, philosophy or kindred subjects, contains a considerable number of proverbs. Yet, few of the writers in the classical period troubled themselves to compile their own collections of aphorisms. The whole proverb literature of the period is reduced to two books, of which one is an original compilation and that in Arabic, and only later translated into Hebrew, and the other is a translation of an Arabic book compiled by an Arab.

The first one is *Mibḥar ha-Peninim* (The Choice of Pearls) by Solomon Ibn Gabirol. About the authorship of the book there was a controversy for a long time. Some ascribed it to Gabirol and some to a later man called Yedayah Bedarsi, who lived during the thirteenth century in the Provence. This Yedayah, on account of his fine Hebrew prose, was named Penini (i. e. pearl producer) and therefore, it was thought that a book with this name rightly belongs to him. It is, however, definitely established now that Gabirol was the author and that it was written in Arabic and only later translated into Hebrew by Judah Ibn Tibbon, the famous translator.

The book is a collection of proverbs and aphorisms which purport to inculcate moral teachings in all phases of conduct. It is thus primarily an ethical book. The proverbs are culled from the entire Arabic literature and arranged according to subjects. There are sixty-four short chapters, each dealing with a certain subject. There are chapters "On Wisdom," "Love of Truth," "Modesty," "Humility," "Love," "Friendship," "On Keeping a Secret," "On Precious Virtues," "Forgiveness," "Haste," and all other possible virtues or vices which respectively lead to a good life or vice versa.

Of the hundreds of proverbs sparkling with wit and wisdom we will select a few at random. Here are two in praise of knowledge: "A wise man was asked, "Why are you wiser than your friends?" He answered: "Because I spent more on oil (the midnight oil) than they on wine." Another one was asked, "Who are more important, wise or rich men?" The answer was, of course, the wise. But the rejoinder was "Why then do we see the wise at the doors of the rich and not vice versa?" To this the reply was given, "Because the wise know the value of riches, but the rich do not know the value of wisdom." On Patience: "Bear the truth even if it is bitter." On Temperance: "A king said to a wise man, 'Were you only to ask me I would support you during your whole life.' Said the wise man, 'And why should I ask? I am richer than you, for I am satisfied with the little I have, while you are not satisfied with the much you possess,' " On Friends: "Friends are of three kinds, some are like food without which you cannot exist, some are like medicine which you need at certain times, and some are like a disease that you never need." On keeping a secret: "The secret, as long as you do not reveal it is your prisoner, but after you revealed it, you are its prisoner," which means that after telling it you will fear the consequences. On Modesty: "What is modesty? Not to do anything in private which one will be ashamed of publicly." On Silence: "Talk little, for the less a man talks the fewer are his errors."

This book was also translated by Joseph Kimḥi into verse, with comments under the name *Shekel Hakodesh* (The Sacred Coin, in reference to the meter in which it is cast, for meter, in Hebrew, is Mishkal). But the added rhyme and meter as well as the comments rather spoiled the original wit and brilliancy and the prose version of Ibn Tibbon is much to be preferred.

The other book is *Musré ha-Pilisufim* (The Moral Teachings of the Philosophers) a collection of apothegms and aphorisms of the sayings of the philosophers compiled in the ninth century by the Syrian, Honein ben Ishak (809–873), the great translator of Greek books into Arabic. The aphorisms are culled mostly from Greek books, but they contain a large number of additions of Arabic and Oriental origin. The book was translated into Hebrew by Judah Al-Ḥarisi under the above-named title.

It consists of three sections or portals divided into chapters. The first is devoted to the praise of knowledge and its various branches, with special attention to music. The second deals with the various phases of life and conduct. The third is a part of a romance on the death of Alexander the Great, giving the contents of the letter sent by him before his death to his mother, her reply and eulogy over him when his body was brought before her, and the eulogies of his friends and companions. Alexander, as is known, was the favorite hero of the Orient and many stories and sayings were spuriously told and ascribed to him.

The aphorisms, on the whole, are given in the name of various Greek philosophers, especially of the most favored of them, as Socrates, Plato and Aristotle. That the greater part of them are spurious, there is no doubt, but that was the Mediæval way. There is an ascetic ring to the book, enjoyment in life is disparaged and the shadow of the other world falls over it. The virtues of moderation, continence, and humility and, above all, the search for wisdom are praised, and naturally, woman comes in for a good deal of blame. It is less orderly arranged than the "Choice of Pearls" and seems to be thrown together without any plan. It contains also a few stories, among them that of the poet Ibycus and the Cranes, known in all European literatures.[1]

We will also quote a few of the aphorisms of this book. "Greed and pride are signs of hidden poverty," meaning of course, poverty of soul. "Life is like a scroll, while unrolling one part, you roll up the other part," which means that the coming experiences make us forget the previous ones. "How can a man revenge himself on his enemies?" "By adding more excellence to his own soul," is the answer. "The wise man understands the fool, for he was a fool in his youth, but the fool never understands the wise man." Diogenes was asked, "When is it good for a man to eat?" The answer was, "The one who has food when he is hungry, the one who has not when he gets it." Ptolemy said, "Man acquires riches, but riches also acquire man." It is an ironical remark meaning that for money you can acquire the services of the best man.

---

[1] The story found in many school books is as follows: The poet, Ibycus, traveling in a lonely place, was attacked by murderers. He looked for help but there was none coming. He finally raised his eyes to the sky and saw cranes coming, and called on them to be the avengers of his blood. Later, his murderers came to the assembly of their people in the city and a crane passed repeatedly over their heads screaming. They remarked mockingly that it must be the avenger of the poet. The remark was overheard and they were brought to trial, confessed and were sentenced to death.

"There is no cure for the fool and it is best to keep at a distance from him."

204. SATIRE AND HUMOUR

Arabic literature of the tenth and eleventh centuries developed a new species of humorous and satirical writing. This was known as the *Maqama*, literally the assembly. It originally meant a description of how several poets came together and rivaled each other in composing odd pieces of humorous poetry. Later it assumed a somewhat changed form, namely, one traveling scholar and poet forms the center of the *Maqama*, and the narrator tells of his exploits. Very often a series of *Maqamas* were joined together, by the device of making the narrator meet the traveling poet or scholar in various places, and tell of his different adventures and tilts with other poets, from which he usually emerges the victor. The great master of this *Maqama* literature was Hariri (1054–1121). His *Maqamas* were full of humor and sparkling wit and were considered the consummation of literary skill.

This kind of literature found imitators among the Jews. The first who composed a similar work in Hebrew was Solomon Ibn Zikbel (twelfth century). His hero, whom he named Asher ben Judah, passes through a series of adventures and strange experiences, in search of a mysterious woman who was supposed to have confessed her love for him in a letter. The adventures and experiences are humoristically described in a series of chapters or *Maqamas*.

The most important work of this kind is the collection of humorous pieces by the name of *Taḥkemoni*, an assembly of wise men—the closest approach to the Arabic word, *Maqama*—written by the poet, Judah Al-Ḥarisi (for his biography see Ch. IX). This traveling poet of whose work we spoke above (Sec. 126) was the best fitted to produce in Hebrew a work which could rival in brilliance and wit that of Ḥariri. As a matter of fact, he at first undertook, at the request of lovers of Hebrew literature in Toledo, to translate the *Maqamas* of Hariri into Hebrew, which work he completed after some time and named *Maḥbarot 'Itiel* (i. e. The Maqamas of Itiel), thus changing the Arabic name of the hero, Abu Said, to the Hebrew 'Itiel, a name found in Proverbs XXX, 1. But, while working on this translation, which he accomplished with great skill, Ḥarisi felt that his mastery of Hebrew is so complete and that his own sense of humor is probably not less keen than that of Hariri, and decided to compose an original book in the same language. Harisi tells us, in his introduction, that he wrote his book in order to show to the world that the Hebrew language is as elastic as the Arabic, and that we can express in it all kinds of thoughts so that there is no need to translate from other languages. On his travels in the East during the years 1218–1220, he found several patrons who gave him financial support and it is to these patrons that he dedicated the book. It seems as if he dedicated the book to two different persons. In the first chapter he dedicates it to the president of the Jewish community at Damascus, Rabbi Josiah, of Davidic descent, who helped him greatly while he stayed in the city. In the introduction, however, he dedicates it again to Samuel Ibn Albarkala, also of the same city. The introduction, most likely, was written later.

The *Tahkemoni* is divided into fifty chapters or portals, each one dealing with a different episode or experience or imaginary subject, but are joined together by the usual *Maqama* device, namely, that the narrator meets everywhere the hero, who is an adventurous scholar. The narrator in the book is Hēman ha-Ezrohi and the hero one by the name of Heber ha-Keni. Both names are Biblical. The first one is mentioned as the author of Psalm 88; the second one is a combination of two different names. Heber the Kenite is represented in the book both as a master of all arts and as a master rogue. He assumes many roles, that of traveling physician, mendicant preacher, poet, astrologer, narrator and many other vocations. There are, however, in the book a number of chapters where the narrator himself tells the story without the coöperation of Heber, thus giving the book a more varied aspect.

The *Tahkemoni* represents a real assortment of various literary wares. There are prayers and sermons for the pious, love ditties and stories for the lover, tales of travel and descriptions of cities and countries for those who enjoy travel, chapters on the history of poetry and rules for poetry making for those interested in literature and a number of wise sayings, proverbs, and fables, riddles and other matters which can not be classified. On account of this peculiar nature the book cannot be summarized, but only generally described. The original form of the Maqama where the literary hero enters into a contest with other poets to show his excellence and skill is well represented in the book; at least nine such contests are found there, and, of course, in all of them, Heber, the hero, is the victor. In these chapters Harisi displays great skill, as the most difficult subjects are drawn upon. Thus, in chapter four, two poets, of which Heber is one, compete as to who can write the most ex-

cellent poetic description of as well as a poem on an insignificant subject. Ḥeber takes the flea and devotes to it a long rhymed prose description and a poem. In chapter five, twelve poets compete, each one taking
a month of the year and extolling it. Chapter eight contains a letter
written by Ḥeber which when read straight is one of praise, but when
read from the bottom up is derogatory and insulting. Another chapter
(XI) contains two letters, one in which every word in it contains the
letter Resh and the other where that letter is not used at all. Thus there
are other contests where poets show their skill, the contestants are sometimes seven, sometimes ten or more. The contest is sometimes expressed
in a series of questions and answers such as chapter thirty-six where
Ḥeber tells Heman how he earned a few good meals and some money
by undertaking to answer all kinds of questions. The series then follows. The answers are all of a moral and proverbial nature.

Another feature closely akin to the first is the debate between two
writers, each undertaking to praise a certain thing. There are about
thirteen such debates on various subjects. Thus there is a debate between body, soul and reason (XIII), between a Rabbanite and Karaite
(XVII), on what constitutes the highest virtue where seven young men
participate (XIX), and also on such subjects as travel (XXVII) and
wine (XXVIII), where both sides are presented. There are debates
between day and night (XXXIX), the pen and sword (XL), man and
woman (XLI) and other subjects.

Besides these subjects there are a large number of miscellanies, a satire
on cantors (XXV), a sermon on temperance in life (2), a speech by a
rooster in his own defense, showing why he should not be slaughtered
(X), and the like. Two other features are especially to be noted, one is
the two chapters on the history of Hebrew poetry (III, XVIII) which
possess both historical and literary value. In them Ḥarisi mentions a
large number of poets and pronounces his judgment upon them. This
helps us to know the time when the poets lived and also how they were
esteemed in the literary circles of that age. The other is chapter eighteen
where Ḥarisi lays down seven rules for composing good poetry. One
of his statements deserves to be quoted. Says Ḥarisi, "People are as a
rule divided into three categories: simple ones, intelligent men, and
poets." Now a poet, in order to please all three classes, must at times
use easy and plain subjects so that the simple should like them, and at
times he must deal with deep subjects and employ chosen words so that
the intelligent be pleased, and above all, his technique must be perfect

and the poems beautiful to please the poets, the best judges. Among Hebrew poets only Judah ha-Levi succeeded in pleasing all the three classes, the others fell short of the mark in one way or another.

The two chapters (XLVII, XLVIII) wherein he describes his travels makes both delightful and useful reading. In them we get a picture of the life of the Jews in the important cities of the East. Harisi, as said, traveled widely and visited Egypt, Palestine, Syria and Babylon. In his descriptions we obtain much information about the scholars, poets and leaders of the Jewish communities he visited, and thus it serves as an excellent complement to the information obtained from the itinerary of Benjamin who visited the same cities fifty years before.

The *Tahkemoni* consists really of two parts, that of the prose which is rhymed and the poetic, namely, the numerous poems, which make up more than half of the book. Harisi's place as Jewish poet has been already discussed (Ch. IX, Sec. 126). As for his prose style, we can say that while in poetry he falls behind the great master, in prose, and especially rhymed prose, he is the master of all. His style is rich, flowing and elastic, his wit keen and description vivid. As Harisi stands at the boundary of two periods in Jewish literature, we can say that although a great part of his literary activity falls within the thirteenth century, he belongs primarily to the classic period, which closed with the twelfth century. He is the last of a long series of poets and writers who, during three centuries, enriched Jewish literature and whose productions made that period the classic one.

ADDITIONS

THE DEVELOPMENT OF THE CONCEPTION OF OLAM HA-BA IN JEWISH APOCALYPTIC LITERATURE AND IN THE TALMUD

Reference was made several times in the chapter to a "New Era" which is to begin at the end of days (p. 6) or to the *Olam ha-Ba* (p. 41), that is the "World to Come" at the appointed time. However, this concept which had played such an important role in the religious life of the Jews during the first century B. C. E. and which later became an integral part also in Rabbinic eschatology so that it was even incorporated in the Mishnah (Sanhedrin, X, 1), deserves a somewhat more detailed treatment. And it is to its elucidation and classification that the following pages are devoted.

As we saw above (p. 6), there were two central concepts in the great complex of ideas which concentrated around the hope for a better future or for the Messianic age, namely, the Last Judgment and the Kingdom of God. We also noted there how these concepts, which are of prophetic origin, were broadened during the period and received new connotations, namely, the first began to be understood not only as the judgment of the enemies of Israel as in Joel, or even of the wicked among the Jews as in Malachi, but as a Day of Judgment of all men, Jews and Gentiles alike. Moreover, the judgment began to be extended even to angels who, according to a belief which prevailed as it seems from olden times and found its expression in the Book of Enoch, rebelled in the early days of the world against the commands of God and were condemned to imprisonment until the Day of Judgment (p. 28).[1] Nay, even the world as a whole is to be judged. This extension of the concept of judgment kept pace with, or rather was the result of, a growing pessimism. The increase of evil in the world during the turbulent times of the two centuries B. C. E. and the burning question of the ages, why do

---

[1] Enoch Ch. XVII, 13–16 speaks even of the punishment of stars which transgressed the command of God and did not come forth at the appointed time.

the wicked prosper and the righteous suffer, which were the prime causes in the rise of this literature, finally led the deeply religious souls to believe that the present world as a whole is corrupt and that there is no remedy for the evil in it except by a complete change. Basing themselves on prophetic utterances which they interpreted literally rather than figuratively, they began to develop a new philosophy of history. The gist of this philosophy is that evil in this world must run its course, and that all is speeding towards an end. Moreover, that all this struggle between good and evil in this world was predetermined to last for a certain time, at the end of which judgment will come and all will be changed completely. The judgment then is the solution to the problem of evil and suffering which is really the substratum of the entire Apocalyptic literature.

The new connotation of the concept of the Last Judgment involved also a change in the concomitant concept, the Kingdom of God. No more did it mean the time when Israel will be triumphant or even that the knowledge of God will cover the earth, views expressed by the prophets, but a time when God will rule the world in a manner totally different than hitherto, when all evil, sin, nay, even death itself will be banished, and all order of nature changed. To express this change briefly, this renovated idea of the Kingdom of God is sometimes characterized by a new creation of heaven and earth and a new order of life. Thus, people began to speak of two ages, namely the present age with all its good and evil, the second predominating, which is to terminate with the Last Judgment, and the age after it, or the age to come; and ultimately of two worlds, "This World" and the "World to Come" (Olam ha-Zeh and Olam ha-Ba).

We will now sketch briefly the various steps of the development of the concept of two worlds. Already in Daniel, VII, 9–15, 23–28, we have the rudimentary conception of two world periods. In these passages we are told that a time is set for the rule of the fourth animal symbolizing the fourth kingdom. That time is when the "Ancient of Days" (God) will sit on his throne of glory and books will be opened before Him. Then we are told further, "One like the Son of Man" will come with the clouds and approach God, and rule and glory shall be turned over to him and to the "people of saints of the Most High" whose rule will be forever over all nations. This is the conception in Daniel of the two periods of world history, the rule of the secular kings up to the Last Judgment and the rule of "the people of saints of the Most High" thereafter. We have no more details about that new period in history and with the exception of the peculiar terms, "one like the Son of Man" and "the people of saints of the Most High," the picture of Messianic times, on the whole, differs little from the traditional one, inasmuch as it is limited to the triumph of the people of Israel after the Day of Judgment. Still, on further analysis of the passage, we can detect several important deviations from the prophetic conception of the Messianic times. First, that the rule of Israel is to follow the judgment to which we find only one parallel in the entire prophetic literature, Joel, III, 9–21. There is a great difference, however, in the conception of the rule between the two passages, for in Joel no rule over all nations is given to Israel, only security from their enemies and stability of government, while in Daniel this rule really begins a new period in human history. Second, the term "one like the Son of Man" undoubtedly refers to the Messiah, but the peculiar appellation and his coming with the clouds impart an aspect of supernaturalness to his personality. Third, the term "the people of saints of the Most High" seems to exclude a large part of the Jewish people from the rule of the new kingdom, as emphasis is laid upon saints.

This rudimentary sketch was enlarged in the later Apocalyptic books. Not only was the conception of the judgment widened, but gradually a current of spiritualization and individualization set in, which reduced the national conception of the Messianic age as a glorious time for Israel to a minimum. The first and also the oldest section of the Book of Enoch (Sec. 23) speaks only of a time set for evil in the world, of the all-embracive Day of Judgment, and of a Messianic kingdom on earth. The fourth section which, as regards the time of composition, follows immediately upon the first, still speaks of a Messiah who will rule in Jerusalem and does not refer to a new creation. The fifth, though, which is the latest of all the sections of the book, a first century B. C. E. production, already speaks of a new heaven and a recreation of the world which will take place after the judgment. Furthermore, it calls the people who will share in this new world the righteous and the elect and asserts that only they will walk in eternal light forever (Enoch, Chas. XCI, XCII). The same view is expressed in IV Ezra in which we are told distinctly that God created not one world but two (Ch. VII, 50) and again that God will renew the creation (Ibid, 75). References to the new creation are also found in the "Book of Jubilees" in a number of places (I, 29; IV, 26), and similarly in other Apocalyptic books.

The origin of this belief can be traced to Isaiah, LXV, 17 which reads, "Behold, I create new heavens and a new earth." There is no doubt that the prophet uses these words as a metaphor to indicate the great changes which will take place in the future as the context clearly shows, but the writers of the Apocalyptic books must have taken them literally. In the "Book of Jubilees," though, the concept retained somewhat of its original metaphorical meaning for the new creation is not pictured there as a catastrophic change but as a gradual one. In the books cited above, however, the new creation is described as a sudden change following immediately upon the Day of Judgment.

The newness of this world consists in the total banishment of sin and corruption from this world, and even death itself. According to this conception the righteous will live forever and, as may be surmised, their existence will be more of a spiritual than a material one (IV Ezra, VII, 114; Enoch, XCII). There are, however, more worldly representations of the life in the new world, such as in the "Book of Jubilees" and in the second section of Enoch (Ch. LXII, 14) which indicate that the earlier conception of a worldly glorious future did not give place to the spiritual without struggle. In fact, these two conceptions continued to exist in literature and in life side by side.

This new conception of "This World" and the "World to Come" also introduced modifications in the concomitant notions of the Messiah, the Messianic kingdom, and resurrection. The Messiah, who for a long time was supposed to be a scion of the House of David, assumes in later Apocalyptic writings a supernatural aspect. The title, "Son of Man," which, as we saw above, was first used in Daniel, as a symbol for the Messiah now became his frequent appellation and he was endowed with a supernatural personality. Some sources even attribute to him preëxistence and speak of his sudden revelation (Enoch, LXII, 3, 5). This view though is not dominant, for side by side with it there persists also the older view which conceived the Messiah as of a human nature, subject to all vicissitudes of life. IV Ezra in which the idea of Olam ha-Ba is dominant still speaks of the death of the Messiah after a period of four hundred glorious years (VII, 29).

As remarked several times, the old Messianic belief which promised a glorious future for the Jewish people struck roots so deep in the consciousness of the people that it could not be lightly set aside by the new spiritualized current of eschatology. Consequently when this new conception of the "World to Come" began to gather force in certain circles, a struggle between the old and the new beliefs arose, and as a result there ensued a compromise. The Messianic kingdom became, not as in the prophetic visions a permanent state, but a temporary affair, merely as a prelude to the "World to Come." In IV Ezra, as stated, the Messianic time is 400 years; in other books different times are given, and we also find different stated periods for the Messianic kingdom in the Talmud and Midrashic literature (see below).

As a result of this compromise between these two currents, the time of the resurrection was shifted from the beginning of the Messianic days to the end, to take place just before the Last Judgment which will initiate the "World to Come." [2]

Thus, the new spiritual concept of the new world with its complex of ideas all of which tended to individualize the hope in the future and to shift the center of that hope from the national and worldly aspects to the individual, or rather to a select group of individuals, namely, the elect, and to the aspect of other-worldliness, found a place both in life and literature. It ultimately gave an impetus to the creation of a new religion in which the ideas involved hold a dominant place.

Judaism, as we know, rejected the entire Apocryphal and Apocalyptic literature, probably for that very tendency, for it saw in it an inclination towards denationalization, a danger to the existence of Israel. It did retain, however, the concept of *Olam ha-Ba,* but it gave it a national aspect. The "World to Come" is primarily the share of Israel. The Mishnah (Sanhedrin X, 1) declares it as a principle that all Israel have a share in the *Olam ha-Ba.* The Gemarah understood the term to mean the world to come after resurrection. Maimonides, though, takes a different view and interprets the term to mean the hereafter. Yet, notwithstanding his great authority, the weight of Talmudic opinion is against his view. Numerous statements in Talmudic tractates distinguish between the "Days of the Messiah" (Yemot ha-Moshiaḥ) and the *Olam ha-Ba,* the latter to exceed in glory the former many times (Sanhedrin 91, b; Pesaḥim, 68a, and other places). The Talmudic view is, however, more worldly, for though the abolition of death is referred to, the general note is that the good which will be bestowed upon those who will share in the "World to Come" is of a physical nature. Yet the purely spiritual life in that world spoken of in the Apocalyptic literature is not entirely unknown to the Rabbis.

[2] On the conflict of conceptions regarding the resurrection whether it will be general or merely for the just, see pp. 5, 31, 36.

Rab, the founder of the leading Babylonian academy, Sura, makes the following statement: "In the 'World to Come' there will be no eating nor drinking, nor will commerce be carried on, nor will there be jealousy, nor hatred, but the righteous, crowned, will sit and enjoy the splendor of the Shekinah" i. e. the presence of God, (Berakot 17a). This, however, is only one statement against many which attribute a more worldly character to the life in the "World to Come."

As regards the duration of the "Days of the Messiah" there are in the Talmud various opinions. One gives the number of years as forty, another as seventy, others, as 365, 400, 2000, and a liberal opinion extends the time even to seven thousand (Sanhedrin 99a: Abodah Zarah, 9a). All these opinions are to be considered as expressions of individual scholars and are based on Agadic interpretation of verses in the Bible. They do not possess by any means any collective authority. They merely indicate the current notions of the "Days of the Messiah" and the period of bliss which is to follow after them.

II

SPECIAL CHARACTERISTICS OF II MACCABEES

The characterization of II Maccabees in the chapter is, on the whole, brief. It will, therefore, not be amiss to add a few more data which will enunciate more clearly the nature of this interesting book, especially the spirit permeating it. First, as to the question of how far the book is really an epitomé of the larger historical work of Jason of Cyrene, as the writer, in his preface, (II, 2–19) professes it to be. A close analysis of the style and contents proves that the writer was not a mere epitomist, for though he undoubtedly shortened Jason's account greatly, he also added some features of his own. There is in a number of places a kind of dual attitude to certain events and persons. This is especially evident in the different characterizations of Antiochus Epiphanes and Nicanor. In Chapter IV that king is described with little animosity and is even endowed with a sense of justice, for we read that he ordered immediately the execution of the governor of Antioch who killed Onias, the deposed high priest who sojourned at the Syrian capital. Likewise is his murder of the Jewish delegates who came to complain about the Hellenist, Menelaus, extenuated by attributing it to the persuasion of one of his councilors, Ptolemy, son of Dorymenes, who was bribed by Menelaus. In Chapter VII, though, the most opprobrious terms are applied to him and similarly in Chapter IX even when the story of the miserable death of this monarch and his repentance of his evil deeds are described, the writer calls him murderer, blasphemous and wicked. The same dualism is seen in regard to Nicanor. In Chapter XIV, he is described as one who admired the courage of the Jews, and especially the manliness of Judah the Maccabee. He even became attached to him and entered into a treaty with him. But at the end of this chapter and in chapter XV, Nicanor is portrayed as an inveterate enemy of the Jews and is called several times "the thrice accursed wretch." Such changes undoubtedly betray two different attitudes towards the enemies of the Jews. It is surmised that the milder one is that of Jason of Cyrene who, as an historian interested in the relation of events, was not prone to indulge in vehement denunciations, while the severer attitude is that of the epitomist who, as can be seen from the whole tenor of the book, was a man of deep piety and an extreme nationalist with strong antipathy and even hatred towards the oppressors of his people. Hence we may assume that the writer added a number of passages.

Another feature which reflects the general tendency of the writer to proclaim the greatness of the God of Israel and His special providence, as manifested in the affairs of this people, is the several descriptions of repentance felt by the leaders of the enemies of the Jews before their death, or in times of defeat. Heliodorus, the emissary of Seleucus IV, sent by him to rob the Temple of its treasures recognizes, after his punishment by the angels in the Holy of Holies, the greatness of God and proclaims it to all (IV, 36). Epiphanes himself, according to the writer, repents of the evil he had done to the Jews and vows to proclaim the holy city free, bestow magnificent presents upon the Temple, become a Jew, and extol the might of God (IX, 13–18). Lysias, after his first defeat by Judah, is likewise made to recognize that "the Hebrews were invincible, thanks to the mighty God who was their ally" (XI, 13). Thus, this glorification of the name of God by the enemies of Israel is repeated frequently and is in agreement with the entire tendency of the book. This tendency embraces not only the exaltation of God but also His Providence over His people and His special interest in them. The writer, therefore, in order to justify his view was forced to offer an explanation for the suffering of Israel and evolve a philosophy. In one place he tells us that it was because of the sins of the people "that the Lord was provoked to anger for a little while, hence his indifference to the place" i.e. to the Temple which was desecrated. He further adds the interesting remark that "the Lord did not choose the nation for the sake of the place; He chose the place for the sake of the nation. Consequently, the place was subject to all the vicissitudes of the nation, and when the people repented, it partook of their prosperity" (V, 17–20). In another place he interrupts his narrative and turns to his readers and appeals to them not to be discouraged by the calamities which befell their people for, "Israel is punished by the way of chastening and not for destruction" (Ib. VI, 13). He considers it a mark of kindness that the impious of Israel are punished at once, and not like with other nations whom God punishes only when their sins have reached the limit. Their punishment then is severe, while that of the Jews is only partial, for though "God chastiseth His own people with calamity, He forsaketh them not." (VI, 12–17)

We can, therefore, see the efforts the epitomist makes in order to solve the problem of the suffering of Israel which occupied the mind of most religious men during the last two centuries of the Second Commonwealth. But as we know, there was also another problem, not less grave than the former, and that was the reward of the righteous who were martyred for the sake of their religion. Our author knows also, as remarked above (p. 10), the solution to this vexing problem, namely resurrection. He inculcates this belief numerous times. It is to be observed that resurrection is limited by the writer to the righteous of Israel only, a view which, as remarked in the previous note, was common in many Apocalyptic writings.

From all that was said we can characterize II Maccabees as an historical book written with a definite aim in view, where the data are frequently used to illustrate the theories underlying it.

We may add that the writer, though engrossed in his theme, paid attention to the literary quality of his work, and that he was not devoid of a sense of humor which he uses occasionally. Thus he concludes his short preface with the following remark: "We have no more to add by way of preface, for it is truly stupid to expatiate in introducing a history and then cut short the history itself."

III

THE CHARACTER OF THE BOOK OF JUBILEES, ITS ORIGINAL LANGUAGE AND PLACE OF COMPOSITION

It was asserted by us in the chapter that the "Book of Jubilees" was written by a rigorous Pharisee in Hebrew and in Palestine. This view, while it is espoused by a number of scholars, both Jews and non-Jews, is by no means unanimous and may, therefore, require some justification.

The questions of the language, authorship, and place of the "Book of Jubilees" were the subject of discussion among scholars for three quarters of a century, and the divergence of opinion is great. Several scholars agree that the book was written by a Hellenistic Jew in Egypt and, of course, in Greek, though they differ on the religious attitude of the author. Another one thinks the author to have been an Essene, and still another considers him a Palestinian Sadducee. It was even suggested that he was a Samaritan, or a Jewish Christian who fought the anti-nomistic tendency of Pauline Christianity. We will not enter into a lengthy discussion on these various theories for that would involve many technical details. Suffice it to say that the last three assertions, namely the Sadducean, Samaritan, and Christian affiliation of the author are excluded by the whole tenor and content of the book. The author could not have been a Sadducee for his agreement with Pharasaic Halakah are by far more numerous than the deviations; besides he enumerates many laws which are of Rabbinic origin and were intended as "fences" around the law, such as riding a horse on the Sabbath and many others. He could not be a Samaritan for Zion is to him holy and "the navel of the earth" (Chas. I, 28, 29; VIII, 19). Nor could he have been a Jewish Christian for there is only one reference in the entire book to the Messiah and he assigns to him a non-important role, though he speaks frequently of the Messianic kingdom. Such could not have been the case were the author a law-observing Christian, for to a follower of this sect the Messiah was the center of the creed.

More weighty and important are the arguments in favor of the authorship by a Hellenistic Jew. These are primarily based on numerous deviations of verses, quoted in the book, from the Hebrew Massoretic text and their agreement with the Septuagint version. There are also agreements with the Samaritan text of the Bible, but in a much lesser degree. Dr. Adolph Büchler is the latest champion of the theory that the book was written in Greek and in Egypt.[1] He marshalls a large number of such agreements with the Septuagint and though he is aware of the argument that their origin may be due to the Greek translator of the "Book of Jubilees" who preferred to use, in a number of cases, the Septuagint rather than the Massoretic text, he rejects this possibility and comes to the above-stated conclusion. He also asserts that the author did not belong to the Pharisees but to some unknown sect. This he bases on the stringency of penalties for offenses which in a few cases exceed those of the Pentateuch and differ with the Talmudic Halakah. The case which Dr. Büchler makes out is undoubtedly worthy of consideration but not sufficient to change the view that the "Book of Jubilees" was written in Hebrew and in Palestine. Against his assumption militates not only the tenor of the book but the fact that the Agadic element of the book which constitutes almost three quarters of its content was retained to a very large extent in later Jewish Agadic works. Not only do the original Hebrew Apocalyptic books, such as the "Testaments of the Twelve Patriarchs" and others contain many of the stories and legends of the "Book of Jubilees" but a number of smaller Midrashim, such as *Midrash Tadshé* and *Midrash wa-Yissau* borrowed from it to a great extent. Besides, much of the Agadic material of our book is scattered in the standard or Large Midrashim. In addition, the *Sefer ha-Yashar* (Sec. 188) and another collection called the "Chronicles of Jeraḥmeel" (Addition to Ch. XIV) have large affinities with this book. Such could not have been the case were the "Book of Jubilees" written in Greek and in Egypt. The fact that of the entire extensive Hellenistic literature, including the works of Philo who was very close to Jewish tradition, there are no traces left in Talmudic and Midrashic literature and the Rabbis passed it over in total silence, argues strongly against any assumption of a Greek original of the "Book of Jubilees," for it could not have been an exception. To this may be added that Palestine was a more likely place for the exotic Agada than philosophic Alexandria.

As for the objection to the supposed affiliation of the author with the Pharisees based on the Halakic deviations in the book, it seems to me that with the exception of the peculiar calendar of 364 days and the celebration of Shabuot on the sixteenth of Siwan instead of on the sixth day, as the Pharisees taught, the other deviations are not formid-

[1] "Studies in the Book of Jubilees" in *Revue des Etudes Juives,* Vol. LXXXII, Paris, 1926.

able. There are only two deviations in regard to punishment of crimes, one for incest, that of stoning for intercourse with a mother-in-law instead of the Biblical penalty of burning, and the other, death by fire for the adulterous married woman instead of the Mishnaic penalty of strangulation. As regards the latter, we must not forget that the Bible does not specify the kind of death, but a Tannaitic interpretation deduced that mode of death. It was, therefore, possible that a different view on the matter existed among certain Pharisees. There remains only the one instance. The stringencies of the author who metes out death to one who marries a Gentile or to one who rides on the Sabbath are easily explained. The "Book of Jubilees," like most Apocalyptic books, is a lay book written not by schoolmen but by pious laymen, and inaccuracies and exaggerations may be expected, especially when the tendency of the author was to inculcate fear of and zeal for the law. The penalties are to be taken more as a means of deterrence than as actually legal decisions and were meant to accentuate the gravity of the offenses. We find numerous such parallels in the Talmud where the expression *Hayab Mitah* (Deserving the Penalty of Death) is used in regard to very slight offenses, as for instance, eating without washing the hands (B. Erubin, 21b) and similar matters. Besides we actually find the interpretation in "Jubilees" of Lev. XVIII, 21, "Thou shalt not give any of thy seed to make them pass through fire to Moloch" to mean, Thou shalt not give thy child in marriage to a Gentile, in the pseudo-Jonathan Targum to that verse. And the Talmud (Megillah 25a) protests against this interpretation which shows that it was current in certain circles. Again the Talmud quotes a case when a man was stoned for riding on the Sabbath remarking that it was not according to law, but as a special measure of deterrence, for the time was one of persecution and there were many transgressors (B. Sanhedrin, 46a). We can thus see the point of view of the author of the "Book of Jubilees" who wrote against transgressions, in times when Hellenism was not as yet stamped out, with the intention of raising the sanctity of the Sabbath to the highest degree. There is, therefore, no reason to question the author's Pharasaism on this score.

IV

DATE OF IV EZRA

Regarding the date and place of IV Ezra, there was, on the whole, until recently very little disagreement among the scholars. All assumed that it belongs to the end of the first century and is of Palestinian origin. A few years ago, however, an attempt was made by a well-known Jewish scholar, A. Kaminka, to antedate it at least six centuries, and because of the scholarship of the savant as well as on account of the novelty of the opinion, we think it deserves a brief discussion.

Dr. A. Kaminka made the claim in the introduction to his Hebrew translation of IV Ezra (Tel-Aviv. 1936) as well as in a series of articles published in the *Monatsschrift,* during the years 1932-1933, that the ground work of the book was written by Shealtiel who was also called Asir, the son of King Jechonaiah, in Babylon in the year 556 B. C. E., but that in the course of time, additions were made to it, the most important though up to the time of Alexander. It seems that the basis for this curious assertion is the fact that the other three versions with the exception of the Latin of the Vulgate read in Ch. III, 1 "I, Salthiel, who am also Ezra." In fact, old Latin manuscripts of the book also retain these words (Salthiel qui et Ezras). It was this curious statement which forced scholars to suppose that the first part (Chas. III-X) was taken from a Salthiel Apocalypse. Kaminka set out to solve this problem and it dawned upon him that since Salthiel is also called Asir in I Chronicles, III, 17 [1] it follows that the original text which he agrees with all scholars was written in Hebrew, read, "I, Asir Shealtiel". He therefore concluded that Asir Shealtiel wrote the book or the larger part of it, and that the later translators, not knowing that Asir is another name of Shealtiel, mistook it for Ezra and hence the puzzling inscription mentioned above. One assumption led to another. Shealtiel lived in Babylon and never came to Palestine, and consequently, the book was written there in the middle of the sixth century B. C. E. It was forgotten for a long time, but when during the early days of the Roman Empire, its legions invaded Mesopotamia, a copy of it was brought to Rome, and there the Latin translation was made. Kaminka therefore differs with other scholars who assert that the Latin translation was made from an earlier Greek which was lost, but claims that it was made from the original Hebrew.

He is, however, not satisfied to base his claim on this conjecture alone and attempts to buttress it by a series of other arguments, some based on linguistic grounds and some on stray incidents in the book. We will not enter into detail but say in general they are far from con-

---

[1] The verse in Chronicles is not definite whether Asir Shealtiel is the name of one person, or that the names really denote two persons, father and son. The Talmud (Sanhedrin 37a) took it as a double name of one person.

vincing, and a single instance will bear out our opinion. Ezra tells that he fasted three times for a period of seven days. Kaminka says that this would imply that he fasted also on the Sabbath. But, argues he, fasting on the Sabbath is already prohibited in the "Book of Jubilees" as well as by the Talmud. He therefore concludes that the book must have been written in earlier times. That such an argument is very slender is evident for the following reasons. First, that we find that Daniel also fasted three weeks in succession and no exception is made for the Sabbaths (Daniel, X, 2, 3). Kaminka makes a distinction between Daniel and Ezra, for the former, he says, fasted three weeks continuously, and since this is impossible he must have eaten on the Sabbath, but such distinction is baseless for all fasting is done only during the day and not at night and there was no continuous fasting. Second, this argument would only posit for IV Ezra a date earlier than the "Book of Jubilees" but not one during Babylonian captivity. Third, fasting on the Sabbath is, on the whole, a light offense and no sin. In fact, the Talmud expressly permits a *Ta'anit Halom* (A fast on account of a bad dream) on the Sabbath (B. Shabbat, 11a), and this was in reality such a fast. Kaminka is, of course, faced by a number of difficulties, for he cannot explain the vision of the eagle (Chas. IX–XII) as originating in the sixth century B. C. E. and relegates it to the time of Alexander. Other passages which enunciate late Apocalyptic doctrines he defers to still later times and thus, as already noted, he merely endeavors to place the ground work in ancient times. Even this assumption forces him though to antedate many eschatological ideas and claim that they were already current among the Jews in very early times, but he does not offer much proof for such assertion.

From all that was said we can safely assert that in spite of the ingenuity of this theory, it is far-fetched, especially the assumption that the Roman soldiers brought a copy of the book to Rome, and does by no means shake our belief in the correctness of the view regarding date and place of IV Ezra, which was stated in our chapter.

V

THE BOOK OF BIBLICAL ANTIQUITIES ASCRIBED TO PHILO

To the Apocryphal and Apocalyptic writings discussed in the chapter there is to be added another work which was inadvertently omitted.

This is "The Book of Biblical Antiquities" by Philo or as it is known under its Latin title *Philonis Judaei Antiquitatum Biblicarum Liber*. Unlike other Apocryphal and Apocalyptic books, it was comparatively unknown until recently, though it was printed as early as 1527 when the editio principes was edited by Johaness Sichardus and published by Adam Petri at Basle. However, for one reason or another, it aroused little interest during the succeeding centuries and was only referred to occasionally. Only toward the end of the last century, an article by Leopold Cohen, a student of Philo's writings and philosophy, in Vol. X of the Jewish Quarterly Review, made known its contents and discussed its date and original language. Cohen also pointed out the fact that it was printed several times during the sixteenth century and gave references to later quotations from the book. He thus brought it to the attention of the scholars, and an English scholar M. R. James, who previously published several Latin fragments containing curious legendary matter about Biblical persons but confessed his ignorance of their source, after being enlightened by Cohen, undertook to translate the book into English and published it in 1917.

The book is found only in a Latin translation of which there are extant Mss. from the twelfth century. References to the book in literature also go back to that century, but earlier references are doubtful. Notwithstanding this fact the book is of early date, for there are numerous facts to prove that the Latin version is a translation from the Greek, and again many linguistic peculiarities indicate that even the Greek was a translation from the Hebrew. In view of the fact that it was considered by the Church as a Biblical Apocryphal book, it could not have been written later than the end of the first century c. e. or the beginning of the second, for subsequent to that time no Christian would have translated a Hebrew book written by a Jew and the Church would not have accepted it as authoritative.

The "Book of Biblical Antiquities" belongs to the class of "Jubilees," for like the latter, the former deals with Biblical history and embellishes it with numerous legends. It does, however, fall much below "Jubilees" in purpose, content, and arrangement. The author of the former had a definite purpose and that was to glorify the law and to prove its eternity and importance and the material is arranged accordingly. The legendary matter in that book is of secondary importance. For this very reason the "Book of Jubilees" terminates with the giving of the Law at Sinai. The author of the "Book of Biblical Antiquities" had no such purpose in mind, but merely aimed at giving a popular history of the Biblical period supplemented and embellished by legends and stories. It is possible that the original covered the entire Biblical period, but the present work contains only the history from Adam to the death of Saul.

In method it resembles to a certain degree the "Book of Jubilees," for like the writer of that book, the author of the "Book of Biblical Antiquities" displays a great predilection for names, speeches, and excessive details of Biblical events and episodes. Thus, the author knows all the names of the sons and daughters who were begotten by Adam after Seth was born. While the Bible merely says "And Adam begot sons and daughters" he states that the number of the sons was twelve and that of the daughters eight, and gives all their names. Similarly, he knows the number and names of the children of Cain begotten by him after Enoch, though the Bible does not mention them, and in this manner he gives long lists of genealogies omitted in the Bible. Moreover, he knows of a census taken by the chiefs of the three families of nations, descendants of the three sons of Noah, namely, Phenech representing the Japheth group, Nembroth (Nimrod) that of Ham, and Jecton (Joktan) that of Shem, in the 340th year after the flood. He is very careful to give us the numbers of each group which are, of course, fabulous.

Whenever an opportunity offers itself, our author launches upon long speeches and euphuistic addresses. Thus, he expands the verse, Gen. VIII, 21, which contains God's promise not to bring a flood upon the world again, into a long oration into which he weaves in some of the principal eschatological ideas. He likewise supplements Ex. II, 1 which reads briefly, "And a man from the house of Levi went and took the daughter of Levi for wife" with a story and a long address by Amram wherein we are informed that the children of Israel decided to decrease the birth of children after the decree issued by Pharaoh that all male children be thrown into the river, and the men separated from their wives. Amram did likewise, but afterwards he rejoined his wife and justified his action in a long speech to the elders. We are told also in this connection of a vision by Miriam in which she foresees the greatness of the child Moses who is about to be born from this reunion. The author also supplies lengthy speeches to Moses and Joshua before their death and to several other Biblical personages on important occasions.

In the narration of the historical events, the author follows, on the whole, the Biblical accounts but adds numerous embellishments. Unlike the author of the "Book of Jubilees," he passes over the history of the patriarchs briefly but he adds some details of their lives in connection with later events. Of the earlier historical episodes he embellishes especially the story of the Tower of Babel, the miraculous escape of Abraham from the lime kiln, the crossing of the Red Sea, the rebellion of Korah, and the death of Moses. He becomes more expansive with the beginning of the period of the Judges in the narrative of which he deviates often from the account of the Bible. Thus, instead of Othniel, the son of Kenaz, who, according to the Book of Judges, was the first judge after Joshua, he makes Kenaz the first judge, omitting Othniel entirely, and tells a number of curious stories about him extolling his courage, heroism, and piety. There are a number of other deviations and embellishments in the successive history. To many of the embellishments and legends we find parallels in the Midrashim and later Agadic collections but some are peculiar to this book. Among the most important of these are: the version of the building of the Tower of Babel, the story of the events preceding the first trial of Abraham, i.e. his being thrown into the lime kiln, the story of the refusal of the sons of Korah to join their father in the rebellion against Moses,[1] and especially the group of stories about Kenaz. Other peculiar Agadic features are: the special importance attached to the rod of Moses, the symbolism of the animals sacrificed by Abraham at his first covenant with God (Gen. XV, 8–13), and similar episodes in the lives of Goliath and Saul. According to the author, the rod of Moses was transported at his death into heaven and is supposed to serve as a reminder to God to mitigate His anger against the Jews when they sin. The animals which Abraham sacrificed at the covenant symbolized, according to our book, not as the Midrash says the kingdoms which were destined to oppress the Jews in later times, but Abraham himself (the dove), the prophets (the turtle dove), the wise men of Israel (the ram), and the masses of the people (the calf). Goliath was the Philistine hero who killed the children of Eli, and Saul, the messenger

---

[1] The Bible itself says, "And the children of Korah did not die" (Num. XXVI, 11), but their escape is variously told. According to one source, the three sons of Korah were saved after they were swallowed up because they repented (Sanhedrin, 110a). Another source has it that these three repented previous to the eruption of the earth (Yalkut, Num. Sec. 752). "Antiquities" has it that all sons, seven in number did not even join the rebellion, which is a novel feature.

who brought the bad tidings to Eli (Samuel, IV, 11-14). Again, the Amelakite, who killed Saul, was the son of Agag, the king of the Amalekites captured by him previously and killed by Samuel. (I Samuel, XV, 24-35).

The author of the "Book of Biblical Antiquities" knows of the beliefs in resurrection, the new world (Olam ha-Ba), the punishment of the wicked in Hell, and other eschatological ideas. He also speaks in glowing terms of Israel, his destiny, the eternity of the law, and the holiness of Palestine. He is likewise acquainted with the important role played by the angels and mentions several by name, and also refers to evil spirits. In short, we have in this book all the important views and notions found in other Apocalyptic writings, but there is no special effort made to inculcate them. They are taken more as a matter of fact, as ideas current and well known.

The book, as a whole, is primarily an Agadic work of early times, the chief purpose of which was to present Biblical history in glorious and exalted terms, though often at the expense of accuracy. As we will see later, (Addition to Ch. XIV), its influence can also be traced in Mediaeval Jewish literature.

CHAPTER II

I

PHARISEES AND SADDUCEES

The account given of the Pharisees and Sadducees in the chapter is very brief and though I still think the views propounded there, with slight modification, are essentially correct, yet in view of the fact that the problem of the nature of these parties received considerable attention during the last eight years, especially by several American Jewish scholars,[1] I believe that a supplement to the statement given above will not be amiss.

First in importance is the question of the origin of the parties and by that we understand the reason or the cause which brought about the division of the larger part of Jewry, during the Second Commonwealth, into two parties or factions. Was it religious diversity or political antagonism, or a combination of both, or a difference of social structure? The sources, especially the principal ones, Josephus and the numerous passages in Talmudic literature including the *Megillat Ta'anit,* are not explicit on the matter. The former represents the controversy between the parties primarily as philosophical-theological, while the religious, i.e. the practical aspect—though he states distinctly that the Sadducees rejected many laws of the Pharisees and much of their legal tradition—(see below), he treats as a secondary issue. The latter, on the other hand, describe the division as concentrating mainly around legal matters, and the theological phase appears, according to them, of second import. However, we do know that both parties did participate in the political life of the Second Commonwealth and that their struggle for mastery was sometimes long and bitter. Yet that does not affect the question of their origin, for in Jewish life religion and state were not separated. Since the sources are not explicit

---

[1] L. Finkelstein in his article "The Pharisees" in the *Harvard Theological Review,* Vol. XXII, 1929; Tchernowitz in *Toldot ha-Halakah,* Vol. II pp. 217–340, N.Y. 1936; S. Zeitlin "ha-Perushim we-ha-Zedukim," *Horeb,* Vol. III, Jerusalem, 1936.

on the matter, and since they are not purely historical but literary, which are subject to interpretation, there arose among scholars a variety of opinions which can be summarized as follows. Most scholars agree that the origin was mainly diversity of religious views and that the political element played only a minor role while a minority with Wellhausen at the head impart to the controversy a political aspect. These were the views on the subject until recently when L. Finkelstein, an able American Jewish scholar, imbued by the spirit of sociological interpretation of history injected into the question the element of social diversity.

The gist of his theory is as follows. The Pharisees were originally an urban and the Sadducees a rural group. However, he says that in the time of Josephus, and probably even earlier, the Pharisees won to themselves through their eschatological and democratic teachings the mass of Judean farmers. As a result, Josephus says of the doctrine of the Sadducees that "it is received but by a few, yet by those still of the greatest dignity." (Ant. B. XVII, 1, 4). The Sadducees who originally hailed from the country ultimately became rich, for Josephus says of them that their followers were only the wealthy (Ibid, XIII, 10, 6). They were rich, as we know, for a long time, for they were the leaders of the government and even the last Hasmonean kings belonged to that party. Yet Finkelstein asserts that they have not lost the boorish manner of the rural peasant and quotes Josephus who says: "The behavior of the Sadducees one toward another is in some degree wild and their conversation with those that are of their own party is as barbarous as if they were strangers to them" (Wars II, VIII, 14).[2] This statement is sufficient proof to him for their origin and to support his theory about the boorish character of the rural population he expatiates about the rudeness of several leading Tannaim who hailed from rural districts. In the different attitudes of the rural and urban population towards life and religion he finds the origin or the cause for the controversy. He supports his view by the common notion among scholars that the Sadducees were more patriotic and cared more for the interests of the nation, while the Pharisees were more zealous for the law than for the national weal and relates these differences to the individualism of the city dweller and to the patriotism of the rural

[2] Finkelstein, following Thackery St. John's translation of Josephus, uses the word *boorish* instead of *wild* employed by Whiston. But wild is a literal translation of the Greek.

man. From this point of view he proceeds to explain all the legal controversies between the Pharisees and Sadducees mentioned in Talmudic literature as well as the theological differences. His explanations are ingenious and skillful, especially those pertaining to the legal matters, but the theory, as a whole, is not convincing and is even untenable.

We will limit our analysis of this theory to three points, for a detailed criticism would turn this addition into a treatise. First, as to the boorishness of the Sadducees, since the author uses it as a major proof for their rural origin. The proof from Josephus is open to grave misgivings, for while in general his testimony of facts is trustworthy, his description is usually colored, especially when he had a certain purpose in presenting an event or a party in a particular light. We will see further on how his entire account of the views of the Sadducees and the Pharisees is dressed in Greek garb. Josephus, who calls himself a Pharisee, was no friend of the Sadducees and hence his description of their behavior. But of greater importance is the possible assumption that his words do not carry exactly the notion of boorish behavior, but may also be interpreted as characterizing the Sadducees as arrogant and haughty which demeanor might have been expected from an aristocratic party, for it is hardly probable that people who were in contact with princes and foreign rulers should have retained the boorishness of distant ancestors for generations. In fact, the Greek word describing the character of the Sadducees is αγριώτερον, i. e. wild or more wild, which carries the notion of arrogance rather than mere boorishness. And just to prove how unreliable Josephus' description is we will point out that the same Josephus who speaks of the Pharisees in the place cited above in glorious terms says of them in another place, "A cunning sect they were and soon deviated to a pitch of open fighting and doing mischief." (Ant. XVII, 2, 4,). We must therefore conclude that our historian was either a man of moods or that he used different sources which express different attitudes. The expression of Josephus is therefore hardly sufficient as proof for the rural origin of the Sadducees.

We will now proceed to examine two more points, one taken from the legal controversies and the other from the theological differences, both of which are explained by Finkelstein on the basis of his theory.

The first was the controversy regarding the libation of water on the altar during the seven days of Succoth which ritual the Pharisees upheld and the Sadducees opposed. The rite is not mentioned in the Bible, but was an innovation introduced during the Second Commonwealth. The Talmud itself is uncertain about its origin and ascribes it to a Sinaitic tradition (Halakah le-Moshe mi-Sinai) as it does often in cases of laws of uncertain origin. Undoubtedly this ritual was introduced as a symbol for the approaching season of rain the prayers for which began, according to one opinion, on the first day of Succoth, and according to another on the last day (Mishnah Ta'anit I, 1). The Sadducees opposed this innovation with special vigor. It is even told that when a Sadducean high priest performed the service on Succoth and he, faithful to the teachings of his party, poured the water on his feet instead of on the altar in order to disparage the Pharasaic ceremony, the people threw their citrons at him (Mishnah Succoth, IV, 5). From a story of Josephus (Ant. XIII, 13. 5), it is to be inferred that this high priest was no other than Alexander Jannaus.

Finkelstein explains this controversy by his theory, namely that the Sadducees who were farmers celebrated Succoth merely as a festival of ingathering, while the urban Pharisees looked upon it mainly as a festival when judgment is pronounced upon rain—in addition to the historical reason connecting it with the Exodus. He avers that the urban population was more in need of rain than the farmers who could wait for some time, while the former needed it for drinking. That this explanation is groundless is evident. To a population which depended entirely on agriculture in a land where irrigation is almost unknown, rain is the greatest blessing and the Bible is full of its promises. We may therefore expect the reverse that the farmers prayed fervently for rain, the season of which began in normal years ten days after Succoth (Ta'anit I, 4). As for the urban population they could well get along for months without rain, for in normal years the collected water in the cisterns lasted till the new rains. Besides, since the urban population spoken of is the one of Jerusalem, we must not forget that the city had water works during the time of the Second Commonwealth, which brought water by pipes from a well at Etom. Ben Sira (Ch. L. 3, 4) tells of Simon the Just—probably the Second, ca. 200—that in his days "a water reservoir was dug, like the sea in its abundance." The supply was sufficient even for a long siege according to the testimony of Tacitus.[3] Our author in order to buttress his theory that the farmers were not in immediate need of rain emphasizes the value of the

[3] Historia, Ch. XII

dew for the Palestinian soil, quoting a few passages of the Bible. But besides that dew is only secondary to rain in the Bible, he forgets that dew is only beneficial when there are already shoots of plants but cannot make the seed grow. For this reason its chief benefits are in the summer to saturate the grass and plants with moisture. The farmers need the rain to make the seeds grow before dew could be of any benefit. The prayer for dew and rain (Tal u-Matar) is not recited until the end of Kislew when there are already shoots on the field.

Again, Finkelstein explains the insertion of the statement that God causes the descent of rain in the second benediction of the *Shemoneh Esré* which speaks of resurrection and which statement is recited from Succoth to Passover by the fact that both were controversial, for the Sadducees denied resurrection (see below) and consequently the Pharisees joined the two pleas in the benediction to vindicate their views. That this is a far-fetched reason is evident for the Sadducees could not have refused a prayer for rain as this was the most important blessing. But he overlooks the Talmudic statement (Ta'anit 2a), "Three keys were not handed over to a messenger, the one of rain, one of birth, and one of resurrection." In these three occurrences, the Jew saw the hand of God. It is enough to glance over Ch. XXXVIII in Job to infer what role rain played in the manifestation of divine power on earth. In fact, the Mishnah (Ta'anit I, 1) uses the term *Geburot Geshamim,* i. e. the Strength of Rain. The second benediction begins with the words *Ata Gibbor* "Thou Who Art Mighty" and is called *Geburot* i. e. a benediction which recites the potence of God, hence rain is joined with resurrection for both are special manifestations of His potence. From all that was said we can clearly see the exceedingly weak side of the theory which undertakes to explain the origin of the parties on the basis of social strata. We will now turn to theology.

That the Sadducees denied resurrection is testified by all sources, by Josephus, the New Testament, and the Talmud, but that they also denied the immortality of the soul is only testified to by Josephus. This last assertion is open to question, as will be seen. Finkelstein, however, assumes the correctness of Josephus' account and proceeds to explain the controversies by his theory. He assumes with certainty, which is absolutely unjustified that both beliefs were imported into Israel from foreign sources. The former was borrowed from Zoroastrianism, the latter from Greek philosophy. The controversy is now clear. The Pharisees as urbanites came in contact with the representatives of the two nations who lived in Jerusalem while the rural Sadducees retained their pristine national beliefs. The logic of this explanation is certainly curious. First, why say that resurrection was borrowed from the Persians and immortality of the soul later from the Greeks? Does not resurrection imply the immortality of the soul, for if the soul is mortal there is no resurrection but a new creation. Besides Parsism definitely speaks of punishment of the souls in Hell and Paradise. Secondly, according to this theory, it is the Pharisees who became Hellenized and not the Sadducees while history tells us definitely that the later Hasmonean kings, leaders of the Sadducees, bore Greek names—true there was also a Pharasaic teacher who called himself by a Greek name, Antigonos of Soko—struck Greek inscriptions upon their coins, built palaces and mausoleums in Greek style, and Aristobolus I, son of John Hyrcanus, was even called "the lover of the Greeks." These and their rich followers did not then come in contact with the Greeks and could not borrow their ideas, but left them as the share of the poorer Pharisees. To assume that is, to say the least, naive. Equally curious is the assertion that the rural origin of the Sadducees accounts for the rejection of the belief in angels. The history of all religions proves the contrary, namely, that belief in mediators and generally the more anthropomorphic conception of religion are rather shared by the rural population than by the urban. The very term paganism testifies to that. We might have analysed our writer's theories of individualism and nationalism, but we consider the foregoing sufficient for our own purpose.

Hayyim Tchernowitz, the second American scholar who dealt extensively with this subject, is more conservative in his views. He assumes with many scholars that the Sadducees were primarily priests, for he agrees with Geiger (Vol. III, Sec. 78) that the name Sadducees or *Zedukim* is derived from Zadok, the head of a family of high priests from the time of Solomon until the Hasmoneans, but also admits that in later times there were laymen among the Sadducees and priests among the Pharisees. In fact, according to his theory, Pharasaism was also founded by priests. He also sees correctly that the difference between the two parties was not as wide as it is usually assumed, and that the Sadducees also had some interpretation of the Bible and partly expanded the law. He further admits that in the long history of the parties there acted a combination of both factors, religious and political. He also subscribes to the general conservative tendency of the Sadducees and the liberal inclination of the Pharisees. All these views are plausible enough but his theory of the origin of the conflict is curious in no less a measure than that of Finkelstein.

He traces the rise of the parties, following Aptowizer who made the suggestion previously, to the rift between two families of priests in early times, that of Zadok who was a descendant of Eliezer, the son of Aaron, and that of the children of Eli, a descendant of Ittamar, the younger son of Aaron. Ebiatar, one of the Ittamar descendants, was high priest in the time of David, but he was removed by Solomon at the advice of his father. Ebiatar retired to his country-place, and thus there arose a party of rural priests who participated little in the service of the Temple, while the Zadokites monopolized the Temple. These two parties of priests had different views about religion, Jewish life, and Temple worship. The Zadokites were less chauvenistic—again because of urbanity—but more anthropomorphistic because they insisted on the *Shekinah* residing on the Ark. Being also the leading priests they were aristocratic and delegated authority to themselves. The Ittamarites were chauvenistic but less anthropomorphistic in their conception of the Godhead, democratic and, of course, held different views about practices of the cult. He finds traces of the rift in several Biblical books but especially in Ezekiel and Jeremiah. Both of these prophets were priests, but the former a Zadokite and the latter an Ittamarite, as he hailed from Anatot, the very city to which Ebiatar retired. Tchernowitz thus makes Ezekiel leader of the Zadokite party and finds in his vision of the future (Chas. XL–XLVIII) traces of Sadducean teaching. He further points to a division between the Zadokite priests and the prophets who were democratic. He therefore surmises that the former rejected many popular customs and prophetic traditions which formed a part of the later Oral Law.

Changes came with the Restoration. This event which intensified the national feeling helped Ezra, the disciple of the prophets, though himself a Zadokite priest, to gain a victory for the national democratic ideas, and due to the spread of learning they became the share not of the priests but of the large masses, and thus the later Pharasaic party was born. The Zadokites retained their views and they also allied themselves with laymen and became the aristocratic party. The conflict later was not between priests and priests but primarily between priests, on the one hand, and scholars who interpreted the law, on the other hand. He attempts to reconcile the two interpretations of the name *Perushim,* namely the one which derives it from the root *Parash* which means to separate and the other from the same root which means also to explain or to interpret. Our writer says that originally the name *Perushim* was applied to the priests who lived outside Jerusalem as separated from the leading priestly stock, but later the name was applied to scholars as interpreters of the Law. He explains quite skilfully the legal controversies and to a degree the theological. We will not enter into an examination of the explanations, but merely remark on the theory as a whole.

It is hardly plausible to assume that there were during such a long time two definite religious currents, and that there should be no reference to it either in the historical or in the prophetic literature, for with the exception of the last chapters in the Book of Ezekiel, there is no mention of the Zadokite priests as a group. Besides, if according to the hypothesis, the Ittamarites or the extra-Jerusalem priests were allied with the prophets, we should have expected the prophets to make a distinction in their invectives against the priests between those who were their allies and their opponents, but no such distinction is found. In addition, if we were to assume with Tchernowitz and others that Ezekiel represents the Zadokite group of priests and Jeremiah the Ittamarite or the early Pharasaic, the question would arise how did it happen that the books of Ezekiel and Jeremiah were both included in the Canon by the same authoritative body whoever they were. The books of the Prophets were canonized before Ben Sira's time (Ecles. XL–6-8) and they were thus stamped as holy and of one spirit. Who were the canonizers, Pharisees or Sadducees? It seems that they were neither, for the former would have excluded Ezekiel and the latter Jeremiah. It is true that later, around the beginning of the Common Era, there arose objections to the Book of Ezekiel and according to a statement in the Talmud (Shabbat, 13b) some wanted to exclude it, but Hananiah ben Hiskiah ben Garon, an outstanding scholar of the time, devoted his energies to the reconciliation of certain teachings in the book with those of the Pentateuch which apparently seemed contradictory. However, this does not answer our query, for whatever the later objections might have been, it is clear that the canonizers saw no rift, on the whole, between the views of Ezekiel and those of Jeremiah, quite contrary to the theory of the early division of the parties advocated by Tchernowitz and others.[4] There are also numerous other

[4] The theory followed by Tchernowitz was first suggested by V. Aptowitzer in his book *Parteipolitik der Hasmonäerzeit*, Vienna, 1927.

difficulties which the theory can hardly surmount, but the above will suffice.

An interesting theory is that of Leszynsky [5] who claims that the Sadducees were like the Karaites and adhered strictly to the Law of Moses, even punctiliously, and what is more they also interpreted the laws in a manner not unlike that of the Karaites. Consequently where the interpretation was not too far from the literal meaning of the words, they at times agreed with the Pharisees. Their main objection was to tradition. By that he means the folk customs and practices which were current among the people, some of which even preceded the Written Law. It is these which, according to his opinion, the term Oral Law connotes and not, as is usually understood, the laws deduced from the interpretation of the Bible. According to him the Pharisees began to use the Midrash method of interpretation only after the Sadducees challenged their oral tradition.

This opposition to oral tradition was smoldering for some time, he asserts, but it broke forth in a more definite manner after the subsiding of the Hellenistic movement. At that time there were a number of the more faithful Jews who reasoned thus. Since all suffering during the persecutions of Antiochus came as a punishment for trangressions of the Law, it follows that henceforth there must be strict adherence to the Law without any additions or changes for these too are against the will of God,[6] and henceforth the opponents of the Oral Tradition became a party. He has great difficulty with the name Sadducees, for according to his theory, the founders of the party must not necessarily have been priests and might have been lay Israelites. Yet he agrees with Geiger that the name is derived from Ẓadok, the founder of the important priestly family. He admits though that the party had a large lay element and that the Pharisees on the other hand had many priests as leaders.

Leszynsky carries his theory further and assumes that the Sadducees believed in angels and spirits, in the Messiah, and in the immortality of the soul. They only rejected resurrection. In short, the Sadducees were pious Jews but refused to recognize the Oral Tradition according to the connotation he gives to that term. There is much that is true in this theory which is to a large extent close to that of Abraham Geiger (Vol. III, Sec. 78), but cannot be accepted as a whole as it contradicts

[5] Die Sadduzäer, Berlin, 1912
[6] Die Sadduzäer, p. 119

the sources. These are made to agree with it only after much casuistry and keen dialectics employed by the propounder.

From all that was said it is evident that the theories which were propounded in recent times did not impair the view which we presented in the chapter. We will restate it more extensively. In spite of the later vehement remarks in the Talmud against the Sadducees, it is to be assumed that the rift between the parties in actual life was not as great as it is usually stated by many scholars. Geiger is certainly right and to a degree also Leszynsky that the Sadducees had certain Halakahs and also interpretations of the laws stated in the Pentateuch, for as we have remarked above (p. 58), the Torah without interpretation can hardly be practiced. Any assertion that the Sadducees clung to the strict letter of the law is therefore groundless. Besides, we could not accept such a wide rift between the parties on historical grounds, for it is hardly possible to believe that two parties, whose religious diversity was as wide as some scholars want us to believe, could have existed for a long time and often mutually carried on the government of a people to whom religion was the most important thing in life without precipitating constant struggle and internecine strife. Yet the case was not so. With the exception of Alexander Jannaus, there was no opposition to the other Hasmonean kings who were Sadducees. Furthermore, in spite of the great influence of the Pharisees upon the masses testified to both by Josephus and the Rabbis, they allowed Sadducees to hold the office of high priest. The Mishnah (Yoma VII, 3) states explicitly that the Pharasaic scholars used to administer an oath to the high priest before the Day of Atonement that he should not deviate from their practices. The reason for the administration of such oath is given in the Gemarah that they suspected the high priest of Sadducean views. Moreover, we find no controversies about the important phases of the dietary laws and other practices for which there is no explicit statement in the Torah. On the contrary we are told that Simeon ben Shataḥ, the leader of the Pharisees, sat at the table with Alexander Jannaus and even said grace at the meal (Barakot, 48a) [7] and we also have a statement that the Bethusians, a faction of the Sadducees, practiced the putting on of phylacteries (Shabbat, 108a). All these prove that the rift between the parties was not as wide as imagined. We have there-

---

[7] It is true that the Talmud does not state that Simeon ate at Jannaus' table but the fact that after drinking a cup of wine he said grace proves that the food was prepared according to the law.

fore to assume that the difference consisted primarily in the degree of interpretation. The Pharisees to whom the study of the Torah was of prime importance kept on developing the law and making it more embracive of all phases of life, and since life is a complex the law had to become more complex and consequently it expanded and interpretation became extensive. That the expansion involved severities and the adding of fences around the law is quite evident. But on the other hand, the close union between law and life also necessitated at times leniencies. To the Sadducees law and life were not so closely united, for a faction of the sect were worldly-minded while the other faction, namely the priestly, laid more emphasis on the cult than on the law as a living force in life. Their general inclination was therefore to interpret the Torah in a more limited way, and as a result the operation of law in life was more circumscribed. They were willing to let the law stay as much as possible within the limits of earlier times with as little addition as possible. To this must be added the influence of the priestly element which, as a rule, are inclined to be conservative in matters of cult. Hence we can see from the description of the sources that the Sadducees were both worldly and conservative, two tendencies apparently opposite, yet they were reconciled in the conduct of that party.

This phenomenon is explained to a large extent by the origin of the party as well as by its composition. In the rise as well as in the continuation of that party there operated not one factor but a combination of factors, both religious and political.

As we know from the history of the Second Commonwealth, the government from early times, at least after Nehemiah, was in the hands of the high priest. Such hierarchies were a common phenomenon in the ancient world, and there were several such autonomous governments under the various empires. A government cannot be conducted by one man and consequently there was formed a party into which there entered laymen, for not all offices can be performed by priests; besides there were also marriage alliances. This party formed the aristocracy of the country. In religious matters, the lay element undoubtedly followed the views of their brethren, the priests. In private life these lay aristocrats allowed themselves much liberty as evidenced by the conduct of Joseph ben Tobias (Ant. B. XII, 4, 6), the practical ruler of Judea at the end of the third century B. C. E. This leniency of the lay element of the ruling party most likely also affected the practices as well as the views of the priests but hardly the ritual of the cult. At the same time there was developing a social and religious power among the people. The *Soferim* had followers, and thus men of learning became popular leaders. Their view of the unity of law and life gradually extended even to matters of cult and encroached not once upon the authority of the priests; and likewise they undoubtedly reproached many times the conduct of the lay leaders of the aristocratic party. Both elements in the ruling party looked therefore askance at the new popular force and its views. The clash between these two parties would probably have occurred earlier if not for the outbreaks of Hellenism and the subsequent events. During the persecutions an inferior priestly family, the Maccabeans, came to power. At first, the Maccabean brothers were supported by all pious men and especially by the scholars, and they likewise allied themselves with them. But when these priests also became rulers, the old aristocratic party was revived and new alliances were made. A secular government necessitates frequently certain transgressions of the law, and Simon and John Hyrcanus undoubtedly committed such transgressions. The fact that the high priest was a warrior certainly did not please the learned men, especially when war, as with the last-named ruler, was more of an offensive nature rather than of a defensive. It is for this reason that the Pharisees advised John Hyrcanus to lay down the crown of priesthood. The reason given by them, according to Josephus and the Talmud (Kidd. 66a), for this advice, namely, that it was because of a circulated rumor that his grandmother was a captive, was only a pretext.

Thus the antagonism between these two parties was increased. But political differences alone could not be a sufficient reason for division in Israel at the time. It was then a combination of both religion and politics. The opposition to the expansion of the law which was smouldering among the priests whose authority was challenged among the scholars even in matters of cult became then stronger, and as a result the entire ruling party repudiated the expanded interpretations of the scholars, and along with them some of their theological teachings, claiming for their own view older origin and declaring the teachings of the popular leaders innovations.

That the repudiation was not as complete as thought we already proved. Besides, it seems to me that this repudiation was more theoretical than practical, for in practice the popular party prevailed. We will take, as an instance, the case of the festival of *Shabuot*. The Pharisees fixed the holiday for the sixth of Siwan, while with the Sadducees the day of the month varied, but was supposed to fall always on Sunday. The reason for the controversy is given, two different interpretations of the verse in Lev. XXIII, 15. But the question arises how was this holiday really celebrated? Was it celebrated on the sixth of Siwan when the Pharisees were in power, and on variable days of the month when the Sadducees prevailed? It is unbelievable that an important holiday had no fixed time. There is no mention of such changes in the entire literature, neither in Rabbinic nor in Josephus. Besides a movable holiday would confuse the pilgrims from other lands who came to celebrate it. In addition, the verse in Joshua, V, 11 supports the Pharasaic view. It is, therefore, right to assume that the holiday was celebrated always according to the Pharasaic view and that the Sadducees repudiated it merely theoretically.

As for the names *Perushim* and *Zaddukim* I still believe that the first is derived from *Parash,* to explain, to interpret, for in later times the expanded interpretation was the main differentiation between the parties, as we find Josephus emphasizing it twice (Bell. II, 8, 14; Vita 38). Less certain is the origin of the second name. The greater number of scholars concur with Geiger that it is derived from the proper name, Zadok, the head of the priestly family. In the chapter, I stated that Zadok was the name of the leader of the opposition in later Maccabean times and supported my view by the story in Aboth de R. Nathan. I believe now that this supposition is untenable and that the former view is to be preferred. It is very plausible to assume that by using that name, the party emphasized the antiquity of its views. However, the derivation of that name is irrelevant. What is important is the nature and character of the views of that party to which our attention was already given.

From the very origin and nature of the parties it follows that the controversies between them should have concentrated primarily on laws affecting public matters and of these mainly the cult. We thus see that out of the thirteen legal controversies eight relate to cult, and four to civil and criminal law, and only one in regard to the Sabbath, which is also a public matter. We have no other controversy which relates to religious practices in the home or of the individual. It is possible that in such matters the rift between the two was not wide.

In matters of belief, there was a real division between the parties, but even there the rift was not as wide as many scholars supposed it to have been on the basis of the description of Josephus. In order to elucidate the real beliefs of the Sadducees, we will have to review briefly the sources. The chief source is, of course, Josephus. This historian speaks of the beliefs of these parties several times. In his earlier description he says as follows: "These, (i. e. the Pharisees), ascribe all to fate and to God, and yet allow, that to act which is right, or the contrary, is principally in the power of men. They say that all souls are incorruptible, but that the souls of good men are only removed into other bodies, but that the souls of bad men are subject to eternal punishment. But the Sadducees take away fate entirely and suppose that God is not concerned in our doing or not doing what is evil, that men may act as they please. They also take away the belief of the immortal duration of the soul, and the punishment and reward in Hades" (Bell. II, 8, 14). From this first description to which he himself often refers in the "Antiquities" we can infer the following beliefs of the parties. The Pharisees believed (a) in a limited freedom of the will and in extended Providence over human affairs; (b) in the immortality of the soul; (c) in reward and punishment after death—the manner of punishment is not given—and (d) in the transmigration of the souls. The Sadducees denied all these, including even Providence and asserted complete freedom of the will. In the second description (Ant. XIII, 5, 9), he discusses only their beliefs in regard to Providence and freedom of the will and repeats in a briefer form what he stated in the "Wars" on that matter with an important omission. He does not state that "God is not concerned in our doing or not doing what is evil." The third description (Ibid, XVIII, 1, 3-5) is longer and while repeating what was said before it adds that the Pharisees believe that there will be reward and punishment after death under the earth, that the wicked "are to be detained in an everlasting prison," and that the righteous will have the power to revive and live again. The addition then consists primarily in the nature of the punishment and in the doctrine of resurrection. He further says that the Sadducees say that the souls die with the bodies and consequently deny all other beliefs connected with this conception.

In Talmudic literature we have only one distinct reference to the heresy of the Sadducees, namely that, according to a statement in *Abot de Rabbi Nathan,* Ch. V, they denied reward and punishment and resurrection. In all other places in the Talmud where heresies and denials of various doctrines are attributed to a *Zeduki,* the name is used in a general sense as an unbeliever and no Sadducean is meant. Very often, the term was inserted instead of another for fear of the censor.

The Gospels refer to the Sadducees as people who deny resurrection and also the existence of angels and spirits. In Matthew, XXII, 23–20, the story is told how one of the Sadducees came to Jesus and asked him mockingly the following question: To which of the brothers will a woman who married seven of them successively, according to the law of levirate marriage, belong on the day of resurrection? Again, in Acts, XXIII, 8 it is said, "The Sadducees say that there is no resurrection, neither angel nor spirit; but the Pharisees confess both."

From a comparison of sources, we note the following facts. All sources agree that the Sadducees denied resurrection, and we can therefore take that for granted. Again, two of the sources agree that they also denied reward and punishment after death in Hell and Paradise, while the third is merely silent about it. Since the later conception of reward and punishment after death, as reflected in the Apocalyptic and Talmudic literature, was so closely connected with the belief in resurrection, it is quite safe to assume that they also rejected this doctrine. We may also consider it very probable that their belief in angels was of a different nature than that of the Pharisees which also prevailed among the people at large. Angels are mentioned in the Bible, yet with the exception of the Book of Daniel where several of them are mentioned by name, such as Michael (Dan. X, 10; XII, 1) and Gabriel (Ibid, VIII, 16) the general term *Malak* may be easily interpreted as messenger or otherwise rationalized. There was, therefore, no need for the Sadducees to believe in a hierarchy of angels on account of the Bible, for they undoubtedly rejected the Book of Daniel wholly or partly, since not only the belief in particular angels is inculcated there but also that of resurrection. We can therefore trust Paul in his testimony about their denial of the belief in angels.[8]

The case is different with the other beliefs. Can we trust the only source, namely Josephus, that the Sadducees denied immortality of the soul altogether and reward and punishment entirely—even in this

[8] This may explain to us the statement in the Mishnah (Yoma, I, 3) that they read before the high priest on the eve of *Yom Kippur* from Daniel, Job, Chronicles, and Ezra. The first was chosen probably because of its theories of resurrection and angels, the second because of its emphasis on complete Providence. The reading was then a test to discover whether the high priest had Sadducean leanings. As for the other books, they were read because of their narrative element.

world—which is of course almost identical with a rejection of divine providence? It seems to me that such assumption is directly contrary to historical truth, Josephus notwithstanding. We already noted above that Josephus' account is dressed in Greek garb and is exceedingly colored for he wanted to give to Jewish opinions the aspect of Greek philosophical discussions. In fact, he likens the Pharisees to the Stoics (Vita, I, 2) and in another place he compares the Essenes to the Pythagoreans (Ant. XV, 10). It remained, therefore, for the Sadducees to be like the Epicureans and he pictures them accordingly. That the description of Josephus of the beliefs of the parties in the "Wars" is modeled after Greek thought can be seen from the following. He speaks of the Pharisees that "they ascribed things to fate and to God" and in another place (Ant. XVIII, 8, 14) he only mentions that they believe in fate. Now we know that the conception of fate was peculiarly Greek and in Jewish belief there is no fate but God, the only master of the universe. There is therefore, no doubt that Josephus merely exchanged the Jewish term *Hashgahah* (Providence) for the Greek fate. Again, he attributes to the Pharisees a belief in the removal of the souls of good men into other bodies, a kind of belief in metempsychosis. But no trace of such doctrine is found in the entire Jewish literature except in the later Kabbala, while it is found in Greek thought especially in connection with reward and punishment. It was taught by Pythagoras and also by Plato, in the tenth book of the Republic and other places. We see then Josephus' exaggerations and irregularities concerning the beliefs of the Pharisees. Similarly there is inaccuracy concerning the doctrines of the Sadducees. These could not teach, as he says, "that God is not concerned in our doing or not doing what is evil." To assert that would have meant denial of the principles not only of prophetic teachings, but of the Pentateuch itself. Is not the whole Pentateuch full of promises of reward for good deeds and punishment for wicked deeds? What are the long passages in Lev. XXVI, 3–46 and Deut. Chas. XXII–XXIII known as *Tokhehot* if not promises of reward and punishment in this world? The same are repeated throughout the Pentateuch. Providence is a fundamental teaching of the Torah and the Sadducees could not deny it without separating themselves from Judaism.

Nor could they deny immortality of the soul altogether, for the prophetic books and the Hagiographa speak of a *Sheol* and some kind of existence after death numerous times, besides the belief in immortality is fundamental to almost all other Oriental religions. The statement of Josephus that the Sadducees say, "The souls die with the bodies" is a mere adjustment of their views to those of the Epicureans.

From what was said, we can safely conclude that the Sadducees did not deny Providence, but most likely said that its sway is more extensive as far as the nation as a whole is concerned and limited as far as the individual—In fact, we find a graded Providence in regard to individuals also with Maimonides (p. 355)—It is likewise plausible to assume that they believed in the continued existence of the soul after death in *Sheol,* but we cannot ascertain the nature of that existence. They certainly believed in reward and punishment, but in this world. It is also very probable that they believed in a Messiah, for it is a fundamental teaching of the prophets, but whether the Messiah was to come from the House of David, or of priestly descent, cannot be ascertained. In the latter case, they undoubtedly explained the prophetic passages about a Messiah from the House of David to refer to Hezekiah as was done by a later Palestinian Amora (San. 99a).

Some scholars, including Tchernowitz assert that the Sadducees rejected all the prophetic and Hagiographic books and accepted as holy only the Pentateuch. This view is supported by the testimony of some Church Fathers.[9] Such an assumption would strengthen the veracity of the report of Josephus. But as stated above, the logic of history is against it. Were this the case the Pharisees and the Sadducees would have been so wide apart as the Jews and Samaritans were, and there could not have been peace in Palestine even for a short time, and both parties certainly could not have carried on together any type of government. Such an hypothesis is preposterous and is contrary to any logical conception of Jewish history during the Second Commonwealth when religion was the very center of the life of the people. True, we find quite a number of divergencies and religious differences of great importance reflected in some of the Apocalyptic books, such as the solar year as the basis of the calendar spoken of in the "Book of Jubilees." But all these were merely literary innovations or desiderata and do by no means warrant that such practices were ever carried out in life. The Sadducees though were a great party and actually controlled the government. The masses certainly would not have tolerated them for any duration of time if they really rejected seventy percent of the Canon which was so holy to them. These then are the views of the Pharisees

---

[9] Quotations in Schürer's *Geschichte,* Eng. tr. div. II, Vol. 2, p. 35.

and Sadducees which seem to be plausible after analysis of the sources on the basis of the logic of history. A more detailed account including explanation of all legal controversies between the parties is out of place in a book of this nature.

II

FRAGMENTS OF A ZADOKITE WORK

In the foregoing essay we discussed the view of the two principal parties or sects in Jewry during the Second Commonwealth, but besides these and the Essenes there were undoubtedly other smaller sects or factions who differed in their religious attitudes from the main currents in Judaism. The time was one of religious differences and favored the formation of numerous schisms and divisions. Unfortunately, the sources are silent about the minor sects with the exception of one which a recently discovered Genizah document not only revealed its existence to us, but to a large degree also its character and teaching. That document was called by Schechter, who discovered, edited, translated, and published it, for want of a better name, "Fragments of a Zadokite Work."

The value of this work cannot be overestimated for it is a first hand literary source dating from the time of the Second Commonwealth and written in Hebrew, which supplies us information about the history of the sect, its character, and its constitution. There are two fragments, a larger one covering sixteen pages and another of only two pages which contain only partly additional matter as one page is only another version of a small part of the first fragment. It is evident that the whole book was still in existence among the Jews in Egypt in the tenth century from which much of the Genizah material dates and that it circulated at least in several copies.

The language is pure Hebrew with a slight admixture of Aramaic, and with the exception of lacunae and some defective writing of words due to the copyist, or to age, or to both, the meaning is easily understood.

The content is briefly as follows: The writer tells us that during the period of 390 years which was the period of God's wrath against Israel there sprouted forth from Israel and Aaron—a term used by the writer to denote both priests and laymen—a root, i. e. a part of the people to inherit the land. For twenty years the people were blinded by the teachings of false leaders. But after that a number at least recognized the teachings of the "righteous teacher," or as he is also called the "only teacher" and they formed that sect concluding a new covenant. The writer then tells us of the low state of religion at the time of the formation of the sect. People turned from the right path, fell into the snares of Belia'al—a name for Satan—which were mainly three, namely adultery, greed, and pollution of the Temple. He is more explicit in his explanation of the term adultery which really means the following of certain views in regard to marriage, such as practice of polygamy and the union of an uncle and niece, which to the sect constitutes adultery, but does not tell us the exact nature of the other two classes of transgressions. He merely mentions that the opponents, whoever they were, spoke against the law of God and that they also oppressed the poor. They were, of course, punished by God who sent the king of Greece to wreak vengeance upon them. From this general calamity, the remnant of the true House of Israel escaped by leaving Judea in order to settle in Damascus. The group that left Judea consisted of priests of the family of Ẓadok (Bené Ẓadok) who, as the writer says basing himself on Ezekiel XLV, 1, are the chosen ones of Israel, Levites, and lay Israelites. He further warns the members of the new covenant to observe the laws, especially those of purity and the Sabbath and also admonishes them to love each other, support the poor, and befriend the stranger. At the end of the eighth page—the part that can be considered as the history of the sect and the polemic against the opponents—the narrative is suddenly interrupted, for a number of pages are missing. The other eight pages are devoted to a description of some of the laws and to the constitution or the order of government of the sect. From the other fragment which continues the story for another page we learn though that the teacher who led the sect to Damascus died there.

In the other part of the larger fragment, we learn the following of the social structure of the sect and its government. It was constituted of four estates: priests, Levites, Israelites, and proselytes; but only the first three participated in the government. The affairs of the sect were placed in the hands of a council of ten, consisting of four from the priests and Levites and six Israelites. All members of the council had to be above twenty-five and younger than sixty, as they were otherwise disqualified from membership.[1] The members of the council were required to be learned in the Law, in accordance with the interpretation of the sect, and besides to be versed in the knowledge of the Book of Hagu, the character of which is unknown to us. We can only surmise that it was a kind of Mishnah of the sect.

The council was headed by an officer who is called by the writer *Mebaḳer,* i. e. a censor, a man between thirty and fifty years of age. He was supposed to be very learned, and his function was to instruct the people and, at times, even the priests in the laws and their performance. He was the practical head of all the settlements of the sects, for it evidently was divided into various communities or *Maḥnot* (Camps). He is therefore called "the censor of all camps." To him new members applied for admission to the sect, and he examined them and assigned them the proper place. He also had the right to expel members who transgressed the law and to readmit them after they repented. He was also the head judge and all controversies were brought before him. He, together with the other members of the council, administered the charity funds of the sect and collected the monthly offerings of the members for that purpose.

The camps were administered by subordinate officers who preferably had to be learned priests conversant with the Bible and also with the Book of Hagu, but if no learned priest could be found, a Levite could take his place. However, if a camp had no learned priest and a case of leprosy occurred which, according to the law (Lev. XIV) had to be examined only by a priest, one was brought from another camp by the censor who instructed him in his duties.[2]

The minimum number required for a camp was ten. The duties of the priests, the heads of the camps, included besides instruction and administration also the taking of a census of the members in the following order: priests first, Levites second, Israelites third, and proselytes fourth. They also, of course, decided litigations which arose in the camp. It seems though that appeals from the decisions of the priests could be taken to the censor.

[1] Cf. Num. VIII, 23 where the term of service for the Levite was from twenty five to fifty, but in Lev. XXVII, 7 we are told that sixty is the age limit for usefulness of a man, and after that age his value is much lower.

[2] I deviated in the description of the functions of the censor and priests from Schechter's interpretation. Schechter makes a priest an associate of the censor. The text does not prove his assertion. The censor was the head of all camps, while a priest administered only single camps, as the text p. 13 lines 1–5 and p. 14 lines 9–12 state explicitly.

The teachings of the sect, both the legal and the theological, are very close to those of the Pharisees and the numerous legal deviations found in the Fragment only point to an extreme pietistic way of life followed by the group which separated them from the body of the Pharisees and ultimately from Israel.

They were very strict in regard to marriage laws, for as was noted, they prohibited polygamy[3] and marriages between uncle and niece. They also differed much from the Pharisees in laws of purity, and though they settled in Damascus, they taught very strict observance of the laws concerning the holiness of the Temple and considered Jerusalem a sacred place, inasmuch as they prohibited marital intercourse within the precincts of the Holy City. Their laws of the Sabbath were more stringent than those of the Pharisees. They prohibited all business conversations on that day, nor did they allow one to walk for more than 1000 cubits out of town. In the Talmud the *Tehum Shabbat* is 2000 cubits. They did allow, however, an animal to pasture for that distance. They, like the Pharisees, prohibited the ordering of a Gentile to perform any work on the Sabbath. They were especially strict in regard to the violation of the Sabbath even if it affected human life, and in contradistinction to Talmudic law prohibited the drawing out of a man from a pit or well by use of ladder and ropes. There are also other deviations from Talmudic Sabbath laws but always tending towards severity. They were likewise strict in laws affecting the relations with Gentiles and required immersion or rubbing with incense for any vessel or garment bought from them, and prohibited the selling of animals to them lest they sacrifice them to their Gods.[4] On the other hand, they admonished not to take anything from them unjustly.

Strictness and severity was enjoined in regard to vows and oaths. The Biblical statement which allows the father to annul the vows of the unmarried daughter and the husband those of his wife they interpreted to mean that only vows against the law can thus be annulled but not otherwise. In this, the teachings of the sect differed with Talmudic law. Likewise do they prohibit all kinds of oaths, whether by the mention of the name of God even in abbreviated form or by the Torah of Moses. There are also severities in regard to testament of witnesses. Like the Talmud, the sect disqualified from testimony trans-

---

[3] Polygamy only and not also divorce as Schechter in his introduction p. xix avers. On this, see Ginzberg in *Monatsschrift,* 1911, p. 691.

[4] With the exception of cleaning garments with incense, the other ordinances are also found in the Talmud.

gressors of the law; but they also barred from bearing testimony any one below twenty, while the Talmud fixes the age at thirteen. From all that was stated and from numerous other deviations it can be seen that the sect not only adopted all Pharasaic interpretations of the law, but went much further.

Close to Pharasaic teachings were also their theological views. They considered the whole Canon holy, believed in the coming of a Messiah, and in resurrection. There is no reference though to reward and punishment after death. However, in regard to the Messianic teachings of the sect there is great diversity among scholars, for the text is in many places defective and the statements are subject to various interpretations. As can be seen from the text the sect had a special reverence for priests and mainly for the sons of Zadok who discovered the Torah after it was hidden from the days of Joshua and the elders. This peculiar assertion comes in connection with the prohibition against polygamy as an explanation why David married many wives. The reason is because he did not know the law since it was hidden in his time. Who this Zadok was cannot be determined. It could not be the first priest, Zadok, recommended by David to Solomon for the high priesthood, for then David and certainly Solomon would have known the Torah. Why then did they not know of the prohibition of polygamy? It must then be another priest by the name of Zadok. Again, the Messiah is referred to several times (Text A, 12, 23; text B, 20, 1) with the title *Mashiah mi Ahron u-mi-Yisrael* (A Messiah from Aaron and Israel).

On the basis of these references as well as due to the fact that the writer quotes the testament of Levi from the "Book of Testaments of the Twelve Patriarchs," where there is also reference to a Messiah from Levi instead of from David, Schechter concludes that this sect also believed in a Messiah from Levi. L. Ginzberg, who devoted a book to the discussion of these fragments, comes after long and detailed analysis to the conclusion that the sect did not deny the Davidic descent of the Messiah. There are difficulties to be met with by either of these views, but in view of the numerous agreements of the teachings of the sect with those of the Pharisees, one is inclined to accept Ginzberg's view, for otherwise the sect would have to disagree also with the teachings of the prophets whom they revered.

The next question is what was the nature of this sect? Schechter identifies it with a sect mentioned by the Karaite writers, especially Kirkisani (Sec. 185). That writer tells of a Zadok who contradicted the Rabbanites and prohibited the marriage of a niece and an uncle. He also said that the Ẓadokites prohibited divorce and had a different calendar. On the basis of these statements, Schechter who, as we have seen, thought that the sect under discussion forbade divorce and that they had a different calendar—a solar like that of the "Book of Jubilees"—concludes that this sect was the very Ẓadokite mentioned by Kirkisani. He furthermore assumes that the polemics of the writer of the Fragment were primarily intended against the Pharisees, though he admits that he also abuses others. As a further step in his theory he supposes that this sect was very close to the Dositheans, a Samaritan sect of whose teachings we have various reports, and that it was finally absorbed by the latter. All these views are hardly plausible, for divorce was not prohibited by the sect, as stated above (p. 506 note 3), nor is the question of the calendar proved by Schechter. Likewise there could be no merger of this sect with the Samaritans for it was as far from them as the Pharisees, for they considered the whole Canon holy, spoke with reverence of the Temple, and enjoined strict observance of its holiness. One is therefore inclined to the view of Ginzberg that it was an unknown sect which followed Pharisaism to the extreme.

There is much difficulty in determining the dates of both the origin of the sect and the composition of the work. The dates given in the beginning of the first fragment are obscure and can be differently interpreted. One thing is certain that the writer was acquainted with the Book of the "Testaments of the Twelve Patriarchs" which he quotes and probably also with the "Book of Jubilees." The date of the former book is the end of the second century B.C.E.; the writer must have lived then at the beginning of the first century. The sect, though, originated earlier. And again one is inclined to accept Ginzberg's view that it arose during the persecutions of Alexander Jannaus (106–76), when the persecutions of the Pharisees by that king were severe. It is not unlikely that a part of the fanatical Pharisees left Judea and went to Damascus. It is also possible that the sect originated earlier during the persecutions of Antiochus, but the latter date is preferable. At any rate, the fragments are of great interest as literary remains of a work written in early times which discloses the views of a sect of whom there is no reference in any other source.

NOTE. The opening paragraph of the first fragment is very obscure. Especially difficult is the following passage: "At the end (Heb. u-be-Kez) of the wrath, three hundred and ninety years after He had delivered them into the hands of Nebuchadnezzar, the king of Babylon, He remembered them and caused a bud to sprout from Israel and Aaron to inherit His land and to rejoice in the good of His earth. And they meditated over their sin and they knew that they were guilty men, and they were like the blind groping in the way twenty years. And God considered their deeds for they sought Him with a perfect heart, and He raised for them a teacher of righteousness to make them walk in the way of His heart." Many scholars among them, also Schechter who discovered the Fragment, believe that the "end of three hundred and ninety years" denotes the date of the beginning of the rise of the sect, and the "twenty years of blindness" they consider the formative years preceding the appearance of the "teacher of righteousness" whom they identify with the founder of the sect.

They are, however, faced with difficulties in the determination of the exact time which is connoted by the "end of the period of 390 years." As is well known the Rabbis figured only four hundred and twenty years for the time of the existence of the Second Temple. If we should assume that the writer of the book agreed in his calculation with the Rabbis, the date of the rise of the sect would be 30 B.C.E. and the appearance of the teacher 10 B.C.E. To such assumption the whole tenor of the content is opposed. On the other hand, to assert that the writer followed the correct chronology—this would fix the dates of the rise of the sect and appearance of the teacher at 196 and 176 B.C.E. respectively—is hardly plausible, for why should we attribute to him greater historical knowledge than to the Rabbis. Besides the words, "And caused a bud to sprout forth to inherit His land" could hardly refer to the sect, for they left Palestine and settled in Damascus.

Ginzberg who, as stated, discussed the entire subject thoroughly in his book *Eine unbekannte jüdische Secte,* published in 1922 offered a very ingenious interpretation of the passage which has an important bearing upon the actual date of the rise of the sect.

According to his analysis, the first paragraph does not refer at all to the history of the sect, but is a kind of survey of the history of Israel and Judah. The three hundred and ninety years which is the Period of Wrath represent according to him the three hundred and ninety years which have passed from the time of the exile of the ten tribes to the rise of the Maccabees, according to Rabbinic chronology as given in the *Seder Olam* (p. 118)—the exact number is five years less. The number three hundred and ninety years is mentioned in Ezekiel, IV, 5 as the period of sin of the House of Israel, i. e. the Ten Tribes. It is, therefore, says Ginzberg, plausible to assume that the same number mentioned in the Fragment constitutes the Period of Wrath, and he interprets *Kez*. not end, but period. That Period of Wrath is equal to that of the time of sin for God's punishment follows the principle of "measure for measure." The words "after He delivered them into the hands of Nebuchadnezzar, King of Babylon," he takes as a gloss by a later writer who did not understand the meaning and took the three hundred and ninety years as a period after the destruction of the Temple, but they were not contained in the original. The "twenty years of blindness" he takes as a symbolic expression for the twenty kings of Israel, from Saul to Hosea ben Elah, the last ruler of the Northern Kingdom. He finds the same expression in an Apocalyptic book, *Assumptio Mosis*. Again the "righteous teacher" is not the founder of the sect, but the priest who found the book of the Law in the time of Josiah (II Kings, XXII, 3–14). Our author supports his views by numerous parallels from the extensive Agadic literature, and evinces great keenness of mind in the propounding of his theory.

This ingenious interpretation of the passage has, as noted, a bearing on the time of origin of the sect, for since the number of three hundred and ninety years does not refer to it, Ginzberg is right in his conclusion that it arose in the reign of Alexander Jannaus, for the whole content of the Fragment supports it. We accordingly followed his view in our description.

However, the interpretation itself, it seems to me, is only partly true. The connotation of the three hundred and ninety years is plausible but the symbolic meaning of the "twenty years of blindness" is far-fetched, the great scholarship of Ginzberg notwithstanding. Likewise, is the explanation that the "righteous teacher" refers to the priest who found the Book of the Law in time of Josiah somewhat stretched.

I venture to suggest that since the three hundred and ninety years are supposed to terminate, according to the theory, with the rise of the Maccabean power, it would be plausible to assume that the "twenty years of blindness" refer to the years of activity of the Hellenists, and that the "righteous teacher" may refer to Matthatias or Judas Maccabee. I also believe that the writer most likely continued to give some additional data on events subsequent to the rise of Maccabean power and ultimately came to the reign of Alexander Jannaus, which is undoubtedly referred to in the bitter tirade against the wicked generation, which follows the opening paragraph. These, though, are missing. We must, therefore, assume a lacuna in the text. We may add that no scholar who discussed the book, not even Ginzberg, succeeded in finding continuity of thought in the two parts of the first page, namely the opening paragraph and the one which follows it.

Chapter IV

ALLEGORISTIC EXEGESIS

We discussed briefly in the chapter the main characteristics of the type of Biblical exegesis which was developed in Alexandria and of which Philo was the chief exponent. As that type of exegesis was an important spiritual and intellectual expression of a large Jewry scattered through the far-flung Hellenic Diaspora, we believe that a few more data bearing on its nature and the spirit which permeated it will not be superfluous.

We said that Philo was the chief exponent of this method of exegesis. This merely implies that his writings which, due to various reasons, escaped the ravages of time, give a clear idea of its aim, purpose, and views, while the works of his predecessors were lost. We know only of one earlier exegete, Aristobolus, of whose writings several longer quotations are cited, as stated above (p. 108), by several Church Fathers. But the works of Philo themselves prove that the allegoristic exegesis was already well developed before his time, for besides the fact that he frequently quotes interpretations with such formulas as "some say" or "some opine," there can be distinguished in his exegesis several sources upon which he drew. Often his views on the same subject stated in different books contradict each other, and this incongruity can be explained only on the theory that some statements represent the view of his source or sources while the others reflect his own.

Allegory, as already pointed out by Zunz (see p. 91) and others, was not during the last two centuries before the Common Era the share of the Jews only but was the common heritage of all the intellectual circles of the ancient world and especially of the Greeks. There was an extensive allegoric exegesis of the writings of Homer and Hesiod. It is no wonder then that the Hellenistic Jews followed suit, for they too could no more accept the Biblical stories, especially the anthropomorphic descriptions of God, literally. These contrasted greatly with their philosophic views. Besides, there was the factor of the apologetic tendency prevalent among the Jews of the Hellenic Diaspora. Many laws, especially the dietary, those of the Sabbath, and others were the target of ridicule by pagan writers. In addition, there was the influence of Palestinian exegesis which, especially in its Agadic aspect, embellished the lives of the Biblical personages with stories and legends and endowed them with excellence of moral qualities and character, and also here and there endeavored to remove the gross conception of the Godhead implied in Biblical anthropomorphic expressions. This Agadic exegesis was carried over to Egypt and served as an impulse and stimulant to further interpretation which ultimately developed into that extensive exegesis in which allegory plays the leading role.

Aristobolus, the only one of the earlier Hellenistic exegetes known to us by name, uses allegory in the proper meaning of the term only to a limited degree. His main concern is to remove anthropomorphisms from the Godhead. Thus he explains that when the Bible uses in regard to God or his activity any form of the verb "to stand" it only means to express by that the constancy and immutability of the laws of nature.[1] Again, by the expression "and God spoke" is meant that He manifested Himself through the works of nature. At times, he employs symbolism, as for instance his remark that the story of the creation of the world in six days has only educational value, as its purpose is to teach men to cultivate orderliness in their activities and thus imitate God in their pursuits and occupations. Only occasionally he uses pure allegory.

Similar use of symbolism we find also with other Hellenistic Jewish writers. The author of the "Letter of Aristeas" (p. 97) explains the two signs by which the Bible distinguishes the animals as clean and are allowed to be eaten by the Jews, namely the cloven-hoof and chewing of the cud, in symbolic manner. The first indicates the ability to distinguish between good and bad, while the second symbolizes the constant recalling by man of his destiny and of the glory of God.

Gradually, however, pure allegory became more and more prevalent, and the tendency grew not only to explain single passages or isolated events but to develop or rather introduce into the Bible a connected ethico-theological system and thus to transform the entire context of the Pentateuch from historical narratives and definite legal commandments into a complex system of ideas and ethical theories. Allegory does not even spare the Patriarchs and other leading personages of the Bible and robs them of their personality. In the earlier Jewish Alex-

---

[1] It is interesting to note that Maimonides in his *Guide of the Perplexed*, Part I, Chas. XIII, XV offers a very similar explanation to God's "standing."

andrian exegesis, which was modeled after the Agada, the Patriarchs typify modes of virtue and are represented as paragons of ethical conduct, but in the later allegoric exegesis they are no more persons but virtues or abstract ideas personified. This type of exegesis was undoubtedly well developed before Philo, but as said, it appears to us in its distinct form in Philo's writings where much of the work of his predecessors was incorporated with additions of his own. It possesses several phases but the important is the ethical. Its main purpose is to prove that the Pentateuch teaches both the history of the spiritual, moral, and intellectual development of man and gives rules for his conduct in life so that he may reach perfection. The first is primarily contained in the narrative part while the second is aimed at by the laws.

Adam and Eve stand in this type of exegesis for man in his two phases, the spiritual and the sensual, and his vicissitudes in striving for perfection are symbolized by the various leading personages whose life story is told in the Book of Genesis. Thus, Philo sees in the three outstanding persons, in the first ten generations until Noah, the lower triad, and in the Patriarchs the higher triad of phases of man's progress towards spiritual perfection. The former, Enosh, Enoch, and Noah represent trust in God, repentance, and justice respectively. Of the latter, Abraham symbolizes instruction, or rather search for knowledge. In his search, he passed through several stages. His living in the land of the Chaldees represents his study of astronomy and astrology—Chaldea was distinguished for these studies. God's command to leave Haran and go to Canaan merely signifies his turning from erroneous beliefs to true ones and attaining higher religious knowledge. Isaac represents the disposition of man to virtue and good as well as heavenly peace. He attains virtue without struggle, as if by intuition. Jacob represents practice of virtue in the life of man. Though a natural disposition to virtue is a high degree of perfection, yet practice and struggle towards a perfect life are still more valuable. When man reaches perfection he becomes Israel, i. e. the man who sees God. This Philo derives from the etymological meaning of the word which he interprets as *Shur El* (See God).[2] Moses represents the highest type of reason. At times though he symbolizes for Philo also different virtues. Again, Sarah—ruler—connotes allegorically philosophy, the ruling form of knowledge, while

---

[2] The Bible itself explains the name Yisrael as striving with God or with an angel (Gen. XXXII, 29), which is correct. Philo, though, seemed to have changed the name to *Yeshrael*.

her servant, Hagar, represents the preparatory sciences, the generally technical and cultural. But when the lower sciences, symbolized by Hagar, want to encroach upon the province of the ruler, then as it is told in the story, they are to be driven out, which means that the time devoted to their study is to be limited and greater devotion paid to philosophy. In this manner, almost all important personages in the Biblical narrative are sublimated by Philo into abstract ideas and principles.

The allegoric method of exegesis made great use of etymology, employing the meaning of the names of Biblical heroes and persons as a support for the interpretations. Very often the etymology of the word suggested the allegory, but frequently the etymology is forced. There are numerous uses of such etymology as a prop or source of allegory. Just to quote a few, Seth, the son of Adam, represents, as the name indicates, the man intoxicated by divine wisdom. Shet is derived by Philo from the root *Shato,* to drink. Jerusalem (Heb. Yerushalayyim) is explained by him as meaning "see peace," namely consisting of two Hebrew words *Re'eh Shalom*. It is, therefore, the city of God, the source of peace. The relation of the Logos (p. 109) to God is as the shadow to the light, and he is, therefore, represented by Bezalel which means etymologically *be-Ẓel-El,* i. e. in the shadow of God.[3] Curiously enough, some such etymological meanings of names are not derived from the original words but from their Greek equivalents and the words are separated into the Greek components. This is explained by the fact that Philo knew little Hebrew and the text of the Septuagint was the Bible he used and studied. But then the question arises, how did the numerous Hebrew etymological interpretations come into his exegesis? The answer to this, according to many scholars, is that that these belong to the works of his predecessors who were conversant with the holy tongue, and were incorporated by Philo in his exegetic works.

In the same manner were the laws explained, allegorized, and sublimated into a set of rules for conduct and ethics. Yet as was pointed out above (p. 92), there was no intention to annul or weaken the obligation to observe the laws minutely, or to assert that the narratives have no historical basis. The exegetes merely aimed to show that the Bible possesses a deeper meaning than the mere literalness of the words

---

[3] The same connotation of the name is found in the Talmud (Berakot, 55a) but merely to prove Bezalel's great wisdom, for he was the master craftsman to whom the work of the Tabernacle was entrusted by Moses (Ex. XXXVI, 2).

implies. That the tendency ultimately led to undervaluation of the laws is another matter, but Philo and probably his predecessors were unconscious of the danger.

From the foregoing we can have a notion of the type of exegesis which formed an important ingredient in the religious views of the Jewish intellectuals in the Hellenic Diaspora. Its influence, however, seemed to have been limited to the lands of the dispersion but made no inroads into the Palestinian schools. There is hardly any trace of both Philo's philosophy and his exegesis in Jewish Agadic literature. There are though numerous resemblances in interpretations of verses, and embellishments of the lives of Biblical persons, found both in the writings of Philo and in the Agada, but in this case it is reasonable to assume that Philo was the borrower. Palestine was the home of Agadic exegesis even in early times, and through the constant intercourse between the Jews of Egypt and Judea this form of explanation of the Bible was transplanted to Alexandria and became current in the learned Jewish circles of that city. Moreover, it was transformed by the Hellenistic Jewish scholars into something different from the original, so that there is only a resemblance between the Agadic element in the exegesis of the Diaspora and that of Palestine but no identity.

Philo and his writings were forgotten by the Jews and, as said, there is hardly any reference to him and his works in the Talmud and Midrashim, but allegoric exegesis did not die out entirely among the Jews. More than a millennium after Philo there arose in the Provence a new school of Jewish allegoric exegesis (Vol. II, Sec. 92), and many allegoric interpretations are also found in mystical books, especially in some parts of the Zohar (Vol. II, Sec. 113). It is difficult to trace the connection between these schools, separated from each other by an interval of more than a millennium, but who knows the way of the spirit and its travels through the ages.

CHAPTER VI

THE YALKUT MAKIRI AND THE
MIDRASH HA-GADOL

In addition to the *Yalkut Shimeoni* spoken of above (p. 150), there is found another Midrashic compilation known as the *Yalkut Makiri,* composed by Makir ben Abba Mari. That compilation is limited only to the Books of the Prophets and to Psalms and Job of the Hagiographa. Parts of that *Yalkut* were published while others are still in manuscript. Thus the *Yalkut Makiri* to Isaiah was published in 1904, the one to Psalms was edited and published by S. Buber in the same year, but the Yalkut to Jeremiah, Ezekiel, the Minor Prophets, and Job are still in manuscript.

The *Yalkut Makiri* differs somewhat from the *Yalkut Shimeoni.* The versions of the quotations from the various Midrashim and Agadic collections in the former have frequently different readings in the passages cited in the latter from the same sources, and some of the Midrashim themselves are mentioned under different titles. The changes in readings are especially numerous in the quotations from *Debarim Rabba,* i. e. the Large Midrash to Deuteronomy, and it is possible that the author had before him a different version of that Midrash.

The time of Makir ben Abba Mari cannot be determined with exactness, but it is assumed, on good grounds, that he lived in the fourteenth century, as the book was already in circulation by the beginning of the following century. Reference to the purchase of the book by a book collector is found on the fly leaf of a manuscript dated 1415.

There is still another Agadic compilation, parts of which were only published recently from a Yemenite manuscript, known as the *Midrash ha-Gadol.* The first to call attention to it was S. Schechter and he also published the part on Genesis in 1902. D. Hoffman edited and published in 1914 the part on Exodus and later the part on Leviticus was edited and published by Rabinowitz. The compilation is limited to the Pentateuch and contains Agadic interpretations, stories and also Halakic passages culled from both Talmuds, numerous Midrashim, and also

517

from the writings of Ḥannanel Gaon, the *Aruk,* the Code of Maimonides, and also from the Zohar. From all these it can be seen that the compiler lived not earlier than the fourteenth century. No sources are given, but it is evident that the author drew upon a large number of Midrashim, earlier and later, for we find statements there from works which we do not possess any more. His compilation is especially valuable for the quotations of such Tannaitic Midrashim which are referred to by earlier authorities but are now lost. Such are the several *Mekilta Midrashim* on the last four books of the Pentateuch originated by the Tanna, Simon ben Yoḥai, the disciple of Akiba. We possessed hitherto a Tannaitic Midrash on Exodus by the name of *Mekilta* (for the meaning, see above p. 69) originated by Rabbi Ishmael, but none by Simon. The quotations are so numerous that David Hoffman was able to compile from these quotations in the *Midrash ha-Gadol* two consecutive versions of *Mekiltot,* one on Exodus (1905) and one on Deuteronomy (1908). The *Midrash ha-Gadol* is also valuable for the determination of some of the sources of Maimonides' legal decisions in his Code, for which hitherto no reference could be found. Rabbi J. Fishman recently pointed out that many of the decisions of Moses ben Maimon which baffled commentators for the reason that they could not find their source in Talmudic literature have their basis in statements found in this Midrash.[1] These statements were undoubtedly taken by the author from earlier Halakic works which Maimonides also possessed.

---

[1] J. Fishman in "Ḥayé ha-Rambam" in the volume *Rabénu Moshe ben Maimon,* pp. 63–85, Jerusalem, 1935.

Chapter IX

NEW DATA ON THE LIFE AND WORKS OF SAMUEL HA-NAGID

Of the three poetical works of Samuel Ibn Nagdila, namely *Ben Tehilim, Ben Mishlé,* and *Ben Kohelet* described in the chapter, there were known until recently small detached parts consisting mostly of several leaves each containing a poem or a section of a poem. In 1934, David Sassoon of London published from a unique manuscript in his possession an almost complete Diwan of these three works. I said almost complete Diwan for the reason that there are several pages missing even in this transcription of the works, inasmuch as at the end of the *Ben Tehilim* there is a lacuna for about two pages and a similar omission can be noted in the midst of *Ben Mishlé*. Disregarding these rather slight omissions we can say that we have now a good edition of the principal poetic works of the Nagid.

The publication of this Diwan throws much light upon both the literary activity of Ibn Nagdila as well as upon numerous phases of his life. We learn that Samuel was a very prolific poet, for the number of poems contained in these three works alone reaches to 1742 distributed as follows: 203 in *Ben Tehilim,* 1127 in *Ben Mishlé,* and 413 in *Ben Kohelet.* Second, we are informed of the manner of the collection of his poems and the names of the collectors and the occasions upon which the various poems were written. Thus, the *Ben Tehilim* was collected by his son, Joseph, who began this work, as he tells us in his preface, at the age of eight and a half, in the year 4804 A. M. or 1044 C. E. and continued it at least until 1056, the year which is generally accepted to be that of Samuel's death, for there is one poem from that date included in this book. The son edited his father's work with great care, for he prefaced each poem with a superscription telling of its nature, and numerous times the occasion which called forth the poem as well as the names of the persons to whom the poems were sent or in whose honor they were written.

Ben Mishlé was copied and collected by the poet's youngest son,

Eliasaf, who was born, as he tells us in the preface, in 1049. He began to copy this work, as he says, at the age of six and a half (1056) and undoubtedly completed it after his father's death. As the *Ben Mishlé* contains mostly rhymed proverbs and short didactic poems there are no superscriptions. Since there is no preface by any collector to the *Ben Kohelet,* we must assume that this work was collected and edited by Samuel himself.

The superscriptions of Joseph to the poems of *Ben Tehilim* are of great interest as they reveal to us the many-sidedness of Samuel's activity and also afford us a glimpse into his inner life and his relations to his children and friends. Thus, we hitherto knew of Samuel as a statesman, diplomat, and expert on finance. The Diwan reveals him to us in a new role as a general and strategist. More than fifteen poems were written by him as hymns of thanks and praise to God after victorious campaigns, and one after he barely escaped from being captured by the enemy during a battle in which his army was defeated. From these poems, we learn that the years between 1039 and 1054 were stormy years for Samuel and that he spent the greater part of them in the field, and among his feats of arms was also the capture of the famous city of Cordova when a rebellious prince escaped thither after his defeat in battle.

His escape from capture by the enemy was commemorated by him not only by the poem referred to above but also by the composition of his code, *Hilkata Gibarata* (Decisive Halakot). He undertook the composition of the book in fulfillment of a vow he had made after his escape. The poem (No. 107 in the Ben Tehilim) tells of the reason which moved him to write the code. He says that he saw that the scholars who preceded him were sparing of words and their Responsa and decisions were written in cryptic language which ultimately caused men to misunderstand them and resulted in erroneous conclusion on the part of some teachers.[1] In order to obviate this obstacle he undertook this work which aimed to tell as clearly as possible the proper decision

---

[1] Sassoon (Diwan p. xxx) and Mann (Texts and Studies Vol. I, p. 631) both assert that the Nagid's purpose in composing his code was to refute the Karaites, and are puzzled by the excerpts which hardly deal with the controversial matter. They rely on line 35 in the poem where the word *Minim* i. e. heretics is found, but they overlooked the lines 29–35 where the poet speaks distinctly of people who misinterpret the words of earlier scholars and circulate erroneous decisions. The word *Minim* does not refer to the Karaites but to the people who mislead others by their decisions. Besides, how could a code based on the decisions of the Geonim refute the teachings of the Karaites who denied all authority to the Geonim?

and the right way in which the laws are to be observed in accordance with the proper interpretation of the Talmud by the Geonim of Babylonia, the birthplace of that work, and especially with those of Rabbi Hai. The book itself is, as noted above (291), not extant but is quoted many times by codifiers during the ages. From these quotations we can see that it dealt with numerous subjects of Jewish law, both purely religious as well as civil and family law. The quotations also prove that it was arranged according to the tractates of the Talmud. There is, therefore, no reason to assume that the Nagid also wrote an abridgment of the Talmud in addition to the code as Sassoon does, though with some hesitation.[2]

From these superscriptions, we also learn that Samuel, in spite of his numerous duties and occupations, did not neglect the interests of his family and devoted much time to the education of his children. In a poem which was written during a serious illness and intended as an ethical testament, Samuel admonishes his son Joseph to be pious, love his friends, and respect them, to be generous to the poor and speak kindly to them, and above all be meek and humble. We have also another poem dealing with ethical instruction to his son. Other superscriptions indicate the close friendship between Samuel and almost all the leading men of his generation, both in Spain and in Babylonia. Numerous poems were sent by him either in exchange for poems by the correspondents, or as offerings on occasion of happy events, such as weddings or birth of children, and, on the contrary, as condolences in time of grief, or finally as peace offerings after quarrels.

Thus, the Diwan shows this remarkable prince of Spanish Jewry in his full glory, and we cannot but wonder at the many-sidedness of this man who, while one hand was occupied in issuing decrees concerning police regulations, taxes, and the observance of Muslim ritual, or at times was busy in drawing the sword in defense of his country, the other penned exquisite poems, wrote rules for minute observances of Jewish laws, or grammatical treatises distinguished by a keen linguistic sense.

[2] Introduction to the Diwan p. xxxiii.

CHAPTER X

CODES AND TALMUDIC COMPENDIA OF THE GAONIC PERIOD

The Cairo *Genizah,* which engaged the attention of Jewish scholars for the last four decades and which, as we have seen, rewarded their labors with the discovery of important documents, is especially rich in literary remains from the Gaonic period. It is, therefore, in this field that the labors and exploits of scholars brought the most fruitful results. The studies of Schechter, Ginzberg, Mann, Levin, Epstein, and others, brought to light hundreds of Gaonic Responsa and numerous parts of Halakic and Agadic books which were hitherto unknown to us, besides letters and other documents of historical and literary value. All these finds revolutionized our knowledge of the history of this period and revealed to us the wide extent of the literary activity of a period which only a few decades ago, was considered very limited in the scope of intellectual productivity. However, since a complete survey of the finds and discoveries of these scholars in the fields of Gaonic literature would fill a volume in itself we shall limit ourselves to the most important of these, especially to codes and Talmudic compendia.

I. The earliest of the hitherto unknown codes emanating from the period is the *Ma'asim li-Bené Erez Yisrael* (A Book of Practical Decisions for Palestinian Jewry). Reference to such a code of collections of practical decisions is found in a Responsum of Hai Gaon. For a long time, this book was considered completely lost, but in 1930 B. M. Lewin, one of the most productive workers in the field of Gaonic literature, published in the *Tarbiz,* a Quarterly appearing in Jerusalem, several fragments containing six leaves from this work which he discovered in an Oxford manuscript from the *Genizah.* Soon afterward J. N. Epstein published in the same Quarterly two more leaves from a manuscript in the Petrograd library, and he was followed by J. Mann, another searcher in the field, who contributed two additional leaves from a *Genizah* manuscript in Cambridge. All these fragments show that the work must have been a code covering a large number of legal subjects.

The discovered fragments deal mostly with family law, but there are also a number of passages which deal with civil law and the ritual. The decisions bear the stamp of Palestinian Halakah, for in a number of cases on which there was a difference of opinion between the Palestinian and Babylonian scholars, the former view is followed, and in general the influence of the Palestinian Talmud is in great evidence. The nature of the decisions as well as the fact that the language is pure Hebrew, and the use of a number of Greek words lead us to conclude that the work was composed not later than the middle of the seventh century, or probably even earlier. At that time Greek was still used by the Jews of Palestine while later it was substituted by Arabic. Also in later times the influence of the Babylonian Talmud became prevalent even in Palestine and affected the practices of the Palestinian Jews as well as the style of legal writing. All legal works of Babylonian Geonim are written in the mixed Hebrew-Aramaic dialect of the Babylonian Talmud. A characteristic of this code is the constant employment of the phrase "such is the practice" and hence its name *Ma'asim* (Practices). This work seems to have been one of the many attempts at codification which were going on in Palestine during the two centuries which elapsed between the redaction of the Palestinian Talmud and the conquest of the land by the Arabs, for as noted above (p. 280), some of the smaller tractates appended to the Babylonian Talmud after its redaction which bear the character of partial codes on some legal subjects are of Palestinian origin.

This code was extensively used by Babylonian Geonim and quotations from it are found in their various works and Responsa though they frequently omitted to name the source and at times they call it *Teshubot Erez Yisrael* (Palestinian Responsa).

II. Another partial code, a Babylonian, is the *Pirḳai ben Baboi* (Chapters of ben Baboi). It seems that Baboi was the name of the father of the author while his own name is unknown. He was, as he tells us, the disciple of Rabbi Aba, who in turn was the disciple of Judai Gaon (fl. 756-770) of Sura from whom we have a number of partial codes (p. 284). Rabbi Aba also compiled a code under the title of *Halaḳot* and several fragments of it were published by Schechter[1] and J. N. Epstein.[2] The code of Rabbi Aba was arranged, as can be seen from the few fragments, on the portions of the Pentateuch like

[1] Hoffman's *Festschrift*, Heb. division, pp. 261–266, Berlin, 1914.
[2] *Publications of the Institute of Jewish Studies at the University of Jerusalem*, Vol. II.

the *Sheiltot* of Rabbi Aḥai (p. 282). However, there are only several fragments of that code, but we have quite a number of leaves from the work of his disciple, Ben Baboi.

The first leaves were published by Harkavy in the annual, *ha-Goren,* from a manuscript in the Petrograd library in the year 1903. L. Ginzberg published later two more leaves and was followed by Schechter, Mann, and Epstein. Ginzberg, in his edition of *Ginzé Schechter* (Treasures from the Schechter Collection) Vol. II, pp. 140–147 and 544–573 collected all the fragments known to him up to the year 1928, but B. M. Lewin published some additional fragments of this work in 1931, some of which are only a different version of those of Ginzberg's in the *Tarbiẓ*. We have thus a considerable number of fragments of this work which reveal to us its character.

These "Chapters of Ben Baboi" were written by him at the beginning of the ninth century and were sent to communities in North Africa and Spain.[3] His purpose was to correct certain legal practices in which these communities followed the Palestinian customs, which differed from the Babylonian. He tells them that the Babylonian practices are the right ones for Rabbi Judai Gaon, the teacher of his teacher, decided in their favor. These fragments deal with synagogue ritual, especially about the addition of *Piyyutim* in the *Shemoneh Esré* prayers and the form of the *Kedushah,* the kind of parchment on which the Holy Scroll may be written, fasting on the Sabbath, the importance of putting on phylacteries, and other matters. These fragments reveal to us the extent of differences in religious practices between Palestine and Babylonia and explain to us many changes in the ritual between the Ashkenazic Jewry and the Sephardic. There is also a polemic note against the Karaites, and we can see in them an effort on the part of the leaders of the great center of Jewish learning, Babylonia, to unify and standardize religious practice in all parts of scattered Jewry.

III. A third work from Gaonic times is a compendium of the Talmud called *Metibot* (Subjects or Discussions). It is one of the earliest compendia which were composed with the purpose of deriving the decision of the law from the long and complicated Talmudic discussion. Its

---

[3] Ginzberg first decided that the "Chapters" were sent by Ben Baboi to Palestine, but in the Fragments discovered by Lewin the writer says as follows, "We heard that God was gracious to you and enabled you to establish schools in all lands of Africa and in many places in Spain." We have, therefore to assume that he wrote to these communities who adopted the Palestinian practices.

earlier version, if B. M. Lewin's supposition is correct,[4] was compiled in the beginning of the second half of the ninth century. In its method the book resembles greatly the later famous compendium of the Talmud of Isaac Al-Fasi. In fact, Al-Fasi quotes the *Metibot* numerous times without mentioning it by name. He, however, was not the only one who refers to this earlier compendium; other codes likewise cite extensive excerpts from it, especially the 'Itur (p. 301). This last code cites the *Metibot* sixty times. As with many of these works also our compendium was thought completely lost until the *Genizah* restored to us many lost literary works. In 1923 Lewin discovered among the manuscripts in the Jewish Theological Seminary in New York two leaves of the compendium. In the years 1928 and 1931 he found eight more leaves in the *Genizah* manuscripts in Oxford and Cambridge. Two additional leaves were found in Cairo by Sh. Asaf. Subsequently, Lewin edited the leaves together with all the excerpts cited in the codes of others in a volume (1934).[5]

The book is still far from complete, but we have sufficient specimens to gauge its nature and character. The distinctive characteristics of this compendium is that it quotes extensively from the Palestinian Talmud. Almost at the end of every section abridged, the author quotes the passage from that Talmud when it adds a point of view not found in the Babylonian Gemarah. From these numerous quotations it is evident that the purpose of the author was to emphasize the importance of the Palestinian Talmud and make its views known as well as to consider them authoritative in legal decisions.

Since we do not know the name of the author, for he is always quoted by the title *Ba'al Metibot* (The Author of the Metibot), the question of the time and place of the composition of the work cannot be determined accurately. However, in view of the fact that the attitude of the Geonim of Sura towards the Palestinian Talmud was a favorable one and they quoted it frequently in their writings, it is plausible to assume that the author was a Babylonian scholar from the Academy of Sura. As to the time of composition, we have to take in consideration the fact that there were two versions of the book, an earlier and a later one. The earlier one found in excerpts quoted in various works must

---

[4] B. M. Lewin, introduction to his edition of the *Metibot,* p. xvii, Jerusalem, 1934.
[5] All the excerpts found in the works of others were collected by Alexander Marx and published in the J.Q.R.N.S. Vol. I.

have preceded the later by forty or fifty years. The date of the earlier one is assumed to be, as said, at the beginning of the second half of the ninth century and that of the later at the end of that century or the beginning of the tenth.[6]

IV. The studies of scholars in the field of Rabbinic literature and the search in the various collections of manuscripts also enriched our knowledge concerning the Talmudic commentary of Rabbi Nissim, called *ha-Mafteah* (The Key) which was discussed above (p. 255). Until recently we possessed only the commentary on three tractates, *Berakot, Shabbat,* and *Erubin* and in Hebrew. In the Genizah, however, L. Ginzberg discovered a number of leaves from that commentary on the tractates *Ketubot, Nedarim,* and *Gittin.*[7] Several years later, J. N. Epstein published[8] from a Yemenite manuscript six leaves containing various selections from that commentary on a number of other tractates, such as *Pesahim, Ta'anit, Megillah,* and *Hagigah* in the order of Moed and on *Yebamot Kiddushin* and *Sotah* in the order of *Nashim,* and *Baba Batra* in the order of *Nezikin.* The discovered parts are written in Arabic. From these discoveries we learn first that Nissim wrote his commentary in Arabic, and that the Hebrew one which we possess is only a translation, and second that his commentary covered most likely the entire Talmud or at least the three orders *Moed, Nashim,* and *Nezikin* plus the tractate *Berakot.*

[6] The determination of the time of composition of the earlier version is deduced from the fact that the author calls the Gaon Sar Shalom (848–853) "our father" and he must have been his son. As for the later version it is concluded that since the latest Gaon quoted there is Zemah (879–885) the recension must have been made after his time.

[7] *Ginzé Schechter* Vol. II, pp. 332–343, New York, 1928.

[8] *Tarbiz,* Vol. 2, No. 1.

Chapter XIV

THE CHRONICLE OF JERAHMEEL

To the class of Mediaeval legendary histories of the type of the "Book of Yashar" belongs also a peculiar collection of historical legends known as the "Chronicle of Jeraḥmeel," published by Gaster in 1899. The Chronicle, however, is not a separate book but forms an important part of a larger work, a compilation of stories and legends by one Eliezer ben Asher ha-Levi, who lived in the Rhine Provinces. The compilation was completed in the year 1325. In his preface, Eliezer tells us that he collected stories, legends, and data from numerous books and combined them into one consecutive narrative. In fact he begins with the creation, continues to the destruction of the Second Temple, and then after reciting tales and legends about the life of Alexander, he passes over centuries and narrates the story of the Crusades. A large part, though, of the compilation was copied verbatim by Eliezer from a Chronicle which was written by one named Jeraḥmeel ben Shlomeh. In this part Eliezer hardly introduced any changes with the exception of a number of extracts from the Yossipon. In several places he interrupts the narrative of Jeraḥmeel by an interpolation from the Yossipon which he, like many Mediaeval writers, calls the "Book of Joseph ben Gorion."

We do not know who that Jeraḥmeel was though we possess several liturgical poems and a number of fragments containing notes on mathematical and astronomical subjects written by him. It is assumed that he lived in the twelfth or eleventh century. The "Chronicle of Jeraḥmeel" is itself a compilation of legends and stories drawn from various sources, Jewish and non-Jewish. He quotes the books of Strabo and of Nicolas of Damascus, and also the "Antiquities of Philo." In fact, a number of chapters in the Chronicle are taken directly from that book. Besides there are incorporated in this work of Jeraḥmeel numerous Apocryphal legends about Biblical personages drawn from sources unknown to us, but to which we find parallels in certain Midrashim, in the "Book of Yashar" and in many Christian Apocryphal and Apocalytic works. A number of chapters bear a striking resemblance

527

to the first part of the Midrash known as *Pirķé de Rabbi Eliezer* (above p. 147) and read like a paraphrase of that Midrash.

The order of the "Chronicle of Jeraḥmeel" is as follows: The first four chapters tell in an embellished manner about the creation of the world and give many details about the things created each day and a special chapter is devoted to the seven planets in which their astronomical position is described. Four more chapters are devoted to the creation of man which is told in an extremely legendary way. All these chapters correspond in their content to the "Chapters of Rabbi Eliezer." From chapter nine the narrative is interrupted by a long excursus on the life of man, beginning with the formation of the foetus in the mother's womb followed by a discussion on the purpose of human life which is the fear of God, and concluded with a discourse on sin and its punishment after death. This excursus, which can be called a treatise on man, extends to Chapter XXII and contains a detailed description of Hell (Gehinom) and Paradise.

The thread of the embellished Biblical narrative is resumed with Chapter XXIII, containing stories about Adam and Eve and their descendants up to Noah. In this Chronicle, Methuselah plays an important role. Chapter XXV relates the story of the fallen angels. The next four chapters (XXVI–XXXI) are excerpted from the "Antiquities of Philo" and deal primarily with the genealogies from Adam to Abraham. Several chapters (XXXIII–XXXVI) deal with the Abraham legends. These are followed by the stories of the wars of Jacob and his children with the Amorites (XXXVI–XXXVIII) and then the testaments of Naphtali and Joseph are given. The narrative is again interrupted by an excerpt from Yossipon on the genealogies of the nations and another excerpt from an unknown source on the history of the building of Rome. Then the history of Moses and Aaron and the death of these leaders is told at length in numerous legends (Chas. XLII–LII), and the narrative then describes the Tabernacle, the plagues, the rebellion of Korah, and arrives at the period of the Judges. At this point (Ch. LVII), the "Antiquities of Philo" are followed up to the story of Jephtah and his daughters. In Jeraḥmeel, like in the former work, Kenaz and his exploits occupy a prominent role (see above p. 484), and likewise the story of Jephtah's daughter is told. From Chapter LX to LXIII we have stories about the various exiles of the Jews and the ten tribes and their sojourn beyond the Sambatyon. These last stories are paralleled by "The Tales of Eldad the Danite" (Sec.

194) and are undoubtedly taken from a collection of his stories. Then follow the histories of Susanna and legends about Nebuchadnezzar. Chapters LXVII to LXXXV are copied from Yossipon telling the stories of Daniel, Esther, and Zerubabel with the embellishments found in the Apocryphal books. From Chapter LXXXV–C the story of the Wars of the Maccabees is told with legendary additions. In fact, this part of the work is entitled "The Book of the Maccabee," but in view of the fact that its contents correspond closely to the narrative in Yossipon, it was undoubtedly taken from there and not from the two books of the Maccabees.

The question arises then was the copying of a large part of the Yossipon done by Jerahmeel or by the later compiler, Eliezer ha-Levi. From the fact that even in the part which belongs to Jerahmeel (Chas. I–LXVI), the later compiler introduced excerpts from Yossipon as he says distinctly, it would be proper to assume that the "Jerahmeel Chronicle" proper is limited to the chapters mentioned above and that the extracts from Yossipon belong to Eliezer.

Now as to the sources of the "Jerahmeel Chronicle." Gaster, who published the Chronicle from manuscript with an English translation and made a thorough study of the work, propounded a theory that the bulk of that Chronicle was copied by Jerahmeel from an ancient Hebrew collection of Biblical legends, composed not later than the seventh century and most likely earlier. The chapters from the "Antiquities of Philo" incorporated in the "Jerahmeel Chronicle" he claims to be the original Hebrew text of that book of which we possess only the Latin, which were incorporated in that collection. We thus have three parts in the "Jerahmeel Chronicle": (1) Portions from the Hebrew original of the "Antiquities of Philo" composed probably in the first century c. e. (2) Apocryphal legends copied from an early Hebrew collection composed not later than the seventh century c. e. (3) Additions of his own.

However, other scholars, such as Perles, Neubauer, and L. Cohen [1] disregard this theory. They claim that Jerahmeel merely translated the chapters XXVI–XXXI which are identical with the "Antiquities" as well as those which he himself says that he excerpted from that book together with many other passages, which bear evidence of having been borrowed from that source, from the Latin translation. Consequently,

---

[1] See L. Cohen's essay "Pseudo-Philo und Jerahmeel" in *Jakob Guttmanns Festschrift*, pp. 173–185, Leipzig, 1914.

the whole theory of Gaster falls to the ground, and we will have to assume that Jeraḥmeel did not have before him any older Hebrew collection of Apocryphal stories. He was merely a good compiler and drew his stories and embellishments from Midrashim, some Agadic legendary books, and from non-Jewish sources. It is also possible that he already utilized some existing collections of legends and stories but certainly not the original Hebrew text of the "Antiquities" or any seventh century collection. The proofs brought by these scholars seem convincing. However, be that as it may, the "Chronicle of Jeraḥmeel" is of great interest to us for it proves the wide spread of numerous cycles of legends and Apocryphal stories in literary circles among the Jews in early Mediaeval times. Besides, the "Chronicle" serves us as a source for many stories and Biblical legends for which we can thus far find no parallel in existing Agadic collections.

SELECTED BIBLIOGRAPHY

(In the Order of the Chapters of the Book)

CHAPTER I

BOUSSET, D. W. *Die jüdische Apokalyptik*. Berlin, 1903.
—— *Die Religion des Judenthums*. 2nd ed. Berlin, 1926.
BÜCHLER, A. "Studies in the Book of Jubilees" in *Revue des etudes juives*. Vol. LXXXII. Nos. 163–164. Paris, 1926.
BURKITT, F. C. *Jewish and Christian Apocalypses*. London, 1914.
CHARLES, R. H. *Religious Development Between the Old and the New Testaments*. N. Y.
—— *The Book of Jubilees*. Eng. Trans. with notes and introduction. London, 1902.
—— *The Book of Enoch*. Eng. Trans. with notes and introduction. Oxford, 1893.
—— *The Testaments of the Twelve Patriarchs*. Eng. Trans. with notes and introduction. Oxford, 1908.
CHURGIN, P. "Sefer Makkabim Bet.," in *Horeb*. Vol. III. Jerusalem, 1937.
HILGENFELD, A. *Die jüdische Apokalyptik*. 1857.
KAMINKA, A. *Sefer Hezyonot Assir Shealtiel*. Hebrew translation of IV. Ezra, with introduction and notes. Tel-Aviv. 1936.
MATTHEWS, G. *The Jewish Apology to the Grecian World in the Apocryphal and Pseudepigraphic Literature*. Chicago, 1910.
SCHÜRER, E. *History of the Jewish People in the Time of Jesus Christ*. Division 2, vol. III. Edinburgh, 1891. German 4th ed. Leipzig, 1909.
WEISS, I. H. *Dor, Dor we-Dorshov*. Vol. I. 2nd ed. New York-Berlin, 1924.
ZÖCKLER, OTTO. *Apokryphen des alten Testaments, Anhang über die pseudoepigraphische Literatur*, München, 1891.

CHAPTER II

FINKELSTEIN, L. "The Pharisees," in *Harvard Theological Review*. 1929.
FRANKEL, Z. *Darké ha-Mishnah*. 2nd edition. Warsaw, 1923.
GINZBERG, L. "Zur Entstehungsgeschichte der Mischnah," in Hoffmann's *Festschrift*. Berlin, 1914.
GRAETZ, H. *Geschichte der Juden von den ältesten Zeiten bis auf die Gegenwart*. Vol. III; Heb. tr. Vol. II. Eng. tr. Vols. I, II.

HERFORD, R. T. *Talmud and Apocrypha*. London, 1933.
HOFFMANN, D. *Die erste Mischnah*. Berlin, 1882.
—— *Zur Einleitung in die halachische Midraschim*. Berlin, 1888.
LAUTERBACH, Z. *Midrash and Mishnah*.
MIELZINER, M. *Introduction to the Talmud*. 2nd edition. New York, 1925.
MOORE, G. F. *Judaism*. 2 vols. Cambridge, 1927.
OPPENHEIM, J. "Toldot ha-Mishnah," in Weiss' *Bet Talmud*. Vols. II, III. Vienna, 1882–3.
STRACK, H. *Einleitung in Talmud und Midrasch*, 5th ed. Berlin, 1920.
TCHERNOWITZ, H. *Toldot ha-Halakah*. Vol. II, pp. 217–338. New York, 1936.
ZEITLIN, S. *The History of the Second Jewish Commonwealth*. New York, 1933.
—— "ha-Perushim" in *Horeb*. Vol. III. Jerusalem, 1937.
WEISS, I. H. *Dor*, Vols. I, II. 2nd ed. New York-Berlin, 1924.

CHAPTER III

BACHER, W. *Die Aggadah der Tannaiten*. Vol. I, Strassburg, 1884; Vol. II, 1890.
BLOCH, J. S. *Einblicke in die Geschichte der Entstehung der talmudischen Literatur*. Wien, 1884.
BRÜLL, J. *Mebo ha-Mishnah*. 2 parts. Frankfort, 1876.
FRANKEL, Z. *Darké ha-Mishnah*. 2nd ed. Warsaw, 1923.
GRAETZ, H. *Geschichte*, Ibidem.
KROCHMAL, N. *More Nebuké ha-Zeman*. Chaps. 14, 15, Lemberg, 1863. Berlin, 1924.
ROSENTHAL, L. A. *Über den Zusammenhang, die Quellen und die Entstehung der Mischnah*. Berlin, 1918.
STEINSCHNEIDER, M. *Jewish Literature*. Hebrew tr. Chap. 5. 2nd ed. Warsaw, 1923.
STRACK, H. Ibidem.
WEISS, I. H. *Ibidem*.
ZUNZ, L. *Die gottesdienstlichen Vorträge der Juden*, Chaps. 3, 4. Berlin, 1832.

CHAPTER IV

BENTWICH, N. *Philo*. Philadelphia, 1912.
—— *Josephus*, Philadelphia, 1914.
BERLINER, A. *Der Targum Onkelos*. Berlin, 1884.
CHURGIN, P. *Targum Jonathan on the Prophets*.
COHN, L.-HEINEMANN, I. *Die Werke Philos*. Trans. with notes and introduction.
DAEHNE, A. F. *Geschichtliche Darstellung der jüdisch-alexandrinischen Philosophie*, 2 vols. Halle, 1831.

Deutsch, E. "On the Targumim," in *Literary Remains*. London, 1874.
Drummond, J. *Philo Judaeus*. 2 vols. London, 1888.
Frankel, Z. "Zur Ethik des jüdisch-alexandrinischen Philosophen Philo." *Monatsschrift*. 1867.
Heinemann, I. *Philos griechische und jüdische Bildung*. Breslau, 1932.
Luzatto, S. D. *Oheb Ger*. Vienna, 1830.
Schürer, E. *Ibidem*.
Stein, Edmund. *Die allegorische Exegese des Philo aus Alexandrien*. Giessen, 1931.
—— *Philo und der Midrasch*. Giessen, 1931.
Steinschneider, M. *Ibidem*, Chap. III.
Thackeray, H. St. John. *Josephus, the Man and the Historian*. New York, 1929.
Zeitlin, S. *Megillat Ta'anit*. ed. with notes and introduction. Philadelphia, 1922.
Zunz, L. *Ibidem*, Chaps. V, IX.

CHAPTER V

Brüll, N. "Die Entstehungsgeschichte des babylonischen Talmuds als Schriftwerkes," in *Jahrbücher*. Vol. II. Frankfurt, a. M, 1876.
Darmstetter, A. *The Talmud*. Philadelphia, 1896.
Deutsch, E. *The Talmud*. Philadelphia, 1897.
Halevi, I. I. *Dorot ha-Rishonim*. Division I. Vol. V.; Division II. Vol. I. Frankfort, 1901.
Mielziner, M. *Ibidem*.
Strack, H. *Ibidem*.
Weiss, I. H. *Dor*, Vol. III.
Yawitz, W. *Toldot Yisrael*. Vols. VI, VII, VIII. Cracow, 1907–09.

CHAPTER VI

Buber, S. *Midrash Tanhuma*. Introduction. Wilna, 1913.
—— *Pesikta de-Rab Kahana*. Introduction. Lyck, 1869.
Friedmann, M. *Pesikta Rabbati*. Introduction. Vienna, 1880.
—— *Seder Eliyahu*. Introduction. Vienna, 1904.
Rapoport, S. J. *Erek Millin*. Vol. I. Articles: "Agada," "Amora." 2nd ed. Warsaw, 1914.
Steinschneider, M. *Ibidem*.
Theodor, J. Article "Midrash Aggadah," in *Jewish Encyclopedia*. Vol. VIII.
Weiss, I. H. *Ibidem*, Vol. III. Chaps. XXI, XXIII.
Zunz, L. *Ibidem*, Chaps. XI–XIX.

CHAPTER VII

Bacher, W. *Nizoné ha-Dikduk*. Tel-Aviv, 1927.
—— "Die hebräische Sprachwissenschaft vom 10-ten bis zum 16-ten Jahr-

hundert," in Winter und Wünsche, *Die Jüdische Literatur,* Vol. II, Trier, 1894.

—— *Leben und Werke des Abulwalid Ibn Ganach,* Leipzig, 1885.

—— *Abraham Ibn Ezra als Grammatiker.* Strassburg, 1882.

DRACHMAN, B. *Die Stellung und Bedeutung des Jehudah Ibn Chajjug in der Geschichte der hebräischen Grammatik.* Breslau, 1884.

EHRENTREU, E. *Untersuchungen über die Massorah.*

EWALD UND DUKES. *Beiträge zur Geschichte der ältesten Auslegung und Spracherklärung des alten Testaments.* Stuttgart, 1844.

FÜRST, J. *Geschichte der hebräischen Lexicographie.* Introduction to his Dictionary. Leipzig, 1876.

GINSBURG, CH. D. *The Massorah.* 3 vols. London, 1880–86.

—— *Introduction to the Hebrew Bible.* London, 1897.

—— *Jacob ben Chaim's Introduction to the Massorah.*

HIRSCHFIELD, H. *Literary History of Hebrew Grammarians and Lexicographers.* London, 1926.

KOHUT, A. Introduction to the *Aruch Completum.* Vienna, 1878.

LEVITA, E. *Massoret ha-Massora,* with Eng. trans. by C. D. Ginsburg. London, 1926.

MALTER, H. *Life and Works of Saadia Gaon.* Philadelphia, 1921.

PINSKER, S. *Mebo le-Nikkud ha-Ashuri.* Vienna, 1863.

RAPOPORT, S. J. Introduction to Ibn Parhon's *Mahberet ha-Aruk.* Ed. Stern, Presburg, 1844.

STEINSCHNEIDER, M. *Bibligraphisches Handbuch über die theoretische und praktische Literatur für hebräische Sprachkunde.* Leipzig, 1859.

CHAPTER VIII

BACHER, W. "Die Bibelexegese vom Anfange des 10-ten bis zum Ende des 15-ten Jahrhunderts," in Winter und Wünsche, *Die Jüdische Literatur.* Vol. II. Trier, 1894.

—— *Die Bibelexegese der jüdischen Religionsphilosophen des Mittelalters vor Maimuni.* Strassburg, 1892.

—— *Ibn Ezras Einleitung zum Pentateuchkommentar.* Wien, 1876.

EWALD UND DUKES. "Saadia als Kommentator," in *Beiträge.*

FRIEDLANDER, M. *Essays on the Writings of Ibn Ezra.* London, 1882.

GEIGER, A. *Parshandata.—Die nordfranzösische Exegetenschule.* Leipzig, 1855.

—— "Joseph Kimhi," "David Kimhi," in *Nachgelassene Schriften, hebräische Abtheilung.* Breslau, 1877.

HARKAVY, A. E. *Studien und Mittheilungen aus der kaiserlichen Bibliothek zu St. Petersburg.* Hefte 3, 5. (Hebrew). Leipzig, 1880; Berlin, 1887.

KRONBERG, N. *Raschi als Exeget.* Halle, 1882.

LIBER, M. *Rashi.* Philadelphia, 1926.

LIPSCHÜTZ, E. M. *Rabbi Shelomo Yizhaki.* Warsaw, 1912.
POZNANSKI, S. Introduction to the edition of *"Kommentar von Eliezer aus Beaugency."* Warsaw, 1913.
STEINSCHNEIDER, M. *Jewish Literature.* (Hebrew translation). pp. 141–146.
WEISS, I. H. "Toldot Rashi," in *Toldot Gedolé Yisrael.* Vienna, 1882.
ZUNZ, L. "Raschi" in *Zeitschrift für die Wissenschaft des Judenthums.* Berlin, 1820.
—— *Zur Geschichte und Literatur,* pp. 60–76, Berlin, 1845.

CHAPTER IX

DAVIDSON, I. Introduction to *Gabirol's Selected Poems.* Philadelphia, 1923.
—— *Mahzor Yannai,* with notes and introduction. New York, 1915.
DUKES, L. *Ehrensäule und Denksteine.* Wien, 1937.
—— *Nahal Kedumim,* Hannover, 1853.
DELITZSCH, FRANZ. *Zur Geschichte der jüdischen Poesie,* Leipzig, 1836.
ELBOGEN, I. *Studien zur Geschichte des jüdischen Gottesdienstes.* Berlin, 1907.
GEIGER, A. *Jüdische Dichtungen der spanischen und italienischen Schule.* Leipzig, 1856.
—— *Salomo ibn Gabirol und seine Dichtungen.* Leipzig, 1867.
HARKAVY, A. E. "Shmuel ha-Nagid" in *Zikron le-Rishonim.* St. Petersburg, 1874.
—— *Rabbi Yehudah ha-Levi,* collected poems ed. with notes and introduction. Warsaw, 1893.
KAHANA, D. *Rabbi Abraham Ibn Ezra,* collected poems ed. with notes and introduction. Warsaw, 1894.
—— *Rabbi Dunash ben Labrat,* a biography. Warsaw, 1894.
—— "Hayé Shlomeh ben Gabirol" in *ha-Shiloah,* vol. I.
—— "Menahem ben Saruk," *Ibid.* vol. XVII.
KAMINKA, A. *Tahkemoni.* ed. with notes and introduction. Warsaw, 1895.
KARPELES, G. *Geschichte der jüdischen Literatur.* vol. II. Berlin, 1886.
KAUFMANN, D. "Jehudah Halevi," in *Gesammelte Schriften.* vol. II. Frankfurt, 1910.
LUZATTO, S. D. *Tal Orot.* Pshemyshl, 1881.
MOSES IBN EZRA, *Shirat Yisrael.* Hebrew translation by Halper.
MUNK, S. *Melanges.* Paris, 1857.
RAPOPORT, S. J. "Toldot Eliezer ha-Kalir," in *Bikkuré ha-Ittim,* 1829, 2nd ed. Warsaw, 1912.
ROSIN, D. *Reime und Gedichte des Abraham ibn Ezra.* Breslau, 1885.
SACHS, M. *Die religiöse Poesie der Juden in Spanien.* Berlin, 1845.
SASOON, D. S. *Diwan of Shemuel Hannaghid,* ed. with introduction and notes, Oxford, 1934.
SIMHONI, J. N. "Yehudah ha-Levi Betor Meshorer Leumi," in *ha-Ibri ha-Hodosh.* pp. 56–78. Berlin, 1912.

—— "Shelomo ibn Gabirol," in *ha-Tekufah.* vols. X, XII, XVI.
STEINSCHNEIDER, M. *Jewish Literature.* Section on poetry.
——*Manna,* Berlin, 1847.
SULZBACH, A. "Die poetische Literatur," in Winter und Wünsche, *Die Jüdische Literatur,* vol. III. Trier, 1896.
ZUNZ, L. *Die Ritus des synagogalen Gottesdienstes.* Berlin, 1859.
—— *Synagogale Poesie des Mittelalters.* Berlin, 1855.
—— *Literaturgeschichte der synagogalen Poesie.* Berlin, 1865.
—— *Zur Geschichte und Literatur,* Berlin, 1845.

CHAPTER X

BACHER, W. "Zum sprachlichen Character des Mischnah Thora," in *Moses ben Maimon, sein Leben, seine Werke und sein Einfluss.* vol. II. Berlin, 1908.
BERLINER, A. *Migdal Hannanel.* Berlin, 1878.
BUCHHOLZ, "Kodifikation des Halachahstoffes," in *Monatsschrift.* vol. XV.
FISHMAN, J. L. "Hayé ha-Rambam, Seforow u-Peulatow," in *Rabbenu Moshe ben Maimon.* Jerusalem, 1936.
FRANKEL, Z. *Entwurf einer Geschichte der Literatur der nachtalmudischen Responsa.* Breslau, 1865.
GINZBERG, L. *Geonica.* vol. I. Chap. 2. New York, 1909.
—— Article "Codification of Law." Jewish Encyclopedia. vol. III.
—— Ginzé Schechter. vol. II. New York, 1928.
GRAETZ, H. *Geschichte.* vols. IV, V; Heb. vols. III, IV; Eng. vol. III.
HERZOG, I. A. "Seder ha-Sefarim be-Mishnah Torah," in *Rabbenu Moshe ben Maimon.* Jerusalem, 1936.
KAMINKA, A. "Die rabbinische Literatur und die Halacha," in Winter und Wünsche *Die jüdische Literatur.* vol. II. Trier, 1894.
LEVIN, B. M. *Metibot,* ed. with notes and introduction. Jerusalem, 1934.
MANN, J. *Texts and Studies,* vol. I. Cincinnati, 1931.
MÜLLER, J. *Mafteah li-Teshubot ha-Geonim.* Berlin, 1891.
MÜNTZ, J. *Moses ben Maimon.* chaps. II, IV. Frankfurt, 1912.
RAPOPORT, S. J. "Rabbenu Nissim." *Bikkure ha-Ittim,* 1832.
—— "Rabbenu Hannanel." *Ibid.,* 1832.
ROSIN, D. *Rabbi Samuel ben Meir.* Breslau, 1880.
SIMHONI, J. N. "Rabbenu Gershom Meor ha-Golah," in *ha-Shiloah.* vol. 28. 1913.
TCHERNOWITZ, H. "le-Seder Sefer ha-Sheiltot," in *ha-Shiloah,* vol. 25.
—— "le-Toldot ha-Shulhan Aruk We-Hit Pa Shtuto," *Ibid.* vol. II–VI.
—— "Sefer Halakot Gedolot," in *ha-Miklat.* vol. III.
WEISS, I. H. *Dor,* vols. III, IV.
—— "Meboot ha-Talmud," in *Bet Talmud.* vols. I, II. Vienna, 1880–81.
ZIEMLICH, B. "Plan und Analogie des Mischnah Thora," in *Moses ben*

Maimon, sein Leben, seine Werke, und sein Einfluss." vol. I. Berlin, 1901.
ZEITLIN, S. *Maimonides.* New York, 1935.

CHAPTER XI

BERNFELD, S. *Daat Elohim.* 2 vols. Warsaw, 1899.
BLOCH, PH. *"Die jüdische Religionsphilosophie,* in Winter und Wünsche, *Die Jüdische Literatur.* vol. III. Trier, 1896.
DIZENDRUCK, Z. "The date of the completion of the More Nebukim" in *Hebrew Union College Annual.* Cincinnati, 1937–38.
EFROS, I. *Philosophical Terms in the More Nebukim.* New York, 1924.
GUTTMANN, J. *Die philosophischen Lehren des Isaac ben Salomon Israeli.* Münster, 1911.
—— *Die Religionsphilosophie des Saadias.* Göttingen, 1882.
—— *Die Philosophie des Salomon Ibn Gabirol.* Göttingen, 1889.
—— *Die Religionsphilosophie des Abraham Ibn Daud.* Göttingen, 1874.
—— ed. *Moses ben Maimon, sein Leben, seine Werke und sein Einfluss.* Leipzig, 1908–1912.
HORWITZ, A. *Die Psychologie bei den jüdischen Religionsphilosophen des Mittelalters von Saadia bis Maimuni,* Breslau, 1908–1912.
HUSIK, I. *History of Mediaeval Jewish Philosophy.* New York, 1918.
JOEL, M. *Beiträge zur Geschichte der Philosophie.* 2 vols. Breslau, 1876.
KAUFMANN, D. *Geschichte der Attributenlehre.* Gotha, 1877.
—— "Die Theologie des Baḥyah Ibn Pakudah" in *Gesammelte Schriften.* vol. II. Frankfurt, 1910.
—— " Judah Halevi" *Ibidem.*
KROCHMAL, N. *More Nebukê ha-Zeman.* Chaps. 17, 18. Lemberg, 1851.
MALTER, H. *Life and Works of Saadia Gaon.* Philadelphia, 1921.
MIRKIN, I. "Ikré ha-pilusufia shel ha-Rambam" in *Moshe ben Maimon.* Jerusalem, 1936.
MUNK, S. *Melanges.* Paris, 1857.
MÜNZ, J. *Moses ben Maimon.* Frankfurt, 1912.
NEUMARK, D. *Toldot ha-Ikkarim.* 2 vols. Odessa, 1913.
—— *Geschichte der jüdischen Philosophie des Mittelalters.* vols. 1, 2. Berlin, 1907.
STEINSCHNEIDER, M. *Jewish Literature.* Sec. "Philosophy and Theology."
WAXMAN, M. *The Philosophy of Don Chasdai Crescas.* Introduction and chaps. 1, 3. New York, 1920.
WISE, S. S. *The Improvement of the Moral Qualities* by Solomon Ibn Gabirol, Eng. transl. with introduction. New York, 1904.
WOLFSON, H. "Judah Halevi and Maimonides," in *J.Q.R. New Series.* vol. III.
ZIPRONI, A. *Kuzari,* ed. with notes and introduction, Warsaw, 1911.

CHAPTER XII

BLOCH, PH. "Die jüdische Mystic," in Winter und Wünsche, *Die Jüdische Literatur*. vol. III. Trier, 1896.

EPSTEIN, A. "Recherches sur le Sefer Yeçira" in *Revue des Etudes Juives*. vols. 28–29.

FRANCK, A. *La Kabbale*. English trans. New York, 1926.

GINZBERG, L. Article "Cabala," *Jewish Encyclopedia*. vol. III.

GINSBURG, CH. D. *The Kabbalah, its Doctrines, Development and Literature*. London, 1865.

GRAETZ, H. *Geschichte*. vol. 7. see especially Note, 3.

JOEL, M. *Religionsphilosophie des Zohar*. Leipzig, 1849.

JELLINEK, A. *Beiträge zur Geschichte der Kabbala*. Leipzig, 1857.

NEUMARK, D. *Toldot ha-Pilusufia be-Yisrael*. vol. I. New York, 1921.

RUBIN, S. *Kabbala und Agada*, Wien, 1895.

ZEITLIN, H. "Mafteaḥ le-Sefer ha-Zohar" in *ha-Teḳufah*. vols. 6–7.

CHAPTER XIII

FÜRST, J. *Geschichte des Karäerthums*. 3 vols. Leipzig, 1865.

GRAETZ, H. *Geschichte*. Hebrew trans. with Harkavy's additions. vols. III, IV.

GOTTLOBER, A. B. *Biḳḳoret le-Toldot ha-Karaim*. Wilna, 1865.

HARKAVY, A. E. Article "Karaites," *Jewish Encyclopedia*. vol. VII.

HANN, J. *Texts and studies*, vol. II. Cincinnati, 1931.

PINSKER, S. *Liḳḳuté Kadmoniyot*. Vienna, 1860.

POZNANSKI, S. Article "Karaites," in *Hastings Encyclopedia of Religion and Ethics*, vol. VII.

—— Articles in J.Q.R. Old Series. vols. X, XVIII, XX.

—— Introduction to edition of *Zeḳer Ẓaddiḳim* by Sultanski, Warsaw, 1920.

—— *The Karaite Literary Opponents of Saadia Gaon*. London, 1908.

STEINSCHNEIDER, M. *Jewish Literature*. Sect. "Karaite Literature."

—— *Hebräische Übersetzungen des Mittelalters*. Berlin, 1893.

—— *Die arabische Literatur der Juden*, Berlin, 1902.

CHAPTER XIV

ASHER, A. *Itinerary of Benjamin of Tudela*. 2 vols. London, 1840.

ELBOGEN, I. "Abraham Ibn Daud als Geschichtsschreiber," in Guttmanns *Festschrift*. Leipzig, 1915.

EPSTEIN, A. "Sources for Geonic Jewish History" in Harkavy's *Sefer ha-Yobel*. St. Petersburg, 1908.

—— *Eldad ha-Dani*. Pressburg, 1891.

GINZBERG, L. *Geonica*. vol. I. chap. 1.

KAHANA, A. *Safrut ha-Historiah ha-Yisraelit.* 2 vols. Warsaw, 1922.
KAUFMANN, D. "Die Chronik des Aḥimaaẓ von Oria" in *Gesammelte Schriften* vol. III. Frankfurt, 1910.
LEWIN, A. "Geschichte, Geographie und Reiseliteratur," in Winter und Wünsche, *Die Jüdische Literatur.* vol. III. Trier, 1896.
LEWIN, B. M. *Iggeret Rab Sherira Gaon.* Jaffa, 1914.
NEUBAUER, A. *Mediaeval Jewish Chronicles.* 2 vols., Oxford, 1893.
SCHECHTER, S. "Khazar Document," in *J.Q.R. New Series.* vol. III.
STEINSCHNEIDER, M. *Jewish Literature.* Sec. "History and Geography."
—— *Geschichtsliteratur der Juden,* Frankfurt, 1905.
ZUNZ, L. "Die geographische Literatur der Juden," in *Gesammelte Schriften.* vol. I. Berlin, 1875.

CHAPTER XV

CARMOLY, E. *La medicine Juive.* Bruxelles, 1844.
STEINSCHNEIDER, M. *Jewish Literature.* Sec. "Science."
—— *Hebräische Übersetzungen des Mittelalters,* Berlin, 1893.
—— *Sabbatai Donolo.* 1868.
VENETIANER, L. *Asaf Judaeus.* Budapest, 1815–17.

CHAPTER XVI

ABRAHAMS, I. *Book of Delight and other Papers.* Philadelphia, 1912.
DAVIDSON, I. *Sefer Sha'ash'uim,* ed. with notes and introduction, Berlin, 1925.
KAMINKA, A. *Taḥḳemoni.* ed. with notes and introduction, Warsaw, 1899.
STEINSCHNEIDER, M. *Jewish Literature.* Sec. "Poetry and Prose."
—— *Manna.* Berlin, 1847.